Software Testing and Analysis: Process, Principles, and Techniques

Software Testing and Analysis: Process, Principles, and Techniques

Mauro Pezzè
Università di Milano Bicocca

Michal Young
University of Oregon

WILEY

Software Testing and Analysis: Process, Principles, and Techniques

Authorised reprint by Wiley India Pvt. Ltd., 4435-36/7, Ansari Road, Daryaganj, New Delhi-110002.

Cover Image: Baris Simsek/iStockphoto

Reprint: 2015

Printed at: Durga Printographics, Delhi.

ISBN: 978-81-265-1773-2

Contents

List of Figures

List of Tables

Preface

This book addresses software test and analysis in the context of an overall effort to achieve quality. It is designed for use as a primary textbook for a course in software test and analysis or as a supplementary text in a software engineering course, and as a resource for software developers.

The main characteristics of this book are:

- It assumes that the reader's goal is to achieve a suitable balance of cost, schedule, and quality. It is not oriented toward critical systems for which ultra-high reliability must be obtained regardless of cost, nor will it be helpful if one's aim is to cut cost or schedule regardless of consequence.

- It presents a selection of techniques suitable for near-term application, with sufficient technical background to understand their domain of applicability and to consider variations to suit technical and organizational constraints. Techniques of only historical interest and techniques that are unlikely to be practical in the near future are omitted.

- It promotes a vision of software testing and analysis as integral to modern software engineering practice, equally as important and technically demanding as other aspects of development. This vision is generally consistent with current thinking on the subject, and is approached by some leading organizations, but is not universal.

- It treats software testing and static analysis techniques together in a coherent framework, as complementary approaches for achieving adequate quality at acceptable cost.

Why This Book?

One cannot "test quality into" a badly constructed software product, but neither can one build quality into a product without test and analysis. The goal of acceptable quality at acceptable cost is both a technical and a managerial challenge, and meeting the goal requires a grasp of both the technical issues and their context in software development.

It is widely acknowledged today that software quality assurance should not be a phase between development and deployment, but rather a set of ongoing activities interwoven with every task from initial requirements gathering through evolution of the deployed product. Realization of this vision in practice is often only partial. It requires careful choices and combinations of techniques fit to the organization, products, and processes, but few people are familiar with the full range of techniques, from inspection to testing to automated analyses. Those best positioned to shape the organization and its processes are seldom familiar with the technical issues, and vice versa. Moreover, there still persists in many organizations a perception that quality assurance requires less skill or background than other aspects of development.

This book provides students with a coherent view of the state of the art and practice, and provides developers and managers with technical and organizational approaches to push the state of practice toward the state of the art.

Who Is This Book For?

Students who read portions of this book will gain a basic understanding of principles and issues in software test and analysis, including an introduction to process and organizational issues. *Developers*, including quality assurance professionals, will find a variety of techniques with sufficient discussion of technical and process issues to support adaptation to the particular demands of their organization and application domain. *Technical managers* will find a coherent approach to weaving software quality assurance into the overall software process. All readers should obtain a clearer view of the interplay among technical and nontechnical issues in crafting an approach to software quality.

Students, developers, and technical managers with a basic background in computer science and software engineering will find the material in this book accessible without additional preparation. Some of the material is technically demanding, but readers may skim it on a first reading to get the big picture, and return to it at need.

A basic premise of this book is that effective quality assurance is best achieved by selection and combination of techniques that are carefully woven into (not grafted onto) a software development process for a particular organization. A software quality engineer seeking technical advice will find here encouragement to consider a wider context and participate in shaping the development process. A manager whose faith lies entirely in process, to the exclusion of technical knowledge and judgment, will find here many connections between technical and process issues, and a rationale for a more comprehensive view.

How to Read This Book

This book is designed to permit selective reading. Most readers should begin with Part I, which presents fundamental principles in a coherent framework and lays the groundwork for understanding the strengths and weaknesses of individual techniques and their application in an effective software process. Part II brings together basic technical background for many testing and analysis methods. Those interested in particular methods may proceed directly to the relevant chapters in Part III of the book. Where there are dependencies, the *Required Background* section at the beginning of a chapter indicates what should be read in preparation. Part IV discusses how to design a systematic testing and analysis process and incorporates it into an overall development process, and may be read either before or after Part III.

Readers new to the field of software test and analysis can obtain an overview by reading Chapters

1	Software Test and Analysis in a nutshell
2	A Framework for Test and Analysis
4	Test and Analysis Activities within a Software Process
10	Functional Testing
11	Combinatorial Testing
14	Model-Based Testing
15	Testing Object-Oriented Software
17	Test Execution
18	Inspection
19	Program Analysis
20	Planning and Monitoring the Process

Notes for Instructors

This book can be used in an introductory course in software test and analysis or as a supplementary text in an undergraduate software engineering course.

An introductory graduate-level or an undergraduate level course in software test and analysis can cover most of the book. In particular, it should include

- All of Part I (Fundamentals of Test and Analysis), which provides a complete overview.
- Most of Part II (Basic Techniques), which provides fundamental background, possibly omitting the latter parts of Chapters 6 (Dependence and Data Flow Models) and 7 (Symbolic Execution and Proof of Properties). These chapters are particularly suited for students who focus on theoretical foundations and those who plan to study analysis and testing more deeply.
- A selection of materials from Parts III (Problems and Methods) and IV (Process).

For a course with more emphasis on techniques than process, we recommend

- Chapter 10 (Functional Testing), to understand how to approach black-box testing.
- The overview section and at least one other section of Chapter 11 (Combinatorial Testing) to grasp some combinatorial techniques.

- Chapter 12 (Structural Testing), through Section 12.3, to introduce the basic coverage criteria.
- Chapter 13 (Data Flow Testing), through Section 13.3, to see an important application of data flow analysis to software testing.
- The overview section and at least one other section of Chapter 14 (Model-based Testing) to grasp the interplay between models and testing.
- Chapter 15 (Testing Object-Oriented Software) to appreciate implications of the object-oriented paradigm on analysis and testing.
- Chapter 17 (Test Execution), to manage an easily overlooked set of problems and costs.
- Chapter 18 (Inspection) to grasp the essential features of inspection and appreciate the complementarity of analysis and test.
- Chapter 19 (Program Analysis) to understand the role of automated program analyses and their relation to testing and inspection techniques.
- Chapters 20 (Planning and Monitoring the Process), 21 (Integration and Component-based Software Testing), and 22 (System, Acceptance, and Regression Testing) to widen the picture of the analysis and testing process.

For a stronger focus on software process and organizational issues, we recommend

- Chapter 10 (Functional Testing), a selection from Chapters 11 and 14 (Combinatorial Testing and Model-Based Testing), and Chapters 15 (Testing Object-Oriented Software), 17 (Test Execution), 18 (Inspection), and 19 (Program Analysis) to provide a basic overview of techniques.
- Part IV, possibly omitting Chapter 23 (Automating Analysis and Test), for a comprehensive view of the quality process.

When used as a supplementary text in an undergraduate software engineering course, Chapters 1 (Software Test and Analysis in a Nutshell), and 2 (A Framework for Test and Analysis) can provide a brief overview of the field. We recommend completing these two essential chapters along with either Chapter 4, or a selection of chapters from Part III, or both, depending on the course schedule. Chapter 4 (Test and Analysis Activities within a Software Process) can be used to understand the essential aspects of a quality process. The following chapters from Part III will help students grasp essential techniques:

- Chapter 10 (Functional Testing) and a selection of techniques from Chapters 11 (Combinatorial Testing) and 14 (Model-Based Testing), to grasp basic black-box testing techniques.
- Chapter 12 (Structural Testing), through Section 12.3, to introduce basic coverage criteria.

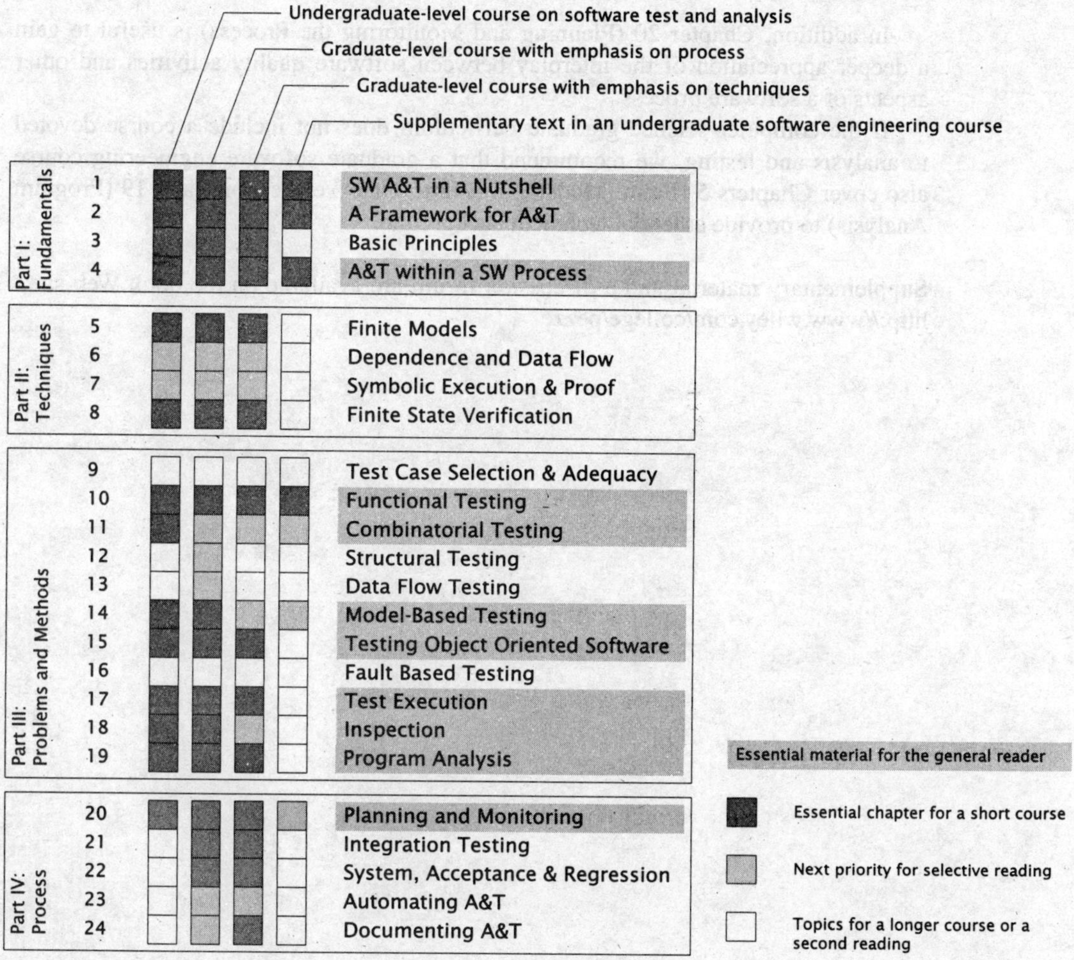

Figure 1: Selecting core material by need

- Chapter 15 (Testing Object-Oriented Software), through Section 15.3, to appreciate implications of the object oriented paradigm on analysis and testing.
- Chapter 17 (Test Execution), to manage an easily overlooked set of problems and costs.
- Chapter 18 (Inspection), to grasp the essential features of inspection.

In addition, Chapter 20 (Planning and Monitoring the Process) is useful to gain a deeper appreciation of the interplay between software quality activities and other aspects of a software process.

If the computer science graduate curriculum does not include a course devoted to analysis and testing, we recommend that a graduate software engineering course also cover Chapters 5 (Finite Models), 8 (Finite State Verification), and 19 (Program Analysis) to provide essential technical background.

Supplementary material and a discussion forum are available on the book Web site, http://www.wiley.com/college/pezze

Part I

Fundamentals of Test and Analysis

Chapter 1

Software Test and Analysis in a Nutshell

Before considering individual aspects and techniques of software analysis and testing, it is useful to view the "big picture" of software quality in the context of a software development project and organization. The objective of this chapter is to introduce the range of software verification and validation (V&V) activities and a rationale for selecting and combining them within a software development process. This overview is necessarily cursory and incomplete, with many details deferred to subsequent chapters.

1.1 Engineering Processes and Verification

Engineering disciplines pair design and construction activities with activities that check intermediate and final products so that defects can be identified and removed. Software engineering is no exception: Construction of high-quality software requires complementary pairing of design and verification activities throughout development.

Verification and design activities take various forms ranging from those suited to highly repetitive construction of noncritical items for mass markets to highly customized or highly critical products. Appropriate verification activities depend on the engineering discipline, the construction process, the final product, and quality requirements.

Repetition and high levels of automation in production lines reduce the need for verification of individual products. For example, only a few key components of products like screens, circuit boards, and toasters are verified individually. The final products are tested statistically. Full test of each individual product may not be economical, depending on the costs of testing, the reliability of the production process, and the costs of field failures.

Even for some mass market products, complex processes or stringent quality requirements may require both sophisticated design and advanced product verification procedures. For example, computers, cars, and aircraft, despite being produced in series, are checked individually before release to customers. Other products are not built in series, but are engineered individually through highly evolved processes and tools. Custom houses, race cars, and software are not built in series. Rather, each house, each racing car, and each software package is at least partly unique in its design and functionality. Such products are verified individually both during and after production to identify and eliminate faults.

Verification of goods produced in series (e.g., screens, boards, or toasters) consists of repeating a predefined set of tests and analyses that indicate whether the products meet the required quality standards. In contrast, verification of a unique product, such as a house, requires the design of a specialized set of tests and analyses to assess the quality of that product. Moreover, the relationship between the test and analysis results and the quality of the product cannot be defined once for all items, but must be assessed for each product. For example, the set of resistance tests for assessing the quality of a floor must be customized for each floor, and the resulting quality depends on the construction methods and the structure of the building.

Verification grows more difficult with the complexity and variety of the products. Small houses built with comparable technologies in analogous environments can be verified with standardized procedures. The tests are parameterized to the particular house, but are nonetheless routine. Verification of a skyscraper or of a house built in an extreme seismic area, on the other hand, may not be easily generalized, instead requiring specialized tests and analyses designed particularly for the case at hand.

Software is among the most variable and complex of artifacts engineered on a regular basis. Quality requirements of software used in one environment may be quite different and incompatible with quality requirements of a different environment or application domain, and its structure evolves and often deteriorates as the software system grows. Moreover, the inherent nonlinearity of software systems and uneven distribution of faults complicates verification. If an elevator can safely carry a load of 1000 kg, it can also safely carry any smaller load, but if a procedure correctly sorts a set of 256 elements, it may fail on a set of 255 or 53 or 12 elements, as well as on 257 or 1023.

The cost of software verification often exceeds half the overall cost of software development and maintenance. Advanced development technologies and powerful supporting tools can reduce the frequency of some classes of errors, but we are far from eliminating errors and producing fault-free software. In many cases new development approaches introduce new subtle kinds of faults, which may be more difficult to reveal and remove than classic faults. This is the case, for example, with distributed software, which can present problems of deadlock or race conditions that are not present in sequential programs. Likewise, object-oriented development introduces new problems due to the use of polymorphism, dynamic binding, and private state that are absent or less pronounced in procedural software.

The variety of problems and the richness of approaches make it challenging to choose and schedule the right blend of techniques to reach the required level of quality within cost constraints. There are no fixed recipes for attacking the problem of verifying a software product. Even the most experienced specialists do not have pre-cooked solutions, but need to design a solution that suits the problem, the requirements, and the development environment.

1.2 Basic Questions

To start understanding how to attack the problem of verifying software, let us consider a hypothetical case. The Board of Governors of Chipmunk Computers, an (imaginary) computer manufacturer, decides to add new online shopping functions to the company Web presence to allow customers to purchase individually configured products. Let us assume the role of quality manager. To begin, we need to answer a few basic questions:

- When do verification and validation start? When are they complete?
- What particular techniques should be applied during development of the product to obtain acceptable quality at an acceptable cost?
- How can we assess the readiness of a product for release?
- How can we control the quality of successive releases?
- How can the development process itself be improved over the course of the current and future projects to improve products and make verification more cost-effective?

1.3 When Do Verification and Validation Start and End?

Although some primitive software development processes concentrate testing and analysis at the end of the development cycle, and the job title "tester" in some organizations still refers to a person who merely executes test cases on a complete product, today it is widely understood that execution of tests is a small part of the verification and validation process required to assess and maintain the quality of a software product.

Verification and validation start as soon as we decide to build a software product, or even before. In the case of Chipmunk Computers, when the Board of Governors asks the information technology (IT) manager for a feasibility study, the IT manager considers not only functionality and development costs, but also the required qualities and their impact on the overall cost.

The Chipmunk software quality manager participates with other key designers in the feasibility study, focusing in particular on risk analysis and the measures needed to assess and control quality at each stage of development. The team assesses the impact of new features and new quality requirements on the full system and considers the contribution of quality control activities to development cost and schedule. For example, migrating sales functions into the Chipmunk Web site will increase the criticality of system availability and introduce new security issues. A feasibility study that ignored quality could lead to major unanticipated costs and delays and very possibly to project failure.

The feasibility study necessarily involves some tentative architectural design, for example, a division of software structure corresponding to a division of responsibility between a human interface design team and groups responsible for core business software ("business logic") and supporting infrastructure, and a rough build plan breaking the project into a series of incremental deliveries. Opportunities and obstacles for cost-effective verification are important considerations in factoring the development effort into subsystems and phases, and in defining major interfaces.

Overall architectural design divides work and separates qualities that can be verified independently in the different subsystems, thus easing the work of the testing team as well as other developers. For example, the Chipmunk design team divides the system into a presentation layer, back-end logic, and infrastructure. Development of the three subsystems is assigned to three different teams with specialized experience, each of which must meet appropriate quality constraints. The quality manager steers the early design toward a separation of concerns that will facilitate test and analysis.

In the Chipmunk Web presence, a clean interface between the presentation layer and back end logic allows a corresponding division between usability testing (which is the responsibility of the human interface group, rather than the quality group) and verification of correct functioning. A clear separation of infrastructure from business logic serves a similar purpose. Responsibility for a small kernel of critical functions is allocated to specialists on the infrastructure team, leaving effectively checkable rules for consistent use of those functions throughout other parts of the system.

Taking into account quality constraints during early breakdown into subsystems allows for a better allocation of quality requirements and facilitates both detailed design and testing. However, many properties cannot be guaranteed by one subsystem alone. The initial breakdown of properties given in the feasibility study will be detailed during later design and may result in "cross-quality requirements" among subsystems. For example, to guarantee a given security level, the infrastructure design team may require verification of the absence of some specific security holes (e.g., buffer overflow) in other parts of the system.

The initial build plan also includes some preliminary decisions about test and analysis techniques to be used in development. For example, the preliminary prototype of Chipmunk on-line sales functionality will not undergo complete acceptance testing, but will be used to validate the requirements analysis and some design decisions. Acceptance testing of the first release will be based primarily on feedback from selected retail stores, but will also include complete checks to verify absence of common security holes. The second release will include full acceptance test and reliability measures.

If the feasibility study leads to a project commitment, verification and validation (V&V) activities will commence with other development activities, and like development itself will continue long past initial delivery of a product. Chipmunk's new Web-based functions will be delivered in a series of phases, with requirements reassessed and modified after each phase, so it is essential that the V&V plan be cost-effective over a series of deliveries whose outcome cannot be fully known in advance. Even when the project is "complete," the software will continue to evolve and adapt to new conditions, such as a new version of the underlying database, or new requirements, such as the opening of a European sales division of Chipmunk. V&V activities continue through each small or large change to the system.

Why Combine Techniques?

No single test or analysis technique can serve all purposes. The primary reasons for combining techniques, rather than choosing a single "best" technique, are

- Effectiveness for different classes of faults. For example, race conditions are very difficult to find with conventional testing, but they can be detected with static analysis techniques.
- Applicability at different points in a project. For example, we can apply inspection techniques very early to requirements and design representations that are not suited to more automated analyses.
- Differences in purpose. For example, systematic (nonrandom) testing is aimed at maximizing fault detection, but cannot be used to measure reliability; for that, statistical testing is required.
- Trade-offs in cost and assurance. For example, one may use a relatively expensive technique to establish a few key properties of core components (e.g., a security kernel) when those techniques would be too expensive for use throughout a project.

1.4 What Techniques Should Be Applied?

The feasibility study is the first step of a complex development process that should lead to delivery of a satisfactory product through design, verification, and validation activities. Verification activities steer the process toward the construction of a product that satisfies the requirements by checking the quality of intermediate artifacts as well as the ultimate product. Validation activities check the correspondence of the intermediate artifacts and the final product to users' expectations.

The choice of the set of test and analysis techniques depends on quality, cost, scheduling, and resource constraints in development of a particular product. For the business logic subsystem, the quality team plans to use a preliminary prototype for validating requirements specifications. They plan to use automatic tools for simple structural checks of the architecture and design specifications. They will train staff for design and code inspections, which will be based on company checklists that identify deviations from design rules for ensuring maintainability, scalability, and correspondence between design and code.

Requirements specifications at Chipmunk are written in a structured, semiformal format. They are not amenable to automated checking, but like any other software artifact they can be inspected by developers. The Chipmunk organization has compiled a checklist based on their rules for structuring specification documents and on experience with problems in requirements from past systems. For example, the checklist for inspecting requirements specifications at Chipmunk asks inspectors to confirm that each specified property is stated in a form that can be effectively tested.

The analysis and test plan requires inspection of requirements specifications, design specifications, source code, and test documentation. Most source code and test documentation inspections are a simple matter of soliciting an off-line review by one other developer, though a handful of critical components are designated for an additional review and comparison of notes. Component interface specifications are inspected by small groups that include a representative of the "provider" and "consumer" sides of the interface, again mostly off-line with exchange of notes through a discussion service. A larger group and more involved process, including a moderated inspection meeting with three or four participants, is used for inspection of a requirements specification.

Chipmunk developers produce functional unit tests with each development work assignment, as well as test oracles and any other scaffolding required for test execution. Test scaffolding is additional code needed to execute a unit or a subsystem in isolation. Test oracles check the results of executing the code and signal discrepancies between actual and expected outputs.

Test cases at Chipmunk are based primarily on interface specifications, but the extent to which unit tests exercise the control structure of programs is also measured. If less than 90% of all statements are executed by the functional tests, this is taken as an indication that either the interface specifications are incomplete (if the missing coverage corresponds to visible differences in behavior), or else additional implementation complexity hides behind the interface. Either way, additional test cases are devised based on a more complete description of unit behavior.

Integration and system tests are generated by the quality team, working from a catalog of patterns and corresponding tests. The behavior of some subsystems or components is modeled as finite state machines, so the quality team creates test suites that exercise program paths corresponding to each state transition in the models.

Scaffolding and oracles for integration testing are part of the overall system architecture. Oracles for individual components and units are designed and implemented by programmers using tools for annotating code with conditions and invariants. The Chipmunk developers use a home-grown test organizer tool to bind scaffolding to code, schedule test runs, track faults, and organize and update regression test suites.

The quality plan includes analysis and test activities for several properties distinct from functional correctness, including performance, usability, and security. Although these are an integral part of the quality plan, their design and execution are delegated in part or whole to experts who may reside elsewhere in the organization. For example, Chipmunk maintains a small team of human factors experts in its software division. The human factors team will produce look-and-feel guidelines for the Web purchasing system, which together with a larger body of Chipmunk interface design rules can be checked during inspection and test. The human factors team also produces and executes a usability testing plan.

Parts of the portfolio of verification and validation activities selected by Chipmunk are illustrated in Figure 1.1. The quality of the final product and the costs of the quality assurance activities depend on the choice of the techniques to accomplish each activity. Most important is to construct a coherent plan that can be monitored. In addition to monitoring schedule progress against the plan, Chipmunk records faults found during each activity, using this as an indicator of potential trouble spots. For example, if the number of faults found in a component during design inspections is high, additional dynamic test time will be planned for that component.

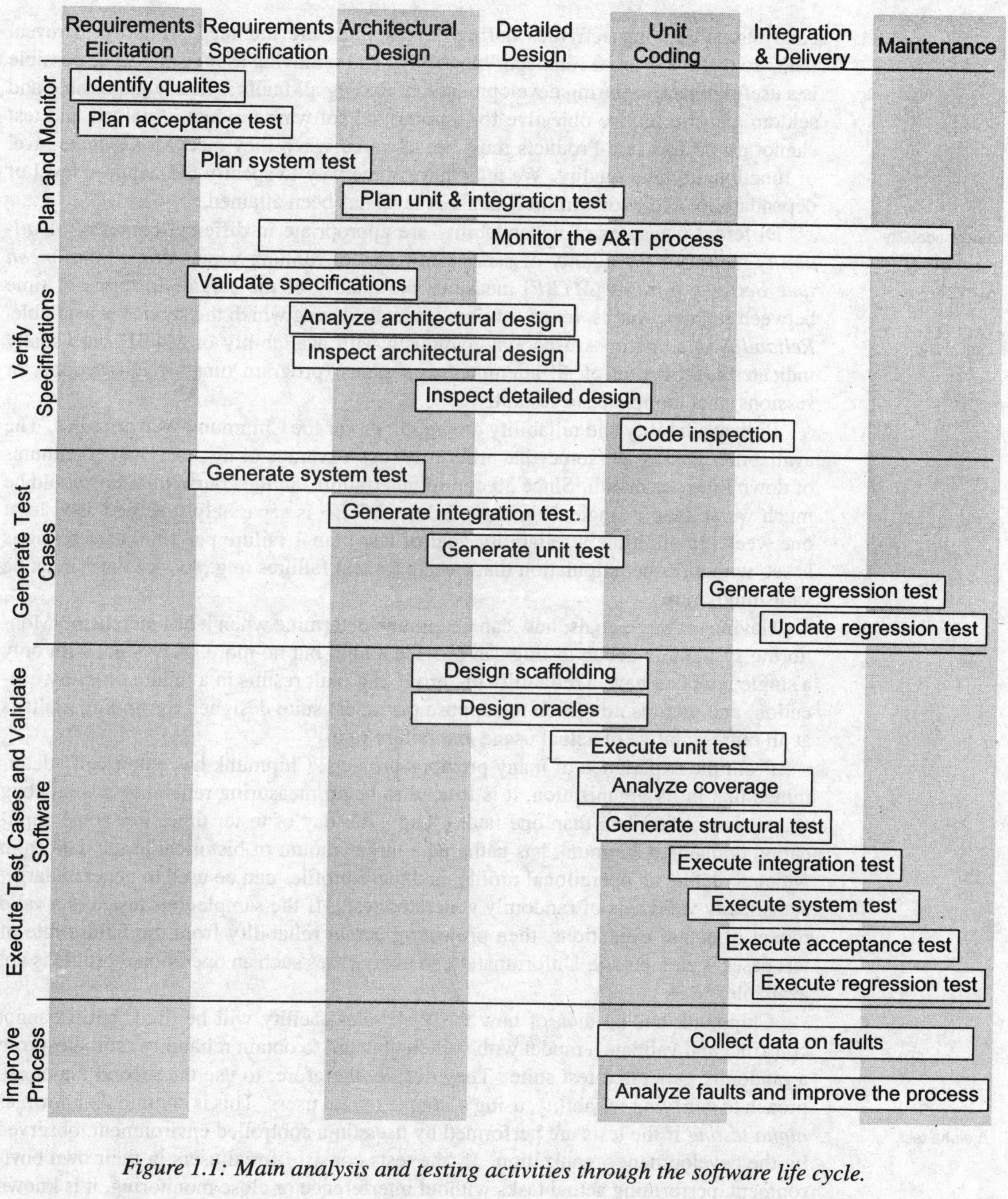

Figure 1.1: Main analysis and testing activities through the software life cycle.

1.5 How Can We Assess the Readiness of a Product?

Analysis and testing activities during development are intended primarily to reveal faults so that they can be removed. Identifying and removing as many faults as possible is a useful objective during development, but finding all faults is nearly impossible and seldom a cost-effective objective for a nontrivial software product. Analysis and test cannot go on forever: Products must be delivered when they meet an adequate level of functionality and quality. We must have some way to specify the required level of dependability and to determine when that level has been attained.

Δ dependability

Δ availability

Δ MTBF

Different measures of dependability are appropriate in different contexts. *Availability* measures the quality of service in terms of running versus down time; *mean time between failures (MTBF)* measures the quality of the service in terms of time between failures, that is, length of time intervals during which the service is available. *Reliability* is sometimes used synonymously with availability or MTBF, but usually indicates the fraction of all attempted operations (program runs, or interactions, or sessions) that complete successfully.

Δ reliability

Both availability and reliability are important for the Chipmunk Web presence. The availability goal is set (somewhat arbitrarily) at an average of no more than 30 minutes of down time per month. Since 30 one-minute failures in the course of a day would be much worse than a single 30-minute failure, MTBF is separately specified as at least one week. In addition, a reliability goal of less than 1 failure per 1000 user sessions is set, with a further stipulation that certain critical failures (e.g., loss of data) must be vanishingly rare.

Having set these goals, how can Chipmunk determine when it has met them? Monitoring systematic debug testing can provide a hint, but no more. A product with only a single fault can have a reliability of zero if that fault results in a failure on every execution, and there is no reason to suppose that a test suite designed for finding faults is at all representative of actual usage and failure rate.

From the experience of many previous projects, Chipmunk has empirically determined that in its organization, it is fruitful to begin measuring reliability when debug testing is yielding less than one fault ("bug") per day of tester time. For some application domains, Chipmunk has gathered a large amount of historical usage data from which to define an operational profile, and these profiles can be used to generate large, statistically valid sets of randomly generated tests. If the sample thus tested is a valid model of actual executions, then projecting actual reliability from the failure rate of test cases is elementary. Unfortunately, in many cases such an operational profile is not available.

Chipmunk has an idea of how the Web sales facility will be used, but it cannot construct and validate a model with sufficient detail to obtain reliability estimates from a randomly generated test suite. They decide, therefore, to use the second major approach to verifying reliability, using a sample of real users. This is commonly known as *alpha testing* if the tests are performed by users in a controlled environment, observed by the development organization. If the tests consist of real users in their own environment, performing actual tasks without interference or close monitoring, it is known as *beta testing*. The Chipmunk team plans a very small alpha test, followed by a longer beta test period in which the software is made available only in retail outlets. To ac-

Δ alpha test

Δ beta test

celerate reliability measurement after subsequent revisions of the system, the beta test version will be extensively instrumented, capturing many properties of a usage profile.

1.6 How Can We Ensure the Quality of Successive Releases?

Software test and analysis does not stop at the first release. Software products often operate for many years, frequently much beyond their planned life cycle, and undergo many changes. They adapt to environment changes—for example, introduction of new device drivers, evolution of the operating system, and changes in the underlying database. They also evolve to serve new and changing user requirements. Ongoing quality tasks include test and analysis of new and modified code, reexecution of system tests, and extensive record-keeping.

Chipmunk maintains a database for tracking problems. This database serves a dual purpose of tracking and prioritizing actual, known program faults and their resolution and managing communication with users who file problem reports. Even at initial release, the database usually includes some known faults, because market pressure seldom allows correcting all known faults before product release. Moreover, "bugs" in the database are not always and uniquely associated with real program faults. Some problems reported by users are misunderstandings and feature requests, and many distinct reports turn out to be duplicates which are eventually consolidated.

Chipmunk designates relatively major revisions, involving several developers, as "point releases," and smaller revisions as "patch level" releases. The full quality process is repeated in miniature for each point release, including everything from inspection of revised requirements to design and execution of new unit, integration, system, and acceptance test cases. A major point release is likely even to repeat a period of beta testing.

point release

patch level release

Patch level revisions are often urgent for at least some customers. For example, a patch level revision is likely when a fault prevents some customers from using the software or when a new security vulnerability is discovered. Test and analysis for patch level revisions is abbreviated, and automation is particularly important for obtaining a reasonable level of assurance with very fast turnaround. Chipmunk maintains an extensive suite of *regression tests*. The Chipmunk development environment supports recording, classification, and automatic re-execution of test cases. Each point release must undergo complete regression testing before release, but patch level revisions may be released with a subset of regression tests that run unattended overnight.

regression test

When fixing one fault, it is all too easy to introduce a new fault or re-introduce faults that have occurred in the past. Chipmunk developers add new regression test cases as faults are discovered and repaired.

1.7 How Can the Development Process Be Improved?

As part of an overall process improvement program, Chipmunk has implemented a quality improvement program. In the past, the quality team encountered the same defects in project after project. The quality improvement program tracks and classifies faults to identify the human errors that cause them and weaknesses in test and analysis that allow them to remain undetected.

Chipmunk quality improvement group members are drawn from developers and quality specialists on several project teams. The group produces recommendations that may include modifications to development and test practices, tool and technology support, and management practices. The explicit attention to buffer overflow in networked applications at Chipmunk is the result of failure analysis in previous projects.

Fault analysis and process improvement comprise four main phases: Defining the data to be collected and implementing procedures for collecting it; analyzing collected data to identify important fault classes; analyzing selected fault classes to identify weaknesses in development and quality measures; and adjusting the quality and development process.

Collection of data is particularly crucial and often difficult. Earlier attempts by Chipmunk quality teams to impose fault data collection practices were a dismal failure. The quality team possessed neither carrots nor sticks to motivate developers under schedule pressure. An overall process improvement program undertaken by the Chipmunk software division provided an opportunity to better integrate fault data collection with other practices, including the normal procedure for assigning, tracking, and reviewing development work assignments. Quality process improvement is distinct from the goal of improving an individual product, but initial data collection is integrated in the same bug tracking system, which in turn is integrated with the revision and configuration control system used by Chipmunk developers.

The quality improvement group defines the information that must be collected for faultiness data to be useful as well as the format and organization of that data. Participation of developers in designing the data collection process is essential to balance the cost of data collection and analysis with its utility, and to build acceptance among developers.

Data from several projects over time are aggregated and classified to identify classes of faults that are important because they occur frequently, because they cause particularly severe failures, or because they are costly to repair. These faults are analyzed to understand how they are initially introduced and why they escape detection. The improvement steps recommended by the quality improvement group may include specific analysis or testing steps for earlier fault detection, but they may also include design rules and modifications to development and even to management practices. An important part of each recommended practice is an accompanying recommendation for measuring the impact of the change.

Summary

The quality process has three distinct goals: improving a software product (by preventing, detecting, and removing faults), assessing the quality of the software product (with respect to explicit quality goals), and improving the long-term quality and cost-effectiveness of the quality process itself. Each goal requires weaving quality assurance and improvement activities into an overall development process, from product inception through deployment, evolution, and retirement.

Each organization must devise, evaluate, and refine an approach suited to that organization and application domain. A well-designed approach will invariably combine several test and analysis techniques, spread across stages of development. An array of fault detection techniques are distributed across development stages so that faults are removed as soon as possible. The overall cost and cost-effectiveness of techniques depends to a large degree on the extent to which they can be incrementally re-applied as the product evolves.

Further Reading

This book deals primarily with software analysis and testing to improve and assess the dependability of software. That is not because qualities other than dependability are unimportant, but rather because they require their own specialized approaches and techniques. We offer here a few starting points for considering some other important properties that interact with dependability. Norman's *The Design of Everyday Things* [Nor90] is a classic introduction to design for usability, with basic principles that apply to both hardware and software artifacts. A primary reference on usability for interactive computer software, and particularly for Web applications, is Nielsen's *Designing Web Usability* [Nie00]. Bishop's text *Computer Security: Art and Science* [Bis02] is a good introduction to security issues. The most comprehensive introduction to software safety is Leveson's *Safeware* [Lev95].

Exercises

1.1. Philip has studied "just-in-time" industrial production methods and is convinced that they should be applied to every aspect of software development. He argues that test case design should be performed just before the first opportunity to execute the newly designed test cases, never earlier. What positive and negative consequences do you foresee for this just-in-time test case design approach?

1.2. A newly hired project manager at Chipmunk questions why the quality manager is involved in the feasibility study phase of the project, rather than joining the team only when the project has been approved, as at the new manager's previous company. What argument(s) might the quality manager offer in favor of her involvement in the feasibility study?

1.3. Chipmunk procedures call for peer review not only of each source code module, but also of test cases and scaffolding for testing that module. Anita argues that inspecting test suites is a waste of time; any time spent on inspecting a test case designed to detect a particular class of fault could more effectively be spent inspecting the source code to detect that class of fault. Anita's project manager, on the other hand, argues that inspecting test cases and scaffolding can be cost-effective when considered over the whole lifetime of a software product. What argument(s) might Anita's manager offer in favor of this conclusion?

1.4. The spiral model of software development prescribes sequencing incremental prototyping phases for risk reduction, beginning with the most important project risks. Architectural design for testability involves, in addition to defining testable interface specifications for each major module, establishing a build order that supports thorough testing after each stage of construction. How might spiral development and design for test be complementary or in conflict?

1.5. You manage an online service that sells downloadable video recordings of classic movies. A typical download takes one hour, and an interrupted download must be restarted from the beginning. The number of customers engaged in a download at any given time ranges from about 10 to about 150 during peak hours. On average, your system goes down (dropping all connections) about two times per week, for an average of three minutes each time. If you can double availability or double mean time between failures, but not both, which will you choose? Why?

1.6. Having no a priori operational profile for reliability measurement, Chipmunk will depend on alpha and beta testing to assess the readiness of its online purchase functionality for public release. Beta testing will be carried out in retail outlets, by retail store personnel, and then by customers with retail store personnel looking on. How might this beta testing still be misleading with respect to reliability of the software as it will be used at home and work by actual customers? What might Chipmunk do to ameliorate potential problems from this reliability misestimation?

1.7. The junior test designers of Chipmunk Computers are annoyed by the procedures for storing test cases together with scaffolding, test results, and related documentation. They blame the extra effort needed to produce and store such data for delays in test design and execution. They argue for reducing the data to store to the minimum required for reexecuting test cases, eliminating details of test documentation, and limiting test results to the information needed for generating oracles. What argument(s) might the quality manager use to convince the junior test designers of the usefulness of storing all this information?

Chapter 2

A Framework for Test and Analysis

The purpose of software test and analysis is either to assess software qualities or else to make it possible to improve the software by finding defects. Of the many kinds of software qualities, those addressed by the analysis and test techniques discussed in this book are the *dependability* properties of the software *product*.

There are no perfect test or analysis techniques, nor a single "best" technique for all circumstances. Rather, techniques exist in a complex space of trade-offs, and often have complementary strengths and weaknesses. This chapter describes the nature of those trade-offs and some of their consequences, and thereby a conceptual framework for understanding and better integrating material from later chapters on individual techniques.

It is unfortunate that much of the available literature treats testing and analysis as independent or even as exclusive choices, removing the opportunity to exploit their complementarities. Armed with a basic understanding of the trade-offs and of strengths and weaknesses of individual techniques, one can select from and combine an array of choices to improve the cost-effectiveness of verification.

2.1 Validation and Verification

While software products and processes may be judged on several properties ranging from time-to-market to performance to usability, the software test and analysis techniques we consider are focused more narrowly on improving or assessing dependability.

Assessing the degree to which a software system actually fulfills its requirements, in the sense of meeting the user's real needs, is called *validation.* Fulfilling requirements is not the same as conforming to a requirements specification. A specification is a statement about a particular proposed solution to a problem, and that proposed solution may or may not achieve its goals. Moreover, specifications are written by people, and therefore contain mistakes. A system that meets its actual goals is *useful*, while a

Δ validation

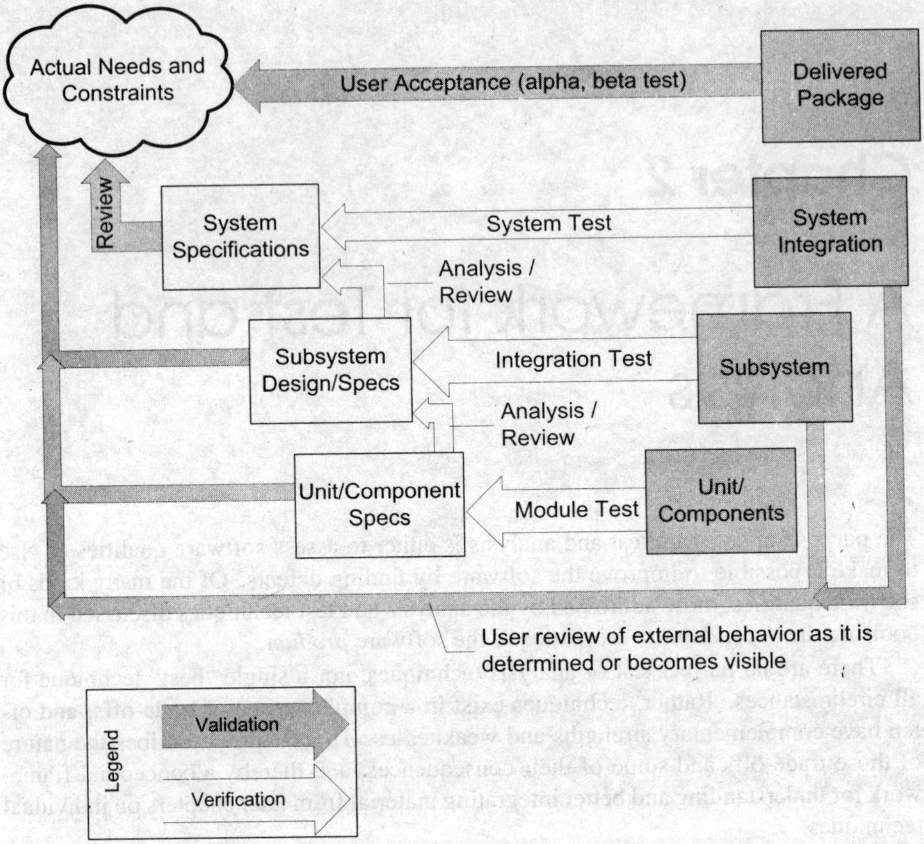

Figure 2.1: Validation activities check work products against actual user requirements, while verification activities check consistency of work products.

Δ dependable

Δ verification

system that is consistent with its specification is *dependable*.[1]

"Verification" is checking the consistency of an implementation with a specification. Here, "specification" and "implementation" are roles, not particular artifacts. For example, an overall design could play the role of "specification" and a more detailed design could play the role of "implementation"; checking whether the detailed design is consistent with the overall design would then be verification of the detailed design. Later, the same detailed design could play the role of "specification" with respect to

[1] A good requirements document, or set of documents, should include both a requirements analysis and a requirements specification, and should clearly distinguish between the two. The requirements analysis describes the problem. The specification describes a proposed solution. This is not a book about requirements engineering, but we note in passing that confounding requirements analysis with requirements specification will inevitably have negative impacts on both validation and verification.

source code, which would be verified against the design. In every case, though, verification is a check of consistency between two descriptions, in contrast to validation which compares a description (whether a requirements specification, a design, or a running system) against actual needs.

Figure 2.1 sketches the relation of verification and validation activities with respect to artifacts produced in a software development project. The figure should not be interpreted as prescribing a sequential process, since the goal of a consistent set of artifacts and user satisfaction are the same whether the software artifacts (specifications, design, code, etc.) are developed sequentially, iteratively, or in parallel. Verification activities check consistency between descriptions (design and specifications) at adjacent levels of detail, and between these descriptions and code.[2] Validation activities attempt to gauge whether the system actually satisfies its intended purpose.

Validation activities refer primarily to the overall system specification and the final code. With respect to overall system specification, validation checks for discrepancies between actual needs and the system specification as laid out by the analysts, to ensure that the specification is an adequate guide to building a product that will fulfill its goals. With respect to final code, validation aims at checking discrepancies between actual need and the final product, to reveal possible failures of the development process and to make sure the product meets end-user expectations. Validation checks between the specification and final product are primarily checks of decisions that were left open in the specification (e.g., details of the user interface or product features). Chapter 4 provides a more thorough discussion of validation and verification activities in particular software process models.

We have omitted one important set of verification checks from Figure 2.1 to avoid clutter. In addition to checks that compare two or more artifacts, verification includes checks for self-consistency and well-formedness. For example, while we cannot judge that a program is "correct" except in reference to a specification of what it should do, we can certainly determine that some programs are "incorrect" because they are ill-formed. We may likewise determine that a specification itself is ill-formed because it is inconsistent (requires two properties that cannot both be true) or ambiguous (can be interpreted to require some property or not), or because it does not satisfy some other well-formedness constraint that we impose, such as adherence to a standard imposed by a regulatory agency.

Validation against actual requirements necessarily involves human judgment and the potential for ambiguity, misunderstanding, and disagreement. In contrast, a specification should be sufficiently precise and unambiguous that there can be no disagreement about whether a particular system behavior is acceptable. While the term *testing* is often used informally both for gauging usefulness and verifying the product, the activities differ in both goals and approach. Our focus here is primarily on dependability, and thus primarily on verification rather than validation, although techniques for validation and the relation between the two is discussed further in Chapter 22.

Dependability properties include correctness, reliability, robustness, and safety. Correctness is absolute consistency with a specification, always and in all circumstances. Correctness with respect to nontrivial specifications is almost never achieved.

[2]This part of the diagram is a variant of the well-known "V model" of verification and validation.

Reliability is a statistical approximation to correctness, expressed as the likelihood of correct behavior in expected use. Robustness, unlike correctness and reliability, weighs properties as more and less critical, and distinguishes which properties should be maintained even under exceptional circumstances in which full functionality cannot be maintained. Safety is a kind of robustness in which the critical property to be maintained is avoidance of particular hazardous behaviors. Dependability properties are discussed further in Chapter 4.

2.2 Degrees of Freedom

Given a precise specification and a program, it seems that one ought to be able to arrive at some logically sound argument or proof that a program satisfies the specified properties. After all, if a civil engineer can perform mathematical calculations to show that a bridge will carry a specified amount of traffic, shouldn't we be able to similarly apply mathematical logic to verification of programs?

For some properties and some very simple programs, it is in fact possible to obtain a logical correctness argument, albeit at high cost. In a few domains, logical correctness arguments may even be cost-effective for a few isolated, critical components (e.g., a safety interlock in a medical device). In general, though, one cannot produce a complete logical "proof" for the full specification of practical programs in full detail. This is not just a sign that technology for verification is immature. It is, rather, a consequence of one of the most fundamental properties of computation.

undecidability

Even before programmable digital computers were in wide use, computing pioneer Alan Turing proved that some problems cannot be solved by any computer program. The universality of computers — their ability to carry out any programmed algorithm, including simulations of other computers — induces logical paradoxes regarding programs (or algorithms) for analyzing other programs. In particular, logical contradictions ensue from assuming that there is some program *P* that can, for some arbitrary program *Q* and input *I*, determine whether *Q* eventually halts. To avoid those logical contradictions, we must conclude that no such program for solving the "halting problem" can possibly exist.

halting problem

Countless university students have encountered the halting problem in a course on the theory of computing, and most of those who have managed to grasp it at all have viewed it as a purely theoretical result that, whether fascinating or just weird, is irrelevant to practical matters of programming. They have been wrong. Almost every interesting property regarding the behavior of computer programs can be shown to "embed" the halting problem, that is, the existence of an infallible algorithmic check for the property of interest would imply the existence of a program that solves the halting problem, which we know to be impossible.

In theory, undecidability of a property *S* merely implies that for each verification technique for checking *S*, there is at least one "pathological" program for which that technique cannot obtain a correct answer in finite time. It does not imply that verification will always fail or even that it will usually fail, only that it will fail in at least one case. In practice, failure is not only possible but common, and we are forced to accept a significant degree of inaccuracy.

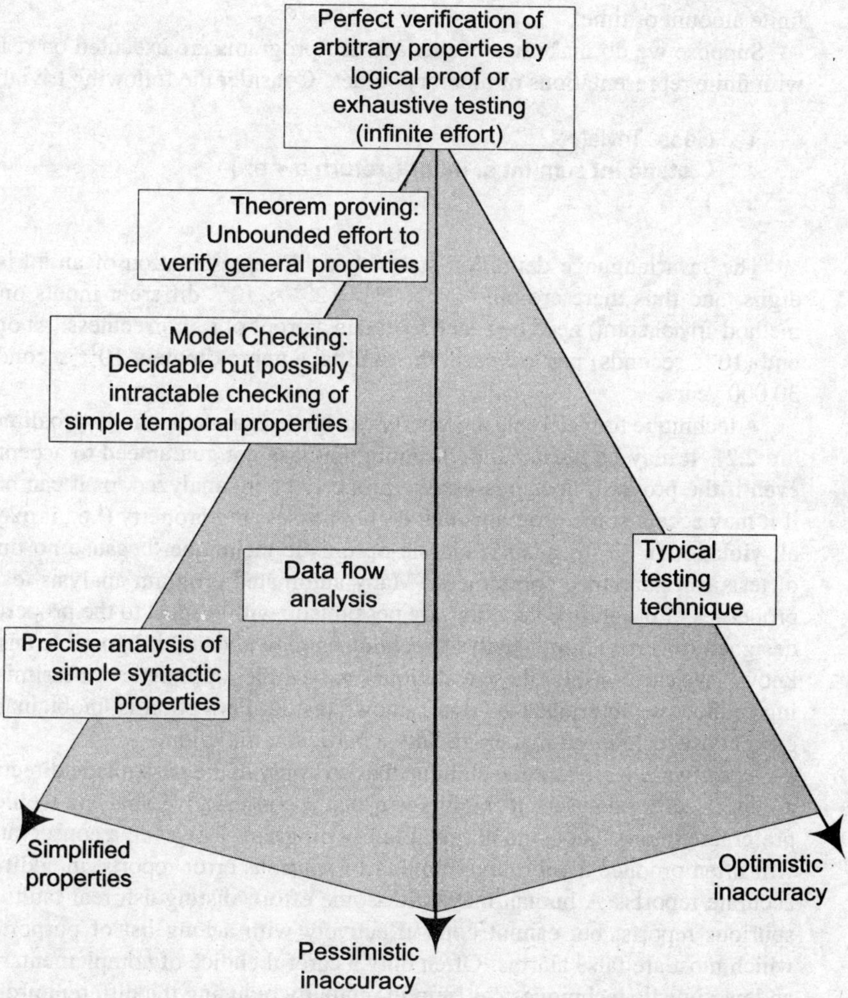

Figure 2.2: Verification trade-off dimensions

Program testing is a verification technique and is as vulnerable to undecidability as other techniques. Exhaustive testing, that is, executing and checking every possible behavior of a program, would be a "proof by cases," which is a perfectly legitimate way to construct a logical proof. How long would this take? If we ignore implementation details such as the size of the memory holding a program and its data, the answer is "forever." That is, for most programs, exhaustive testing cannot be completed in any finite amount of time.

Suppose we do make use of the fact that programs are executed on real machines with finite representations of memory values. Consider the following trivial Java class:

```
class Trivial{
    static int sum(int a, int b) { return a + b; }
}
```

The Java language definition states that the representation of an int is 32 binary digits, and thus there are only $2^{32} \times 2^{32} = 2^{64} \approx 10^{21}$ different inputs on which the method Trivial.sum() need be tested to obtain a proof of its correctness. At one nanosecond (10^{-9} seconds) per test case, this will take approximately 10^{12} seconds, or about 30,000 years.

Δ pessimistic

Δ optimistic

A technique for verifying a property can be inaccurate in one of two directions (Figure 2.2). It may be *pessimistic*, meaning that it is not guaranteed to accept a program even if the program does possess the property being analyzed, or it can be *optimistic* if it may accept some programs that do not possess the property (i.e., it may not detect all violations). Testing is the classic optimistic technique, because no finite number of tests can guarantee correctness. Many automated program analysis techniques for properties of program behaviors[3] are pessimistic with respect to the properties they are designed to verify. Some analysis techniques may give a third possible answer, "don't know." We can consider these techniques to be either optimistic or pessimistic depending on how we interpret the "don't know" result. Perfection is unobtainable, but one can choose techniques that err in only a particular direction.

A software verification technique that errs only in the pessimistic direction is called a *conservative* analysis. It might seem that a conservative analysis would always be preferable to one that could accept a faulty program. However, a conservative analysis will often produce a very large number of spurious error reports, in addition to a few accurate reports. A human may, with some effort, distinguish real faults from a few spurious reports, but cannot cope effectively with a long list of purported faults of which most are false alarms. Often only a careful choice of complementary optimistic and pessimistic techniques can help in mutually reducing the different problems of the techniques and produce acceptable results.

In addition to pessimistic and optimistic inaccuracy, a third dimension of compromise is possible: substituting a property that is more easily checked, or constraining the class of programs that can be checked. Suppose we want to verify a property *S*, but we are not willing to accept the optimistic inaccuracy of testing for *S*, and the only

[3]Why do we bother to say "properties of program behaviors" rather than "program properties?" Because simple syntactic properties of program text, such as declaring variables before they are used or indenting properly, can be decided efficiently and precisely.

A Note on Terminology

Many different terms related to *pessimistic* and *optimistic* inaccuracy appear in the literature on program analysis. We have chosen these particular terms because it is fairly easy to remember which is which. Other terms a reader is likely to encounter include:

Safe: A *safe* analysis has no optimistic inaccuracy; that is, it accepts only correct programs. In other kinds of program analysis, safety is related to the goal of the analysis. For example, a safe analysis related to a program optimization is one that allows that optimization only when the result of the optimization will be correct.

Sound: Soundness is a term to describe evaluation of formulas. An analysis of a program P with respect to a formula F is *sound* if the analysis returns *True* only when the program actually does satisfy the formula. If satisfaction of a formula F is taken as an indication of correctness, then a *sound* analysis is the same as a *safe* or *conservative* analysis.

If the sense of F is reversed (i.e., if the truth of F indicates a fault rather than correctness) then a *sound* analysis is not necessarily *conservative*. In that case it is allowed optimistic inaccuracy but must not have pessimistic inaccuracy. (Note, however, that use of the term *sound* has not always been consistent in the software engineering literature. Some writers use the term *unsound* as we use the term *optimistic*.)

Complete: Completeness, like soundness, is a term to describe evaluation of formulas. An analysis of a program P with respect to a formula F is *complete* if the analysis always returns *True* when the program actually does satisfy the formula. If satisfaction of a formula F is taken as an indication of correctness, then a *complete* analysis is one that admits only optimistic inaccuracy. An analysis that is sound but incomplete is a conservative analysis.

available static analysis techniques for S result in such huge numbers of spurious error messages that they are worthless. Suppose we know some property S' that is a sufficient, but not necessary, condition for S (i.e., the validity of S' implies S, but not the contrary). Maybe S' is so much simpler than S that it can be analyzed with little or no pessimistic inaccuracy. If we check S' rather than S, then we may be able to provide precise error messages that describe a real violation of S' rather than a potential violation of S.

Many examples of substituting simple, checkable properties for actual properties of interest can be found in the design of modern programming languages. Consider, for example, the property that each variable should be initialized with a value before its value is used in an expression. In the C language, a compiler cannot provide a precise static check for this property, because of the possibility of code like the following:

```
int i, sum;
int first=1;
for (i=0; i<10; ++i) {
    if (first) {
        sum=0; first=0;
    }
    sum += i;
}
```

It is impossible in general to determine whether each control flow path can be executed, and while a human will quickly recognize that the variable sum is initialized on the first iteration of the loop, a compiler or other static analysis tool will typically not be able to rule out an execution in which the initialization is skipped on the first iteration. Java neatly solves this problem by making code like this illegal; that is, the rule is that a variable must be initialized on *all* program control paths, whether or not those paths can ever be executed.

Software developers are seldom at liberty to design new restrictions into the programming languages and compilers they use, but the same principle can be applied through external tools, not only for programs but also for other software artifacts. Consider, for example, the following condition that we might wish to impose on requirements documents:

(1) Each significant domain term shall appear with a definition in the glossary of the document.

This property is nearly impossible to check automatically, since determining whether a particular word or phrase is a "significant domain term" is a matter of human judgment. Moreover, human inspection of the requirements document to check this requirement will be extremely tedious and error-prone. What can we do? One approach is to separate the decision that requires human judgment (identifying words and phrases as "significant") from the tedious check for presence in the glossary.

(1a) Each significant domain term shall be set off in the requirements document by the use of a standard style *term*. The default visual representation of the *term* style is a single underline in printed documents and purple text in on-line displays.

(1b) Each word or phrase in the *term* style shall appear with a definition in the glossary of the document.

Property (1a) still requires human judgment, but it is now in a form that is much more amenable to inspection. Property (1b) can be easily automated in a way that will be completely precise (except that the task of determining whether definitions appearing in the glossary are clear and correct must also be left to humans).

As a second example, consider a Web-based service in which user sessions need not directly interact, but they do read and modify a shared collection of data on the server. In this case a critical property is maintaining integrity of the shared data. Testing for this property is notoriously difficult, because a "race condition" (interference between writing data in one process and reading or writing related data in another process) may cause an observable failure only very rarely.

Fortunately, there is a rich body of applicable research results on concurrency control that can be exploited for this application. It would be foolish to rely primarily on direct testing for the desired integrity properties. Instead, one would choose a (well-known, formally verified) concurrency control protocol, such as the two-phase locking protocol, and rely on some combination of static analysis and program testing to check conformance to that protocol. Imposing a particular concurrency control protocol substitutes a much simpler, *sufficient* property (two-phase locking) for the complex property of interest (serializability), at some cost in generality; that is, there are programs that violate two-phase locking and yet, by design or dumb luck, satisfy serializability of data access.

It is a common practice to further impose a global order on lock accesses, which again simplifies testing and analysis. Testing would identify execution sequences in which data is accessed without proper locks, or in which locks are obtained and relinquished in an order that does not respect the two-phase protocol or the global lock order, even if data integrity is not violated on that particular execution, because the locking protocol failure indicates the potential for a dangerous race condition in some other execution that might occur only rarely or under extreme load.

With the adoption of coding conventions that make locking and unlocking actions easy to recognize, it may be possible to rely primarily on flow analysis to determine conformance with the locking protocol, with the role of dynamic testing reduced to a "back-up" to raise confidence in the soundness of the static analysis. Note that the critical decision to impose a particular locking protocol is *not* a post-hoc decision that can be made in a testing "phase" at the end of development. Rather, the plan for verification activities with a suitable balance of cost and assurance is part of system design.

2.3 Varieties of Software

The software testing and analysis techniques presented in the main parts of this book were developed primarily for procedural and object-oriented software. While these "generic" techniques are at least partly applicable to most varieties of software, particular application domains (e.g., real-time and safety-critical software) and construction methods (e.g., concurrency and physical distribution, graphical user interfaces) call for particular properties to be verified, or the relative importance of different properties, as well as imposing constraints on applicable techniques. Typically a software system does not fall neatly into one category but rather has a number of relevant characteristics that must be considered when planning verification.

As an example, consider a physically distributed (networked) system for scheduling a group of individuals. The possibility of concurrent activity introduces considerations that would not be present in a single-threaded system, such as preserving the integrity of data. The concurrency is likely to introduce nondeterminism, or else introduce an obligation to show that the system is deterministic, either of which will almost certainly need to be addressed through some formal analysis. The physical distribution may make it impossible to determine a global system state at one instant, ruling out some simplistic approaches to system test and, most likely, suggesting an approach in which dynamic testing of design conformance of individual processes is combined with static analysis of their interactions. If in addition the individuals to be coordinated are fire trucks, then the criticality of assuring prompt response will likely lead one to choose a design that is amenable to strong analysis of worst-case behavior, whereas an average-case analysis might be perfectly acceptable if the individuals are house painters.

As a second example, consider the software controlling a "soft" dashboard display in an automobile. The display may include ground speed, engine speed (rpm), oil pressure, fuel level, and so on, in addition to a map and navigation information from a global positioning system receiver. Clearly usability issues are paramount, and may even impinge on safety (e.g., if critical information can be hidden beneath or among less critical information). A disciplined approach will not only place a greater emphasis on validation of usability throughout development, but to the extent possible will also attempt to codify usability guidelines in a form that permits verification. For example, if the usability group determines that the fuel gauge should always be visible when the fuel level is below a quarter of a tank, then this becomes a specified property that is subject to verification. The graphical interface also poses a challenge in effectively checking output. This must be addressed partly in the architectural design of the system, which can make automated testing feasible or not depending on the interfaces between high-level operations (e.g., opening or closing a window, checking visibility of a window) and low-level graphical operations and representations.

Summary

Verification activities are comparisons to determine the consistency of two or more software artifacts, or self-consistency, or consistency with an externally imposed criterion. Verification is distinct from validation, which is consideration of whether software fulfills its actual purpose. Software development always includes some validation and some verification, although different development approaches may differ greatly in their relative emphasis.

Precise answers to verification questions are sometimes difficult or impossible to obtain, in theory as well as in practice. Verification is therefore an art of compromise, accepting some degree of optimistic inaccuracy (as in testing) or pessimistic inaccuracy (as in many static analysis techniques) or choosing to check a property that is only an approximation of what we really wish to check. Often the best approach will not be exclusive reliance on one technique, but careful choice of a portfolio of test and analysis techniques selected to obtain acceptable results at acceptable cost, and addressing particular challenges posed by characteristics of the application domain or software.

Further Reading

The "V" model of verification and validation (of which Figure 2.1 is a variant) appears in many software engineering textbooks, and in some form can be traced at least as far back as Myers' classic book [Mye79]. The distinction between validation and verification as given here follow's Boehm [Boe81], who has most memorably described validation as "building the right system" and verification as "building the system right."

The limits of testing have likewise been summarized in a famous aphorism, by Dijkstra [Dij72] who pronounced that "Testing can show the presence of faults, but not their absence." This phrase has sometimes been interpreted as implying that one should always prefer formal verification to testing, but the reader will have noted that we do not draw that conclusion. Howden's 1976 paper [How76] is among the earliest treatments of the implications of computability theory for program testing.

A variant of the diagram in Figure 2.2 and a discussion of pessimistic and optimistic inaccuracy were presented by Young and Taylor [YT89]. A more formal characterization of conservative abstractions in static analysis, called abstract interpretation, was introduced by Cousot and Cousot in a seminal paper that is, unfortunately, nearly unreadable [CC77]. We enthusiastically recommend Jones's lucid introduction to abstract interpretation [JN95], which is suitable for readers who have a firm general background in computer science and logic but no special preparation in programming semantics.

There are few general treatments of trade-offs and combinations of software testing and static analysis, although there are several specific examples, such as work in communication protocol conformance testing [vBDZ89, FvBK+91]. The two-phase locking protocol mentioned in Section 2.2 is described in several texts on databases; Bernstein et al. [BHG87] is particularly thorough.

Exercises

2.1. The Chipmunk marketing division is worried about the start-up time of the new version of the RodentOS operating system (an (imaginary) operating system of Chipmunk). The marketing division representative suggests a software requirement stating that the start-up time shall not be annoying to users.

Explain why this simple requirement is not verifiable and try to reformulate the requirement to make it verifiable.

2.2. Consider a simple specification language *SL* that describes systems diagrammatically in terms of *functions*, which represent data transformations and correspond to nodes of the diagram, and *flows*, which represent data flows and correspond to arcs of the diagram.[4] Diagrams can be hierarchically refined by associating a function F (a node of the diagram) with an *SL* specification that details function F. Flows are labeled to indicate the type of data.

Suggest some checks for self-consistency for *SL*.

2.3. A calendar program should provide *timely* reminders; for example, it should remind the user of an upcoming event early enough for the user to take action, but not too early. Unfortunately, "early enough" and "too early" are qualities that can only be validated with actual users. How might you derive verifiable dependability properties from the timeliness requirement?

2.4. It is sometimes important in multi-threaded applications to ensure that a sequence of accesses by one thread to an aggregate data structure (e.g., some kind of table) appears to other threads as an atomic transaction. When the shared data structure is maintained by a database system, the database system typically uses concurrency control protocols to ensure the atomicity of the transactions it manages. No such automatic support is typically available for data structures maintained by a program in main memory.

Among the options available to programmers to ensure serializability (the illusion of atomic access) are the following:

- The programmer could maintain very coarse-grain locking, preventing any interleaving of accesses to the shared data structure, even when such interleaving would be harmless. (For example, each transaction could be encapsulated in an single synchronized Java method.) This approach can cause a great deal of unnecessary blocking between threads, hurting performance, but it is almost trivial to verify either automatically or manually.
- Automated static analysis techniques can sometimes verify serializability with finer-grain locking, even when some methods do not use locks at all. This approach can still reject some sets of methods that would ensure serializability.
- The programmer could be required to use a particular concurrency control protocol in his or her code, and we could build a static analysis tool that checks for conformance with that protocol. For example, adherence to the common two-phase-locking protocol, with a few restrictions, can be checked in this way.
- We might augment the data accesses to build a *serializability graph* structure representing the "happens before" relation among transactions in testing. It can be shown that the transactions executed in serializable manner if and only if the serializability graph is acyclic.

[4]Readers expert in Structured Analysis may have noticed that *SL* resembles a simple Structured Analysis specification

Compare the relative positions of these approaches on the three axes of verification techniques: pessimistic inaccuracy, optimistic inaccuracy, and simplified properties.

2.5. When updating a program (e.g., for removing a fault, changing or adding a functionality), programmers may introduce new faults or expose previously hidden faults. To be sure that the updated version maintains the functionality provided by the previous version, it is common practice to reexecute the test cases designed for the former versions of the program. Reexecuting test cases designed for previous versions is called regression testing.

When testing large complex programs, the number of regression test cases may be large. If updated software must be expedited (e.g., to repair a security vulnerability before it is exploited), test designers may need to select a subset of regression test cases to be reexecuted.

Subsets of test cases can be selected according to any of several different criteria. An interesting property of some regression test selection criteria is that they do not to exclude any test case that could possibly reveal a fault.

How would you classify such a property according to the sidebar of page 21?

Chapter 3

Basic Principles

Mature engineering disciplines are characterized by basic principles. Principles provide a rationale for defining, selecting, and applying techniques and methods. They are valid beyond a single technique and over a time span in which techniques come and go, and can help engineers study, define, evaluate, and apply new techniques.

Analysis and testing (A&T) has been common practice since the earliest software projects. A&T activities were for a long time based on common sense and individual skills. It has emerged as a distinct discipline only in the last three decades.

This chapter advocates six principles that characterize various approaches and techniques for analysis and testing: sensitivity, redundancy, restriction, partition, visibility, and feedback. Some of these principles, such as partition, visibility, and feedback, are quite general in engineering. Others, notably sensitivity, redundancy, and restriction, are specific to A&T and contribute to characterizing A&T as a discipline.

3.1 Sensitivity

Human developers make errors, producing faults in software. Faults may lead to failures, but faulty software may not fail on every execution. The sensitivity principle states that it is better to fail every time than sometimes.

Consider the cost of detecting and repairing a software fault. If it is detected immediately (e.g., by an on-the-fly syntactic check in a design editor), then the cost of correction is very small, and in fact the line between fault prevention and fault detection is blurred. If a fault is detected in inspection or unit testing, the cost is still relatively small. If a fault survives initial detection efforts at the unit level, but triggers a failure detected in integration testing, the cost of correction is much greater. If the first failure is detected in system or acceptance testing, the cost is very high indeed, and the most costly faults are those detected by customers in the field.

A fault that triggers a failure on every execution is unlikely to survive past unit testing. A characteristic of faults that escape detection until much later is that they trigger failures only rarely, or in combination with circumstances that seem unrelated or are difficult to control. For example, a fault that results in a failure only for some unusual configurations of customer equipment may be difficult and expensive to detect.

A fault that results in a failure randomly but very rarely — for example, a race condition that only occasionally causes data corruption — may likewise escape detection until the software is in use by thousands of customers, and even then be difficult to diagnose and correct.

The small C program in Figure 3.1 has three faulty calls to string copy procedures. The call to strcpy, strncpy, and stringCopy all pass a source string "Muddled," which is too long to fit in the array middle. The vulnerability of strcpy is well known, and is the culprit in the by-now-standard buffer overflow attacks on many network services. Unfortunately, the fault may or may not cause an observable failure depending on the arrangement of memory (in this case, it depends on what appears in the position that would be middle[7], which will be overwritten with a newline character). The standard recommendation is to use strncpy in place of strcpy. While strncpy avoids overwriting other memory, it truncates the input without warning, and sometimes without properly null-terminating the output. The replacement function stringCopy, on the other hand, uses an assertion to ensure that, if the target string is too long, the program always fails in an observable manner.

The sensitivity principle says that we should try to make these faults easier to detect by making them cause failure more often. It can be applied in three main ways: at the design level, changing the way in which the program fails; at the analysis and testing level, choosing a technique more reliable with respect to the property of interest; and at the environment level, choosing a technique that reduces the impact of external factors on the results.

Replacing strcpy and strncpy with stringCopy in the program of Figure 3.1 is a simple example of application of the sensitivity principle in design. Run-time array bounds checking in many programming languages (including Java but not C or C++) is an example of the sensitivity principle applied at the language level. A variety of tools and replacements for the standard memory management library are available to enhance sensitivity to memory allocation and reference faults in C and C++.

The fail-fast property of Java iterators is another application of the sensitivity principle. A Java iterator provides a way of accessing each item in a collection data structure. Without the fail-fast property, modifying the collection while iterating over it could lead to unexpected and arbitrary results, and failure might occur rarely and be hard to detect and diagnose. A fail-fast iterator has the property that an immediate and observable failure (throwing ConcurrentModificationException) occurs when the illegal modification occurs. Although fail-fast behavior is not guaranteed if the update occurs in a different thread, a fail-fast iterator is far more sensitive than an iterator without the fail-fast property.

So far, we have discussed the sensitivity principle applied to design and code: always privilege design and code solutions that lead to consistent behavior, that is, such that fault occurrence does not depend on uncontrolled execution conditions that may mask faults, thus resulting in random failures. The sensitivity principle can also be applied to test and analysis techniques. In this case, we privilege techniques that cause faults to consistently manifest in failures.

Deadlock and race conditions in concurrent systems may depend on the relative speed of execution of the different threads or processes, and a race condition may lead

```
/**
 * Worse than broken: Are you feeling lucky?
 */

#include <assert.h>

  char before[ ] = "=Before=";
  char middle[ ] = "Middle";
  char after[ ] = "=After=";

void show() {
   printf("%s\n%s\n%s\n", before, middle, after);
}

void stringCopy(char *target, const char *source, int howBig);

int main(int argc, char *argv) {
   show();
   strcpy(middle, "Muddled");     /* Fault, but may not fail */
   show();
   strncpy(middle, "Muddled", sizeof(middle)); /* Fault, may not fail */
   show();
   stringCopy(middle, "Muddled",sizeof(middle)); /* Guaranteed to fail */
   show();
}

/* Sensitive version of strncpy; can be counted on to fail
 * in an observable way EVERY time the source is too large
 * for the target, unlike the standard strncpy or strcpy.
 */
void stringCopy(char *target, const char *source, int howBig) {
   assert(strlen(source) < howBig);
   strcpy(target, source);
}
```

Figure 3.1: Standard C functions strcpy *and* strncpy *may or may not fail when the source string is too long. The procedure* stringCopy is sensitive: *It is guaranteed to fail in an observable way if the source string is too long.*

to an observable failure only under rare conditions. Testing a concurrent system on a single configuration may fail to reveal deadlocks and race conditions. Repeating the tests with different configurations and system loads may help, but it is difficult to predict or control the circumstances under which failure occurs. We may observe that testing is not sensitive enough for revealing deadlocks and race conditions, and we may substitute other techniques that are more sensitive and less dependent on factors outside the developers' and testers' control. Model checking and reachability analysis techniques are limited in the scope of the faults they can detect, but they are very sensitive to this particular class of faults, having the advantage that they attain complete independence from any particular execution environment by systematically exploring all possible interleavings of processes.

Test adequacy criteria identify partitions of the input domain of the unit under test that must be sampled by test suites. For example, the statement coverage criterion requires each statement to be exercised at least once, that is, it groups inputs according to the statements they execute. Reliable criteria require that inputs belonging to the same class produce the same test results: They all fail or they all succeed. When this happens, we can infer the correctness of a program with respect to the a whole class of inputs from a single execution. Unfortunately, general reliable criteria do not exist[1].

Code inspection can reveal many subtle faults. However, inspection teams may produce completely different results depending on the cohesion of the team, the discipline of the inspectors, and their knowledge of the application domain and the design technique. The use of detailed checklists and a disciplined review process may reduce the influence of external factors, such as teamwork attitude, inspectors' discipline, and domain knowledge, thus increasing the predictability of the results of inspection. In this case, sensitivity is applied to reduce the influence of external factors.

Similarly, skilled test designers can derive excellent test suites, but the quality of the test suites depends on the mood of the designers. Systematic testing criteria may not do better than skilled test designers, but they can reduce the influence of external factors, such as the tester's mood.

3.2 Redundancy

Redundancy is the opposite of independence. If one part of a software artifact (program, design document, etc.) constrains the content of another, then they are not entirely independent, and it is possible to check them for consistency.

The concept and definition of redundancy are taken from information theory. In communication, redundancy can be introduced into messages in the form of error-detecting and error-correcting codes to guard against transmission errors. In software test and analysis, we wish to detect faults that could lead to differences between intended behavior and actual behavior, so the most valuable form of redundancy is in the form of an explicit, redundant statement of intent.

Where redundancy can be introduced or exploited with an automatic, algorithmic check for consistency, it has the advantage of being much cheaper and more thorough

[1]Existence of a general, reliable test coverage criterion would allow us to prove the equivalence of programs. Readers interested in this topic will find more information in Chapter 9.

than dynamic testing or manual inspection. Static type checking is a classic application of this principle: The type declaration is a statement of intent that is at least partly redundant with the use of a variable in the source code. The type declaration constrains other parts of the code, so a consistency check (type check) can be applied.

An important trend in the evolution of programming languages is introduction of additional ways to declare intent and automatically check for consistency. For example, Java enforces rules about explicitly declaring each exception that can be thrown by a method.

Checkable redundancy is not limited to program source code, nor is it something that can be introduced only by programming language designers. For example, software design tools typically provide ways to check consistency between different design views or artifacts. One can also intentionally introduce redundancy in other software artifacts, even those that are not entirely formal. For example, one might introduce rules quite analogous to type declarations for semistructured requirements specification documents, and thereby enable automatic checks for consistency and some limited kinds of completeness.

When redundancy is already present — as between a software specification document and source code — then the remaining challenge is to make sure the information is represented in a way that facilitates cheap, thorough consistency checks. Checks that can be implemented by automatic tools are usually preferable, but there is value even in organizing information to make inconsistency easier to spot in manual inspection.

Of course, one cannot always obtain cheap, thorough checks of source code and other documents. Sometimes redundancy is exploited instead with run-time checks. Defensive programming, explicit run-time checks for conditions that should always be true if the program is executing correctly, is another application of redundancy in programming.

3.3 Restriction

When there are no acceptably cheap and effective ways to check a property, sometimes one can change the problem by checking a different, more restrictive property or by limiting the check to a smaller, more restrictive class of programs.

Consider the problem of ensuring that each variable is initialized before it is used, on every execution. Simple as the property is, it is not possible for a compiler or analysis tool to precisely determine whether it holds. See the program in Figure 3.2 for an illustration. Can the variable k ever be uninitialized the first time i is added to it? If someCondition(0) always returns true, then k will be initialized to zero on the first time through the loop, before k is incremented, so perhaps there is no potential for a run-time error — but method someCondition could be arbitrarily complex and might even depend on some condition in the environment. Java's solution to this problem is to enforce a stricter, simpler condition: A program is not permitted to have any syntactic control paths on which an uninitialized reference could occur, regardless of whether those paths could actually be executed. The program in Figure 3.2 has such a path, so the Java compiler rejects it.

Java's rule for initialization before use is a program source code restriction that

```
/** A trivial method with a potentially uninitialized variable.
 * Maybe someCondition(0) is always true, and therefore k is
 * always initialized before use ... but it's impossible, in
 * general, to know for sure. Java rejects the method.
 */
static void questionable() {
    int k;
    for (int i=0; i < 10; ++i) {
        if (someCondition(i)) {
            k = 0;
        } else {
            k += i;
        }
    }
    System.out.println(k);
    }
}
```

Figure 3.2: Can the variable k *ever be uninitialized the first time* i *is added to it? The property is undecidable, so Java enforces a simpler, stricter property.*

enables precise, efficient checking of a simple but important property by the compiler. The choice of programming language(s) for a project may entail a number of such restrictions that impact test and analysis. Additional restrictions may be imposed in the form of programming standards (e.g., restricting the use of type casts or pointer arithmetic in C), or by tools in a development environment. Other forms of restriction can apply to architectural and detailed design.

Consider, for example, the problem of ensuring that a transaction consisting of a sequence of accesses to a complex data structure by one process appears to the outside world as if it had occurred atomically, rather than interleaved with transactions of other processes. This property is called *serializability*: The end result of a set of such transactions should appear as if they were applied in some serial order, even if they didn't.

One way to ensure serializability is to make the transactions really serial (e.g., by putting the whole sequence of operations in each transaction within a Java synchronized block), but that approach may incur unacceptable performance penalties. One would like to allow interleaving of transactions that don't interfere, while still ensuring the appearance of atomic access, and one can devise a variety of locking and versioning techniques to achieve this. Unfortunately, checking directly to determine whether the serializability property has been achieved is very expensive at run-time, and precisely checking whether it holds on all possible executions is impossible. Fortunately, the problem becomes much easier if we impose a particular locking or versioning scheme on the program at design time. Then the problem becomes one of proving, on the one hand, that the particular concurrency control protocol has the desired property, and then checking that the program obeys the protocol. Database researchers have completed the first step, and some of the published and well-known concurrency control protocols are trivial to check at run-time and simple enough that (with some modest additional restrictions) they can be checked even by source code analysis.

From the above examples it should be clear that the restriction principle is useful mainly during design and specification; it can seldom be applied post hoc on a complete software product. In other words, restriction is mainly a principle to be applied in design for test. Often it can be applied not only to solve a single problem (like detecting potential access of uninitialized variables, or nonserializable execution of transactions) but also at a more general, architectural level to simplify a whole set of analysis problems.

Stateless component interfaces are an example of restriction applied at the architectural level. An interface is stateless if each service request (method call, remote procedure call, message send and reply) is independent of all others; that is, the service does not "remember" anything about previous requests. Stateless interfaces are far easier to test because the correctness of each service request and response can be checked independently, rather than considering all their possible sequences or interleavings. A famous example of simplifying component interfaces by making them stateless is the Hypertext Transport Protocol (HTTP) 1.0 of the World-Wide-Web, which made Web servers not only much simpler and more robust but also much easier to test.

3.4 Partition

Partition, often also known as "divide and conquer," is a general engineering principle. Dividing a complex problem into subproblems to be attacked and solved independently is probably the most common human problem-solving strategy. Software engineering in particular applies this principle in many different forms and at almost all development levels, from early requirements specifications to code and maintenance. Analysis and testing are no exception: the partition principle is widely used and exploited.

Partitioning can be applied both at process and technique levels. At the process level, we divide complex activities into sets of simple activities that can be attacked independently. For example, testing is usually divided into unit, integration, subsystem, and system testing. In this way, we can focus on different sources of faults at different steps, and at each step, we can take advantage of the results of the former steps. For instance, we can use units that have been tested as stubs for integration testing. Some static analysis techniques likewise follow the modular structure of the software system to divide an analysis problem into smaller steps.

Many static analysis techniques first construct a model of a system and then analyze the model. In this way they divide the overall analysis into two subtasks: first simplify the system to make the proof of the desired properties feasible and then prove the property with respect to the simplified model. The question "Does this program have the desired property?" is decomposed into two questions, "Does this model have the desired property?" and "Is this an accurate model of the program?"

Since it is not possible to execute the program with every conceivable input, systematic testing strategies must identify a finite number of classes of test cases to execute. Whether the classes are derived from specifications (functional testing) or from program structure (structural testing), the process of enumerating test obligations proceeds by dividing the sources of information into significant elements (clauses or special values identifiable in specifications, statements or paths in programs), and creating test cases that cover each such element or certain combinations of elements.

3.5 Visibility

Visibility means the ability to measure progress or status against goals. In software engineering, one encounters the visibility principle mainly in the form of process visibility, and then mainly in the form of schedule visibility: ability to judge the state of development against a project schedule. Quality process visibility also applies to measuring achieved (or predicted) quality against quality goals. The principle of visibility involves setting goals that can be assessed as well as devising methods to assess their realization.

Visibility is closely related to observability, the ability to extract useful information from a software artifact. The architectural design and build plan of a system determines what will be observable at each stage of development, which in turn largely determines the visibility of progress against goals at that stage.

A variety of simple techniques can be used to improve observability. For example, it is no accident that important Internet protocols like HTTP and SMTP (Simple Mail Transport Protocol, used by Internet mail servers) are based on the exchange of simple textual commands. The choice of simple, human-readable text rather than a more compact binary encoding has a small cost in performance and a large payoff in observability, including making construction of test drivers and oracles much simpler. Use of human-readable and human-editable files is likewise advisable wherever the performance cost is acceptable.

A variant of observability through direct use of simple text encodings is providing readers and writers to convert between other data structures and simple, human-readable and editable text. For example, when designing classes that implement a complex data structure, designing and implementing also a translation from a simple text format to the internal structure, and vice versa, will often pay back handsomely in both ad hoc and systematic testing. For similar reasons it is often useful to design and implement an equality check for objects, even when it is not necessary to the functionality of the software product.

3.6 Feedback

Feedback is another classic engineering principle that applies to analysis and testing. Feedback applies both to the process itself (process improvement) and to individual techniques (e.g., using test histories to prioritize regression testing).

Systematic inspection and walkthrough derive part of their success from feedback. Participants in inspection are guided by checklists, and checklists are revised and refined based on experience. New checklist items may be derived from root cause analysis, analyzing previously observed failures to identify the initial errors that lead to them.

Summary

Principles constitute the core of a discipline. They form the basis of methods, techniques, methodologies and tools. They permit understanding, comparing, evaluating and extending different approaches, and they constitute the lasting basis of knowledge of a discipline.

The six principles described in this chapter are

- Sensitivity: better to fail every time than sometimes,
- Redundancy: making intentions explicit,
- Restriction: making the problem easier,
- Partition: divide and conquer,
- Visibility: making information accessible, and
- Feedback: applying lessons from experience in process and techniques.

Principles are identified heuristically by searching for a common denominator of techniques that apply to various problems and exploit different methods, sometimes borrowing ideas from other disciplines, sometimes observing recurrent phenomena. Potential principles are validated by finding existing and new techniques that exploit the underlying ideas. Generality and usefulness of principles become evident only with time. The initial list of principles proposed in this chapter is certainly incomplete. Readers are invited to validate the proposed principles and identify additional principles.

Further Reading

Analysis and testing is a relatively new discipline. To our knowledge, the principles underlying analysis and testing have not been discussed in the literature previously. Some of the principles advocated in this chapter are shared with other software engineering disciplines and are discussed in many books. A good introduction to software engineering principles is the third chapter of Ghezzi, Jazayeri, and Mandrioli's book on software engineering [GJM02].

Exercises

3.1. Indicate which principles guided the following choices:

1. Use an externally readable format also for internal files, when possible.
2. Collect and analyze data about faults revealed and removed from the code.
3. Separate test and debugging activities; that is, separate the design and execution of test cases to reveal failures (test) from the localization and removal of the corresponding faults (debugging).
4. Distinguish test case design from execution.
5. Produce complete fault reports.
6. Use information from test case design to improve requirements and design specifications.
7. Provide interfaces for fully inspecting the internal state of a class.

3.2. A simple mechanism for augmenting fault tolerance consists of replicating computation and comparing the obtained results. Can we consider redundancy for fault tolerance an application of the redundancy principle?

3.3. A system safety specification describes prohibited behaviors (what the system must never do). Explain how specified safety properties can be viewed as an implementation of the redundancy principle.

3.4. Process visibility can be increased by extracting information about the progress of the process. Indicate some information that can be easily produced to increase process visibility.

Chapter 4

Test and Analysis Activities Within a Software Process

Dependability and other qualities of software are not ingredients that can be added in a final step before delivery. Rather, software quality results from a whole set of interdependent activities, among which analysis and testing are necessary but far from sufficient. And while one often hears of a testing "phase" in software development, as if testing were a distinct activity that occurred at a particular point in development, one should not confuse this flurry of test execution with the whole process of software test and analysis any more than one would confuse program compilation with programming.

Testing and analysis activities occur throughout the development and evolution of software systems, from early in requirements engineering through delivery and subsequent evolution. Quality depends on every part of the software process, not only on software analysis and testing; no amount of testing and analysis can make up for poor quality arising from other activities. On the other hand, an essential feature of software processes that produce high-quality products is that software test and analysis is thoroughly integrated and not an afterthought.

4.1 The Quality Process

One can identify particular activities and responsibilities in a software development process that are focused primarily on ensuring adequate dependability of the software product, much as one can identify other activities and responsibilities concerned primarily with project schedule or with product usability. It is convenient to group these quality assurance activities under the rubric "quality process," although we must also recognize that quality is intertwined with and inseparable from other facets of the overall process. Like other parts of an overall software process, the quality process provides a framework for selecting and arranging activities aimed at a particular goal, while also considering interactions and trade-offs with other important goals. All software development activities reflect constraints and trade-offs, and quality activities are no exception. For example, high dependability is usually in tension with time to market, and in most cases it is better to achieve a reasonably high degree of dependability on a tight schedule than to achieve ultra-high dependability on a much longer schedule, although the opposite is true in some domains (e.g., certain medical devices).

The quality process should be structured for completeness, timeliness, and cost-effectiveness. Completeness means that appropriate activities are planned to detect each important class of faults. What the important classes of faults are depends on the application domain, the organization, and the technologies employed (e.g., memory leaks are an important class of faults for C++ programs, but seldom for Java programs). Timeliness means that faults are detected at a point of high leverage, which in practice almost always means that they are detected as early as possible. Cost-effectiveness means that, subject to the constraints of completeness and timeliness, one chooses activities depending on their cost as well as their effectiveness. Cost must be considered over the whole development cycle and product life, so the dominant factor is likely to be the cost of repeating an activity through many change cycles.

Activities that one would typically consider as being in the domain of quality assurance or quality improvement, that is, activities whose primary goal is to prevent or detect faults, intertwine and interact with other activities carried out by members of a software development team. For example, architectural design of a software system has an enormous impact on the test and analysis approaches that will be feasible and on their cost. A precise, relatively formal architectural model may form the basis for several static analyses of the model itself and of the consistency between the model and its implementation, while another architecture may be inadequate for static analysis and, if insufficiently precise, of little help even in forming an integration test plan.

The intertwining and mutual impact of quality activities on other development activities suggests that it would be foolish to put off quality activities until late in a project. The effects run not only from other development activities to quality activities but also in the other direction. For example, early test planning during requirements engineering typically clarifies and improves requirements specifications. Developing a test plan during architectural design may suggest structures and interfaces that not only facilitate testing earlier in development, but also make key interfaces simpler and more precisely defined.

There is also another reason for carrying out quality activities at the earliest opportunity and for preferring earlier to later activities when either could serve to detect the same fault: The single best predictor of the cost of repairing a software defect is the time between its introduction and its detection. A defect introduced in coding is far cheaper to repair during unit test than later during integration or system test, and most expensive if it is detected by a user of the fielded system. A defect introduced during requirements engineering (e.g., an ambiguous requirement) is relatively cheap to repair at that stage, but may be hugely expensive if it is only uncovered by a dispute about the results of a system acceptance test.

4.2 Planning and Monitoring

Process visibility is a key factor in software process in general, and software quality processes in particular. A process is visible to the extent that one can answer the question, "How does our progress compare to our plan?" Typically, schedule visibility is a main emphasis in process design ("Are we on schedule? How far ahead or behind?"), but in software quality process an equal emphasis is needed on progress against quality goals. If one cannot gain confidence in the quality of the software system long before it reaches final testing, the quality process has not achieved adequate visibility.

process visibility

A well-designed quality process balances several activities across the whole development process, selecting and arranging them to be as cost-effective as possible, and to improve early visibility. Visibility is particularly challenging and is one reason (among several) that quality activities are usually placed as early in a software process as possible. For example, one designs test cases at the earliest opportunity (not "just in time") and uses both automated and manual static analysis techniques on software artifacts that are produced before actual code.

Early visibility also motivates the use of "proxy" measures, that is, use of quantifiable attributes that are not identical to the properties that one really wishes to measure, but that have the advantage of being measurable earlier in development. For example, we know that the number of faults in design or code is not a true measure of reliability. Nonetheless, one may count faults uncovered in design inspections as an early indicator of potential quality problems, because the alternative of waiting to receive a more accurate estimate from reliability testing is unacceptable.

Quality goals can be achieved only through careful planning of activities that are matched to the identified objectives. Planning is integral to the quality process and is elaborated and revised through the whole project. It encompasses both an overall strategy for test and analysis, and more detailed test plans.

The overall analysis and test strategy identifies company- or project-wide standards that must be satisfied: procedures for obtaining quality certificates required for certain classes of products, techniques and tools that must be used, and documents that must be produced. Some companies develop and certify procedures following international standards such as ISO 9000 or SEI Capability Maturity Model, which require detailed documentation and management of analysis and test activities and well-defined phases, documents, techniques, and tools. A&T strategies are described in detail in Chapter 20, and a sample strategy document for the Chipmunk Web presence is given in Chapter 24.

A&T strategy

The initial build plan for Chipmunk Web-based purchasing functionality includes an analysis and test plan. A complete analysis and test plan is a comprehensive description of the quality process and includes several items: It indicates objectives and scope of the test and analysis activities; it describes documents and other items that must be available for performing the planned activities, integrating the quality process with the software development process; it identifies items to be tested, thus allowing for simple completeness checks and detailed planning; it distinguishes features to be tested from those not to be tested; it selects analysis and test activities that are considered essential for success of the quality process; and finally it identifies the staff involved in analysis and testing and their respective and mutual responsibilities.

A&T plan

The final analysis and test plan includes additional information that illustrates constraints, pass and fail criteria, schedule, deliverables, hardware and software requirements, risks, and contingencies. Constraints indicate deadlines and limits that may be derived from the hardware and software implementation of the system under analysis and the tools available for analysis and testing. Pass and fail criteria indicate when a test or analysis activity succeeds or fails, thus supporting monitoring of the quality process. The schedule describes the individual tasks to be performed and provides a feasible schedule. Deliverables specify which documents, scaffolding and test cases must be produced, and indicate the quality expected from such deliverables. Hardware, environment and tool requirements indicate the support needed to perform the scheduled activities. The risk and contingency plan identifies the possible problems and provides recovery actions to avoid major failures. The test plan is discussed in more detail in Chapter 20.

4.3 Quality Goals

Process visibility requires a clear specification of goals, and in the case of quality process visibility this includes a careful distinction among dependability qualities. A team that does not have a clear idea of the difference between reliability and robustness, for example, or of their relative importance in a project, has little chance of attaining either. Goals must be further refined into a clear and reasonable set of objectives. If an organization claims that nothing less than 100% reliability will suffice, it is not setting an ambitious objective. Rather, it is setting no objective at all, and choosing not to make reasoned trade-off decisions or to balance limited resources across various activities. It is, in effect, abrogating responsibility for effective quality planning, and leaving trade-offs among cost, schedule, and quality to an arbitrary, ad hoc decision based on deadline and budget alone.

The relative importance of qualities and their relation to other project objectives varies. Time-to-market may be the most important property for a mass market product, usability may be more prominent for a Web based application, and safety may be the overriding requirement for a life-critical system.

Product qualities are the goals of software quality engineering, and process qualities are means to achieve those goals. For example, development processes with a high degree of visibility are necessary for creation of highly dependable products. The process goals with which software quality engineering is directly concerned are often on the "cost" side of the ledger. For example, we might have to weigh stringent reliability objectives against their impact on time-to-market, or seek ways to improve time-to-market without adversely impacting robustness.

internal and external qualities

Software product qualities can be divided into those that are directly visible to a client and those that primarily affect the software development organization. Reliability, for example, is directly visible to the client. Maintainability primarily affects the development organization, although its consequences may indirectly affect the client as well, for example, by increasing the time between product releases. Properties that are directly visible to users of a software product, such as dependability, latency, usability, and throughput, are called *external* properties. Properties that are not directly visible to end users, such as maintainability, reusability, and traceability, are called *internal* properties, even when their impact on the software development and evolution processes may indirectly affect users.

The external properties of software can ultimately be divided into dependability (does the software do what it is intended to do?) and usefulness. There is no precise way to distinguish these, but a rule of thumb is that when software is not dependable, we say it has a fault, or a defect, or (most often) a bug, resulting in an undesirable behavior or failure.

dependability

It is quite possible to build systems that are very reliable, relatively free from hazards, and completely useless. They may be unbearably slow, or have terrible user interfaces and unfathomable documentation, or they may be missing several crucial features. How should these properties be considered in software quality? One answer is that they are not part of quality at all unless they have been explicitly specified, since quality is the presence of specified properties. However, a company whose products are rejected by its customers will take little comfort in knowing that, by some definitions, they were high-quality products.

usefulness

We can do better by considering quality as fulfillment of required and desired properties, as distinguished from specified properties. For example, even if a client does not explicitly specify the required performance of a system, there is always *some* level of performance that is required to be useful.

One of the most critical tasks in software quality analysis is making desired properties explicit, since properties that remain unspecified (even informally) are very likely to surface unpleasantly when it is discovered that they are not met. In many cases these implicit requirements can not only be made explicit, but also made sufficiently precise that they can be made part of dependability or reliability. For example, while it is better to explicitly recognize usability as a requirement than to leave it implicit, it is better yet to augment[1] usability requirements with specific interface standards, so that a deviation from the standards is recognized as a defect.

4.4 Dependability Properties

The simplest of the dependability properties is correctness: A program or system is correct if it is consistent with its specification. By definition, a specification divides all possible system behaviors[2] into two classes, *successes* (or correct executions) and *failures*. All of the possible behaviors of a correct system are successes.

correctness

A program cannot be mostly correct or somewhat correct or 30% correct. It is absolutely correct on all possible behaviors, or else it is not correct. It is very easy to achieve correctness, since every program is correct with respect to some (very bad)

[1] Interface standards augment, rather than replace, usability requirements because conformance to the standards is not sufficient assurance that the requirement is met. This is the same relation that other specifications have to the user requirements they are intended to fulfill. In general, verifying conformance to specifications does not replace validating satisfaction of requirements.

[2] We are simplifying matters somewhat by considering only specifications of behaviors. A specification may also deal with other properties, such as the disk space required to install the application. A system may thus also be "incorrect" if it violates one of these static properties.

specification. Achieving correctness with respect to a useful specification, on the other hand, is seldom practical for nontrivial systems. Therefore, while correctness may be a noble goal, we are often interested in assessing some more achievable level of dependability.

reliability

Reliability is a statistical approximation to correctness, in the sense that 100% reliability is indistinguishable from correctness. Roughly speaking, reliability is a measure of the likelihood of correct function for some "unit" of behavior, which could be a single use or program execution or a period of time. Like correctness, reliability is relative to a specification (which determines whether a unit of behavior is counted as a success or failure). Unlike correctness, reliability is also relative to a particular usage profile. The same program can be more or less reliable depending on how it is used.

availability

Particular measures of reliability can be used for different units of execution and different ways of counting success and failure. *Availability* is an appropriate measure when a failure has some duration in time. For example, a failure of a network router may make it impossible to use some functions of a local area network until the service is restored; between initial failure and restoration we say the router is "down" or "unavailable." The availability of the router is the time in which the system is "up" (providing normal service) as a fraction of total time. Thus, a network router that averages 1 hour of down time in each 24-hour period would have an availability of $\frac{23}{24}$, or 95.8%.

MTBF

Mean time between failures (MTBF) is yet another measure of reliability, also using time as the unit of execution. The hypothetical network switch that typically fails once in a 24-hour period and takes about an hour to recover has a mean time between failures of 23 hours. Note that availability does not distinguish between two failures of 30 minutes each and one failure lasting an hour, while MTBF does.

The definitions of correctness and reliability have (at least) two major weaknesses. First, since the success or failure of an execution is relative to a specification, they are only as strong as the specification. Second, they make no distinction between a failure that is a minor annoyance and a failure that results in catastrophe. These are simplifying assumptions that we accept for the sake of precision, but in some circumstances — particularly, but not only, for critical systems — it is important to consider dependability properties that are less dependent on specification and that do distinguish among failures depending on severity.

safety

hazards

Software safety is an extension of the well-established field of system safety into software. Safety is concerned with preventing certain undesirable behaviors, called *hazards*. It is quite explicitly not concerned with achieving any useful behavior apart from whatever functionality is needed to prevent hazards. Software safety is typically a concern in "critical" systems such as avionics and medical systems, but the basic principles apply to any system in which particularly undesirable behaviors can be distinguished from run-of-the-mill failure. For example, while it is annoying when a word processor crashes, it is much more annoying if it irrecoverably corrupts document files. The developers of a word processor might consider safety with respect to the hazard of file corruption separately from reliability with respect to the complete functional requirements for the word processor.

Just as correctness is meaningless without a specification of allowed behaviors, safety is meaningless without a specification of hazards to be prevented, and in practice the first step of safety analysis is always finding and classifying hazards. Typically, hazards are associated with some system in which the software is embedded (e.g., the medical device), rather than the software alone. The distinguishing feature of safety is that it is concerned *only* with these hazards, and not with other aspects of correct functioning.

The concept of safety is perhaps easier to grasp with familiar physical systems. For example, lawn-mowers in the United States are equipped with an interlock device, sometimes called a "dead-man switch." If this switch is not actively held by the operator, the engine shuts off. The dead-man switch does not contribute in any way to cutting grass; its sole purpose is to prevent the operator from reaching into the mower blades while the engine runs.

One is tempted to say that safety is an aspect of correctness, because a good system specification would rule out hazards. However, safety is best considered as a quality distinct from correctness and reliability for two reasons. First, by focusing on a few hazards and ignoring other functionality, a separate safety specification can be much simpler than a complete system specification, and therefore easier to verify. To put it another way, while a good system specification *should* rule out hazards, we cannot be confident that either specifications or our attempts to verify systems are good enough to provide the degree of assurance we require for hazard avoidance. Second, even if the safety specification were redundant with regard to the full system specification, it is important because (by definition) we regard avoidance of hazards as more crucial than satisfying other parts of the system specification.

Correctness and reliability are contingent upon normal operating conditions. It is not reasonable to expect a word processing program to save changes normally when the file does not fit in storage, or to expect a database to continue to operate normally when the computer loses power, or to expect a Web site to provide completely satisfactory service to all visitors when the load is 100 times greater than the maximum for which it was designed. Software that fails under these conditions, which violate the premises of its design, may still be "correct" in the strict sense, yet the manner in which the software fails is important. It is acceptable that the word processor fails to write the new file that does not fit on disk, but unacceptable to also corrupt the previous version of the file in the attempt. It is acceptable for the database system to cease to function when the power is cut, but unacceptable for it to leave the database in a corrupt state. And it is usually preferable for the Web system to turn away some arriving users rather than becoming too slow for all, or crashing. Software that gracefully degrades or fails "softly" outside its normal operating parameters is *robust*.

robustness

Software safety is a kind of robustness, but robustness is a more general notion that concerns not only avoidance of hazards (e.g., data corruption) but also partial functionality under unusual situations. Robustness, like safety, begins with explicit consideration of unusual and undesirable situations, and should include augmenting software specifications with appropriate responses to undesirable events.

Figure 4.1 illustrates the relation among dependability properties.

Quality analysis should be part of the feasibility study. The sidebar on page 47

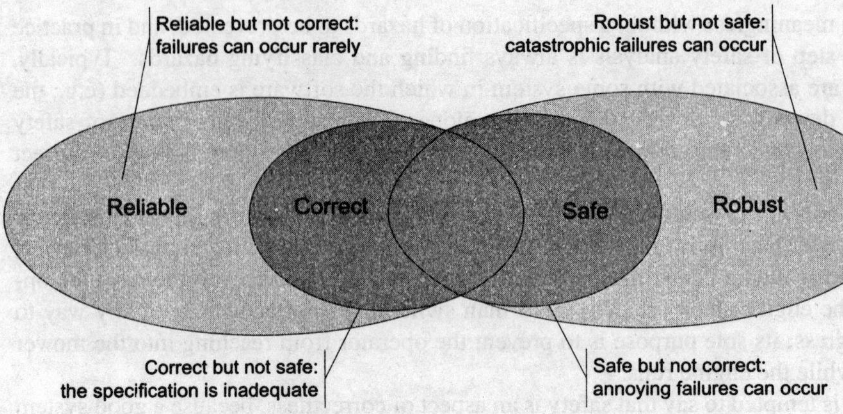

Figure 4.1: Relation among dependability properties

shows an excerpt of the feasibility study for the Chipmunk Web presence. The primary quality requirements are stated in terms of dependability, usability, and security. Performance, portability and interoperability are typically not primary concerns at this stage, but they may come into play when dealing with other qualities.

4.5 Analysis

Analysis techniques that do not involve actual execution of program source code play a prominent role in overall software quality processes. Manual inspection techniques and automated analyses can be applied at any development stage. They are particularly well suited at the early stages of specifications and design, where the lack of executability of many intermediate artifacts reduces the efficacy of testing.

Inspection, in particular, can be applied to essentially any document including requirements documents, architectural and more detailed design documents, test plans and test cases, and of course program source code. Inspection may also have secondary benefits, such as spreading good practices and instilling shared standards of quality. On the other hand, inspection takes a considerable amount of time and requires meetings, which can become a scheduling bottleneck. Moreover, re-inspecting a changed component can be as expensive as the initial inspection. Despite the versatility of inspection, therefore, it is used primarily where other techniques are either inapplicable or where other techniques do not provide sufficient coverage of common faults.

Automated static analyses are more limited in applicability (e.g., they can be applied to some formal representations of requirements models but not to natural language documents), but are selected when available because substituting machine cycles for human effort makes them particularly cost-effective. The cost advantage of automated static analyses is diminished by the substantial effort required to formalize and properly structure a model for analysis, but their application can be further mo-

Excerpt of Web Presence Feasibility Study

Purpose of this document

This document was prepared for the Chipmunk IT management team. It describes the results of a feasibility study undertaken to advise Chipmunk corporate management whether to embark on a substantial redevelopment effort to add online shopping functionality to the Chipmunk Computers' Web presence.

Goals

The primary goal of a Web presence redevelopment is to add online shopping facilities. Marketing estimates an increase of 15% over current direct sales within 24 months and an additional 8% savings in direct sales support costs from shifting telephone price inquiries to online price inquiries. [. . .]

Architectural Requirements

The logical architecture will be divided into three distinct subsystems: human interface, business logic, and supporting infrastructure. Each major subsystem must be structured for phased development, with initial features delivered 6 months from inception, full features at 12 months, and a planned revision at 18 months from project inception. [. . .]

Quality Requirements

Dependability: With the introduction of direct sales and customer relationship management functions, dependability of Chipmunk's Web services becomes business-critical. A critical core of functionality will be identified, isolated from less critical functionality in design and implementation, and subjected to the highest level of scrutiny. We estimate that this will be approximately 20% of new development and revisions, and that the V&V costs for those portions will be approximately triple the cost of V&V for noncritical development.

Usability: The new Web presence will be, to a much greater extent than before, the public face of Chipmunk Computers. [. . .]

Security: Introduction of online direct ordering and billing raises a number of security issues. Some of these can be avoided initially by contracting with one of several service companies that provide secure credit card transaction services. Nonetheless, order tracking, customer relationship management, returns, and a number of other functions that cannot be effectively outsourced raise significant security and privacy issues. Identifying and isolating security concerns will add a significant but manageable cost to design validation. [. . .]

tivated by their ability to thoroughly check for particular classes of faults for which checking with other techniques is very difficult or expensive. For example, finite state verification techniques for concurrent systems requires construction and careful structuring of a formal design model, and addresses only a particular family of faults (faulty synchronization structure). Yet it is rapidly gaining acceptance in some application domains because that family of faults is difficult to detect in manual inspection and resists detection through dynamic testing.

Sometimes the best aspects of manual inspection and automated static analysis can be obtained by carefully decomposing properties to be checked. For example, suppose a desired property of requirements documents is that each special term in the application domain appear in a glossary of terms. This property is not directly amenable to an automated static analysis, since current tools cannot distinguish meaningful domain terms from other terms that have their ordinary meanings. The property can be checked with manual inspection, but the process is tedious, expensive, and error-prone. A hybrid approach can be applied if each domain term is marked in the text. Manually checking that domain terms are marked is much faster and therefore less expensive than manually looking each term up in the glossary, and marking the terms permits effective automation of cross-checking with the glossary.

4.6 Testing

Despite the attractiveness of automated static analyses when they are applicable, and despite the usefulness of manual inspections for a variety of documents including but not limited to program source code, dynamic testing remains a dominant technique. A closer look, though, shows that dynamic testing is really divided into several distinct activities that may occur at different points in a project.

Tests are executed when the corresponding code is available, but testing activities start earlier, as soon as the artifacts required for designing test case specifications are available. Thus, acceptance and system test suites should be generated before integration and unit test suites, even if executed in the opposite order.

Early test design has several advantages. Tests are specified independently from code and when the corresponding software specifications are fresh in the mind of analysts and developers, facilitating review of test design. Moreover, test cases may highlight inconsistencies and incompleteness in the corresponding software specifications. Early design of test cases also allows for early repair of software specifications, preventing specification faults from propagating to later stages in development. Finally, programmers may use test cases to illustrate and clarify the software specifications, especially for errors and unexpected conditions.

No engineer would build a complex structure from parts that have not themselves been subjected to quality control. Just as the "earlier is better" rule dictates using inspection to reveal flaws in requirements and design before they are propagated to program code, the same rule dictates module testing to uncover as many program faults as possible before they are incorporated in larger subsystems of the product. At Chipmunk, developers are expected to perform functional and structural module testing before a work assignment is considered complete and added to the project baseline. The test driver and auxiliary files are part of the work product and are expected to make re-execution of test cases, including result checking, as simple and automatic as possible, since the same test cases will be used over and over again as the product evolves.

4.7 Improving the Process

While the assembly-line, mass production industrial model is inappropriate for software, which is at least partly custom-built, there is almost always some commonality among projects undertaken by an organization over time. Confronted by similar problems, developers tend to make the same kinds of errors over and over, and consequently the same kinds of software faults are often encountered project after project. The quality process, as well as the software development process as a whole, can be improved by gathering, analyzing, and acting on data regarding faults and failures.

The goal of quality process improvement is to find cost-effective countermeasures for classes of faults that are expensive because they occur frequently, or because the failures they cause are expensive, or because, once detected, they are expensive to repair. Countermeasures may be either prevention or detection and may involve either quality assurance activities (e.g., improved checklists for design inspections) or other aspects of software development (e.g., improved requirements specification methods).

The first part of a process improvement feedback loop, and often the most difficult to implement, is gathering sufficiently complete and accurate raw data about faults and failures. A main obstacle is that data gathered in one project goes mainly to benefit other projects in the future and may seem to have little direct benefit for the current project, much less to the persons asked to provide the raw data. It is therefore helpful to integrate data collection as well as possible with other, normal development activities, such as version and configuration control, project management, and bug tracking. It is also essential to minimize extra effort. For example, if revision logs in the revision control database can be associated with bug tracking records, then the time between checking out a module and checking it back in might be taken as a rough guide to cost of repair.

Raw data on faults and failures must be aggregated into categories and prioritized. Faults may be categorized along several dimensions, none of them perfect. Fortunately, a flawless categorization is not necessary; all that is needed is some categorization scheme that is sufficiently fine-grained and tends to aggregate faults with similar causes and possible remedies, and that can be associated with at least rough estimates of relative frequency and cost. A small number of categories — maybe just one or two — are chosen for further study.

The analysis step consists of tracing several instances of an observed fault or failure back to the human error from which it resulted, or even further to the factors that led to that human error. The analysis also involves the reasons the fault was not detected and eliminated earlier (e.g., how it slipped through various inspections and levels of testing). This process is known as "root cause analysis," but the ultimate aim is for the most cost-effective countermeasure, which is sometimes but not always the ultimate root cause. For example, the persistence of security vulnerabilities through buffer overflow errors in network applications may be attributed at least partly to widespread

root cause analysis

use of programming languages with unconstrained pointers and without array bounds checking, which may in turn be attributed to performance concerns and a requirement for interoperability with a large body of legacy code. The countermeasure could involve differences in programming methods (e.g., requiring use of certified "safe" libraries for buffer management), or improvements to quality assurance activities (e.g., additions to inspection checklists), or sometimes changes in management practices.

4.8 Organizational Factors

The quality process includes a wide variety of activities that require specific skills and attitudes and may be performed by quality specialists or by software developers. Planning the quality process involves not only resource management but also identification and allocation of responsibilities.

A poor allocation of responsibilities can lead to major problems in which pursuit of individual goals conflicts with overall project success. For example, splitting responsibilities of development and quality-control between a development and a quality team, and rewarding high productivity in terms of lines of code per person-month during development may produce undesired results. The development team, not rewarded to produce high-quality software, may attempt to maximize productivity to the detriment of quality. The resources initially planned for quality assurance may not suffice if the initial quality of code from the"very productive" development team is low. On the other hand, combining development and quality control responsibilities in one undifferentiated team, while avoiding the perverse incentive of divided responsibilities, can also have unintended effects: As deadlines near, resources may be shifted from quality assurance to coding, at the expense of product quality.

Conflicting considerations support both the separation of roles (e.g., recruiting quality specialists), and the mobility of people and roles (e.g, rotating engineers between development and testing tasks).

At Chipmunk, responsibility for delivery of the new Web presence is distributed among a development team and a quality assurance team. Both teams are further articulated into groups. The quality assurance team is divided into the analysis and testing group, responsible for the dependability of the system, and the usability testing group, responsible for usability. Responsibility for security issues is assigned to the infrastructure development group, which relies partly on external consultants for final tests based on external attack attempts.

Having distinct teams does not imply a simple division of all tasks between teams by category. At Chipmunk, for example, specifications, design, and code are inspected by mixed teams; scaffolding and oracles are designed by analysts and developers; integration, system, acceptance, and regression tests are assigned to the test and analysis team; unit tests are generated and executed by the developers; and coverage is checked by the testing team before starting integration and system testing. A specialist has been hired for analyzing faults and improving the process. The process improvement specialist works incrementally while developing the system and proposes improvements at each release.

Summary

Test and analysis activities are not a late phase of the development process, but rather a wide set of activities that pervade the whole process. Designing a quality process with a suitable blend of test and analysis activities for the specific application domain, development environment, and quality goals is a challenge that requires skill and experience.

A well-defined quality process must fulfill three main goals: improving the software product during and after development, assessing its quality before delivery, and improving the process within and across projects. These challenging goals can be achieved by increasing visibility, scheduling activities as early as practical, and monitoring results to adjust the process. Process visibility — that is, measuring and comparing progress to objectives — is a key property of the overall development process. Performing A&T activities early produces several benefits: It increases control over the process, it hastens fault identification and reduces the costs of fault removal, it provides data for incrementally tuning the development process, and it accelerates product delivery. Feedback is the key to improving the process by identifying and removing persistent errors and faults.

Further Reading

Qualities of software are discussed in many software engineering textbooks; the discussion in Chapter 2 of Ghezzi, Jazayeri, and Mandrioli [GJM02] is particularly useful. Process visibility is likewise described in software engineering textbooks, usually with an emphasis on schedule. Musa [Mus04] describes a quality process oriented particularly to establishing a quantifiable level of reliability based on models and testing before release. Chillarege et al. [CBC+92] present principles for gathering and analyzing fault data, with an emphasis on feedback within a single process but applicable also to quality process improvement.

Exercises

4.1. We have stated that 100% reliability is indistinguishable from correctness, but they are not quite identical. Under what circumstance might an incorrect program be 100% reliable? *Hint:* Recall that a program may be more or less reliable depending on how it is used, but a program is either correct or incorrect regardless of usage.

4.2. We might measure the reliability of a network router as the fraction of all packets that are correctly routed, or as the fraction of total service time in which packets are correctly routed. When might these two measures be different?

4.3. If I am downloading a very large file over a slow modem, do I care more about the availability of my internet service provider or its mean time between failures?

4.4. Can a system be correct and yet unsafe?

4.5. Under what circumstances can making a system more safe make it less reliable?

4.6. Software application domains can be characterized by the relative importance of schedule (calendar time), total cost, and dependability. For example, while all three are important for game software, schedule (shipping product in September to be available for holiday purchases) has particular weight, while dependability can be somewhat relaxed. Characterize a domain you are familiar with in these terms.

4.7. Consider responsiveness as a desirable property of an Internet chat program. The informal requirement is that messages typed by each member of a chat session appear instantaneously on the displays of other users. Refine this informal requirement into a concrete specification that can be verified. Is anything lost in the refinement?

4.8. Identify some correctness, robustness and safety properties of a word processor.

Part II

Basic Techniques

Chapter 5

Finite Models

From wind-tunnels to Navier-Stokes equations to circuit diagrams to finite-element models of buildings, engineers in all fields of engineering construct and analyze models. Fundamentally, modeling addresses two problems in engineering. First, analysis and test cannot wait until the actual artifact is constructed, whether that artifact is a building or a software system. Second, it is impractical to test the actual artifact as thoroughly as we wish, whether that means subjecting it to all foreseeable hurricane and earthquake forces, or to all possible program states and inputs. Models permit us to start analysis earlier and repeat it as a design evolves, and allows us to apply analytic methods that cover a much larger class of scenarios than we can explicitly test. Importantly, many of these analyses may be automated.

This chapter presents some basic concepts in models of software and some families of models that are used in a wide variety of testing and analysis techniques. Several of the analysis and testing techniques described in subsequent chapters use and specialize these basic models. The fundamental concepts and trade-offs in the design of models is necessary for a full understanding of those test and analysis techniques, and is a foundation for devising new techniques and models to solve domain-specific problems.

5.1 Overview

A model is a representation that is simpler than the artifact it represents but preserves (or at least approximates) some important attributes of the actual artifact. Our concern in this chapter is with models of program execution, and not with models of other (equally important) attributes such as the effort required to develop the software or its usability. A good model of (or, more precisely, a good class of models) must typically be: model

Compact: A model must be representable and manipulable in a reasonably compact form. What is "reasonably compact" depends largely on how the model will be used. Models intended for human inspection and reasoning must be small enough to be comprehensible. Models intended solely for automated analysis may be far too large and complex for human comprehension, but must still be sufficiently small or regular for computer processing.

Predictive: A model used in analysis or design must represent some salient characteristics of the modeled artifact well enough to distinguish between "good" and "bad" outcomes of analysis, with respect to those characteristics.

Typically, no single model represents all characteristics well enough to be useful for all kinds of analysis. One does not, for example, use the same model to predict airflow over an aircraft fuselage and to design internal layout for efficient passenger loading and safe emergency exit.

Semantically meaningful: Beyond distinguishing between predictions of success and failure, it is usually necessary to interpret analysis results in a way that permits diagnosis of the causes of failure. If a finite-element model of a building predicts collapse in a category five hurricane, we want to know enough about that collapse to suggest revisions to the design. Likewise, if a model of an accounting system predicts a failure when used concurrently by several clients, we need a description of that failure sufficient to suggest possible revisions.

Sufficiently general: Models intended for analysis of some important characteristic (e.g., withstanding earthquakes or concurrent operation by many clients) must be general enough for practical use in the intended domain of application.

We may sometimes tolerate limits on design imposed by limitations of our modeling and analysis techniques. For example, we may choose a conventional bridge design over a novel design because we have confidence in analysis techniques for the former but not the latter, and we may choose conventional concurrency control protocols over novel approaches for the same reason. However, if a program analysis technique for C programs is applicable only to programs without pointer variables, we are unlikely to find much use for it.

Since design models are intended partly to aid in making and evaluating design decisions, they should share these characteristics with models constructed primarily for analysis. However, some kinds of models — notably the widely used UML design notations — are designed primarily for human communication, with less attention to semantic meaning and prediction.

Models are often used indirectly in evaluating an artifact. For example, some models are not themselves analyzed, but are used to guide test case selection. In such cases, the qualities of being predictive and semantically meaningful apply to the model together with the analysis or testing technique applied to another artifact, typically the actual program or system.

Graph Representations

We often use directed graphs to represent models of programs. Usually we draw them as "box and arrow" diagrams, but to reason about them it is important to understand that they have a well-defined mathematical meaning, which we review here.

A directed graph is composed of a set of nodes N and a relation E on the set (that is, a set of ordered pairs), called the edges. It is conventional to draw the nodes as points or shapes and to draw the edges as arrows. For example:

Nodes: $\{a,b,c\}$
Edges: $\{(a,b),(a,c),(c,a)\}$

Drawn as

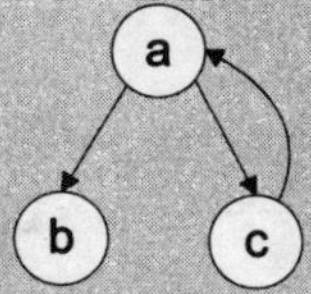

Or drawn as

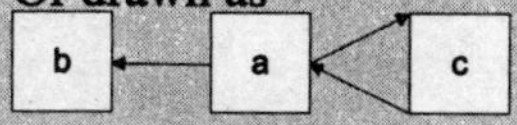

Typically, the nodes represent entities of some kind, such as procedures or classes or regions of source code. The edges represent some relation among the entities. For example, if we represent program control flow using a directed graph model, an edge (a,b) would be interpreted as the statement "program region a can be directly followed by program region b in program execution."

We can label nodes with the names or descriptions of the entities they represent. If nodes a and b represent program regions containing assignment statements, we might draw the two nodes and an edge (a,b) connecting them in this way:

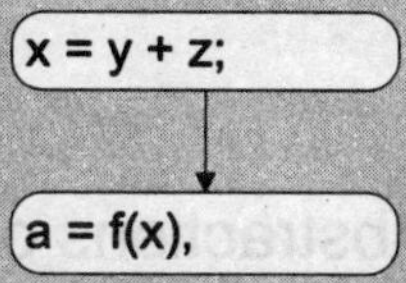

Sometimes we draw a single diagram to represent more than one directed graph, drawing the shared nodes only once. For example, we might draw a single diagram in which we express both that class B extends (is a subclass of) class A and that class B has a field that is an object of type C. We can do this by drawing edges in the "extends" relation differently than edges in the "includes" relation.

Nodes and edges of "extends" relation
$\langle\{A,B,C\},\{(A,B)\}\rangle$

Nodes and edges of "includes" relation
$\langle\{A,B,C\},\{(B,C)\}\rangle$

Drawn together

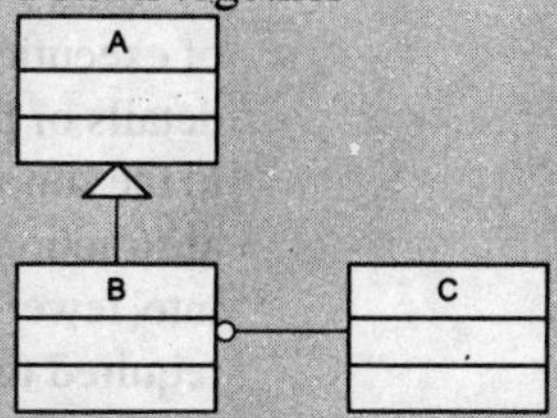

Drawings of graphs can be refined in many ways, for example, depicting some relations as attributes rather than directed edges. Important as these presentation choices may be for clear communication, only the underlying sets and relations matter for reasoning about models.

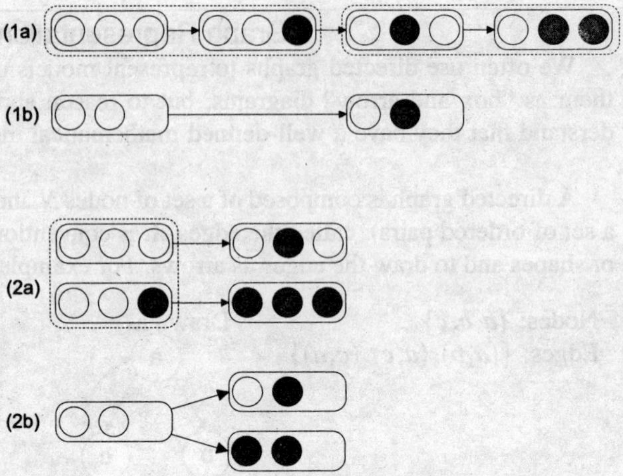

Figure 5.1: Abstraction elides details of execution states and in so doing may cause an abstract model execution state to represent more than one concrete program execution state. In the illustration, program state is represented by three attributes, each with two possible values, drawn as light or dark circles. Abstract model states retain the first two attributes and elide the third. The relation between (1a) and (1b) illustrates coarsening of the execution model, since the first and third program execution steps modify only the omitted attribute. The relation between (2a) and (2b) illustrates introduction of nondeterminism, because program execution states with different successor states have been merged.

5.2 Finite Abstractions of Behavior

A single program execution can be viewed as a sequence of states alternating with actions (e.g., machine operations).[1] The possible behaviors of a program are a set of such sequences. If we abstract from the physical limits of a particular machine, for all but the most trivial programs the set of possible execution sequences is infinite. That whole set of states and transitions is called the *state space* of the program. Models of program execution are abstractions of that space.

state space

States in the state space of program execution are related to states in a finite model of execution by an abstraction function. Since an abstraction function suppresses some details of program execution, it lumps together execution states that differ with respect to the suppressed details but are otherwise identical. Figure 5.1 illustrates two effects of abstraction: The execution model is coarsened (sequences of transitions are collapsed into fewer execution steps), and nondeterminism is introduced (because information required to make a deterministic choice is sacrificed).

Finite models of program execution are inevitably imperfect. Collapsing the po-

[1] We put aside, for the moment, the possibility of parallel or concurrent execution. Most but not all models of concurrent execution reduce it to an equivalent serial execution in which operation by different procedures are interleaved, but there also exist models for which our treatment here is insufficient.

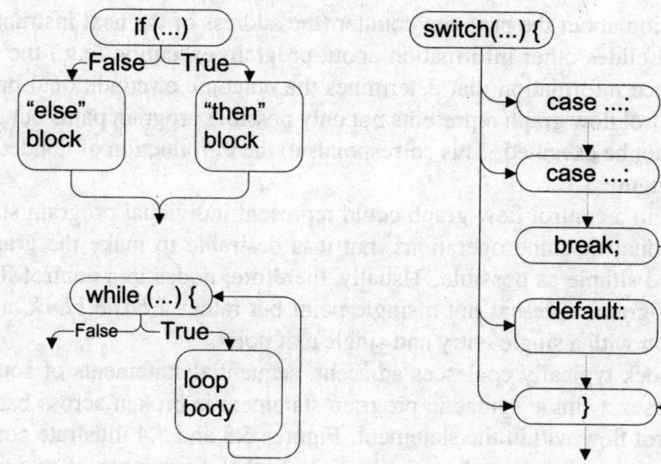

Figure 5.2: Building blocks for constructing intraprocedural control flow graphs. Other control constructs are represented analogously. For example, the for *construct of C, C++, and Java is represented as if the initialization part appeared before a* while *loop, with the increment part at the end of the* while *loop body.*

tentially infinite states of actual execution into a finite number of representative model states necessarily involves omitting some information. While one might hope that the omitted information is irrelevant to the property one wishes to verify, this is seldom completely true. In Figure 5.1, parts 2(a) and 2(b) illustrate how abstraction can cause a set of deterministic transitions to be modeled by a nondeterministic choice among transitions, thus making the analysis imprecise. This in turn can lead to "false alarms" in analysis of models.

5.3 Control Flow Graphs

It is convenient and intuitive to construct models whose states are closely related to locations in program source code. In general, we will associate an abstract state with a whole region (that is, a set of locations) in a program. We know that program source code is finite, so a model that associates a finite amount of information with each of a finite number of program points or regions will also be finite.

Control flow of a single procedure or method can be represented as an *intraprocedural control flow graph*, often abbreviated as *control flow graph* or *CFG*. The intraprocedural control flow graph is a directed graph in which nodes represent regions of the source code and directed edges represent the possibility that program execution proceeds from the end of one region directly to the beginning of another, either through sequential execution or by a branch. Figure 5.2 illustrates the representation of typical control flow constructs in a control flow graph.

Δ control flow graph

In terms of program execution, we can say that a control flow graph model retains some information about the program counter (the address of the next instruction to be executed), and elides other information about program execution (e.g., the values of variables). Since information that determines the outcome of conditional branches is elided, the control flow graph represents not only possible program paths but also some paths that cannot be executed. This corresponds to the introduction of nondeterminism illustrated in Figure 5.1.

The nodes in a control flow graph could represent individual program statements, or even individual machine operations, but it is desirable to make the graph model as compact and simple as possible. Usually, therefore, nodes in a control flow graph model of a program represent not a single point but rather a *basic block*, a maximal program region with a single entry and single exit point.

Δ basic block

A basic block typically coalesces adjacent, sequential statements of source code, but in some cases a single syntactic program statement is broken across basic blocks to model control flow within the statement. Figures 5.3 and 5.4 illustrate construction of a control flow graph from a Java method. Note that a sequence of two statements within the loop has been collapsed into a single basic block, but the for statement and the complex predicate in the if statement have been broken across basic blocks to model their internal flow of control.

Some analysis algorithms are simplified by introducing a distinguished node to represent procedure entry and another to represent procedure exit. When these distinguished start and end nodes are used in a CFG, a directed edge leads from the start node to the node representing the first executable block, and a directed edge from each procedure exit (e.g., each return statement and the last sequential block in the program) to the distinguished end node. Our practice will be to draw a start node identified with the procedure or method signature, and to leave the end node implicit.

The intraprocedural control flow graph may be used directly to define thoroughness criteria for testing (see Chapters 9 and 12). Often the control flow graph is used to define another model, which in turn is used to define a thoroughness criterion. For example, some criteria are defined by reference to linear code sequences and jumps (LCSAJs), which are essentially subpaths of the control flow graph from one branch to another. Figure 5.5 shows the LCSAJs derived from the control flow graph of Figure 5.4.

For use in analysis, the control flow graph is usually augmented with other information. For example, the data flow models described in the next chapter are constructed using a CFG model augmented with information about the variables accessed and modified by each program statement.

Not all control flow is represented explicitly in program text. For example, if an empty string is passed to the collapseNewlines method of Figure 5.3, the exception java.lang.StringIndexOutOfBoundsException will be thrown by String.charAt, and execution of the method will be terminated. This could be represented in the CFG as a directed edge to an exit node. However, if one includes such implicit control flow edges for every possible exception (for example, an edge from each reference that might lead to a null pointer exception), the CFG becomes rather unwieldy.

More fundamentally, it may not be simple or even possible to determine which of the implicit control flow edges can actually be executed. We can reason about the call to argStr.charAt(cIdx) within the body of the for loop and determine that cIdx must

```
/**
 * Remove/collapse multiple newline characters.
 *
 * @param String string to collapse newlines in.
 * @return String
 */
public static String collapseNewlines(String argStr)
{
    char last = argStr.charAt(0);
    StringBuffer argBuf = new StringBuffer();

    for (int cIdx = 0 ; cIdx < argStr.length(); cIdx++)
    {
        char ch = argStr.charAt(cIdx);
        if (ch != '\n' || last != '\n')
        {
            argBuf.append(ch);
            last = ch;
        }
    }

    return argBuf.toString();
}
```

Figure 5.3: A Java method to collapse adjacent newline characters, from the StringUtilities class of the Velocity project of the open source Apache project. (c) 2001 Apache Software Foundation, used with permission.

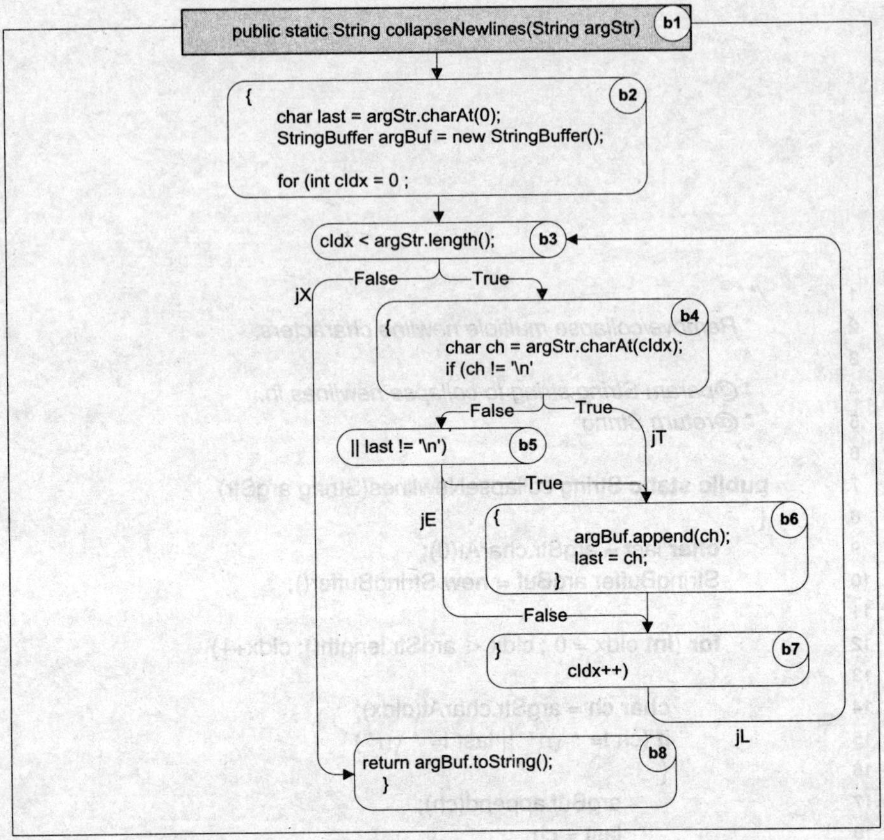

Figure 5.4: A control flow graph corresponding to the Java method in Figure 5.3. The for *statement and the predicate of the* if *statement have internal control flow branches, so those statements are broken across basic blocks.*

From	*Sequence of Basic Blocks*								*To*
entry	b1	b2	b3						jX
entry	b1	b2	b3	b4					jT
entry	b1	b2	b3	b4	b5				jE
entry	b1	b2	b3	b4	b5	b6	b7		jL
jX								b8	return
jL			b3	b4					jT
jL			b3	b4	b5				jE
jL			b3	b4	b5	b6	b7		jL

Figure 5.5: Linear code sequences and jumps (LCSAJs) corresponding to the Java method in Figure 5.3 and the control flow graph in Figure 5.4. Note that proceeding to the next sequential basic block is not considered a "jump" for purposes of identifying LCSAJs.

always be within bounds, but we cannot reasonably expect an automated tool for extracting control flow graphs to perform such inferences. Whether to include some or all implicit control flow edges in a CFG representation therefore involves a trade-off between possibly omitting some execution paths or representing many spurious paths. Which is preferable depends on the uses to which the CFG representation will be put.

Even the representation of explicit control flow may differ depending on the uses to which a model is put. In Figure 5.3, the for statement has been broken into its constituent parts (initialization, comparison, and increment for next iteration), each of which appears at a different point in the control flow. For some kinds of analysis, this breakdown would serve no useful purpose. Similarly, a complex conditional expression in Java or C is executed by "short-circuit" evaluation, so the single expression i > 0 && i < 10 can be broken across two basic blocks (the second test is not executed if the first evaluates to false). If this fine level of execution detail is not relevant to an analysis, we may choose to ignore short-circuit evaluation and treat the entire conditional expression as if it were fully evaluated.

5.4 Call Graphs

The intraprocedural control flow graph represents possible execution paths through a single procedure or method. interprocedural control flow can also be represented as a directed graph. The most basic model is the *call graph*, in which nodes represent procedures (methods, C functions, etc.) and edges represent the "calls" relation. For example, a call graph representation of the program that includes the collapseNewlines method above would include a node for StringUtils. collapseNewlines with a directed edge to method String.charAt.

Call graph representations present many more design issues and trade-offs than intraprocedural control flow graphs; consequently, there are many variations on the basic call graph representation. For example, consider that in object-oriented languages, method calls are typically made through object references and may be bound to methods in different subclasses depending on the current binding of the object. A call graph for programs in an object-oriented language might therefore represent the *calls* relation to each of the possible methods to which a call might be dynamically bound. More often, the call graph will explicitly represent only a call to the method in the declared class of an object, but it will be part of a richer representation that includes inheritance relations. Constructing an abstract model of executions in the course of analysis will involve interpreting this richer structure.

Figure 5.6 illustrates overestimation of the *calls* relation due to dynamic dispatch. The static call graph includes calls through dynamic bindings that never occur in execution. A.foo() calls b.bar(), and b's declared class is C, and S inherits from C and overrides bar(). The call graph includes a possible call from A.foo() to S.bar(). It might very well include that call even if a more precise analysis could show that b can never actually be bound to an object of subclass S, because in general such analysis is very expensive or even impossible.

If a call graph model represents different behaviors of a procedure depending on where the procedure is called, we call it *context-sensitive*. For example, a context-

```
public class C {

    public static C cFactory(String kind) {
        if (kind == "C") return new C();
        if (kind == "S") return new S();
        return null;
    }

    void foo() {
        System.out.println("You called the parent's method");
    }

    public static void main(String args[]) {
        (new A()).check();
    }
}

class S extends C {
    void foo() {
        System.out.println("You called the child's method");
    }
}

class A {
    void check() {
        C myC = C.cFactory("S");
        myC.foo();
    }
}
```

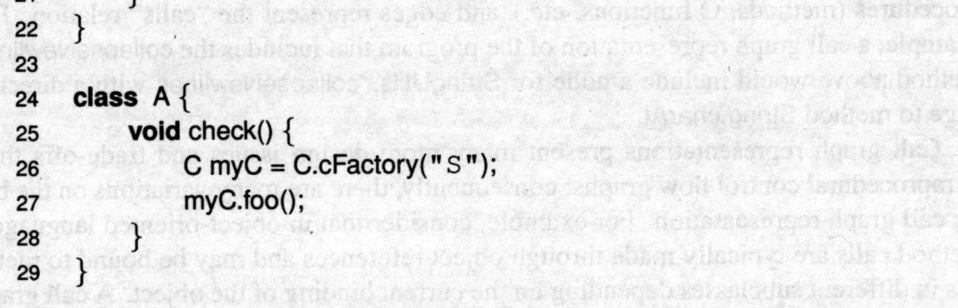

Figure 5.6: Overapproximation in a call graph. Although the method A.check() *can never actually call* C.foo(), *a typical call graph construction will include it as a possible call.*

sensitive model of collapseNewlines might distinguish between one call in which the argument string cannot possibly be empty, and another in which it could be. Context-sensitive analyses can be more precise than context-insensitive analyses when the model includes some additional information that is shared or passed among procedures. Information not only about the immediate calling context, but about the entire chain of procedure calls may be needed, as illustrated in Figure 5.7. In that case the cost of context-sensitive analysis depends on the number of paths from the root (main program) to each lowest level procedure. The number of paths can be exponentially larger than the number of procedures, as illustrated in Figure 5.8.

The Java compiler uses a typical call graph model to enforce the language rule that all checked exceptions are either handled or declared in each method. The throws clauses in a method declaration are provided by the programmer, but if they were not, they would correspond exactly to the information that a context insensitive analysis of exception propagation would associate with each procedure (which is why the compiler can check for completeness and complain if the programmer omits an exception that can be thrown).

5.5 Finite State Machines

Most of the models discussed above can be extracted from programs. Often, though, models are constructed prior to or independent of source code, and serve as a kind of specification of allowed behavior. Finite state machines of various kinds are particularly widely used.

In its simplest form, a finite state machine (FSM) is a finite set of states and a set of transitions among states, that is, a directed graph in which nodes represent program states and edges represent operations that transform one program state into another. Since there may be infinitely many program states, the finite set of state nodes must be an abstraction of the concrete program states.

A transition from one state node a to another state node b denotes the possibility that a concrete program state corresponding to a can be followed immediately by a concrete program state corresponding to b. Usually we label the edge to indicate a program operation, condition, or event associated with the transition. We may label transitions with both an external event or a condition (what must happen or be true for the program to make a corresponding state change) and with a program operation that can be thought of as a "response" to the event. Such a finite state machine with *event / response* labels on transitions is called a Mealy machine. Mealy machine

Figure 5.9 illustrates a specification for a converter among Dos, Unix, and Macintosh line end conventions in the form of a Mealy machine. An "event" for this specification is reading a character or encountering end-of-file. The possible input characters are divided into four categories: carriage return, line feed, end-of-file, and everything else. The states represent both program control points and some information that may be stored in program variables.

There are three kinds of correctness relations that we may reason about with respect to finite state machine models, illustrated in Figure 5.10. The first is internal properties, such as completeness and determinism. Second, the possible executions of a model,

```java
public class Context {
    public static void main(String args[]) {
        Context c = new Context();
        c.foo(3);
        c.bar(17);
    }

    void foo(int n) {
        int[]  myArray = new int[ n ];
        depends( myArray, 2) ;
    }

    void bar(int n) {
        int[]  myArray = new int[ n ];
        depends( myArray, 16) ;
    }

    void depends( int[] a, int n ) {
        a[n] = 42;
    }
}
```

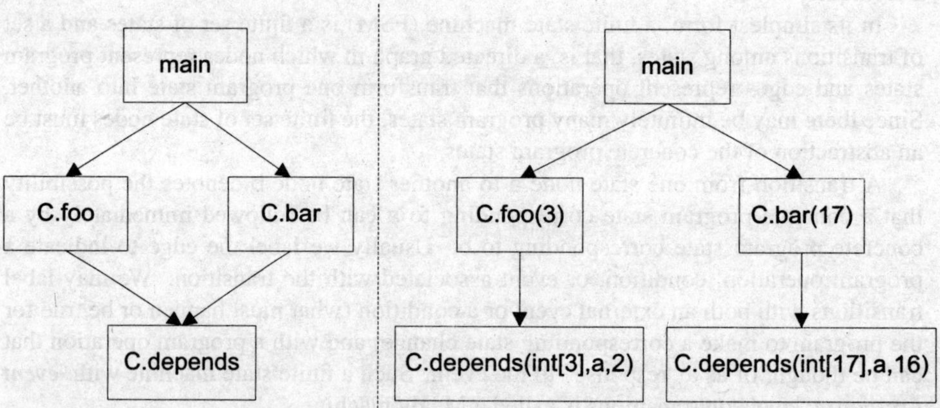

Figure 5.7: The Java code above can be represented by the context-insensitive call graph at left. However, to capture the fact that method depends *never attempts to store into a nonexistent array element, it is necessary to represent parameter values that differ depending on the context in which* depends *is called, as in the context-sensitive call graph on the right.*

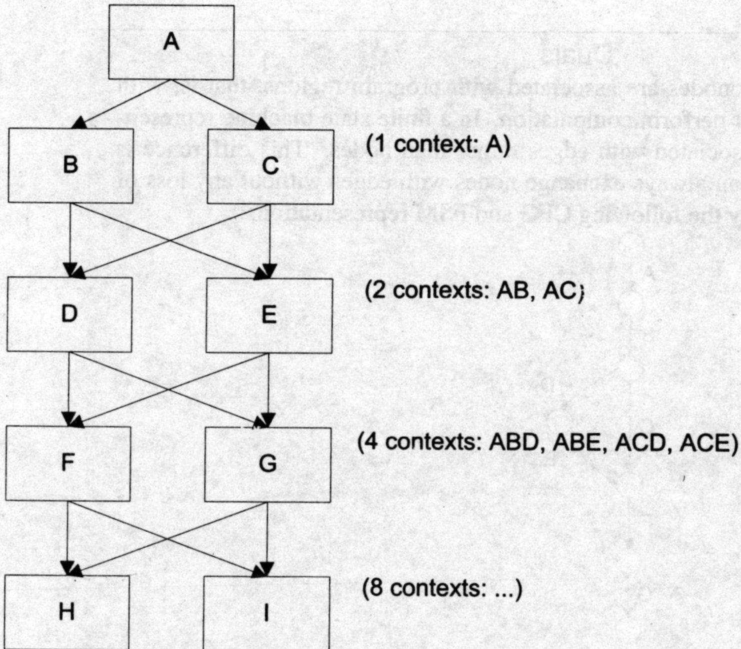

Figure 5.8: The number of paths in a call graph — and therefore the number of calling contexts in a context-sensitive analysis — can be exponentially larger than the number of procedures, even without recursion.

Duals

In a control flow graph, nodes are associated with program regions, that is, with blocks of program code that perform computation. In a finite state machine representation, computations are associated with edges rather than nodes. This difference is unimportant, because one can always exchange nodes with edges without any loss of information, as illustrated by the following CFG and FSM representations:

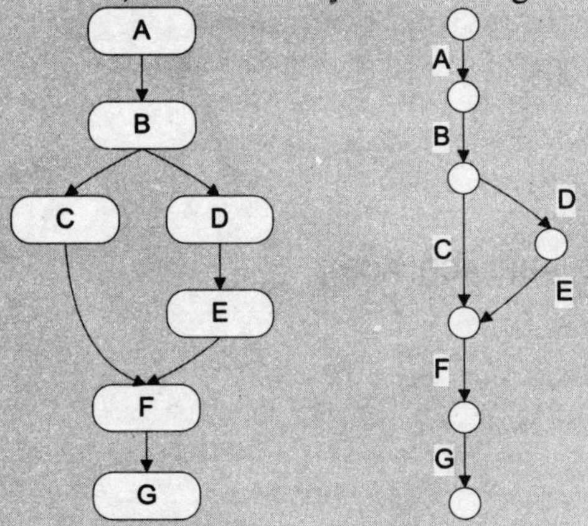

The graph on the right is called the *dual* of the graph on the left. Taking the dual of the graph on the right, one obtains again the graph on the left.

The choice between associating nodes or edges with computations performed by a program is only a matter of convention and convenience, and is not an important difference between CFG and FSM models. In fact, aside from this minor difference in customary presentation, the control flow graph is a particular kind of finite state machine model in which the abstract states preserve some information about control flow (program regions and their execution order) and elide all other information about program state.

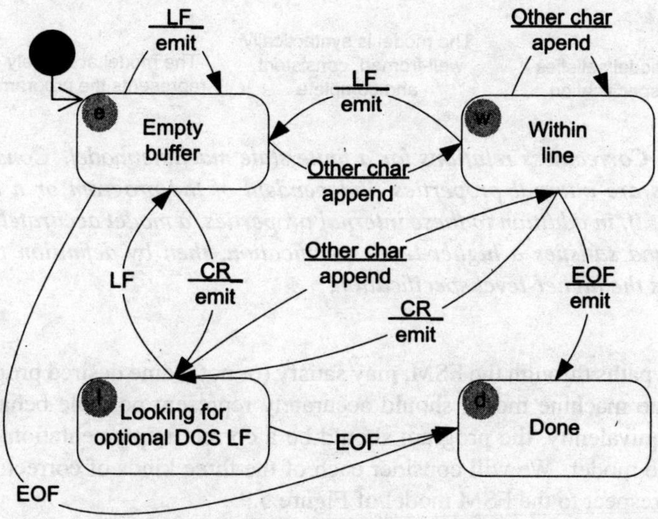

	LF	CR	EOF	other
e	e / emit	l / emit	d / –	w / append
w	e / emit	l / emit	d / emit	w / append
l	e / –		d / –	w / append

***Figure 5.9:** Finite state machine (Mealy machine) description of line-end conversion procedure, depicted as a state transition diagram (top) and as a state transition table (bottom). An omission is obvious in the tabular representation, but easy to overlook in the state transition diagram.*

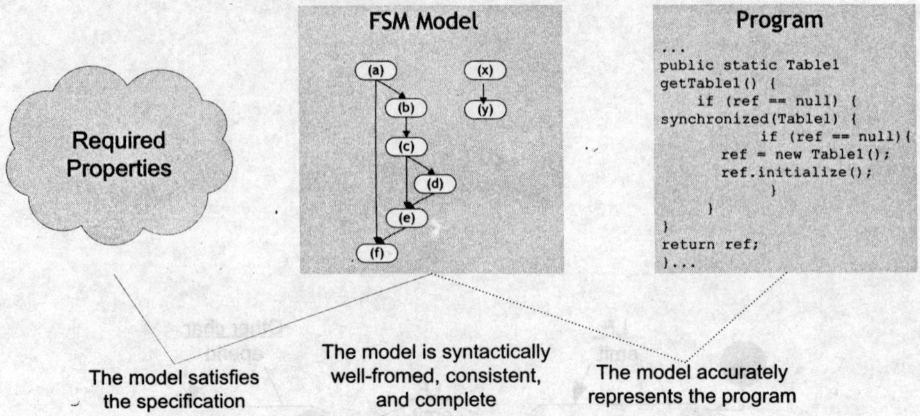

Figure 5.10: Correctness relations for a finite state machine model. Consistency and completeness are internal properties, independent of the program or a higher-level specification. If, in addition to these internal properties, a model accurately represents a program and satisfies a higher-level specification, then by definition the program itself satisfies the higher-level specification.

described by paths through the FSM, may satisfy (or not) some desired property. Third, the finite state machine model should accurately represent possible behaviors of the program. Equivalently, the program should be a correct implementation of the finite state machine model. We will consider each of the three kinds of correctness relation in turn with respect to the FSM model of Figure 5.9.

Many details are purposely omitted from the FSM model depicted in Figure 5.9, but it is also incomplete in an undesirable way. Normally, we require a finite state machine specification to be complete in the sense that it prescribes the allowed behavior(s) for any possible sequence of inputs or events. For the line-end conversion specification, the state transition diagram does not include a transition from state *l* on carriage return; that is, it does not specify what the program should do if it encounters a carriage return immediately after a line feed.

An alternative representation of finite state machines, including Mealy machines, is the state transition table, also illustrated in Figure 5.9. There is one row in the transition table for each state node and one column for each event or input. If the FSM is complete and deterministic, there should be exactly one transition in each table entry. Since this table is for a Mealy machine, the transition in each table entry indicates both the next state and the response (e.g., *d / emit* means "emit and then proceed to state *d*"). The omission of a transition from state *l* on a carriage return is glaringly obvious when the state transition diagram is written in tabular form.

Analysis techniques for verifying properties of models will be presented in subsequent chapters. For the current example, we illustrate with informal reasoning. The desired property of this program and of its FSM models is that, for every possible execution, the output file is identical to the input file except that each line ending is replaced by the line-end convention of the target format. Note, however, that the *emit* action is responsible for emitting a line ending along with whatever text has been accumulated in a buffer. While *emit* is usually triggered by a line ending in the input, it is also used to reproduce any text in the buffer when end-of-file is reached. Thus, if the last line of an input file is not terminated with a line ending, a line ending will nonetheless be added. This discrepancy between specification and implementation is somewhat easier to detect by examining the FSM model than by inspecting the program text.

To consider the third kind of correctness property, consistency between the model and the implementation, we must define what it means for them to be consistent. The most general way to define consistency is by considering behaviors. Given a way to compare a sequence of program actions to a path through the finite state machine (which in general will involve interpreting some program events and discarding others), a program is consistent with a finite state machine model if every possible program execution corresponds to a path through the model.[2]

Matching sequences of program actions to paths through a finite state machine model is a useful notion of consistency if we are testing the program, but it is not a practical way to reason about all possible program behaviors. For that kind of reasoning, it is more helpful to also require a relation between states in the finite state machine model and concrete program execution states.

It should be possible to describe the association of concrete program states with abstract FSM states by an *abstraction function*. The abstraction function maps each concrete program state to exactly one FSM state. Moreover, if some possible step *op* in program execution takes the concrete program state from some state *before* to some state *after*, then one of two conditions must apply: If the FSM model does not include transitions corresponding to *op*, then program state *before* and program state *after* must be associated with the same abstract state in the model. If the FSM does include transitions corresponding to *op*, then there must be a corresponding transition in the FSM model that connects program state *before* to program state *after*.

Using the second notion of conformance, we can reason about whether the implementation of the line-end conversion program of Figure 5.11 is consistent with the FSM of Figure 5.9 or Figure 5.12. Note that, in contrast to the control flow graph models considered earlier, most of the interesting "state" is in the variables pos and atCR. We posit that the abstraction function might be described by the following table:

Abstract state	*Concrete state*		
	Lines	atCR	pos
e (Empty buffer)	2 – 12	0	0
w (Within line)	12	0	> 0
l (Looking for LF)	12	1	0
d (Done)	35	–	–

[2]As with other abstraction functions used in reasoning about programs, the mapping is from concrete representation to abstract representation, and not from abstract to concrete. This is because the mapping from concrete to abstract is many-to-one, and its inverse is therefore not a mathematical function (which by definition maps each object in the domain set into a single object in the range).

```
/** Convert each line from standard input */
void transduce() {

    #define BUFLEN 1000
    char buf[BUFLEN];   /* Accumulate line into this buffer   */
    int   pos = 0;          /* Index for next character in buffer */

    char inChar; /* Next character from input */

    int atCR = 0; /* 0="within line", 1="optional DOS LF" */

    while ((inChar = getchar()) != EOF ) {
      switch (inChar) {
      case LF:
        if (atCR) {   /* Optional DOS LF */
          atCR = 0;
        } else {        /* Encountered CR within line */
          emit(buf, pos);
          pos = 0;
        }
        break;
      case CR:
        emit(buf, pos);
        pos = 0;
        atCR = 1;
        break;
      default:
        if (pos >= BUFLEN-2) fail("Buffer overflow");
        buf[pos++] = inChar;
      } /* switch */
    }
    if (pos > 0) {
      emit(buf, pos);
    }
}
```

Figure 5.11: Procedure to convert among Dos, Unix, and Macintosh line ends.

	LF	CR	EOF	other
e	e / emit	l / emit	d / –	w / append
w	e / emit	l / emit	d / emit	w / append
l	e / –	l / emit	d / –	w / append

Figure 5.12: Completed finite state machine (Mealy machine) description of line-end conversion procedure, depicted as a state-transition table (bottom). The omitted transition in Figure 5.9 has been added.

With this state abstraction function, we can check conformance between the source code and each transition in the FSM. For example, the transition from state *e* to state *l* is interpreted to mean that, if execution is at the head of the loop with pos equal to zero and atCR also zero (corresponding to state *e*), and the next character encountered is a carriage return, then the program should perform operations corresponding to the *emit* action and then enter a state in which pos is zero and atCR is 1 (corresponding to state *l*). It is easy to verify that this transition is implemented correctly. However, if we examine the transition from state *l* to state *w*, we will discover that the code does not correspond because the variable atCR is not reset to zero, as it should be. If the program encounters a carriage return, then some text, and then a line feed, the line feed will be discarded — a program fault.

The fault in the conversion program was actually detected by the authors through testing, and not through manual verification of correspondence between each transition and program source code. Making the abstraction function explicit was nonetheless important to understanding the nature of the error and how to repair it.

Summary

Models play many of the same roles in software development as in engineering of other kinds of artifacts. Models must be much simpler than the artifacts they describe, but must preserve enough essential detail to be useful in making choices. For models of software execution, this means that a model must abstract away enough detail to represent the potentially infinite set of program execution states by a finite and suitably compact set of model states.

Some models, such as control flow graphs and call graphs, can be extracted from programs. The key trade-off for these extracted models is precision (retaining enough information to be predictive) versus the cost of producing and storing the model. Other models, including many finite state machine models, may be constructed before the program they describe, and serve as a kind of intermediate-level specification of intended behavior. These models can be related to both a higher-level specification of intended behavior and the actual program they are intended to describe.

The relation between finite state models and programs is elaborated in Chapter 6. Analysis of models, particularly those involving concurrent execution, is described further in Chapter 8.

Further Reading

Finite state models of computation have been studied at least since the neural models of McColloch and Pitts [MP43], and modern finite state models of programs remain close to those introduced by Mealy [Mea55] and Moore [Moo56]. Lamport [Lam89] provides the clearest and most accessible introduction the authors know regarding what a finite state machine model "means" and what it means for a program to conform to it. Guttag [Gut77] presents an early explication of the abstraction relation between a model and a program, and why the abstraction function goes from concrete to abstract and not vice versa. Finite state models have been particularly important in development of reasoning and tools for concurrent (multi-threaded, parallel, and distributed) systems; Pezzè, Taylor, and Young [PTY95] overview finite models of concurrent programs.

Exercises

5.1. We construct large, complex software systems by breaking them into manageable pieces. Likewise, models of software systems may be decomposed into more manageable pieces. Briefly describe how the requirements of model compactness, predictiveness, semantic meaningfulness, and sufficient generality apply to approaches for modularizing models of programs. Give examples where possible.

5.2. Models are used in analysis, but construction of models from programs often requires some form of analysis. Why bother, then? If one is performing an initial analysis to construct a model to perform a subsequent analysis, why not just merge the initial and subsequent analysis and dispense with defining and constructing the model? For example, if one is analyzing Java code to construct a call graph and class hierarchy that will be used to detect overriding of inherited methods, why not just analyze the source code directly for method overriding?

5.3. Linear code sequence and jump (LCSAJ) makes a distinction between "sequential" control flow and other control flow. Control flow graphs, on the other hand, make no distinction between sequential and nonsequential control flow. Considering the criterion of model predictiveness, is there a justification for this distinction?

5.4. What upper bound can you place on the number of basic blocks in a program, relative to program size?

5.5. A directed graph is a set of nodes and a set of directed edges. A mathematical relation is a set of ordered pairs.

1. If we consider a directed graph as a representation of a relation, can we ever have two distinct edges from one node to another?
2. Each ordered pair in the relation corresponds to an edge in the graph. Is the set of nodes superfluous? In what case might the set of nodes of a directed graph be different from the set of nodes that appear in the ordered pairs?

5.6. We have described how abstraction can introduce nondeterminism by discarding some of the information needed to determine whether a particular state transition is possible. In addition to introducing spurious transitions, abstraction can introduce states that do not correspond to any possible program execution state — we say such states are *infeasible*. Can we still have an abstraction function from concrete states to model states if some of the model states are infeasible?

5.7. Can the number of basic blocks in the control flow graph representation of a program ever be greater than the number of program statements? If so, how? If not, why not?

Chapter 6

Dependence and Data Flow Models

The control flow graph and state machine models introduced in the previous chapter capture one aspect of the dependencies among parts of a program. They explicitly represent control flow but deemphasize transmission of information through program variables. Data flow models provide a complementary view, emphasizing and making explicit relations involving transmission of information.

Models of data flow and dependence in software were originally developed in the field of compiler construction, where they were (and still are) used to detect opportunities for optimization. They also have many applications in software engineering, from testing to refactoring to reverse engineering. In test and analysis, applications range from selecting test cases based on dependence information (as described in Chapter 13) to detecting anomalous patterns that indicate probable programming errors, such as uses of potentially uninitialized values. Moreover, the basic algorithms used to construct data flow models have even wider application and are of particular interest because they can often be quite efficient in time and space.

6.1 Definition-Use Pairs

The most fundamental class of data flow model associates the point in a program where a value is produced (called a "definition") with the points at which the value may be accessed (called a "use"). Associations of definitions and uses fundamentally capture the flow of information through a program, from input to output.

Definitions occur where variables are declared or initialized, assigned values, or received as parameters, and in general at all statements that change the value of one or more variables. Uses occur in expressions, conditional statements, parameter passing, return statements, and in general in all statements whose execution extracts a value from a variable. For example, in the standard greatest common divisor (GCD) algorithm of Figure 6.1, line 1 contains a definition of parameters x and y, line 3 contains a use of variable y, line 6 contains a use of variable tmp and a definition of variable y,

```
1    public int gcd(int x, int y) {       /* A: def x,y  */
2        int tmp;                         /*    def tmp  */
3        while (y != 0) {                 /* B: use y    */
4            tmp = x % y;                 /* C: use x,y, def tmp */
5            x = y;                       /* D: use y, def x  */
6            y = tmp;                     /* E: use tmp, def y */
7        }
8        return x;                        /* F: use x */
9    }
```

Figure 6.1: Java implementation of Euclid's algorithm for calculating the greatest common denominator of two positive integers. The labels A–F are provided to relate statements in the source code to graph nodes in subsequent figures.

and the return in line 8 is a use of variable x.

Each definition-use pair associates a definition of a variable (e.g., the assignment to y in line 6) with a use of the same variable (e.g., the expression y != 0 in line 3). A single definition can be paired with more than one use, and vice versa. For example, the definition of variable y in line 6 is paired with a use in line 3 (in the loop test), as well as additional uses in lines 4 and 5. The definition of x in line 5 is associated with uses in lines 4 and 8.

Δ kill

Δ definition-clear path

A definition-use pair is formed only if there is a program path on which the value assigned in the definition can reach the point of use without being overwritten by another value. If there is another assignment to the same value on the path, we say that the first definition is *killed* by the second. For example, the declaration of tmp in line 2 is not paired with the use of tmp in line 6 because the definition at line 2 is killed by the definition at line 4. A *definition-clear* path is a path from definition to use on which the definition is not killed by another definition of the same variable. For example, with reference to the node labels in Figure 6.2, path E,B,C,D is a definition-clear path from the definition of y in line 6 (node E of the control flow graph) to the use of y in line 5 (node D). Path A,B,C,D,E is not a definition-clear path with respect to tmp because of the intervening definition at node C.

Δ direct data dependence

Definition-use pairs record a kind of program dependence, sometimes called direct data dependence. These dependencies can be represented in the form of a graph, with a directed edge for each definition-use pair. The data dependence graph representation of the GCD method is illustrated in Figure 6.3 with nodes that are program statements. Different levels of granularity are possible. For use in testing, nodes are typically basic blocks. Compilers often use a finer-grained data dependence representation, at the level of individual expressions and operations, to detect opportunities for performance-improving transformations.

The data dependence graph in Figure 6.3 captures only dependence through flow of data. Dependence of the body of the loop on the predicate governing the loop is not represented by data dependence alone. Control dependence can also be represented with a graph, as in Figure 6.5, which shows the control dependencies for the GCD

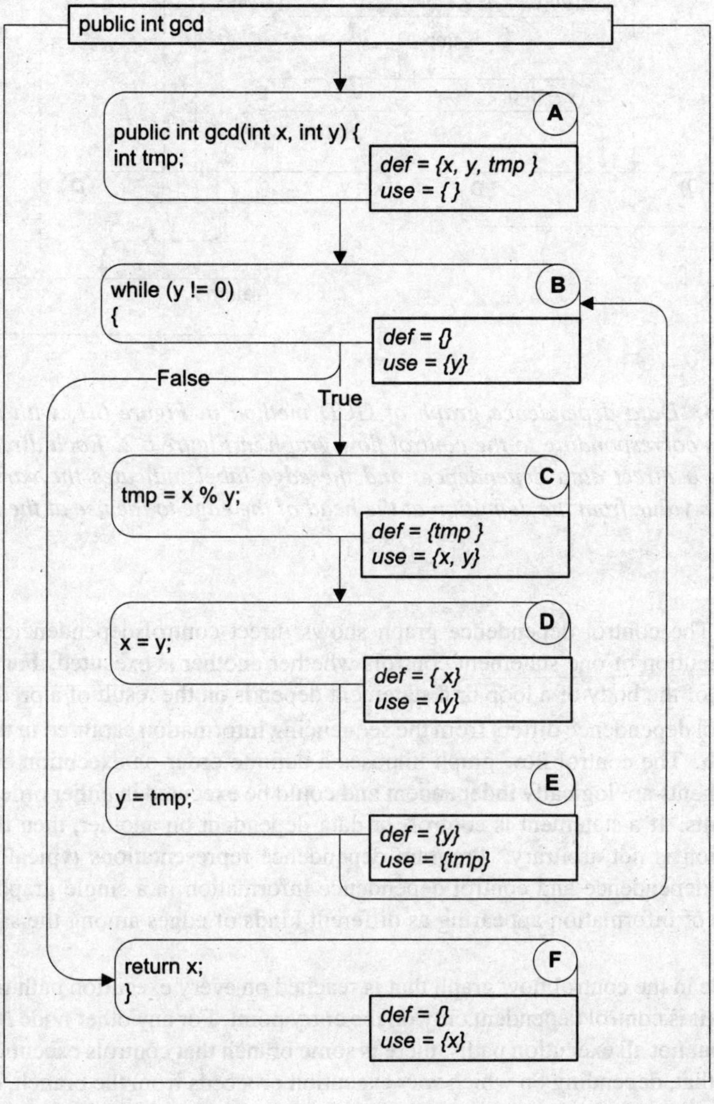

Figure 6.2: Control flow graph of GCD method in Figure 6.1.

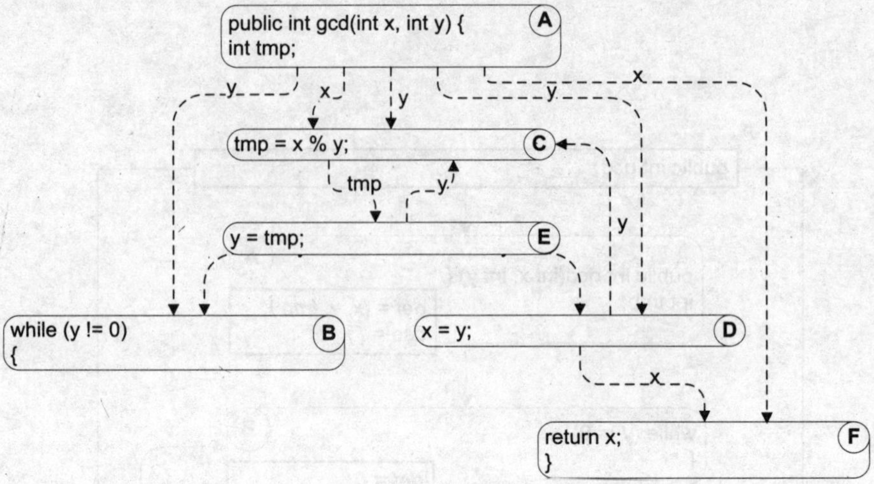

Figure 6.3: Data dependence graph of GCD method in Figure 6.1, with nodes for statements corresponding to the control flow graph in Figure 6.2. Each directed edge represents a direct data dependence, and the edge label indicates the variable that transmits a value from the definition at the head of the edge to the use at the tail of the edge.

method. The control dependence graph shows direct control dependencies, that is, where execution of one statement controls whether another is executed. For example, execution of the body of a loop or if statement depends on the result of a predicate.

Control dependence differs from the sequencing information captured in the control flow graph. The control flow graph imposes a definite order on execution even when two statements are logically independent and could be executed in either order with the same results. If a statement is control- or data-dependent on another, then their order of execution is not arbitrary. Program dependence representations typically include both data dependence and control dependence information in a single graph with the two kinds of information appearing as different kinds of edges among the same set of nodes.

A node in the control flow graph that is reached on every execution path from entry point to exit is control dependent only on the entry point. For any other node *N*, reached on some but not all execution paths, there is some branch that controls execution of *N* in the sense that, depending on which way execution proceeds from the branch, execution of *N* either does or does not become inevitable. It is this notion of control that control dependence captures.

Δ dominator

The notion of dominators in a rooted, directed graph can be used to make this intuitive notion of "controlling decision" precise. Node *M* dominates node *N* if every path from the root of the graph to *N* passes through *M*. A node will typically have many dominators, but except for the root, there is a unique *immediate dominator* of node *N*, which is closest to *N* on any path from the root and which is in turn dominated

Δ immediate dominator

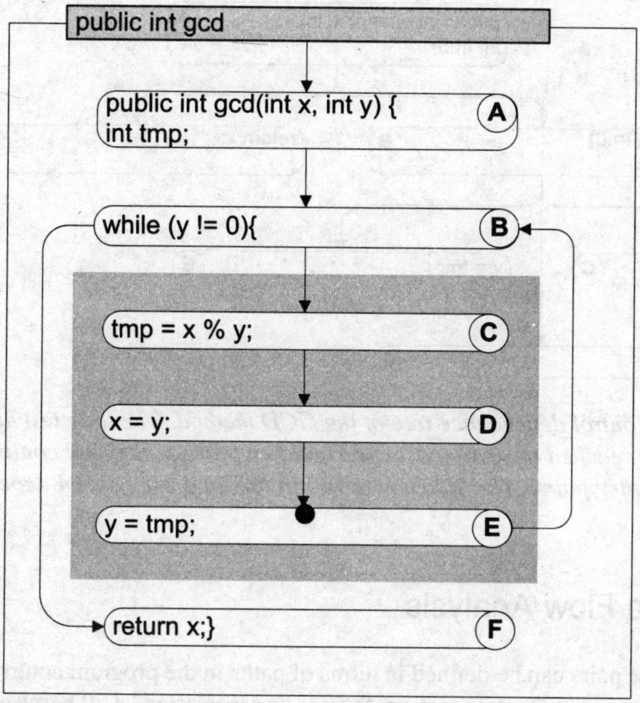

Figure 6.4: Calculating control dependence for node E in the control flow graph of the GCD method. Nodes C, D, and E in the gray region are post-dominated by E; that is, execution of E is inevitable in that region. Node B has successors both within and outside the gray region, so it controls whether E is executed; thus E is control-dependent on B.

by all the other dominators of *N*. Because each node (except the root) has a unique immediate dominator, the immediate dominator relation forms a tree.

The point at which execution of a node becomes inevitable is related to paths from a node to the end of execution — that is, to dominators that are calculated in the reverse of the control flow graph, using a special "exit" node as the root. Dominators in this direction are called post-dominators, and dominators in the normal direction of execution can be called pre-dominators for clarity.

Δ post-dominator

Δ pre-dominator

We can use post-dominators to give a more precise definition of control dependence. Consider again a node *N* that is reached on some but not all execution paths. There must be some node *C* with the following property: *C* has at least two successors in the control flow graph (i.e., it represents a control flow decision); *C* is not post-dominated by *N* (*N* is not already inevitable when *C* is reached); and there is a successor of *C* in the control flow graph that is post-dominated by *N*. When these conditions are true, we say node *N* is control-dependent on node *C*. Figure 6.4 illustrates the control dependence calculation for one node in the GCD example, and Figure 6.5 shows the control dependence relation for the method as a whole.

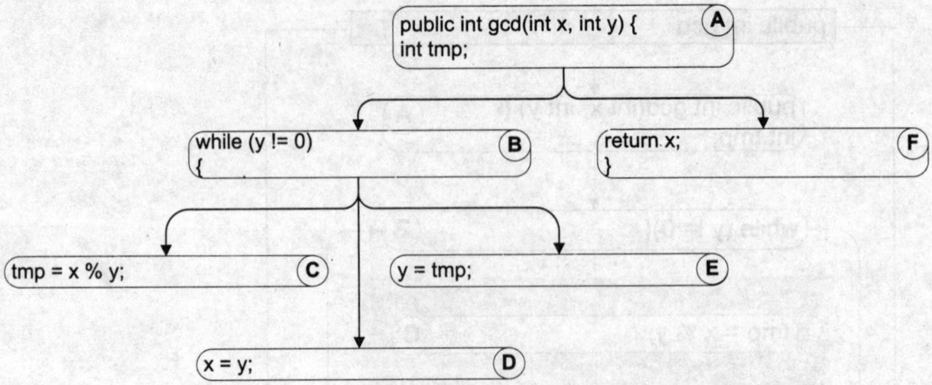

Figure 6.5: Control dependence tree of the GCD method. The loop test and the return statement are reached on every possible execution path, so they are control-dependent only on the entry point. The statements within the loop are control-dependent on the loop test.

6.2 Data Flow Analysis

Definition-use pairs can be defined in terms of paths in the program control flow graph. As we have seen in the former section, there is an association (d, u) between a definition of variable v at d and a use of variable v at u if and only if there is at least one control flow path from d to u with no intervening definition of v. We also say that definition v_d *reaches* u, and that v_d is a *reaching definition* at u. If, on the other hand, a control flow path passes through another definition e of the same variable v, we say that v_e *kills* v_d at that point.

Δ reaching definition

It would be possible to compute definition-use pairs by searching the control flow graph for individual paths of the form described above. However, even if we consider only loop-free paths, the number of paths in a graph can be exponentially larger than the number of nodes and edges. Practical algorithms therefore cannot search every individual path. Instead, they summarize the reaching definitions at a node over all the paths reaching that node.

An efficient algorithm for computing reaching definitions (and several other properties, as we will see below) is based on the way reaching definitions at one node are related to reaching definitions at an adjacent node. Suppose we are calculating the reaching definitions of node n, and there is an edge (p, n) from an immediate predecessor node p. We observe:

- If the predecessor node p can assign a value to variable v, then the definition v_p reaches n. We say the definition v_p is *generated* at p.
- If a definition v_d of variable v reaches a predecessor node p, and if v is not redefined at that node (in which case we say the v_d is *killed* at that point), then the definition is propagated on from p to n.

These observations can be stated in the form of an equation describing sets of reaching definitions. For example, reaching definitions at node E in Figure 6.2 are those at node D, except that D adds a definition of y and replaces (kills) an earlier definition of y:

$$Reach(E) = (Reach(D) \setminus \{x_A\}) \cup \{x_D\}$$

This rule can be broken down into two parts to make it a little more intuitive and more efficient to implement. The first part describes how node E receives values from its predecessor D, and the second describes how it modifies those values for its successors:

$$\begin{aligned} Reach(E) &= ReachOut(D) \\ ReachOut(D) &= (Reach(D) \setminus \{x_A\}) \cup \{x_D\} \end{aligned}$$

In this form, we can easily express what should happen at the head of the while loop (node B in Figure 6.2), where values may be transmitted both from the beginning of the procedure (node A) and through the end of the body of the loop (node E). The beginning of the procedure (node A) is treated as an initial definition of parameters and local variables. (If a local variable is declared but not initialized, it is treated as a definition to the special value "uninitialized.")

$$\begin{aligned} Reach(B) &= ReachOut(A) \cup ReachOut(E) \\ ReachOut(A) &= gen(A) = \{x_A, y_A, tmp_A\} \\ ReachOut(E) &= (ReachIn(E) \setminus \{y_A\}) \cup \{y_E\} \end{aligned}$$

In general, for any node n with predecessors $pred(n)$,

$$\begin{aligned} Reach(n) &= \bigcup_{m \in pred(n)} ReachOut(m) \\ ReachOut(n) &= (ReachIn(n) \setminus kill(n)) \cup gen(n) \end{aligned}$$

Remarkably, the reaching definitions can be calculated simply and efficiently, first initializing the reaching definitions at each node in the control flow graph to the empty set, and then applying these equations repeatedly until the results stabilize. The algorithm is given as pseudocode in Figure 6.6.

Algorithm *Reaching definitions*

Input: A controi flow graph $G = (\text{nodes}, \text{edges})$
pred$(n) = \{m \in \text{nodes} \mid (m,n) \in \text{edges}\}$
succ$(m) = \{n \in \text{nodes} \mid (m,n) \in \text{edges}\}$
gen$(n) = \{v_n\}$ if variable v is defined at n, otherwise $\{\}$
kill(n) = all other definitions of v if v is defined at n, otherwise $\{\}$

Output: Reach(n) = the reaching definitions at node n

```
for n ∈ nodes loop
    ReachOut(n) = {} ;
end loop;
workList = nodes ;
while (workList ≠ {}) loop
    // Take a node from worklist (e.g., pop from stack or queue)
    n = any node in workList ;
    workList = workList \ {n} ;

    oldVal = ReachOut(n) ;

    // Apply flow equations, propagating values from predecessars
    Reach(n) = ∪_{m∈pred(n)} ReachOut(m);
    ReachOut(n) = (Reach(n) \ kill(n)) ∪ gen(n) ;
    if ( ReachOut(n) ≠ oldVal ) then
        // Propagate changed value to successor nodes
        workList = workList ∪ succ(n)
    end if;
end loop;
```

Figure 6.6: An iterative work-list algorithm to compute reaching definitions by applying each flow equation until the solution stabilizes.

6.3 Classic Analyses: Live and Avail

Reaching definition is a classic data flow analysis adapted from compiler construction to applications in software testing and analysis. Other classical data flow analyses from compiler construction can likewise be adapted. Moreover, they follow a common pattern that can be used to devise a wide variety of additional analyses.

Available expressions is another classical data flow analysis, used in compiler construction to determine when the value of a subexpression can be saved and reused rather than recomputed. This is permissible when the value of the subexpression remains unchanged regardless of the execution path from the first computation to the second.

Available expressions can be defined in terms of paths in the control flow graph. An expression is *available* at a point if, for all paths through the control flow graph from procedure entry to that point, the expression has been computed and not subsequently modified. We say an expression is *generated* (becomes available) where it is computed and is *killed* (ceases to be available) when the value of any part of it changes (e.g., when a new value is assigned to a variable in the expression).

As with reaching definitions, we can obtain an efficient analysis by describing the relation between the available expressions that reach a node in the control flow graph and those at adjacent nodes. The expressions that become available at each node (the *gen* set) and the expressions that change and cease to be available (the *kill* set) can be computed simply, without consideration of control flow. Their propagation to a node from its predecessors is described by a pair of set equations:

$$
\begin{aligned}
Avail(n) &= \bigcap_{m \in pred(n)} AvailOut(m) \\
AvailOut(n) &= (Avail(n) \setminus kill(n)) \cup Gen(n)
\end{aligned}
$$

The similarity to the set equations for reaching definitions is striking. Both propagate sets of values along the control flow graph in the direction of program execution (they are *forward* analyses), and both combine sets propagated along different control flow paths. However, reaching definitions combines propagated sets using set union, since a definition can reach a use along *any* execution path. Available expressions combines propagated sets using set intersection, since an expression is considered available at a node only if it reaches that node along *all* possible execution paths. Thus we say that, while reaching definitions is a *forward, any-path* analysis, available expressions is a *forward, all-paths* analysis. A work-list algorithm to implement available expressions analysis is nearly identical to that for reaching definitions, except for initialization and the flow equations, as shown in Figure 6.7.

forward analysis

any-path analysis

all-paths analysis

Applications of a forward, all-paths analysis extend beyond the common subexpression detection for which the Avail algorithm was originally developed. We can think of available expressions as tokens that are propagated from where they are generated through the control flow graph to points where they might be used. We obtain different analyses by choosing tokens that represent some other property that becomes true (is generated) at some points, may become false (be killed) at some other points, and is

```
Algorithm Available expressions

Input:   A control flow graph G = (nodes, edges), with a distinguished root node start.
         pred(n) = {m ∈ nodes | (m,n) ∈ edges}
         succ(m) = {n ∈ nodes | (m,n) ∈ edges}
         gen(n) = all expressions e computed at node n
         kill(n) = expressions e computed anywhere, whose value is changed at n;
             kill(start) is the set of all e.

Output:  Avail(n) = the available expressions at node n


for n ∈ nodes loop
    AvailOut(n) = set of all e defined anywhere ;
end loop;
workList = nodes ;
while (workList ≠ {}) loop
    // Take a node from worklist (e.g., pop from stack or queue)
    n = any node in workList ;
    workList = workList \ {n} ;
    oldVal = AvailOut(n) ;
    // Apply flow equations, propagating values from predecessors
    Avail(n) = ⋂_{m∈pred(n)} AvailOut(m);
    AvailOut(n) = (Avail(n) \ kill(n)) ∪ gen(n) ;
    if ( AvailOut(n) ≠ oldVal ) then
        // Propagate changes to successors
        workList = workList ∪ succ(n)
    end if;
end loop;
```

Figure 6.7: An iterative work-list algorithm for computing available expressions.

```
/** A trivial method with a potentially uninitialized variable.
 * Java compilers reject the program. The compiler uses
 * data flow analysis to determine that there is a potential
 * (syntactic) execution path on which k is used before it
 * has been assigned an initial value.
 */
static void questionable() {
    int k;
    for (int i=0; i < 10; ++i) {
        if (someCondition(i)) {
            k = 0;
        } else {
            k += i;
        }
    }
    System.out.println(k);
}
}
```

Figure 6.8: Function questionable *(repeated from Chapter 3) has a potentially uninitialized variable, which the Java compiler can detect using data flow analysis.*

evaluated (used) at certain points in the graph. By associating appropriate sets of tokens in gen and kill sets for a node, we can evaluate other properties that fit the pattern

> "*G* occurs on all execution paths leading to *U*, and there is no intervening occurrence of *K* between the last occurrence of *G* and *U*."

G, *K*, and *U* can be any events we care to check, so long as we can mark their occurrences in a control flow graph.

An example problem of this kind is variable initialization. We noted in Chapter 3 that Java requires a variable to be initialized before use on all execution paths. The analysis that enforces this rule is an instance of Avail. The tokens propagated through the control flow graph record which variables have been assigned initial values. Since there is no way to "uninitialize" a variable in Java, the kill sets are empty. Figure 6.8 repeats the source code of an example program from Chapter 3. The corresponding control flow graph is shown with definitions and uses in Figure 6.9 and annotated with gen and kill sets for the initialized variable check in Figure 6.10.

Reaching definitions and available expressions are forward analyses; that is, they propagate values in the direction of program execution. Given a control flow graph model, it is just as easy to propagate values in the opposite direction, backward from nodes that represent the next steps in computation. *Backward* analyses are useful for determining what happens after an event of interest. Live variables is a backward analysis that determines whether the value held in a variable may be subsequently

backward analysis

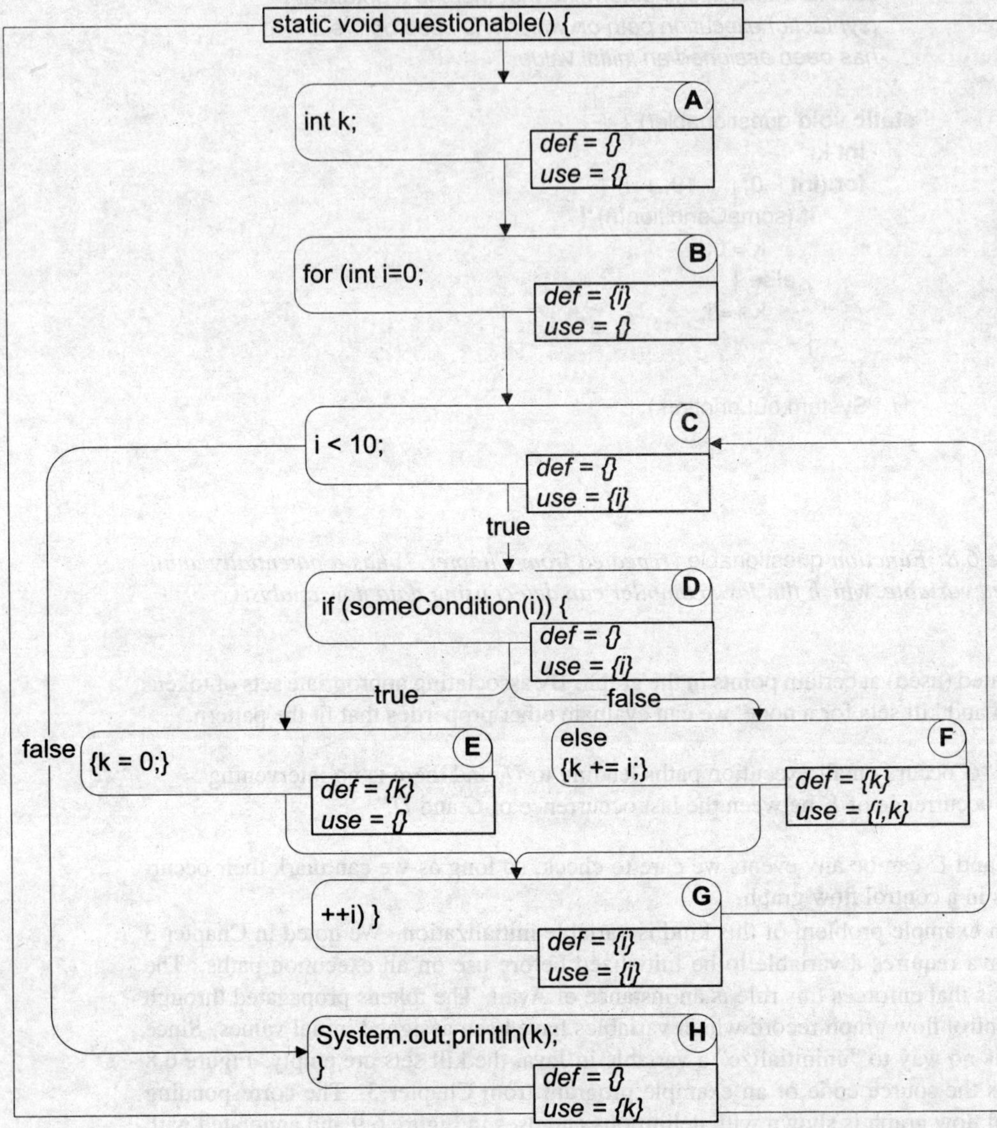

Figure 6.9: Control flow graph of the source code in Figure 6.8, annotated with variable definitions and uses.

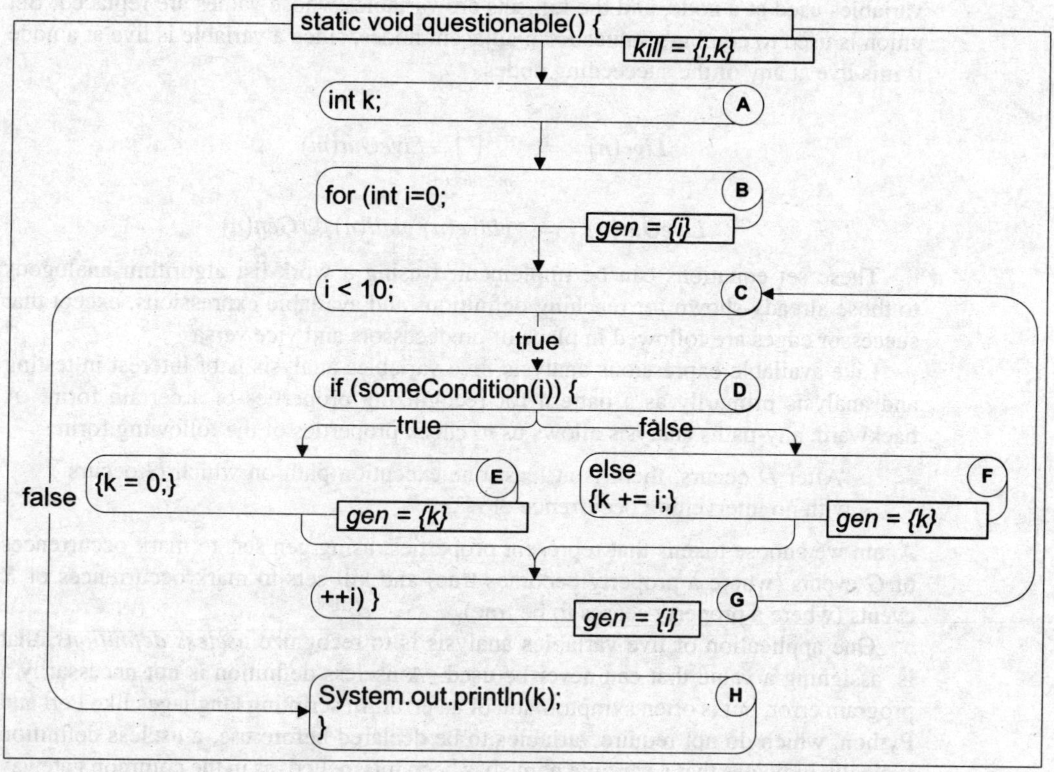

Figure 6.10: Control flow graph of the source code in Figure 6.8, annotated with gen and kill sets for checking variable initialization using a forward, all-paths Avail *analysis. (Empty gen and kill sets are omitted.) The* Avail *set flowing from node G to node C will be* $\{i,k\}$*, but the* Avail *set flowing from node B to node C is* $\{i\}$*. The all-paths analysis intersects these values, so the resulting* $Avail(C)$ *is* $\{i\}$*. This value propagates through nodes C and D to node F, which has a use of k as well as a definition. Since* $k \notin Avail(F)$*, a possible use of an uninitialized variable is detected.*

used. Because a variable is considered live if there is any possible execution path on which it is used, a *backward, any-path* analysis is used.

A variable is live at a point in the control flow graph if, on some execution path, its current value may be used before it is changed. Live variables analysis can be expressed as set equations as before. Where *Reach* and *Avail* propagate values to a node from its predecessors, *Live* propagates values from the successors of a node. The gen sets are variables used at a node, and the kill sets are variables whose values are replaced. Set union is used to combine values from adjacent nodes, since a variable is live at a node if it is live at any of the succeeding nodes.

$$Live(n) = \bigcup_{m \in succ(n)} LiveOut(m)$$

$$LiveOut(n) = (Live(n) \setminus kill(n)) \cup Gen(n)$$

These set equations can be implemented using a work-list algorithm analogous to those already shown for reaching definitions and available expressions, except that successor edges are followed in place of predecessors and vice versa.

Like available expressions analysis, live variables analysis is of interest in testing and analysis primarily as a pattern for recognizing properties of a certain form. A backward, any-paths analysis allows us to check properties of the following form:

> "After *D* occurs, there is at least one execution path on which *G* occurs with no intervening occurrence of *K*."

Again we choose tokens that represent properties, using gen sets to mark occurrences of *G* events (where a property becomes true) and kill sets to mark occurrences of *K* events (where a property ceases to be true).

One application of live variables analysis is to recognize *useless definitions*, that is, assigning a value that can never be used. A useless definition is not necessarily a program error, but is often symptomatic of an error. In scripting languages like Perl and Python, which do not require variables to be declared before use, a useless definition typically indicates that a variable name has been misspelled, as in the common gateway interface (CGI) script of Figure 6.11.

We have so far seen a forward, any-path analysis (reaching definitions), a forward, all-paths analysis (available definitions), and a backward, any-path analysis (live variables). One might expect, therefore, to round out the repertoire of patterns with a backward, all-paths analysis, and this is indeed possible. Since there is no classical name for this combination, we will call it "inevitability" and use it for properties of the form

> "After *D* occurs, *G* always occurs with no intervening occurrence of *K*"

or, informally,

> "*D* inevitably leads to *G* before *K*"

Examples of inevitability checks might include ensuring that interrupts are reenabled after executing an interrupt-handling routine in low-level code, files are closed after opening them, and so on.

```
class SampleForm(FormData):
    """ Used with Python cgi module
        to hold and validate data
        from HTML form """

    fieldnames = ('name', 'email', 'comment')

    # Trivial example of validation. The bug would be
    # harder to see in a real validation method.
    def validate(self):
        valid = 1;
        if self.name == "" : valid = 0
        if self.email == "" : vald = 0
        if self.comment == "" : valid = 0
        return valid
```

Figure 6.11: Part of a CGI program (Web form processing) in Python. The misspelled variable name in the data validation method will be implicitly declared and will not be rejected by the Python compiler or interpreter, which could allow invalid data to be treated as valid. The classic live variables data flow analysis can show that the assignment to valid *is a useless definition, suggesting that the programmer probably intended to assign the value to a different variable.*

6.4 From Execution to Conservative Flow Analysis

Data flow analysis algorithms can be thought of as a kind of simulated execution. In place of actual values, much smaller sets of possible values are maintained (e.g., a single bit to indicate whether a particular variable has been initialized). All possible execution paths are considered at once, but the number of different states is kept small by associating just one summary state at each program point (node in the control flow graph). Since the values obtained at a particular program point when it is reached along one execution path may be different from those obtained on another execution path, the summary state must combine the different values. Considering flow analysis in this light, we can systematically derive a conservative flow analysis from a dynamic (that is, run-time) analysis.

As an example, consider the "taint-mode" analysis that is built into the programming language Perl. Taint mode is used to prevent some kinds of program errors that result from neglecting to fully validate data before using it, particularly where invalidated data could present a security hazard. For example, if a Perl script wrote to a file whose name was taken from a field in a Web form, a malicious user could provide a full path to sensitive files. Taint mode detects and prevents use of the "tainted" Web form input in a sensitive operation like opening a file. Other languages used in CGI scripts do not provide such a monitoring function, but we will consider how an analogous static analysis could be designed for a programming language like C.

When Perl is running in taint mode, it tracks the sources from which each variable value was derived, and distinguishes between safe and tainted data. Tainted data is any input (e.g., from a Web form) and any data derived from tainted data. For example, if a tainted string is concatenated with a safe string, the result is a tainted string. One exception is that pattern matching always returns safe strings, even when matching against tainted data — this reflects the common Perl idiom in which pattern matching is used to validate user input. Perl's taint mode will signal a program error if tainted data is used in a potentially dangerous way (e.g., as a file name to be opened).

Perl monitors values dynamically, tagging data values and propagating the tags through computation. Thus, it is entirely possible that a Perl script might run without errors in testing, but an unanticipated execution path might trigger a taint mode program error in production use. Suppose we want to perform a similar analysis, but instead of checking whether "tainted" data is used unsafely on a particular execution, we want to ensure that tainted data can never be used unsafely on any execution. We may also wish to perform the analysis on a language like C, for which run-time tagging is not provided and would be expensive to add. So, we can consider deriving a conservative, static analysis that is like Perl's taint mode except that it considers all possible execution paths.

A data flow analysis for taint would be a forward, any-path analysis with tokens representing tainted variables. The gen set at a program point would be a set containing any variable that is assigned a tainted value at that point. Sets of tainted variables would be propagated forward to a node from its predecessors, with set union where a node in the control flow graph has more than one predecessor (e.g., the head of a loop).

There is one fundamental difference between such an analysis and the classic data flow analyses we have seen so far: The gen and kill sets associated with a program point are not constants. Whether or not the value assigned to a variable is tainted (and thus whether the variable belongs in the gen set or in the kill set) depends on the set of tainted variables at that program point, which will vary during the course of the analysis.

There is a kind of circularity here — the gen set and kill set depend on the set of tainted variables, and the set of tainted variables may in turn depend on the gen and kill set. Such circularities are common in defining flow analyses, and there is a standard approach to determining whether they will make the analysis unsound. To convince ourselves that the analysis is sound, we must show that the output values computed by each flow equation are monotonically increasing functions of the input values. We will say more precisely what "increasing" means below.

The determination of whether a computed value is tainted will be a simple function of the set of tainted variables at a program point. For most operations of one or more arguments, the output is tainted if any of the inputs are tainted. As in Perl, we may designate one or a few operations (operations used to check an input value for validity) as taint removers. These special operations always return an untainted value regardless of their inputs.

Suppose we evaluate the taintedness of an expression with the input set of tainted variables being $\{a,b\}$, and again with the input set of tainted variables being $\{a,b,c\}$. Even without knowing what the expression is, we can say with certainty that if the expression is tainted in the first evaluation, it must also be tainted in the second evalu-

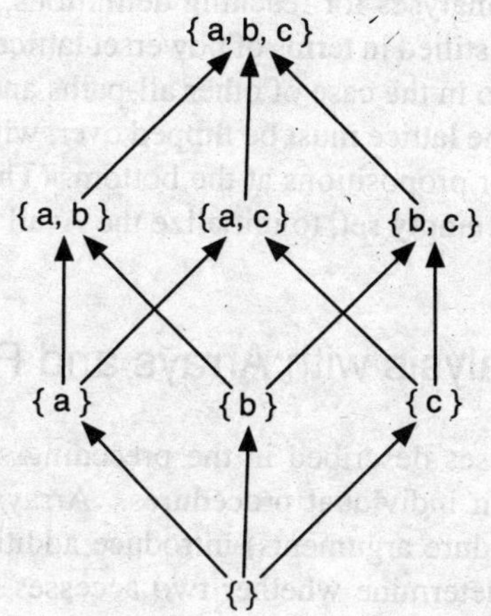

Figure 6.12: The powerset lattice of set $\{a, b, c\}$. The powerset contains all subsets of the set and is ordered by set inclusion.

ation, in which the set of tainted input variables is larger. This also means that adding elements to the input tainted set can only add elements to the gen set for that point, or leave it the same, and conversely the kill set can only grow smaller or stay the same. We say that the computation of tainted variables at a point increases monotonically.

To be more precise, the monotonicity argument is made by arranging the possible values in a lattice. In the sorts of flow analysis framework considered here, the lattice is almost always made up of subsets of some set (the set of definitions, or the set of tainted variables, etc.); this is called a powerset lattice because the powerset of set A is the set of all subsets of A. The bottom element of the lattice is the empty set, the top is the full set, and lattice elements are ordered by inclusion as in Figure 6.12. If we can follow the arrows in a lattice from element x to element y (e.g., from $\{a\}$ to $\{a, b, c\}$), then we say $y > x$. A function f is monotonically increasing if

powerset lattice

$$y \geq x \Rightarrow f(y) \geq f(x)$$

Not only are all of the individual flow equations for taintedness monotonic in this sense, but in addition the function applied to merge values where control flow paths come together is also monotonic:

$$A \supseteq B \Rightarrow A \cup C \supseteq B \cup C$$

If we have a set of data flow equations that is monotonic in this sense, and if we begin by initializing all values to the bottom element of the lattice (the empty set in this case), then we are assured that an iterative data flow analysis will converge on a unique minimum solution to the flow equations.

The standard data flow analyses for reaching definitions, live variables, and available expressions can all be justified in terms of powerset lattices. In the case of available expressions, though, and also in the case of other all-paths analyses such as the one we have called "inevitability," the lattice must be flipped over, with the empty set at the top and the set of all variables or propositions at the bottom. (This is why we used the set of all tokens, rather than the empty set, to initialize the Avail sets in Figure 6.7.)

6.5 Data Flow Analysis with Arrays and Pointers

The models and flow analyses described in the preceding section have been limited to simple scalar variables in individual procedures. Arrays and pointers (including object references and procedure arguments) introduce additional issues, because it is not possible in general to determine whether two accesses refer to the same storage location. For example, consider the following code fragment:

```
a[i] = 13;
k = a[j];
```

Are these two lines a definition-use pair? They are if the values of i and j are equal, which might be true on some executions and not on others. A static analysis cannot, in general, determine whether they are always, sometimes, or never equal, so a source of imprecision is necessarily introduced into data flow analysis.

Pointers and object references introduce the same issue, often in less obvious ways. Consider the following snippet:

```
a[2] = 42;
i = b[2];
```

It seems that there cannot possibly be a definition-use pair involving these two lines, since they involve none of the same variables. However, arrays in Java are dynamically allocated objects accessed through pointers. Pointers of any kind introduce the possibility of *aliasing*, that is, of two different names referring to the same storage location. For example, the two lines above might have been part of the following program fragment:

```
int [ ] a = new int[3];
int [ ] b = a;
a[2] = 42;
i = b[2];
```

Δ alias

Here a and b are *aliases*, two different names for the same dynamically allocated array object, and an assignment to part of a is also an assignment to part of b.

The same phenomenon, and worse, appears in languages with lower-level pointer manipulation. Perhaps the most egregious example is pointer arithmetic in C:

```
p = &b;
*(p + i) = k;
```

It is impossible to know which variable is defined by the second line. Even if we know the value of i, the result is dependent on how a particular compiler arranges variables in memory.

Dynamic references and the potential for aliasing introduce uncertainty into data flow analysis. In place of a definition or use of a single variable, we may have a potential definition or use of a whole set of variables or locations that could be aliases of each other. The proper treatment of this uncertainty depends on the use to which the analysis will be put. For example, if we seek strong assurance that v is always initialized before it is used, we may not wish to treat an assignment to a potential alias of v as initialization, but we may wish to treat a use of a potential alias of v as a use of v.

A useful mental trick for thinking about treatment of aliases is to translate the uncertainty introduced by aliasing into uncertainty introduced by control flow. After all, data flow analysis already copes with uncertainty about which potential execution paths will actually be taken; an infeasible path in the control flow graph may add elements to an any-paths analysis or remove results from an all-paths analysis. It is usually appropriate to treat uncertainty about aliasing consistently with uncertainty about control flow. For example, considering again the first example of an ambiguous reference:

```
a[i] = 13;
k = a[j];
```

We can imagine replacing this by the equivalent code:

```
a[i] = 13;
if (i == j) {
    k = a[i];
} else {
    k = a[j];
}
```

In the (imaginary) transformed code, we could treat all array references as distinct, because the possibility of aliasing is fully expressed in control flow. Now, if we are using an any-path analysis like reaching definitions, the potential aliasing will result in creating a definition-use pair. On the other hand, an assignment to a[j] would not kill a previous assignment to a[i]. This suggests that, for an any-path analysis, gen sets should include everything that might be referenced, but kill sets should include only what is definitely referenced.

If we were using an all-paths analysis, like available expressions, we would obtain a different result. Because the sets of available expressions are intersected where control flow merges, a definition of a[i] would make only that expression, and none of its potential aliases, available. On the other hand, an assignment to a[j] would kill a[i]. This suggests that, for an all-paths analysis, gen sets should include only what is definitely referenced, but kill sets should include all the possible aliases.

Even in analysis of a single procedure, the effect of other procedures must be considered at least with respect to potential aliases. Consider, for example, this fragment of a Java method:

```
public void transfer (CustInfo fromCust, CustInfo toCust) {

    PhoneNum fromHome = fromCust.gethomePhone();
    PhoneNum fromWork = fromCust.getworkPhone();

    PhoneNum toHome = toCust.gethomePhone();
    PhoneNum toWork = toCust.getworkPhone();
```

We cannot determine whether the two arguments fromCust and toCust are references to the same object without looking at the context in which this method is called. Moreover, we cannot determine whether fromHome and fromWork are (or could be) references to the same object without more information about how CustInfo objects are treated elsewhere in the program.

Sometimes it is sufficient to treat all nonlocal information as unknown. For example, we could treat the two CustInfo objects as potential aliases of each other, and similarly treat the four PhoneNum objects as potential aliases. Sometimes, though, large sets of aliases will result in analysis results that are so imprecise as to be useless. Therefore data flow analysis is often preceded by an interprocedural analysis to calculate sets of aliases or the locations that each pointer or reference can refer to.

6.6 Interprocedural Analysis

Most important program properties involve more than one procedure, and as mentioned earlier, some interprocedural analysis (e.g., to detect potential aliases) is often required as a prelude even to intraprocedural analysis. One might expect the interprocedural analysis and models to be a natural extension of the intraprocedural analysis, following procedure calls and returns like intraprocedural control flow. Unfortunately, this is seldom a practical option.

If we were to extend data flow models by following control flow paths through procedure calls and returns, using the control flow graph model and the call graph model together in the obvious way, we would observe many spurious paths. Figure 6.13 illustrates the problem: Procedure foo and procedure bar each make a call on procedure sub. When procedure call and return are treated as if they were normal control flow, in addition to the execution sequences (A,X,Y,B) and (C,X,Y,D), the combined graph contains the impossible paths (A,X,Y,D) and (C,X,Y,B).

context-sensitive analysis

It is possible to represent procedure calls and returns precisely, for example by making a copy of the called procedure for each point at which it is called. This would result in a *context-sensitive* analysis. The shortcoming of context sensitive analysis was already mentioned in the previous chapter: The number of different contexts in which a procedure must be considered could be exponentially larger than the number of procedures. In practice, a context-sensitive analysis can be practical for a small group of closely related procedures (e.g., a single Java class), but is almost never a practical option for a whole program.

Some interprocedural properties are quite independent of context and lend themselves naturally to analysis in a hierarchical, piecemeal fashion. Such a hierarchical

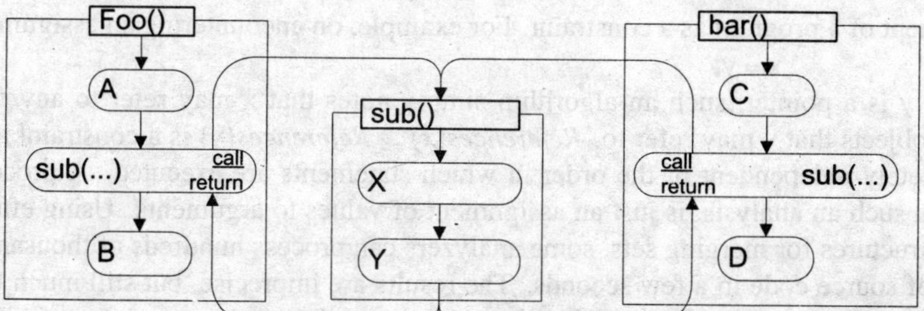

Figure 6.13: Spurious execution paths result when procedure calls and returns are treated as normal edges in the control flow graph. The path (A,X,Y,D) appears in the combined graph, but it does not correspond to an actual execution order.

analysis can be both precise and efficient. The analyses that are provided as part of normal compilation are often of this sort. The unhandled exception analysis of Java is a good example: Each procedure (method) is required to declare the exceptions that it may throw without handling. If method M calls method N in the same or another class, and if N can throw some exception, then M must either handle that exception or declare that it, too, can throw the exception. This analysis is simple and efficient because, when analyzing method M, the internal structure of N is irrelevant; only the results of the analysis at N (which, in Java, is also part of the signature of N) are needed.

Two conditions are necessary to obtain an efficient, hierarchical analysis like the exception analysis routinely carried out by Java compilers. First, the information needed to analyze a calling procedure must be small: It must not be proportional either to the size of the called procedure, or to the number of procedures that are directly or indirectly called. Second, it is essential that information about the called procedure be independent of the caller; that is, it must be context-independent. When these two conditions are true, it is straightforward to develop an efficient analysis that works upward from leaves of the call graph. (When there are cycles in the call graph from recursive or mutually recursive procedures, an iterative approach similar to data flow analysis algorithms can usually be devised.)

Unfortunately, not all important properties are amenable to hierarchical analysis. Potential aliasing information, which is essential to data flow analysis even within individual procedures, is one of those that are not. We have seen that potential aliasing can depend in part on the arguments passed to a procedure, so it does not have the context-independence property required for an efficient hierarchical analysis. For such an analysis, additional sacrifices of precision must be made for the sake of efficiency.

Even when a property is context-dependent, an analysis for that property may be context-insensitive, although the context-insensitive analysis will necessarily be less precise as a consequence of discarding context information. At the extreme, a linear time analysis can be obtained by discarding both context and control flow information.

flow-insensitive

Context- and flow-insensitive algorithms for pointer analysis typically treat each statement of a program as a constraint. For example, on encountering an assignment

```
x = y;
```

where y is a pointer, such an algorithm simply notes that x may refer to any of the same objects that y may refer to. $References(x) \supseteq References(y)$ is a constraint that is completely independent of the order in which statements are executed. A procedure call, in such an analysis, is just an assignment of values to arguments. Using efficient data structures for merging sets, some analyzers can process hundreds of thousands of lines of source code in a few seconds. The results are imprecise, but still much better than the worst-case assumption that any two compatible pointers might refer to the same object.

The best approach to interprocedural pointer analysis will often lie somewhere between the astronomical expense of a precise, context- and flow-sensitive pointer analysis and the imprecision of the fastest context- and flow-insensitive analyses. Unfortunately, there is not one best algorithm or tool for all uses. In addition to context and flow sensitivity, important design trade-offs include the granularity of modeling references (e.g., whether individual fields of an object are distinguished) and the granularity of modeling the program heap (that is, which allocated objects are distinguished from each other).

Summary

Data flow models are used widely in testing and analysis, and the data flow analysis algorithms used for deriving data flow information can be adapted to additional uses. The most fundamental model, complementary to models of control flow, represents the ways values can flow from the points where they are defined (computed and stored) to points where they are used.

Data flow analysis algorithms efficiently detect the presence of certain patterns in the control flow graph. Each pattern involves some nodes that initiate the pattern and some that conclude it, and some nodes that may interrupt it. The name "data flow analysis" reflects the historical development of analyses for compilers, but patterns may be used to detect other control flow patterns.

An any-path analysis determines whether there is any control flow path from the initiation to the conclusion of a pattern without passing through an interruption. An all-paths analysis determines whether every path from the initiation necessarily reaches a concluding node without first passing through an interruption. Forward analyses check for paths in the direction of execution, and backward analyses check for paths in the opposite direction. The classic data flow algorithms can all be implemented using simple work-list algorithms.

A limitation of data flow analysis, whether for the conventional purpose or to check other properties, is that it cannot distinguish between a path that can actually be executed and a path in the control flow graph that cannot be followed in any execution. A related limitation is that it cannot always determine whether two names or expressions refer to the same object.

Fully detailed data flow analysis is usually limited to individual procedures or a few closely related procedures (e.g., a single class in an object-oriented program). Analyses that span whole programs must resort to techniques that discard or summarize some information about calling context, control flow, or both. If a property is independent of calling context, a hierarchical analysis can be both precise and efficient. Potential aliasing is a property for which calling context is significant. There is therefore a trade-off between very fast but imprecise alias analysis techniques and more precise but much more expensive techniques.

Further Reading

Data flow analysis techniques were originally developed for compilers, as a systematic way to detect opportunities for code-improving transformations and to ensure that those transformations would not introduce errors into programs (an all-too-common experience with early optimizing compilers). The compiler construction literature remains an important source of reference information for data flow analysis, and the classic "Dragon Book" text [ASU86] is a good starting point.

Fosdick and Osterweil recognized the potential of data flow analysis to detect program errors and anomalies that suggested the presence of errors more than two decades ago [FO76]. While the classes of data flow anomaly detected by Fosdick and Osterweil's system has largely been obviated by modern strongly typed programming languages, they are still quite common in modern scripting and prototyping languages. Olender and Osterweil later recognized that the power of data flow analysis algorithms for recognizing execution patterns is not limited to properties of data flow, and developed a system for specifying and checking general sequencing properties [OO90, OO92].

Interprocedural pointer analyses — either directly determining potential aliasing relations, or deriving a "points-to" relation from which aliasing relations can be derived — remains an area of active research. At one extreme of the cost-versus-precision spectrum of analyses are completely context- and flow-insensitive analyses like those described by Steensgaard [Ste96]. Many researchers have proposed refinements that obtain significant gains in precision at small costs in efficiency. An important direction for future work is obtaining acceptably precise analyses of a portion of a large program, either because a whole program analysis cannot obtain sufficient precision at acceptable cost or because modern software development practices (e.g., incorporating externally developed components) mean that the whole program is never available in any case. Rountev et al. present initial steps toward such analyses [RRL99]. A very readable overview of the state of the art and current research directions (circa 2001) is provided by Hind [Hin01].

Exercises

6.1. For a graph $G = (N, V)$ with a root $r \in N$, node m dominates node n if every path from r to n passes through m. The root node is dominated only by itself.

The relation can be restated using flow equations.

(a) When dominance is restated using flow equations, will it be stated in the form of an any-path problem or an all-paths problem? Forward or backward? What are the tokens to be propagated, and what are the gen and kill sets?

(b) Give a flow equation for $Dom(n)$.

(c) If the flow equation is solved using an iterative data flow analysis, what should the set $Dom(n)$ be initialized to at each node n?

(d) Implement an iterative solver for the dominance relation in a programming language of your choosing.

The first line of input to your program is an integer between 1 and 100 indicating the number k of nodes in the graph. Each subsequent line of input will consist of two integers, m and n, representing an edge from node m to node n. Node 0 designates the root, and all other nodes are designated by integers between 0 and $k-1$. The end of the input is signaled by the pseudo-edge $(-1, -1)$.

The output of your program should be a sequences of lines, each containing two integers separated by blanks. Each line represents one edge of the *Dom* relation of the input graph.

(e) The *Dom* relation itself is not a tree. The immediate dominators relation is a tree. Write flow equations to calculate immediate dominators, and then modify the program from part (d) to compute the immediate dominance relation.

6.2. Write flow equations for inevitability, a backward, all-paths intraprocedural analysis. Event (or program point) q is inevitable at program point p if every execution path from p to a normal exit point passes through q.

6.3. The Java language automatically initializes fields of objects, in contrast to local variables of methods that the programmer is responsible for initializing. Given what you know of intra- and interprocedural data flow analysis, explain why the language designers may have made these design choices.

6.4. Show the data and control dependence graphs for the binary search program of Figure 7.1 on page 103.

Chapter 7

Symbolic Execution and Proof of Properties

Symbolic execution builds predicates that characterize the conditions under which execution paths can be taken and the effect of the execution on program state. Extracting predicates through symbolic execution is the essential bridge from the complexity of program behavior to the simpler and more orderly world of logic. It finds important applications in program analysis, in generating test data, and in formal verification[1] (proofs) of program correctness.

Conditions under which a particular control flow path is taken can be determined through symbolic execution. This is useful for identifying infeasible program paths (those that can never be taken) and paths that could be taken when they should not. It is fundamental to generating test data to execute particular parts and paths in a program.

Deriving a logical representation of the effect of execution is essential in methods that compare a program's possible behavior to a formal specification. We have noted in earlier chapters that proving the correctness of a program is seldom an achievable or useful goal. Nonetheless the basic methods of formal verification, including symbolic execution, underpin practical techniques in software analysis and testing. Symbolic execution and the techniques of formal verification find use in several domains:

- **Rigorous proofs of properties of (small) critical subsystems, such as a safety kernel of a medical device;**

- **Formal verification of critical properties (e.g., security properties) that are particularly resistant to dynamic testing;**

- **Formal verification of algorithm descriptions and logical designs that are much less complex than their implementations in program code.**

---

[1]**Throughout this book we use the term *verification* in the broad sense of checking whether a program or system is consistent with some form of specification. The broad sense of verification includes, for example, inspection techniques and program testing against informally stated specifications. The term *formal verification* is used in the scientific literature in a much narrower sense to denote techniques that construct a mathematical proof of consistency between some formal representation of a program or design and a formal specification.**

More fundamentally, the techniques of formal reasoning are a conceptual foundation for a variety of analysis techniques, ranging from informal reasoning about program behavior and correctness to automated checks for certain classes of errors.

7.1 Symbolic State and Interpretation

Tracing execution is familiar to any programmer who has attempted to understand the behavior of source code by simulating execution. For example, one might trace a single statement in the binary search routine of Figure 7.1 as shown on the left side of Figure 7.2. One can just as easily use symbolic values like L and H in place of concrete values, as shown on the right side of Figure 7.2. Tracing execution with symbolic values and expressions is the basis of symbolic execution.

When tracing execution with concrete values, it is clear enough what to do with a branch statement, for example, an if or while test: The test predicate is evaluated with the current values, and the appropriate branch is taken. If the values bound to variables are symbolic expressions, however, both the *True* and *False* outcomes of the decision may be possible. Execution can be traced through the branch in either direction, and execution of the test is interpreted as adding a constraint to record the outcome. For example, consider

```
while (high >= low) {
```

Suppose the symbolic state after one loop iteration is

$$\begin{aligned} & \text{low} = 0 \\ \wedge\ & \text{high} = \tfrac{H-1}{2} - 1 \\ \wedge\ & \text{mid} = \tfrac{H-1}{2} \end{aligned}$$

If we trace execution of the test assuming a *True* outcome (leading to a second iteration of the loop), the loop condition becomes a constraint in the symbolic state immediately after the while test:

$$\begin{aligned} & \text{low} = 0 \\ \wedge\ & \text{high} = \tfrac{H-1}{2} - 1 \\ \wedge\ & \text{mid} = \tfrac{H-1}{2} \\ \wedge\ & \tfrac{H-1}{2} - 1 \geq 0 \end{aligned}$$

Later, when we consider the branch assuming a *False* outcome of the test, the new constraint is negated and becomes $\neg(\frac{H-1}{2} - 1 \geq 0)$ or, equivalently, $\frac{H-1}{2} - 1 < 0$.

Execution can proceed in this way down any path in the program. One can think of "satisfying" the predicate by finding concrete values for the symbolic variables that make it evaluate to *True*; this corresponds to finding data values that would force execution of that program path. If no such satisfying values are possible, then that execution path cannot be executed with any data values; we say it is an infeasible path.

```

/** Binary search for key in sorted array dictKeys, returning
 * corresponding value from dictValues or null if key does
 * not appear in dictKeys. Standard binary search algorithm
 * as described in any elementary text on data structures and algorithms.
**/

char * binarySearch( char *key, char *dictKeys[ ], char *dictValues[ ],
                     int dictSize) {

    int low = 0;
    int high = dictSize - 1;
    int mid;
    int comparison;

    while (high >= low) {
        mid = (high + low) / 2;
        comparison = strcmp( dictKeys[mid], key );
        if (comparison < 0) {
            /* dictKeys[mid] too small; look higher */
            low = mid + 1;
        } else if ( comparison > 0) {
            /* dictKeys[mid] too large; look lower */
            high = mid - 1;
        } else {
            /* found */
            return dictValues[mid];
        }
    }
    return 0;    /* null means not found */
}

```

Figure 7.1: Binary search procedure.

before

low	12
high	15
mid	–

mid = (high + low) / 2;

after

low	12
high	15
mid	13

before

low	L
high	H
mid	–

mid = (high + low) / 2;

after

low	L
high	H
mid	$\frac{L+H}{2}$

Figure 7.2: Hand-tracing an execution step with concrete values (left) and symbolic values (right).

7.2 Summary Information

If there were only a finite number of execution paths in a program, then in principle a symbolic executor could trace each of them and obtain a precise representation of a predicate that characterizes each one. From even a few execution steps in the preceding small example, one can see that the representation of program state will quickly become unwieldy. Moreover, there are a potentially infinite number of program execution paths to consider. An automated symbolic executor can cope with much more complex symbolic expressions than a human, but even an automated tool will not get far with brute force evaluation of every program path.

Since the representation of program state is a logical predicate, there is an alternative to keeping a complete representation of the state at every point: a *weaker* predicate can always be substituted for the complete representation. That is, if the representation of the program state at some point in execution is P, and if $W \Rightarrow P$, then substituting W for P will result in a predicate that still correctly describes the execution state, but with less precision. We call W a *summary* of P.

Consider the computation of mid in line 17 of the binary search example from Figure 7.1. If we are reasoning about the performance of binary search, the fact that the value of mid lies halfway between the values of low and high is important, but if we are reasoning about functional correctness it matters only that mid lies somewhere between them. Thus, if we had $\text{low} = L \wedge \text{high} = H \wedge \text{mid} = M$, and if we could show $L \leq H$, we could replace $M = (L+H)/2$ by the weaker condition $L \leq M \leq H$.

Note that the weaker predicate $L \leq \text{mid} \leq H$ is chosen based on what must be true for the program to execute correctly. This is not information that can be derived automatically from source code; it depends as well on our understanding of the code and our rationale for believing it to be correct. A predicate stating what *should* be true at a given point can be expressed in the form of an assertion. When we assert that predicate W is true at a point in a program, we mark our intention both to verify it at that point (by showing that W is implied by the predicates that describe the program state at that point) and to replace part of the program state description P by W at that point.

One of the prices of weakening the predicate in this way will be that satisfying the predicate is no longer sufficient to find data that forces the program execution along that path. If the complete predicate P is replaced by a weaker predicate W, then test data that satisfies W is necessary to execute the path, but it may not be sufficient. Showing that W cannot be satisfied is still tantamount to showing that the execution path is infeasible.

7.3 Loops and Assertions

The number of execution paths through a program with one or more loops is potentially infinite, or at least unimaginably huge. This may not matter for symbolic execution along a single, relatively simple execution path. It becomes a major obstacle if symbolic execution is used to reason about a path involving several iterations of a loop, or to reason about all possible program executions.

To reason about program behavior in a loop, we can place within the loop an assertion that states a predicate that is expected to be true each time execution reaches that point. Such an assertion is called an *invariant*. Each time program execution reaches the invariant assertion, we can weaken the description of program state. If the program state is represented by P, and the assertion is W, we must first ascertain $W \Rightarrow P$ (the assertion is satisfied along that path), and then we can substitute W for P.

Δ loop invariant

Suppose every loop contained such an assertion, and suppose in addition there was an assertion at the beginning of the program (perhaps just the trivial predicate *True*) and a final assertion at the end. In that case, every possible execution path would consist of a sequence of segments from one assertion to the next. The assertion at the beginning of a segment is the *precondition* for that segment, and the assertion at the end of the segment is the *postcondition*. If we were able to execute each such segment independently, starting with only the precondition and then checking that the assertion at the end of the segment is satisfied, we would have shown that every assertion is satisfied on every possible program execution — that is, we would have verified correct execution on an infinite number of program paths by verifying the finite number of segments from which the paths are constructed.

Δ precondition

Δ postcondition

We illustrate the technique by using assertions to check the logic of the binary search algorithm implemented by the program in Figure 7.1. The first precondition and the final postcondition serve as a specification of correct behavior as a kind of contract: If the client ensures the precondition, the program will ensure the postcondition.

The binary search procedure depends on the array dictKeys being sorted. Thus we might have a precondition assertion like the following:

$$\forall i, j, 0 \le i < j < \text{size} : dictKeys[i] \le dictKeys[j]$$

Here we interpret $s \le t$ for strings as indicating lexical order consistent with the C library strcmp; that is, we assume that $s \le t$ whenever strcmp(s,t) ≤ 0. For convenience we will abbreviate the predicate above as *sorted*.

We can associate the following assertion with the while statement at line 16:

$$\forall i, 0 \le i < \text{size} : \text{dictkeys}[i] = \text{key} \Rightarrow \text{low} \le i \le \text{high}$$

In other words, we assert that the key can appear only between low and high, if it appears anywhere in the array. We will abbreviate this condition as *inrange*.

Inrange must be true when we first reach the loop, because at that point the range low...high is the same as 0...size − 1. For each path through the body of the loop, the symbolic executor would begin with the invariant assertion above, and determine that it is true again after following that path. We say the invariant is *preserved*.

While the *inrange* predicate should be true on each iteration, it is not the complete loop invariant. The *sorted* predicate remains true and will be used in reasoning. In principle it is also part of the invariant, although in informal reasoning we may not bother to write it down repeatedly. The full invariant is therefore *sorted* ∧ *inrange*.

Let us consider the path from line 16 through line 21 and back to the loop test. We begin by assuming that the loop invariant assertion holds at the beginning of the segment. Where expressions in the invariant refer to program variables whose values may change, they are replaced by symbols representing the initial values of those variables. The variable bindings will be

$$\begin{aligned} & \text{low} = L \\ \wedge\ & \text{high} = H \end{aligned}$$

We need not introduce symbols to represent the values of dictKeys, dictVals, key, or size. Since those variables are not changed in the procedure, we can use the variable names directly. The condition, instantiated with symbolic values, will be

$$\begin{aligned} & \forall i, j, 0 \le i < j < \text{size} : \mathit{dictKeys}[i] \le \mathit{dictKeys}[j] \\ \wedge\ & \forall k, 0 \le k < \text{size} : \text{dictkeys}[k] = \text{key} \Rightarrow L \le k \le H \end{aligned}$$

Passing through the while test into the body of the loop adds the clause $H \ge L$ to this condition. Execution of line 17 adds a binding of $\lfloor (H+L)/2 \rfloor$ to variable mid, where $\lfloor x \rfloor$ is the integer obtained by rounding x toward zero. As we have discussed, this can be simplified with an assertion so that the bindings and condition become

$$\begin{aligned} & \text{low} = L && \textit{(bindings)} \\ \wedge\ & \text{high} = H && \\ \wedge\ & \text{mid} = M && \\ \wedge\ & \forall i, j, 0 \le i < j < \text{size} : \text{dictKeys}[i] \le \text{dictKeys}[j] && \textit{(sorted)} \\ \wedge\ & \forall k, 0 \le k < \text{size} : \text{dictkeys}[k] = \text{key} \Rightarrow L \le k \le H && \textit{(inrange)} \\ \wedge\ & H \ge M \ge L && \end{aligned}$$

Tracing the execution path into the first branch of the if statement to line 21, we add the constraint that strcmp(dictKeys[mid], key) returns a negative value, which we interpret as meaning the probed entry is lexically less than the string value of the key. Thus we arrive at the symbolic constraint

$$\begin{aligned} & \text{low} = L \\ \wedge\ & \text{high} = H \\ \wedge\ & \text{mid} = M \\ \wedge\ & \forall i,j, 0 \le i < j < \text{size} : \text{dictKeys}[i] \le \text{dictKeys}[j] \\ \wedge\ & \forall k, 0 \le k < \text{size} : \text{dictkeys}[k] = \text{key} \Rightarrow L \le k \le H \\ \wedge\ & H \ge M \ge L \\ \wedge\ & \text{dictKeys}[M] < \text{key} \end{aligned}$$

The assignment in line 21 then modifies a variable binding without otherwise disturbing the conditions, giving us

$$\begin{aligned} & \text{low} = M+1 \\ \wedge\ & \text{high} = H \\ \wedge\ & \text{mid} = M \\ \wedge\ & \forall i,j, 0 \le i < j < \text{size} : \text{dictKeys}[i] \le \text{dictKeys}[j] \\ \wedge\ & \forall k, 0 \le k < \text{size} : \text{dictkeys}[k] = \text{key} \Rightarrow L \le k \le H \\ \wedge\ & H \ge M \ge L \\ \wedge\ & \text{dictKeys}[M] < \text{key} \end{aligned}$$

Finally, we trace execution back to the while test at line 16. Now our obligation is to show that the invariant still holds when instantiated with the changed set of variable bindings. The *sorted* condition has not changed, and showing that it is still true is trivial. The interesting part is the *inrange* predicate, which is instantiated with a new value for low and thus becomes

$$\forall k, 0 \le k < \text{size} : \text{dictkeys}[k] = \text{key} \Rightarrow M+1 \le k \le H$$

Now the verification step is to show that this predicate is a logical consequence of the predicate describing the program state. This step requires purely logical and mathematical reasoning, and might be carried out either by a human or by a theorem-proving tool. It no longer depends in any way upon the program. The task performed by the symbolic executor is essentially to transform a question about a program (is the invariant preserved on a particular path?) into a question of logic alone.

The path through the loop on which the probed key is too large, rather than too small, proceeds similarly. The path on which the probed key matches the sought key returns from the procedure, and our obligation there (trivial in this case) is to verify that the contract of the procedure has been met.

The other exit from the procedure occurs when the loop terminates without locating a matching key. The contract of the procedure is that it should return the null pointer (represented in the C language by 0) only if the key appears nowhere in dictKeys[0..size-1]. Since the null pointer is returned whenever the loop terminates, the postcondition of the loop is that key is not present in dictKeys.

The loop invariant is used to show that the postcondition holds when the loop terminates. What symbolic execution can verify immediately after a loop is that the invariant is true but the loop test is false. Thus we have

$$
\begin{array}{lll}
 & \text{low} = L & \textit{(bindings)} \\
\wedge & \text{high} = H & \\
\wedge & \forall i, j, 0 \leq i < j < \text{size} : \text{dictKeys}[i] \leq \text{dictKeys}[j] & \textit{(sorted)} \\
\wedge & \forall k, 0 \leq k < \text{size} : \text{dictkeys}[k] = \text{key} \Rightarrow L \leq k \leq H & \textit{(inrange)} \\
\wedge & L > H &
\end{array}
$$

Knowing that presence of the key in the array implies $L \leq H$, and that in fact $L > H$, we can conclude that the key is not present. Thus the postcondition is established, and the procedure fulfills its contract by returning the null pointer in this case.

Finding and verifying a complete set of assertions, including an invariant assertion for each loop, is difficult in practice. Even the small example above is rather tedious to verify by hand. More realistic examples can be quite demanding even with the aid of symbolic execution tools. If it were easy or could be fully automated, we might routinely use this method to prove the correctness of programs. Writing down a full set of assertions formally, and rigorously verifying them, is usually reserved for small and extremely critical modules, but the basic approach we describe here can also be applied in a much less formal manner and is quite useful in finding holes in an informal correctness argument.

7.4 Compositional Reasoning

The binary search procedure is very simple. There is only one loop, containing a single if statement. It was not difficult to reason about individual paths through the control flow. If the procedure contained nested loops or more conditional branches, we could in principle still proceed in that manner as long as each cycle in the control flow graph were broken by at least one assertion. It would, however, be very difficult to think about programs in this manner and to choose appropriate assertions. It is better if our approach follows the hierarchical structure of the program, both at a small scale (e.g., control flow within a single procedure) and at larger scales (across multiple procedures, classes, subsystems, etc.).

The steps for verifying the binary search procedure above already hint at a hierarchical approach. The loop invariant was not placed just anywhere in the loop. We associated it with the beginning of the loop so that we could follow a standard style of reasoning that allows us to compose facts about individual pieces of a program to derive facts about larger pieces. In this hierarchical or compositional style, the effect of any program block is described by a *Hoare triple*:

Hoare triple

$$(\!|\, \textit{pre} \,|\!)\ \text{block}\ (\!|\, \textit{post} \,|\!)$$

The meaning of this triple is that if the program is in a state satisfying the precondition *pre* at entry to the block, then after execution of the block it will be in a state satisfying the postcondition *post*.

There are standard templates, or schemata, for reasoning with triples. In the previous section we were following this schema for reasoning about while loops:

$$\frac{(\!|I \wedge C|\!)\ S\ (\!|I|\!)}{(\!|I|\!)\ \text{while(C) \{ S \}}\ (\!|I \wedge \neg C|\!)}$$

The formula above the line is the premise of an inference, and the formula below the line is the conclusion. An inference rule states that if we can verify the premise, then we can infer the conclusion. The premise of this inference rule says that the loop body preserves invariant I: If the invariant I is true before the loop, and if the condition C governing the loop is also true, then the invariant is established again after executing the loop body S. The conclusion says that the loop as a whole takes the program from a state in which the invariant is true to a state satisfying a postcondition composed of the invariant and the negation of the loop condition.

The important characteristic of these rules is that they allow us to compose proofs about small parts of the program into proofs about larger parts. The inference rule for while allows us to take a triple about the body of a loop and infer a triple about the whole loop. There are similar rules for building up triples describing other kinds of program blocks. For example:

$$\frac{(\!|P \wedge C|\!)\ \textit{thenpart}\ (\!|Q|\!) \qquad (\!|P \wedge \neg C|\!)\ \textit{elsepart}\ (\!|Q|\!)}{(\!|P|\!)\ \text{if (C) \{}\textit{thenpart}\text{ \} else \{ }\textit{elsepart}\text{ \}}\ (\!|Q|\!)}$$

This style of reasoning essentially lets us summarize the effect of a block of program code by a precondition and a postcondition. Most importantly, we can summarize the effect of a whole procedure in the same way. The *contract* of the procedure is a precondition (what the calling client is required to provide) and a postcondition (what the called procedure promises to establish or return). Once we have characterized the contract of a procedure in this way, we can use that contract wherever the procedure is called. For example, we might summarize the effect of the binary search procedure this way:

contract

$$(\!|\forall i,j, 0 \le i < j < \text{size} : \text{keys}[i] \le \text{keys}[j]|\!)$$
$$\text{s = binarySearch(k, keys, vals, size)}$$
$$(\!|\ \begin{array}{l} (\text{s} = v \wedge \exists i, 0 \le i < \text{size} : \text{keys}[i] = \text{k} \wedge \text{vals}[i] = v) \\ \vee\ \ (\text{s} = 0 \wedge \nexists i, 0 \le i < \text{size} : \text{keys}[i] = \text{k}) \end{array}\ |\!)$$

7.5 Reasoning about Data Structures and Classes

The contract of the binary search procedure can be specified in a relatively simple, self-contained manner. Imagine, though, that it is part of a module that maintains a dictionary structure (e.g., the relation between postal codes and the nearest airport with air-freight capability). In that case, the responsibility for keeping the table in sorted order would belong to the module itself, and not to its clients. If implemented in a modern object-oriented language, the data structure would not even be visible to the client, but would rather be encapsulated within a class.

Modular reasoning about programs must follow the modular structure of program designs, with the same layering of design secrets. We must have ways of specifying contracts for classes and other modules that do not expose what the program constructs encapsulate. Fortunately there are well-developed methods for modular specification and verification of modules that encapsulate data structures.

A data structure module provides a collection of procedures (methods) whose specifications are strongly interrelated. Their contracts with clients are specified by relating them to an abstract model of their (encapsulated) inner state. For example, the behavior of a dictionary object can be abstractly modeled as a set of $\langle key, value\rangle$ pairs. Reflecting the desired encapsulation and information hiding, the abstract model of the value of a dictionary structure is the same whether the structure is implemented using sorted arrays, a hash table, or a tree.

A module may be required to establish and preserve certain structural characteristics of the data structure it maintains. For example, if the dictionary structure is maintained as a pair of sorted arrays, then it is the responsibility of the dictionary module to maintain the arrays in sorted order. If the structure is a balanced search tree, then the responsibility is to properly initialize and maintain the tree structure. This is called a *structural invariant*, and it is directly analogous to a loop invariant. When reasoning about a loop invariant, we begin by showing that it is established when execution first reaches the loop; this corresponds to showing that the data structure is properly initialized. The methods of the data structure module correspond to paths through the body of the loop. Each method must preserve the structural invariant; that is, if the invariant holds before invocation of the method, then it must still hold when the method returns.

structural invariant

The second responsibility of a class or other data structure module is that its behavior must faithfully reflect the abstract model. To make this precise, one posits an *abstraction function* that maps concrete object states to abstract model states. The abstraction function for a dictionary object would map the object to a set of $\langle key, value\rangle$ pairs. Using the conventional notation ϕ for an abstraction function, the contract of the get method of java.util.Map might include a pre- and postcondition that can be expressed as the Hoare triple

abstraction function

$$(|\langle k, v\rangle \in \phi(\text{dict})|)$$
o = dict.get(k)
$$(|o = v|)$$

Explicit consideration of the abstract model, abstraction function, and structural invariant of a class or other data structure model is the basis not only of formal or informal reasoning about correctness, but also of designing test cases and test oracles.

Summary

Symbolic execution is a bridge from an operational view of program execution to logical and mathematical statements. The basic symbolic execution technique is like hand execution using symbols rather than concrete values. To use symbolic execution for loops, procedure calls, and data structures encapsulated in modules (e.g., classes), it is necessary to proceed hierarchically, composing facts about small parts into facts about larger parts. Compositional reasoning is closely tied to strategies for specifying intended behavior.

Symbolic execution is a fundamental technique that finds many different applications. Test data generators use symbolic execution to derive constraints on input data. Formal verification systems combine symbolic execution to derive logical predicates with theorem provers to prove them. Many development tools use symbolic execution techniques to perform or check program transformations, for example, unrolling a loop for performance or refactoring source code.

Human software developers can seldom carry out symbolic execution of program code in detail, but often use it (albeit informally) for reasoning about algorithms and data structure designs. The approach to specifying preconditions, postconditions, and invariants is also widely used in programming, and is at least partially supported by tools for run-time checking of assertions.

Further Reading

The techniques underlying symbolic execution were developed by Floyd [Flo67] and Hoare [Hoa69], although the fundamental ideas can be traced all the way back to Turing and the beginnings of modern computer science. Hantler and King [HK76] provide an excellent clear introduction to symbolic execution in program verification. Kemmerer and Eckman [KE85] describe the design of an actual symbolic execution system, with discussion of many pragmatic details that are usually glossed over in theoretical descriptions.

Generation of test data using symbolic execution was pioneered by Clarke [Cla76], and Howden [How77, How78] described an early use of symbolic execution to test programs. The *PREfix* tool described by Bush, Pincus, and Sielaff [BPS00] is a modern application of symbolic testing techniques with several refinements and simplifications for adequate performance on large programs.

Exercises

7.1. We introduce symbols to represent variables whose value may change, but we do not bother to introduce symbols for variables whose value remains unchanged in the code we are symbolically executing. Why are new symbols necessary in the former case but not in the latter?

7.2. Demonstrate that the statement return dictValues[mid] at line 27 of the binary search program of Figure 7.1 always returns the value of the input key.

7.3. Compute an upper bound to the number of iterations through the while loop of the binary search program of Figure 7.1.

7.4. The body of the loop of the binary search program of Figure 7.1 can be modified as follows:

```
if (comparison < 0) {
    /* dictKeys[mid] too small; look higher */
    low = mid + 1;
}
if ( comparison > 0 ) {
    /* dictKeys[mid] too large; look lower */
    high = mid - 1;
}
if  ( comparison = 0 ) {
    /* found */
    return dictValues[mid];
}
```

Demonstrate that the path that traverses the false branch of all three statements is infeasible.

7.5. Write the pre- and postconditions for a program that finds the index of the maximum element in a nonempty set of integers.

Chapter 8

Finite State Verification

Finite state verification techniques are intermediate in power and cost between construction of simple control and data flow models, on the one hand, and reasoning with the full strength of symbolic execution and theorem proving on the other. They automatically explore finite but potentially very large representations of program behavior to address important properties. They are particularly useful for checking properties for which testing is inadequate. For example, synchronization faults in multi-threaded programs may trigger failures very rarely, or under conditions that are nearly impossible to re-create in testing, but finite state verification techniques can detect them by exhaustively considering *all* possible interleavings of concurrent processes. Finite state verification can similarly be used to systematically explore possible instantiations of a data model.

8.1 Overview

Most important properties of program execution are undecidable in general, but finite state verification can automatically prove some significant properties of a finite model of the infinite execution space. Of course, there is no magic: We must carefully reconcile and balance trade-offs among the generality of the properties to be checked, the class of programs or models that can be checked, computational effort, and human effort to use the techniques.

Symbolic execution and formal reasoning can prove many properties of program behavior, but the power to prove complex properties is obtained at the cost of devising complex conditions and invariants and expending potentially unbounded computational effort. Construction of control and data flow models, on the other hand, can be fully and efficiently automated, but is typically limited to very simple program properties. Finite state verification borrows techniques from symbolic execution and formal verification, but like control and data flow analysis, applies them to models that abstract the potentially infinite state space of program behavior into finite representations. Finite state verification techniques fall between basic flow analyses and full-blown formal verification in the richness of properties they can address and in the human guidance and computational effort they require.

Since even simple properties of programs are undecidable in general, one cannot expect an algorithmic technique to provide precise answers in all cases. Often finite state verification is used to augment or substitute for testing when the optimistic inaccuracy of testing (due to examining only a sample of the program state space) is unacceptable. Techniques are therefore often designed to provide results that are tantamount to formal proofs of program properties. In trade for this assurance, both the programs and properties that can be checked are severely restricted. Restrictions on program constructs typically appear in procedures for deriving a finite state model from a program, generating program code from a design model, or verifying consistency between a program and a separately constructed model.

Finite state verification techniques include algorithmic checks, but it is misleading to characterize them as completely automated. Human effort and considerable skill are usually required to prepare a finite state model and a suitable specification for the automated analysis step. Very often there is an iterative process in which the first several attempts at verification produce reports of impossible or unimportant faults, which are addressed by repeatedly refining the specification or the model.

The automated step can be computationally costly, and the computational cost can impact the cost of preparing the model and specification. A considerable amount of manual effort may be expended just in obtaining a model that can be analyzed within available time and memory, and tuning a model or specification to avoid combinatorial explosion is itself a demanding task. The manual task of refining a model and specification to obtain either assurance or useful reports of real faults in design or coding is much less expensive if the analysis step is near-interactive than if it requires several minutes or hours.

Some analysis techniques perform quite tolerably on small models, but their computational demands grow very rapidly with model size. These may be perfectly acceptable for a simple model of a critical component, such as a protocol whose description does not depend on the size of the system in which it is implemented. In other cases, scalability of the finite state verification technique is likely to be a limiting factor in its useful application.

Finite state verification techniques vary widely in the balance they strike on issues of generality, precision, automation, computational effort, and scalability. A core idea shared by all is that a question about a program is translated into a simpler question about a finite state model of the program, as illustrated in Figure 8.1. Ultimately, one question about the program (Does it conform to the property we want to check?) is divided into two (Does the model conform to the simpler property we can check? Is it an accurate model of the program?)

The model may be derived from an actual program, like the control flow and data flow models described in prior chapters, or from some other design artifact (e.g., a program specification). Restrictions on the program may be required to derive a model automatically from a program. It is also possible to derive program code from annotated models.[1] If either the model or the program is derived automatically from the other, we may be able to do so in a way that guarantees consistency between the two.

[1]Note that one may independently derive several different models from one program, but deriving one program from several different models is much more difficult.

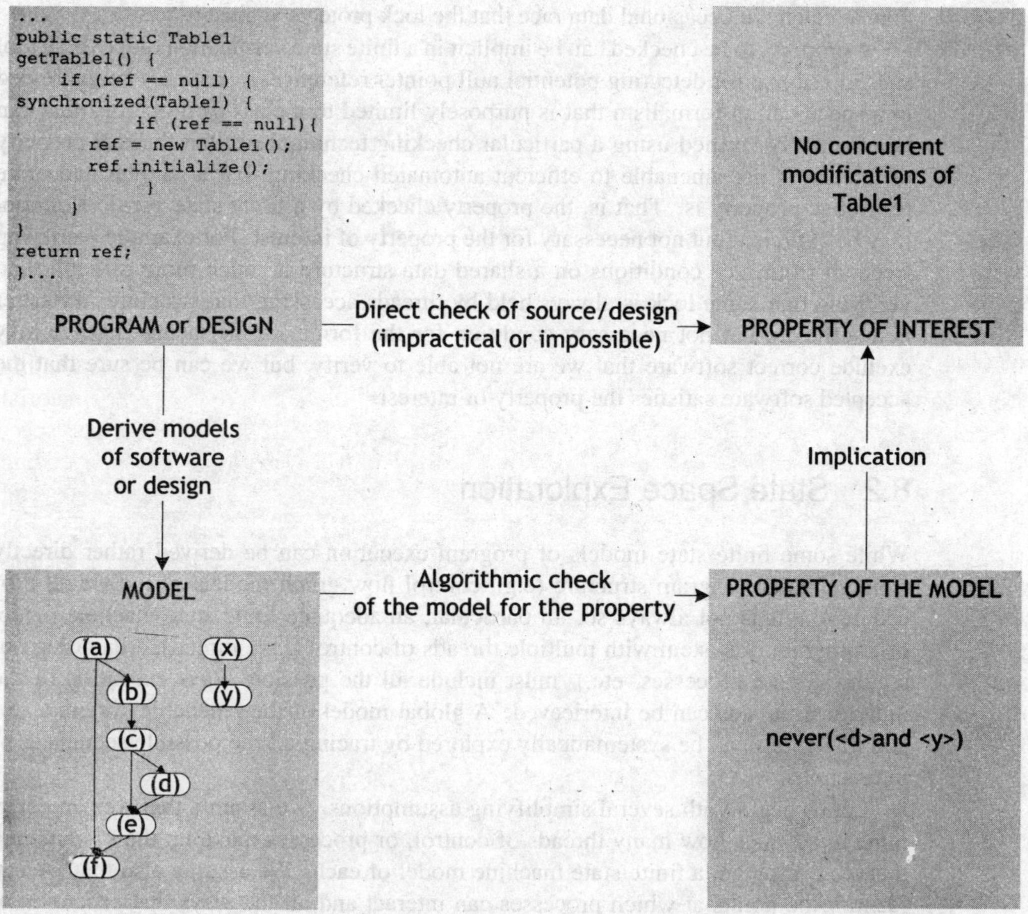

Figure 8.1: The finite state verification framework.

We may also be able to check consistency automatically even if the derivation is not automatic. Alternatively, the accuracy of the model may be assessed by conformance testing, treating the model as a kind of specification. The combination of finite state verification and conformance testing is often more effective than directly testing for the property of interest, because a discrepancy that is easily discovered in conformance testing may very rarely lead to a run-time violation of the property (e.g., it is much easier to detect that a particular lock is not held during access to a shared data structure than to catch the occasional data race that the lock protects against).

A property to be checked can be implicit in a finite state verification tool (e.g., a tool specialized just for detecting potential null pointer references), or it may be expressed in a specification formalism that is purposely limited to a class of properties that can be effectively verified using a particular checking technique. Often the real property of interest is not amenable to efficient automated checking, but a simpler and more restrictive property is. That is, the property checked by a finite state verification tool may be sufficient but not necessary for the property of interest. For example, verifying freedom from race conditions on a shared data structure is much more difficult than verifying that some lock is always held by threads accessing that structure; the latter is a sufficient but not necessary condition for the former. This means that we may exclude correct software that we are not able to verify, but we can be sure that the accepted software satisfies the property of interest.

8.2 State Space Exploration

While some finite state models of program execution can be derived rather directly from syntactic program structure (e.g., control flow graph models of individual procedures), this is not always so. In particular, an adequate finite state machine model of a program or system with multiple threads of control (Java threads, Ada tasks, operating system processes, etc.) must include all the possible ways execution of the individual threads can be interleaved. A global model of the reachable system states and transitions can be systematically explored by tracing all the possible sequences of interactions.

Let us begin with several simplifying assumptions. We assume that we can determine in advance how many threads of control, or processes make up the system, and that we can obtain a finite state machine model of each. We assume also that we can identify the points at which processes can interact and all the ways that execution of one process may affect another. A state of the whole system model, then, is a tuple representing the state of each individual process model, and a transition in the system model is a transition of one or more of the individual processes, acting individually or in concert.

From one global system state, several different individual or joint transitions of the component processes may be possible. That is, execution in the global model is nondeterministic. This should be no surprise, as it reflects the real situation in multi-threaded software, with execution dependent on uncontrolled factors like the arrival of asynchronous interrupts, process scheduler decisions, and the relative execution speed of different processes. It is these unpredictable and uncontrollable factors that make effectively testing programs and systems with multiple threads of control difficult. A test case may run correctly a million times in a test configuration and fail the first time a client uses it.

Given an appropriate model and an execution rule, exploring all the possible states reachable by the system is a completely mechanical process. If "good" states can be easily distinguished from "bad" states, then the whole process of exploring and checking the state space model can be automatic. Even the simplest and most brute-force state space exploration tools can systematically check many times more states in a minute than a person could in a month.

We illustrate with a simple and somewhat contrived example. In a certain multi-threaded module of the Chipmunk on-line purchasing system, there is an in-memory data structure that is initialized by reading configuration tables at system start-up. Initialization of the data structure must appear atomic (the structure should not be accessed while initialization is underway). Moreover, it must be reinitialized on occasion. The structure is kept in memory, rather than read from a database on each use, because it is small, changes rarely, and is accessed very frequently. A Chipmunk programmer has noticed that obtaining a monitor lock for each and every access (which is what a Java "synchronized" method does) substantially reduces concurrency and slows user response time. The programmer has recently learned of the double-checked locking idiom to avoid unnecessary locking during data structure initialization. Unfortunately, the programmer does not fully comprehend the double-check idiom and its underlying assumptions, and produces the faulty implementation excerpted in Figure 8.2.

The fault in this example is simple: The double-check idiom is applicable only to initialization, not to modification of a structure after initialization.[2] However, it is not easy for a person to comprehend all the possible ways that multiple threads could interleave while concurrently executing these methods, and it is surprisingly easy to convince oneself that the faulty implementation avoids race conditions. Moreover, it is extremely difficult to find them with conventional testing. Even under heavy load, the potential race condition in the code of Figure 8.2 very rarely leads to run-time failure and may not appear at all depending on the scheduling policies and resources of a particular Java run-time system.

A potential failure is simple to find by systematically tracing through all the possible interleavings of two threads. We begin by constructing a finite state machine model of each individual thread. For method lookup in Figure 8.2, the state machines in Figure 8.3 describe the actions of an individual thread executing methods lookup and reInit, but we do not know in advance how many distinct threads might be executing concurrently.

Java threading rules ensure that in a system state in which one thread has obtained a monitor lock, the other thread cannot make a transition to obtain the same lock. We can observe that the locking prevents both threads from concurrently calling the initialize method. However, another race condition is possible, between two concurrent threads each executing the lookup method.

---

[2]In fact even a correctly implemented double-check pattern can fail in Java due to properties of the Java memory model, as discussed below.

```
/** A singleton class with mis-application of double-check pattern. */
class Table1 {
    private static Table1 ref = null; // Singleton instance
    private boolean needsInit = true; // To trigger lazy re-initializatiion
    private ElementClass [ ] theValues;

    private Table1() { } // Initialization is separate

    /** Initialization with double-check pattern. */
    public static Table1 getTable1() {
        if (ref == null) { synchedInitialize(); }
        return ref;
    }

    private static synchronized void synchedInitialize() {
        if (ref == null) {
            Table1 tmp = new Table1();
            tmp.initialize();
            ref = tmp; }
    }

    /** Trigger re-initialization on next access */
    public void reinit() { needsInit = true; }

    /** Initialize or re-initialize. Must appear atomic to lookup. */
    private synchronized void  initialize() {
    ...
        needsInit = false;
    }

    /** Lookup value, lazily re-init. (WRONG!) */
    public int lookup(int i) {
        if (needsInit) {
            synchronized(this) {
                if (needsInit) {
                    this.initialize();
                }
            }
        }
        return theValues[i].getX() + theValues[i].getY();
    }

...
}
```

Figure 8.2: Double-check pattern, misapplied to reinitialization.

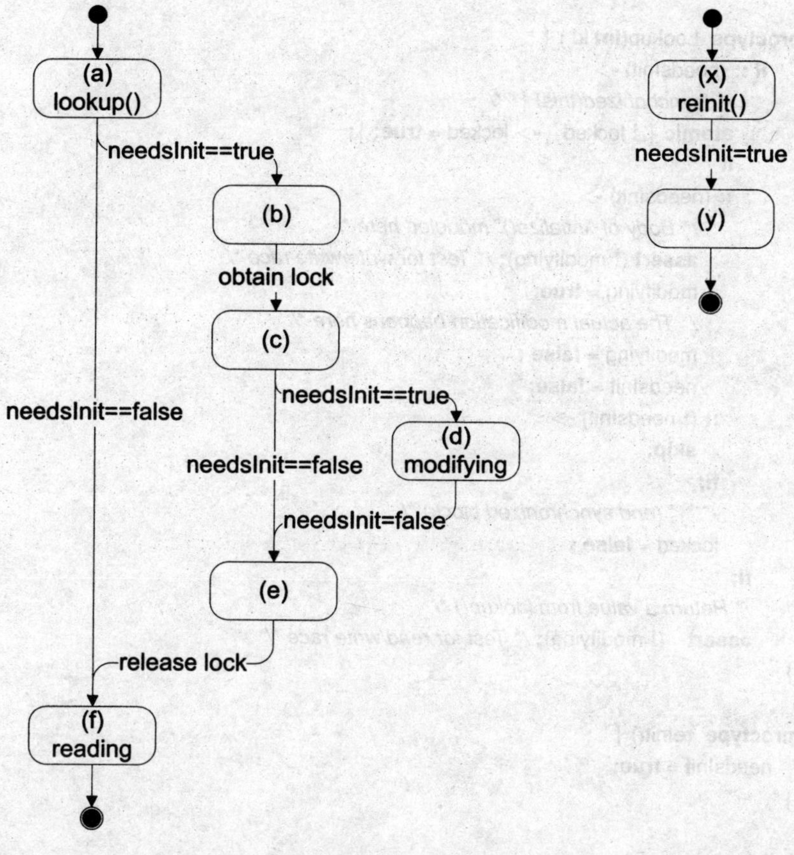

Figure 8.3: Finite state models of individual threads executing the lookup *and* reInit *methods from Figure 8.2. Each state machine may be replicated to represent concurrent threads executing the same method.*

```
bool needsInit = true,   /* Models variable by same name */
     locked = false,     /* To model synchronized block */
     modifying = false; /* To test for race condition  */

proctype Lookup(int id ) {
    if :: (needsInit) ->
        /* "synchonized(this) { " */
        atomic { ! locked   -> locked = true; };
        if
        :: (needsInit) ->
            /* Body of "intialize()" modeled here */
            assert (! modifying); /* Test for write/write race */
            modifying = true;
            /* The actual modification happens here */
            modifying = false ;
            needsInit = false;
        :: (! needsInit) ->
            skip;
        fi;
        /* "}" (end synchronized block) */
        locked = false ;
    fi;
    /* Return a value from lookup() */
    assert   (! modifying); /* Test for read/write race */
}

proctype reInit() {
    needsInit = true;
}

init {
    run reInit();
    run Lookup(1);
    run Lookup(2);
}
```

Figure 8.4: Promela finite state model of faulty double-check implementation.

```
Depth=      10 States=       51 Transitions=       92 Memory= 2.302
pan: assertion violated  !(modifying) (at depth 17)
pan: wrote pan_in.trail
(Spin Version 4.2.5 -- 2 April 2005)

...

        0.16 real          0.00 user          0.03 sys
```

Figure 8.5: Excerpts of Spin verification tool transcript. Spin has performed a depth-first search of possible executions of the model, exploring 10 states and 51 state transitions in 0.16 seconds before finding a sequence of 17 transitions from the initial state of the model to a state in which one of the assertions in the model evaluates to False.

Tracing possible executions by hand — "desk checking" multi-threaded execution — is capable in principle of finding the race condition between two concurrent threads executing the lookup method, but it is at best tedious and in general completely impractical. Fortunately, it can be automated, and many state space analysis tools can explore millions of states in a short time. For example, a model of the faulty code from Figure 8.2 was coded in the Promela modeling language and submitted to the Spin verification tool. In a few seconds, Spin systematically explored the state space and reported a race condition, as shown in Figure 8.5.

A few seconds of automated analysis to find a critical fault that can elude extensive testing seems a very attractive option. Indeed, finite state verification should be a key component of strategies for eliminating faults in multi-threaded and distributed programs, as well as some kinds of security problems (which are similarly resistant to systematic sampling in conventional program testing) and some other domains. On the other hand, we have so far glossed over several limitations and problems of state space exploration, each of which also appears in other forms of finite state verification. We will consider two fundamental and related issues in the following sections: the size of the state space to be explored, and the challenge of obtaining a model that is sufficiently precise without making the state space explosion worse.

The Promela Modeling Language

The Promela language for finite state models of communicating processes, which is interpreted by the verification tool Spin, is described in a book and on-line references (see *Further Reading* at the end of this chapter). Here we present a very brief and partial introduction to aid in reading the example code of Figure 8.4.

A Promela program describes a set of *processes*, roughly analogous to threads in Java. A single *process type* (proctype) can be instantiated more than once with run statements to create multiple instances of a process, much as thread objects can be created from a class in a Java program. A Promela model consists of some global data type and variable declarations, followed by some process type declarations, and finally a "main" process init.

Many lexical conventions of Promela are borrowed from the C language, and should be familiar to C and Java programmers. Comments are enclosed in /* and */, syntactic nesting is indicated by braces { and }, and assignment is indicated by a single = while an equality comparison is indicated by ==. As in C, nonzero values are interpreted as *True* and zero is Boolean *False*.

Promela borrows syntax and semantics for "guarded commands" from Communicating Sequential Processes (CSP), a formal notation for describing communicating processes. A guarded command in Promela is written *expression* -> *statements* and means that the *statements* can be executed only when the guarding *expression* is true. If the *expression* evaluates to zero or is otherwise disabled, execution of the guarded statement is blocked. Thus, the statement

```
atomic { ! locked -> locked = true; }
```

in Figure 8.4 can be used to represent acquiring a monitor lock, because execution blocks at this point until locked has the value *False*. The guard is enclosed in an atomic block to prevent another process taking the lock between evaluation of the guard condition and execution of the statement.

The concept of enabling or blocking in guarded commands is used in conditional and looping constructs. Alternatives in an if...fi construct, marked syntactically with ::, begin with guarded commands. If none of the alternatives is enabled (all of the guards evaluate to *False*), then the whole if construct blocks. If more than one of the guarded alternatives is enabled, the if construct does not necessarily choose the first among them, as a programmer might expect from analogous if...else if... constructs in conventional programming languages. *Any* of the enabled alternatives can be nondeterministically chosen for execution; in fact the Spin tool will consider the possible consequences of each choice. The do...od construct similarly chooses nondeterministically among enabled alternatives, but repeats until a break or goto is evaluated in one of the guarded commands.

The simplest way to check properties of a Promela model is with assertions, like the two assert statements in Figure 8.4. Spin searches for any possible execution sequence in which an assertion can be violated. Sequencing properties can also be specified in the form of temporal logic formulas, or encoded as state machines.

```
preparing trail, please wait...done
Starting :init: with pid 0
spin: warning, "pan_in", proctype Lookup,
     'int   id' variable is never used
Starting reInit with pid 1
  1: proc  0 (:init:) line  33 "pan_in" (state 1) [(run reInit())]
Starting Lookup with pid 2
  2: proc  0 (:init:) line  34 "pan_in" (state 2) [(run Lookup(1))]
Starting Lookup with pid 3
  3: proc  0 (:init:) line  35 "pan_in" (state 3) [(run Lookup(2))]
  4: proc  3 (Lookup) line   7 "pan_in" (state 1) [(needsInit)]
  5: proc  3 (Lookup) line   9 "pan_in" (state 2) [(!(locked))]
        <merge 0 now @3>
  5: proc  3 (Lookup) line   9 "pan_in" (state 3) [locked = 1]
  6: proc  3 (Lookup) line  11 "pan_in" (state 5) [(needsInit)]
  7: proc  3 (Lookup) line  13 "pan_in" (state 6) [assert(!(modifying))]
  8: proc  3 (Lookup) line  14 "pan_in" (state 7) [modifying = 1]
  9: proc  3 (Lookup) line  16 "pan_in" (state 8) [modifying = 0]
 10: proc  3 (Lookup) line  17 "pan_in" (state 9) [needsInit = 0]
 11: proc  3 (Lookup) line  22 "pan_in" (state 14) [locked = 0]
 12: proc  1 (reInit) line  29 "pan_in" (state 1) [needsInit = 1]
 13: proc  2 (Lookup) line   7 "pan_in" (state 1) [(needsInit)]
 14: proc  2 (Lookup) line   9 "pan_in" (state 2) [(!(locked))]
        <merge 0 now @3>
 14: proc  2 (Lookup) line   9 "pan_in" (state 3) [locked = 1]
 15: proc  2 (Lookup) line  11 "pan_in" (state 5) [(needsInit)]
 16: proc  2 (Lookup) line  13 "pan_in" (state 6) [assert(!(modifying))]
 17: proc  2 (Lookup) line  14 "pan_in" (state 7) [modifying = 1]
spin: trail ends after 17 steps
#processes: 4
 17: proc  3 (Lookup) line  25 "pan_in" (state 17)
 17: proc  2 (Lookup) line  16 "pan_in" (state 8)
 17: proc  1 (reInit) line  30 "pan_in" (state 2)
 17: proc  0 (:init:) line  36 "pan_in" (state 4)
4 processes created
Exit-Status 0
```

Figure 8.6: A Spin guided simulation trace describes each of the 17 steps from the initial model state to the state in which the assertion !(modifying) *is violated. For example, in step 8, one of the two processes (threads) simulating execution of the* Lookup *method sets the global variable* modifying *to True, represented as the integer value 1. A graphical representation of this trace is presented in Figure 8.7.*

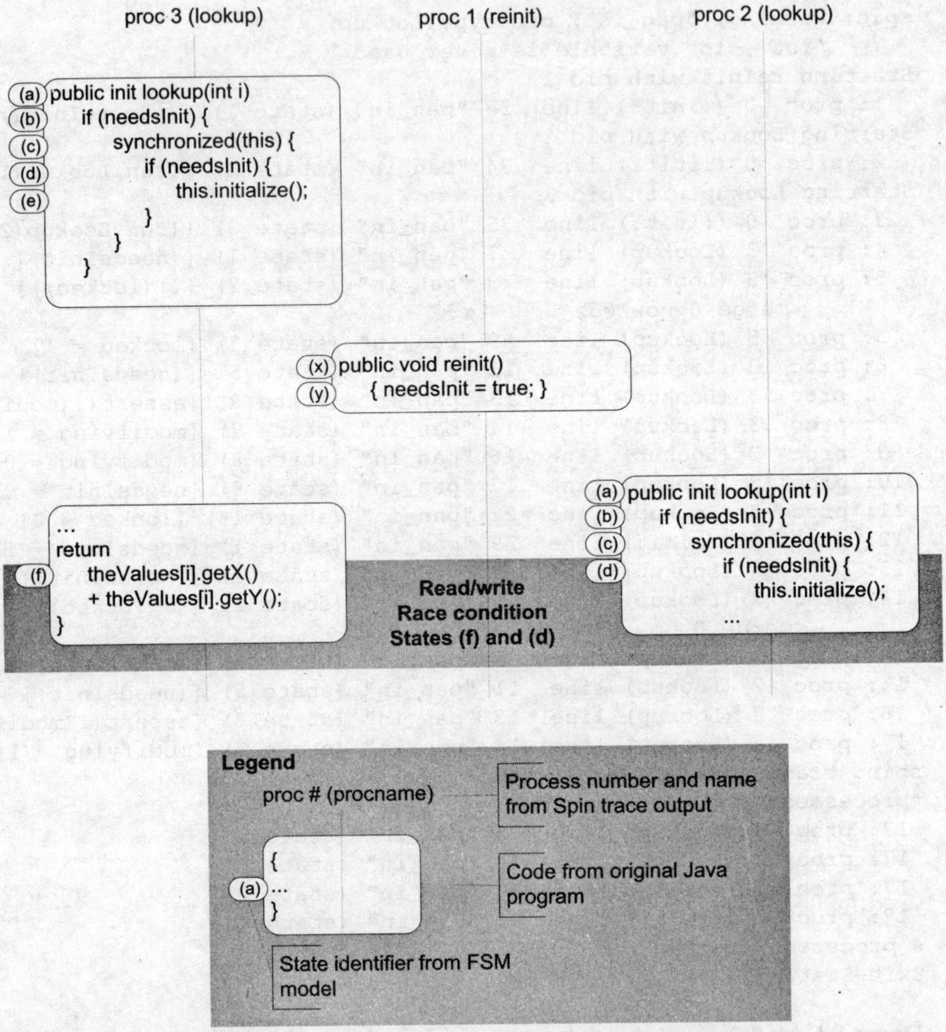

Figure 8.7: A graphical interpretation of Spin guided simulation output (Figure 8.6) in terms of Java source code (Figure 8.2) and state machines (Figure 8.3).

Safety and Liveness Properties

Properties of concurrent systems can be divided into simple safety properties, sequencing safety properties, and liveness properties.

Simple safety properties divide states of the system into "good" (satisfying the property) and "bad" (violating the property). They are easiest to specify, and least expensive to check, because we can simply provide a predicate to be evaluated at each state. Often simple safety properties relate the local state of one process to local states of other processes. For example, the assertion assert(! modifying) in the Promela code of Figure 8.4 states a mutual exclusion property between two instances of the lookup process. When simple safety properties are expressed in temporal logic, they have the form $\Box p$, where p is a simple predicate with no temporal modalities.

Safety properties about sequences of events are similar, but treat the history of events preceding a state as an attribute of that state. For example, an assertion that two operations a and b strictly alternate is a safety property about the history of those events; a "bad" state is one in which a or b is about to be performed out of order. Sequencing properties can be specified in temporal logic, but do not require it: They are always equivalent to simple safety properties embedded in an "observer" process. Checking a sequencing property adds the same degree of complexity to the verification process as adding an explicit observer process, whether there is a real observer (which is straightforward to encode for some kinds of model, and nearly impossible for others) or whether the observer is implicit in the checking algorithm (as it would be using a temporal logic predicate with the Spin tool).

True liveness properties, sometimes called "eventuality" properties, are those that can only be violated by an infinite length execution. For example, if we assert that p must *eventually* be true ($\Diamond p$), the assertion is violated only by an execution that runs forever with p continuously false. Liveness properties are useful primarily as a way of abstracting over sequences of unknown length. For example, *fairness* properties are an important class of liveness properties. When we say, for example, that a mutual exclusion protocol must be fair, we do not generally mean that all processes have an equal chance to obtain a resource; we merely assert that no process can be starved forever. Liveness properties (including fairness properties) must generally be stated in temporal logic, or encoded directly in a Büchi automaton that appears similar to a deterministic finite state acceptor but has different rules for acceptance. A finite state verification tool finds violations of liveness properties by searching for execution loops in which the predicate that should eventually be true remains false; this adds considerably to the computational cost of verification.

A common mnemonic for safety and liveness is that safety properties say "nothing bad happens," while liveness properties say "something good eventually happens."

Properties involving real time (e.g., "the stop signal is sent within 5 seconds of receiving the damage signal") are technically safety properties in which the "bad thing" is expiration of a timer. However, naive models involving time are so expensive that it is seldom practical to simply add a clock to a model and use simple safety properties. Usually it is best to keep reasoning about time separate from verifying untimed properties with finite state verification.

8.3 The State Space Explosion Problem

The finite state model of faulty code described in the previous section is very simple: two processes concurrently executing the lookup method, another executing the trivial reInit method, and an even more trivial administrative process to start them. While it is quite tedious to trace out all the potential interleavings of these processes by hand,[3] an automated verification tool can do so almost instantaneously.

Unfortunately, larger and more complex models may cause the same tools to grind for hours or days without producing a result, typically ending by exhausting all available memory. The number of states in a concurrent system with P processes, each with K individual states, is at most the number of possible P-tuples of K values, that is, K^P. Synchronization and other dependencies among processes will limit the number of reachable states to a somewhat smaller number. Nonetheless, the number of reachable states does typically grow exponentially with the number of processes.

Figure 8.8 and the sidebar on page 127 illustrate state space explosion with the classical dining philosophers problem. This exponential blow-up in the number of reachable states is not just an artifact of a naive modeling methodology. It has been proved, in a variety of models of concurrent execution, that decision procedures even for very simple properties like freedom from deadlock or race conditions is PSPACE-complete. This means that in the worst case, exponential complexity is almost certainly unavoidable in any procedure that can answer the kinds of questions we use state space exploration to answer.

The known complexity results strongly imply that, in the worst case, no finite state verification technique can be practical. Worst case complexity results, however, say nothing about the performance of verification techniques on typical problems. Experience with a variety of automated techniques tells us a fair amount about what to expect: Many techniques work very well when applied on well-designed models, within a limited domain, but no single finite state verification technique gives satisfactory results on all problems. Moreover, crafting a model that accurately and succinctly captures the essential structure of a system, and that can be analyzed with reasonable performance by a given verification tool, requires creativity and insight as well as understanding of the verification approach used by that tool.

[3] It is a useful exercise to try this, because even though the number of reachable states is quite small, it is remarkably difficult to enumerate them by hand without making mistakes. Programmers who attempt to devise clever protocols for concurrent operation face the same difficulty, and if they do not use some kind of automated formal verification, it is not an exaggeration to say they almost never get it right.

An Illustration of State Space Explosion

Consider the classic dining philosophers problem, in which an equal number of philosophers and forks are arranged around a table. A philosopher must lift both adjacent forks before eating. A Promela model of the dining philosophers problem is shown in Figure 8.8. With 5 philosophers and 5 forks, Spin finds the potential deadlock in less than a second of search, exploring only 145 unique states of the system. With 10 philosophers and 10 forks, Spin with default settings begins to cut off the search at a depth of 9999 execution steps, but still finds the deadlock at a depth of 9995 steps, generating 18,313 unique states while executing a depth-first search. With 15 philosophers and 15 forks, Spin explores 148,897 states before finding a deadlock, and again the error trace it creates is too long to be useful in diagnosis. Spin can be instructed to use a breadth-first search or iterate to find a shorter error trace, but these options cause it to generate over half a million unique states and exhaust its default allocation of memory. A version of the model with 10 forks and only 9 philosophers generates 404,796 unique states with the default settings, with an inconclusive result since it finds no errors but terminates the search at depth 9999 (after 195 minutes on the same computer that analyzed the first example in a few seconds). One can increase the allocation of memory and wait longer for a result, but from the rate of growth it is evident that an approach of buying bigger and faster machines will not scale to a much larger model.

Fortunately, the deadlock produced by a system of just three philosophers is a perfectly good representation of the potential deadlock in a system of 10 or 15 or 100 philosopher processes. State space enumeration is most effective when the essential structure of a system can be represented by a much smaller model.

```
mtype = { Up, Down, /* Fork operations      */
          Thinking, Hungry, Eating /* What philosophers do */ }

proctype fork(chan opChannel) {
    do
    :: opChannel?Up;    /* First I can be lifted ...  */
       opChannel?Down; /* Then I can be set down ...  */
    od;                 /* Then lifted again, and so on */
}

proctype philosopher(chan leftFork, rightFork) {
    show mtype   myState = Thinking;
    do
    :: myState = Hungry;
       leftFork!Up;
       rightFork!Up;
       myState = Eating;
       rightFork!Down;
       leftFork!Down;
       myState = Thinking;
    od;
}

#define NumSeats 10
chan forkInterface[NumSeats] = [0] of {mtype} ;
init {
    int i = 0;
    do :: i < NumSeats ->
          run fork( forkInterface[i] );
          i = i+1;
       :: i >= NumSeats -> break;
    od;
    i = 0;
    do :: i < NumSeats   ->
          run philosopher( forkInterface[i], forkInterface[ (i+1)%NumSeats ]);
          i = i+1;
       :: i >= NumSeats-1   -> break;
    od;
}
```

Figure 8.8: The classic dining philosophers problem in Promela. The number of unique states explored before finding the potential deadlock (with default settings) grows from 145 with 5 philosophers, to 18,313 with 10 philosophers, to 148,897 with 15 philosophers.

8.4 The Model Correspondence Problem

In the simple examples above, we have written Promela models by hand to verify concurrent execution in Java programs. One may ask how we can be sure that the Promela models accurately represent the possible behaviors of the Java programs, particularly if there are conceptual errors in the design of the Java programs. This is a serious problem, and it has no fully satisfactory solution.

We could verify correspondence between a finite state model and a program in one of three ways. First, we could automatically extract a model from the program source code (or compiled code, e.g., Java byte code), using procedures that we have verified once and for all. Second, we could turn the derivation relation around, producing program source code automatically from a model, treating the model as a kind of design document. The third option is to apply some combination of static analysis and testing to verify correspondence between model and program.

Automatically extracting models from programs is an attractive option, with the important advantage that the correctness of the extraction tool can be verified once and for all. In this approach, sophisticated and expensive verification can be justified and carried out by tool developers who are much more expert in finite state verification than users of the tool. The previous section strongly hints at the chief obstacle to model extraction: A model that blindly mirrors all details of program execution is likely to suffer from a much worse state space explosion than a model that has been carefully crafted to capture just the relevant essence of synchronization structure. A model that omits some crucial detail, on the other hand, can produce so many "false alarm" reports (failures that are possible in the model but not in the program) that the results are useless. The challenge for automatic model extraction, then, is to capture just enough of the relevant detail to be accurate, while abstracting enough to keep state space explosion under control.

Some abstraction of program details can be completely automated. For example, dependence analysis can be used to identify portions of the program that are irrelevant to checking a particular property. For this reason, it is often worthwhile to extract different models from the same program, to check different properties of interest. Where the required level of detail cannot be determined a priori by program analysis, sometimes a coarse initial model can be iteratively refined until either a verification or a counter-example is achieved. This is discussed further in Section 8.7.

Human cleverness in model design and automated support for model extraction are not mutually exclusive. For example, an important tactic in building finite state models is abstracting data values. It would be far too expensive to represent all the possible states of a queue of integers, for instance, but one might be able to capture enough information in the predicate isEmpty(Q). Sometimes a choice of predicates is strongly suggested by control structure of the program, and may even be found automatically by a model extraction tool. In other cases the user may be able to provide much better predicates to guide automated model extraction.

One can also reverse the model extraction process, starting with a finite state model and generating program code. Usually what can be generated is not the whole application, but it may be a component or skeleton in which the relevant behavior is localized. Essentially, this is equivalent to requiring the developer to manually distinguish the finite state model from other aspects of the application, but it can be much easier to specify how the finite state model is combined with other application details than to specify how the finite state model is extracted from the completed application. Program generation from (verifiable) finite state models, like program generation in general, is most applicable within constrained or well-understood application domains.

If a model is automatically extracted, or a program is automatically generated from a model, then correspondence between model and program can be verified once and for all by verifying the method of derivation. If, however, the derivation method is at least partly manual, then it will be necessary to gain confidence in their consistency by some other approach. Static program analysis can be helpful, but in the worst case a static analysis that verifies consistency between a model and a program can be as complex as a static analysis for extracting a model. More typically, conformance is verified by testing.

The details of an approach to conformance testing depend primarily on the form of the model and on what can be observed from program execution. A typical scenario is that the program model is equivalent to a deterministic finite state machine (FSM), and the only relevant observable aspect of program execution is a set of events (e.g., system calls or instrumented points) that correspond to event labels in the FSM model. A single execution is then consistent with the model if the observed sequence of execution events corresponds to a sequence of state transitions in a traversal of the model. The basic approach can be extended in several ways, for example, by testing against each of several communicating state machines separately or in parallel, by checking portions of program state against model state, or by considering multiple possible traversals in parallel if the model is inherently nondeterministic or the correspondence between observed program events and model state transitions is ambiguous. There is a well-developed body of testing techniques based on state machine models, some of which are discussed further in Chapter 14.

One may ask what advantage finite state verification has over simply testing the program for the property of interest, if we must still resort to conformance testing to verify the accuracy of a model. For example, if we are using finite state verification to show absence of race conditions, and then testing the program for conformance to the verified model, why not simply use testing to check for race conditions directly in the program?

In fact, the combination of finite state verification with testing can be both less expensive and more effective than testing alone. Consider again our simple example of misapplication of the double-check pattern in Figure 8.2. Tens of thousands of test executions can fail to reveal the race condition in this code, depending on the way threads are scheduled on a particular hardware platform and Java virtual machine implementation. Testing for a discrepancy between model and program, on the other hand, is fairly straightforward because the model of each individual state machine can be checked independently (in fact all but one are trivial). The complexity that stymies testing comes from nondeterministic interleaving of their execution, but this interleaving is completely irrelevant to conformance testing.

```
/** Trivial race between two increments. A version of this program
 * appears in many books on concurrency or operating systems; it is
 * the "hello world" of race conditions.
 */
class Unsafe   implements Runnable {
    static int i = 1;   /* Before increments, value is 1. And after? */

    /** Each thread increments i by 1 */
    public void run() {
        i = i + 1;
    }

    /** Two threads interleave their updates */
    public static void main(String[] argv) {
        Unsafe unsafe = new Unsafe();
        Thread racerP = new Thread(unsafe);
        racerP.start();
        Thread racerQ = new Thread(unsafe);
        racerQ.start();

        /* Wait for both to finish */
        try {
            racerP.join(); racerQ.join();
        } catch (InterruptedException e) {
            System.err.println("Unexpected interruption");
        }

        /* What values could i possibly have? */
        System.out.println("i:  " + i);
    }

}
```

Figure 8.9: A simple data race in Java. The possible ending values of i *depend on how the statement* i = i+1 *in one thread is interleaved with the same sequence in the other thread.*

8.5 Granularity of Modeling

Showing that each thread or process in a program performs actions in an order consistent with its FSM model, and that the effect of each sequence of actions is modeled correctly, is not quite enough. We also need to consider the granularity of those actions — the points at which actions from one thread can be interrupted by actions of another.

Consider the trivial program of Figure 8.9. The race condition is apparent: Both threads RacerP and RacerQ increment shared variable i. The possible ending values

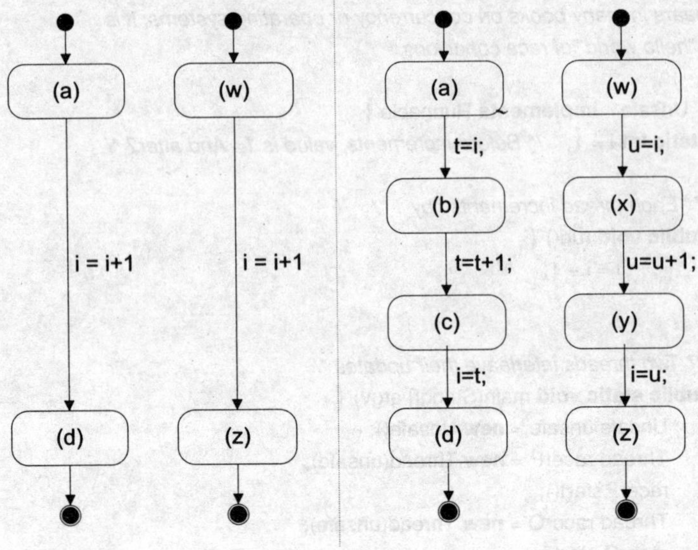

Figure 8.10: Coarse and fine-grain models of the same program from Figure 8.9. In the coarse-grain model, i *will be increased by 2, but other outcomes are possible in the finer grain model in which the shared variable* i *is loaded into temporary variable or register, updated locally, and then stored.*

of i depend on whether i=i+1 is an atomic (indivisible) action, or a sequence of smaller operations. The coarse-grain FSM of Figure 8.10 treats each statement as an atomic action, while the fine-grain FSM in the same figure breaks the increment operation into separate load, add, and store steps. Only the finer grain FSM can reveal the "lost update" problem illustrated in Figure 8.11.

Even representing each memory access as an individual action is not always sufficient. Programming language definitions usually allow compilers to perform some rearrangements in the order of instructions. What appears to be a simple store of a value into a memory cell may be compiled into a store into a local register, with the actual store to memory appearing later (or not at all, if the value is replaced first). Two loads or stores to different memory locations may also be reordered for reasons of efficiency. Moreover, when a machine instruction to store a value into memory is executed by a parallel or distributed computer, the value may initially be placed in the cache memory of a local processor, and only later written into a memory area accessed by other processors. These reorderings are not under programmer control, nor are they directly visible, but they can lead to subtle and unpredictable failures in multi-threaded programs.

As an example, consider once again the flawed program of Figure 8.2. Suppose we corrected it to use the double-check idiom only for lazy initialization and not for updates of the data structure. It would still be wrong, and unfortunately it is unlikely

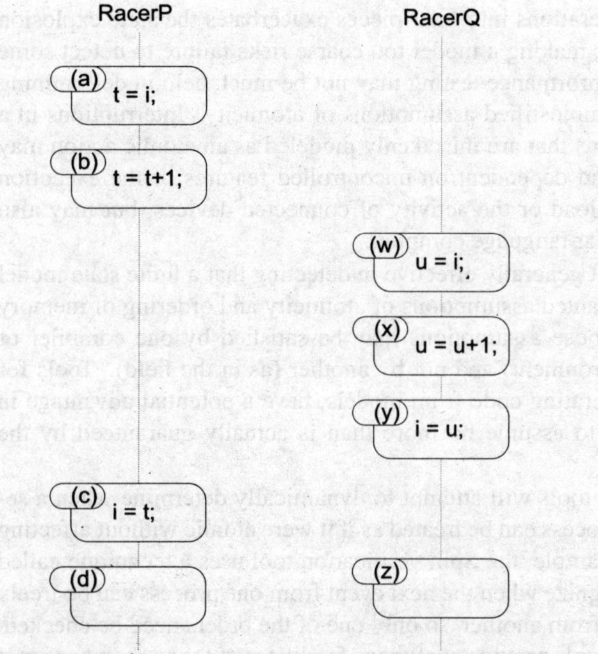

Figure 8.11: The lost update problem, in which only one of the two increments affects the final value of i. *The illustrated sequence of operations from the program of Figure 8.9 can be found using the finer grain model of Figure 8.10, but is not revealed by the coarser grain model.*

we would discover the flaw through finite state verification. Our model in Promela assumes that memory accesses occur in the order given in the Java program, but Java does not guarantee that they will be executed in that order. In particular, while the programmer may assume that initialization invoked in line 18 of the Java program is completed before field ref is set in line 19, Java makes no such guarantee.

Breaking sequences of operations into finer pieces exacerbates the state explosion problem, but as we have seen, making a model too coarse risks failure to detect some possible errors. Moreover, conformance testing may not be much help in determining whether a model depends on unjustified assumptions of atomicity. Interruptions in a sequence of program operations that are mistakenly modeled as an atomic action may not only be extremely rare and dependent on uncontrolled features of the execution environment, such as system load or the activity of connected devices, but may also depend on details of a particular language compiler.

Conformance testing is not generally effective in detecting that a finite state model of a program relies on unwarranted assumptions of atomicity and ordering of memory accesses, particularly when those assumptions may be satisfied by one compiler or machine (say, in the test environment) and not by another (as in the field). Tools for extracting models, or for generating code from models, have a potential advantage in that they can be constructed to assume no more than is actually guaranteed by the programming language.

Many state space analysis tools will attempt to dynamically determine when a sequence of operations in one process can be treated as if it were atomic without affecting the results of analysis. For example, the Spin verification tool uses a technique called partial order reduction to recognize when the next event from one process can be freely reordered with the next event from another, so only one of the orders need be checked. Many finite state verification tools provide analogous facilities, and though they cannot completely compensate for the complexity of a model that is more fine-grained than necessary, they reduce the penalty imposed on the cautious model-builder.

8.6 Intensional Models

The computational cost of enumerating reachable states, particularly the storage required to recognize states that have already been explored, is often a limiting factor in applying finite state verification tools. Sometimes (but not always) this expense can be significantly reduced by using intensional (symbolic) representations that describe sets of reachable states without enumerating each one individually.

The idea of symbolic or intensional representations can be illustrated with sets of integers. Consider the set

$$\{2,4,6,8,10,12,14,16,18\}$$

The *extensional* representation, given above, lists the elements of the set. The same set can be represented *intensionally* as

$$\{x \in \mathbb{N} \mid \; x \bmod 2 = 0 \;\wedge\; 0 < x < 20\}$$

The predicate $x \bmod 2 = 0 \ \wedge \ 0 < x < 20$, which is true for elements included in the set and false for excluded elements, is called a *characteristic function*. The length of the representation of the characteristic function does not necessarily grow with the size of the set it describes. For example, the set

$$\{x \in \mathbb{N} \mid \ x \bmod 2 = 0 \ \wedge \ 0 < x < 80\}$$

contains four times as many elements as the one above, and yet the length of the representation is the same.

It could be advantageous to use similarly compact representations for sets of reachable states and transitions among them. For example, ordered binary decision diagrams (OBDDs) are a representation of Boolean functions that can be used to describe the characteristic function of a transition relation. Transitions in the model state space are pairs of states (the state before and the state after executing the transition), and the Boolean function represented by the OBDD takes a pair of state descriptions and returns *True* exactly if there is a transition between such a pair of states. The OBDD is built by an iterative procedure that corresponds to a breadth-first expansion of the state space (i.e., creating a representation of the whole set of states reachable in $k+1$ steps from the set of states reachable in k steps). If the OBDD representation does not grow too large to be manipulated in memory, it stabilizes when all the transitions that can occur in the next step are already represented in the OBDD form.

Finding a compact intensional representation of the model state space is not, by itself, enough. In addition we must have an algorithm for determining whether that set satisfies the property we are checking. For example, an OBDD can be used to represent not only the transition relation of a set of communicating state machines, but also a class of temporal logic specification formulas. The OBDD representations of model and specification can be combined to produce a representation of just the set of transitions leading to a violation of the specification. If that set is empty, the property has been verified. This approach is known as symbolic model checking, and has been spectacularly successful in dealing with some models of concurrent system (primarily for hardware, but sometimes also for software).

Encoding transition relations as OBDDs can be divided into two parts: representing transition relations as Boolean functions, and representing Boolean functions as OBDDs. Representing Boolean functions as OBDDs is straightforward, as illustrated in Figure 8.12. Essentially the BDD is a decision tree that has been transformed into an acyclic graph by merging nodes leading to identical subtrees. The merging is made efficient by ordering the decisions in the same way on all paths from the root of the decision tree to the leaves, which represent outcomes. Constructing the representation of transition relations as Boolean functions, on the other hand, can be quite involved. Figure 8.13 illustrates some of the basic ideas.

In the worst case, intensional representations are no more compact than listing the elements of a set. In fact, information theory tells us that if we have a large set S of states, a representation capable of distinguishing each subset of S (all elements of 2^S) cannot be more compact on average than the representation that simply lists elements of the chosen subset. When intensional representations work well, it is because we do not produce arbitrary sets of reachable states; rather, there is a good deal of structure and regularity in the state space, and that regularity is exploited in symbolic representations.

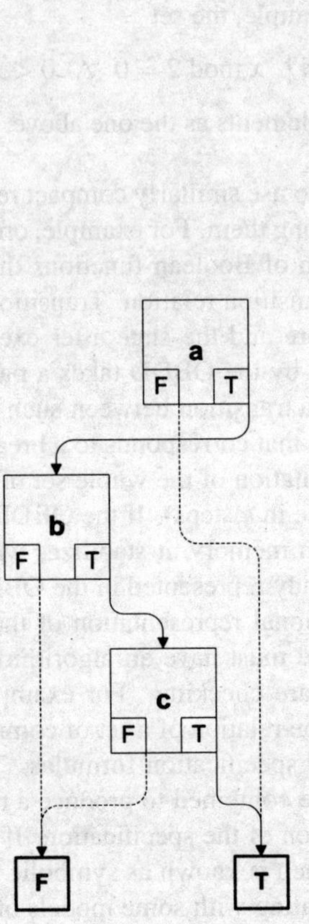

***Figure 8.12:** Ordered binary decision diagram (OBDD) encoding of the Boolean proposition $a \Rightarrow b \wedge c$, which is equivalent to $\neg a \vee (b \wedge c)$. The formula and OBDD structure can be thought of as a function from the Boolean values of a, b, and c to a single Boolean value True or False.*

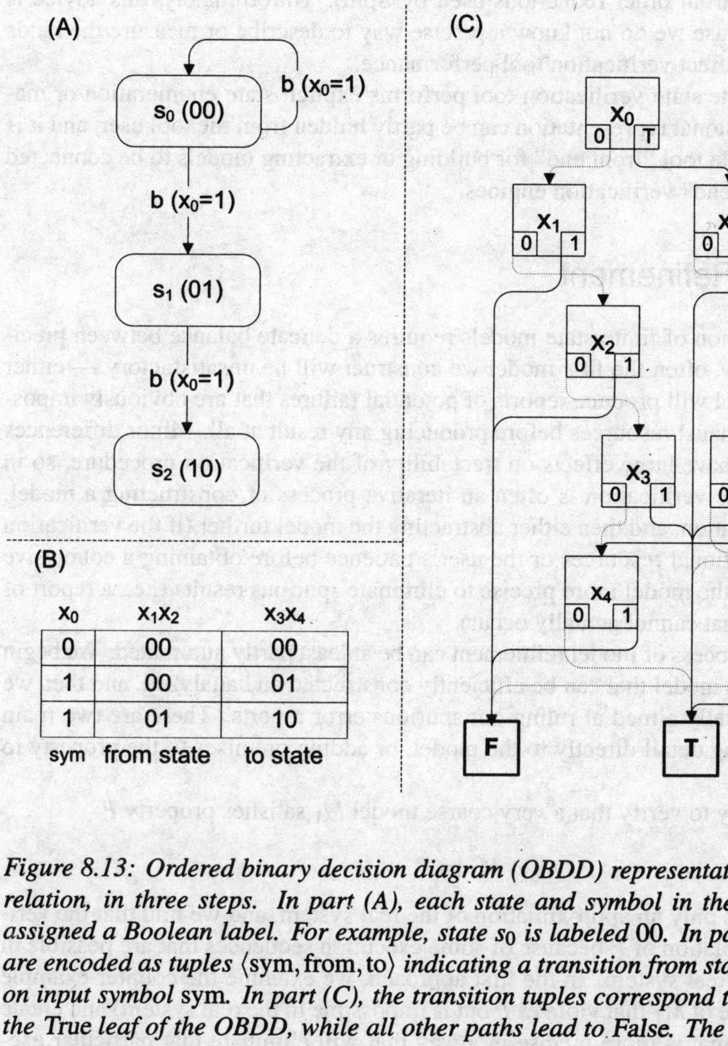

x_0	x_1x_2	x_3x_4
0	00	00
1	00	01
1	01	10
sym	from state	to state

Figure 8.13: Ordered binary decision diagram (OBDD) representation of a transition relation, in three steps. In part (A), each state and symbol in the state machine is assigned a Boolean label. For example, state s_0 is labeled 00. *In part (B), transitions are encoded as tuples* ⟨sym, from, to⟩ *indicating a transition from state* from *to state* to *on input symbol* sym. *In part (C), the transition tuples correspond to paths leading to the True leaf of the OBDD, while all other paths lead to False. The OBDD represents a characteristic function that takes valuations of $x_0 \ldots x_4$ and returns* True *only if it corresponds to a state transition.*

A good rule of thumb is that finite state verification tools that use intensional representations (typically called symbolic model checkers) are more effective, the more regularity is captured in the model, while an explicit model checker (like Spin) is apt to be at least as effective where little regularity can be captured, or where the kinds of regularity that can be captured can also be exploited in explicit state space exploration (e.g., the partial order reductions used by Spin). Unfortunately, this advice is rather vague, because we do not know a precise way to describe or measure the kinds of regularity that affect verification tool performance.

Whether a finite state verification tool performs explicit state enumeration or manipulates an intensional representation can be partly hidden from the tool user, and it is possible for a single tool "front end" for building or extracting models to be connected to multiple "back end" verification engines.

8.7 Model Refinement

Because construction of finite state models requires a delicate balance between precision and efficiency, often the first model we construct will be unsatisfactory — either the verification tool will produce reports of potential failures that are obviously impossible, or it will exhaust resources before producing any result at all. Minor differences in the model can have large effects on tractability of the verification procedure, so in practice finite state verification is often an iterative process of constructing a model, attempting verification, and then either abstracting the model further (if the verification exhausts computational resources or the user's patience before obtaining a conclusive result) or making the model more precise to eliminate spurious results (i.e., a report of a potential error that cannot actually occur).

An iterative process of model refinement can be at least partly automated. We begin with a very coarse model that can be efficiently constructed and analyzed, and then we add detail specifically aimed at ruling out spurious error reports. There are two main approaches: adding detail directly to the model, or adding premises to the property to be checked.

Initially, we try to verify that a very coarse model M_1 satisfies property P:

$$M_1 \models P$$

However, M is only an approximation of the real system, and we find that the verification finds a violation of P because of some execution sequences that are possible in M_1 but not in the real system. In the first approach, we examine the counter-example (an execution trace of M_1 that violates P but is impossible in the real system) and create a new model M_2 that is more precise in a way that will eliminate that particular execution trace (and many similar traces). We attempt verification again with the refined model:

$$M_2 \models P$$

If verification fails again, we repeat the process to obtain a new model M_3, and so on, until verification succeeds with some "good enough" model M_k or we obtain a counter-example that corresponds to an execution of the actual program.

One kind of model that can be iteratively refined in this way is *Boolean programs*. The initial Boolean program model of an (ordinary) program omits all variables; branches (if, while, etc.) refer to a dummy Boolean variable whose value is unknown. Boolean programs are refined by adding variables, with assignments and tests — but only Boolean variables. For instance, if a counter-example produced by trying to verify a property of a pump controller shows that the waterLevel variable cannot be ignored, a Boolean program might be refined by adding a Boolean variable corresponding to a predicate in which waterLevel is tested (say, waterLevel < highLimit), rather than adding the variable waterLevel itself. For some kinds of interprocedural control flow analysis, it is possible to completely automate the step of choosing additional Boolean variables to refine M_i into M_{i+1} and eliminate some spurious executions.

In the second approach, M remains fixed,[4] but premises that constrain executions to be checked are added to the property P. When bogus behaviors of M violate P, we add a constraint C_1 to rule them out and try the modified verification problem:

$$M \models C_1 \Rightarrow P$$

If the modified verification problem fails because of additional bogus behaviors, we try again with new constraints C_2:

$$M \models (C_1 \wedge C_2) \Rightarrow P$$

so on until verification either succeeds or produces a valid counter-example.

The FLAVERS finite state verification tool is an example of the second approach, adding constraints to refine a model of concurrent execution. A FLAVERS model approximates concurrent execution with a pairwise "may immediately precede" (MIP) relation among operations in different threads. Because MIP relates only pairs of individual process states, rather than k-tuples for a model with k processes, its size is only quadratic in the size of the state machine model, rather than exponential in the number of processes. Moreover, a reasonably good approximation of the MIP relation can be obtained in cubic time.[5]

If one thinks of each MIP edge in the program model as representing possible interruption of one thread and continuation of another, it is apparent that paths combining transitions within individual processes and MIP transitions between processes can represent all paths through the global state space. Many additional paths, which would not appear in a more precise global model of possible executions, are also represented. The overapproximation leads to spurious error reports involving impossible execution paths.

Additional spurious error reports result from eliding details of data variables. In the Boolean programs approach to model refinement, we would refine the model by

[4]In practice the model M may be augmented slightly to facilitate observing significant events in the constraint, but the augmentation does not restrict or change the possible behaviors of the model M.

[5]Published algorithms for computing the "may immediately precede" relation, or the closely related "may happen in parallel" (MHP) relation, range from $O(n^3)$ to $O(n^6)$ where n is the sum of the sizes of the individual state machine models or control flow graphs. They differ depending on the thread interactions under consideration (e.g., a MIP calculation for Ada tasks would use diffferent constraints than a MIP calculation for Java threads) as well as algorithmic approach.

expanding the finite state representation of the process. With FLAVERS, in contrast, information about the variable value is represented in a separate constraint state machine, which may be provided by the user or extracted automatically from the program to be verified. Only violations of property P that satisfy all the constraints C_i are reported. The same approach of adding constraints is used to eliminate spurious error reports resulting from the MIP overestimation of possible concurrency.

8.8 Data Model Verification with Relational Algebra

Many information systems have relatively simple logic and algorithms, with much of their complexity in the structure of the data they maintain. A *data model* is a key design description for such systems. It is typically described, for example, in the class and object diagrams of a Unified Modeling Language (UML) design document, possibly augmented by assertions in the Object Constraint Language (OCL). The finite state verification techniques we have described are suited to reasoning about complex or subtle program logic, but are quite limited in dealing with complex data. Fortunately, suitable finite state verification techniques can also be devised for reasoning about data models.

The data model consists of sets of data and relations among them. Often a data model describes many individual relations and constraints; the challenge is in knowing whether all of the individual constraints are consistent, and whether together they ensure the desired properties of the system as a whole. Constructing and testing a portion or partial version of the system may provide some increased confidence in the realizability of the system, but even with incremental development it can happen that a fundamental problem in the data model is discovered only after a great deal of development effort has been invested in the flawed model. Reasoning about the model itself is a more timely and cost-effective way to find and correct these flaws.

Let us consider, for example, a simple Web site with a data model described as sets and relations as follows:

- A set of *pages*, divided among *restricted*, *unrestricted*, and *maintenance* pages. Unrestricted pages are freely accessible, while restricted pages are accessible only to registered users, and pages in maintenance are currently inaccessible to both sets of users.

- A set of *users*, classified as *administrator*, *registered*, and *unregistered* users.

- A set of *links* relations among pages. Different relations describe different kinds of links. *Private* links lead to *restricted* pages, *public* links lead to *unrestricted* pages, and *maintenance* links lead to pages undergoing maintenance.

- A set of *access rights* relations between users and pages, relating different classes of users to the pages they can access. *Unregistered users* can access only unrestricted pages, *registered* users can access both restricted and unrestricted pages, and an *administrator* can access all pages, including pages under maintenance.

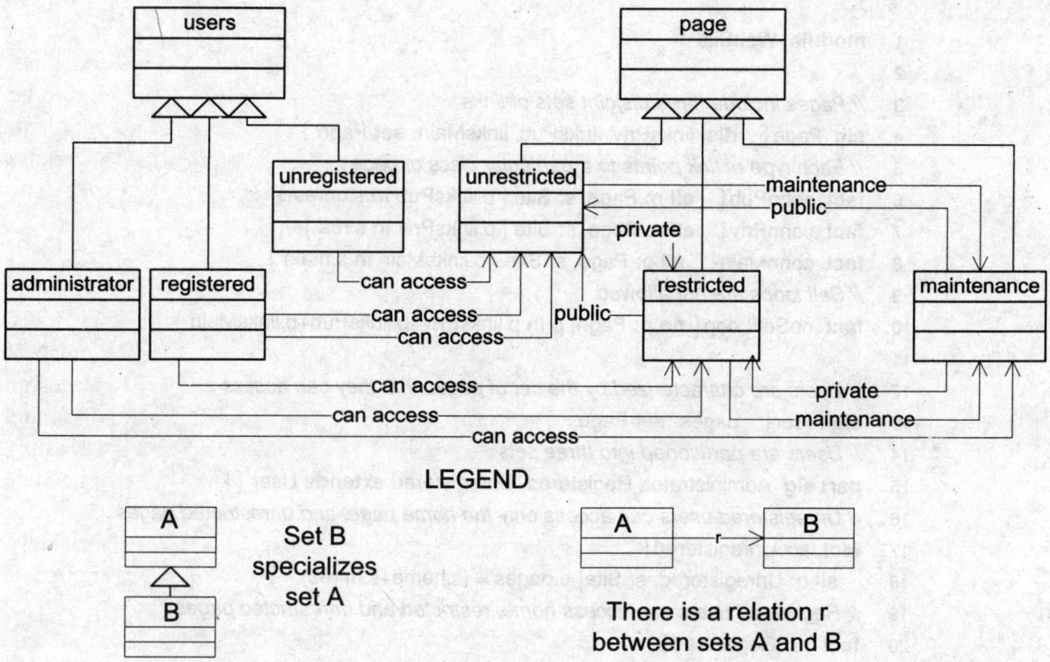

Figure 8.14: The data model of a simple Web site.

So far we have identified the sets involved in the relations, which we call their *signature*. To complete the description we need to indicate the rules that constrain relations among specific elements. For example we may:

- Exclude self loops from "links" relations; that is, specify that a page should not be directly linked to itself.
- Allow at most one type of link between two pages. Note that relations need not be symmetric; that is, the relation between *A* and *B* is distinct from the relation between *B* and *A*, so there can be a link of type *private* from *A* to *B* and a link of type *public* from *B* back to *A*.
- Require the Web site to be connected; that is, require that there be at least one way of following links from the home page to each other page of the site.

A data model can be visualized as a diagram with nodes corresponding to sets and edges representing relations, as in Figure 8.14.

```
module WebSite

// Pages include three disjoint sets of links
sig Page{  disj linksPriv, linksPub, linksMain: set Page }
// Each type of link points to a particular class of page
fact connPub{  all p: Page, s: Site | p.linksPub in s.unres }
fact connPriv{  all p: Page, s: Site | p.linksPriv in s.res }
fact connMain{  all p: Page, s: Site | p.linksMain in s.main }
// Self loops are not allowed
fact noSelfLoop{ no p: Page| p in p.linksPriv+p.linksPub+p.linksMain }

// Users are characterized by the set of pages that they can access
sig User{  pages: set Page  }
// Users are partitioned into three sets
part sig Administrator, Registered, Unregistered extends User {}
// Unregistered users can access only the home page, and unrestricted pages
fact accUnregistered{
   all u: Unregistered, s: Site| u.pages = (s.home+s.unres)  }
// Registered users can access home, restricted and unrestricted pages
fact accRegistered{
   all u: Registered, s: Site|
         u.pages = (s.home+s.res+s.unres)
}
// Administrators can access all pages
fact accAdministrator{
   all u: Administrator, s: Site|
         u.pages = (s.home+s.res+s.unres+s.main)
}

// A web site includes one home page and three disjoint sets
// of pages: restricted, unrestricted and maintenance
static sig Site{
   home: Page,
   disj res, unres, main: set Page
} {
   // All pages are accessible from the home page ('^' is transitive closure)
   all p: (res+unres+main)| p in home.^(linksPub+linksPriv+linksMain)
}

```

Figure 8.15: Alloy model of a Web site with different kinds of pages, users, and access rights (data model part). Continued in Figure 8.16.

```
module WebSite
...
// We consider one Web site that includes one home page
// and some other pages
fun initSite() {
        one s: Site| one s.home and
                some s.res and
                some s.unres and
                some s.main
}

// We consider one administrator and some registered and unregistered users
fun initUsers() {one Administrator and
                some Registered and
                some Unregistered}

fun init() {
    initSite() and initUsers()
}

// ANALYSIS

// Verify if there exists a solution
// with sets of cardinality at most 5
run init for 5

// check if unregistered users can visit all unrestrited pages,
// i.e., all unrestricted pages are connected to the home page with
// at least a path of public links.
// Perform analysis with sets of at most 3 objects.
// '*' indicates the transtivie closure including the source element.

assert browsePub{
    all p: Page, s: Site| p in s.unres implies s.home in p.* linksPub
}
check browsePub for 3
```

Figure 8.16: Alloy model of a Web site with different kinds of pages, users, and access rights, continued from Figure 8.15.

We can reason about sets and relations using mathematical laws. For example, set union and set intersection obey many of the same algebraic laws as addition and subtraction of integers:

$A \cup B = B \cup A$	commutative law
$A \cap B = B \cap A$	" "
$(A \cup B) \cup C = A \cup (B \cup C)$	associative law
$(A \cap B) \cap C = A \cap (B \cap C)$	" "
$A \cap (B \cup C) = (A \cap B) \cup (A \cap C)$	distributive law
etc.	

These and many other laws together make up *relational algebra*, which is used extensively in database processing and has many other uses.

It would be inconvenient to write down a data model directly as a collection of mathematical formulas. Instead, we use some notation whose meaning is the same as the mathematical formulas, but is easier to write, maintain, and comprehend. *Alloy* is one such modeling notation, with the additional advantage that it can be processed by a finite state verification tool.

The definition of the data model as sets and relations can be formalized and verified with relational algebra by specifying signatures and constraints. Figure 8.15 presents a formalization of the data model of the Web site in *Alloy*. Keyword sig (signature) identifies three sets: Pages, User, and Site. The definition of set Pages also defines three disjoint relations among pages: linksPriv (private links), linksPub (public links), and linksMain (maintenance links). The definition of User also defines a relation between users and pages. User is partitioned into three disjoint sets (Administrator, Registered, and Unregistered). The definition of Site aggregates pages into the site and identifies the home page. Site is defined static since it is a fixed classification of objects.

The keyword facts introduces constraints.[6] The constraints connPub, connPriv and connMain restrict the target of the links relations, while noSelfLoop excludes links from a page to itself. The constraints accAdministrator, accRegistered, and accUnregistered map users to pages. The constraint that follows the definition of Site forces the Web site to be connected by requiring each page to belong to the transitive closure of links starting from the Web page (operator '^').

A relational algebra specification may be over- or underconstrained. Overconstrained specifications are not satisfiable by any implementation, while underconstrained specifications allow undesirable implementations; that is, implementations that violate important properties.

In general, specifications identify infinite sets of solutions, each characterized by a different set of objects and relations (e.g., the infinite set of Web sites with different sets of pages, users and correct relations among them). Thus in general, properties of a relational specification are undecidable because proving them would require examining an infinite set of possible solutions. While attempting to prove absence of a solution may be inconclusive, often a (counter) example that invalidates a property can be found within a finite set of small models.

We can verify a specification over a finite set of solutions by limiting the cardinality

[6]The order in which relations and constraints are given is irrelevant. We list constraints after the relations they refer to.

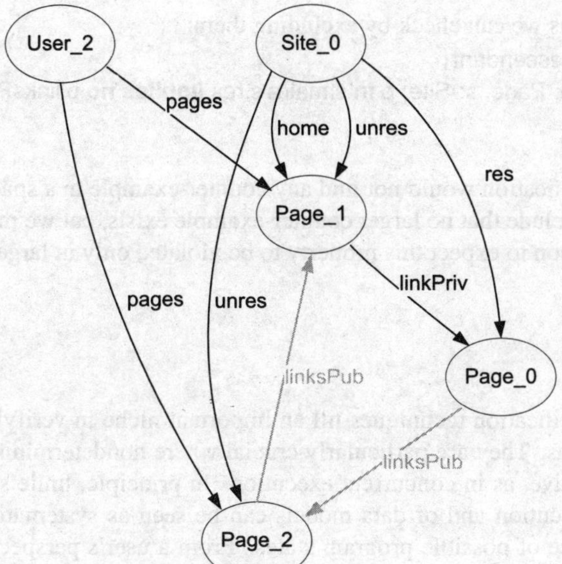

Figure 8.17: A Web site that violates the "browsability" property, because public page Page_2 *is not reachable from the home page using only unrestricted links. This diagram was generated by the Alloy tool.*

of the sets. In the example, we first verify that the model admits solutions for sets with at most five elements (run init for 5 issued after an initialization of the system.) A positive outcome indicates that the specification is not overconstrained — there are no logical contradictions. A negative outcome would not allow us to conclude that no solution exists, but tells us that no "reasonably small" solution exists.

We then verify that the example is not underconstrained with respect to property browsePub that states that unregistered users must be able to visit all unrestricted pages by accessing the site from the home page. The property is asserted by requiring that all unrestricted pages belong to the reflexive transitive closure of the linkPub relation from the home page (here we use operator '*' instead of '^' because the home page is included in the closure). If we check whether the property holds for sets with at most three elements (check browsePub for 3) we obtain a counter-example like the one shown in Figure 8.17, which shows how the property can be violated.

The simple Web site in the example consists of two unrestricted pages (page_1, the home page, and page_2), one restricted page (page_0), and one unregistered user (user_2). User_2 cannot visit one of the unrestricted pages (page_2) because the only path from the home page to page_2 goes through the restricted page page_0. The property is violated because unrestricted browsing paths can be "interrupted" by restricted pages or pages under maintenance, for example, when a previously unrestricted page is reserved or disabled for maintenance by the administrator.

The problem appears only when there are public links from maintenance or reserved pages, as we can check by excluding them:

```
fact descendant{
   all p: Page, s: Site| p in s.main+s.res implies no p.linksPub
}
```

This new specification would not find any counter-example in a space of cardinality 3. We cannot conclude that no larger counter-example exists, but we may be satisfied that there is no reason to expect this property to be violated only in larger models.

Summary

Finite state verification techniques fill an important niche in verifying critical properties of programs. They are particularly crucial where nondeterminism makes program testing ineffective, as in concurrent execution. In principle, finite state verification of concurrent execution and of data models can be seen as systematically exploring an enormous space of possible program states. From a user's perspective, the challenge is to construct a suitable model of the software that can be analyzed with reasonable expenditure of human and computational resources, captures enough significant detail for verification to succeed, and can be shown to be consistent with the actual software.

Further Reading

There is a large literature on finite state verification techniques reaching back at least to the 1960s, when Bartlett et al. [BSW69] employed what is recognizably a manual version of state space exploration to justify the corrrectness of a communication protocol. A number of early state space verification tools were developed initially for communication protocol verification, including the Spin tool. Holzmann's journal description of Spin's design and use [Hol97], though now somewhat out of date, remains an adequate introduction to the approach, and a full primer and reference manual [Hol03] is available in book form.

The ordered binary decision diagram representation of Boolean functions, used in the first symbolic model checkers, was introduced by Randal Bryant [Bry86]. The representation of transition relations as OBDDs in this chapter is meant to illustrate basic ideas but is simplified and far from complete; Bryant's survey paper [Bry92] is a good source for understanding applications of OBDDs, and Huth and Ryan [HR00] provide a thorough and clear step-by-step description of how OBDDs are used in the SMV symbolic model checker.

Model refinement based on iterative refinements of an initial coarse model was introduced by Ball and Rajamani in the tools Slam [BR01a] and Bebop [BR01b], and by Henzinger and his colleagues in Blast [HJMS03]. The complementary refinement approach of FLAVERS was introduced by Dwyer and colleagues [DCCN04].

Automated analysis of relational algebra for data modeling was introduced by Daniel Jackson and his students with the Alloy notation and associated tools [Jac02].

Exercises

8.1. We stated, on the one hand, that finite state verification falls between basic flow analysis and formal verification in power and cost, but we also stated that finite state verification techniques are often designed to provide results that are tantamount to formal proofs of program properties. Are these two statements contradictory? If not, how can a technique that is less powerful than formal verification produce results that are tantamount to formal proofs?

8.2. Construct an ordered binary decision diagram (OBDD) for the proposition

$$x \Rightarrow y \vee z$$

8.3. (a) How does the size of the OBDD representation of

$$(x \vee y) \wedge \neg(x \wedge y \wedge z)$$

differ depending on which variable (x, y, or z) is first in the variable ordering (i.e., appears in the root node of the OBDD representation)? Is the size of the OBDD equivalent for some different orderings of the variables? Why or why not?

(b) Predict whether the order of variables would make a difference for

$$(x \vee y \vee z) \wedge \neg(x \wedge y \wedge z)$$

8.4. A property like "if the button is pressed, then eventually the elevator will come" is classified as a liveness property. However, the stronger real-time version "if the button is pressed, then the elevator will arrive within 30 seconds" is technically a safety property rather than a liveness property. Why?

Part III

Problems and Methods

Chapter 9

Test Case Selection and Adequacy

A key problem in software testing is selecting and evaluating test cases. This chapter introduces basic approaches to test case selection and corresponding adequacy criteria. It serves as a general introduction to the problem and provides a conceptual framework for functional and structural approaches described in subsequent chapters.

Required Background

- Chapter 2
  The fundamental problems and limitations of test case selection are a consequence of the undecidability of program properties. A grasp of the basic problem is useful in understanding Section 9.3.

9.1 Overview

Experience suggests that software that has passed a thorough set of systematic tests is likely to be more dependable than software that has been only superficially or haphazardly tested. Surely we should require that each software module or subsystem undergo thorough, systematic testing before being incorporated into the main product. But what do we mean by thorough testing? What is the criterion by which we can judge the adequacy of a suite of tests that a software artifact has passed?

Ideally, we should like an "adequate" test suite to be one that ensures correctness of the product. Unfortunately, that goal is not attainable. The difficulty of proving that some set of test cases is adequate in this sense is equivalent to the difficulty of proving that the program is correct. In other words, we could have "adequate" testing in this sense only if we could establish correctness without any testing at all.

In practice we settle for criteria that identify inadequacies in test suites. For example, if the specification describes different treatment in two cases, but the test suite does not check that the two cases are in fact treated differently, then we may conclude that the test suite is inadequate to guard against faults in the program logic. If no test in the test suite executes a particular program statement, we might similarly conclude that the test suite is inadequate to guard against faults in that statement. We may use a whole set of (in)adequacy criteria, each of which draws on some source of information about the program and imposes a set of obligations that an adequate set of test cases ought to satisfy. If a test suite fails to satisfy some criterion, the obligation that has not been satisfied may provide some useful information about improving the test suite. If a set of test cases satisfies all the obligations by all the criteria, we still do not know definitively that it is a well-designed and effective test suite, but we have at least some evidence of its thoroughness.

9.2 Test Specifications and Cases

A test case includes not only input data but also any relevant execution conditions and procedures, and a way of determining whether the program has passed or failed the test on a particular execution. The term *input* is used in a very broad sense, which may include all kinds of stimuli that contribute to determining program behavior. For example, an interrupt is as much an input as is a file. The pass/fail criterion might be given in the form of expected output, but could also be some other way of determining whether a particular program execution is correct.

A test case specification is a requirement to be satisfied by one or more actual test cases. The distinction between a test case specification and a test case is similar to the distinction between a program specification and a program. A test case specification might be met by several different test cases, and vice versa. Suppose, for example, we are testing a program that sorts a sequence of words. "The input is two or more words" would be a test case specification, while test cases with the input values "alpha beta" and "Milano Paris London" would be two among many test cases satisfying the test case specification. A test case with input "Milano Paris London" would satisfy both the test case specification "the input is two or more words" and the test case specification "the input contains a mix of lower- and upper-case alphabetic characters."

Characteristics of the input are not the only thing that might be mentioned in a test case specification. A complete test case specification includes pass/fail criteria for judging test execution and may include requirements, drawn from any of several sources of information, such as system, program, and module interface specifications; source code or detailed design of the program itself; and records of faults encountered in other software systems.

Test specifications drawn from system, program, and module interface specifications often describe program inputs, but they can just as well specify any observable behavior that could appear in specifications. For example, the specification of a database system might require certain kinds of robust failure recovery in case of power loss, and test specifications might therefore require removing system power at certain critical points in processing. If a specification describes inputs and outputs, a test specification could prescribe aspects of the input, the output, or both. If the specification is modeled as an extended finite state machine, it might require executions corresponding to particular transitions or paths in the state-machine model. The general term for such

Testing Terms

While the informal meanings of words like "test" may be adequate for everyday conversation, in this context we must try to use terms in a more precise and consistent manner. Unfortunately, the terms we will need are not always used consistently in the literature, despite the existence of an IEEE standard that defines several of them. The terms we will use are defined as follows.

Test case: A *test case* is a set of inputs, execution conditions, and a pass/fail criterion. (This usage follows the IEEE standard.)

Test case specification: A test case specification is a requirement to be satisfied by one or more actual test cases. (This usage follows the IEEE standard.)

Test obligation: A test obligation is a partial test case specification, requiring some property deemed important to thorough testing. We use the term *obligation* to distinguish the requirements imposed by a test adequacy criterion from more complete test case specifications.

Test suite: A *test suite* is a set of test cases. Typically, a method for functional testing is concerned with creating a test suite. A test suite for a program, system, or individual unit may be made up of several test suites for individual modules, subsystems, or features. (This usage follows the IEEE standard.)

Test or test execution: We use the term *test* or *test execution* to refer to the activity of executing test cases and evaluating their results. When we refer to "a test," we mean execution of a single test case, except where context makes it clear that the reference is to execution of a whole test suite. (The IEEE standard allows this and other definitions.)

Adequacy criterion: A test adequacy criterion is a predicate that is true (satisfied) or false (not satisfied) of a ⟨program, test suite⟩ pair. Usually a test adequacy criterion is expressed in the form of a rule for deriving a set of test obligations from another artifact, such as a program or specification. The adequacy criterion is then satisfied if every test obligation is satisfied by at least one test case in the suite.

test specifications is *functional testing,* although the term *black-box testing* and more specific terms like *specification-based testing* and *model-based testing* are also used.

Test specifications drawn from program source code require coverage of particular elements in the source code or some model derived from it. For example, we might require a test case that traverses a loop one or more times. The general term for testing based on program structure is *structural testing,* although the term *white-box testing* or *glass-box testing* is sometimes used.

Previously encountered faults can be an important source of information regarding useful test cases. For example, if previous products have encountered failures or security breaches due to buffer overflows, we may formulate test requirements specifically to check handling of inputs that are too large to fit in provided buffers. These fault-based test specifications usually draw also from interface specifications, design models, or source code, but add test requirements that might not have been otherwise considered. A common form of fault-based testing is fault-seeding, purposely inserting faults in source code and then measuring the effectiveness of a test suite in finding the seeded faults, on the theory that a test suite that finds seeded faults is likely also to find other faults.

Test specifications need not fall cleanly into just one of the categories. For example, test specifications drawn from a model of a program might be considered specification-based if the model is produced during program design, or structural if it is derived from the program source code.

Consider the Java method of Figure 9.1. We might apply a general rule that requires using an empty sequence wherever a sequence appears as an input; we would thus create a test case specification (a test obligation) that requires the empty string as input.[1] If we are selecting test cases structurally, we might create a test obligation that requires the first clause of the if statement on line 15 to evaluate to true and the second clause to evaluate to false, and another test obligation on which it is the second clause that must evaluate to true and the first that must evaluate to false.

9.3 Adequacy Criteria

We have already noted that adequacy criteria are just imperfect but useful indicators of inadequacies, so we may not always wish to use them directly to generate test specifications from which actual test cases are drawn. We will use the term *test obligation* for test specifications imposed by adequacy criteria, to distinguish them from test specifications that are actually used to derive test cases. Thus, the usual situation will be that a set of test cases (a test suite) is created using a set of test specifications, but then the adequacy of that test suite is measured using a different set of test obligations.

We say a test suite satisfies an adequacy criterion if all the tests succeed and if every test obligation in the criterion is satisfied by at least one of the test cases in the test suite. For example, the statement coverage adequacy criterion is satisfied by a particular test suite for a particular program if each executable statement in the program (i.e., excluding comments and declarations) is executed by at least one test case in the

[1] Constructing and using catalogs of general rules like this is described in Chapter 10.

```java
/**
 * Remove/collapse multiple spaces.
 *
 * @param String string to remove multiple spaces from.
 * @return String
 */
public static String collapseSpaces(String argStr)
{
    char last = argStr.charAt(0);
    StringBuffer argBuf = new StringBuffer();

    for (int cIdx = 0 ; cIdx < argStr.length(); cIdx++)
    {
        char ch = argStr.charAt(cIdx);
        if (ch != ' ' || last != ' ')
        {
            argBuf.append(ch);
            last = ch;
        }
    }

    return argBuf.toString();
}
```

Figure 9.1: A Java method for collapsing sequences of blanks, excerpted from the StringUtils class of Velocity version 1.3.1, an Apache Jakarta project. © Apache Group, used by permission.

test suite. A fault-based adequacy criterion that seeds a certain set of faults would be satisfied if, for each of the seeded faults, there is a test case that passes for the original program but fails for the program with (only) that seeded fault.

It is quite possible that *no* test suite will satisfy a particular test adequacy criterion for a particular program. For example, if the program contains statements that can never be executed (perhaps because it is part of a sanity check that can be executed only if some other part of the program is faulty), then no test suite can satisfy the statement coverage criterion. Analogous situations arise regardless of the sources of information used in devising test adequacy criteria. For example, a specification-based criterion may require combinations of conditions drawn from different parts of the specification, but not all combinations may be possible.

One approach to overcoming the problem of unsatisfiable test obligations is to simply exclude any unsatisfiable obligation from a criterion. For example, the statement coverage criterion can be modified to require execution only of statements that can be executed. The question of whether a particular statement or program path is executable, or whether a particular combination of clauses in a specification is satisfiable, or whether a program with a seeded error actually behaves differently from the original program, are all provably undecidable in the general case. Thus, while tools may be some help in distinguishing feasible from infeasible test obligations, in at least some cases the distinction will be left to fallible human judgment.

If the number of infeasible test obligations is modest, it can be practical to identify each of them, and to ameliorate human fallibility through peer review. If the number of infeasible test obligations is large, it becomes impractical to carefully reason about each to avoid excusing an obligation that is feasible but difficult to satisfy. A common practice is to measure the extent to which a test suite approaches an adequacy criterion. For example, if an adequacy criterion based on control flow paths in a program unit induced 100 distinct test obligations, and a test suite satisfied 85 of those obligations, then we would say that we had reached 85% coverage of the test obligations.

Quantitative measures of test coverage are widely used in industry. They are simple and cheap to calculate, provide some indication of progress toward thorough testing, and project an aura of objectivity. In managing software development, anything that produces a number can be seductive. One must never forget that coverage is a rough proxy measure for the thoroughness and effectiveness of test suites. The danger, as with any proxy measure of some underlying goal, is the temptation to improve the proxy measure in a way that does not actually contribute to the goal. If, for example, 80% coverage of some adequacy criterion is required to declare a work assignment complete, developers under time pressure will almost certainly yield to the temptation to design tests specifically to that criterion, choosing the simplest test cases that achieve the required coverage level. One cannot entirely avoid such distortions, but to the extent possible one should guard against them by ensuring that the ultimate measure of performance is preventing faults from surviving to later stages of development or deployment.

9.4 Comparing Criteria

It would be useful to know whether one test adequacy criterion was more effective than another in helping find program faults, and whether its extra effectiveness was worthwhile with respect to the extra effort expended to satisfy it. One can imagine two kinds of answers to such a question, empirical and analytical. An empirical answer would be based on extensive studies of the effectiveness of different approaches to testing in industrial practice, including controlled studies to determine whether the relative effectiveness of different testing methods depends on the kind of software being tested, the kind of organization in which the software is developed and tested, and a myriad of other potential confounding factors. The empirical evidence available falls short of providing such clear-cut answers. An analytical answer to questions of relative effectiveness would describe conditions under which one adequacy criterion is guaranteed to be more effective than another, or describe in statistical terms their relative effectiveness.

Analytic comparisons of the strength of test coverage depends on a precise definition of what it means for one criterion to be "stronger" or "more effective" than another. Let us first consider single test suites. In the absence of specific information, we cannot exclude the possibility that any test case can reveal a failure. A test suite T_A that does not include all the test cases of another test suite T_B may fail revealing the potential failure exposed by the test cases that are in T_B but not in T_A. Thus, if we consider only the guarantees that a test suite provides, the only way for one test suite T_A to be stronger than another suite T_B is to include all test cases of T_B plus additional ones.

Many different test suites might satisfy the same coverage criterion. To compare criteria, then, we consider all the possible ways of satisfying the criteria. If every test suite that satisfies some criterion A is a superset of some test suite that satisfies criterion B, or equivalently, every suite that satisfies A also satisfies B, then we can say that A "subsumes" B.

Δ subsumes

Test coverage criterion A *subsumes* test coverage criterion B iff, for every program P, every test set satisfying A with respect to P also satisfies B with respect to P.

In this case, if we satisfy criterion C_1, there is no point in measuring adequacy with respect to C_2. For example, a structural criterion that requires exploring all outcomes of conditional branches subsumes statement coverage. Likewise, a specification-based criterion that requires use of a set of possible values for attribute A and, independently, for attribute B, will be subsumed by a criterion that requires all combinations of those values.

Consider again the example of Figure 9.1. Suppose we apply an adequacy criterion that imposes an obligation to execute each statement in the method. This criterion can be met by a test suite containing a single test case, with the input value (value of argStr) being "doesn'tEvenHaveSpaces." Requiring both the true and false branches of each test to be taken subsumes the previous criterion and forces us to at least provide an input with a space that is not copied to the output, but it can still be satisfied by a suite with just one test case. We might add a requirement that the loop be iterated zero times, once, and several times, thus requiring a test suite with at least three test cases. The obligation to execute the loop body zero times would force us to add a test case with the empty string as input, and like the specification-based obligation to consider an empty sequence, this would reveal a fault in the code.

Should we consider a more demanding adequacy criterion, as indicated by the subsumes relation among criteria, to be a better criterion? The answer would be "yes" if we were comparing the guarantees provided by test adequacy criteria: If criterion *A* subsumes criterion *B*, and if any test suite satisfying *B* in some program is guaranteed to find a particular fault, then any test suite satisfying *A* is guaranteed to find the same fault in the program. This is not as good as it sounds, though. Twice nothing is nothing. Adequacy criteria do not provide useful guarantees for fault detection, so comparing guarantees is not a useful way to compare criteria.

A better statistical measure of test effectiveness is whether the probability of finding at least one program fault is greater when using one test coverage criterion than another. Of course, such statistical measures can be misleading if some test coverage criteria require much larger numbers of test cases than others. It is hardly surprising if a criterion that requires at least 300 test cases for program *P* is more effective, on average, than a criterion that requires at least 50 test cases for the same program. It would be better to know, if we have 50 test cases that satisfy criterion *B*, is there any value in finding 250 test cases to finish satisfying the "stronger" criterion *A*, or would it be just as profitable to choose the additional 250 test cases at random?

Although theory does not provide much guidance, empirical studies of particular test adequacy criteria do suggest that there is value in pursuing stronger criteria, particularly when the level of coverage attained is very high. Whether the extra value of pursuing a stronger adequacy criterion is commensurate with the cost almost certainly depends on a plethora of particulars, and can only be determined by monitoring results in individual organizations.

Open Research Issues

A good deal of theoretical research has been done on what one can conclude about test effectiveness from test adequacy criteria. Most of the results are negative. In general, one cannot be certain that a test suite that meets any practical test adequacy criterion ensures correctness, or even that it is more effective at finding faults than another test suite that does not meet the criterion. While theoretical characterization of test adequacy criteria and their properties was once an active research area, interest has waned, and it is likely that future theoretical progress must begin with a quite different conception of the fundamental goals of a theory of test adequacy.

The trend in research is toward empirical, rather than theoretical, comparison of the effectiveness of particular test selection techniques and test adequacy criteria. Empirical approaches to measuring and comparing effectiveness are still at an early stage. A major open problem is to determine when, and to what extent, the results of an empirical assessment can be expected to generalize beyond the particular programs and test suites used in the investigation. While empirical studies have to a large extent displaced theoretical investigation of test effectiveness, in the longer term useful empirical investigation will require its own theoretical framework.

Further Reading

Goodenough and Gerhart made the original attempt to formulate a theory of "adequate" testing [GG75]; Weyuker and Ostrand extended this theory to consider when a set of test obligations is adequate to ensure that a program fault is revealed [WO80]. Gourlay's exposition of a mathematical framework for adequacy criteria is among the most lucid developments of purely analytic characterizations [Gou83]. Hamlet and Taylor show that, if one takes statistical confidence in (absolute) program correctness as the goal, none of the standard coverage testing techniques improve on random testing [HT90], from which an appropriate conclusion is that confidence in absolute correctness is not a reasonable goal of systematic testing. Frankl and Iakounenko's study of test effectiveness [FI98] is a good example of the development of empirical methods for assessing the practical effectiveness of test adequacy criteria.

Related Topics

Test adequacy criteria and test selection techniques can be categorized by the sources of information they draw from. Functional testing draws from program and system specifications, and is described in Chapters 10, 11, and 14. Structural testing draws from the structure of the program or system, and is described in Chapters 12 and 13. The techniques for testing object-oriented software described in Chapter 15 draw on both functional and structural approaches. Selection and adequacy criteria based on consideration of hypothetical program faults are described in Chapter 16.

Exercises

9.1. Deterministic finite state machines (FSMs), with states representing classes of program states and transitions representing external inputs and observable program actions or outputs, are sometimes used in modeling system requirements. We can design test cases consisting of sequences of program inputs that trigger FSM transitions and the predicted program actions expected in response. We can also define test coverage criteria relative to such a model. Which of the following coverage criteria subsume which others?

State coverage: For each state in the FSM model, there is a test case that visits that state.

Transition coverage: For each transition in the FSM model, there is a test case that traverses that transition.

Path coverage: For all finite-length subpaths from a distinguished start state in the FSM model, there is at least one test case that includes a corresponding subpath.

State-pair coverage: For each state r in the FSM model, for each state s reachable from r along some sequence of transitions, there is at least one test case that passes through state r and then reaches state s.

9.2. Adequacy criteria may be derived from specifications (functional criteria) or code (structural criteria). The presence of infeasible elements in a program may make it impossible to obtain 100% coverage. Since we cannot possibly cover infeasible elements, we might define a coverage criterion to require 100% coverage of feasible elements (e.g., execution of all program statements that can actually be reached in program execution). We have noted that feasibility of program elements is undecidable in general. Suppose we instead are using a functional test adequacy criterion, based on logical conditions describing inputs and outputs. It is still possible to have infeasible elements (logical condition A might be inconsitent with logical condition B, making the conjunction $A \wedge B$ infeasible). Would you expect distinguishing feasible from infeasible elements to be easier or harder for functional criteria, compared to structural criteria? Why?

9.3. Suppose test suite A satisfies adequacy criterion C_1. Test suite B satisfies adequacy criterion C_2, and C_2 subsumes C_1. Can we be certain that faults revealed by A will also be revealed by B?

Chapter 10

Functional Testing

A functional specification is a description of intended program[1] behavior, distinct from the program itself. Whatever form the functional specification takes — whether formal or informal — it is the most important source of information for designing tests. Deriving test cases from program specifications is called functional testing.

Functional testing, or more precisely, functional test case design, attempts to answer the question "What test cases shall I use to exercise my program?" considering only the specification of a program and not its design or implementation structure. Being based on program specifications and not on the internals of the code, functional testing is also called specification-based or black-box testing.

Functional testing is typically the base-line technique for designing test cases, for a number of reasons. Functional test case design can (and should) begin as part of the requirements specification process, and continue through each level of design and interface specification; it is the only test design technique with such wide and early applicability. Moreover, functional testing is effective in finding some classes of fault that typically elude so-called white-box or glass-box techniques of structural or fault-based testing. Functional testing techniques can be applied to any description of program behavior, from an informal partial description to a formal specification, and at any level of granularity from module to system testing. Finally, functional test cases are typically less expensive to design and execute than white-box tests.

10.1 Overview

In testing and analysis aimed at verification[2] — that is, at finding any discrepancies between what a program does and what it is intended to do — one must obviously refer to requirements as expressed by users and specified by software engineers. A

[1]We use the term *program* generically for the artifact under test, whether that artifact is a complete application or an individual unit together with a test harness. This is consistent with usage in the testing research literature.

[2]Here we focus on software verification as opposed to validation (see Chapter 2). The problems of validating the software and its specifications, that is, checking the program behavior and its specifications with respect to the users' expectations, is treated in Chapter 22.

functional specification, that is, a description of the expected behavior of the program, is the primary source of information for test case specification.

Δ black-box testing

Functional testing, also known as black-box or specification-based testing, denotes techniques that derive test cases from functional specifications. Usually functional testing techniques produce test case specifications that identify classes of test cases and are instantiated to produce individual test cases.

The core of functional test case design is partitioning[3] the possible behaviors of the program into a finite number of homogeneous classes, where each such class can reasonably be expected to be consistently correct or incorrect. In practice, the test case designer often must also complete the job of formalizing the specification far enough to serve as the basis for identifying classes of behaviors. An important side benefit of test design is highlighting the weaknesses and incompleteness of program specifications.

Deriving functional test cases is an analytical process that decomposes specifications into test cases. The myriad aspects that must be taken into account during functional test case specification makes the process error prone. Even expert test designers can miss important test cases. A methodology for functional test design helps by decomposing the functional test design process into elementary steps. In this way, it is possible to control the complexity of the process and to separate human intensive activities from activities that can be automated.

Sometimes, functional testing can be fully automated. This is possible, for example, when specifications are given in terms of some formal model, such as a grammar or an extended state machine specification. In these (exceptional) cases, the creative work is performed during specification and design of the software. The test designer's job is then limited to the choice of the test selection criteria, which defines the strategy for generating test case specifications. In most cases, however, functional test design is a human intensive activity. For example, when test designers must work from informal specifications written in natural language, much of the work is in structuring the specification adequately for identifying test cases.

10.2 Random versus Partition Testing Strategies

With few exceptions, the number of potential test cases for a given program is unimaginably huge — so large that for all practical purposes it can be considered infinite. For example, even a simple function whose input arguments are two 32-bit integers has $2^{64} \approx 10^{54}$ legal inputs. In contrast to input spaces, budgets and schedules are finite, so any practical method for testing must select an infinitesimally small portion of the complete input space.

Some test cases are better than others, in the sense that some reveal faults and others do not.[4] Of course, we cannot know in advance which test cases reveal faults. At a minimum, though, we can observe that running the same test case again is less likely

[3]We are using the term *partition* in a common but rather sloppy sense. A true partition would form disjoint classes, the union of which is the entire space. Partition testing separates the behaviors or input space into classes whose union is the entire space, but the classes may not be disjoint.

[4]Note that the relative value of different test cases would be quite different if our goal were to measure dependability, rather than finding faults so that they can be repaired.

Functional vs. Structural Testing

Test cases and test suites can be derived from several sources of information, including specifications (functional and model-based testing), detailed design and source code (structural testing), and hypothesized defects (fault-based testing). Functional test case design is an indispensable base of a good test suite, complemented but never replaced by structural and fault-based testing, because there are classes of faults that only functional testing effectively detects. Omission of a feature, for example, is unlikely to be revealed by techniques that refer only to the code structure.

Consider a program that is supposed to accept files in either plain ASCII text, or HTML, or PDF formats and generate standard Postscript. Suppose the programmer overlooks the PDF functionality, so that the program accepts only plain text and HTML files. Intuitively, a functional testing criterion would require at least one test case for each item in the specification, regardless of the implementation; that is, it would require the program to be exercised with at least one ASCII, one HTML, and one PDF file, thus easily revealing the failure due to the missing code. In contrast, criteria based solely on the code would not require the program to be exercised with a PDF file, since each part of the code can be exercised without attempting to use that feature. Similarly, fault-based techniques, based on potential faults in design or coding, would not have any reason to indicate a PDF file as a potential input even if "missing case" were included in the catalog of potential faults.

Functional specifications often address semantically rich domains, and we can use domain information in addition to the cases explicitly enumerated in the program specification. For example, while a program may manipulate a string of up to nine alphanumeric characters, the program specification may reveal that these characters represent a postal code, which immediately suggests test cases based on postal codes of various localities. Suppose the program logic distinguishes only two cases, depending on whether they are found in a table of U.S. zip codes. A structural testing criterion would require testing of valid and invalid U.S. zip codes, but only consideration of the specification and richer knowledge of the domain would suggest test cases that reveal missing logic for distinguishing between U.S.-bound mail with invalid U.S. zip codes and mail bound for other countries.

Functional testing can be applied at any level of granularity where some form of specification is available, from overall system testing to individual units, although the level of granularity and the type of software influence the choice of the specification styles and notations, and consequently the functional testing techniques that can be used.

In contrast, structural and fault-based testing techniques are invariably tied to program structures at some particular level of granularity and do not scale much beyond that level. The most common structural testing techniques are tied to fine-grain program structures (statements, classes, etc.) and are applicable only at the level of modules or small collections of modules (small subsystems, components, or libraries).

to reveal a fault than running a different test case, and we may reasonably hypothesize that a test case that is very different from the test cases that precede it is more valuable than a test case that is very similar (in some sense yet to be defined) to others.

As an extreme example, suppose we are allowed to select only three test cases for a program that breaks a text buffer into lines of 60 characters each. Suppose the first test case is a buffer containing 40 characters, and the second is a buffer containing 30 characters. As a final test case, we can choose a buffer containing 16 characters or a buffer containing 100 characters. Although we cannot prove that the 100-character buffer is the better test case (and it might not be; the fact that 16 is a power of 2 might have some unforeseen significance), we are naturally suspicious of a set of tests that is strongly biased toward lengths less than 60.

Accidental bias may be avoided by choosing test cases from a random distribution. Random sampling is often an inexpensive way to produce a large number of test cases. If we assume absolutely no knowledge on which to place a higher value on one test case than another, then random sampling maximizes value by maximizing the number of test cases that can be created (without bias) for a given budget. Even if we do possess some knowledge suggesting that some cases are more valuable than others, the efficiency of random sampling may in some cases outweigh its inability to use any knowledge we may have.

Consider again the line-break program, and suppose that our budget is one day of testing effort rather than some arbitrary number of test cases. If the cost of random selection and actual execution of test cases is small enough, then we may prefer to run a large number of random test cases rather than expending more effort on each of a smaller number of test cases. We may in a few hours construct programs that generate buffers with various contents and lengths up to a few thousand characters, as well as an automated procedure for checking the program output. Letting it run unattended overnight, we may execute a few million test cases. If the program does not correctly handle a buffer containing a sequence of more than 60 nonblank characters (a single "word" that does not fit on a line), we are likely to encounter this case by sheer luck if we execute enough random tests, even without having explicitly considered this case.

Even a few million test cases is an infinitesimal fraction of the complete input space of most programs. Large numbers of random tests are unlikely to find failures at single points (singularities) in the input space. Consider, for example, a simple procedure for returning the two roots of a quadratic equation $ax^2+bx+c=0$ and suppose we choose test inputs (values of the coefficients a, b, and c) from a uniform distribution ranging from -10.0 to 10.0. While uniform random sampling would certainly cover cases in which $b^2-4ac>0$ (where the equation has no real roots), it would be very unlikely to test the case in which $a=0$ and $b=0$, in which case a naive implementation of the quadratic formula

$$x = \frac{-b \pm \sqrt{b^2-4ac}}{2a}$$

will divide by zero (see Figure 10.1).

Of course, it is unlikely that anyone would test *only* with random values. Regardless of the overall testing strategy, most test designers will also try some "special" values. The test designer's intuition comports with the observation that random sam-

```
/** Find the two roots of ax^2 + bx + c,
 * that is, the values of x for which the result is 0.
 */
class Roots {
    double root_one, root_two;
    int num_roots;
    public roots(double a, double b, double c) {
        double q;
        double r;
        // Apply the textbook quadratic formula:
        // Roots = -b +- sqrt(b^2 - 4ac) / 2a
        q = b*b - 4*a*c;
        if (q > 0 && a != 0) {
            // If b^2 > 4ac, there are two distinct roots
            num_roots = 2;
            r = (double) Math.sqrt(q) ;
            root_one =  ((0-b) + r)/(2*a);
            root_two =  ((0-b) - r)/(2*a);
        } else if (q==0) { // (BUG HERE)
            // The equation has exactly one root
            num_roots = 1;
            root_one = (0-b)/(2*a);
            root_two = root_one;
        } else {
            // The equation has no roots if b^2 < 4ac
            num_roots = 0;
            root_one = -1;
            root_two = -1;
        }
    }
    public int num_roots() { return num_roots; }
    public double first_root()  { return root_one; }
    public double second_root() { return root_two; }
}
```

Figure 10.1: The Java class roots*, which finds roots of a quadratic equation. The case analysis in the implementation is incomplete: It does not properly handle the case in which $b^2 - 4ac = 0$ and $a = 0$. We cannot anticipate all such faults, but experience teaches that boundary values identifiable in a specification are disproportionately valuable. Uniform random generation of even large numbers of test cases is ineffective at finding the fault in this program, but selection of a few "special values" based on the specification quickly uncovers it.*

pling is an ineffective way to find singularities in a large input space. The observation about singularities can be generalized to any characteristic of input data that defines an infinitesimally small portion of the complete input data space. If again we have just three real-valued inputs a, b, and c, there is an infinite number of choices for which $b = c$, but random sampling is unlikely to generate any of them because they are an infinitesimal part of the complete input data space.

The observation about special values and random samples is by no means limited to numbers. Consider again, for example, breaking a text buffer into lines. Since line breaks are permitted at blanks, we would consider blanks a "special" value for this problem. While random sampling from the character set is likely to produce a buffer containing a sequence of at least 60 nonblank characters, it is much less likely to produce a sequence of 60 blanks.

The reader may justifiably object that a reasonable test designer would not create text buffer test cases by sampling uniformly from the set of all characters. The designer would instead classify characters depending on their treatment, lumping alphabetic characters into one class and white space characters into another. In other words, a test designer will *partition* the input space into classes and will then generate test data in a manner that is likely to choose data from each partition. Test designers seldom use pure random sampling; usually they exploit some knowledge of application semantics to choose samples that are more likely to include "special" or trouble-prone regions of the input space.

Partition testing separates the input space into classes whose union is the entire space, but the classes may not be disjoint (and thus the term *partition* is not mathematically accurate, although it has become established in testing terminology). Figure 10.2 illustrates a desirable case: All inputs that lead to a failure belong to at least one class that contains only inputs that lead to failures. In this case, sampling each class in the quasi-partition selects at least one input that leads to a failure, revealing the fault. We could easily turn the quasi-partition of Figure 10.2 into a true partition, by considering intersections among the classes, but sampling in a true partition would not improve the efficiency or effectiveness of testing.

Δ partition testing

Δ specification-based testing

Δ functional testing

A testing method that divides the infinite set of possible test cases into a finite set of classes, with the purpose of drawing one or more test cases from each class, is called a *partition testing* method. When partitions are chosen according to information in the specification, rather than the design or implementation, it is called *specification-based partition testing*, or more briefly, *functional testing*. Note that not all testing of product functionality is "functional testing." Rather, the term is used specifically to refer to systematic testing based on a functional specification. It excludes ad hoc and random testing, as well as testing based on the structure of a design or implementation.

Partition testing typically increases the cost of each test case, since in addition to generation of a set of classes, creation of test cases from each class may be more expensive than generating random test data. In consequence, partition testing usually produces fewer test cases than random testing for the same expenditure of time and money. Partitioning can therefore be advantageous only if the average value (fault detection effectiveness) is greater.

If we were able to group together test cases with such perfect knowledge that the outcome of test cases in each class were uniform (either all successes or all failures),

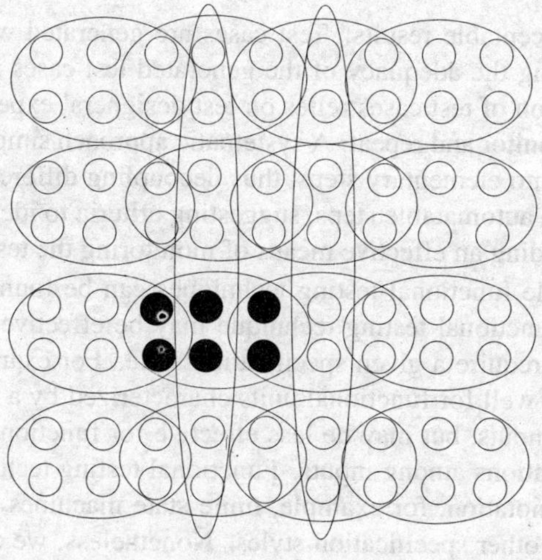

Figure 10.2: A quasi-partition of a program's input space. Black circles represent inputs that lead to failures. All elements of the input domain belong to at least one class, but classes are not disjoint.

then partition testing would be at its theoretical best. In general we cannot do that, nor can we even quantify the uniformity of classes of test cases. Partitioning by any means, including specification-based partition testing, is always based on experience and judgment that leads one to believe that certain classes of test case are "more alike" than others, in the sense that failure-prone test cases are likely to be concentrated in some classes. When we appealed earlier to the test designer's intuition that one should try boundary cases and special values, we were actually appealing to a combination of experience (many failures occur at boundary and special cases) and knowledge that identifiable cases in the specification often correspond to classes of input that require different treatment by an implementation.

Given a fixed budget, the optimum may not lie in only partition testing or only random testing, but in some mix that makes use of available knowledge. For example, consider again the simple numeric problem with three inputs, *a*, *b*, and *c*. We might consider a few special cases of each input, individually and in combination, and we might consider also a few potentially significant relationships (e.g., $a = b$). If no faults are revealed by these few test cases, there is little point in producing further arbitrary partitions — one might then turn to random generation of a large number of test cases.

10.3 A Systematic Approach

Deriving test cases from functional specifications is a complex analytical process that partitions the input space described by the program specification. Brute force generation of test cases, that is, direct generation of test cases from program specifications, seldom produces acceptable results: Test cases are generated without particular criteria, and determining the adequacy of the generated test cases is almost impossible. Brute force generation of test cases relies on test designers' expertise and is a process that is difficult to monitor and repeat. A systematic approach simplifies the overall process by dividing it into elementary steps, thus decoupling different activities, dividing brain-intensive from automatable steps, suggesting criteria to identify adequate sets of test cases, and providing an effective means of monitoring the testing activity.

Although suitable functional testing techniques can be found for any granularity level, a particular functional testing technique may be effective only for some kinds of software or may require a given specification style. For example, a combinatorial approach may work well for functional units characterized by a large number of relatively independent inputs, but may be less effective for functional units characterized by complex interrelations among inputs. Functional testing techniques designed for a given specification notation, for example, finite state machines or grammars, are not easily applicable to other specification styles. Nonetheless, we can identify a general pattern of activities that captures the essential steps in a variety of different functional test design techniques. By describing particular functional testing techniques as instantiations of this general pattern, relations among the techniques may become clearer, and the test designer may gain some insight into adapting and extending these techniques to the characteristics of other applications and situations.

Figure 10.3 identifies the general steps of systematic approaches. The steps may be difficult or trivial depending on the application domain and the available program specifications. Some steps may be omitted depending on the application domain, the available specifications and the test designers' expertise. Instances of the process can be obtained by suitably instantiating different steps. Although most techniques are presented and applied as stand-alone methods, it is also possible to mix and match steps from different techniques, or to apply different methods for different parts of the system to be tested.

Identify Independently Testable Features Functional specifications can be large and complex. Usually, complex specifications describe systems that can be decomposed into distinct features. For example, the specification of a Web site may include features for searching the site database, registering users' profiles, getting and storing information provided by the users in different forms, and so on. The specification of each of these features may comprise several functionalities. For example, the search feature may include functionalities for editing a search pattern, searching the database with a given pattern, and so on. Although it is possible to design test cases that exercise several functionalities at once, designing different test cases for different functionalities can simplify the test generation problem, allowing each functionality to be examined separately. Moreover, it eases locating faults that cause the revealed failures. It is thus recommended to devise separate test cases for each functionality of the system, whenever possible.

The preliminary step of functional testing consists in partitioning the specifications into features that can be tested separately. This can be an easy step for well-designed, modular specifications, but informal specifications of large systems may be difficult to

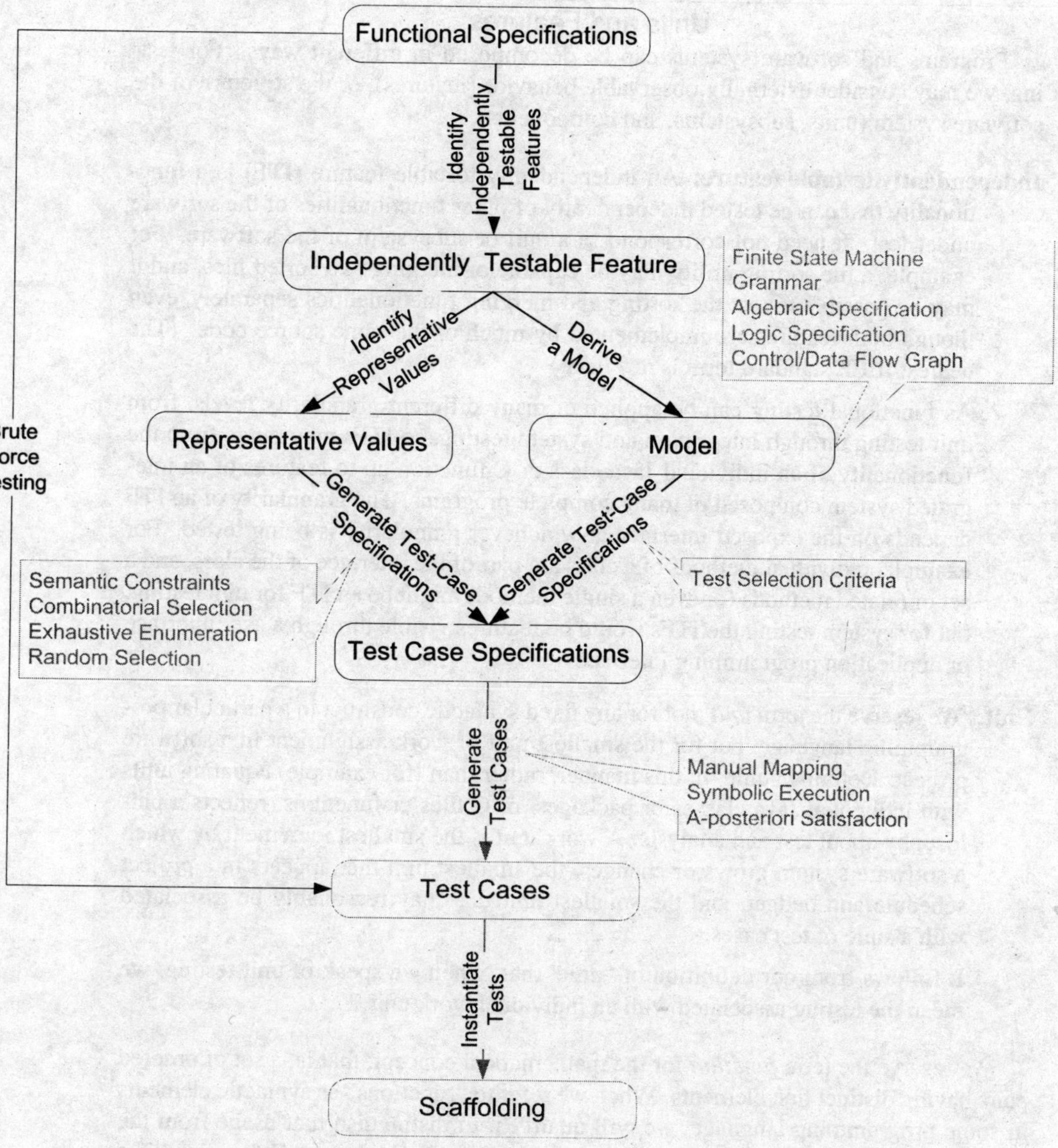

Figure 10.3: The main steps of a systematic approach to functional program testing.

Units and Features

Programs and software systems can be decomposed in different ways. For testing, we may consider externally observable behavior (features), or the structure of the software system (units, subsystems, and components).

Independently testable feature: An independently testable feature (ITF) is a functionality that can be tested independently of other functionalities of the software under test. It need not correspond to a unit or subsystem of the software. For example, a file sorting utility may be capable of merging two sorted files, and it may be possible to test the sorting and merging functionalities separately, even though both features are implemented by much of the same source code. (The nearest IEEE standard term is *test item.*)

As functional testing can be applied at many different granularity levels, from unit testing through integration and system testing, so ITFs may range from the functionality of an individual Java class or C function up to features of an integrated system composed of many complete programs. The granularity of an ITF depends on the exposed interface at whichever granularity is being tested. For example, individual methods of a class are part of the interface of the class, and a set of related methods (or even a single method) might be an ITF for unit testing, but for system testing the ITFs would be features visible through a user interface or application programming interface.

Unit: We reserve the term *unit,* not for any fixed syntactic construct in a particular programming language, but for the smallest unit of work assignment in a software project. Defining "unit" in this manner, rather than (for example) equating units with individual Java classes or packages, or C files or functions, reflects a philosophy about test and analysis. A work unit is the smallest increment by which a software system grows or changes, the smallest unit that appears in a project schedule and budget, and the smallest unit that may reasonably be associated with a suite of test cases.

It follows from our definition of "unit" that, when we speak of unit testing, we mean the testing associated with an individual work unit.

We reserve the term *function* for the mathematical concept, that is, a set of ordered pairs having distinct first elements. When we refer to "functions" as syntactic elements in some programming language, we will qualify it to distinguish that usage from the mathematical concept. A "function" is a set of ordered pairs but a "C function" is a syntactic element in the C programming language.

decompose into independently testable features. Some degree of formality, at least to the point of careful definition and use of terms, is usually required.

Identification of functional features that can be tested separately is different from module decomposition. In both cases we apply the divide and conquer principle, but in the former case, we partition specifications according to the functional behavior as perceived by the users of the software under test,[5] while in the latter, we identify logical units that can be implemented separately. For example, a Web site may require a *sort* function, as a service routine, that does not correspond to an external functionality. The sort function may be a functional feature at module testing, when the program under test is the sort function itself, but is not a functional feature at system test, while deriving test cases from the specifications of the whole Web site. On the other hand, the registration of a new user profile can be identified as one of the functional features at system-level testing, even if such functionality is spread across several modules. Thus, identifying functional features does not correspond to identifying single modules at the design level, but rather to suitably slicing the specifications to attack their complexity incrementally.

Independently testable features are described by identifying all the inputs that form their execution environments. Inputs may be given in different forms depending on the notation used to express the specifications. In some cases they may be easily identifiable. For example, they can be the input alphabet of a finite state machine specifying the behavior of the system. In other cases, they may be hidden in the specification. This is often the case for informal specifications, where some inputs may be given explicitly as parameters of the functional unit, but other inputs may be left implicit in the description. For example, a description of how a new user registers at a Web site may explicitly indicate the data that constitutes the user profile to be inserted as parameters of the functional unit, but may leave implicit the collection of elements (e.g., database) in which the new profile must be inserted.

Trying to identify inputs may help in distinguishing different functions. For example, trying to identify the inputs of a graphical tool may lead to a clearer distinction between the graphical interface per se and the associated callbacks to the application. With respect to the Web-based user registration function, the data to be inserted in the database are part of the execution environment of the functional unit that performs the insertion of the user profile, while the combination of fields that can be used to construct such data is part of the execution environment of the functional unit that takes care of the management of the specific graphical interface.

Identify Representative Classes of Values or Derive a Model The execution environment of the feature under test determines the form of the final test cases, which are given as combinations of values for the inputs to the unit. The next step of a testing process consists of identifying which values of each input should be selected to form test cases. Representative values can be identified directly from informal specifications expressed in natural language. Alternatively, representative values may be selected in-

[5] Here the word "user" designates the individual using the specified service. It can be the user of the system, when dealing with a system specification, but it can be another module of the system, when dealing with detailed design specifications.

directly through a model, which can either be produced only for the sake of testing or be available as part of the specification. In both cases, the aim of this step is to identify the values for each input in isolation, either explicitly through enumeration or implicitly trough a suitable model, but not to select suitable combinations of such values (i.e., test case specifications). In this way, we separate the problem of identifying the representative values for each input from the problem of combining them to obtain meaningful test cases, thus splitting a complex step into two simpler steps.

Most methods that can be applied to informal specifications rely on explicit enumeration of representative values by the test designer. In this case, it is very important to consider all possible cases and take advantage of the information provided by the specification. We may identify different categories of expected values, as well as boundary and exceptional or erroneous values. For example, when considering operations on a nonempty list of elements, we may distinguish the cases of the empty list (an error value) and a singleton element (a boundary value) as special cases. Usually this step determines characteristics of values (e.g., any list with a single element) rather than actual values.

Implicit enumeration requires the construction of a (partial) model of the specifications. Such a model may be already available as part of a specification or design model, but more often it must be constructed by the test designer, in consultation with other designers. For example, a specification given as a finite state machine implicitly identifies different values for the inputs by means of the transitions triggered by the different values. In some cases, we can construct a partial model as a means of identifying different values for the inputs. For example, we may derive a grammar from a specification and thus identify different values according to the legal sequences of productions of the given grammar.

Directly enumerating representative values may appear simpler and less expensive than producing a suitable model from which values may be derived. However, a formal model may also be valuable in subsequent steps of test case design, including selection of combinations of values. Also, a formal model may make it easier to select a larger or smaller number of test cases, balancing cost and thoroughness, and may be less costly to modify and reuse as the system under test evolves. Whether to invest effort in producing a model is ultimately a management decision that depends on the application domain, the skills of test designers, and the availability of suitable tools.

Generate Test Case Specifications Test specifications are obtained by suitably combining values for all inputs of the functional unit under test. If representative values were explicitly enumerated in the previous step, then test case specifications will be elements of the Cartesian product of values selected for each input. If a formal model was produced, then test case specifications will be specific behaviors or combinations of parameters of the model, and a single test case specification could be satisfied by many different concrete inputs. Either way, brute force enumeration of all combinations is unlikely to be satisfactory.

The number of combinations in the Cartesian product of independently selected values grows as the product of the sizes of the individual sets. For a simple functional unit with five inputs each characterized by six values, the size of the Cartesian product is $6^5 = 7776$ test case specifications, which may be an impractical number for test cases for a simple functional unit. Moreover, if (as is usual) the characteristics are not completely orthogonal, many of these combinations may not even be feasible.

Consider the input of a procedure that searches for occurrences of a complex pattern in a Web database. Its input may be characterized by the length of the pattern and the presence of special characters in the pattern, among other aspects. Interesting values for the length of the pattern may be zero, one, or many. Interesting values for the presence of special characters may be zero, one, or many. However, the combination of value "zero" for the length of the pattern and value "many" for the number of special characters in the pattern is clearly impossible.

The test case specifications represented by the Cartesian product of all possible inputs must be restricted by ruling out illegal combinations and selecting a practical subset of the legal combinations. Illegal combinations are usually eliminated by constraining the set of combinations. For example, in the case of the complex pattern presented above, we can constrain the choice of one or more special characters to a positive length of the pattern, thus ruling out the illegal cases of patterns of length zero containing special characters.

Selection of a practical subset of legal combination can be done by adding information that reflects the hazard of the different combinations as perceived by the test designer or by following combinatorial considerations. In the former case, for example, we can identify exceptional values and limit the combinations that contain such values. In the pattern example, we may consider only one test for patterns of length zero, thus eliminating many combinations that would otherwise be derived for patterns of length zero. Combinatorial considerations reduce the set of test cases by limiting the number of combinations of values of different inputs to a subset of the inputs. For example, we can generate only tests that exhaustively cover all combinations of values for inputs considered pair by pair.

Depending on the technique used to reduce the space represented by the Cartesian product, we may be able to estimate the number of generated test cases generated and modify the selected subset of test cases according to budget considerations. Subsets of combinations of values (i.e., potential special cases) can often be derived from models of behavior by applying suitable test selection criteria that identify subsets of interesting behaviors among all behaviors represented by a model, for example by constraining the iterations on simple elements of the model itself. In many cases, test selection criteria can be applied automatically.

Generate Test Cases and Instantiate Tests The test generation process is completed by turning test case specifications into test cases and instantiating them. Test case specifications can be turned into test cases by selecting one or more test cases for each test case specification. Test cases are implemented by creating the scaffolding required for their execution.

10.4 Choosing a Suitable Approach

In the next chapters we will see several approaches to functional testing, each applying to different kinds of specifications. Given a specification, there may be one or more techniques well suited for deriving functional test cases, while some other techniques may be hard or even impossible to apply or may lead to unsatisfactory results. Some techniques can be interchanged; that is, they can be applied to the same specification and lead to similar results. Other techniques are complementary; that is, they apply to different aspects of the same specification or at different stages of test case generation.

The choice of approach for deriving functional test cases depends on several factors: the nature of the specification, form of the specification, expertise and experience of test designers, structure of the organization, availability of tools, budget and quality constraints, and costs of designing and implementing scaffolding.

Nature and form of the specification Different approaches exploit different characteristics of the specification. For example, the presence of several constraints on the input domain may suggest using a partitioning method with constraints, such as the category-partition method described in Chapter 11, while unconstrained combinations of values may suggest a pairwise combinatorial approach. If transitions among a finite set of system states are identifiable in the specification, a finite state machine approach may be indicated, while inputs of varying and unbounded size may be tackled with grammar-based approaches. Specifications given in a specific format (e.g., as decision structures) suggest corresponding techniques. For example, functional test cases for SDL[6] specifications of protocols are often derived with finite state machine-based criteria.

Experience of test designers and organization The experience of testers and company procedures may drive the choice of the testing technique. For example, test designers expert in category partition may prefer that technique over a catalog-based approach when both are applicable, while a company that works in a specific application area may require the use of domain-specific catalogs.

Tools Some techniques may require the use of tools, whose availability and cost should be taken into account when choosing a testing technique. For example, several tools are available for deriving test cases from SDL specifications. The availability of one of these tools may suggest the use of SDL for capturing a subset of the requirements expressed in the specification.

Budget and quality constraints Different quality and budget constraints may lead to different choices. For example, if the primary constraint is rapid, automated testing, and reliability requirements are not stringent, random test case generation may be appropriate. In contrast, thorough testing of a safety critical application may require the

[6]SDL (Specification Description Language) is a formal specification notation based on extended finite state machines, widely used in telecommunication systems and standardized by the International Telecommunication Union.

use of sophisticated methods for functional test case generation. When choosing an approach, it is important to evaluate all relevant costs. For example, generating a large number of random test cases may necessitate design and construction of sophisticated test oracles, or the cost of training to use a new tool may exceed the advantages of adopting a new approach.

Scaffolding costs Each test case specification must be converted to a concrete test case, executed many times over the course of development, and checked each time for correctness. If generic scaffolding code required to generate, execute, and judge the outcome of a large number of test cases can be written just once, then a combinatorial approach that generates a large number of test case specifications is likely to be affordable. If each test case must be realized in the form of scaffolding code written by hand — or worse, if test execution requires human involvement — then it is necessary to invest more care in selecting small suites of test case specifications.

Many engineering activities require careful analysis of trade-offs. Functional testing is no exception: Successfully balancing the many aspects is a difficult and often underestimated problem that requires skilled designers. Functional testing is not an exercise of choosing the optimal approach, but a complex set of activities for finding a suitable combination of models and techniques that yield a set of test cases to satisfy cost and quality constraints. This balancing extends beyond test design to software design for test. Appropriate design not only improves the software development process, but can greatly facilitate the job of test designers and lead to substantial savings.

Open Research Issues

Functional testing is by far the most common way of deriving test cases in industry, but neither industrial practice nor research has established general and satisfactory methodologies. Research in functional testing is increasingly active and progressing in many directions.

Deriving test cases from formal models is an active research area. In the past three decades, formal methods have been studied mainly as a means of proving software properties. Recently, attention has moved toward using formal methods for deriving test cases. There are three main open research topics in this area:

- *Definition of techniques for automatically deriving test cases from particular formal models.* Formal methods present new challenges and opportunities for deriving test cases. We can both adapt existing techniques borrowed from other disciplines or research areas and define new techniques for test case generation. Formal notations can support automatic generation of test cases, thus opening additional problems and research challenges.

- *Adaptation of formal methods to be more suitable for test case generation.*. As illustrated in this chapter, test cases can be derived in two broad ways, either by identifying representative values or by deriving a model of the unit under test. A variety of formal models could be used in testing. The research challenge lies in identifying a trade-off between costs of creating formal models and savings in automatically generating test cases.

- *Development of a general framework for deriving test cases from a range of formal specifications.* Currently research addresses techniques for generating test cases from individual formal methods. Generalization of techniques will allow more combinations of formal methods and testing.

Another important research area is fed by interest in different specification and design paradigms (e.g., software architectures, software design patterns, and service-oriented applications). Often these approaches employ new graphical or textual notations. Research is active in investigating different approaches to automatically or semi-automatically deriving test cases from these artifacts and studying the effectiveness of existing test case generation techniques.

Increasing size and complexity of software systems is a challenge to testing. Existing functional testing techniques do not take advantage of test cases available for parts of the artifact under test. Compositional approaches for deriving test cases for a given system taking advantage of test cases available for its subsystems is an important open research problem.

Further Reading

Functional testing techniques, sometimes called black-box testing or specification-based testing, are presented and discussed by several authors. Ntafos [DN81] makes the case for random rather than systematic testing; Frankl, Hamlet, Littlewood, and Strigini [FHLS98] is a good starting point to the more recent literature considering the relative merits of systematic and statistical approaches.

Related topics

Readers interested in practical technique for deriving functional test specifications from informal specifications and models may continue with the next two chapters, which describe several functional testing techniques. Readers interested in the complementarities between functional and structural testing may continue with Chapters 12 and 13, which describe structural and data flow testing.

Exercises

10.1. In the Extreme Programming (XP) methodology (see the sidebar on page 381), a written description of a desired feature may be a single sentence, and the first step to designing the implementation of that feature is designing and implementing a set of test cases. Does this aspect of the XP methodology contradict our assertion that test cases are a formalization of specifications?

10.2. (a) Compute the probability of selecting a test case that reveals the fault in line 19 of program *Root* of Figure 10.1 by randomly sampling the input domain, assuming that type double has range $-2^{31} \ldots 2^{31}-1$.

(b) Compute the probability of randomly selecting a test case that reveals a fault if lines 13 and 19 were both missing the condition $a \neq 0$.

10.3. Identify independently testable units in the following specification.

Desk calculator *Desk calculator* performs the following algebraic operations: *sum*, *subtraction*, *product*, *division*, and *percentage* on *integers* and *real numbers*. Operands must be of the same type, except for percentage, which allows the first operator to be either integer or real, but requires the second to be an integer that indicates the percentage to be computed. Operations on integers produce integer results. Program *Calculator* can be used with a textual interface that provides the following commands:

Mx=N, where Mx is a memory location, that is, M0 ... M9, and N is a number. Integers are given as nonempty sequences of digits, with or without sign. Real numbers are given as nonempty sequences of digits that include a dot ".", with or without sign. Real numbers can be terminated with an optional exponent, that is, character "E" followed by an integer. The command displays the stored number.

Mx=display, where Mx is a memory location and *display* indicates the value shown on the last line.

operand1 operation operand2, where *operand1* and *operand2* are numbers or memory locations or *display* and *operation* is one of the following symbols: "+", "-", "*", "/", "%", where each symbol indicates a particular operation. Operands must follow the type conventions. The command displays the result or the string *Error*.

or with a graphical interface that provides a display with 12 characters and the following keys:

[0], [1], [2], [3], [4], [5], [6], [7], [8], [9], the 10 digits

[+], [-], [*], [/], [%], the operations

[=] to display the result of a sequence of operations

[C] , to clear display

[M], [M+], [MS], [MR], [MC], where [M] is pressed before a digit to indicate the target memory, 0…9, keys [M+], [MS], [MR], [MC] pressed after [M] and a digit indicate the operation to be performed on the target memory: add display to memory, store display in memory, retrieve memory; that is, move the value in memory to the display and clear memory.
Example: [5] [+] [1] [0] [M] [3] [MS] [8] [0] [−] [M] [3] [MR] [=] prints 65 (the value 15 is stored in memory cell 3 and then retrieved to compute 80 − 15).

Chapter 11

Combinatorial Testing

Requirements specifications typically begin in the form of natural language statements. The flexibility and expressiveness of natural language, which are so important for human communication, represent an obstacle to automatic analysis. Combinatorial approaches to functional testing consist of a manual step of structuring the specification statement into a set of properties or attributes that can be systematically varied and an automatizable step of producing combinations of choices.

Simple "brute force" synthesis of test cases by test designers squanders the intelligence of expert staff on tasks that can be partly automated. Even the most expert of test designers will perform suboptimally and unevenly when required to perform the repetitive and tedious aspects of test design, and quality will vary widely and be difficult to monitor and control. In addition, estimation of the effort and number of test cases required for a given functionality will be subjective.

Combinatorial approaches decompose the "brute force" work of the test designers into steps, to attack the problem incrementally by separating analysis and synthesis activities that can be quantified and monitored, and partially supported by tools. They identify the variability of elements involved in the execution of a given functionality, and select representative combinations of relevant values for test cases. Repetitive activities such as the combination of different values can be easily automated, thus allowing test designers to focus on more creative and difficult activities.

Required Background

- Chapter 10
  Understanding the limits of random testing and the needs of a systematic approach motivates the study of combinatorial as well as model-based testing techniques. The general functional testing process illustrated in Section 10.3 helps position combinatorial techniques within the functional testing process.

11.1 Overview

In this chapter, we introduce three main techniques that are successfully used in industrial environments and represent modern approaches to systematically derive test cases from natural language specifications: the category-partition approach to identifying attributes, relevant values, and possible combinations; combinatorial sampling to test a large number of potential interactions of attributes with a relatively small number of inputs; and provision of catalogs to systematize the manual aspects of combinatorial testing.

The category-partition approach separates identification of the values that characterize the input space from the combination of different values into complete test cases. It provides a means of estimating the number of test cases early, size a subset of cases that meet cost constraints, and monitor testing progress.

Pairwise and n-way combination testing provide systematic ways to cover interactions among particular attributes of the program input space with a relatively small number of test cases. Like the category-partition method, it separates identification of characteristic values from generation of combinations, but it provides greater control over the number of combinations generated.

The manual step of identifying attributes and representative sets of values can be made more systematic using catalogs that aggregate and synthesize the experience of test designers in a particular organization or application domain. Some repetitive steps can be automated, and the catalogs facilitate training for the inherently manual parts.

These techniques address different aspects and problems in designing a suite of test cases from a functional specification. While one or another may be most suitable for a specification with given characteristics, it is also possible to combine ideas from each.

11.2 Category-Partition Testing

Category-partition testing is a method for generating functional tests from informal specifications. The following steps comprise the core part of the category-partition method:

A. Decompose the specification into independently testable features: Test designers identify features to be tested separately, and identify parameters and any other elements of the execution environment the unit depends on. Environment dependencies are treated identically to explicit parameters. For each parameter and environment element, test designers identify the elementary *parameter characteristics*, which in the category-partition method are usually called *categories*.

Δ parameter characteristic

Δ category

Δ classes of values

Δ choice

B. Identify Representative Values: Test designers select a set of representative classes of values for each parameter characteristic. Values are selected in isolation, independent of other parameter characteristics. In the category-partition method, classes of values are called *choices,* and this activity is called *partitioning the categories into choices.*

C. Generate Test Case Specifications: Test designers impose semantic constraints on values to indicate invalid combinations and restrict valid combinations (e.g., limiting combinations involving exceptional and invalid values).

Categories, choices, and constraints can be provided to a tool to automatically generate a set of test case specifications. Automating trivial and repetitive activities such as these makes better use of human resources and reduces errors due to distraction. Just as important, it is possible to determine the number of test cases that will be generated (by calculation, or by actually generating them) before investing human effort in test execution. If the number of derivable test cases exceeds the budget for test execution and evaluation, test designers can reduce the number of test cases by imposing additional semantic constraints. Controlling the number of test cases *before* test execution begins is preferable to ad hoc approaches in which one may at first create very thorough test suites and then test less and less thoroughly as deadlines approach.

We illustrate the category-partition method using a specification of a feature from the direct sales Web site of Chipmunk Computers. Customers are allowed to select and price custom configurations of Chipmunk Computers. A *configuration* is a set of selected options for a particular model of computer. Some combinations of model and options are not valid (e.g., digital LCD monitor with analog video card), so configurations are tested for validity before they are priced. The *check configuration* function (Figure 11.1) is given a model number and a set of components, and returns the Boolean value *True* if the configuration is valid or *False* otherwise. This function has been selected by the test designers as an independently testable feature.

A. Identify Independently Testable Features and Parameter Characteristics We assume that step *A* starts by selecting the *Check configuration* feature to be tested independently of other features. This entails choosing to separate testing of the configuration check per se from its presentation through a user interface (e.g., a Web form), and depends on the architectural design of the software system.

Step *A* requires the test designer to identify the parameter characteristics, that is, the elementary characteristics of the parameters and environment elements that affect the unit's execution. A single parameter may have multiple elementary characteristics. A quick scan of the functional specification would indicate *model* and *components* as the parameters of *check configuration*. More careful consideration reveals that what is "valid" must be determined by reference to additional information. In fact, the functional specification assumes the existence of a database of models and components. The database is an environment element that, though not explicitly mentioned in the functional specification, is required for executing and thus testing the feature, and partly determines its behavior. Note that our goal is not to test a particular configuration of the system with a fixed database, but to test the generic system that may be configured through different database contents.

Having identified *model*, *components*, and *product database* as the parameters and environment elements required to test the *check configuration* functionality, the test designer would next identify the parameter characteristics of each.

Model may be represented as an integer, but we know that it is not to be used arithmetically, but rather serves as a key to the database and other tables. The specification

Check Configuration: Check the validity of a computer configuration. The parameters of *check configuration* are:

Model: A model identifies a specific product and determines a set of constraints on available components. Models are characterized by logical slots for components, which may or may not be implemented by physical slots on a bus. Slots may be required or optional. Required slots must be assigned a suitable component to obtain a legal configuration, while optional slots may be left empty or filled depending on the customer's needs.

Example: The required "slots" of the Chipmunk C20 laptop computer include a screen, a processor, a hard disk, memory, and an operating system. (Of these, only the hard disk and memory are implemented using actual hardware slots on a bus.) The optional slots include external storage devices such as a CD/DVD writer.

Set of Components: A set of $\langle slot, component \rangle$ pairs, which must correspond to the required and optional slots associated with the model. A component is a choice that can be varied within a model and that is not designed to be replaced by the end user. Available components and a default for each slot is determined by the model. The special value "empty" is allowed (and may be the default selection) for optional slots.

In addition to being compatible or incompatible with a particular model and slot, individual components may be compatible or incompatible with each other.

Example: The default configuration of the Chipmunk C20 includes 20 gigabytes of hard disk; 30 and 40 gigabyte disks are also available. (Since the hard disk is a required slot, "empty" is not an allowed choice.) The default operating system is RodentOS 3.2, personal edition, but RodentOS 3.2 mobile server edition may also be selected. The mobile server edition requires at least 30 gigabytes of of hard disk.

Figure 11.1: Functional specification of the feature Check configuration *of the Web site of a computer manufacturer.*

mentions that a model is characterized by a set of slots for required components and a set of slots for optional components. We may identify *model number*, *number of required slots*, and *number of optional slots* as characteristics of parameter *model*.

Parameter *components* is a collection of $\langle slot, selection \rangle$ pairs. The size of a collection is always an important characteristic, and since components are further categorized as required or optional, the test designer may identify *number of required components with nonempty selection* and *number of optional components with nonempty selection* as characteristics. The matching between the tuple passed to *check configuration* and the one actually required by the selected model is important and may be identified as category *correspondence of selection with model slots*. The actual selections are also significant, but for now the test designer simply identifies *required component selection* and *optional component selection*, postponing selection of relevant values to the next stage in test design.

The environment element *product database* is also a collection, so *number of models in the database* and *number of components in the database* are parameter characteristics. Actual values of database entries are deferred to the next step in test design.

There are no hard-and-fast rules for choosing categories, and it is not a trivial task. Categories reflect the test designer's judgment regarding which classes of values may be treated differently by an implementation, in addition to classes of values that are explicitly identified in the specification. Test designers must also use their experience and knowledge of the application domain and product architecture to look under the surface of the specification and identify hidden characteristics. For example, the specification fragment in Figure 11.1 makes no distinction between configurations of models with several required slots and models with none, but the experienced test designer has seen enough failures on "degenerate" inputs to test empty collections wherever a collection is allowed.

The number of options that can (or must) be configured for a particular model of computer may vary from model to model. However, the category-partition method makes no direct provision for structured data, such as sets of $\langle slot, selection \rangle$ pairs. A typical approach is to "flatten" collections and describe characteristics of the whole collection as parameter characteristics. Typically the size of the collection (the length of a string, for example, or in this case the number of required or optional slots) is one characteristic, and descriptions of possible combinations of elements (occurrence of special characters in a string, for example, or in this case the selection of required and optional components) are separate parameter characteristics.

Suppose the only significant variation among $\langle slot, selection \rangle$ pairs was between pairs that are compatible and pairs that are incompatible. If we treated each pair as a separate characteristic, and assumed n slots, the category-partition method would generate all 2^n combinations of compatible and incompatible slots. Thus we might have a test case in which the first selected option is compatible, the second is compatible, and the third incompatible, and a different test case in which the first is compatible but the second and third are incompatible, and so on. Each of these combinations could be combined in several ways with other parameter characteristics. The number of combinations quickly explode. Moreover, since the number of slots is not actually fixed, we cannot even place an upper bound on the number of combinations that must be considered. We will therefore choose the flattening approach and select possible

Identifying and Bounding Variation

It may seem that drawing a boundary between a fixed program and a variable set of parameters would be the simplest of tasks for the test designer. It is not always so.

Consider a program that produces HTML output. Perhaps the HTML is based on a template, which might be encoded in constants in C or Java code, or might be provided through an external data file, or perhaps both: it could be encoded in a C or source code file that is generated at compile time from a data file. If the HTML template is identified in one case as a parameter to varied in testing, it seems it should be so identified in all three of these variations, or even if the HTML template is embedded directly in print statements of the program, or in an XSLT transformation script.

The underlying principle for identifying parameters to be varied in testing is anticipation of variation in use. Anticipating variation is likewise a key part of architectural and detailed design of software. In a well-designed software system, module boundaries reflect "design secrets," permitting one part of a system to be modified (and retested) with minimum impact on other parts. The most frequent changes are facilitated by making them input or configurable options. The best software designers identify and document not only what is likely to change, but how often and by whom. For example, a configuration or template file that may be modified by a user will be clearly distinguished from one that is considered a fixed part of the system.

Ideally the scope of anticipated change is both clearly documented and consonant with the program design. For example, we expect to see client-customizable aspects of HTML output clearly isolated and documented in a configuration file, not embedded in an XSLT script file and certainly not scattered about in print statements in the code. Thus, the choice to encode something as "data" rather than "program" should at least be a good hint that it may be a parameter for testing, although further consideration of the scope of variation may be necessary. Conversely, defining the parameters for variation in test design can be part of the architectural design process of setting the scope of variation anticipated for a given product or release.

patterns for the collection as a whole.

Should the representative values of the flattened collection of pairs be *one compatible selection, one incompatible selection, all compatible selections, all incompatible selections,* or should we also include *mix of 2 or more compatible and 2 or more incompatible selections*? Certainly the latter is more thorough, but whether there is sufficient value to justify the cost of this thoroughness is a matter of judgment by the test designer.

We have oversimplified by considering only whether a selection is compatible with a slot. It might also happen that the selection does not appear in the database. Moreover, the selection might be incompatible with the model, or with a selected component of another slot, in addition to the possibility that it is incompatible with the slot for which it has been selected. If we treat each such possibility as a separate parameter characteristic, we will generate many combinations, and we will need semantic constraints to rule out combinations like *there are three options, at least two of which are compatible with the model and two of which are not, and none of which appears in the database*. On the other hand, if we simply enumerate the combinations that do make sense and are worth testing, then it becomes more difficult to be sure that no important combinations have been omitted. Like all design decisions, the way in which collections and complex data are broken into parameter characteristics requires judgment based on a combination of analysis and experience.

B. Identify Representative Values This step consists of identifying a list of representative values (more precisely, a list of classes of values) for each of the parameter characteristics identified during step *A*. Representative values should be identified for each category independently, ignoring possible interactions among values for different categories, which are considered in the next step.

Representative values may be identified by manually applying a set of rules known as boundary value testing or erroneous condition testing. The boundary value testing rule suggests selection of extreme values within a class (e.g., maximum and minimum values of the legal range), values outside but as close as possible to the class, and "interior" (non-extreme) values of the class. Values near the boundary of a class are often useful in detecting "off by one" errors in programs. The erroneous condition rule suggests selecting values that are outside the normal domain of the program, since experience suggests that proper handling of error cases is often overlooked.

Table 11.1 summarizes the parameter characteristics and the corresponding value choices identified for feature *Check configuration.*[1] For numeric characteristics whose legal values have a lower bound of 1, i.e., *number of models in database* and *number of components in database*, we identify 0, the erroneous value, 1, the boundary value, and *many*, the class of values greater than 1, as the relevant value classes. For numeric characteristics whose lower bound is zero, i.e., *number of required slots for selected model* and *number of optional slots for selected model*, we identify 0 as a boundary value, 1 and *many* as other relevant classes of values. Negative values are impossible here, so we do not add a negative error choice. For numeric characteristics whose legal values have definite lower and upper-bounds, i.e., *number of optional components with*

[1] At this point, readers may ignore the items in square brackets, which indicate constraints identified in step *C* of the category-partition method.

non-empty selection and *number of optional components with non-empty selection*, we identify boundary and (when possible) erroneous conditions corresponding to both lower and upper bounds.

Identifying relevant values is an important but tedious task. Test designers may improve manual selection of relevant values by using the catalog approach described in Section 11.4, which captures the informal approaches used in this section with a systematic application of catalog entries.

C. Generate Test Case Specifications A test case specification for a feature is given as a combination of value classes, one for each identified parameter characteristic. Unfortunately, the simple combination of all possible value classes for each parameter characteristic results in an unmanageable number of test cases (many of which are impossible) even for simple specifications. For example, in the Table 11.1 we find 7 categories with 3 value classes, 2 categories with 6 value classes, and one with four value classes, potentially resulting in $3^7 \times 6^2 \times 4 = 314{,}928$ test cases, which would be acceptable only if the cost of executing and checking each individual test case were very small. However, not all combinations of value classes correspond to reasonable test case specifications. For example, it is not possible to create a test case from a test case specification requiring a *valid* model (a model appearing in the database) where the database contains zero models.

The category-partition method allows one to omit some combinations by indicating value classes that need not be combined with all other values. The label [*error*] indicates a value class that need be tried only once, in combination with non-error values of other parameters. When [*error*] constraints are considered in the category-partition specification of Table 11.1, the number of combinations to be considered is reduced to $1\times3\times3\times1\times1\times3\times5\times5\times2\times2+11 = 2711$. Note that we have treated "component not in database" as an error case, but have treated "incompatible with slot" as a normal case of an invalid configuration; once again, some judgment is required.

Although the reduction from 314,928 to 2,711 is impressive, the number of derived test cases may still exceed the budget for testing such a simple feature. Moreover, some values are not erroneous per se, but may only be useful or even valid in particular combinations. For example, the number of optional components with non-empty selection is relevant to choosing useful test cases only when the number of optional slots is greater than 1. A number of non-empty choices of required component greater than zero does not make sense if the number of required components is zero.

Erroneous combinations of valid values can be ruled out with the *property* and *if-property* constraints. The *property* constraint groups values of a single parameter characteristic to identify subsets of values with common properties. The *property* constraint is indicated with label *property PropertyName*, where *PropertyName* identifies the property for later reference. For example, property *RSNE* (required slots non-empty) in Table 11.1 groups values that correspond to non-empty sets of required slots for the parameter characteristic *Number of Required Slots for Selected Model (#SMRS)*, i.e., values *1* and *many*. Similarly, property *OSNE* (optional slots non-empty) groups non-empty values for the parameter characteristic *Number of Optional Slots for Selected Model (#SMOS)*.

Parameter: Model

Model number

malformed	[error]
not in database	[error]
valid	

Number of required slots for selected model (#SMRS)

0	[single]
1	[property **RSNE**] [single]
many	[property **RSNE**], [property **RSMANY**]

Number of optional slots for selected model (#SMOS)

0	[single]
1	[property **OSNE**] [single]
many	[property **OSNE**][property **OSMANY**]

Parameter: Components

Correspondence of selection with model slots

omitted slots	[error]
extra slots	[error]
mismatched slots	[error]
complete correspondence	

Number of required components with non-empty selection

0	[if **RSNE**] [error]
$<$ number of required slots	[if **RSNE**] [error]
$=$ number of required slots	[if **RSMANY**]

Number of optional components with non-empty selection

0	
$<$ number of optional slots	[if **OSNE**]
$=$ number of optional slots	[if **OSMANY**]

Required component selection

some default	[single]
all valid	
≥ 1 incompatible with slot	
≥ 1 incompatible with another selection	
≥ 1 incompatible with model	
≥ 1 not in database	[error]

Optional component selection

some default	[single]
all valid	
≥ 1 incompatible with slot	
≥ 1 incompatible with another selection	
≥ 1 incompatible with model	
≥ 1 not in database	[error]

Environment element: Product database

Number of models in database (#DBM)

0	[error]
1	[single]
many	

Number of components in database (#DBC)

0	[error]
1	[single]
many	

Table 11.1: Categories and value classes derived with the category-partition method from the specification of Figure 11.1

The *if-property* constraint bounds the choices of values for a parameter characteristic that can be combined with a particular value selected for a different parameter characteristic. The *if-property* constraint is indicated with label *if PropertyName*, where *PropertyName* identifies a property defined with the *property* constraint. For example, the constraint *if RSNE* attached to value *0* of parameter characteristic *Number of required components with non-empty selection* limits the combination of this value with values *1* and *many* of the parameter characteristics *Number of Required Slots for Selected Model (#SMRS)*. In this way, we rule out illegal combinations like *Number of required components with non-empty selection = 0* with *Number of Required Slots for Selected Model (#SMRS) = 0*.

The *property* and *if-property* constraints introduced in Table 11.1 further reduce the number of combinations to be considered to $1 \times 3 \times 1 \times 1 \times (3+2+1) \times 5 \times 5 \times 2 \times 2 + 11 = 1811$.

The number of combinations can be further reduced by iteratively adding *property* and *if-property* constraints and by introducing the new *single* constraint, which is indicated with label *single* and acts like the *error* constraint, i.e., it limits the number of occurrences of a given value in the selected combinations to *1*.

Test designers can introduce new *property*, *if-property*, and *single* constraints to reduce the total number of combinations when needed to meet budget and schedule limits. Placement of these constraints reflects the test designer's judgment regarding combinations that are least likely to require thorough coverage.

The *single* constraints introduced in Table 11.1 reduces the number of combinations to be considered to $1 \times 1 \times 1 \times 1 \times 1 \times 3 \times 4 \times 4 \times 1 \times 1 + 19 = 67$, which may be a reasonable balance between cost and quality for the considered functionality. The number of combinations can also be reduced by applying the pairwise and n-way combination testing techniques, as explained in the next section.

The set of combinations of value classes for the parameter characteristics can be turned into test case specifications by simply instantiating the identified combinations. Table 11.2 shows an excerpt of test case specifications. The error tag in the last column indicates test case specifications corresponding to the *error* constraint. Corresponding test cases should produce an error indication. A dash indicates no constraints on the choice of values for the parameter or environment element.

Choosing meaningful names for parameter characteristics and value classes allows (semi)automatic generation of test case specifications.

11.3 Pairwise Combination Testing

However one obtains sets of value classes for each parameter characteristic, the next step in producing test case specifications is selecting combinations of classes for testing. A simple approach is to exhaustively enumerate all possible combinations of classes, but the number of possible combinations rapidly explodes.

Some methods, such as the category-partition method described in the previous section, take exhaustive enumeration as a base approach to generating combinations, but allow the test designer to add constraints that limit growth in the number of combinations. This can be a reasonable approach when the constraints on test case generation

Model#	# required slots	# optional slots	# Corr. w/ model slots	# required components	# optional components	Required components selection	Optional components selection	# Models in DB	# Components in DB	Exp result
malformed	many	many	same	EQR	0	all valid	all valid	many	many	Err
Not in DB	many	many	same	EQR	0	all valid	all valid	many	many	Err
valid	0	many	same	-	0	all valid	all valid	many	many	OK
...					...					...
valid	many	many	same	EQR	EQO	in-other	in-mod	many	many	OK
valid	many	many	same	EQR	EQO	in-mod	all valid	many	many	OK
valid	many	many	same	EQR	EQO	in-mod	in-slot	many	many	OK
valid	many	many	same	EQR	EQO	in-mod	in-other	many	many	OK
valid	many	many	same	EQR	EQO	in-mod	in-mod	many	many	OK

Legend

EQR	= # req slot
EQO	= # opt slot
in-mod	≥1 incompat w/ model
in-other	≥1 incompat w/ another slot
in-slot	≥1 incompat w/ slot

Table 11.2: An excerpt of test case specifications derived from the value classes given in Table 11.1

Display Mode	**Language**	**Fonts**
full-graphics	English	Minimal
text-only	French	Standard
limited-bandwidth	Spanish	Document-loaded
	Portuguese	

Color	**Screen size**
Monochrome	Hand-held
Color-map	Laptop
16-bit	Full-size
True-color	

Table 11.3: Parameters and values controlling Chipmunk Web site display

reflect real constraints in the application domain, and eliminate many redundant combinations (for example, the "error" entries in category-partition testing). It is less satisfactory when, lacking real constraints from the application domain, the test designer is forced to add arbitrary constraints (e.g., "single" entries in the category-partition method) whose sole purpose is to reduce the number of combinations.

Consider the parameters that control the Chipmunk Web site display, shown in Table 11.3. Exhaustive enumeration produces 432 combinations, which is too many if the test results (e.g., judging readability) involve human judgment. While the test designer might hypothesize some constraints, such as observing that monochrome displays are limited mostly to hand-held devices, radical reductions require adding several "single" and "property" constraints without any particular rationale.

Exhaustive enumeration of all n-way combinations of value classes for n parameters, on the one hand, and coverage of individual classes, on the other, are only the extreme ends of a spectrum of strategies for generating combinations of classes. Between them lie strategies that generate all pairs of classes for different parameters, all triples, and so on. When it is reasonable to expect some potential interaction between parameters (so coverage of individual value classes is deemed insufficient), but covering all combinations is impractical, an attractive alternative is to generate k-way combinations for $k < n$, typically pairs or triples.

How much does generating possible pairs of classes save, compared to generating all combinations? We have already observed that the number of all combinations is the product of the number of classes for each parameter, and that this product grows exponentially with the number of parameters. It turns out that the number of combinations needed to cover all possible pairs of values grows only logarithmically with the number of parameters — an enormous saving.

A simple example may suffice to gain some intuition about the efficiency of generating tuples that cover pairs of classes, rather than all combinations. Suppose we have just the three parameters *display mode, screen size,* and *fonts* from Table 11.3. If we consider only the first two, *display mode* and *screen size*, the set of all pairs and the set

Display mode × Screen size		*Fonts*
Full-graphics	Hand-held	Minimal
Full-graphics	Laptop	Standard
Full-graphics	Full-size	Document-loaded
Text-only	Hand-held	Standard
Text-only	Laptop	Document-loaded
Text-only	Full-size	Minimal
Limited-bandwidth	Hand-held	Document-loaded
Limited-bandwidth	Laptop	Minimal
Limited-bandwidth	Full-size	Standard

Table 11.4: Covering all pairs of value classes for three parameters by extending the cross-product of two parameters

of all combinations are identical, and contain $3 \times 3 = 9$ pairs of classes. When we add the third parameter, *fonts*, generating all combinations requires combining each value class from *fonts* with every pair of *display mode* × *screen size*, a total of 27 tuples; extending from n to $n+1$ parameters is multiplicative. However, if we are generating pairs of values from *display mode*, *screen size*, and *fonts*, we can add value classes of *fonts* to existing elements of *display mode* × *screen size* in a way that covers all the pairs of *fonts* × *screen size* and all the pairs of *fonts* × *display mode* without increasing the number of combinations at all (see Table 11.4). The key is that each tuple of three elements contains three pairs, and by careful selecting value classes of the tuples we can make each tuple cover up to three different pairs.

Table 11.3 shows 17 tuples that cover all pairwise combinations of value classes of the five parameters. The entries not specified in the table ("–") correspond to open choices. Each of them can be replaced by any legal value for the corresponding parameter. Leaving them open gives more freedom for selecting test cases.

Generating combinations that efficiently cover all pairs of classes (or triples, or ...) is nearly impossible to perform manually for many parameters with many value classes (which is, of course, exactly when one really needs to use the approach). Fortunately, efficient heuristic algorithms exist for this task, and they are simple enough to incorporate in tools.

The tuples in Table 11.3 cover all pairwise combinations of value choices for the five parameters of the example. In many cases not all choices may be allowed. For example, the specification of the Chipmunk Web site display may indicate that monochrome displays are limited to hand-held devices. In this case, the tuples covering the pairs ⟨*Monochrome*, *Laptop*⟩ and ⟨*Monochrome*, *Full-size*⟩, i.e., the fifth and ninth tuples of Table 11.3, would not correspond to legal inputs. We can restrict the set of legal combinations of value classes by adding suitable constraints. Constraints can be expressed as tuples with wild-cards that match any possible value class. The patterns describe combinations that should be omitted from the sets of tuples.

Language	Color	Display Mode	Fonts	Screen Size
English	Monochrome	Full-graphics	Minimal	Hand-held
English	Color-map	Text-only	Standard	Full-size
English	16-bit	Limited-bandwidth	–	Full-size
English	True-color	Text-only	Document-loaded	Laptop
French	Monochrome	Limited-bandwidth	Standard	Laptop
French	Color-map	Full-graphics	Document-loaded	Full-size
French	16-bit	Text-only	Minimal	–
French	True-color	–	–	Hand-held
Spanish	Monochrome	–	Document-loaded	Full-size
Spanish	Color-map	Limited-bandwidth	Minimal	Hand-held
Spanish	16-bit	Full-graphics	Standard	Laptop
Spanish	True-color	Text-only	–	Hand-held
Portuguese	Monochrome	Text-only	–	–
Portuguese	Color-map	–	Minimal	Laptop
Portuguese	16-bit	Limited-bandwidth	Document-loaded	Hand-held
Portuguese	True-color	Full-graphics	Minimal	Full-size
Portuguese	True-color	Limited-bandwidth	Standard	Hand-held

Table 11.5: Covering all pairs of value classes for the five parameters

For example, the constraints

$$OMIT\langle *, *, *, Monochrome, Laptop\rangle$$

$$OMIT\langle *, *, *, Monochrome, Full\text{-}size\rangle$$

indicate that tuples containing the pair ⟨*Monochrome*, *Hand-held*⟩ as values for the fourth and fifth parameter are not allowed in the relation of Table 11.3.

Tuples that cover all pairwise combinations of value classes without violating the constraints can be generated by simply removing the illegal tuples and adding legal tuples that cover the removed pairwise combinations. Open choices must be bound consistently in the remaining tuples, e.g., tuple

⟨*Portuguese*, *Monochrome*, *Text-only*, -, -⟩

must become

⟨*Portuguese*, *Monochrome*, *Text-only*, -, *Hand-held*⟩

Constraints can also be expressed with sets of tables to indicate only the legal combinations, as illustrated in Table 11.6, where the first table indicates that the value class *Hand-held* for parameter *Screen* can be combined with any value class of parameter *Color*, including *Monochrome*, while the second table indicates that the value classes *Laptop* and *Full-size* for parameter *Screen size* can be combined with all values classes except *Monochrome* for parameter *Color*.

Hand-held devices

Display Mode	Language	Fonts
full-graphics	English	Minimal
text-only	French	Standard
limited-bandwidth	Spanish	Document-loaded
	Portuguese	

Color	Screen size
Color-map	Hand-held
16-bit	
True-color	

Laptop and Full-size devices

Display Mode	Language	Fonts
full-graphics	English	Minimal
text-only	French	Standard
limited-bandwidth	Spanish	Document-loaded
	Portuguese	

Color	Screen size
Monochrome	Laptop
Color-map	Full size
16-bit	
True-color	

Table 11.6: Pairs of tables that indicate valid value classes for the Chipmunk Web site display

If constraints are expressed as a set of tables that give only legal combinations, tuples can be generated without changing the heuristic. Although the two approaches express the same constraints, the number of generated tuples can be different, since different tables may indicate overlapping pairs and thus result in a larger set of tuples. Other ways of expressing constraints may be chosen according to the characteristics of the specification and the preferences of the test designer.

So far we have illustrated the combinatorial approach with pairwise coverage. As previously mentioned, the same approach can be applied for triples or larger combinations. Pairwise combinations may be sufficient for some subset of the parameters, but not enough to uncover potential interactions among other parameters. For example, in the Chipmunk display example, the fit of text fields to screen areas depends on the combination of language, fonts, and screen size. Thus, we may prefer exhaustive coverage of combinations of these three parameters, but be satisfied with pairwise coverage of other parameters. In this case, we first generate tuples of classes from the parameters to be most thoroughly covered, and then extend these with the parameters which require less coverage.

11.4 Catalog-Based Testing

The test design techniques described above require judgment in deriving value classes. Over time, an organization can build experience in making these judgments well. Gathering this experience in a systematic collection can speed up the process and routinize many decisions, reducing human error and better focusing human effort. Catalogs capture the experience of test designers by listing all cases to be considered for each possible type of variable that represents logical inputs, outputs, and status of the computation. For example, if the computation uses a variable whose value must belong to a range of integer values, a catalog might indicate the following cases, each corresponding to a relevant test case:

1. The element immediately preceding the lower bound of the interval
2. The lower bound of the interval
3. A non-boundary element within the interval
4. The upper bound of the interval
5. The element immediately following the upper bound

The catalog would in this way cover the intuitive cases of erroneous conditions (cases 1 and 5), boundary conditions (cases 2 and 4), and normal conditions (case 3).

The catalog-based approach consists in *unfolding* the specification, i.e., decomposing the specification into elementary items, deriving an initial set of test case specifications from pre-conditions, post-conditions, and definitions, and completing the set of test case specifications using a suitable test catalog.

STEP 1: identify elementary items of the specification The initial specification is transformed into a set of elementary items. Elementary items belong to a small set of basic types:

Preconditions represent the conditions on the inputs that must be satisfied before invocation of the unit under test. Preconditions may be checked either by the unit under test (*validated preconditions*) or by the caller (*assumed preconditions*).

Postconditions describe the result of executing the unit under test.

Variables indicate the values on which the unit under test operates. They can be input, output, or intermediate values.

Operations indicate the main operations performed on input or intermediate variables by the unit under test

Definitions are shorthand used in the specification

cgi_decode: Function cgi_decode translates a cgi-encoded string to a plain ASCII string, reversing the encoding applied by the common gateway interface (CGI) of most Web servers.

CGI translates spaces to '+', and translates most other non-alphanumeric characters to hexadecimal escape sequences. cgi_decode maps '+' to ' ', "%xy" (where x and y are hexadecimal digits) to to the corresponding ASCII character, and other alphanumeric characters to themselves.

INPUT: encoded A string of characters, representing the input CGI sequence. It can contain:

- alphanumeric characters
- the character '+'
- the substring "%xy", where x and y are hexadecimal digits.

encoded is terminated by a null character.

OUTPUT: decoded A string containing the plain ASCII characters corresponding to the input CGI sequence.

- Alphanumeric characters are copied into the output in the corresponding position
- A blank is substituted for each '+' character in the input.
- A single ASCII character with hexadecimal value xy_{16} is substituted for each substring "%xy" in the input.

OUTPUT: return value cgi_decode returns

- 0 for success
- 1 if the input is malformed

Figure 11.2: An informal (and imperfect) specification of C function cgi_decode

As in other approaches that begin with an informal description, it is not possible to give a precise recipe for extracting the significant elements. The result will depend on the capability and experience of the test designer.

Consider the informal specification of a function for converting URL-encoded form data into the original data entered through an html form. An informal specification is given in Figure 11.2.[2]

The informal description of cgi_decode uses the concept of hexadecimal digit, hexadecimal escape sequence, and element of a cgi encoded sequence. This leads to the identification of the following three definitions:

[2] The informal specification is ambiguous and inconsistent, i.e., it is the kind of spec one is most likely to encounter in practice.

DEF 1 *hexadecimal digits* are: '0', '1', '2', '3', '4', '5', '6', '7', '8', '9', 'A', 'B', 'C', 'D', 'E', 'F', 'a', 'b', 'c', 'd', 'e', 'f'

DEF 2 a *CGI-hexadecimal* is a sequence of three characters: "%xy", where x and y are hexadecimal digits

DEF 3 a *CGI item* is either an alphanumeric character, or character '+', or a CGI-hexadecimal

In general, every concept introduced in the description to define the problem can be represented as a definition.

The description of cgi_decode mentions some elements that are inputs and outputs of the computation. These are identified as the following variables:

VAR 1 Encoded: string of ASCII characters

VAR 2 Decoded: string of ASCII characters

VAR 3 return value: Boolean

Note the distinction between a variable and a definition. Encoded and decoded are actually used or computed, while *hexadecimal digits*, *CGI-hexadecimal*, and *CGI item* are used to describe the elements but are not objects in their own right. Although not strictly necessary for the problem specification, explicit identification of definitions can help in deriving a richer set of test cases.

The description of cgi_decode indicates some conditions that must be satisfied upon invocation, represented by the following preconditions:

PRE 1 *(Assumed)* the input string Encoded is a null-terminated string of characters.

PRE 2 *(Validated)* the input string Encoded is a sequence of CGI items.

In general, preconditions represent all the conditions that should be true for the intended functioning of a module. A condition is labeled as *validated* if it is checked by the module (in which case a violation has a specified effect, e.g., raising an exception or returning an error code). *Assumed* preconditions must be guaranteed by the caller, and the module does not guarantee a particular behavior in case they are violated.

The description of cgi_decode indicates several possible results. These can be represented as a set of postconditions:

POST 1 if the input string Encoded contains alphanumeric characters, they are copied to the corresponding position in the output string.

POST 2 if the input string Encoded contains '+' characters, they are replaced by ASCII space characters in the corresponding positions in the output string.

POST 3 if the input string Encoded contains CGI-hexadecimals, they are replaced by the corresponding ASCII characters.

POST 4 if the input string Encoded is a valid sequence, cgi_decode returns 0.

POST 5 if the input string Encoded contains a malformed CGI-hexadecimal, i.e., a substring "%xy", where either x or y is absent or are not hexadecimal digits, cgi_decode returns 1

POST 6 if the input string Encoded contains any illegal character, cgi_decode returns 1.

The postconditions should, together, capture all the expected outcomes of the module under test. When there are several possible outcomes, it is possible to capture all of them in one complex postcondition or in several simple postconditions; here we have chosen a set of simple contingent postconditions, each of which captures one case. The informal specification does not distinguish among cases of malformed input strings, but the test designer may make further distinctions while refining the specification.

Although the description of cgi_decode does not mention explicitly how the results are obtained, we can easily deduce that it will be necessary to scan the input sequence. This is made explicit in the following operation:

OP 1 Scan the input string Encoded.

In general, a description may refer either explicitly or implicitly to elementary operations which help to clearly describe the overall behavior, like definitions help to clearly describe variables. As with variables, they are not strictly necessary for describing the relation between pre- and postconditions, but they serve as additional information for deriving test cases.

The result of step 1 for cgi_decode is summarized in Figure 11.3.

STEP 2 Derive a first set of test case specifications from preconditions, postconditions and definitions The aim of this step is to explicitly describe the partition of the input domain:

Validated Preconditions: A simple precondition, i.e., a precondition that is expressed as a simple Boolean expression without *and* or *or*, identifies two classes of input: values that satisfy the precondition and values that do not. We thus derive two test case specifications.

A compound precondition, given as a Boolean expression with *and* or *or*, identifies several classes of inputs. Although in general one could derive a different test case specification for each possible combination of truth values of the elementary conditions, usually we derive only a subset of test case specifications using the modified condition decision coverage (*MC/DC*) approach, which is illustrated in Section 14.3 and in Chapter 12. In short, we derive a set of combinations of elementary conditions such that each elementary condition can be shown to independently affect the outcome of each decision. For each elementary condition *C*, there are two test case specifications in which the truth values of all conditions except *C* are the same, and the compound condition as a whole evaluates to *True* for one of those test cases and *False* for the other.

PRE 1	(*Assumed*) the input string Encoded is a null-terminated string of characters
PRE 2	(*Validated*) the input string Encoded is a sequence of CGI items
POST 1	if the input string Encoded contains alphanumeric characters, they are copied to the output string in the corresponding positions.
POST 2	if the input string Encoded contains '+' characters, they are replaced in the output string by ASCII space characters in the corresponding positions
POST 3	if the input string Encoded contains CGI-hexadecimals, they are replaced by the corresponding ASCII characters.
POST 4	if the input string Encoded is well-formed, cgi_decode returns 0
POST 5	if the input string Encoded contains a malformed CGI hexadecimal, i.e., a substring "%xy", where either x or y are absent or are not hexadecimal digits, cgi_decode returns 1
POST 6	if the input string Encoded contains any illegal character, cgi_decode returns 1
VAR 1	Encoded: a string of ASCII characters
VAR 2	Decoded: a string of ASCII characters
VAR 3	Return value: a Boolean
DEF 1	hexadecimal digits are ASCII characters in range ['0' .. '9', 'A' .. 'F', 'a' .. 'f']
DEF 2	CGI-hexadecimals are sequences "%xy", where x and y are hexadecimal digits
DEF 3	A CGI item is an alphanumeric character, or '+', or a CGI-hexadecimal
OP 1	Scan Encoded

Figure 11.3: Elementary items of specification cgi_decode

Assumed Preconditions: We do not derive test case specifications for cases that violate assumed preconditions, since there is no defined behavior and thus no way to judge the success of such a test case. We also do not derive test cases when the whole input domain satisfies the condition, since test cases for these would be redundant. We generate test cases from assumed preconditions only when the MC/DC criterion generates more than one class of valid combinations (i.e., when the condition is a logical disjunction of more elementary conditions).

Postconditions: In all cases in which postconditions are given in a conditional form, the condition is treated like a validated precondition, i.e., we generate a test case specification for cases that satisfy and cases that do not satisfy the condition.

Definition: Definitions that refer to input or output values and are given in conditional form are treated like validated preconditions. We generate a set of test case specification for cases that satisfy and cases that do not satisfy the specification. The test cases are generated for each variable that refers to the definition.

The elementary items of the specification identified in step 1 are scanned sequentially and a set of test cases is derived applying these rules. While scanning the specifications, we generate test case specifications incrementally. When new test case specifications introduce a refinement of an existing case, or vice versa, the more general case becomes redundant and can be eliminated. For example, if an existing test case specification requires a non-empty set, and we have to add two test case specifications that require a size that is a power of two and one which is not, the existing test case specification can be deleted because the new test cases must include a non-empty set.

Scanning the elementary items of the cgi_decode specification given in Figure 11.3, we proceed as follows:

PRE 1: The first precondition is a simple assumed precondition. We do not generate any test case specification. The only condition would be "encoded: a null terminated string of characters," but this matches every test case and thus it does not identify a useful test case specification.

PRE 2: The second precondition is a simple validated precondition. We generate two test case specifications, one that satisfies the condition and one that does not:

TC-PRE2-1 Encoded: a sequence of CGI items

TC-PRE2-2 Encoded: not a sequence of CGI items

All postconditions in the cgi_decode specification are given in a conditional form with a simple condition. Thus, we generate two test case specifications for each of them. The generated test case specifications correspond to a case that satisfies the condition and a case that violates it.

POST 1:

TC-POST1-1 Encoded: contains one or more alphanumeric characters

TC-POST1-2 Encoded: does not contain any alphanumeric characters

POST 2:

TC-POST2-1 Encoded: contains one or more character '+'

TC-POST2-2 Encoded: does not any contain character '+'

POST 3:

TC-POST3-1 Encoded: contains one or more CGI-hexadecimals

TC-POST3-2 Encoded: does not contain any CGI-hexadecimal

POST 4: We do not generate any new useful test case specifications, because the two specifications are already covered by the specifications generated from *PRE 2*.

POST 5: We generate only the test case specification that satisfies the condition. The test case specification that violates the specification is redundant with respect to the test case specifications generated from *POST 3*

TC-POST5-1 : Encoded contains one or more malformed CGI-hexadecimals

POST 6: As for *POST 5*, we generate only the test case specification that satisfies the condition. The test case specification that violates the specification is redundant with respect to several of the test case specifications generated so far.

TC-POST6-1 Encoded: contains one or more illegal characters

None of the definitions in the specification of cgi_decode is given in conditional terms, and thus no test case specifications are generated at this step.

The test case specifications generated from postconditions refine test case specification TC-PRE2-1, which can thus be eliminated from the checklist. The result of step 2 for cgi_decode is summarized in Figure 11.4.

STEP 3 Complete the test case specifications using catalogs The aim of this step is to generate additional test case specifications from variables and operations used or defined in the computation. The catalog is scanned sequentially. For each entry of the catalog we examine the elementary components of the specification and add cases to cover all values in the catalog. As when scanning the test case specifications during step 2, redundant test case specifications are eliminated.

Table 11.7 shows a simple catalog that we will use for the cgi_decode example. A catalog is structured as a list of kinds of elements that can occur in a specification. Each catalog entry is associated with a list of generic test case specifications appropriate for that kind of element. We scan the specification for elements whose type is compatible with the catalog entry, then generate the test cases defined in the catalog for that entry. For example, the catalog of Table 11.7 contains an entry for Boolean variables. When we find a Boolean variable in the specification, we instantiate the catalog entry by generating two test case specifications, one that requires a *True* value and one that requires a *False* value.

Each generic test case in the catalog is labeled *in*, *out*, or *in/out*, meaning that a test case specification is appropriate if applied to an input variable, or to an output

PRE 2		*Validated*) the input string Encoded is a sequence of CGI items
	[TC-PRE2-2]	Encoded: not a sequence of CGI items
POST 1		if the input string Encoded contains alphanumeric characters, they are copied to the output string in the corresponding positions
	[TC-POST1-1]	Encoded: contains alphanumeric characters
	[TC-POST1-2]	Encoded: does not contain alphanumeric characters
POST 2		if the input string Encoded contains '+' characters, they are replaced in the output string by ' ' in the corresponding positions
	[TC-POST2-1]	Encoded: contains '+'
	[TC-POST2-2]	Encoded: does not contain '+'
POST 3		if the input string Encoded contains CGI-hexadecimals, they are replaced by the corresponding ASCII characters.
	[TC-POST3-1]	Encoded: contains CGI-hexadecimals
	[TC-POST3-2]	Encoded: does not contain a CGI-hexadecimal
POST 4		if the input string Encoded is well-formed, cgi_decode returns 0
POST 5		if the input string Encoded contains a malformed CGI-hexadecimal, i.e., a substring "%xy", where either x or y are absent or non hexadecimal digits, cgi_decode returns 1
	[TC-POST5-1]	Encoded: contains malformed CGI-hexadecimals
POST 6		if the input string Encoded contains any illegal character, cgi_decode returns a positive value
	[TC-POST6-1]	Encoded: contains illegal characters
VAR 1		Encoded: a string of ASCII characters
VAR 2		Decoded: a string of ASCII characters
VAR 3		Return value: a Boolean
DEF 1		hexadecimal digits are in range ['0' .. '9', 'A' .. 'F', 'a' .. 'f']
DEF 2		CGI-hexadecimals are sequences '%xy', where x and y are hexadecimal digits
DEF 3		CGI items are either alphanumeric characters, or '+', or CGI-hexadecimals
OP 1		Scan Encoded

Figure 11.4: Test case specifications for cgi_decode *generated after step 2*

Boolean		
	[in/out]	True
	[in/out]	False
Enumeration		
	[in/out]	Each enumerated value
	[in]	Some value outside the enumerated set
Range $L \dots U$		
	[in]	$L-1$ (the element immediately preceding the lower bound)
	[in/out]	L (the lower bound)
	[in/out]	A value between L and U
	[in/out]	U (the upper bound)
	[in]	$U+1$ (the element immediately following the upper bound)
Numeric Constant C		
	[in/out]	C (the constant value)
	[in]	$C-1$ (the element immediately preceding the constant value)
	[in]	$C+1$ (the element immediately following the constant value)
	[in]	Any other constant compatible with C
Non-Numeric Constant C		
	[in/out]	C (the constant value)
	[in]	Any other constant compatible with C
	[in]	Some other compatible value
Sequence		
	[in/out]	Empty
	[in/out]	A single element
	[in/out]	More than one element
	[in/out]	Maximum length (if bounded) or very long
	[in]	Longer than maximum length (if bounded)
	[in]	Incorrectly terminated
Scan with action on elements P		
	[in]	P occurs at beginning of sequence
	[in]	P occurs in interior of sequence
	[in]	P occurs at end of sequence
	[in]	PP occurs contiguously
	[in]	P does not occur in sequence
	[in]	pP where p is a proper prefix of P
	[in]	Proper prefix p occurs at end of sequence

Table 11.7: Part of a simple test catalog.

variable, or in both cases. In general, erroneous values should be used when testing the behavior of the system with respect to input variables, but are usually impossible to produce when testing the behavior of the system with respect to output variables. For example, when the value of an input variable can be chosen from a set of values, it is important to test the behavior of the system for all enumerated values and some values outside the enumerated set, as required by entry *ENUMERATION* of the catalog. However, when the value of an output variable belongs to a finite set of values, we should derive a test case for each possible outcome, but we cannot derive a test case for an impossible outcome, so entry *ENUMERATION* of the catalog specifies that the choice of values outside the enumerated set is limited to input variables. Intermediate variables, if present, are treated like output variables.

Entry *Boolean* of the catalog applies to Return value (VAR 3). The catalog requires a test case that produces the value *True* and one that produces the value *False*. Both cases are already covered by test cases *TC-PRE2-1* and *TC-PRE2-2* generated for precondition *PRE 2*, so no test case specification is actually added.

Entry *Enumeration* of the catalog applies to any variable whose values are chosen from an explicitly enumerated set of values. In the example, the values of CGI item (DEF 3) and of improper CGI hexadecimals in POST 5 are defined by enumeration. Thus, we can derive new test case specifications by applying entry *enumeration* to POST 5 and to any variable that can contain CGI items.

The catalog requires creation of a test case specification for each enumerated value and for some excluded values. For encoded, which should consist of CGI-items as defined in DEF 3, we generate a test case specification where a CGI-item is an alphanumeric character, one where it is the character '+', one where it is a CGI-hexadecimal, and one where it is an illegal value. We can easily ascertain that all the required cases are already covered by test case specifications for *TC-POST1-1*, *TC-POST1-2*, *TC-POST2-1*, *TC-POST2-2*, *TC-POST3-1*, and *TC-POST3-2*, so any additional test case specifications would be redundant.

From the enumeration of malformed CGI-hexadecimals in POST 5, we derive the following test cases: %y, %x, %ky, %xk, %xy (where x and y are hexadecimal digits and k is not). Note that the first two cases, %x (the second hexadecimal digit is missing) and %y (the first hexadecimal digit is missing) are identical, and %x is distinct from %xk only if %x are the last two characters in the string. A test case specification requiring a correct pair of hexadecimal digits (%xy) is a value out of the range of the enumerated set, as required by the catalog.

The added test case specifications are:

TC-POST5-2 encoded: terminated with %x, where x is a hexadecimal digit

TC-POST5-3 encoded: contains %ky, where k is not a hexadecimal digit and y is a hexadecimal digit.

TC-POST5-4 encoded: contains %xk, where x is a hexadecimal digit and k is not.

The test case specification corresponding to the correct pair of hexadecimal digits is redundant, having already been covered by TC-POST3-1. The test case TC-POST5-1 can now be eliminated because it is more general than the combination of TC-POST5-2, TC-POST5-3, and TC-POST5-4.

Entry *Range* applies to any variable whose values are chosen from a finite range. In the example, ranges appear three times in the definition of hexadecimal digit. Ranges also appear implicitly in the reference to alphanumeric characters (the alphabetic and numeric ranges from the ASCII character set) in DEF 3. For hexadecimal digits we will try the special values '/' and ':' (the characters that appear before '0' and after '9' in the ASCII encoding), the values '0' and '9' (upper and lower bounds of the first interval), some value between '0' and '9'; similarly '@', 'G', 'A', 'F', and some value between 'A' and 'F' for the second interval; and '`', 'g', 'a', 'f', and some value between 'a' and 'f' for the third interval.

These values will be instantiated for variable encoded, and result in 30 additional test case specifications (5 values for each subrange, giving 15 values for each hexadecimal digit and thus 30 for the two digits of CGI-hexadecimal). The full set of test case specifications is shown in Table 11.8. These test case specifications are more specific than (and therefore replace) test case specifications TC-POST3-1, TC-POST5-3, and TC-POST5-4.

For alphanumeric characters we will similarly derive boundary, interior and excluded values, which result in 15 additional test case specifications, also given in Table 11.8. These test cases are more specific than (and therefore replace) TC-POST1-1, TC-POST1-2, and TC-POST6-1.

Entry *Numeric Constant* does not apply to any element of this specification.

Entry *Non-Numeric Constant* applies to '+' and '%', occurring in DEF 3 and DEF 2 respectively. Six test case specifications result, but all are redundant.

Entry *Sequence* applies to encoded (VAR 1), decoded (VAR 2), and cgi-item (DEF 2). Six test case specifications result for each, of which only five are mutually nonredundant and not already in the list. From VAR 1 (encoded) we generate test case specifications requiring an empty sequence, a sequence containing a single element, and a very long sequence. The catalog entry requiring more than one element generates a redundant test case specification, which is discarded. We cannot produce reasonable test cases for incorrectly terminated strings (the behavior would vary depending on the contents of memory outside the string), so we omit that test case specification.

All test case specifications that would be derived for decoded (VAR 2) would be redundant with respect to test case specifications derived for encoded (VAR 1).

From CGI-hexadecimal (DEF 2) we generate two additional test case specifications for variable encoded: a sequence that terminates with '%' (the only way to produce a one-character subsequence beginning with '%') and a sequence containing '%xyz', where x, y, and z are hexadecimal digits.

Entry *Scan* applies to Scan Encoded (OP 1) and generates 17 test case specifications. Three test case specifications (alphanumeric, '+', and CGI item) are generated for each of the first 5 items of the catalog entry. One test case specification is generated for each of the last two items of the catalog entry when *Scan* is applied to CGI item. The last two items of the catalog entry do not apply to alphanumeric characters and '+', since they have no non-trivial prefixes. Seven of the 17 are redundant. The ten generated test case specifications are summarized in Table 11.8.

TC-POST2-1	Encoded contains character '+'
TC-POST2-2	Encoded does not contain character '+'
TC-POST3-2	Encoded does not contain a CGI-hexadecimal
TC-POST5-2	Encoded terminates with %*x*
TC-VAR1-1	Encoded is the empty sequence
TC-VAR1-2	Encoded is a sequence consisting of a single character
TC-VAR1-3	Encoded is a very long sequence
Encoded contains ...	
TC-DEF2-1	... '%/*y*'
TC-DEF2-2	... '%0*y*'
TC-DEF2-3	... '%*xy*', with *x* in ['1'..'8']
TC-DEF2-4	... '%9*y*'
TC-DEF2-5	... '%:*y*'
TC-DEF2-6	... '%@*y*'
TC-DEF2-7	... '%A*y*'
TC-DEF2-8	... '%*xy*', with *x* in ['B'..'E']
TC-DEF2-9	... '%F*y*'
TC-DEF2-10	... '%G*y*'
TC-DEF2-11	... '%`*y*'
TC-DEF2-12	... '%a*y*'
TC-DEF2-13	... '%*xy*', with *x* in ['b'..'e']
TC-DEF2-14	... '%f*y*'
TC-DEF2-15	... '%g*y*'
TC-DEF2-16	... '%*x*/'
TC-DEF2-17	... '%*x*0'
TC-DEF2-18	... '%*xy*', with *y* in ['1'..'8']
TC-DEF2-19	... '%*x*9'
TC-DEF2-20	... '%*x*:'
TC-DEF2-21	... '%*x*@'
TC-DEF2-22	... '%*x*A'
TC-DEF2-23	... '%*xy*', with *y* in ['B'..'E']
TC-DEF2-24	... '%*x*F'
TC-DEF2-25	... '%*x*G'
TC-DEF2-26	... '%*x*`'
TC-DEF2-27	... '%*x*a'
TC-DEF2-28	... '%*xy*', with *y* in ['b'..'e']
TC-DEF2-29	... '%*x*f'
TC-DEF2-30	... '%*x*g'
TC-DEF2-31	... '%$'
TC-DEF2-32	... '%*xyz*'
TC-DEF3-1	... '/'
TC-DEF3-2	... '0'
TC-DEF3-3	... c, with c in ['1'..'8']
TC-DEF3-4	... '9'
TC-DEF3-5	... ':'
TC-DEF3-6	... '@'
TC-DEF3-7	... 'A'
TC-DEF3-8	... *a*, with *a* in ['B'..'Y']
TC-DEF3-9	... 'Z'
TC-DEF3-10	... '['
TC-DEF3-11	... '\'
TC-DEF3-12	... 'a'
TC-DEF3-13	... *a*, with *a* in ['b'..'y']
TC-DEF3-14	... 'z'
TC-DEF3-15	... '{'
TC-OP1-1	... '^*a*'
TC-OP1-2	... '^+'
TC-OP1-3	... ^%*xy*'
TC-OP1-4	... '*a*$'
TC-OP1-5	... '+$'
TC-OP1-6	... '%*xy*$'
TC-OP1-7	... '*aa*'
TC-OP1-8	... '++'
TC-OP1-9	... '%*xy*%*zw*'
TC-OP1-10	... '%*x*%*yz*'

Where w, x, y, z are hexadecimal digits, *a* is an alphanumeric character, ^ represents the beginning of the string, and $ represents the end of the string.

Table 11.8: Summary table: Test case specifications for cgi_decode *generated with a catalog.*

Test catalogs, like other check lists used in test and analysis (e.g., inspection check lists), are an organizational asset that can be maintained and enhanced over time. A good test catalog will be written precisely and suitably annotated to resolve ambiguity. Catalogs should also be specialized to an organization and application domain, typically using a process such as defect causal analysis or root cause analysis (Chapters 20 and 18). Entries are added to detect particular classes of faults that have been encountered frequently or have been particularly costly to remedy in previous projects. Refining check lists is a typical activity carried out as part of process improvement. When a test reveals a program fault, it is useful to make a note of which catalog entries the test case originated from, as an aid to measuring the effectiveness of catalog entries. Catalog entries that are not effective should be removed.

Open research issues

In the last decades, structured languages replaced natural language in software specifications, and today unstructured specifications written in natural language are becoming less common. Unstructured natural language specifications are still commonly used in informal development environments that lack expertise and tools, and often do not adopt rigorous development methodologies. Deriving structure from natural language is not a main focus of the research community, which pays more attention to exploiting formal and semi-formal models that may be produced in the course of a project.

Combinatorial methods per se is a niche research area that attracts relatively little attention from the research community. One issue that has received too little attention to date is adapting combinatorial test techniques to cope with constantly changing specifications.

Further Reading

Category partition testing is described by Ostrand and Balcer [OB88]. The combinatorial approach described in this chapter is due to Cohen, Dalal, Fredman, and Patton [CDFP97]; the algorithm described by Cohen et al. is patented by Bellcore. Catalog-based testing of subsystems is described in Marick's *The Craft of Software Testing* [Mar97].

Related topics

Readers interested in learning additional functional testing techniques may continue with the next Chapter that describes model-based testing techniques. Readers interested in the complementarities between functional and structural testing as well as readers interested in testing the decision structures and control and data flow graphs may continue with the following chapters that describe structural and data flow testing. Readers interested in the quality of specifications may proceed to Chapter 18, which describes inspection techniques.

Exercises

11.1. When designing a test suite with the category partition method, sometimes it is useful to determine the number of test case specifications that would be generated from a set of parameter characteristics (categories) and value classes (choices) without actually generating or enumerating them. Describe how to quickly determine the number of test cases in these cases:

(a) Parameter characteristics and value classes are given, but no constraints (*error*, *single*, *property*, or *if-property*) are used.

(b) Only the constraints *error* and *single* are used (without *property* and *if-property*).

When the *property* and *if-property* are also used, they can interact in ways that make a quick closed-form calculation of the number of test cases difficult or impossible.

(c) Sketch an algorithm for counting the number of test cases that would be generated when *if* and *if-property* are used. Your algorithm should be simple, and may not be more efficient than actually generating each test case specification.

11.2. Suppose we have a tool to generate combinatorial tests with pairwise coverage from a specification of the same form as category partition specifications, and it interprets property constraints and single and error cases in the same way. Also assume the tool for pairwise testing never generates two identical test case specifications. Given the same specification of parameter values and constraints, can a suite of test case specifications generated by the pairwise tool ever be larger than the set of test case specifications generated by the tool for category partition testing?

11.3. Suppose we are constructing a tool for combinatorial testing. Our tool will read a specification in exactly the same form as the input of a tool for the category partition method, except that it will achieve pairwise coverage rather than exhaustive coverage of values. However, we notice that it is sometimes not possible to cover all pairs of choices. For example, we might encounter the following specification:

C1

V1 [property P1]
V2 [property P2]

C2

V3 [property P3]
V4 [property P4]

C3

V5 [if P1]
V6 [if P4]

Our tool prints a warning that it is unable to create any complete test case specification that pairs value V2 with V3.

(a) Explain why the values V2 and V3 cannot be paired in a test case specification.

(b) Suppose the parameter characteristic V3 were instead described as follows:

C3

V5 [if P1]
V6 [if P4]
V7 [error]

Would it be satisfactory to cover the test obligation $\langle C1 = V2, C2 = V3 \rangle$ with the complete test case specification $\langle C1 = V2, C2 = V3, C3 = V7 \rangle$? In general, should values marked *error* be used to cover pairs of parameter characteristics?

(c) Suppose, instead, the otherwise unconstrained value V7 is marked *single*, like this:

C3

V5 [if P1]
V6 [if P4]
V7 [single]

Would it be a good idea to use V7 to complete a test case specification matching V2 with V3? Does your answer depend on whether the *single* constraint has been used just to reduce the total number of test cases or to identify situations that are really treated as special cases in the program specification and code?

11.4. Derive parameter characteristics, representative values, and semantic constraints from the following specification of an *Airport connection check* function, suitable for generating a set of test case specifications using the category partition method.

Airport connection check: The airport connection check is part of an (imaginary) travel reservation system. It is intended to check the validity of a single connection between two flights in an itinerary. It is described here at a fairly abstract level, as it might be described in a preliminary design before concrete interfaces have been worked out.

Specification Signature: Valid_Connection (Arriving_Flight: flight, Departing_Flight: flight) returns Validity_Code

Validity_Code 0 (OK) is returned if Arriving_Flight and Departing_Flight make a valid connection (the arriving airport of the first is the departing airport of the second) and there is sufficient time between arrival and departure according to the information in the airport database described below.

Otherwise, a validity code other than 0 is returned, indicating why the connection is not valid.

Data types

Flight: A "flight" is a structure consisting of

- A unique identifying flight code, three alphabetic characters followed by up to four digits. (The flight code is not used by the *valid connection* function.)
- The originating airport code (3 characters, alphabetic)
- The scheduled departure time of the flight (in universal time)
- The destination airport code (3 characters, alphabetic)
- The scheduled arrival time at the destination airport.

Validity Code: The validity code is one of a set of integer values with the following interpretations

0: The connection is valid.

10: Invalid airport code (airport code not found in database)

15: Invalid connection, too short: There is insufficient time between arrival of first flight and departure of second flight.

16: Invalid connection, flights do not connect. The destination airport of Arriving_Flight is not the same as the originating airport of Departing_Flight.

20: Another error has been recognized (e.g., the input arguments may be invalid, or an unanticipated error was encountered).

Airport Database

The Valid_Connection function uses an internal, in-memory table of airports which is read from a configuration file at system initialization. Each record in the table contains the following information:

- Three-letter airport code. This is the key of the table and can be used for lookups.
- Airport zone. In most cases the airport zone is a two-letter country code, e.g., "us" for the United States. However, where passage from one country to another is possible without a passport, the airport zone represents the complete zone in which passport-free travel is allowed. For example, the code "eu" represents the European countries which are treated as if they were a single country for purposes of travel.
- Domestic connect time. This is an integer representing the minimum number of minutes that must be allowed for a domestic connection at the airport. A connection is "domestic" if the originating and destination airports of both flights are in the same airport zone.
- International connect time. This is an integer representing the minimum number of minutes that must be allowed for an inter-

national connection at the airport. The number -1 indicates that international connections are not permitted at the airport. A connection is "international" if any of the originating or destination airports are in different zones.

11.5. Derive a set of test cases for the *Airport Connection Check* example of Exercise 11.4 using the catalog based approach.
Extend the catalog of Table 11.7 as needed to deal with specification constructs.

Chapter 12

Structural Testing

The structure of the software itself is a valuable source of information for selecting test cases and determining whether a set of test cases has been sufficiently thorough. We can ask whether a test suite has "covered" a control flow graph or other model of the program.[1] It is simplest to consider structural coverage criteria as addressing the test adequacy question: "Have we tested enough." In practice we will be interested not so much in asking whether we are done, but in asking what the unmet obligations with respect to the adequacy criteria suggest about additional test cases that may be needed; that is, we will often treat the adequacy criterion as a heuristic for test case selection or generation. For example, if one statement remains unexecuted despite execution of all the test cases in a test suite, we may devise additional test cases that exercise that statement. Structural information should not be used as the primary answer to the question, "How shall I choose tests," but it is useful in combination with other test selection criteria (particularly functional testing) to help answer the question "What additional test cases are needed to reveal faults that may not become apparent through black-box testing alone."

Required Background

- Chapter 5

  The material on control flow graphs and related models of program structure is required to understand this chapter.

- Chapter 9

  The introduction to test case adequacy and test case selection in general sets the context for this chapter. It is not strictly required for understanding this chapter, but is helpful for understanding how the techniques described in this chapter should be applied.

[1]In this chapter we use the term *program* generically for the artifact under test, whether that artifact is a complete application or an individual unit together with a test harness. This is consistent with usage in the testing research literature.

12.1 Overview

Testing can reveal a fault only when execution of the faulty element causes a failure. For example, if there were a fault in the statement at line 31 of the program in Figure 12.1, it could be revealed only with test cases in which the input string contains the character % followed by two hexadecimal digits, since only these cases would cause this statement to be executed. Based on this simple observation, a program has not been adequately tested if some of its elements have not been executed.[2] Control flow testing criteria are defined for particular classes of elements by requiring the execution of all such elements of the program. Control flow elements include statements, branches, conditions, and paths.

Unfortunately, a set of correct program executions in which all control flow elements are exercised does not guarantee the absence of faults. Execution of a faulty statement may not always result in a failure. The state may not be corrupted when the statement is executed with some data values, or a corrupt state may not propagate through execution to eventually lead to failure. Let us assume, for example, to have erroneously typed 6 instead of 16 in the statement at line 31 of the program in Figure 12.1. Test cases that execute the faulty statement with value 0 for variable digit_high would not corrupt the state, thus leaving the fault unrevealed despite having executed the faulty statement.

The statement at line 26 of the program in Figure 12.1 contains a fault, since variable eptr used to index the input string is incremented twice without checking the size of the string. If the input string contains a character % in one of the last two positions, eptr* will point beyond the end of the string when it is later used to index the string. Execution of the program with a test case where string encoded terminates with character % followed by at most one character causes the faulty statement to be executed. However, due to the memory management of C programs, execution of this faulty statement may not cause a failure, since the program will read the next character available in memory, ignoring the end of the string. Thus, this fault may remain hidden during testing despite having produced an incorrect intermediate state. Such a fault could be revealed using a dynamic memory checking tool that identifies memory violations.

Control flow testing complements functional testing by including cases that may not be identified from specifications alone. A typical case is implementation of a single item of the specification by multiple parts of the program. For example, a good specification of a table would leave data structure implementation decisions to the programmer. If the programmer chooses a hash table implementation, then different portions of the insertion code will be executed depending on whether there is a hash collision. Selection of test cases from the specification would not ensure that both the collision case and the noncollision case are tested. Even the simplest control flow testing criterion would require that both of these cases are tested.

On the other hand, test suites satisfying control flow adequacy criteria could fail in revealing faults that can be caught with functional criteria. The most notable example is the class of so-called *missing path* faults. Such faults result from the missing im-

[2]This is an oversimplification, since some of the elements may not be executed by any possible input. The issue of infeasible elements is discussed in Section 12.8

```
  #include "hex_values.h"
  /**
  * @title cgi_decode
  * @desc
  *     Translate a string from the CGI encoding to plain ascii text
  *      '+' becomes space, %xx becomes byte with hex value xx,
  *      other alphanumeric characters map to themselves
  *
  *     returns 0 for success, positive for erroneous input
  *           1 = bad hexadecimal digit
  */
  int cgi_decode(char *encoded, char *decoded) {
    char *eptr = encoded;
    char *dptr = decoded;
★   int ok=0;
★   while (*eptr) {
      char c;
★     c = *eptr;
      /* Case 1: '+' maps to blank */
★     if (c == '+') {
★       *dptr = ' ';
★     } else if (c == '%') {
        /* Case 2: '%xx' is hex for character xx */
★       int   digit_high = Hex_Values[*(++eptr)];
★       int   digit_low  = Hex_Values[*(++eptr)];
        /* Hex_Values maps illegal digits to -1 */
★       if (    digit_high == -1 || digit_low == -1 ) {
          /* *dptr='?'; */
★         ok=1; /* Bad return code */
        } else {
★         *dptr = 16* digit_high + digit_low;
        }
        /* Case 3: All other characters map to themselves */
★     } else {
★       *dptr = *eptr;
      }
★     ++dptr;
★     ++eptr;
    }
★   *dptr = '\0';                /* Null terminator for string */
★   return ok;
  }
```

Figure 12.1: The C function cgi_decode*, which translates a cgi-encoded string to a plain ASCII string (reversing the encoding applied by the common gateway interface of most Web servers).*

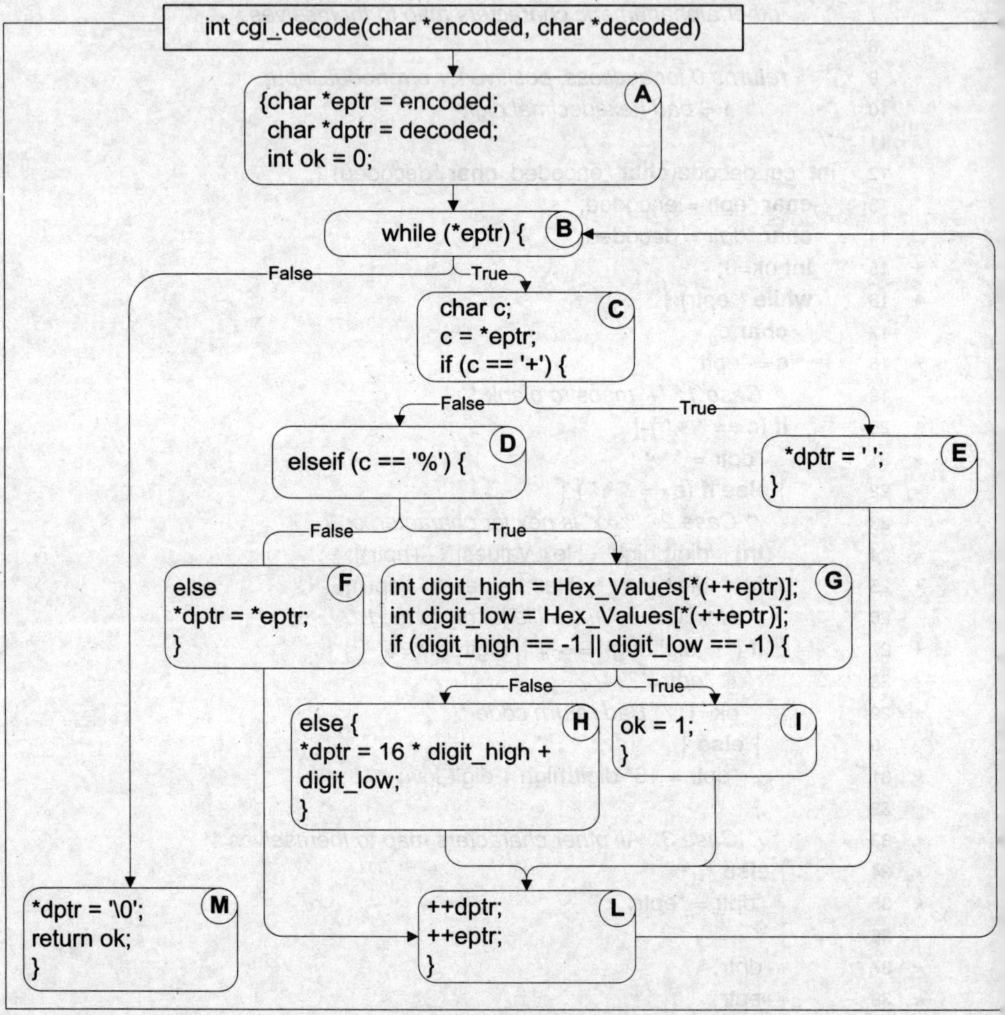

Figure 12.2: Control flow graph of function cgi_decode from Figure 12.1

$$
\begin{aligned}
T_0 &= \{\ \text{" ", "test", "test+case\%1Dadequacy"}\ \} \\
T_1 &= \{\ \text{"adequate+test\%0Dexecution\%7U"}\ \} \\
T_2 &= \{\ \text{"\%3D", "\%A", "a+b", "test"}\ \} \\
T_3 &= \{\ \text{" ", "+\%0D+\%4J"}\ \} \\
T_4 &= \{\ \text{"first+test\%9Ktest\%K9"}\ \}
\end{aligned}
$$

Table 12.1: Sample test suites for C function cgi_decode *from Figure 12.1*

plementation of some items in the specification. For example, the program in Figure 12.1 transforms all hexadecimal ASCII codes to the corresponding characters. Thus, it is not a correct implementation of a specification that requires control characters to be identified and skipped. A test suite designed only to adequately cover the control structure of the program will not explicitly include test cases to test for such faults, since no elements of the structure of the program correspond to this feature of the specification.

In practice, control flow testing criteria are used to evaluate the thoroughness of test suites derived from functional testing criteria by identifying elements of the programs not adequately exercised. Unexecuted elements may be due to natural differences between specification and implementation, or they may reveal flaws of the software or its development process: inadequacy of the specifications that do not include cases present in the implementation; coding practice that radically diverges from the specification; or inadequate functional test suites.

Control flow adequacy can be easily measured with automatic tools. The degree of control flow coverage achieved during testing is often used as an indicator of progress and can be used as a criterion of completion of the testing activity.[3]

12.2 Statement Testing

The most intuitive control flow elements to be exercised are statements, that is, nodes of the control flow graph. The statement coverage criterion requires each statement to be executed at least once, reflecting the idea that a fault in a statement cannot be revealed without executing the faulty statement.

Δ statement adequacy criterion

Let T be a test suite for a program P. T satisfies the statement adequacy criterion for P, iff, for each statement S of P, there exists at least one test case in T that causes the execution of S.

This is equivalent to stating that every node in the control flow graph model of program P is visited by some execution path exercised by a test case in T.

Δ statement coverage

The statement coverage $C_{Statement}$ of T for P is the fraction of statements of program P executed by at least one test case in T.

$$C_{Statement} = \frac{\text{number of executed statements}}{\text{number of statements}}$$

[3]Application of test adequacy criteria within the testing process is discussed in Chapter 20.

T satisfies the statement adequacy criterion if $C_{Statement} = 1$. The ratio of visited control flow graph nodes to total nodes may differ from the ratio of executed statements to all statements, depending on the granularity of the control flow graph representation. Nodes in a control flow graph often represent *basic blocks* rather than individual statements, and so some standards (notably *DOD-178B*) refer to basic block coverage, thus indicating node coverage for a particular granularity of control flow graph. For the standard control flow graph models discussed in Chapter 5, the relation between coverage of statements and coverage of nodes is monotonic: If the statement coverage achieved by test suite T_1 is greater than the statement coverage achieved by test suite T_2, then the node coverage is also greater. In the limit, statement coverage is 1 exactly when node coverage is 1.

Δ basic block coverage

Let us consider, for example, the program of Figure 12.1. The program contains 18 statements. A test suite T_0

$$T_0 = \{\text{" ", "test", "test+case\%1Dadequacy"}\}$$

does not satisfy the statement adequacy criterion because it does not execute statement ok = 1 at line 29. The test suite T_0 results in statement coverage of .94 (17/18), or node coverage of .91 (10/11) relative to the control flow graph of Figure 12.2. On the other hand, a test suite with only test case

$$T_1 = \{\text{"adequate+test\%0Dexecution\%7U"}\}$$

causes all statements to be executed and thus satisfies the statement adequacy criterion, reaching a coverage of 1.

Coverage is not monotone with respect to the size of test suites; test suites that contain fewer test cases may achieve a higher coverage than test suites that contain more test cases. T_1 contains only one test case, while T_0 contains three test cases, but T_1 achieves a higher coverage than T_0. (Test suites used in this chapter are summarized in Table 12.1.)

Criteria can be satisfied by many test suites of different sizes. A test suite Both T_1 and Both T_1 and

$$T_2 = \{\text{"\%3D", "\%A", "a+b", "test"}\}$$

cause all statements to be executed and thus satisfy the statement adequacy criterion for program cgi_decode, although one consists of a single test case and the other consists of four test cases.

Notice that while we typically wish to limit the size of test suites, in some cases we may prefer a larger test suite over a smaller suite that achieves the same coverage. A test suite with fewer test cases may be more difficult to generate or may be less helpful in debugging. Let us suppose, for example, that we omitted the 1 in the statement at line 31 of the program in Figure 12.1. Both test suites T_1 and T_2 would reveal the fault, resulting in a failure, but T_2 would provide better information for localizing the fault, since the program fails only for test case "%1D", the only test case of T_2 that exercises the statement at line 31.

On the other hand, a test suite obtained by adding test cases to T_2 would satisfy the statement adequacy criterion, but would not have any particular advantage over T_2 with respect to the total effort required to reveal and localize faults. Designing complex test cases that exercise many different elements of a unit is seldom a good way to optimize a test suite, although it may occasionally be justifiable when there is large and unavoidable fixed cost (e.g., setting up equipment) for each test case regardless of complexity.

Control flow coverage may be measured incrementally while executing a test suite. In this case, the contribution of a single test case to the overall coverage that has been achieved depends on the order of execution of test cases. For example, in test suite T_2, execution of test case "%1D" exercises 16 of the 18 statements of the program cgi_decode, but it exercises only 1 new statement if executed after "%A." The increment of coverage due to the execution of a specific test case does not measure the absolute efficacy of the test case. Measures independent from the order of execution may be obtained by identifying *independent statements*. However, in practice we are only interested in the coverage of the whole test suite, and not in the contribution of individual test cases.

12.3 Branch Testing

A test suite can achieve complete statement coverage without executing all the possible branches in a program. Consider, for example, a faulty program cgi_decode′ obtained from program cgi_decode by removing line 34. The control flow graph of program cgi_decode′ is shown in Figure 12.3. In the new program there are no statements following the false branch exiting node *D*. Thus, a test suite that tests only translation of specially treated characters but not treatment of strings containing other characters that are copied without change satisfies the statement adequacy criterion, but would not reveal the missing code in program cgi_decode′. For example, a test suite T_3

$$T_3 = \{\text{" "}, \text{"+\%0D+\%4J"}\}$$

satisfies the statement adequacy criterion for program cgi_decode′ but does not exercise the false branch from node D in the control flow graph model of the program.

The branch adequacy criterion requires each branch of the program to be executed by at least one test case.

Δ branch adequacy criterion

Let T be a test suite for a program P. T satisfies the branch adequacy criterion for P, iff, for each branch B of P, there exists at least one test case in T that causes execution of B.

This is equivalent to stating that every edge in the control flow graph model of program P belongs to some execution path exercised by a test case in T.

Δ branch coverage

The branch coverage C_{Branch} of T for P is the fraction of branches of program P executed by at least one test case in T.

$$C_{Branch} = \frac{\text{number of executed branches}}{\text{number of branches}}$$

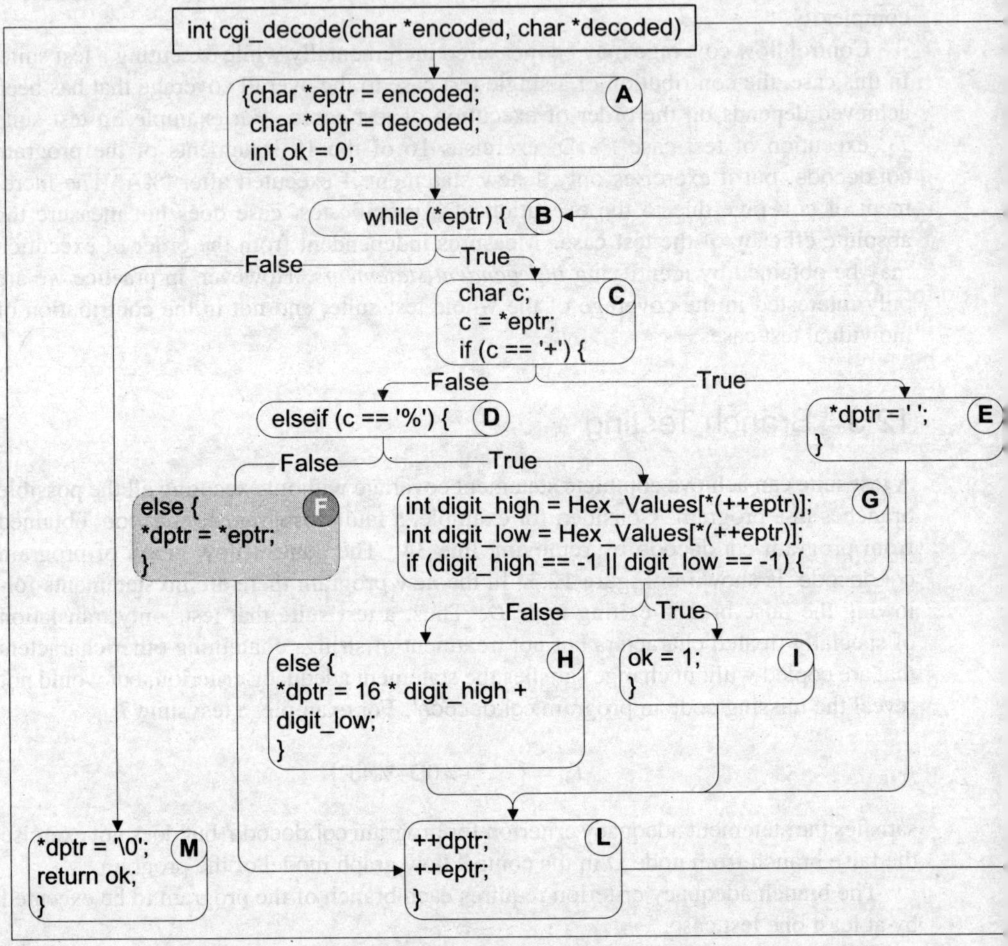

Figure 12.3: The control flow graph of C function cgi_decode′ *which is obtained from the program of Figure 12.1 after removing node F.*

T satisfies the branch adequacy criterion if $C_{Branch} = 1$.

Test suite T_3 achieves branch coverage of .88 since it executes 7 of the 8 branches of program cgi_decode′. Test suite T_2 satisfies the branch adequacy criterion, and would reveal the fault. Intuitively, since traversing all edges of a graph causes all nodes to be visited, test suites that satisfy the branch adequacy criterion for a program P also satisfy the statement adequacy criterion for the same program.[4] The contrary is not true, as illustrated by test suite T_3 for the program cgi_decode′ presented earlier.

12.4 Condition Testing

Branch coverage is useful for exercising faults in the way a computation has been decomposed into cases. Condition coverage considers this decomposition in more detail, forcing exploration not only of both possible results of a Boolean expression controlling a branch, but also of different combinations of the individual conditions in a compound Boolean expression.

Assume, for example, that we have forgotten the first operator '−' in the conditional statement at line 27 resulting in the faulty expression

```
(digit_high == 1 || digit_low == -1).
```

As trivial as this fault seems, it can easily be overlooked if only the outcomes of complete Boolean expressions are explored. The branch adequacy criterion can be satisfied, and both branches exercised, with test suites in which the first comparison evaluates always to *False* and only the second is varied. Such tests do not systematically exercise the first comparison and will not reveal the fault in that comparison. Condition adequacy criteria overcome this problem by requiring different basic conditions of the decisions to be separately exercised. The basic conditions, sometimes also called elementary conditions, are comparisons, references to Boolean variables, and other Boolean-valued expressions whose component subexpressions are not Boolean values.

The simplest condition adequacy criterion, called basic condition coverage requires each basic condition to be covered. Each basic condition must have a *True* and a *False* outcome at least once during the execution of the test suite.

Δ basic condition adequacy criterion

A test suite T for a program P covers all basic conditions of P, that is, it satisfies the basic condition adequacy criterion, iff each basic condition in P has a *true* outcome in at least one test case in T and a *false* outcome in at least one test case in T.

Δ basic condition coverage

The basic condition coverage $C_{Basic\_Condition}$ of T for P is the fraction of the total number of truth values assumed by the basic conditions of program P during the execution of all test cases in T.

$$C_{\text{Basic\_Condition}} = \frac{\text{total number of truth values assumed by all basic conditions}}{2 \times \text{number of basic conditions}}$$

[4]We can consider entry and exit from the control flow graph as branches, so that branch adequacy will imply statement adequacy even for units with no other control flow.

T satisfies the basic condition adequacy criterion if $C_{Basic\_Conditions} = 1$. Notice that the total number of truth values that the basic conditions can take is twice the number of basic conditions, since each basic condition can assume value *true* or *false*. For example, the program in Figure 12.1 contains five basic conditions, which in sum may take ten possible truth values. Three basic conditions correspond to the simple decisions at lines 18, 22, and 24 — decisions that each contain only one basic condition. Thus they are covered by any test suite that covers all branches. The remaining two conditions occur in the compound decision at line 27. In this case, test suites T_1 and T_3 cover the decisions without covering the basic conditions. Test suite T_1 covers the decision since it has an outcome *True* for the substring *%0D* and an outcome *False* for the substring *%7U* of test case "adequate+test%0Dexecution%7U." However test suite T_1 does not cover the first condition, since it has only outcome *True*. To satisfy the basic condition adequacy criterion, we need to add an additional test case that produces outcome *false* for the first condition (e.g., test case "basic%K7").

The basic condition adequacy criterion can be satisfied without satisfying branch coverage. For example, the test suite

$$T_4 = \{\text{"first+test\%9Ktest\%K9"}\}$$

satisfies the basic condition adequacy criterion, but not the branch condition adequacy criterion, since the outcome of the decision at line 27 is always *False*. Thus branch and basic condition adequacy criteria are not directly comparable.

Δ branch and condition adequacy

An obvious extension that includes both the basic condition and the branch adequacy criteria is called *branch and condition adequacy criterion*, with the obvious definition: A test suite satisfies the branch and condition adequacy criterion if it satisfies both the branch adequacy criterion and the condition adequacy criterion.

Δ compound condition adequacy

A more complete extension that includes both the basic condition and the branch adequacy criteria is the *compound condition adequacy criterion*,[5] which requires a test for each possible evaluation of compound conditions. It is most natural to visualize compound condition adequacy as covering paths to leaves of the evaluation tree for the expression. For example, the compound condition at line 27 would require covering the three paths in the following tree:

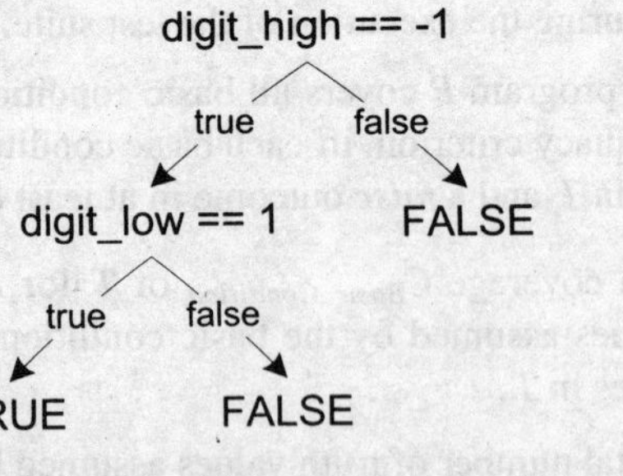

Notice that due to the left-to-right evaluation order and short-circuit evaluation of logical *OR* expressions in the C language, the value *True* for the first condition does

[5] Compound condition adequacy is also known as multiple condition coverage.

not need to be combined with both values *False* and *True* for the second condition. The number of test cases required for compound condition adequacy can, in principle, grow exponentially with the number of basic conditions in a decision (all 2^N combinations of N basic conditions), which would make compound condition coverage impractical for programs with very complex conditions. Short-circuit evaluation is often effective in reducing this to a more manageable number, but not in every case. The number of test cases required to achieve compound condition coverage even for expressions built from N basic conditions combined only with short-circuit Boolean operators like the `&&` and `||` of C and Java can still be exponential in the worst case.

Consider the number of cases required for compound condition coverage of the following two Boolean expressions, each with five basic conditions. For the expression `a && b && c && d && e`, compound condition coverage requires:

Test Case	a	b	c	d	e
(1)	*True*	*True*	*True*	*True*	*True*
(2)	*True*	*True*	*True*	*True*	*False*
(3)	*True*	*True*	*True*	*False*	–
(4)	*True*	*True*	*False*	–	–
(5)	*True*	*False*	–	–	–
(6)	*False*	–	–	–	–

For the expression `(((a || b) && c) || d) && e`, however, compound condition adequacy requires many more combinations:

Test Case	a	b	c	d	e
(1)	*True*	–	*True*	–	*True*
(2)	*False*	*True*	*True*	–	*True*
(3)	*True*	–	*False*	*True*	*True*
(4)	*False*	*True*	*False*	*True*	*True*
(5)	*False*	*False*	–	*True*	*True*
(6)	*True*	–	*True*	–	*False*
(7)	*False*	*True*	*True*	–	*False*
(8)	*True*	–	*False*	*True*	*False*
(9)	*False*	*True*	*False*	*True*	*False*
(10)	*False*	*False*	–	*True*	*False*
(11)	*True*	–	*False*	*False*	–
(12)	*False*	*True*	*False*	*False*	–
(13)	*False*	*False*	–	*False*	–

An alternative approach that can be satisfied with the same number of test cases for Boolean expressions of a given length regardless of short-circuit evaluation is the *modified condition/decision coverage* or MC/DC, also known as the *modified condition adequacy criterion*. The modified condition/decision criterion requires that each basic condition be shown to independently affect the outcome of each decision. That is, for each basic condition C, there are two test cases in which the truth values of all evaluated conditions except C are the same, and the compound condition as a whole evaluates to *True* for one of those test cases and *False* for the other. The modified condition adequacy criterion can be satisfied with $N+1$ test cases, making it an attrac-

Δ modified condition/decision coverage (MC/DC)

tive compromise between number of required test cases and thoroughness of the test. It is required by important quality standards in aviation, including RTCA/DO-178B, "Software Considerations in Airborne Systems and Equipment Certification," and its European equivalent EUROCAE ED-12B.

Recall the expression `(((a || b) && c) || d) && e`, which required 13 different combinations of condition values for compound condition adequacy. For modified condition/decision adequacy, only 6 combinations are required. Here they have been numbered for easy comparison with the previous table:

	a	b	c	d	e	Decision
(1)	*True*	–	*True*	–	*True*	*True*
(2)	*False*	*True*	*True*	–	*True*	*True*
(3)	*True*	–	*False*	*True*	*True*	*True*
(6)	*True*	–	*True*	–	*False*	*False*
(11)	*True*	–	*False*	*False*	–	*False*
(13)	*False*	*False*	–	*False*	–	*False*

The values underlined in the table independently affect the outcome of the decision. Note that the same test case can cover the values of several basic conditions. For example, test case (1) covers value *True* for the basic conditions a, c and e. Note also that this is not the only possible set of test cases to satisfy the criterion; a different selection of Boolean combinations could be equally effective.

12.5 Path Testing

Decision and condition adequacy criteria force consideration of individual program decisions. Sometimes, though, a fault is revealed only through exercise of some sequence of decisions (i.e., a particular path through the program). It is simple (but impractical, as we will see) to define a coverage criterion based on complete paths rather than individual program decisions

Δ path adequacy criterion

A test suite T for a program P satisfies the path adequacy criterion iff, for each path p of P, there exists at least one test case in T that causes the execution of p.

This is equivalent to stating that every path in the control flow graph model of program P is exercised by a test case in T.

Δ path coverage

The path coverage C_{Path} of T for P is the fraction of paths of program P executed by at least one test case in T.

$$C_{Path} = \frac{\text{number of executed paths}}{\text{number of paths}}$$

Unfortunately, the number of paths in a program with loops is unbounded, so this criterion cannot be satisfied for any but the most trivial programs. For a program with loops, the denominator in the computation of the path coverage becomes infinite, and thus path coverage is zero no matter how many test cases are executed.

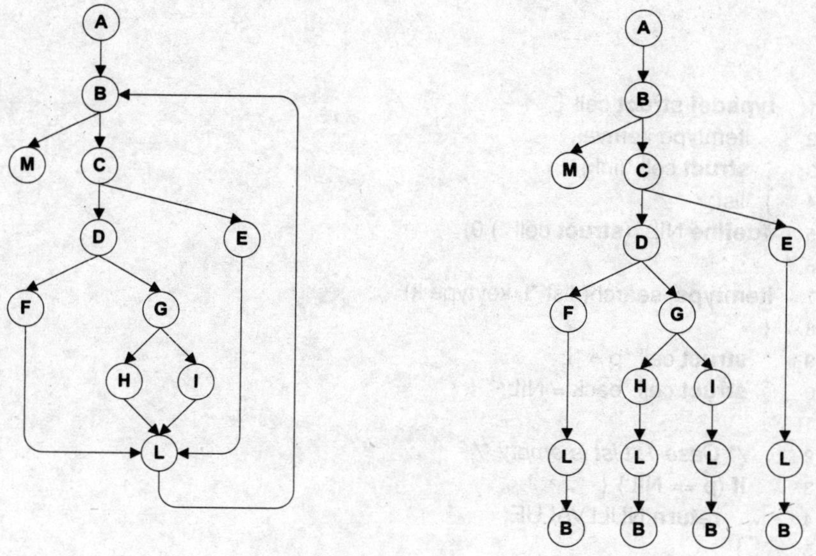

(i) (ii)

Figure 12.4: Deriving a tree from a control flow graph to derive subpaths for boundary/interior testing. Part (i) is the control flow graph of the C function cgi_decode, *identical to Figure 12.1 but showing only node identifiers without source code. Part (ii) is a tree derived from part (i) by following each path in the control flow graph up to the first repeated node. The set of paths from the root of the tree to each leaf is the required set of subpaths for boundary/interior coverage.*

To obtain a practical criterion, it is necessary to partition the infinite set of paths into a finite number of classes and require only that representatives from each class be explored. Useful criteria can be obtained by limiting the number of paths to be covered. Relevant subsets of paths to be covered can be identified by limiting the number of traversals of loops, the length of the paths to be traversed, or the dependencies among selected paths.

The boundary interior criterion groups together paths that differ only in the subpath they follow when repeating the body of a loop.

Δ boundary interior criterion

Figure 12.4 illustrates how the classes of subpaths distinguished by the boundary interior coverage criterion can be represented as paths in a tree derived by "unfolding" the control flow graph of function *cgi_decode*.

Figures 12.5 – 12.7 illustrate a fault that may not be uncovered using statement or decision testing, but will assuredly be detected if the boundary interior path criterion is satisfied. The program fails if the loop body is executed exactly once — that is, if the search key occurs in the second position in the list.

Although the boundary/interior coverage criterion bounds the number of paths that must be explored, that number can grow quickly enough to be impractical. The number

```
typedef struct cell {
   itemtype itemval;
   struct cell *link;
} *list;
#define NIL ((struct cell *) 0)

itemtype search( list *l, keytype k)
{
   struct cell *p = *l;
   struct cell *back = NIL;

   /* Case 1: List is empty */
   if (p == NIL) {
      return NULLVALUE;
   }

   /* Case 2: Key is at front of list */
   if (k == p->itemval) {
      return p->itemval;
   }

   /* Default: Simple (but buggy) sequential search */
   p=p->link;
   while (1) {
      if (p == NIL) {
         return NULLVALUE;
      }
      if (k==p->itemval) {   /* Move to front */
         back->link = p->link;
         p->link = *l;
         *l = p;
         return p->itemval;
      }
      back=p; p=p->link;
   }
}
```

Figure 12.5: A C function for searching and dynamically rearranging a linked list, excerpted from a symbol table package. Initialization of the back *pointer is missing, causing a failure only if the search key is found in the second position in the list.*

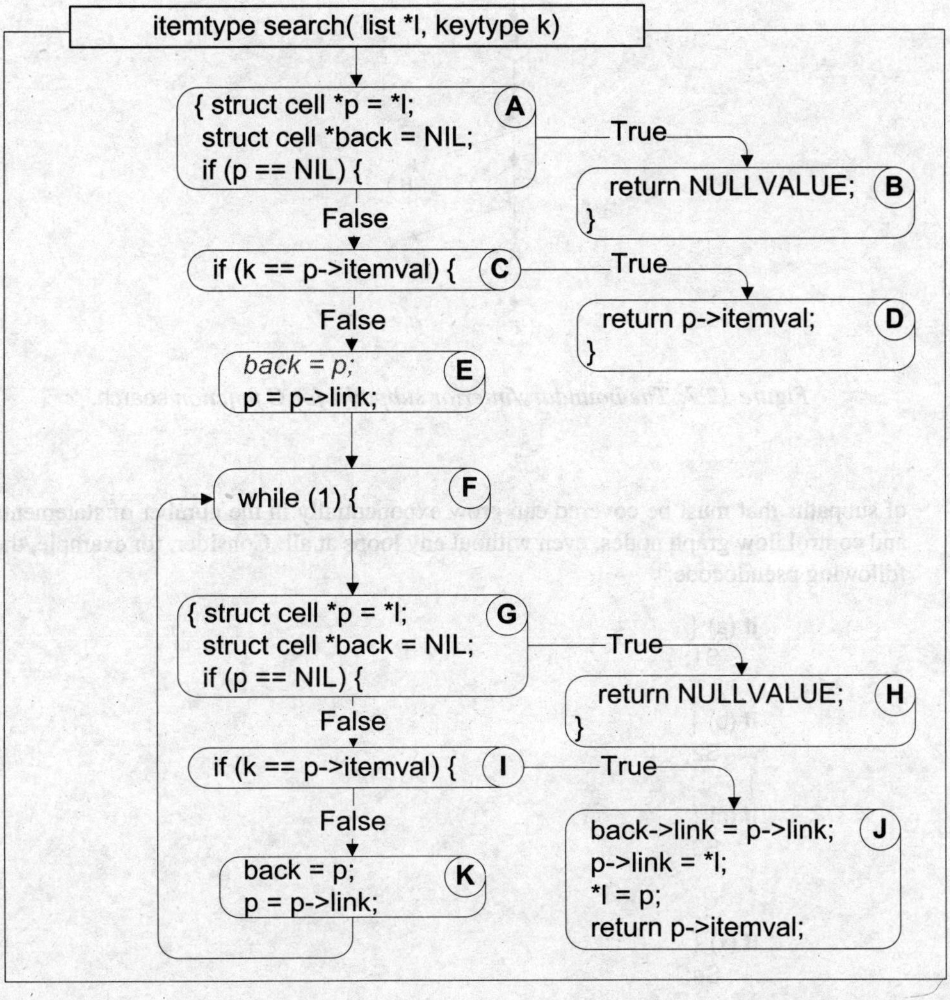

Figure 12.6: The control flow graph of C function search *with move-to-front feature.*

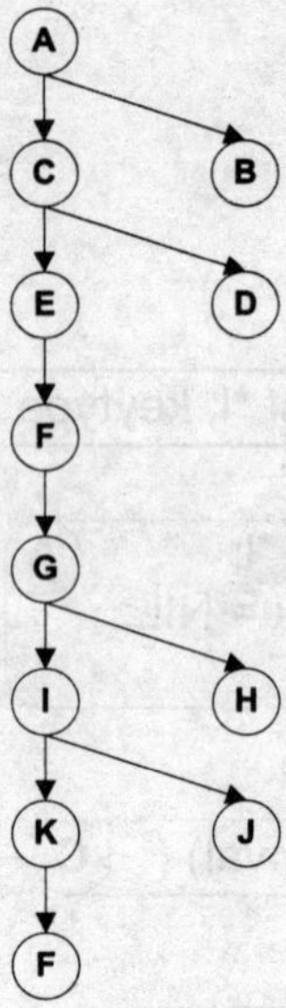

Figure 12.7: The boundary/interior subpaths for C function search.

of subpaths that must be covered can grow exponentially in the number of statements and control flow graph nodes, even without any loops at all. Consider, for example, the following pseudocode:

```
if (a) {
    S1;
}
if (b) {
    S2;
}
if (c) {
    S3;
}
...
if (x) {
    Sn;
}
```

The subpaths through this control flow can include or exclude each of the statements S_i, so that in total N branches result in 2^N paths that must be traversed. Moreover, choosing input data to force execution of one particular path may be very difficult, or even impossible if the conditions are not independent.[6]

Since coverage of non-looping paths is expensive, we can consider a variant of

[6] Section 12.8 discusses infeasible paths.

the boundary/interior criterion that treats loop boundaries similarly but is less stringent with respect to other differences among paths.

A test suite T for a program P satisfies the loop boundary adequacy criterion iff, for each loop l in P,

Δ loop boundary adequacy criterion

- In at least one execution, control reaches the loop, and then the loop control condition evaluates to *False* the first time it is evaluated.[7]
- In at least one execution, control reaches the loop, and then the body of the loop is executed exactly once before control leaves the loop.
- In at least one execution, the body of the loop is repeated more than once.

One can define several small variations on the loop boundary criterion. For example, we might excuse from consideration loops that are always executed a definite number of times (e.g., multiplication of fixed-size transformation matrices in a graphics application). In practice we would like the last part of the criterion to be "many times through the loop" or "as many times as possible," but it is hard to make that precise (how many is "many?").

It is easy enough to define such a coverage criterion for loops, but how can we justify it? Why should we believe that these three cases — zero times through, once through, and several times through — will be more effective in revealing faults than, say, requiring an even and an odd number of iterations? The intuition is that the loop boundary coverage criteria reflect a deeper structure in the design of a program. This can be seen by their relation to the reasoning we would apply if we were trying to formally verify the correctness of the loop. The basis case of the proof would show that the loop is executed zero times only when its postcondition (what should be true immediately following the loop) is already true. We would also show that an invariant condition is established on entry to the loop, that each iteration of the loop maintains this invariant condition, and that the invariant together with the negation of the loop test (i.e., the condition on exit) implies the postcondition. The loop boundary criterion does not require us to explicitly state the precondition, invariant, and postcondition, but it forces us to exercise essentially the same cases that we would analyze in a proof.

There are additional path-oriented coverage criteria that do not explicitly consider loops. Among these are criteria that consider paths up to a fixed length. The most common such criteria are based on *Linear Code Sequence and Jump (LCSAJ)*. An LCSAJ is defined as a body of code through which the flow of control may proceed sequentially, terminated by a jump in the control flow. Coverage of LCSAJ sequences of length 1 is almost, but not quite, equivalent to branch coverage. Stronger criteria can be defined by requiring N consecutive LCSAJs to be covered. The resulting criteria are also referred to as TER_{N+2}, where N is the number of consecutive LCSAJs to be covered. Conventionally, TER_1 and TER_2 refer to statement and branch coverage, respectively.

Δ linear code sequence and jump (LCSAJ)

The number of paths to be exercised can also be limited by identifying a subset that can be combined (in a manner to be described shortly) to form all the others.

[7]For a *while* or *for* loop, this is equivalent to saying that the loop body is executed zero times.

Such a set of paths is called a basis set, and from graph theory we know that every connected graph with n nodes, e edges, and c connected components has a basis set of only $e-n+c$ independent subpaths. Producing a single connected component from a program flow graph by adding a "virtual edge" from the exit to the entry, the formula becomes $e-n+2$, which is called the cyclomatic complexity of the control flow graph. Cyclomatic testing consists of attempting to exercise any set of execution paths that is a basis set for the control flow graph.

Δ cyclomatic testing

To be more precise, the sense in which a basis set of paths can be combined to form other paths is to consider each path as a vector of counts indicating how many times each edge in the control flow graph was traversed. For example, the third element of the vector might be the number of times a particular branch is taken. The basis set is combined by adding or subtracting these vectors (and not, as one might intuitively expect, by concatenating paths). Consider again the pseudocode

```
if (a) {
    S1;
}
if (b) {
    S2;
}
if (c) {
    S3;
}
...
if (x) {
    Sn;
}
```

While the number of distinct paths through this code is exponential in the number of if statements, the number of basis paths is small: only $n+1$ if there are n if statements. We can represent one basis set (of many possible) for a sequence of four such if statements by indicating whether each predicate evaluates to *True* or *False*:

1	*False*	*False*	*False*	*False*
2	*True*	*False*	*False*	*False*
3	*False*	*True*	*False*	*False*
4	*False*	*False*	*True*	*False*
5	*False*	*False*	*False*	*True*

The path represented as $\langle True, False, True, False\rangle$ is formed from these by adding paths 2 and 4 and then subtracting path 1.

Cyclomatic testing does not require that any particular basis set is covered. Rather, it counts the number of independent paths that have actually been covered (i.e., counting a new execution path as progress toward the coverage goal only if it is independent of all the paths previously exercised), and the coverage criterion is satisfied when this count reaches the cyclomatic complexity of the code under test.

12.6 Procedure Call Testing

The criteria considered to this point measure coverage of control flow within individual procedures. They are not well suited to integration testing or system testing. It is difficult to steer fine-grained control flow decisions of a unit when it is one small part of a larger system, and the cost of achieving fine-grained coverage for a system or major component is seldom justifiable. Usually it is more appropriate to choose a coverage granularity commensurate with the granularity of testing. Moreover, if unit testing has been effective, then faults that remain to be found in integration testing will be primarily interface faults, and testing effort should focus on interfaces between units rather than their internal details.

In some programming languages (FORTRAN, for example), a single procedure may have multiple entry points, and one would want to test invocation through each of the entry points. More common are procedures with multiple exit points. For example, the code of Figure 12.5 has four different return statements. One might want to check that each of the four returns is exercised in the actual context in which the procedure is used. Each of these would have been exercised already if even the simplest statement coverage criterion were satisfied during unit testing, but perhaps only in the context of a simple test driver; testing in the real context could reveal interface faults that were previously undetected.

Δ procedure entry and exit testing

Exercising all the entry points of a procedure is not the same as exercising all the calls. For example, procedure *A* may call procedure *C* from two distinct points, and procedure *B* may also call procedure *C*. In this case, coverage of calls of *C* means exercising calls at all three points. If the component under test has been constructed in a bottom-up manner, as is common, then unit testing of *A* and *B* may already have exercised calls of *C*. In that case, even statement coverage of *A* and *B* would ensure coverage of the calls relation (although not in the context of the entire component).

Δ call coverage

The search function in Figure 12.5 was originally part of a symbol table package in a small compiler. It was called at only one point, from one other C function in the same unit.[8] That C function, in turn, was called from tens of different points in a scanner and a parser. Coverage of calls requires exercising each statement in which the parser and scanner access the symbol table, but this would almost certainly be satisfied by a set of test cases exercising each production in the grammar accepted by the parser.

When procedures maintain internal state (local variables that persist from call to call), or when they modify global state, then properties of interfaces may only be revealed by sequences of several calls. In object-oriented programming, local state is manipulated by procedures called *methods*, and systematic testing necessarily concerns sequences of method calls on the same object. Even simple coverage of the "calls" relation becomes more challenging in this environment, since a single call point may be dynamically bound to more than one possible procedure (method). While these complications may arise even in conventional procedural programs (e.g., using function pointers in C), they are most prevalent in object-oriented programming. Not surprisingly, then, approaches to systematically exercising sequences of procedure calls are

[8]The "unit" in this case is the C source file, which provided a single data abstraction through several related C functions, much as a C++ or Java class would provide a single abstraction through several methods. The search function was analogous in this case to a private (internal) method of a class.

beginning to emerge mainly in the field of object-oriented testing, and we therefore cover them in Chapter 15.

12.7 Comparing Structural Testing Criteria

The power and cost of the structural test adequacy criteria described in this chapter can be formally compared using the *subsumes* relation introduced in Chapter 9. The relations among these criteria are illustrated in Figure 12.8. They are divided into two broad categories: practical criteria that can always be satisfied by test sets whose size is at most a linear function of program size; and criteria that are of mainly theoretical interest because they may require impractically large numbers of test cases or even (in the case of path coverage) an infinite number of test cases.

The hierarchy can be roughly divided into a part that relates requirements for covering program paths and another part that relates requirements for covering combinations of conditions in branch decisions. The two parts come together at branch coverage. Above branch coverage, path-oriented criteria and condition-oriented criteria are generally separate, because there is considerable cost and little apparent benefit in combining them. Statement coverage is at the bottom of the subsumes hierarchy for systematic coverage of control flow. Applying any of the structural coverage criteria, therefore, implies at least executing all the program statements.

Procedure call coverage criteria are not included in the figure, since they do not concern internal control flow of procedures and are thus incomparable with the control flow coverage criteria.

12.8 The Infeasibility Problem

Sometimes *no* set of test cases is capable of satisfying some test coverage criterion for a particular program, because the criterion requires execution of a program element that can never be executed. This is true even for the statement coverage criterion, weak as it is. Unreachable statements can occur as a result of defensive programming (e.g., checking for error conditions that never occur) and code reuse (reusing code that is more general than strictly required for the application). Large amounts of "fossil" code may accumulate when a legacy application becomes unmanageable. In that case, they may indicate serious maintainability problems, but some unreachable code is common even in well-designed, well-maintained systems, and must be accommodated in testing processes that otherwise require satisfaction of coverage criteria.

Stronger coverage criteria tend to call for coverage of more elements that may be infeasible. For example, in discussing multiple condition coverage, we implicitly assumed that basic conditions were independent and could therefore occur in any combination. In reality, basic conditions may be comparisons or other relational expressions and may be interdependent in ways that make certain combinations infeasible. For example, in the expression (a > 0 && a < 10), it is not possible for both basic conditions to be *False*. Fortunately, short-circuit evaluation rules ensure that the combination

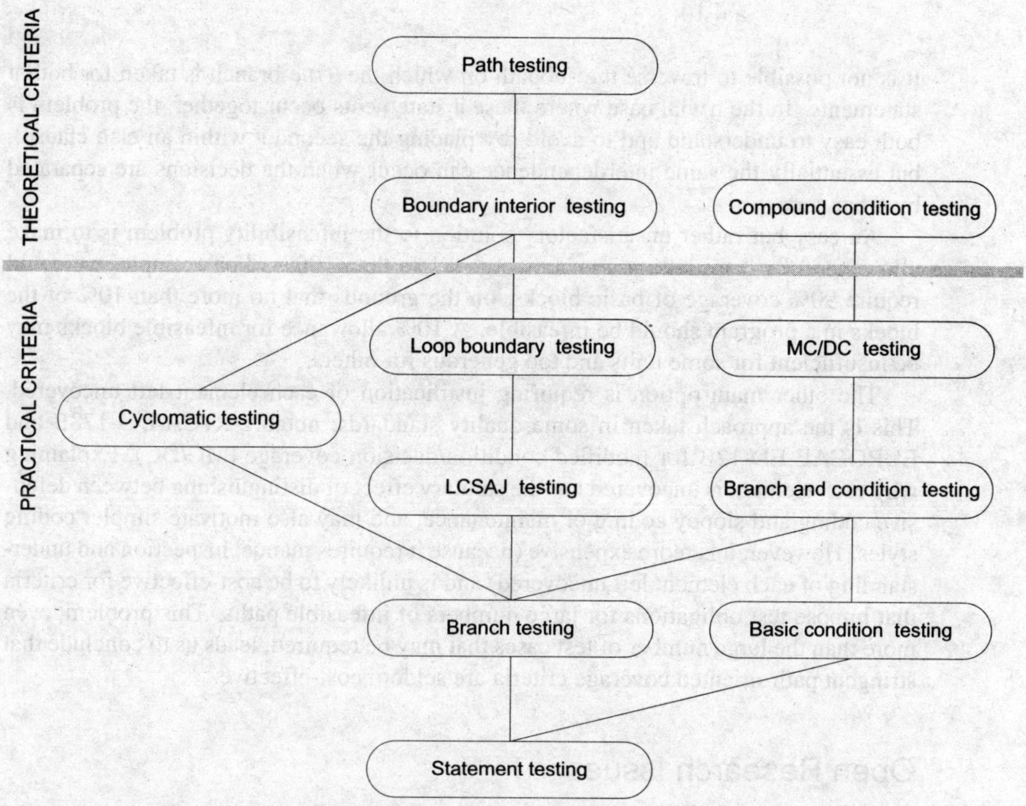

Figure 12.8: The subsumption relation among structural test adequacy criteria described in this chapter.

⟨*False*, *False*⟩ is not required for multiple condition coverage of this particular expression in a C or Java program.

The infeasibility problem is most acute for path-based structural coverage criteria, such as the boundary/interior coverage criterion. Consider, for example, the following simple code sequence:

```
if (a < 0) {
    a = 0;
}
if (a > 10) {
    a = 10;
}
```

It is not possible to traverse the subpath on which the *True* branch is taken for both if statements. In the trivial case where these if statements occur together, the problem is both easy to understand and to avoid (by placing the second if within an else clause), but essentially the same interdependence can occur when the decisions are separated by other code.

An easy but rather unsatisfactory solution to the infeasibility problem is to make allowances for it by setting a coverage goal less than 100%. For example, we could require 90% coverage of basic blocks, on the grounds that no more than 10% of the blocks in a program should be infeasible. A 10% allowance for infeasible blocks may be insufficient for some units and too generous for others.

The other main option is requiring justification of each element left uncovered. This is the approach taken in some quality standards, notably RTCA/DO-178B and EUROCAE ED-12B for modified condition/decision coverage (MC/DC). Explaining why each element is uncovered has the salutary effect of distinguishing between defensive coding and sloppy coding or maintenance, and may also motivate simpler coding styles. However, it is more expensive (because it requires manual inspection and understanding of each element left uncovered) and is unlikely to be cost-effective for criteria that impose test obligations for large numbers of infeasible paths. This problem, even more than the large number of test cases that may be required, leads us to conclude that stringent path-oriented coverage criteria are seldom cost-effective.

Open Research Issues

Devising and comparing structural criteria was a hot topic in the 1980s. It is no longer an active research area for imperative programming, but new programming paradigms or design techniques present new challenges. Polymorphism, dynamic binding, and object-oriented and distributed code open new problems and require new techniques, as discussed in other chapters. Applicability of structural criteria to architectural design descriptions is still under investigation. Usefulness of structural criteria for implicit control flow has been addressed only recently.

Early testing research, including research on structural coverage criteria, was concerned largely with improving the fault-detection effectiveness of testing. Today, the most pressing issues are cost and schedule. Better automated techniques for identifying infeasible paths will be necessary before more stringent structural coverage criteria can be seriously considered in any but the most critical of domains. Alternatively, for many applications it may be more appropriate to gather evidence of feasibility from actual product use; this is called *residual* test coverage monitoring and is a topic of current research.

Further Reading

The main structural adequacy criteria are presented in Myers' *The Art of Software Testing* [Mye79], which has been a preeminent source of information for more than two decades. It is a classic despite its age, which is evident from the limited set of techniques addressed and the programming language used in the examples. The excellent survey by Adrion et al. [ABC82] remains the best overall survey of testing techniques, despite similar age. Frankl and Weyuker [FW93] provide a modern treatment of the subsumption hierarchy among structural coverage criteria.

Boundary/interior testing is presented by Howden [How75]. Woodward et al. [WHH80] present LCSAJ testing. Cyclomatic testing is described by McCabe [McC83]. Residual test coverage measurement is described by Pavlopoulou and Young [PY99].

Related Topics

Readers with a strong interest in coverage criteria should continue with the next chapter, which presents data flow testing criteria. Others may wish to proceed to Chapter 15, which addresses testing object-oriented programs. Readers wishing a more comprehensive view of unit testing may continue with Chapters 17 on test scaffolding and test data generation. Tool support for structural testing is discussed in Chapter 23.

Exercises

12.1. Let us consider the following loop, which appears in C lexical analyzers generated by the tool flex:[9]

```
for ( n = 0;
        n < max_size && (c = getc( yyin )) != EOF && c != '\n';
        ++n )
            buf[n] = (char) c;
```

Devise a set of test cases that satisfy the compound condition adequacy criterion and a set of test cases that satisfy the modified condition adequacy criterion with respect to this loop.

[9] Flex is a widely used generator of lexical analyzers. Flex was written by Vern Paxson and is compatible with the original AT&T lex written by M.E. Lesk. This excerpt is from version 2.5.4 of flex, distributed with the Linux operating system.

12.2. The following if statement appears in the Java source code of Grappa,[10] a graph layout engine distributed by AT&T Laboratories:

```
if(pos < parseArray.length
    && (parseArray[pos] == '{'
        || parseArray[pos] == '}'
        || parseArray[pos] == '|')) {
    continue;
}
```

(a) Derive a set of test case specifications and show that it satisfies the MC/DC criterion for this statement. For brevity, abbreviate each of the basic conditions as follows:

Room for pos < parseArray.length
Open for parseArray[pos] == '{'
Close for parseArray[pos] == '}'
Bar for parseArray[pos] == '|'

(b) Do the requirements for compound condition coverage and modified condition/decision coverage differ in this case? Aside from increasing the number of test cases, what difference would it make if we attempted to exhaustively cover all combinations of truth values for the basic conditions?

12.3. Prove that the number of test cases required to satisfy the modified condition adequacy criterion for a predicate with N basic conditions is $N+1$.

12.4. The number of basis paths (cyclomatic complexity) does not depend on whether nodes of the control flow graph are individual statements or basic blocks that may contain several statements. Why?

12.5. Derive the subsumption hierarchy for the call graph coverage criteria described in this chapter, and justify each of the relationships.

12.6. If the modified condition/decision adequacy criterion requires a test case that is not feasible because of interdependent basic conditions, should this always be taken as an indication of a defect in design or coding? Why or why not?

[10]The statement appears in file Table.java. This source code is copyright 1996, 1997, 1998 by AT&T Corporation. Grappa is distributed as open source software, available at the time of this writing from `http://www.graphviz.org`. Formatting of the line has been altered for readability in this printed form.

Chapter 13

Data Flow Testing

Exercising every statement or branch with test cases is a practical goal, but exercising every path is impossible. Even the number of simple (that is, loop-free) paths can be exponential in the size of the program. Path-oriented selection and adequacy criteria must therefore select a tiny fraction of control flow paths. Some control flow adequacy criteria, notably the loop boundary interior condition, do so heuristically. Data flow test adequacy criteria improve over pure control flow criteria by selecting paths based on how one syntactic element can affect the computation of another.

Required Background

- Chapter 6

  At least the basic data flow models presented in Chapter 6, Section 6.1, are required to understand this chapter, although algorithmic details of data flow analysis can be deferred. Section 6.5 of that chapter is important background for Section 13.4 of the current chapter. The remainder of Chapter 6 is useful background but not strictly necessary to understand and apply data flow testing.

- Chapter 9

  The introduction to test case adequacy and test case selection in general sets the context for this chapter. It is not strictly required for understanding this chapter, but is helpful for understanding how the techniques described in this chapter should be applied.

- Chapter 12

  The data flow adequacy criteria presented in this chapter complement control flow adequacy criteria. Knowledge about control flow adequacy criteria is desirable but not strictly required for understanding this chapter.

13.1 Overview

We have seen in Chapter 12 that structural testing criteria are practical for single elements of the program, from simple statements to complex combinations of conditions, but become impractical when extended to paths. Even the simplest path testing criteria require covering large numbers of paths that tend to quickly grow far beyond test suites of acceptable size for nontrivial programs.

Close examination of paths that need to be traversed to satisfy a path selection criterion often reveals that, among a large set of paths, only a few are likely to uncover faults that could have escaped discovery using condition testing coverage. Criteria that select paths based on control structure alone (e.g., boundary interior testing) may not be effective in identifying these few significant paths because their significance depends not only on control flow but on data interactions.

Data flow testing is based on the observation that computing the wrong value leads to a failure only when that value is subsequently used. Focus is therefore moved from control flow to data flow. Data flow testing criteria pair variable definitions with uses, ensuring that each computed value is actually used, and thus selecting from among many execution paths a set that is more likely to propagate the result of erroneous computation to the point of an observable failure.

Consider, for example, the C function cgi_decode of Figure 13.1, which decodes a string that has been transmitted through the Web's Common Gateway Interface. Data flow testing criteria would require one to execute paths that first define (change the value of) variable eptr (e.g., by incrementing it at line 37) and then use the new value of variable eptr (e.g., using variable eptr to update the array indexed by dptr at line 34). Since a value defined in one iteration of the loop is used on a subsequent iteration, we are obliged to execute more than one iteration of the loop to observe the propagation of information from one iteration to the next.

13.2 Definition-Use Associations

Data flow testing criteria are based on data flow information — variable *definitions* and *uses*. Table 13.1 shows definitions and uses for the program cgi_decode of Figure 13.1. Recall that when a variable occurs on both sides of an assignment, it is first used and then defined, since the value of the variable before the assignment is used for computing the value of the variable after the assignment. For example, the ++eptr increment operation in C is equivalent to the assignment eptr = eptr + 1, and thus first uses and then defines variable eptr.

We will initially consider treatment of arrays and pointers in the current example in a somewhat ad hoc fashion and defer discussion of the general problem to Section 13.4. Variables eptr and dptr are used for indexing the input and output strings. In program cgi_decode, we consider the variables as both indexes (eptr and dptr) and strings (*eptr and *dptr). The assignment *dptr = *eptr is treated as a definition of the string *dptr as well as a use of the index dptr, the index eptr, and the string *eptr, since the result depends on both indexes as well as the contents of the source string. A change to an index is treated as a definition of both the index and the string, since a

```
/* External file hex_values.h defines Hex_Values[128]
 * with value 0 to 15 for the legal hex digits (case-insensitive)
 * and value -1 for each illegal digit including special characters
 */

#include "hex_values.h"
/**    Translate a string from the CGI encoding to plain ascii text.
 *     '+' becomes space, %xx becomes byte with hex value xx,
 *     other alphanumeric characters map to themselves.
 *    Returns 0 for success, positive for erroneous input
 *          1 = bad hexadecimal digit
 */
int cgi_decode(char *encoded, char *decoded) {
  char *eptr = encoded;
  char *dptr = decoded;
  int ok=0;
  while (*eptr) {
    char c;
    c = *eptr;

    if (c == '+') {   /* Case 1: '+' maps to blank */
      *dptr = ' ';
    } else if (c == '%') { /* Case 2: '%xx' is hex for character xx */
      int  digit_high = Hex_Values[*(++eptr)];
      int  digit_low  = Hex_Values[*(++eptr)];
      if (   digit_high == -1 || digit_low == -1 ) {
        /* *dptr='?'; */
        ok=1; /* Bad return code */
      } else {
        *dptr = 16* digit_high + digit_low;
      }
    } else { /* Case 3: All other characters map to themselves */
      *dptr = *eptr;
    }
    ++dptr;
    ++eptr;
  }
  *dptr = '\0';                      /* Null terminator for string */
  return ok;
}
```

Figure 13.1: The C function cgi_decode*, which translates a cgi-encoded string to a plain ASCII string (reversing the encoding applied by the common gateway interface of most Web servers). This program is also used in Chapter 12 and also presented in Figure 12.1 of Chapter 12.*

Variable	Definitions	Uses
encoded	14	15
decoded	14	16
*eptr	15, 25, 26, 37	18, 20, 25, 26, 34
eptr	15, 25, 26, 37	15, 18, 20, 25, 26, 34, 37
*dptr	16, 23, 31, 34, 36, 39	40
dptr	16 36	16, 23, 31, 34, 36, 39
ok	17, 29	40
c	20	22, 24
digit_high	25	27, 31
digit_low	26	27, 31
Hex_Values	–	25, 26

Table 13.1: Definitions and uses for C function cgi_decode. *eptr *and* *dptr *indicate the strings, while* eptr *and* dptr *indicate the indexes.*

change of the index changes the value accessed by it. For example, in the statement at line 36 (++dptr), we have a use of variable dptr followed by a definition of variables dptr and *dptr.

It is somewhat counterintuitive that we have definitions of the string *eptr, since it is easy to see that the program is scanning the encoded string without changing it. For the purposes of data flow testing, though, we are interested in interactions between computation at different points in the program. Incrementing the index eptr is a "definition" of *eptr in the sense that it can affect the value that is next observed by a use of *eptr.

Δ DU pair

Pairing definitions and uses of the same variable v identifies potential data interactions through v — definition-use pairs (DU pairs). Table 13.2 shows the DU pairs in program cgi_decode of Figure 13.1. Some pairs of definitions and uses from Table 13.1 do not occur in Table 13.2, since there is no definition-clear path between the two statements. For example, the use of variable eptr at line 15 cannot be reached from the increment at line 37, so there is no DU pair $\langle 37, 15 \rangle$. The definitions of variables *eptr and eptr at line 25, are paired only with the respective uses at line 26, since successive definitions of the two variables at line 26 kill the definition at line 25 and eliminate definition-clear paths to any other use.

Δ DU path

A DU pair requires the existence of at least one *definition-clear path* from definition to use, but there may be several. Additional uses on a path do not interfere with the pair. We sometimes use the term *DU path* to indicate a particular definition-clear path between a definition and a use. For example, let us consider the definition of *eptr at line 37 and the use at line 34. There are infinitely many paths that go from line 37 to the use at line 34. There is one DU path that does not traverse the loop while going from 37 to 34. There are infinitely many paths from 37 back to 37, but only two DU paths, because the definition at 37 kills the previous definition at the same point.

Data flow testing, like other structural criteria, is based on information obtained through static analysis of the program. We discard definitions and uses that cannot be statically paired, but we may select pairs even if none of the statically identifiable

Variable	DU Pairs
*eptr	⟨ 15, 18 ⟩, ⟨ 15, 20 ⟩, ⟨ 15, 25 ⟩, ⟨ 15, 34 ⟩ ⟨ 25, 26 ⟩, ⟨ 26, 37 ⟩ ⟨ 37, 18 ⟩, ⟨ 37, 20 ⟩, ⟨ 37, 25 ⟩, ⟨ 37, 34 ⟩
eptr	⟨ 15, 15 ⟩, ⟨ 15, 18 ⟩, ⟨ 15, 20 ⟩, ⟨ 15, 25 ⟩, ⟨ 15, 34 ⟩, ⟨ 15, 37 ⟩, ⟨ 25, 26 ⟩, ⟨ 26, 37 ⟩ ⟨ 37, 18 ⟩, ⟨ 37, 20 ⟩, ⟨ 37, 25 ⟩, ⟨ 37, 34 ⟩, ⟨ 37, 37 ⟩
*dptr	⟨ 39, 40 ⟩
dptr	⟨ 16, 16 ⟩, ⟨ 16, 23 ⟩, ⟨ 16, 31 ⟩, ⟨ 16, 34 ⟩, ⟨ 16, 36 ⟩, ⟨ 16, 39 ⟩, ⟨ 36, 23 ⟩, ⟨ 36, 31 ⟩, ⟨ 36, 34 ⟩, ⟨ 36, 36 ⟩, ⟨ 36, 39 ⟩
ok	⟨ 17, 40 ⟩, ⟨ 29, 40 ⟩
c	⟨ 20, 22 ⟩, ⟨ 20 24 ⟩
digit_high	⟨ 25, 27 ⟩, ⟨ 25, 31 ⟩
digit_low	⟨ 26, 27 ⟩, ⟨ 26, 31 ⟩
encoded	⟨ 14, 15⟩
decoded	⟨ 14, 16⟩

Table 13.2: DU pairs for C function cgi_decode. *Variable* Hex_Values *does not appear because it is not defined (modified) within the procedure.*

definition-clear paths is actually executable. In the current example, we have made use of information that would require a quite sophisticated static data flow analyzer, as discussed in Section 13.4.

13.3 Data Flow Testing Criteria

Various data flow testing criteria can be defined by requiring coverage of DU pairs in various ways.

The *All DU pairs adequacy criterion* requires each DU pair to be exercised in at least one program execution, following the idea that an erroneous value produced by one statement (the definition) might be revealed only by its use in another statement.

A test suite T for a program P satisfies the all DU pairs adequacy criterion iff, for each DU pair *du* of P, at least one test case in T exercises *du*.

Δ all DU pairs adequacy criterion

The corresponding coverage measure is the proportion of covered DU pairs:

The all DU pairs coverage $C_{DU\ pairs}$ of T for P is the fraction of DU pairs of program P exercised by at least one test case in T.

Δ all DU pairs coverage

$$C_{DU\ pairs} = \frac{\text{number of exercised DU pairs}}{\text{number of DU pairs}}$$

The all DU pairs adequacy criterion assures a finer grain coverage than statement and branch adequacy criteria. If we consider, for example, function cgi_decode, we can easily see that statement and branch coverage can be obtained by traversing the while loop no more than once, for example, with the test suite $T_{branch} = \{$"+", "%3D", "%FG", "t"$\}$ while several DU pairs cannot be covered without executing the while loop at least twice. The pairs that may remain uncovered after statement and branch coverage correspond to occurrences of different characters within the source string, and not only at the beginning of the string. For example, the DU pair ⟨37, 25⟩ for variable *eptr can be covered with a test case $TC_{DU\,pairs}$"test%3D" where the hexadecimal escape sequence occurs inside the input string, but not with "%3D." The test suite $T_{DU\,pairs}$ obtained by adding the test case $TC_{DU\,pairs}$ to the test suite T_{branch} satisfies the all DU pairs adequacy criterion, since it adds both the cases of a hexadecimal escape sequence and an ASCII character occurring inside the input string.

One DU pair might belong to many different execution paths. The *All DU paths adequacy criterion* extends the all DU pairs criterion by requiring each simple (non looping) DU path to be traversed at least once, thus including the different ways of pairing definitions and uses. This can reveal a fault by exercising a path on which a definition of a variable should have appeared but was omitted.

Δ all DU paths adequacy criterion

A test suite T for a program P satisfies the all DU paths adequacy criterion iff, for each simple DU path dp of P, there exists at least one test case in T that exercises a path that includes dp.

The corresponding coverage measure is the fraction of covered simple DU paths:

Δ all DU paths coverage

The all DU pair coverage $C_{DU\,paths}$ of T for P is the fraction of simple DU paths of program P executed by at least one test case in T.

$$C_{DU\,paths} = \frac{\text{number of exercised simple DU paths}}{\text{number of simple DU paths}}$$

The test suite $T_{DU\,pairs}$ does not satisfy the all DU paths adequacy criterion, since both DU pairs $\langle 37,37\rangle$ for variable eptr and $\langle 36,23\rangle$ for variable dptr correspond each to two simple DU paths, and in both cases one of the two paths is not covered by test cases in $T_{DU\,pairs}$. The uncovered paths correspond to a test case that includes character '+' occurring within the input string (e.g., test case $TC_{DU\,paths}$ = "test+case").

Although the number of simple DU paths is often quite reasonable, in the worst case it can be exponential in the size of the program unit. This can occur when the code between the definition and use of a particular variable is essentially irrelevant to that variable, but contains many control paths, as illustrated by the example in Figure 13.2: The code between the definition of ch in line 2 and its use in line 12 does not modify ch, but the all DU paths coverage criterion would require that each of the 256 paths be exercised.

We normally consider both *All DU paths* and *All DU pairs adequacy criteria* as relatively powerful and yet practical test adequacy criteria, as depicted in Figure 12.8 on page 231. However, in some cases, even the all DU pairs criterion may be too costly. In these cases, we can refer to a coarser grain data flow criterion, the *All definitions adequacy criterion*, which requires pairing each definition with at least one use.

Δ all definitions adequacy criterion

A test suite T for a program P satisfies the all definitions adequacy criterion for P iff, for each definition def of P, there exists at least one test case in T that exercises a DU pair that includes def.

```
void countBits(char ch) {
    int count = 0;
    if (ch & 1) ++count;
    if (ch & 2) ++count;
    if (ch & 4) ++count;
    if (ch & 8) ++count;
    if (ch & 16) ++count;
    if (ch & 32) ++count;
    if (ch & 64) ++count;
    if (ch & 128) ++count;
    printf("'%c' (0X%02x) has %d bits set to 1\n",
        ch, ch, count);
}
```

Figure 13.2: A C procedure with a large number of DU paths. The number of DU paths for variable ch *is exponential in the number of* if *statements, because the use in each increment and in the final print statement can be paired with any of the preceding definitions. The number of DU paths for variable* count *is the same as the number of DU pairs. For variable* ch*, there is only one DU pair, matching the procedure header with the final print statement, but there are 256 definition-clear paths between those statements — exponential in the number of intervening* if *statements.*

The corresponding coverage measure is the proportion of covered definitions, where we say a definition is covered only if the value is used before being killed:

Δ all definitions coverage

The all definitions coverage C_{Def} of T for P is the fraction of definitions of program P covered by at least one test case in T.

$$C_{defs} = \frac{\text{number of covered definitions}}{\text{number of definitions}}$$

13.4 Data Flow Coverage with Complex Structures

Like all static analysis techniques, data flow analysis approximates the effects of program executions. It suffers imprecision in modeling dynamic constructs, in particular dynamic access to storage, such as indexed access to array elements or pointer access to dynamically allocated storage. We have seen in Chapter 6 (page 94) that the proper treatment of potential aliases involving indexes and pointers depends on the use to which analysis results will be put. For the purpose of choosing test cases, some risk of underestimating alias sets may be preferable to gross overestimation or very expensive analysis.

The precision of data flow analysis depends on the precision of alias information used in the analysis. Alias analysis requires a trade-off between precision and compu-

```
void pointer_abuse() {
    int i=5, j=10, k=20;
    int *p, *q;
    p = &j + 1;
    q = &k;
    *p = 30;
    *q = *q + 55;
    printf("p=%d, q=%d\n", *p, *q);
}
```

Figure 13.3: Pointers to objects in the program stack can create essentially arbitrary definition-use associations, particularly when combined with pointer arithmetic as in this example.

tational expense, with significant overestimation of alias sets for approaches that can be practically applied to real programs. In the case of data flow testing, imprecision can be mitigated by specializing the alias analysis to identification of definition-clear paths between a potentially matched definition and use. We do not need to compute aliases for all possible behaviors, but only along particular control flow paths. The risk of underestimating alias sets in a local analysis is acceptable considering the application in choosing good test cases rather than offering hard guarantees of a property.

In the cgi_decode example we have made use of information that would require either extra guidance from the test designer or a sophisticated tool for data flow and alias analysis. We may know, from a global analysis, that the parameters encoded and decoded never refer to the same or overlapping memory regions, and we may infer that initially eptr and dptr likewise refer to disjoint regions of memory, over the whole range of values that the two pointers take. Lacking this information, a simple static data flow analysis might consider *dptr a potential alias of *eptr and might therefore consider the assignment *dptr = *eptr a potential definition of both *dptr and *eptr. These spurious definitions would give rise to infeasible DU pairs, which produce test obligations that can never be satisfied. A local analysis that instead assumes (without verification) that *eptr and *dptr are distinct could fail to require an important test case if they can be aliases. Such underestimation may be preferable to creating too many infeasible test obligations.

A good alias analysis can greatly improve the applicability of data flow testing but cannot eliminate all problems. Undisciplined use of dynamic access to storage can make precise alias analysis extremely hard or impossible. For example, the use of pointer arithmetic in the program fragment of Figure 13.3 results in aliases that depend on the way the compiler arranges variables in memory.

13.5 The Infeasibility Problem

Not all elements of a program are executable, as discussed in Section 12.8 of Chapter 12. The path-oriented nature of data flow testing criteria aggravates the problem since infeasibility creates test obligations not only for isolated unexecutable elements, but also for infeasible combinations of feasible elements.

Complex data structures may amplify the infeasibility problem by adding infeasible paths as a result of alias computation. For example, while we can determine that x[i] is an alias of x[j] exactly when i = j, we may not be able to determine whether i can be equal to j in any possible program execution.

Fortunately, the problem of infeasible paths is usually modest for the all definitions and all DU pairs adequacy criteria, and one can typically achieve levels of coverage comparable to those achievable with simpler criteria like statement and branch adequacy during unit testing. The all DU paths adequacy criterion, on the other hand, often requires much larger numbers of control flow paths. It presents a greater problem in distinguishing feasible from infeasible paths and should therefore be used with discretion.

Open Research Issues

Data flow test adequacy criteria are close to the border between techniques that can be applied at low cost with simple tools and techniques that offer more power but at much higher cost. While in principle data flow test coverage can be applied at modest cost (at least up to the all DU adequacy criterion), it demands more sophisticated tool support than test coverage monitoring tools based on control flow alone.

Fortunately, data flow analysis and alias analysis have other important applications. Improved support for data flow testing may come at least partly as a side benefit of research in the programming languages and compilers community. In particular, finding a good balance of cost and precision in data flow and alias analysis across procedure boundaries (interprocedural or “whole program” analysis) is an active area of research.

The problems presented by pointers and complex data structures cannot be ignored. In particular, modern object-oriented languages like Java use reference semantics — an object reference is essentially a pointer — and so alias analysis (preferably interprocedural) is a prerequisite for applying data flow analysis to object-oriented programs.

Further Reading

The concept of test case selection using data flow information was apparently first suggested in 1976 by Herman [Her76], but that original paper is not widely accessible. The more widely known version of data flow test adequacy criteria was developed independently by Rapps and Weyuker [RW85] and by Laski and Korel [LK83]. The variety of data flow testing criteria is much broader than the handful of criteria described in this chapter; Clarke et al. present a formal comparison of several criteria [CPRZ89]. Frankl and Weyuker consider the problem of infeasible paths and how they affect the relative power of data flow and other structural test adequacy criteria [FW93].

Marx and Frankl consider the problem of aliases and application of alias analysis on individual program paths [MF96]. A good example of modern empirical research on costs and effectiveness of structural test adequacy criteria, and data flow test coverage in particular, is Frankl and Iakounenko [FI98].

Related Topics

The next chapter discusses model-based testing. Section 14.4 shows how control and data flow models can be used to derive test cases from specifications. Chapter 15 illustrates the use of data flow analysis for structural testing of object oriented programs.

Readers interested in the use of data flow for program analysis can proceed with Chapter 19.

Exercises

13.1. Sometimes a distinction is made between uses of values in predicates (*p-uses*) and other "computational" uses in statements (*c-uses*). New criteria can be defined using that distinction, for example:

all p-use some c-use: for all definitions and uses, exercise all (def, p-use) pairs and at least one (def, c-use) pair

all c-use some p-use: for all definitions and uses, exercise all (def, c-use) pairs and at least one (def, p-use) pair

(a) provide a precise definition of these criteria.

(b) describe the differences in the test suites derived applying the different criteria to function cgi_decode in Figure 13.1.

13.2. Demonstrate the subsume relation between all p-use some c-use, all c-use some p-use, all DU pairs, all DU paths and all definitions.

13.3. How would you treat the buf array in the transduce procedure shown in Figure 16.1?

Chapter 14

Model-Based Testing

Models are often used to express requirements, and embed both structure and fault information that can help generate test case specifications. Control flow and data flow testing are based on models extracted from program code. Models can also be extracted from specifications and design, allowing us to make use of additional information about intended behavior. Model-based testing consists in using or deriving models of expected behavior to produce test case specifications that can reveal discrepancies between actual program behavior and the model.

Required Background

- Chapter 10
  The rationale of systematic approaches to functional testing is a key motivation for the techniques presented in this chapter.
- Chapters 12 and 13
  The material on control and data flow graphs is required to understand Section 14.4, but it is not necessary to comprehend the rest of the chapter.

14.1 Overview

Combinatorial approaches to specification-based testing (Chapter 11) primarily select combinations of orthogonal choices. They can accommodate constraints among choices, but their strength is in systematically distributing combinations of (purportedly) independent choices. The human effort in applying those techniques is primarily in characterizing the elements to be combined and constraints on their combination, often starting from informal or semistructured specifications.

Specifications with more structure can be exploited to help test designers identify input elements, constraints, and significant combinations. The structure may be explicit and available in a specification, for example, in the form of a finite state machine or grammar. It may be derivable from a semiformal model, such as class and object diagrams, with some guidance by the designer. Even if the specification is expressed in natural language, it may be worthwhile for the test designer to manually derive one or more models from it, to make the structure explicit and suitable for automatic derivation of test case specifications.

Models can be expressed in many ways. Formal models (e.g., finite state machines or grammars) provide enough information to allow one to automatically generate test cases. Semiformal models (e.g, class and object diagrams) may require some human judgment to generate test cases. This chapter discusses some of the most common models used to express requirements specifications. Models used for object-oriented design are discussed in Chapter 15.

Models can provide two kinds of help. They describe the structure of the input space and thus allow test designers to take advantage of work done in software requirements analysis and design. Moreover, discrepancies from the model can be used as an implicit fault model to help identify boundary and error cases.

The utility of models for generating test cases is an important factor in determining the cost-effectiveness of producing formal or semiformal specifications. The return on investment for model building should be evaluated not only in terms of reduced specification errors and avoided misinterpretation, but also improved effectiveness and reduced effort and cost in test design.

14.2 Deriving Test Cases from Finite State Machines

Finite state machines are often used to specify sequences of interactions between a system and its environment. State machine specifications in one form or another are common for control and reactive systems, such as embedded systems, communication protocols, menu-driven applications, and threads of control in a system with multiple threads or processes.

Specifications may be expressed directly as some form of finite state machine. For example, embedded control systems are frequently specified with Statecharts, communication protocols are commonly described with SDL diagrams, and menu driven applications are sometimes modeled with simple diagrams representing states and transitions.

Sometimes the finite state essence of systems is left implicit in informal specifications. For instance, the informal specification of feature *Maintenance* of the Chipmunk Web site given in Figure 14.1 describes a set of interactions between the maintenance system and its environment that can be modeled as transitions through a finite set of process states. The finite state nature of the interaction is made explicit by the finite state machine shown in Figure 14.2. Note that some transitions appear to be labeled by conditions rather than events, but they can be interpreted as shorthand for an event in which the condition becomes true or is discovered (e.g., "lack component" is shorthand for "discover that a required component is not in stock").

Many control or interactive systems have a potentially infinite set of states. Fortunately, the non-finite state parts of the specification are often simple enough that finite state machines remain a useful model for testing as well as specification. For example, communication protocols are frequently specified using finite state machines, often

Maintenance: The *Maintenance* function records the history of items undergoing maintenance.

If the product is covered by warranty or maintenance contract, maintenance can be requested either by calling the maintenance toll free number, or through the Web site, or by bringing the item to a designated maintenance station.

If the maintenance is requested by phone or Web site and the customer is a US or EU resident, the item is picked up at the customer site, otherwise, the customer shall ship the item with an express courier.

If the maintenance contract number provided by the customer is not valid, the item follows the procedure for items not covered by warranty.

If the product is not covered by warranty or maintenance contract, maintenance can be requested only by bringing the item to a maintenance station. The maintenance station informs the customer of the estimated costs for repair. Maintenance starts only when the customer accepts the estimate. If the customer does not accept the estimate, the product is returned to the customer.

Small problems can be repaired directly at the maintenance station. If the maintenance station cannot solve the problem, the product is sent to the maintenance regional headquarters (if in US or EU) or to the maintenance main headquarters (otherwise).

If the maintenance regional headquarters cannot solve the problem, the product is sent to the maintenance main headquarters.

Maintenance is suspended if some components are not available.

Once repaired, the product is returned to the customer.

Figure 14.1: Functional specification of feature Maintenance *of the Chipmunk Web site.*

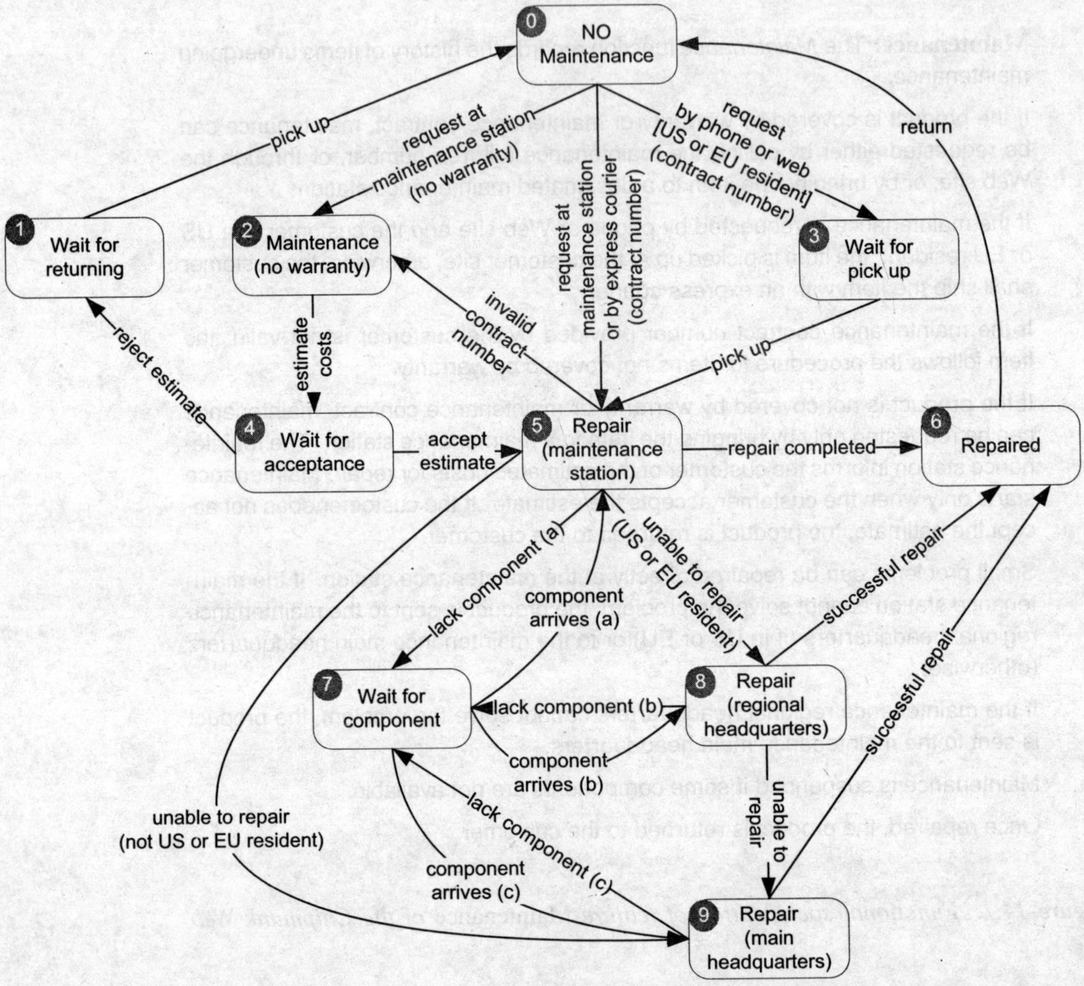

Figure 14.2: A finite state machine corresponding to functionality Maintenance *specified in Figure 14.1*

	T-Cover
TC-1	0 – 2 – 4 – 1 – 0
TC-2	0 – 5 – 2 – 4 – 5 – 6 – 0
TC-3	0 – 3 – 5 – 9 – 6 – 0
TC-4	0 – 3 – 5 – 7 – 5 – 8 – 7 – 8 – 9 – 7 – 9 – 6 – 0

States numbers refer to Figure 14.2. For example, TC-1 represents the path (0,2), (2,4), (4,1), (1,0).

Table 14.1: A test suite satisfying the transition coverage criterion with respect to the finite state machine of Figure 14.2

with some extensions that make them not truly finite state. Even a state machine that simply receives a message on one port and then sends the same message on another port is not really finite state unless the set of possible messages is finite, but is often rendered as a finite state machine, ignoring the contents of the exchanged messages.

State-machine specifications can be used both to guide test selection and in construction of an oracle that judges whether each observed behavior is correct. There are many approaches for generating test cases from finite state machines, but most are variations on a basic strategy of checking each state transition. One way to understand this basic strategy is to consider that each transition is essentially a specification of a precondition and postcondition, for example, a transition from state S to state T on stimulus i means "*if* the system is in state S and receives stimulus i, *then* after reacting it will be in state T." For instance, the transition labeled *accept estimate* from state *Wait for acceptance* to state *Repair (maintenance station)* of Figure 14.2 indicates that if an item is on hold waiting for the customer to accept an estimate of repair costs, and the customer accepts the estimate, then the item is designated as eligible for repair.

A faulty system could violate any of these precondition, postcondition pairs, so each should be tested. For example, the state *Repair (maintenance station)* can be arrived at through three different transitions, and each should be checked.

Details of the approach taken depend on several factors, including whether system states are directly observable or must be inferred from stimulus/response sequences, whether the state machine specification is complete as given or includes additional, implicit transitions, and whether the size of the (possibly augmented) state machine is modest or very large.

The *transition coverage* criterion requires each transition in a finite state model to be traversed at least once. Test case specifications for transition coverage are often given as state sequences or transition sequences. For example, the test suite *T-Cover* in Table 14.1 is a set of four paths, each beginning at the initial state, which together cover all transitions of the finite state machine of Figure 14.2. *T-Cover* thus satisfies the transition coverage criterion.

Δ transition coverage

The transition coverage criterion depends on the assumption that the finite state machine model is a sufficient representation of all the "important" state, for example, that transitions out of a state do not depend on how one reached that state. Although it can be considered a logical flaw, in practice one often finds state machines that exhibit "history sensitivity," (i.e., the transitions from a state depend on the path by which one reached that state). For example, in Figure 14.2, the transition taken from state *Wait for component* when the component becomes available depends on how the state was entered. This is a flaw in the model — there really should be three distinct *Wait for component* states, each with a well-defined action when the component becomes available. However, sometimes it is more expedient to work with a flawed state machine model than to repair it, and in that case test suites may be based on more than the simple transition coverage criterion.

Coverage criteria designed to cope with history sensitivity include *single state path coverage*, *single transition path coverage*, and *boundary interior loop coverage*. Each of these criteria requires execution of paths that include certain subpaths in the FSM. The *single state path coverage* criterion requires each subpath that traverses states at most once to be included in a path that is exercised. The *single transition path coverage* criterion requires each subpath that traverses transitions at most once to be included in a path that is exercised. The *boundary interior loop coverage* criterion requires each distinct loop of the state machine to be exercised the minimum, an intermediate, and the maximum or a large number of times[1]. These criteria may be practical for very small and simple finite state machine specifications, but since the number of even simple paths (without repeating states) can grow exponentially with the number of states, they are often impractical.

Δ single state path coverage

Δ single transition path coverage

Δ boundary interior loop coverage

Specifications given as finite state machines are typically incomplete: They do not include a transition for every possible (state, stimulus) pair. Often the missing transitions are implicitly error cases. Depending on the system, the appropriate interpretation may be that these are *don't care* transitions (since no transition is specified, the system may do anything or nothing), *self* transitions (since no transition is specified, the system should remain in the same state), or (most commonly) *error* transitions that enter a distinguished state and possibly trigger some error-handling procedure. In at least the latter two cases, thorough testing includes the implicit as well as the explicit state transitions. No special techniques are required: The implicit transitions are simply added to the representation before test cases are selected.

The presence of implicit transitions with a *don't care* interpretation is typically an implicit or explicit statement that those transitions are impossible (e.g., because of physical constraints). For example, in the specification of the maintenance procedure of Figure 14.2, the effect of event *lack of component* is specified only for the states that represent repairs in progress because only in those states might we discover a needed is missing.

Sometimes it is possible to test *don't care* transitions even if they are believed to be impossible in the fielded system, because the system does not prevent the triggering event from occurring in a test configuration. If it is not possible to produce test cases for the *don't care* transitions, then it may be appropriate to pass them to other validation or verification activities, for example, by including explicit assumptions in a requirements or specification document that will undergo inspection.

[1] The boundary interior path coverage was originally proposed for structural coverage of program control flow, and is described in Chapter 12.

Terminology: Predicates and Conditions

A *predicate* is a function with a Boolean (*True* or *False*) value. When the input argument of the predicate is clear, particularly when it describes some property of the input of a program, we often leave it implicit. For example, the actual representation of account types in an information system might be as three-letter codes, but in a specification we may not be concerned with that representation — we know only that there is some predicate *educational-account* that is either *True* or *False*.

A *basic condition* is a single predicate that cannot be decomposed further.

A *complex condition* is made up of basic conditions, combined with Boolean connectives.

The *Boolean connectives* include "and" ($\wedge$), "or" ($\vee$), "not" ($\neg$), and several less common derived connectives such as "implies" and "exclusive or."

14.3 Testing Decision Structures

Specifications are often expressed as decision structures, such as sets of conditions on input values and corresponding actions or results. A model of the decision structure can be used to choose test cases that may reveal discrepancies between the decisions actually made in the code and the intended decision structure.

The example specification of Figure 14.3 describes outputs that depend on type of account (either educational, or business, or individual), amount of current and yearly purchases, and availability of special prices. These can be considered as Boolean conditions, for example, the condition *educational account* is either true or false (even if the type of account is actually represented in some other manner). Outputs can be described as Boolean expressions over the inputs, for example, the output *no discount* can be associated with the Boolean expression

$$
\begin{array}{rl}
(& \text{individual account} \\
\wedge\neg & \text{current purchase} > \text{tier 1 individual threshold} \\
\wedge\neg & \text{special offer price} < \text{individual scheduled price} \quad) \\
\vee\ (& \text{business account} \\
\wedge\neg & \text{current purchase} > \text{tier 1 business threshold} \\
\wedge\neg & \text{current purchase} > \text{tier 1 business yearly threshold} \\
\wedge\neg & \text{special offer price} < \text{business scheduled price} \quad)
\end{array}
$$

When functional specifications can be given as Boolean expressions, we can apply any of the condition testing approaches described in Chapter 12, Section 12.4. A good test suite should at least exercise all elementary conditions occurring in the expression. For simple conditions we might derive test case specifications for all possible combinations of truth values of the elementary conditions. For complex formulas, when testing all 2^n combinations of n elementary conditions is apt to be too expensive, the modified decision/condition coverage criterion (page 12.4) derives a small set of test conditions such that each elementary condition independently affects the outcome.

We can produce different models of the decision structure of a specification depending on the original specification and on the technique we want to use for deriving

Pricing: The *pricing* function determines the adjusted price of a configuration for a particular customer. The scheduled price of a configuration is the sum of the scheduled price of the model and the scheduled price of each component in the configuration. The adjusted price is either the scheduled price, if no discounts are applicable, or the scheduled price less any applicable discounts.

There are three price schedules and three corresponding discount schedules, *Business*, *Educational*, and *Individual*. The Business price and discount schedules apply only if the order is to be charged to a business account in good standing. The Educational price and discount schedules apply to educational institutions. The Individual price and discount schedules apply to all other customers. Account classes and rules for establishing business and educational accounts are described further in [...].

A discount schedule includes up to three discount levels, in addition to the possibility of "no discount." Each discount level is characterized by two threshold values, a value for the current purchase (configuration schedule price) and a cumulative value for purchases over the preceding 12 months (sum of adjusted price).

Educational prices The adjusted price for a purchase charged to an educational account in good standing is the scheduled price from the educational price schedule. No further discounts apply.

Business account discounts Business discounts depend on the size of the current purchase as well as business in the preceding 12 months. A tier 1 discount is applicable if the scheduled price of the current order exceeds the tier 1 current order threshold, or if total paid invoices to the account over the preceding 12 months exceeds the tier 1 year cumulative value threshold. A tier 2 discount is applicable if the current order exceeds the tier 2 current order threshold, or if total paid invoices to the account over the preceding 12 months exceeds the tier 2 cumulative value threshold. A tier 2 discount is also applicable if both the current order and 12 month cumulative payments exceed the tier 1 thresholds.

Individual discounts Purchase by individuals and by others without an established account in good standing is based on current value alone (not on cumulative purchases). A tier 1 individual discount is applicable if the scheduled price of the configuration in the current order exceeds the tier 1 current order threshold. A tier 2 individual discount is applicable if the scheduled price of the configuration exceeds the tier 2 current order threshold.

Special-price nondiscountable offers Sometimes a complete configuration is offered at a special, non-discountable price. When a special, nondiscountable price is available for a configuration, the adjusted price is the nondiscountable price or the regular price after any applicable discounts, whichever is less.

Figure 14.3: The functional specification of feature Pricing *of the Chipmunk Web site.*

test cases. If the original specification is expressed informally as in Figure 14.3, we can transform it into either a Boolean expression, a graph, or a tabular model before applying a test case generation technique.

Techniques for deriving test case specifications from decision structures were originally developed for graph models, and in particular cause-effect graphs, which have been used since the early 1970s. Cause-effect graphs are tedious to derive and do not scale well to complex specifications. Tables, on the other hand, are easy to work with and scale well.

The rows of a *decision table* represent basic conditions, and columns represent combinations of basic conditions. The last row of the table indicates the expected outputs for each combination. Cells of the table are labeled either *True*, *False*, or **don't care** (usually written –), to indicate the truth value of the basic condition. Thus, each column is equivalent to a logical expression joining the required values (negated, in the case of *False* entries) and omitting the basic conditions with **don't care** values.[2]

Decision tables can be augmented with a set of *constraints* that limit the possible combinations of basic conditions. A constraint language can be based on Boolean logic. Often it is useful to add some shorthand notations for common combinations such as *at-most-one(C1, ..., Cn)* and *exactly-one(C1, ..., Cn)*, which are tedious to express with the standard Boolean connectives.

Figure 14.4 shows the decision table for the functional specification of feature *pricing* of the Chipmunk Web site presented in Figure 14.3.

The informal specification of Figure 14.3 identifies three customer profiles: *educational*, *business*, and *individual*. Figure 14.4 has only rows *Educational account (EduAc)* and *Business account (BusAc)*. The choice *individual* corresponds to the combination *False*, *False* for choices *EduAc* and *BusAc*, and is thus redundant. The informal specification of Figure 14.3 indicates different discount policies depending on the relation between the current purchase and two progressive thresholds for the current purchase and the yearly cumulative purchase. These cases correspond to rows 3 through 6 of Figure 14.4. Conditions on thresholds that do not correspond to individual rows in the table can be defined by suitable combinations of values for these rows. Finally, the informal specification of Figure 14.3 distinguishes the cases in which special offer prices do not exceed either the scheduled or the tier 1 or tier 2 prices. Rows 7 through 9 of the table, suitably combined, capture all possible cases of special prices without redundancy.

Constraints formalize the compatibility relations among different basic conditions listed in the table. For example, a cumulative purchase exceeding threshold tier 2 also exceeds threshold tier 1.

The *basic condition adequacy criterion* requires generation of a test case specification for each column in the table. *Don't care* entries of the table can be filled out arbitrarily, as long as constraints are not violated.

Δ basic condition coverage

The *compound condition adequacy criterion* requires a test case specification for each combination of truth values of basic conditions. The compound condition ade-

Δ compound condition coverage

[2] The set of columns sharing a label is therefore equivalent to a logical expression in sum-of-products form.

	Education		Individual					
EduAc	T	T	F	F	F	F	F	F
BusAc	-	-	F	F	F	F	F	F
CP > CT1	-	-	F	F	T	T	-	-
YP > YT1	-	-	-	-	-	-	-	-
CP > CT2	-	-	-	-	F	F	T	T
YP > YT2	-	-	-	-	-	-	-	-
SP > Sc	F	T	F	T	-	-	-	-
SP > T1	-	-	-	-	F	T	-	-
SP > T2	-	-	-	-	-	-	F	T
Out	Edu	SP	ND	SP	T1	SP	T2	SP

	Business											
EduAc	-	-	-	-	-	-	-	-	-	-	-	-
BusAc	T	T	T	T	T	T	T	T	T	T	T	T
CP > CT1	F	F	T	T	F	F	T	T	-	-	-	-
YP > YT1	F	F	F	F	T	T	T	T	-	-	-	-
CP > CT2	-	-	F	F	-	-	-	-	T	T	-	-
YP > YT2	-	-	-	-	F	F	-	-	-	-	T	T
SP > Sc	F	T	-	-	-	-	-	-	-	-	-	-
SP > T1	-	-	F	T	F	T	-	-	-	-	-	-
SP > T2	-	-	-	-	-	-	F	T	F	T	F	T
Out	ND	SP	T1	SP	T1	SP	T2	SP	T2	SP	T2	SP

Constraints

at-most-one(EduAc, BusAc)
at-most-one(YP < YT1, YP > YT2)
YP > YT2 ⇒ YP > YT1
at-most-one(CP < CT1, CP > CT2)
CP > CT2 ⇒ CP > CT1
at-most-one(SP < T1, SP > T2)
SP > T2 ⇒ SP > T1

Abbreviations

EduAc	Educational account	Edu	Educational price
BusAc	Business account	ND	No discount
CP > CT1	Current purchase greater than threshold 1	T1	Tier 1
YP > YT1	Year cumulative purchase greater than threshold 1	T2	Tier 2
CP > CT2	Current purchase greater than threshold 2	SP	Special Price
YP > YT2	Year cumulative purchase greater than threshold 2		
SP > Sc	Special Price better than scheduled price		
SP > T1	Special Price better than tier 1		
SP > T2	Special Price better than tier 2		

Figure 14.4: A decision table for the functional specification of feature Pricing *of the Chipmunk Web site of Figure 14.3.*

quacy criterion generates a number of cases exponential in the number of basic conditions (2^n combinations for n conditions) and can thus be applied only to small sets of basic conditions.

For the *modified condition/decision adequacy criterion* (MC/DC), each column in the table represents a test case specification. In addition, for each of the original columns, MC/DC generates new columns by modifying each of the cells containing *True* or *False*. If modifying a truth value in one column results in a test case specification consistent with an existing column (agreeing in all places where neither is *don't care*), the two test cases are represented by one merged column, provided they can be merged without violating constraints.

Δ modified condition/decision coverage

The MC/DC criterion formalizes the intuitive idea that a thorough test suite would not only test *positive* combinations of values — combinations that lead to specified outputs — but also *negative* combinations of values — combinations that differ from the specified ones — thus, they should produce different outputs, in some cases among the specified ones, in some other cases leading to error conditions.

Applying MC/DC to column 1 of Figure 14.4 generates two additional columns: one for *Educational Account* = *False* and *Special Price better than scheduled price* = *False*, and the other for *Educational Account* = *True* and *Special Price better than scheduled price* = *True*. Both columns are already in the table (columns 3 and 2, respectively) and thus need not be added.

Similarly, from column 2, we generate two additional columns corresponding to *Educational Account* = *False* and *Special Price better than scheduled price* = *True*, and *Educational Account* = *True* and *Special Price better than scheduled price* = *False*, also already in the table.

Generation of a new column for each possible variation of the Boolean values in the columns, varying exactly one value for each new column, produces 78 new columns, 21 of which can be merged with columns already in the table. Figure 14.5 shows a table obtained by suitably joining the generated columns with the existing ones. Many **don't care** cells from the original table are assigned either *True* or *False* values, to allow merging of different columns or to obey constraints. The few **don't-care** entries left can be set randomly to obtain a complete test case.

There are many ways of merging columns that generate different tables. The table in Figure 14.5 may not be the optimal one — the one with the fewest columns. The objective in test design is not to find an optimal test suite, but rather to produce a cost effective test suite with an acceptable trade-off between the cost of generating and executing test cases and the effectiveness of the tests.

The table in Figure 14.5 fixes the entries as required by the constraints, while the initial table in Figure 14.4 does not. Keeping constraints separate from the table corresponding to the initial specification increases the number of **don't care** entries in the original table, which in turn increases the opportunity for merging columns when generating new cases with the MC/DC criterion. For example, if *business account (BusAc)* = *False*, the constraint at-most-one(EduAc, BusAc) can be satisfied by assigning either *True* or *False* to entry *educational account*. Fixing either choice prematurely may later make merging with a newly generated column impossible.

EduAc	T	T	F	F	F	F	F	F	F	F	F	F	F	F	F
BusAc	F	F	F	F	F	F	F	F	T	T	T	T	T	T	T
CP > CT1	T	T	F	F	T	T	T	T	F	F	T	T	F	F	T
YP > YT1	F	-	F	-	-	F	T	T	F	F	F	F	T	T	T
CP > CT2	F	F	F	F	F	F	T	T	F	F	F	F	F	F	F
YP > YT2	-	-	-	-	-	-	-	-	-	-	-	-	F	F	F
SP > Sc	F	T	F	T	F	T	-	-	F	T	F	-	F	T	-
SP > T1	F	T	F	T	F	T	F	T	F	T	F	T	F	T	F
SP > T2	F	-	F	-	F	-	F	T	F	-	F	-	F	-	F
Out	Edu	SP	ND	SP	T1	SP	T2	SP	ND	SP	T1	SP	T1	SP	T2

EduAc	F	F	F	F	F	T	T	T	T	F	-
BusAc	T	T	T	T	T	F	F	F	F	F	F
CP > CT1	T	T	T	F	F	F	F	T	-	-	F
YP > YT1	T	F	F	T	T	T	-	-	-	T	T
CP > CT2	F	T	T	F	F	F	F	T	T	F	F
YP > YT2	F	-	-	T	T	F	-	-	-	T	F
SP > Sc	T	-	T	-	T	F	T	-	-	-	-
SP > T1	T	F	T	F	T	F	-	-	T	T	T
SP > T2	T	F	T	F	T	F	F	F	T	T	-
Out	SP	T2	SP	T2	SP	Edu	SP	Edu	SP	SP	SP

Abbreviations

EduAc	Educational account	Edu	Educational price
BusAc	Business account	ND	No discount
CP > CT1	Current purchase greater than threshold 1	T1	Tier 1
YP > YT1	Year cumulative purchase greater than threshold 1	T2	Tier 2
CP > CT2	Current purchase greater than threshold 2	SP	Special Price
YP > YT2	Year cumulative purchase greater than threshold 2		
SP > Sc	Special Price better than scheduled price		
SP > T1	Special Price better than tier 1		
SP > T2	Special Price better than tier 2		

Figure 14.5: The set of test cases generated for feature Pricing *of the Chipmunk Web site applying the modified adequacy criterion.*

14.4 Deriving Test Cases from Control and Data Flow Graphs

Functional specifications are seldom given as control or data flow graphs, but sometimes they describe a set of mutually dependent steps to be executed in a given (partial) order, and can thus be modeled with flow graphs.

The specification in Figure 14.6 describes the Chipmunk functionality that prepares orders for shipping. The specification indicates a set of steps to check the validity of fields in the order form. Type and validity of some of the values depend on other fields in the form. For example, shipping methods are different for domestic and international customers, and payment methods depend on customer type.

The informal specification in Figure 14.6 can be modeled with a control flow graph, where the nodes represent computations and branches represent control flow consistent with the dependencies among computations, as illustrated in Figure 14.7. Given a control or a data flow graph model, we can generate test case specifications using the criteria originally devised for structural testing and described in Chapters 12 and 13.

Control flow testing criteria require test cases that exercise all elements of a particular kind in a graph model. The *node adequacy criterion* requires each node to be exercised at least once, and corresponds to statement testing. It is easy to verify that test suite *T-node* in Figure 14.8, consisting of test case specifications TC-1 and TC-2, causes all nodes of the control flow graph of Figure 14.7 to be traversed, and thus *T-node* satisfies the node adequacy criterion.

Δ node adequacy criterion

The *branch adequacy criterion* requires each branch to be exercised at least once: each edge of the graph must be traversed by at least one test case. Test suite *T-branch* (Figure 14.9) covers all branches of the control flow graph of Figure 14.7 and thus satisfies the branch adequacy criterion.

Δ branch adequacy criterion

In principle, other test adequacy criteria described in Chapters 12 and 13 can be applied to more complex control structures derived from specifications, such as loops. A good functional specification should rarely result in a complex control structure, but data flow testing may be useful at a much coarser structure (e.g., to test interaction of transactions through a database).

14.5 Deriving Test Cases from Grammars

Functional specifications for complex documents or domain-specific notations, as well as for conventional compilers and interpreters, are often structured as an annotated grammar or set of regular expressions. Test suites can be systematically derived from these grammatical structures.

The informal specification of the Chipmunk Web site advanced search, shown in Figure 14.10, defines the syntax of a search pattern. Not surprisingly, this specification can easily be expressed as a grammar. Figure 14.11 expresses the specification as a grammar in Backus Naur Form (BNF).

A second example is given in Figure 14.12, which specifies a *product configuration* of the Chipmunk Web site. In this case, the syntactic structure of *product configuration*

Process shipping order: The *Process shipping order* function checks the validity of orders and prepares the receipt.

A valid order contains the following data:

cost of goods If the cost of goods is less than the minimum processable order (*MinOrder*), then the order is invalid.

shipping address The address includes name, address, city, postal code, and country.

preferred shipping method If the address is domestic, the shipping method must be either *land freight*, or *expedited land freight*, or *overnight air*. If the address is international, the shipping method must be either *air freight* or *expedited air freight*; a shipping cost is computed based on address and shipping method.

type of customer A customer can be *individual*, *business*, or *educational*.

preferred method of payment Individual customers can use only credit cards, while business and educational customers can choose between *credit card* and *invoice*.

card information If the method of payment is credit card, fields credit card number, name on card, expiration date, and billing address, if different from shipping address, must be provided. If credit card information is not valid, the user can either provide new data or abort the order.

The outputs of *Process shipping order* are

validity Validity is a Boolean output that indicates whether the order can be processed.

total charge The total charge is the sum of the value of goods and the computed shipping costs (only if validity = true).

payment status If all data are processed correctly and the credit card information is valid or the payment method is by invoice, payment status is set to valid, the order is entered, and a receipt is prepared; otherwise validity = false.

Figure 14.6: Functional specification of the feature Process shipping order *of the Chipmunk Web site.*

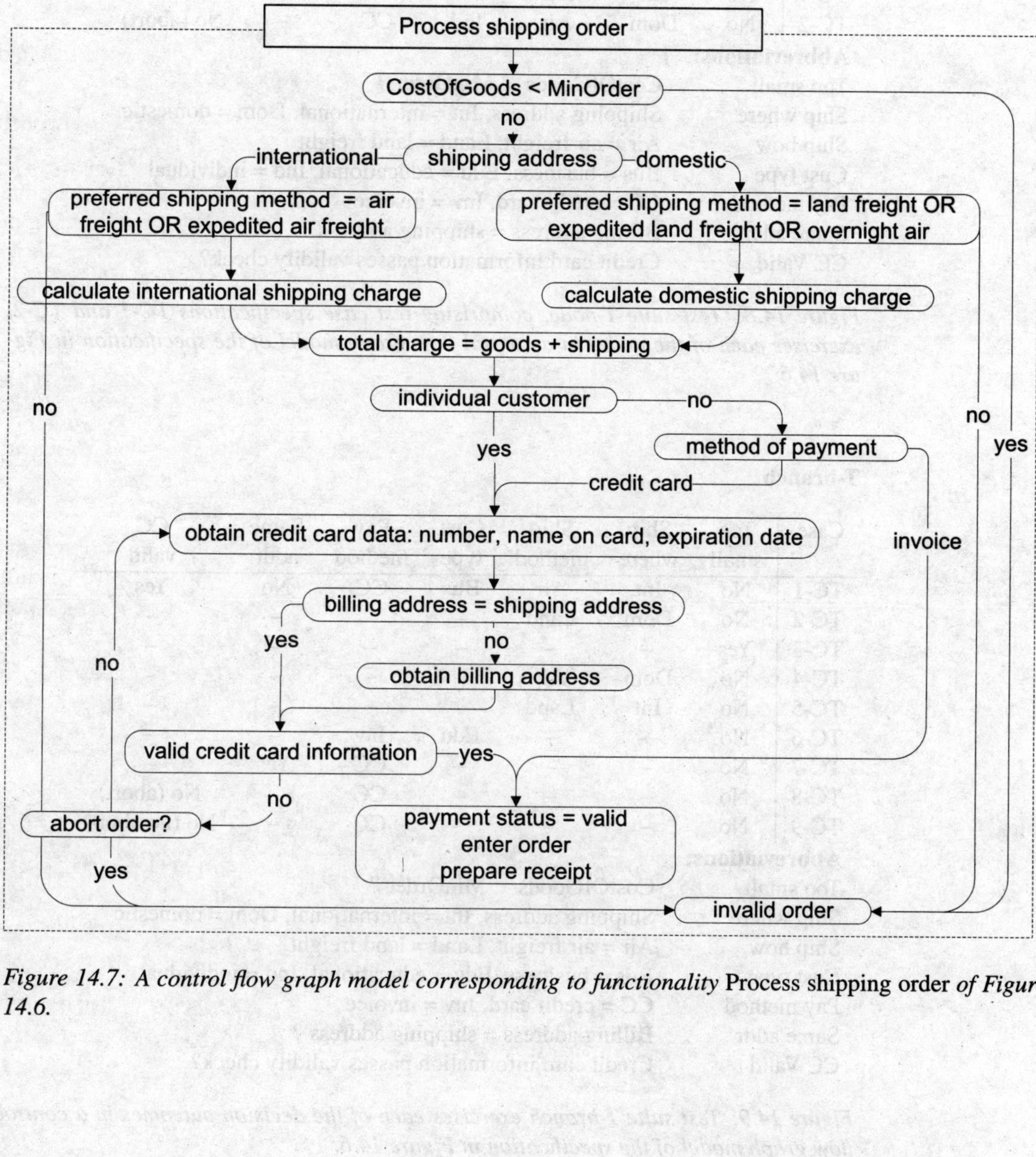

Figure 14.7: A control flow graph model corresponding to functionality Process shipping order *of Figure 14.6.*

T-node

Case	Too small	Ship where	Ship method	Cust type	Pay method	Same addr	CC valid
TC-1	No	Int	Air	Bus	CC	No	Yes
TC-2	No	Dom	Air	Ind	CC	–	No (abort)

Abbreviations:

Too small	CostOfGoods < MinOrder ?
Ship where	Shipping address, Int = international, Dom = domestic
Ship how	Air = air freight, Land = land freight
Cust type	Bus = business, Edu = educational, Ind = individual
Pay method	CC = credit card, Inv = invoice
Same addr	Billing address = shipping address ?
CC Valid	Credit card information passes validity check?

Figure 14.8: Test suite T-node, comprising test case specifications TC-1 and TC-2, exercises each of the nodes in a control flow graph model of the specification in Figure 14.6.

T-branch

Case	Too small	Ship where	Ship method	Cust type	Pay method	Same addr	CC valid
TC-1	No	Int	Air	Bus	CC	No	Yes
TC-2	No	Dom	Land	–	–	–	–
TC-3	Yes	–	–	–	–	–	–
TC-4	No	Dom	Air	–	–	–	–
TC-5	No	Int	Land	–	–	–	–
TC-6	No	–	–	Edu	Inv	–	–
TC-7	No	–	–	–	CC	Yes	–
TC-8	No	–	–	–	CC	–	No (abort)
TC-9	No	–	–	–	CC	–	No (no abort)

Abbreviations:

Too small	CostOfGoods < MinOrder ?
Ship where	Shipping address, Int = international, Dom = domestic
Ship how	Air = air freight, Land = land freight
Cust type	Bus = business, Edu = educational, Ind = individual
Pay method	CC = credit card, Inv = invoice
Same addr	Billing address = shipping address ?
CC Valid	Credit card information passes validity check?

Figure 14.9: Test suite T-branch exercises each of the decision outcomes in a control flow graph model of the specification in Figure 14.6.

Advanced search: The *Advanced search* function allows for searching elements in the Web site database.

The key for searching can be:

a simple string, i.e., a simple sequence of characters

a compound string, i.e.,

- a string terminated with character *, used as wild character, or
- a string composed of substrings included in braces and separated with commas, used to indicate alternatives

a combination of strings, i.e., a set of strings combined with the Boolean operators NOT, AND, OR, and grouped within parentheses to change the priority of operators.

Examples:

laptop The routine searches for string "laptop"

{DVD*,CD*} The routine searches for strings that start with substring "DVD" or "CD" followed by any number of characters.

NOT (C2021*) AND C20* The routine searches for strings that start with substring "C20" followed by any number of characters, except substring "21."

Figure 14.10: Functional specification of the feature Advanced search *of the Chipmunk Web site.*

⟨*search*⟩ ::= ⟨*search*⟩ ⟨*binop*⟩ ⟨*term*⟩ | `not` ⟨*search*⟩ | ⟨*term*⟩

⟨*binop*⟩ ::= `and` | `or`

⟨*term*⟩ ::= ⟨*regexp*⟩ | `(` ⟨*search*⟩ `)`

⟨*regexp*⟩ ::= *Char* ⟨*regexp*⟩ | *Char* | `{` ⟨*choices*⟩ `}` | `*`

⟨*choices*⟩ ::= ⟨*regexp*⟩ | ⟨*regexp*⟩ `,` ⟨*choices*⟩

Figure 14.11: BNF description of functionality Advanced search

is described by an XML schema, which defines an element *Model* of type *ProductConfigurationType*. XML schemata are essentially a variant of BNF, so it is not difficult to render the schema in the same BNF notation, as shown in Figure 14.11.

Grammars are well suited to represent inputs of varying and unbounded size, with recursive structures and boundary conditions. These characteristics are not easily addressed with the fixed lists of parameters required by conventional combinatoric techniques described in Chapter 11, or by other model-based techniques presented in this chapter.

Δ production coverage criterion

Generating test cases from grammar specifications is straightforward and can easily be automated. Each test case is a string generated from the grammar. To produce a string, we start from a non terminal symbol and progressively apply productions to substitute substrings for non terminals occurring in the current string, until we obtain a string composed only of terminal symbols.

In general, we must choose among several applicable production rules at each step. A simple criterion requires each production to be exercised at least once in producing a set of test cases.

The number and complexity of the generated test cases depend on the order of application of the productions. If we first apply productions with non terminals on the right-hand side, we generate a smaller set of large test cases. First applying productions with only terminals on the right-hand side generates larger sets of smaller test cases. An algorithm that favors non terminals applied to the BNF for *advanced search* of Figure 14.10, exercises all the productions to generate the single test case

not Char {, Char} and (Char or Char)*

The derivation tree for this test case is given in Figure 14.14. It shows that each production of the BNF is exercised at least once.

Δ boundary condition grammar-based criterion

The simple production coverage criterion is subsumed by a richer criterion that applies boundary conditions on the number of times each recursive production is applied successively. To generate test cases for boundary conditions we need to choose a minimum and maximum number of applications of each recursive production and then generate a test case for the minimum, maximum, one greater than minimum and one smaller than maximum. The approach is essentially similar to boundary interior path testing of program loops (see Section 12.5 of Chapter 12, page 222), where the "loop" in this case is in repeated applications of a production.

To apply the boundary condition criterion, we need to annotate recursive productions with limits. Names and limits are shown in Figure 14.15, which extends the grammar of Figure 14.13. Alternatives within compound productions are broken out into individual productions. Production names are added for reference, and limits are added to recursive productions. In the example of Figure 14.15, the limit of productions *compSeq1* and *optCompSeq1* is set to 16; we assume that each model can have at most 16 required and 16 optional components.

The boundary condition grammar-based criterion would extend the minimal set by adding test cases that cover the following choices:

- zero required components (*compSeq1* applied 0 times)
- one required component (*compSeq1* applied 1 time)

```
<?xml version="1.0" encoding="ISO-8859-1" ?>
<xsd:schema xmlns:xsd="http://www.w3.org/2000/08/XMLSchema">

<xsd:annotation>
  <xsd:documentation>
      Chipmunk Computers - Product Configuration Schema
      Copyright 2001 D. Seville, Chipmunk Computers Inc.
  </xsd:documentation>
</xsd:annotation>

<xsd:element name="Model" type="ProductConfigurationType"/>

<xsd:complexType name="ProductConfigurationType">
  <xsd:attribute name="modelNumber"
                 type="xsd:string" use="required"/>
    <xsd:element name="Component"
                 minoccurs="0" maxoccurs="unbounded">
        <xsd:sequence>
            <xsd:element name="ComponentType" type="string"/>
            <xsd:element name="ComponentValue" type="string"/>
        </xsd:sequence>
    </xsd:element>
  <xsd:element name="OptionalComponent"
               minoccurs="0" maxoccurs="unbounded">
    <xsd:element name="ComponentType" type="string"/>
  </xsd:element>
</xsd:complexType>
</xsd:schema>
```

Figure 14.12: An XML schema description of a Product configuration *on the Chipmuk Web site. Items are enclosed in matching tags (⟨tag⟩ text ⟨/tag⟩) or incorporated in a self-terminating tag (⟨tag attribute="value" /⟩). The schema describes type* ProductConfigurationType *as a tuple composed of a required field* modelNumber *of type string; a set (possibly empty) of Components, each of which is composed of two string-valued fields* ComponentType *and* ComponentValue*; and a possibly empty set of* OptionalComponents, *each of which is composed of a single string-valued* ComponentType.

⟨*Model*⟩ ::= ⟨*modelNumber*⟩ ⟨*compSequence*⟩ ⟨*optCompSequence*⟩

⟨*compSequence*⟩ ::= ⟨*Component*⟩ ⟨*compSequence*⟩ | `empty`

⟨*optCompSequence*⟩ ::= ⟨*OptionalComponent*⟩ ⟨*optCompSequence*⟩ | `empty`

⟨*Component*⟩ ::= ⟨*ComponentType*⟩ ⟨*ComponentValue*⟩

⟨*OptionalComponent*⟩ ::= ⟨*ComponentType*⟩

⟨*modelNumber*⟩ ::= `string`

⟨*ComponentType*⟩ ::= `string`

⟨*ComponentValue*⟩ ::= `string`

Figure 14.13: BNF description of Product configuration.

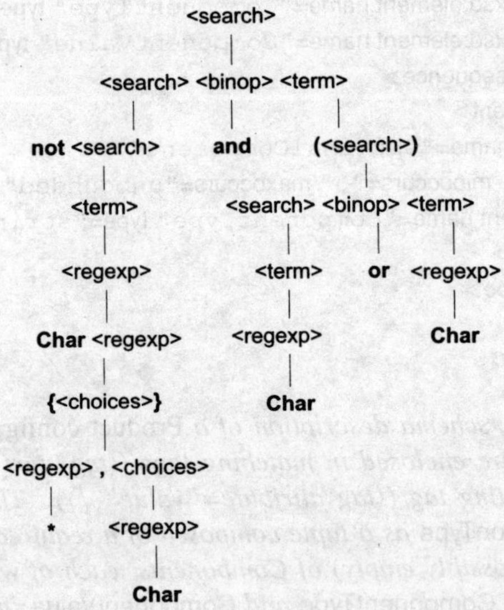

Figure 14.14: The derivation tree of a test case for functionality Advanced Search *derived from the BNF specification of Figure 14.11.*

Model	$\langle$*Model*$\rangle$	::=	$\langle$*modelNumber*$\rangle$ $\langle$*compSequence*$\rangle$ $\langle$*optCompSequence*$\rangle$
compSeq1 limit=16	$\langle$*compSequence*$\rangle$	::=	$\langle$*Component*$\rangle$ $\langle$*compSequence*$\rangle$
compSeq2	$\langle$*compSequence*$\rangle$	::=	`empty`
optCompSeq1 limit=16	$\langle$*optCompSequence*$\rangle$	::=	$\langle$*OptionalComponent*$\rangle$ $\langle$*optCompSequence*$\rangle$
optCompSeq2	$\langle$*optCompSequence*$\rangle$	::=	`empty`
Comp	$\langle$*Component*$\rangle$	::=	$\langle$*ComponentType*$\rangle$ $\langle$*ComponentValue*$\rangle$
OptComp	$\langle$*OptionalComponent*$\rangle$	::=	$\langle$*ComponentType*$\rangle$
modNum	$\langle$*modelNumber*$\rangle$	::=	`string`
CompTyp	$\langle$*ComponentType*$\rangle$	::=	`string`
CompVal	$\langle$*ComponentValue*$\rangle$	::=	`string`

Figure 14.15: The BNF description of Product Configuration *extended with production names and limits.*

- fifteen required components (*compSeq1* applied $n-1$ times)
- sixteen required components (*compSeq1* applied n times)
- zero optional components (*optCompSeq1* applied 0 times)
- one optional component (*optCompSeq1* applied 1 time)
- fifteen optional components (*optCompSeq1* applied $n-1$ times)
- sixteen optional components (*optCompSeq1* applied n times)

Probabilistic grammar-based criteria assign probabilities to productions, indicating which production to select at each step to generate test cases. Unlike names and limits, probabilities are attached to grammar productions as a separate set of annotations. We can generate several sets of test cases from the same grammar with different sets of probabilities, called "seeds." Figure 14.16 shows a sample seed for the grammar that specifies the product configuration functionality of the Chipmunk Web site presented in Figure 14.15.

Δ probabilistic grammar-based criteria

Probabilities are interpreted as weights that determine how frequently each production is used to generate a test case. The equal weight for *compSeq1* and *optCompSeq1* in Figure 14.16 indicates that test cases are generated by balancing use of these two productions; they contain approximately the same number of required and optional components. Weight 0 disables the productions, which are then applied only when application of competing productions reaches the limit indicated in the grammar.

weight	Model	1
weight	compSeq1	10
weight	compSeq2	0
weight	optCompSeq1	10
weight	optCompSeq2	0
weight	Comp	1
weight	OptComp	1
weight	modNum	1
weight	CompTyp	1
weight	CompVal	1

Figure 14.16: Sample seed probabilities for BNF productions of Product configuration.

Open Research Issues

As long as there have been models of software, there has been model-based testing. A recent and ongoing ferment of activity in model-based testing is partly the result of wider use of models throughout software development. Ongoing research will certainly include test design based on software architecture, domain-specific models, and models of emerging classes of systems such as service-oriented architectures and adaptive systems, as well as additional classes of systems and models that we cannot yet anticipate.

As well as following the general trend toward greater use of models in development, though, research in model-based testing reflects greater understanding of the special role that models of software can play in test design and in combining conventional testing with analysis. A model is often the best way — perhaps the only way — to divide one property to be verified into two, one part that is best verified with static analysis and another part that is best verified with testing. Conformance testing of all kinds exploits models in this way, focusing analysis techniques where they are most necessary (e.g., nondeterministic scheduling decisions in concurrent software) and using testing to cost-effectively verify consistency between model and program.

Models are also used to specify and describe system structure at levels of organization beyond those that are directly accommodated in conventional programming languages (e.g., components and subsystems). Analysis, and to a lesser extent testing, have been explicit concerns in development of architecture description languages. Still there remains a divide between models developed primarily for people to communicate and record design decisions (e.g., UML) and models developed primarily for verification (e.g., various FSM notations). Today we see a good deal of research re-purposing design models for test design, which involves adding or disambiguating the semantics of notations intended for human communication. A challenge for future design notations is to provide a better foundation for analysis and testing without sacrificing the characteristics that make them useful for communicating and recording design decisions.

An important issue in modeling, and by extension in model-based testing, is how to use multiple model "views" to together form a comprehensive model of a program. More work is needed on test design that uses more than one modeling view, or on the potential interplay between test specifications derived from different model views of the same program.

As with many other areas of software testing and analysis, more empirical research is also needed to characterize the cost and effectiveness of model-based testing approaches. Perhaps even more than in other areas of testing research, this is not only a matter of carrying out experiments and case studies, but is at least as much a matter of understanding how to pose questions that can be effectively answered by experiments and whose answers generalize in useful ways.

Further Reading

Myers' classic text [Mye79] describes a number of techniques for testing decision structures. Richardson, O'Malley, and Tittle [ROT89] and Stocks and Carrington [SC96] among others attempt to generate test cases based on the structure of (formal) specifications. Beizer's *Black Box Testing* [Bei95] is a popular presentation of techniques for testing based on control and data flow structure of (informal) specifications.

Test design based on finite state machines has long been important in the domain of communication protocol development and conformance testing; Fujiwara, von Bochmann, Amalou, and Ghedamsi [FvBK+91] is a good introduction. Gargantini and Heitmeyer [GH99] describe a related approach applicable to software systems in which the finite state machine is not explicit but can be derived from a requirements specification.

Generating test suites from context-free grammars is described by Celentano et al. [CCD+80] and apparently goes back at least to Hanford's test generator for an IBM PL/I compiler [Han70]. The probabilistic approach to grammar-based testing is described by Sirer and Bershad [SB99], who use annotated grammars to systematically generate tests for Java virtual machine implementations.

Heimdahl et al. [HDW04] provide a cautionary note regarding how naive model-based testing can go wrong, while a case study by Pretschner et al. [PPW+05] suggests that model based testing is particularly effective in revealing errors in informal specifications.

Related Topics

Readers interested in testing based on finite state machines may proceed to Chapter 15, in which finite state models are applied to testing object-oriented programs.

Exercises

14.1. Derive sets of test cases for functionality *Maintenance* from the FSM specification in Figure 14.2.

(a) Derive a test suite that satisfies the *Transition Coverage* criterion.

(b) Derive a test suite that satisfies the *Single State Path Coverage* criterion.

(c) Indicate at least one element of the program that must be covered by a test suite satisfying the *Single Transition Path Coverage*, but need not be covered by a test suite that satisfies the *Single State Path Coverage* criterion. Derive a test case that covers that element.

(d) Describe at least one element that must be covered by a test suite that satisfies both the *Single Transition Path Coverage* and *Boundary Interior Loop Coverage* criteria, but need not be covered by a test suite that satisfies the *Transition Coverage* and *Single State Path Coverage* criteria. Derive a test case that covers that element.

14.2. Discuss how the test suite derived for functionality *Maintenance* applying *Transition Coverage* to the FSM specification of Figure 14.2 (Exercise 14.1) must be modified under the following assumptions.

(a) How must it be modified if the implicit transitions ar error conditions?

(b) How must it be modified if the implicit transitions are self-transitions?

14.3. Finite state machine specifications are often augumented with variables that may be tested and changed by state transitions. The same system can often be described by a machine with more or fewer states, depending on how much information is represented by the states themselves and how much is represented by extra variables. For example, in Figure 5.9 (page 69), the state of the buffer (empty or not) is represented directly by the states, but we could also represent that information with a variable empty and merge states *Empty buffer* and *Within line* of the finite state machine into a single *Gathering* state to obtain a more compact finite state machine, as in this diagram:

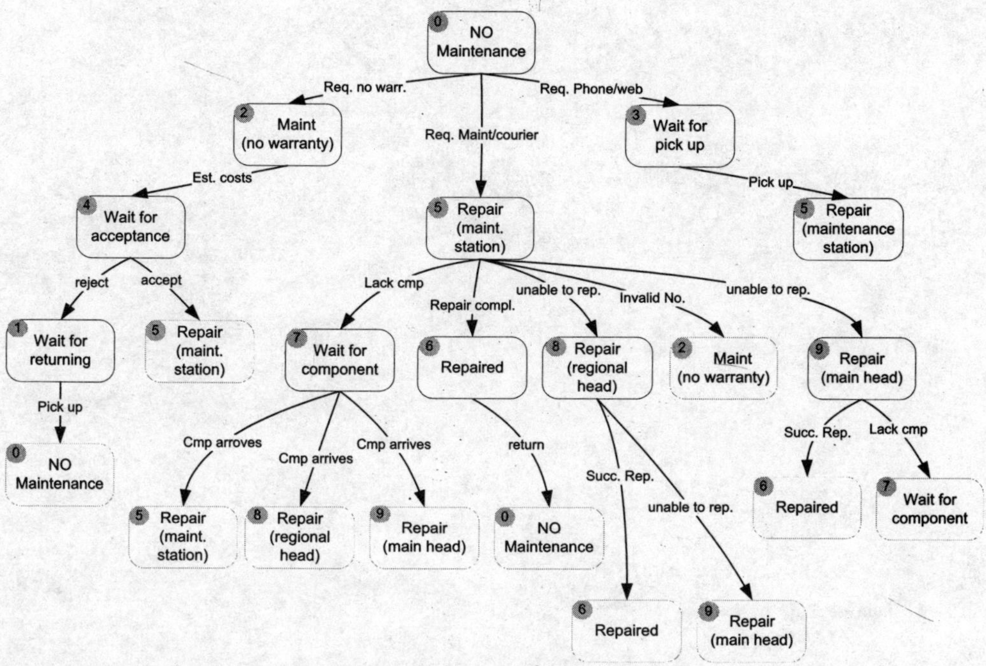

For the following questions, consider only scalar variables with a limited set of possible values, like the Boolean variable empty in the example.

(a) How can we systematically transform a test case for one version of the specification into a test suite for the other? Under what conditions is this transformation possible? Consider transformation in both directions, merging states by adding variables and splitting states to omit variables.

(b) If a test suite satisfies the transition coverage criterion for the version with more states, will a corresponding test suite (converting each test case as you described in part (a)) necessarily satisfy the transition coverage criterion for the version with a suite that satisfies the transition coverage criterion for the version with fewer states?

(c) Conversely, if a test suite satisfies the transition coverage criterion for the version of the specification with fewer states, will a corresponding test suite (converted as you described in part (a)) necessarily satisfy the transition coverage criterion for the version with more states?

(d) How might you combine transition coverage with decision structure testing methods to select test suites independently from the information coded explicitly in the states or implicitly in the state variable?

For the following questions, consider only scalar variables with a limited set of possible values, like the Boolean variable empty in the example.

(a) How can we systematically transform a test case for one version of the specification into a test suite for the other? Under what conditions is this transformation possible? Consider transformation in both directions, merging states by adding variables and splitting states to omit variables.

(b) If a test suite satisfies the transition coverage criterion for the version with more states, will a corresponding test suite (converting each test case as you described in part (a)) necessarily satisfy the transition coverage criterion for the version with a suite that satisfies the transition coverage criterion for the version with fewer states?

(c) Conversely, if a test suite satisfies the transition coverage criterion for the version of the specification with fewer states, will a corresponding test suite (converted as you described in part (a)) necessarily satisfy the transition coverage criterion for the version with more states?

(d) How might you combine transition coverage with decision structure testing methods to select test suites independently from the information coded explicitly in the states or implicitly in the state variable?

Chapter 15

Testing Object-Oriented Software

Systematic testing of object-oriented software is fundamentally similar to systematic testing approaches for procedural software: We begin with functional tests based on specification of intended behavior, add selected structural test cases based on the software structure, and work from unit testing and small-scale integration testing toward larger integration and then system testing. Nonetheless, the differences between procedural software and object-oriented software are sufficient to make specialized techniques appropriate.

Required Background

- Chapters 11, 12, 13, and 14

  This chapter builds on basic functional, structural, and model-based testing techniques, including data flow testing techniques. Some basic techniques, described more thoroughly in earlier chapters, are recapped very briefly here to provide flexibility in reading order.

- Chapter 5

  Many of the techniques described here employ finite state machines for modeling object state.

15.1 Overview

Object-oriented software differs sufficiently from procedural software to justify reconsidering and adapting approaches to software test and analysis. For example, methods in object-oriented software are typically shorter than procedures in other software, so faults in complex intraprocedural logic and control flow occur less often and merit less attention in testing. On the other hand, short methods together with encapsulation of object state suggest greater attention to interactions among method calls, while polymorphism, dynamic binding, generics, and increased use of exception handling introduce new classes of fault that require attention.

Some traditional test and analysis techniques are easily adapted to object-oriented software. For example, code inspection can be applied to object-oriented software much as it is to procedural software, albeit with different checklists. In this chapter we will be concerned mostly with techniques that require more substantial revision (like conventional structural testing techniques) and with the introduction of new techniques for coping with problems associated with object-oriented software.

15.2 Issues in Testing Object-Oriented Software

The characteristics of object-oriented software that impact test design are summarized in the sidebar on page 273 and discussed in more detail below.

state-dependent behavior

The behavior of object-oriented programs is inherently stateful: The behavior of a method depends not only on the parameters passed explicitly to the method, but also on the state of the object. For example, method CheckConfiguration() of class Model, shown in Figure 15.1, returns *True* or *False* depending on whether all components are bound to compatible slots in the current object state.

encapsulation

In object-oriented programs, *public* and *private* parts of a class (fields and methods) are distinguished. Private state and methods are inaccessible to external entities, which can only change or inspect private state by invoking public methods.[1] For example, the instance variable modelID of class Model in Figure 15.1 is accessible by external entities, but slots and legalConfig are accessible only within methods of the same class. The constructor Model() and the method checkConfiguration() can be used by external entities to create new objects and to check the validity of the current configuration, while method openDB() can be invoked only by methods of this class.

Encapsulated information creates new problems in designing oracles and test cases. Oracles must identify incorrect (hidden) state, and test cases must exercise objects in different (hidden) states.

inheritance

Object-oriented programs include classes that are defined by extending or specializing other classes through *inheritance*. For example, class Model in Figure 15.1 extends class CompositeItem, as indicated in the class declaration. A child class can inherit variables and methods from its ancestors, overwrite others, and add yet others. For example, the class diagram of Figure 15.3 shows that class Model inherits the instance variables sku, units and parts, and methods validItem(), getUnitPrice() and getExtendedPrice(). It overwrites methods getHeightCm(), getWidthCm(), getDepthCm() and getWeightGm(). It adds the instance variables baseWeight, modelID, heightCm, widthCm, DepthCm, slots and legalConfig, and the methods selectModel(), deselectModel(), addComponent(), removeComponent() and isLegalConfiguration().

[1] Object-oriented languages differ with respect to the categories of accessibility they provide. For example, nothing in Java corresponds exactly to the "friend" functions in C++ that are permitted to access the private state of other objects. But while details vary, encapsulation of state is fundamental to the object-oriented programming paradigm, and all major object-oriented languages have a construct comparable to Java's private field declarations.

Summary: Relevant Characteristics of Object-Oriented Software

State Dependent Behavior: Testing techniques must consider the state in which methods are invoked. Testing techniques that are oblivious to state (e.g., traditional coverage of control structure) are not effective in revealing state-dependent faults.

Encapsulation: The effects of executing object-oriented code may include outputs, modification of object state, or both. Test oracles may require access to private (encapsulated) information to distinguish between correct and incorrect behavior.

Inheritance: Test design must consider the effects of new and overridden methods on the behavior of inherited methods, and distinguish between methods that require new test cases, ancestor methods that can be tested by reexecuting existing test cases, and methods that do not need to be retested.

Polymorphism and Dynamic Binding: A single method call may be dynamically bound to different methods depending on the state of the computation. Tests must exercise different bindings to reveal failures that depend on a particular binding or on interactions between bindings for different calls.

Abstract Classes: Abstract classes cannot be directly instantiated and tested, yet they may be important interface elements in libraries and components. It is necessary to test them without full knowledge of how they may be instantiated.

Exception Handling: Exception handling is extensively used in modern object-oriented programming. The textual distance between the point where an exception is thrown and the point where it is handled, and the dynamic determination of the binding, makes it important to explicitly test exceptional as well as normal control flow.

Concurrency: Modern object-oriented languages and toolkits encourage and sometimes even require multiple threads of control (e.g., the Java user interface construction toolkits AWT and Swing). Concurrency introduces new kinds of possible failures, such as deadlock and race conditions, and makes the behavior of a system dependent on scheduler decisions that are not under the tester's control.

```
public class Model extends Orders.CompositeItem {
    public String modelID; // Database key for slots
    private int baseWeight; // Weight excluding optional components
    private int heightCm, widthCm, depthCm; // Dimensions if boxed
    private Slot[] slots; // Component slots

    private boolean legalConfig = false; // memoized result of isLegalConf
    private static final String NoModel = "NO MODEL SELECTED";
...
    /** Constructor, which should be followed by selectModel */
    public Model(Orders.Order _order) {
        super(_order);
        modelID = NoModel;
    }
...
    /** Is the current binding of components to slots a legal
      * configuration? Memo-ize the result for repeated calls */
    public boolean isLegalConfiguration() {
        if (! legalConfig) {
            checkConfiguration();
        }
        return legalConfig;
    }

    /** Are all required slots filled with compatible components?
      * It is impossible to assign an incompatible component,
      * so just to check that every required slot is filled. */
    private void checkConfiguration() {
        legalConfig = true;
        for (int i=0; i < slots.length; ++i) {
            Slot slot = slots[i];
            if (slot.required && ! slot.isBound()) {
                legalConfig = false;
            }
        }
    }
...
}
```

Figure 15.1: Part of a Java implementation of class Model.

```
public class Model   extends Orders.CompositeItem {
...
    /** Bind a component to a slot.
     * @param slotIndex Which slot (integer index)?
     * @param sku   Key to component database.
     * Choices should be constrained by web interface, so we don't
     * need to be graceful in handling bogus parameters.
     */
    public void addComponent(int slotIndex, String sku) {
        Slot slot =slots[slotIndex];
        if (componentDB.contains(sku)) {
            Component comp = new Component(order, sku);
            if (comp.isCompatible(slot.slotID)) {
                slot.bind(comp);
                // Note this cannot have made the
                // configuration illegal.
            } else {
                slot.unbind();
                legalConfig = false;
            }
        } else {
            slot.unbind();
            legalConfig = false;
        }
    }


    /** Unbind a component from a slot. */
    public void removeComponent(int slotIndex) {
        // assert slotIndex in 0..slots.length
        if (slots[slotIndex].isBound()) {
                slots[slotIndex].unbind();
            }
        legalConfig = false;
    }
...
}
```

Figure 15.2: More of the Java implementation of class Model. *Because of the way method* isLegalConfig *is implemented (see Figure 15.1), all methods that modify slots must reset the private variable* legalConfig.

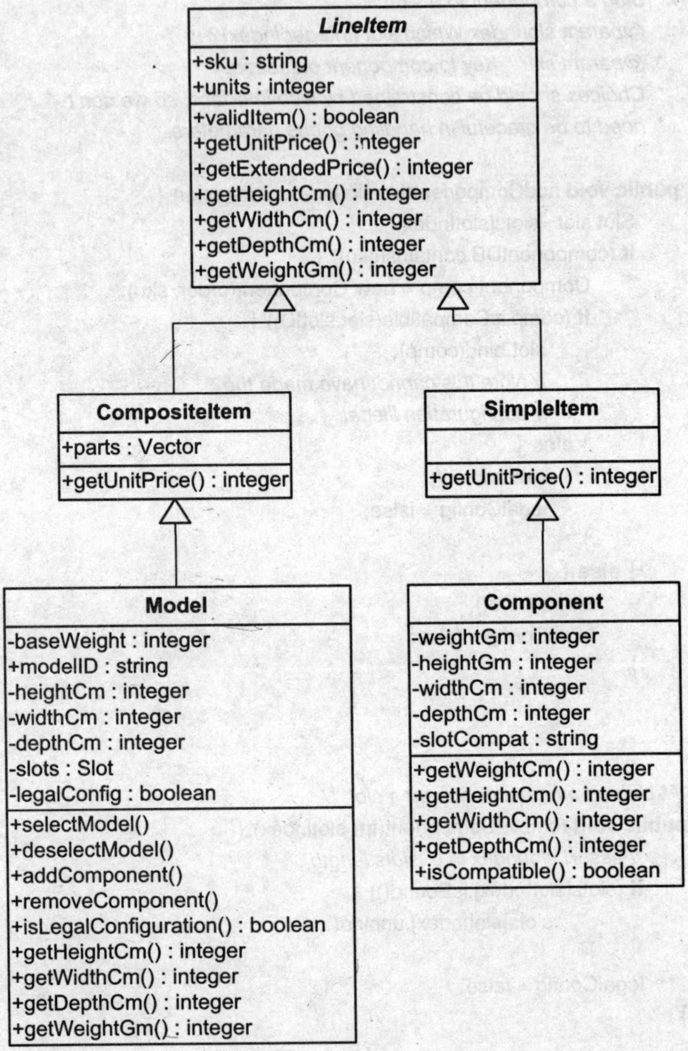

Figure 15.3: An excerpt from the class diagram of the Chipmunk Web presence that shows the hierarchy rooted in class LineItem.

Inheritance brings in optimization issues. Child classes may share several methods with their ancestors. Sometimes an inherited method must be retested in the child class, despite not having been directly changed, because of interaction with other parts of the class that have changed. Many times, though, one can establish conclusively that the behavior of an inherited method is really unchanged and need not be retested. In other cases, it may be necessary to rerun tests designed for the inherited method, but not necessary to design new tests.

Most object-oriented languages allow variables to dynamically change their type, as long as they remain within a hierarchy rooted at the declared type of the variable. For example, variable subsidiary of method getYTDPurchased() in Figure 15.4 can be dynamically bound to different classes of the Account hierarchy, and thus the invocation of method subsidiary.getYTDPurchased() can be bound dynamically to different methods. polymorphism dynamic binding

Dynamic binding to different methods may affect the whole computation. Testing a call by considering only one possible binding may not be enough. Test designers need testing techniques that select subsets of possible bindings that cover a sufficient range of situations to reveal faults in possible combinations of bindings.

Some classes in an object-oriented program are intentionally left incomplete and cannot be directly instantiated. These abstract classes[2] must be extended through subclasses; only subclasses that fill in the missing details (e.g., method bodies) can be instantiated. For example, both classes LineItem of Figure 15.3 and Account of Figure 15.4 are abstract. abstract classes

If abstract classes are part of a larger system, such as the Chipmunk Web presence, and if they are not part of the public interface to that system, then they can be tested by testing all their child classes: classes Model, Component, CompositeItem, and SimpleItem for class LineItem and classes USAccount, UKAccount, JPAccount, EUAccount and OtherAccount for class Account. However, we may need to test an abstract class either prior to implementing all child classes, for example if not all child classes will be implemented by the same engineers in the same time frame, or without knowing all its implementations, for example if the class is included in a library whose reuse cannot be fully foreseen at development time. In these cases, test designers need techniques for selecting a representative set of instances for testing the abstract class.

Exceptions were originally introduced in programming languages independently of object-oriented features, but they play a central role in modern object-oriented programming languages and in object-oriented design methods. Their prominent role in object-oriented programs, and the complexity of propagation and handling of exceptions during program execution, call for careful attention and specialized techniques in testing. exceptions

The absence of a main execution thread in object-oriented programs makes them well suited for concurrent and distributed implementations. Although many object-oriented programs are designed for and executed in sequential environments, the design concurrency

[2]Here we include the Java interface construct as a kind of abstract class.

```java
public abstract class Account {
...
    /**
     * The YTD Purchased amount for an account is the YTD
     * total of YTD purchases of all customers using this account
     * plus the YTD purchases of all subsidiaries of this account;
     * currency is currency of this account.
     */
    public int getYTDPurchased() {

        if (ytdPurchasedValid) { return ytdPurchased; }

        int totalPurchased = 0;
        for (Enumeration e = subsidiaries.elements() ; e.hasMoreElements(); )
            {
                Account subsidiary = (Account) e.nextElement();
                totalPurchased += subsidiary.getYTDPurchased();
            }
        for (Enumeration e = customers.elements(); e.hasMoreElements(); )
            {
                Customer aCust = (Customer) e.nextElement();
                totalPurchased += aCust.getYearlyPurchase();
            }
        ytdPurchased = totalPurchased;
        ytdPurchasedValid = true;
        return totalPurchased;
    }
...
}
```

Figure 15.4: Part of a Java implementation of Class Account. *The abstract class is specialized by the regional markets served by Chipmunk into* USAccount, UKAccount, JPAccount, EUAccount *and* OtherAccount, *which differ with regard to shipping methods, taxes, and currency. A corporate account may be associated with several individual customers, and large companies may have different subsidiaries with accounts in different markets. Method* getYTDPurchased() *sums the year-to-date purchases of all customers using the main account and the accounts of all subsidiaries.*

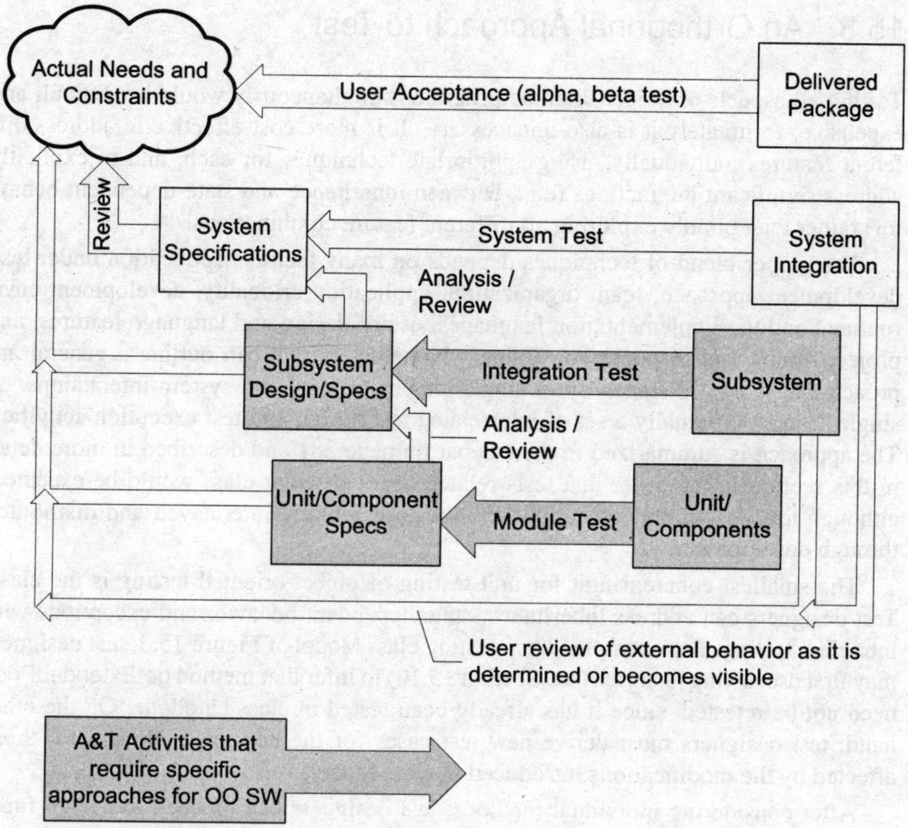

Figure 15.5: The impact of object-oriented design and coding on analysis and testing.

of object-oriented applications for concurrent and distributed environments is becoming very frequent.

Object-oriented design and programming greatly impact analysis and testing. However, test designers should not make the mistake of ignoring traditional technology and methodologies. A specific design approach mainly affects detailed design and code, but there are many aspects of software development and quality assurance that are largely independent of the use of a specific design approach. In particular, aspects related to planning, requirements analysis, architectural design, deployment and maintenance can be addressed independently of the design approach. Figure 15.5 indicates the scope of the impact of object-oriented design on analysis and testing.

15.3 An Orthogonal Approach to Test

Testing all aspects of object-oriented programs simultaneously would be difficult and expensive; fortunately it is also unnecessary. It is more cost-effective to address different features individually, using appropriate techniques for each, and to explicitly address significant interactions (e.g., between inheritance and state-dependent behavior) rather than blindly exploring all different feature combinations.

The proper blend of techniques depends on many factors: application under test, development approach, team organization, application criticality, development environment and the implementation languages, use of design and language features, and project timing and resource constraints. Nonetheless, we can outline a general approach that works in stages, from single classes to class and system interactions. A single "stage" is actually a set of interrelated test design and test execution activities. The approach is summarized in the sidebar on page 281 and described in more detail in this section in the order that tests related to a particular class would be executed, although test design and execution activities are actually interleaved and distributed through development.

The smallest coherent unit for unit testing of object-oriented testing is the class. Test designers can address inheritance, state-dependent behavior and exceptions with intraclass testing. For example, when testing class Model of Figure 15.3, test designers may first use testing histories (see Section 15.10) to infer that method getExtendedPrice need not be retested, since it has already been tested in class LineItem. On the other hand, test designers must derive new test cases for the new methods and for those affected by the modifications introduced in class Model.

After considering individual methods, test designers can proceed to design functional test cases from the statechart specification of class Model (see Section 15.5) and structural test cases from data flow information (see Section 15.7). To execute test cases, test designers may decide to use equivalent scenarios as oracles (see Section 15.8). Test designers will then create test cases for exceptions thrown or handled by the class under test (see Section 15.12). Class Model does not make polymorphic calls, so no additional test cases need be designed to check behavior with variable bindings to different classes.

Integration (interclass) tests must be added to complete the testing for hierarchy, polymorphism, and exception-related problems. For example, when testing integration of class Model within the Chipmunk Web presence, test designers will identify class Slot as a predecessor in the integration order and will test it first, before testing its integration with class Model (see Sections 15.5 and 15.7). They will also derive test cases for completing the test of exceptions (see Section 15.12) and polymorphism (see Section 15.9).

System and acceptance testing check overall system behavior against user and system requirements. Since these requirements are (at least in principle) independent of the design approach, system and acceptance testing can be addressed with traditional techniques. For example, to test the business logic subsystem of the Chipmunk Web presence, test designers may decide to derive test cases from functional specifications using category-partition and catalog based methods (see Chapter 11).

Steps in Object-Oriented Software Testing

Object-oriented testing can be broken into three phases, progressing from individual classes toward consideration of integration and interactions.

Intraclass: Testing classes in isolation (unit testing)

1. If the class-under-test is abstract, derive a set of instantiations to cover significant cases. Instantiations may be taken from the application (if available) and/or created just for the purpose of testing.
2. Design test cases to check correct invocation of inherited and overridden methods, including constructors. If the class-under-test extends classes that have previously been tested, determine which inherited methods need to be retested and which test cases from ancestor classes can be reused.
3. Design a set of intraclass test cases based on a state machine model of specified class behavior.
4. Augment the state machine model with structural relations derived from class source code and generate additional test cases to cover structural features.
5. Design an initial set of test cases for exception handling, systematically exercising exceptions that should be thrown by methods in the class under test and exceptions that should be caught and handled by them.
6. Design an initial set of test cases for polymorphic calls (calls to superclass or interface methods that can be bound to different subclass methods depending on instance values).

Interclass: Testing class integration (integration testing)

1. Identify a hierarchy of clusters of classes to be tested incrementally.
2. Design a set of functional interclass test cases for the cluster-under-test.
3. Add test cases to cover data flow between method calls.
4. Integrate the intraclass exception-handling test sets with interclass exception-handling test cases for exceptions propagated across classes.
5. Integrate the polymorphism test sets with tests that check for interclass interactions of polymorphic calls and dynamic bindings.

System and Acceptance: Apply standard functional and acceptance testing techniques to larger components and the whole system.

15.4 Intraclass Testing

Unit and integration testing aim to expose faults in individual program units and in their interactions, respectively. The meaning of "unit" is the smallest development work assignment for a single programmer that can reasonably be planned and tracked. In procedural programs, individual program units might be single functions or small sets of strongly related functions and procedures, often included in a single file of source code. In object-oriented programs, small sets of strongly related functions or procedures are naturally identified with *classes*, which are generally the smallest work units that can be systematically tested.

Treating an individual method as a unit is usually not practical because methods in a single class interact by modifying object state and because the effect of an individual method is often visible only through its effect on other methods. For example, method check_configuration of class computer, shown in Figure 15.1, can be executed only if the object is in a given state, and its result depends on the current configuration. The method may execute correctly in a given state (i.e., for a given configuration), but may not execute correctly in a different state (e.g., accepting malformed configurations or rejecting acceptable configurations). Moreover, method check_configuration might produce an apparently correct output (return value) but leave the object in an incorrect state.

15.5 Testing with State Machine Models

Since the state of an object is implicitly part of the input and output of methods, we need a way to systematically explore object states and transitions. This can be guided by a state machine model, which can be derived from module specifications.

A state machine model can be extracted from an informal, natural language specification of intended behavior, even when the specification does not explicitly describe states and transitions. States can be inferred from descriptions of methods that act differently or return different results, depending on the state of the object; this includes any description of when it is allowable to call a method. Of course, one wants to derive only a reasonable number of abstract states as representatives of a much larger number of concrete states, and some judgment is required to choose the grouping. For example, if an object kept an integer count, we might choose "zero" and "nonzero" as representative states, rather than creating a different state for every possible value. The principle to observe is that we are producing a model of how one method affects another, so the states should be refined just enough to capture interactions. Extracting a state machine from an informal specification, and then creating test cases (sequences of method calls) to cover transitions in that model, are illustrated in the sidebar on page 283.

statechart (state diagram)

Sometimes an explicit state machine model is already available as part of a specification or design. If so, it is likely to be in the form of a statechart (also known as a *state diagram* in the UML family of notations). Statecharts include standard state transition diagrams, but also provide hierarchical structuring constructs. The structuring facilities of statecharts can be used to organize and hide complexity, but this complexity must be exposed to be tested.

From Informal Specs to Transition Coverage

An Informal Specification of Class *Slot*

Slot represents a configuration choice in all instances of a particular model of computer. It may or may not be implemented as a physical slot on a bus. A given model may have zero or more slots, each of which is marked as required or optional. If a slot is marked as "required," it must be bound to a suitable component in all legal configurations.

Class Slot offers the following services:

Incorporate: Make a slot part of a model, and mark it as either required or optional. All instances of a model incorporate the same slots.
Example: We can incorporate a required primary battery slot and an optional secondary battery slot on the Chipmunk C20 laptop that includes two battery slots. The C20 laptop may then be sold with one battery or two batteries, but it is not sold without at least the primary battery.

Bind: Associate a compatible component with a slot. *Example:* We can bind slot primary battery to a Blt4, Blt6, or Blt8 lithium battery or to a Bcdm4 nickel cadmium battery. We cannot bind a disk drive to the battery slot.

Unbind: The unbind operation breaks the binding of a component to a slot, reversing the effect of a previous bind operation.

IsBound: Returns true if a component is currently bound to a slot, or false if the slot is currently empty.

The Corresponding Finite State Machine

A simple analysis of the informal specification of class Slot allows one to identify states and transitions. Often an analysis of natural language specifications will reveal ambiguities that must be resolved one way or the other in the model; these may suggest additional test cases to check the interpretation, or lead to refinement of the specification, or both. For class slot, we infer that the bind operation makes sense only after the slot has been incorporated in a model, and that it is initially empty.

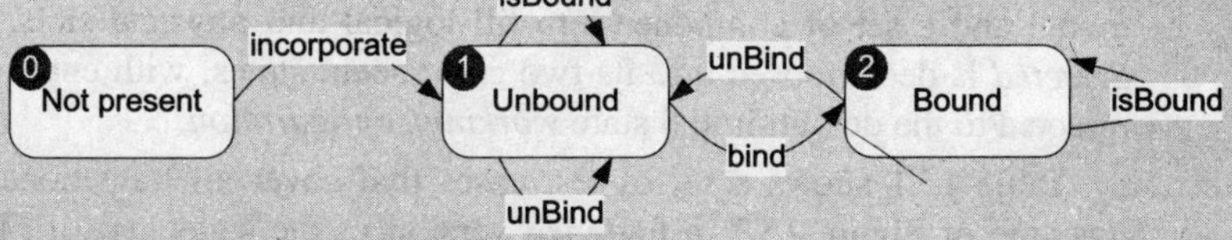

The Generated Test Case Specifications

A single test case will be given as a sequence of method calls. For class Slot, the following test cases suffice to execute each transition in the state machine model:

TC-1 incorporate, isBound, bind, isBound
TC-2 incorporate, unBind, bind, unBind, isBound

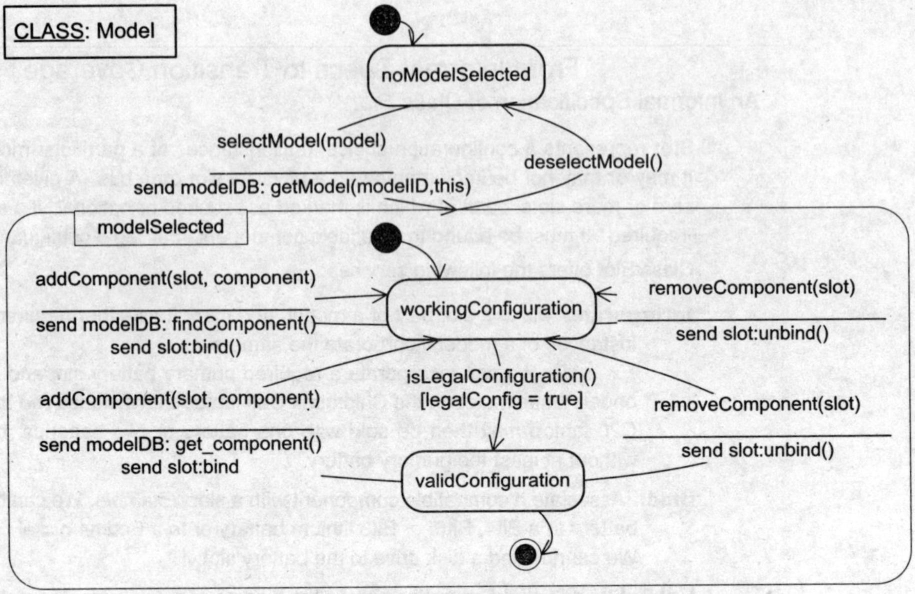

Figure 15.6: Statechart specification of class Model.

The most common structuring mechanism in statecharts is grouping of states in superstates (also called OR-states). A transition from a superstate is equivalent to a transition from every state contained within it. A transition to a superstate is equivalent to a transition to the initial state within the superstate. We can obtain an ordinary state machine by "flattening" the statechart hierarchy, replacing transitions to and from superstates to transitions among elementary states.

superstate (OR-state)

Figure 15.6 shows a statechart specification for class Model of the business logic of the Chipmunk Web presence. Class Model provides methods for selecting a computer model and a set of components to fill logical and physical slots. The state *model-Selected* is decomposed into its two component states, with entries to *modelSelected* directed to the default initial state *workingConfiguration*.

Table 15.1 shows a set of test cases that cover all transitions of the finite state machine of Figure 15.7, a flattened version of the statechart of Figure 15.6. Notice that transition *selectModel* of the statechart corresponds to a single transition in the FSM, since entry to the superstate is directed to the default initial state, while transition *deselectModel* of the statechart corresponds to two transitions in the FSM, one for each of the two children states, since the superstate can be exited while in either component state.

In covering the state machine model, we have chosen sets of transition sequences that together exercise each individual transition at least once. This is the transition adequacy criterion introduced in Chapter 14. The stronger history-sensitive criteria described in that chapter are also applicable in principle, but are seldom used because

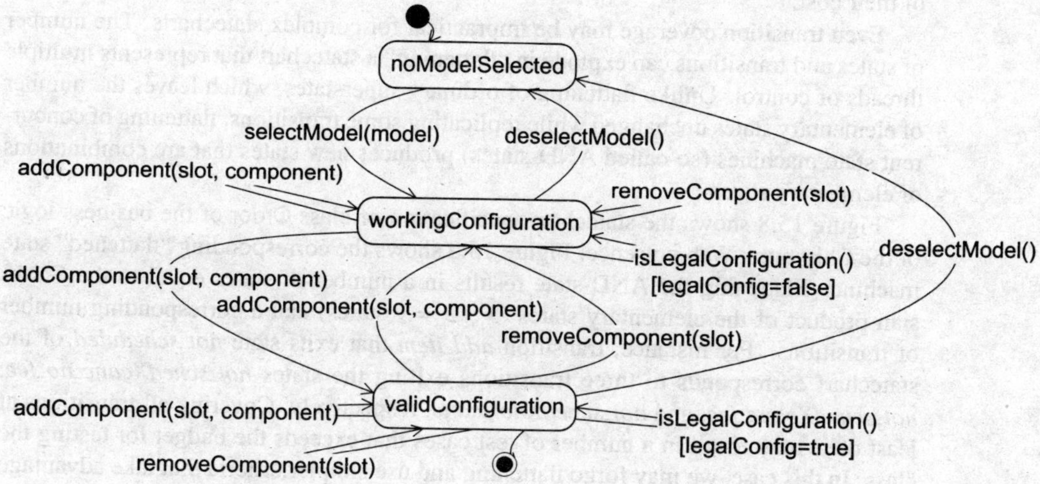

Figure 15.7: Finite state machine corresponding to the statechart of Figure 15.6.

Test Case TC_A
selectModel(M1)
addComponent(S1,C1)
addComponent(S2,C2)
isLegalConfiguration()

Test Case TC_B
selectModel(M1)
deselectModel()
selectModel(M2)
addComponent(S1,C1)
addComponent(S2,C2)
removeComponent(S1)
isLegalConfiguration()

Test Case TC_C
selectModel(M1)
addComponent(S1,C1)
removeComponent(S1)
addComponent(S1,C2)
isLegalConfiguration()

Test Case TC_D
selectModel(M1)
addComponent(S1,C1)
addComponent(S2,C2)
addComponent(S3,C3)
deselectModel()
selectModel(M1)
addComponent(S1,C1)
isLegalConfiguration()

Test Case TC_E
selectModel(M1)
addComponent(S1,C1)
addComponent(S2,C2)
addComponent(S3,C3)
removeComponent(S2)
addComponent(S2,C4)
isLegalConfiguration()

Table 15.1: A set of test cases that satisfies the transition coverage *criterion for the statechart of Figure 15.6.*

of their cost.

Even transition coverage may be impractical for complex statecharts. The number of states and transitions can explode in "flattening" a statechart that represents multiple threads of control. Unlike flattening of ordinary superstates, which leaves the number of elementary states unchanged while replicating some transitions, flattening of concurrent state machines (so-called AND-states) produces new states that are combinations of elementary states.

Figure 15.8 shows the statechart specification of class Order of the business logic of the Chipmunk Web presence. Figure 15.9 shows the corresponding "flattened" state machine. Flattening the AND-state results in a number of states equal to the Cartesian product of the elementary states ($3 \times 3 = 9$ states) and a corresponding number of transitions. For instance, transition *add_item* that exits state *not_scheduled* of the statechart corresponds to three transitions exiting the states *not_schedXcanc_no_fee*, *not_schedXcanc_fee*, and *not_schedXnot_canc*, respectively. Covering all transitions at least once may result in a number of test cases that exceeds the budget for testing the class. In this case, we may forgo flattening and use simpler criteria that take advantage of the hierarchical structure of the statechart.

Δ simple transition coverage

Table 15.2 shows a test suite that satisfies the *simple transition coverage* adequacy criterion, which requires the execution of all transitions that appear in the statechart. The criterion requires that each statechart transition is exercised at least once, but does not guarantee that transitions are exercised in all possible states. For example, transition *add_item*, which leaves the initial state, is exercised from at least one substate, but not from all possible substates as required by the transition coverage adequacy criterion.

15.6 Interclass Testing

Interclass testing is the first level of integration testing for object-oriented software. While intraclass testing focuses on single classes, interclass testing checks interactions among objects of different classes. As in integration testing of imperative programs, test designers proceed incrementally, starting from small clusters of classes.

Since the point of interclass testing is to verify interactions, it is useful to model potential interactions through a use/include relation. Classes A and B are related by the use/include relation if objects of class A make method calls on objects of class B, or if objects of class A contain references to objects of class B. Inheritance is ignored (we do not consider a subclass to use or include its ancestors), and abstract classes, which cannot directly participate in interactions, are omitted. Derivation of the use/include relation from a conventional UML class diagram is illustrated in Figures 15.10 and 15.11.

Interclass testing strategies usually proceed bottom-up, starting from classes that depend on no others. The implementation-level use/include relation among classes typically parallels the more abstract, logical *depends* relation among modules (see sidebar on page 292), so a bottom-up strategy works well with cluster-based testing. For example, we can start integrating class SlotDB with class Slot, and class Component with class ComponentDB, and then proceed incrementally integrating classes ModelDB and Model, up to class Order.

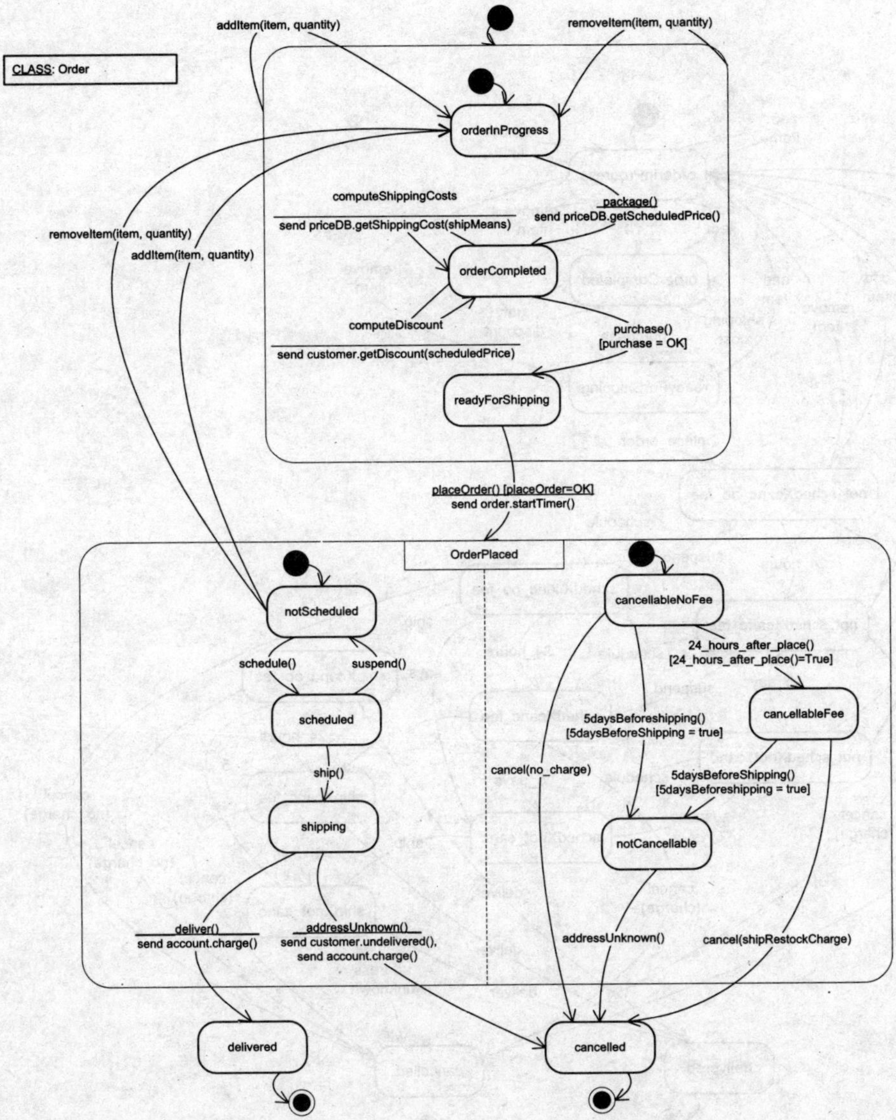

Figure 15.8: Statechart specification of class Order. *This is a conceptual model in which both methods of class* Order *and method calls by class* Order *are represented as transitions with names that differ from method names in the implementation (e.g., 5DaysBeforeShipping is not a legal method or field name).*

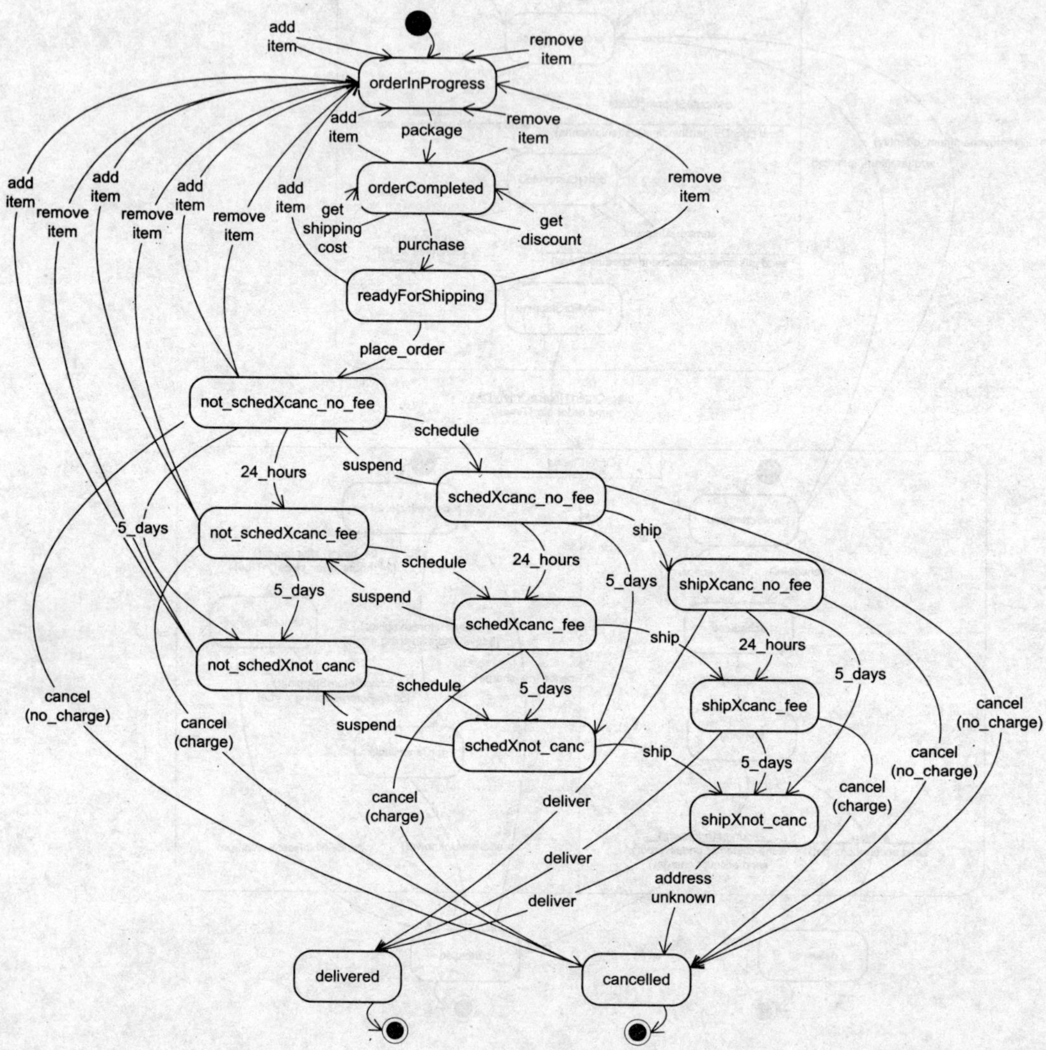

Figure 15.9: Finite state machine corresponding to the statechart of Figure 15.8.

Test Case TC_A
add_item()
add_item()
package()
get_shipping_cost()
get_discount()
purchase()
place_order()
24_hours()
5_days()
schedule()
ship()
deliver()

Test Case TC_B
add_item()
add_item()
remove_item()
add_item()
package()
get_shipping_cost()
get_discount()
purchase()
place_order()
24_hours()
5_days()
schedule()
ship()
deliver()

Test Case TC_C
add_item()
add_item()
package()
get_shipping_cost()
get_discount()
purchase()
place_order()
add_item()
package()
get_shipping_cost()
get_discount()
purchase()
place_order()
24_hours()
5_days()
schedule()
ship()
deliver()

Test Case TC_D
add_item()
add_item()
package()
get_shipping_cost()
get_discount()
purchase()
place_order()
remove item()
add_item()
package()
get_shipping_cost()
get_discount()
purchase()
place_order()
24_hours()
5_days()
schedule()
ship()
deliver()

Test Case TC_E
add_item()
add_item()
package()
get_shipping_cost()
get_discount()
purchase()
place_order()
schedule()
suspend()
5_days()
schedule()
ship()
deliver()

Test Case TC_F
add_item()
add_item()
package()
get_shipping_cost()
get_discount()
purchase()
place_order()
schedule()
cancel()

Test Case TC_G
add_item()
add_item()
package()
get_shipping_cost()
get_discount()
purchase()
place_order()
schedule()
ship()
address unknown()

Test Case TC_H
add_item()
add_item()
package()
get_shipping_cost()
get_discount()
purchase()
place_order()
schedule()
5_days()
address_unknown()

Test Case TC_I
add_ item()
add_item()
package()
get_shipping_cost()
get_discount()
purchase()
place_order()
schedule()
24_hours()
cancel()

Table 15.2: A test suite that satisfies the simple transition coverage *adequacy criterion for the statechart of Figure 15.8. Transitions are indicated without parameters for simplicity.*

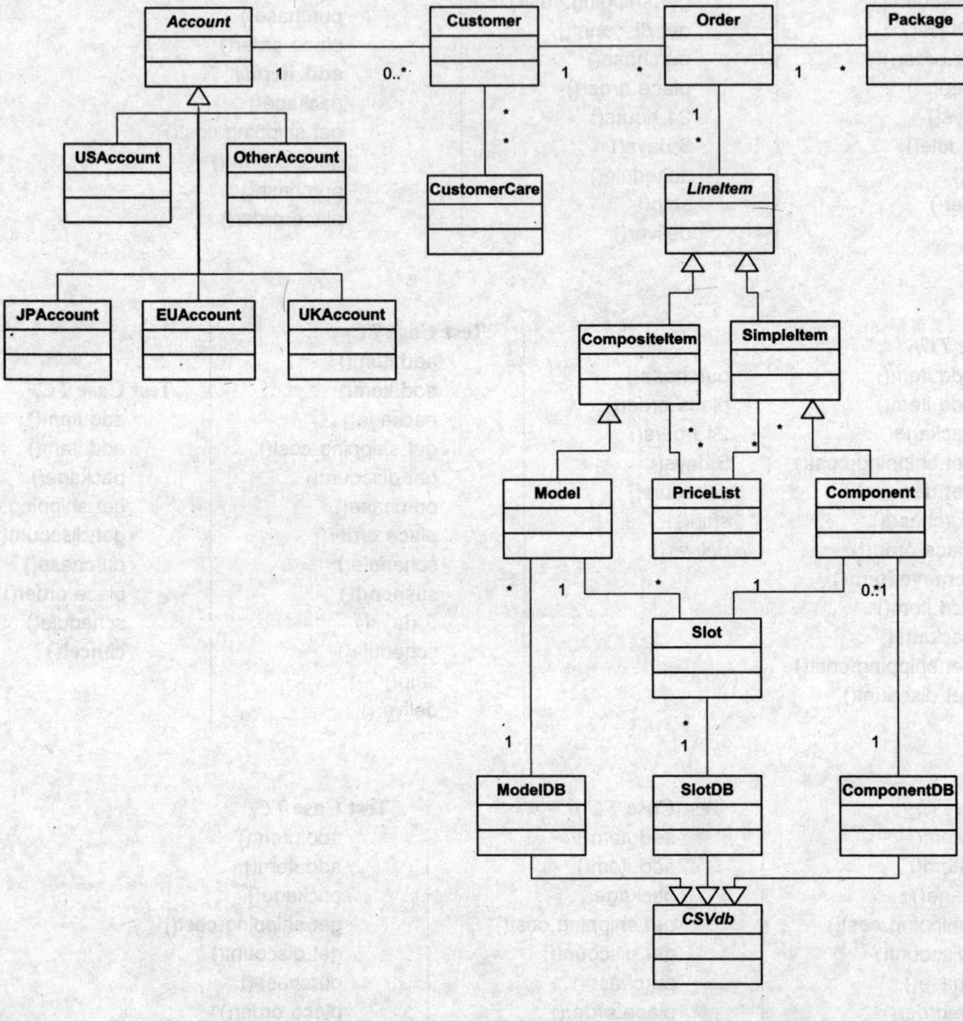

Figure 15.10: Part of a class diagram of the Chipmunk Web presence. Classes Account, LineItem, *and* CSVdb *are abstract.*

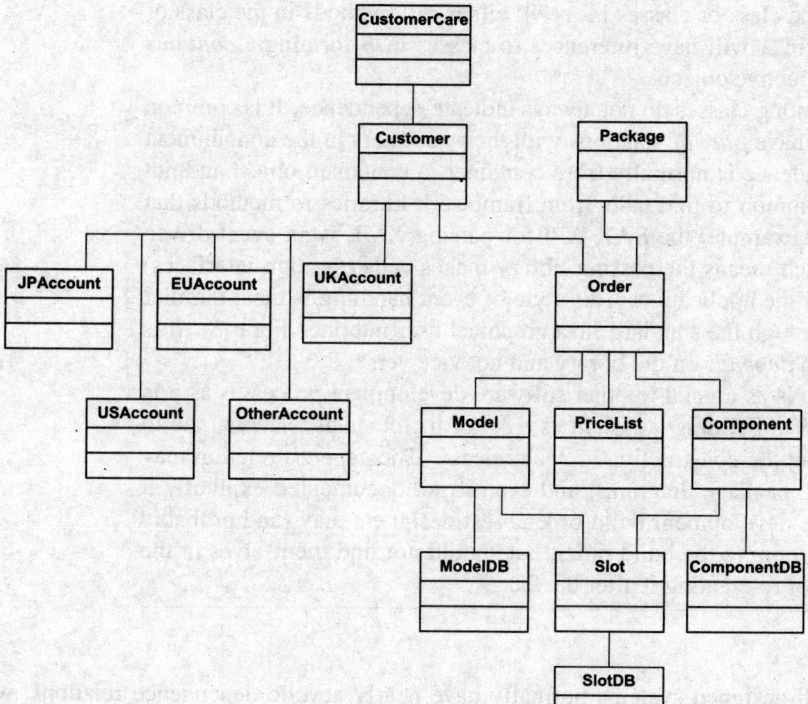

Figure 15.11: Use/include relation for the class diagram in Figure 15.10. Abstract classes are not included. Two classes are related if one uses or includes the other. Classes that are higher in the diagram include or use classes that are lower in the diagram.

Dependence

The hierarchy of clusters for interclass testing is based on a conceptual relation of *dependence*, and not directly on concrete relations among implementation classes (or implementation-level design documentation).

Module *A depends on* module *B* if the functionality of *B* must be present for the functionality of *A* to be provided.

If *A* and *B* are implemented as classes or clusters of closely related classes, it is likely that the logical *depends* relation will be reflected in concrete relations among the classes. Typically, the class or classes in *A* will either call methods in the class or classes in *B*, or classes in *A* will have references to classes in *B* forming a *contains* relation among their respective objects.

Concrete relations among classes do not always indicate dependence. It is common for contained objects to have *part-of* relations with their ancestors in the containment hierarchy, but the dependence is normally from container to contained object and not vice versa. It is also common to find calls from framework libraries to methods that use those libraries. For example, the SAX API for parsing XML is an event-driven parsing framework, which means the parsing library makes calls (through interfaces) on methods provided by the application. This style of event handling is most familiar to Java programmers through the standard Java graphical user interface libraries. It is clear that the application *depends* on the library and not vice versa.

The *depends* relation is as crucial to other software development processes as it is to testing. It is essential to building a system as a set of incremental releases, and to scheduling and managing the construction of each release. The *depends* relation may be documented in UML package diagrams, and even if not documented explicitly it is surely manifest in the development build order. Test designers may (and probably should) be involved in defining the build order, but should not find themselves in the position of discovering or re-creating it after the fact.

Well-designed systems normally have nearly acyclic dependence relations, with dependence loops limited to closely related clusters. When there are larger loops in the relation, or when a use/include relation among classes runs contrary to the *depends* relation (e.g., an "up-call" to an ancestor in the *depends* relation), the loop can be broken by substituting a stub for the ancestor class. Thus, we always work with an acyclic graph of clusters.

In principle, while climbing the dependence relation, a thorough interclass testing should consider all combinations of possible interactions. If, for example, a test case for class Order includes a call to a method of class Model, and the called method calls a method of class Slot, each call should be exercised for all relevant states of the different classes, as identified during intraclass testing. However, this suffers from the same kind of combinatorial explosion that makes flattening concurrent state diagrams impractical. We need to select a subset of interactions among the possible combinations of method calls and class states. An arbitrary or random selection of interactions may be an acceptable solution, but in addition one should explicitly test any significant interaction scenarios that have been previously identified in design and analysis.

Interaction scenarios may have been recorded in the form of UML interaction diagrams, expressed as *sequence* or *collaboration diagrams*. These diagrams describe interactions among objects and can be considered essentially as test scenarios created during the course of design.

In addition to testing the scenarios spelled out in sequence or collaboration diagrams, the test designer can vary those scenarios to consider illegal or unexpected interaction sequences. For example, replacing a single interaction in a sequence diagram with another interaction that should not be permitted at that point yields a test case that checks error handling.

Figure 15.12 shows a possible pattern of interactions among objects, when a customer assembling an order O first selects the computer model C20, then adds a hard disk HD60 that is not compatible with the slots of the selected model, and then adds "legal" hard disk HD20. The sequence diagram indicates the sequence of interactions among objects and suggests possible testing scenarios. For example, it suggests adding a component after having selected a model. In other words, it indicates interesting states of objects of type ModelDB and Slots when testing class Model.

Unlike statecharts, which should describe all possible sequences of transitions that an object can undergo, interaction diagrams illustrate selected interactions that the designers considered significant because they were typical, or perhaps because they were difficult to understand. Deriving test cases from interaction diagrams is useful as a way of choosing some significant cases among the enormous variety of possible interaction sequences, but it is insufficient as a way of ensuring thorough testing. Integration tests should at the very least repeat coverage of individual object states and transitions in the context of other parts of the cluster under test.

15.7 Structural Testing of Classes

In testing procedural code, we take specifications as the primary source of information for test design (*functional* testing), and then we analyze implementation structure and add test cases as needed to cover additional variation (*structural* testing). The same approach applies to object-oriented programs and for the same reasons. The techniques described in previous sections are all based on specification of intended behavior. They should be augmented (but never replaced) by structural techniques.

If we compare the implementation of class Model shown in Figures 15.1 and 15.2 with its specification in Figures 15.3 and 15.6, we notice that the code uses an instance variable legalConfig and an internal (private) method checkConfiguration to optimize the implementation of method isLegalConfiguration. The functional test cases shown in Table 15.1 do not include method checkConfiguration, though some of them will call it indirectly through isLegalConfiguration. An alert test designer will note that every modification of the object state that could possibly invalidate a configuration should reset the hidden legalConfig variable to *False*, and will derive structural test cases to cover behaviors not sufficiently exercised by functional test cases.

The chief difference between functional testing techniques for object-oriented software and their counterparts for procedural software (Chapters 10, 11, and 14) is the central role of object state and of sequences of method invocations to modify and ob-

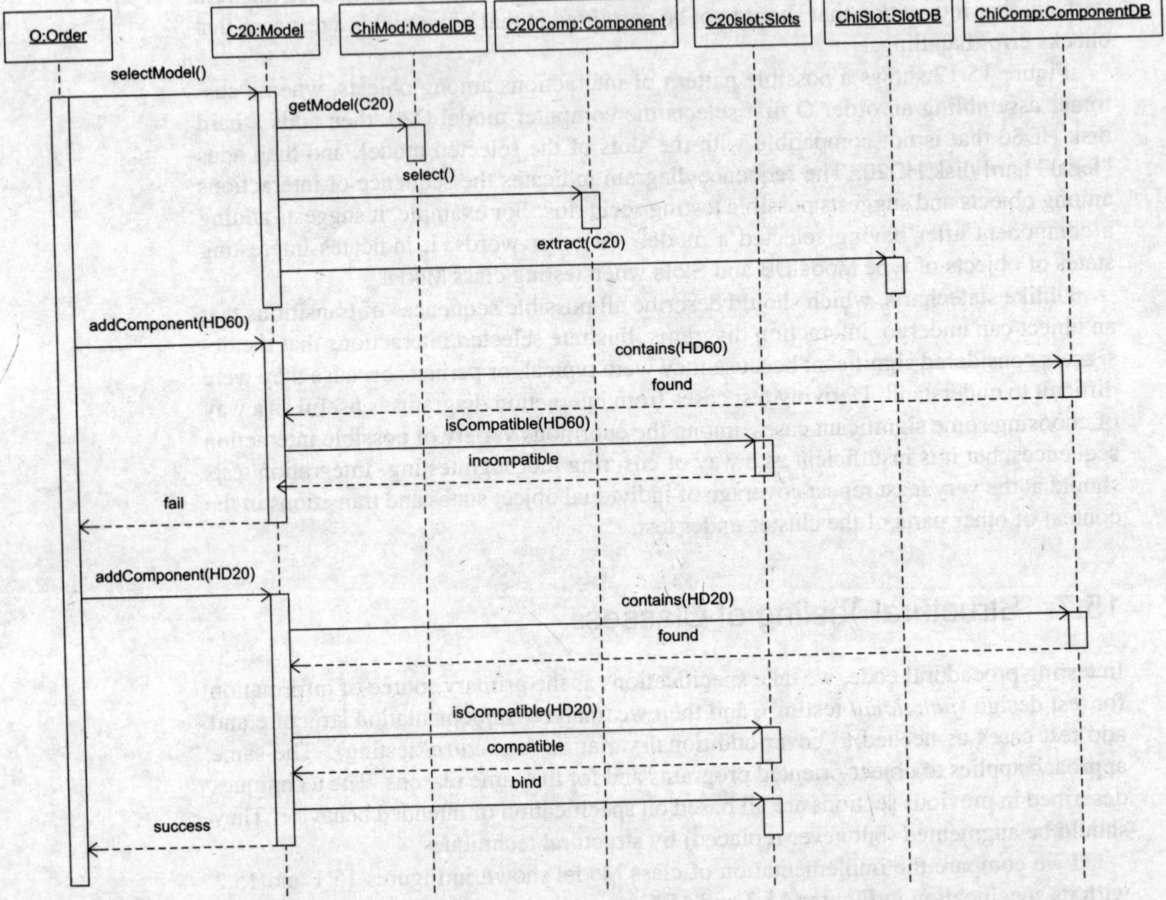

Figure 15.12: A (partial) sequence diagram that specifies the interactions among objects of type Order, Model, ModelDB, Component, ComponentDB, Slots, *and* SlotDB, *to select a computer, add an illegal component, and then add a legal one.*

serve object state. Similarly, structural test design must be extended beyond consideration of control and data flow in a single method to take into account how sequences of method invocations interact. For example, tests of isLegalConfiguration would not be sufficient without considering the prior state of private variable legalConfig.

Since the state of an object is comprised of the values of its instance variables, the number of possible object states can be enormous. We might choose to consider only the instance variables that do not appear in the specification, and add only those to the state machine representation of the object state. In the class Model example, we will have to add only the state of the Boolean variable legalConfig, which can at most double the number of states (and at worst quadruple the number of transitions). While we can model the concrete values of a single Boolean variable like legalConfig, this approach would not work if we had a dozen such variables, or even a single integer variable introduced in the implementation. To reduce the enormous number of states obtained by considering the combinations of all values of the instance variables, we could select a few representative values.

intraclass structural testing

Another way to reduce the number of test cases based on interaction through instance variable values while remaining sensitive enough to catch many common oversights is to model not the values of the variables, but the points at which the variables receive those values. This is the same intuition behind data flow testing described in Chapter 13, although it requires some extension to cover sequences in which one method defines (sets) a variable and another uses that variable. Definition-use pairs for the instance variables of an object are computed on an intraclass control flow graph that joins all the methods of a single class, and thus allows pairing of definitions and uses that occur in different methods.

Figure 15.13 shows a partial intraclass control flow graph of class Model. Each method is modeled with a standard control flow graph (CFG), just as if it were an independent procedure, except that these are joined to allow paths that invoke different methods in sequence. To allow sequences of method calls, the class itself is modeled with a node class Model connected to the CFG of each method. Method Model includes two extra statements that correspond to the declarations of variables legalConfig and modelDB that are initialized when the constructor is invoked.[3]

Sometimes definitions and uses are made through invocation of methods of other classes. For example, method addComponent calls method contains of class componentDB. Moreover, some variables are structured; for example, the state variable slot is a complex object. For the moment, we simply "unfold" the calls to external methods, and we treat arrays and objects as if they were simple variables.

A test case to exercise a definition-use pair (henceforth *DU pair*) is a sequence of method invocations that starts with a constructor, and includes the definition followed by the use without any intervening definition (a *definition-clear path*). A suite of test cases can be designed to satisfy a data flow coverage criterion by covering all such pairs. In that case we say the test suite satisfies the all DU pairs adequacy criterion.

Δ all DU pairs adequacy criterion

Consider again the private variable legalConfig in class Model, Figures 15.1 and 15.2. There are two uses of legalConfig, both in method isLegalConfiguration, one

[3]We have simplified Figure 15.13 by omitting methods getHeightCm, getWidthCm, getDepthCm, and getWeightGm, since they depend only on the constructor and do not affect other methods. Exception handlers are excluded since they will be treated separately, as described in Section 15.12.

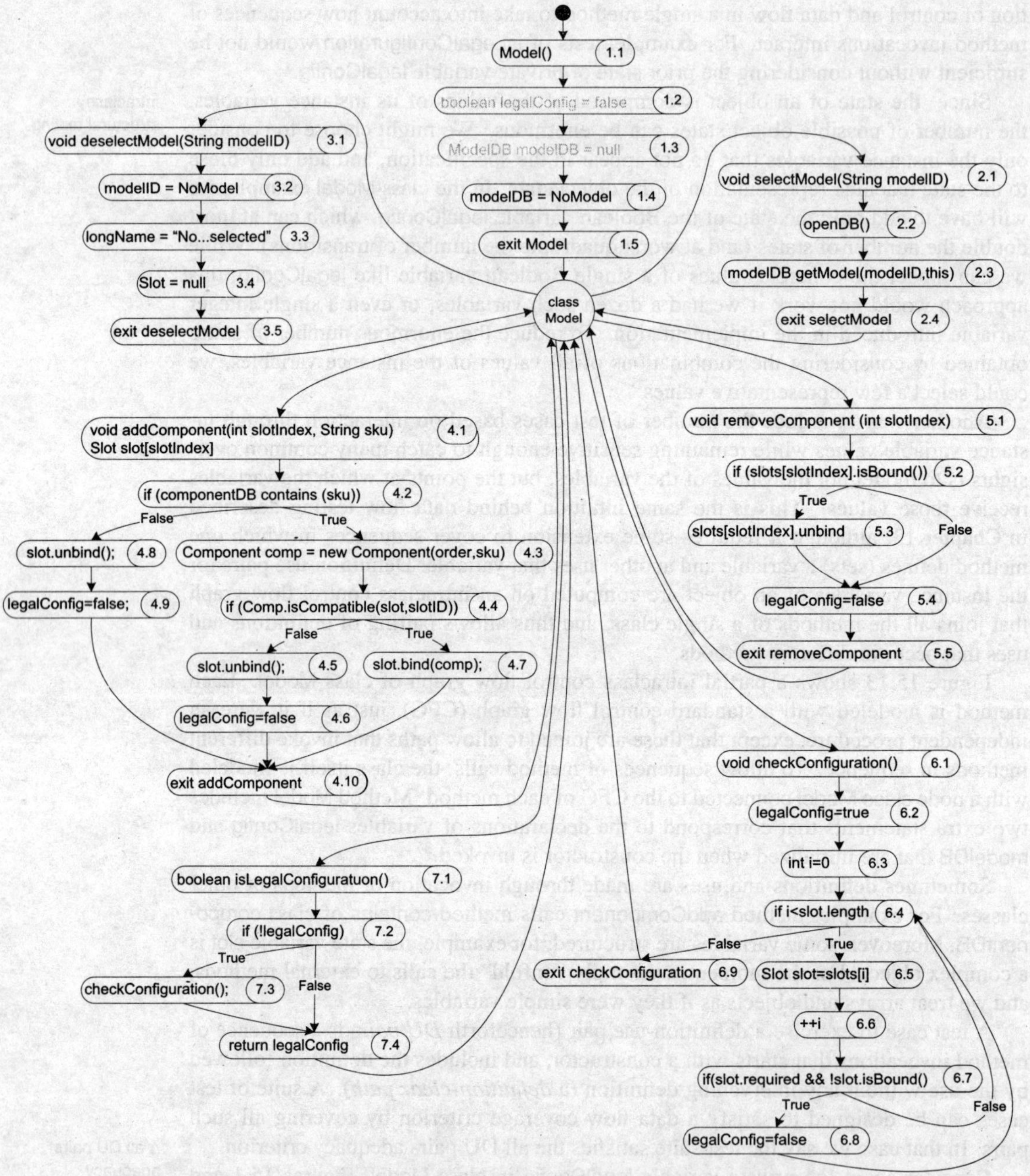

Figure 15.13: A partial intraclass control flow graph for the implementation of class Model *in Figures 15.1 and 15.2.*

in the if and one in the return statement; and there are several definitions in methods addComponent, removeComponent, checkConfiguration and in the constructor, which initializes legalConfig to *False*. The all DU pairs adequacy criterion requires a test case to exercise each definition followed by each use of legalConfig with no intervening definitions.

Specifications do not refer to the variable legalConfig and thus do not directly consider method interactions through legalConfig or contribute to defining test cases to exercise such interactions. This is the case, for example, in the invocation of method checkConfiguration in isLegalConfiguration: The specification suggests that a single invocation of method isLegalConfiguration can be sufficient to test the interactions involving this method, while calls to method checkConfiguration in isLegalConfiguration indicate possible failures that may be exposed only after two calls of method isLegalConfiguration. In fact, a first invocation of isLegalConfiguration with value *True* for legalConfig implies a call to checkConfiguration and consequent new definitions of legalConfig. Only a second call to isLegalConfiguration would exercise the use of the new value in the if statement, thus revealing failures that may derive from bad updates of legalConfig in checkConfiguration.

The all DU pairs adequacy criterion ensures that every assignment to a variable is tested at each of the uses of that variable, but like other structural coverage criteria it is not particularly good at detecting missing code. For example, if the programmer omitted an assignment to legalConfig, there would be no DU pair connecting the missing assignment to the use. However, assignments to legalConfig are correlated with updates to slots, and all DU pairs coverage with respect to slots is likely to reveal a missing assignment to the Boolean variable. Correlation among assignments to related fields is a common characteristic of the structure of object-oriented software.

Method calls and complex state variables complicate data flow analysis of object-oriented software, as procedure calls and structured variables do in procedural code. As discussed in Chapters 6 and 13, there is no universal recipe to deal with interclass calls. Test designers must find a suitable balance between costs and benefits.

interclass structural testing

A possible approach to deal with interclass calls consists in proceeding incrementally following the dependence relation, as we did for functional interclass testing. The dependence relation that can be derived from code may differ from the dependence relation derived from specifications. However, we can still safely assume that well-designed systems present at most a small number of easily breakable cycles. The dependencies of the implementation and specification of class Model are the same and are shown in Figure 15.11.

Leaf classes of the dependence hierarchy can be analyzed in isolation by identifying definitions and uses of instance variables, as just shown. The data flow information collected on leaf classes can be summarized by marking methods that access but do not modify the state as *Inspectors*; methods that modify, but do not otherwise access the state, as *Modifiers*; and methods that both access and modify the state as *Inspector/Modifiers*.

Δ inspector
Δ modifier
Δ inspector/modifiers

When identifying inspectors, modifiers and inspector/modifiers, we consider the whole object state. Thus, we mark a method as inspector/modifier even if it uses just one instance variable and modifies a different one. This simplification is crucial to scalability, since distinguishing uses and definitions of each individual variable would quickly lead to an unmanageable amount of information while climbing the dependence hierarchy.

If methods contain more than one execution path, we could summarize the whole method as an inspector, modifier, or inspector/modifier, or we could select a subset of paths to be considered independently. A single method might include Inspector, Modifier, and Inspector/Modifier paths.

Once the data flow information of leaf classes has been summarized, we can proceed with classes that only use or contain leaf classes. Invocations of modifier methods and inspector/modifiers of leaf classes are considered as definitions. Invocations of inspectors and inspector/modifiers are treated as uses. When approximating inspector/modifiers as uses, we assume that the method uses the values of the instance variables for computing the new state. This is a common way of designing methods, but some methods may fall outside this pattern. Again, we trade precision for scalability and reduced cost.

We can then proceed incrementally analyzing classes that depend only on classes already analyzed, until we reach the top of the hierarchy. In this way, each class is always considered in isolation, and the summary of information at each step prevents exponential growth of information, thus allowing large classes to be analyzed, albeit at a cost in precision.

Figure 15.14 shows the summary information for classes Slot, ModelDB, and Model. The summary information for classes Slot and ModelDB can be used for computing structural coverage of class Model without unfolding the method calls. The summary information for class Model can be used to compute structural coverage for class Order without knowing the structure of the classes used by class Order. Method checkConfiguration is not included in the summary information because it is private. The three paths in checkConfiguration are included in the summary information of the calling method isLegalConfiguration.

While summary information is usually derived from child classes, sometimes it is useful to provide the same information without actually performing the analysis, as we have done when analyzing class Model. This is useful when we cannot perform data flow analysis on the child classes, as when child classes are delivered as a closed component without source code, or are not available yet because the development is still in progress.

15.8 Oracles for Classes

Unit (intraclass) and integration (interclass) testing require suitable scaffolding to exercise the classes under test (drivers and stubs) and to inspect the test results (oracles). Constructing stubs and drivers for object-oriented software is essentially similar to the same task for procedural programs, and as in procedural programs, stubs can be avoided to the extent that the order of test execution is aligned with the build order of the software system. Oracles, however, can be more difficult to construct, owing to encapsulation of object state.

The effect of executing a method or a whole sequence of methods in a test case

Class Slot

Slot()	modifier
bind()	modifier
unbind()	modifier
isBound()	inspector

Class ModelDB

ModelDB()	modifier
getModel()	inspector
findModel()	inspector

Class Model

Model()	modifier
selectModel()	modifier
deselectModel()	modifier
addComponent() [1,2,8,9,10]	inspector/modifier
addComponent() [1,2,3,4,5,6,10]	inspector/modifier
addComponent() [1,2,3,4,7,10]	inspector/modifier
removeComponent() [1,2,3,4,5]	inspector/modifier
removeComponent() [1,2,4,5]	inspector/modifier
isLegalConfiguration() [1,2,3,[1,2,3,4,9],4]	inspector/modifier
isLegalConfiguration() [1,2,3,[1,2,3,4,5,6,7,4,9],4]	inspector/modifier
isLegalConfiguration() [1,2,3,[1,2,3,4,5,6,7,8,4,9],4]	inspector/modifier
isLegalConfiguration() [1,2,4]	modifier

Figure 15.14: Summary information for structural interclass testing for classes Slot, ModelDB, *and* Model. *Lists of CFG nodes in square brackets indicate different paths, when methods include more than one part.*

is not only the outputs produced, but also the state of the objects after execution. For example, if method deselectModel of class Model does not clear the array slots, it is erroneous, even if it produces the expected visible outputs. Thus, oracles need to check the validity of both output and state. Unfortunately for the oracle builder, though, the state of objects may not be directly accessible. For example, variable slots is private and thus cannot be directly accessed by an oracle outside the class under test.

One approach to building oracles is to break the encapsulation, for example, by modifying the source code to allow inspection of private variables. If we violate encapsulation by modifying code just for the purpose of testing, rather than leaving the modifications in the actual delivered code, then we risk differences in behavior between what is tested and what is used. We may mask faults, or we may inadvertently insert faults not present in the original code, particularly if we make modifications by hand. Even a small difference in performance can be important in a real-time system or in a multi-threaded system sensitive to scheduler decisions.

Modifications that remain in the code, or (better) design rules that require programmers to provide observability interfaces, avoid discrepancies between the production code and the tested code. This is a particularly attractive option if the interface for observing object state can be separated from the main class, as one can for example do with a C++ friend class.[4] An observability interface can be a collection of observer methods, or a single method to produce a representation of the full object state. Often an interface that produces a readable, canonical representation of an object value will be useful in debugging as well as in testing.

A second alternative is not to reveal the internal state of an object per se, but to provide a way of determining whether two objects are equivalent. Here "equivalent" does not mean that the internal states of two objects are identical, but that they represent the same abstract value. For example, we might consider the Java Vector class as representing a sequence. If so, then not only might two vectors with different capacities be considered equivalent, but we might even consider a vector object and a linked list object to be equivalent if they contain the same elements in the same order.

equivalent scenarios

An (abstract) check for equivalence can be used in a test oracle if test cases exercise two sequences of method calls that should (or should not) produce the same object state. Comparing objects using this *equivalent scenarios* approach is particularly suitable when the classes being tested are an instance of a fairly simple abstract data type, such as a dictionary structure (which includes hash tables, search trees, etc.), or a sequence or collection.

Table 15.3 shows two sequences of method invocations, one equivalent and one non-equivalent to test case TC_E for class Model. The equivalent sequence is obtained by removing "redundant" method invocations — invocations that brings the system to a previous state. In the example, method deselectModel cancels the effect of previous invocations of method selectModel and addComponent. The nonequivalent sequence is obtained by selecting a legal subset of method invocations that bring the object to a different state.

[4]A "friend" class in C++ is permitted direct access to private variables in another class. There is no direct equivalent in Java or SmallTalk, although in Java one could obtain a somewhat similar effect by using package visibility for variables and placing oracles in the same package.

Test Case TC_E	**Scenario** TC_{E1}	**Scenario** TC_{E2}
selectModel(M1) addComponent(S1,C1) addComponent(S2,C2) isLegalConfiguration() deselectModel() selectModel(M2) addComponent(S1,C1) isLegalConfiguration()	selectModel(M2) addComponent(S1,C1) isLegalConfiguration()	selectModel(M2) addComponent(S1,C1) addComponent(S2,C2) isLegalConfiguration()
	EQUIVALENT	NON-EQUIVALENT

Table 15.3: Equivalent and nonequivalent scenarios (invocation sequences) for test case TC_E *from Table 15.1 for class* Model.

Producing equivalent sequences is often quite simple. While finding nonequivalent sequences is even easier, choosing a few good ones is difficult. One approach is to hypothesize a fault in the method that "generated" the test case, and create a sequence that could be equivalent if the method contained that fault. For example, test case TC_E was designed to test method deselectModel. The nonequivalent sequence of Table 15.3 leads to a state that could be produced if method deselectModel did not clear all slots, leaving component C2 bound to slot S2 in the final configuration.

One sequence of method invocations is equivalent to another if the two sequences lead to the same object state. This does not necessarily mean that their concrete representation is bit-for-bit equal. For example, method addComponent binds a component to a slot by creating a new Slot object (Figure 15.2). Starting from two identical Model objects, and calling addComponent on both with exactly the same parameters, would result in two objects that represent the same information but that nonetheless would contain references to distinct Slot objects. The default equals method inherited from class Object, which makes a bit-for-bit comparison, would not consider them equivalent. A good practice is to add a suitable observer method to a class (e.g., by overriding the default equals method in Java).

15.9 Polymorphism and Dynamic Binding

Limited use of polymorphism and dynamic binding is easily addressed by unfolding polymorphic calls, considering each method that can be dynamically bound to each polymorphic call. Complete unfolding is impractical when many references may each be bound to instances of several subclasses.

Consider, for example, the code fragment in Figure 15.15. Object Account may by an instance of any of the classes USAccount, UKAccount, EUAccount, JPAccount, or OtherAccount. Method validateCredit can be dynamically bound to methods validateCredit of any of the classes EduCredit, BizCredit, or IndividualCredit, each implementing different credit policies. Parameter creditCard may be dynamically bound to VISACard,

```
abstract class Credit {
  ...
    abstract boolean validateCredit( Account a, int amt, CreditCard c);
  ...
}
```

Figure 15.15: A method call in which the method itself and two of its parameters can be dynamically bound to different classes.

AmExpCard, or ChipmunkCard, each with different characteristics. Even in this simple example, replacing the calls with all possible instances results in 45 different cases (5 possible types of account × 3 possible types of credit × 3 possible credit cards).

The explosion in possible combinations is essentially the same combinatorial explosion encountered if we try to cover all combinations of attributes in functional testing, and the same solutions are applicable. The combinatorial testing approach presented in Chapter 11 can be used to choose a set of combinations that covers each pair of possible bindings (e.g., Business account in Japan, Education customer using Chipmunk Card), rather than all possible combinations (Japanese business customer using Chipmunk card). Table 15.4 shows 15 cases that cover all pairwise combinations of calls for the example of Figure 15.15.

Account	Credit	creditCard
USAccount	EduCredit	VISACard
USAccount	BizCredit	AmExpCard
USAccount	individualCredit	ChipmunkCard
UKAccount	EduCredit	AmExpCard
UKAccount	BizCredit	VISACard
UKAccount	individualCredit	ChipmunkCard
EUAccount	EduCredit	ChipmunkCard
EUAccount	BizCredit	AmExpCard
EUAccount	individualCredit	VISACard
JPAccount	EduCredit	VISACard
JPAccount	BizCredit	ChipmunkCard
JPAccount	individualCredit	AmExpCard
OtherAccount	EduCredit	ChipmunkCard
OtherAccount	BizCredit	VISACard
OtherAccount	individualCredit	AmExpCard

Table 15.4: A set of test case specifications that cover all pairwise combinations of the possible polymorphic bindings of Account, Credit, *and* creditCard.

The combinations in Table 15.4 were of dynamic bindings in a single call. Bindings in a sequence of calls can also interact. Consider, for example, method getYTDPurchased of class Account shown in Figure 15.4 on page 278, which computes the total yearly purchase associated with one account to determine the applicable discount. Chipmunk offers tiered discounts to customers whose total yearly purchase reaches a threshold, considering all subsidiary accounts.

The total yearly purchase for an account is computed by method getYTDPurchased, which sums purchases by all customers using the account and all subsidiaries. Amounts are always recorded in the local currency of the account, but getYTDPurchased sums the purchases of subsidiaries even when they use different currencies (e.g., when some are bound to subclass USAccount and others to EUAccount). The intra- and interclass testing techniques presented in the previous section may fail to reveal this type of fault. The problem can be addressed by selecting test cases that cover combinations of polymorphic calls and bindings. To identify sequential combinations of bindings, we must first identify individual polymorphic calls and binding sets, and then select possible sequences.

Let us consider for simplicity only the method getYTDPurchased. This method is called once for each customer and once for each subsidiary of the account and in both cases can be dynamically bound to methods belonging to any of the subclasses of Account (UKAccount, EUAccount, and so on). At each of these calls, variable totalPurchased is used and changed, and at the end of the method it is used twice more (to set an instance variable and to return a value from the method).

Data flow analysis may be used to identify potential interactions between possible bindings at a point where a variable is modified and points where the same value is used. Any of the standard data flow testing criteria could be extended to consider each possible method binding at the point of definition and the point of use. For instance, a single definition-use pair becomes $n \times m$ pairs if the point of definition can be bound in n ways and the point of use can be bound in m ways. If this is impractical, a weaker but still useful alternative is to vary both bindings independently, which results in m or n pairs (whichever is greater) rather than their product. Note that this weaker criterion would be very likely to reveal the fault in getYTDPurchased, provided the choices of binding at each point are really independent rather than going through the same set of choices in lockstep. In many cases, binding sets are not mutually independent, so the selection of combinations is limited.

15.10 Inheritance

Inheritance does not introduce new classes of faults except insofar as it is associated with polymorphism and dynamic binding, which we have already discussed, and exception handling, which is discussed in Section 15.12. It does provide an opportunity for optimization by reusing test cases and even test executions. Subclasses share methods with ancestors. Identifying which methods do not need to be retested and which test cases can be reused may significantly reduce testing effort.

Methods of a subclass can be categorized as

New: if they are newly defined in the subclass — that is, they do not occur in the ancestor. New methods include those with the same name but different parameters than methods in ancestor classes.

Method	Intra funct	Intra struct	Inter funct	Inter struct
LineItem	$\langle TS_{LI1}, Y\rangle$	$\langle TS_{LI2}, Y\rangle$	$\langle TS_{LI3}, Y\rangle$	$\langle TS_{LI4}, Y\rangle$
validItem	$\langle TS_{vI1}, N\rangle$	$\langle -,-\rangle$	$\langle -,-\rangle$	$\langle -,-\rangle$
getUnitPrice	$\langle TS_{gUP1}, N\rangle$	$\langle -,-\rangle$	$\langle TS_{gUP3}, N\rangle$	$\langle -,-\rangle$
getExtendedPrice	$\langle TS_{gXP1}, Y\rangle$	$\langle TS_{gXP2}, Y\rangle$	$\langle TS_{gXP3}, Y\rangle$	$\langle TS_{gXP4}, Y\rangle$
getWeightGm	$\langle TS_{gWG1}, N\rangle$	$\langle -,-\rangle$	$\langle -,-\rangle$	$\langle -,-\rangle$
getHeightCm	$\langle TS_{gHC1}, N\rangle$	$\langle -,-\rangle$	$\langle -,-\rangle$	$\langle -,-\rangle$
getWidthCm	$\langle TS_{gWC1}, N\rangle$	$\langle -,-\rangle$	$\langle -,-\rangle$	$\langle -,-\rangle$
getDepthCm	$\langle TS_{gDC1}, N\rangle$	$\langle -,-\rangle$	$\langle -,-\rangle$	$\langle -,-\rangle$

Legend: $\langle TS_I, B\rangle$ refers to test set I, to be executed if $B = Y$.
$\langle -,-\rangle$ means no applicable tests.

Table 15.5: Testing history for class LineItem

Recursive: if they are inherited from the ancestor without change — that is, they occur only in the ancestor.

Redefined: if they are overridden in the subclass, that is, both occur in the subclass.

Abstract new: if they are newly defined and abstract in the subclass.

Abstract recursive: if they are inherited from the ancestor, where they are abstract.

Abstract redefined: if they are redefined in the subclass, and they are abstract in the ancestor.

When testing a base class, one that does not specialize a previously tested class, we can summarize the testing information in a simple table that indicates the sets of generated and executed test cases. Such a table is called a *testing history*.

testing history

In general we will have four sets of test cases for a method: *intraclass functional*, *intraclass structural*, *interclass functional*, and *interclass structural*. For methods that do not call methods in other classes, we will have only *intraclass test cases*, since no integration test focuses on such methods. For abstract methods, we will only have *functional test cases*, since we do not have the code of the method. Each set of test cases is marked with a flag that indicates whether the test set can be executed.

Table 15.5 shows a testing history for class LineItem, whose code is shown in Figure 15.16. Methods validItem, getWeightGm, getHeightCm, getWidthCm, and getDepthCm are abstract and do not interact with external classes; thus we only have intraclass functional test cases that cannot be directly executed. Method getUnitPrice is abstract, but from the specifications (not shown here) we can infer that it interacts with other classes; thus we have both intra- and interclass functional test cases. Both the constructor and method getExtendedPrice are implemented and interact with other classes (Order and AccountType, respectively), and thus we have all four sets of test cases.

New and abstract new methods need to be tested from scratch, thus we need to derive the needed test cases and execute them. We report the testing activity in the testing history of the new class by adding a new row and new test cases. Recursive and

```java
/** One line item of a customer order (abstract). */
public abstract class LineItem {

    /** The order this LineItem belongs to. */
    protected Order order;

    /** Constructor links item to owning order. Must call in subclasses. */
    public LineItem(Order _order) { order = _order; }

    /** Stock-keeping unit (sku) is unique key to all product databases. */
    public String sku;

    /** Number of identical units to be purchased. */
    public int units=1;

    /** Has this line item passed all validation tests? */
    public abstract boolean validItem();

    /** Price of a single item. */
    public abstract int getUnitPrice(AccountType accountType);

    /** Extended price for number of units */
    public int getExtendedPrice(AccountType accountType)
    {    return units * this.getUnitPrice(accountType);    }

    // Dimensions for packing and shipping (required of all top-level items)
    /** Weight in grams */
    public abstract int getWeightGm();
    /** Height in centimeters */
    public abstract int getHeightCm();
    /** Width in Centimeters. */
    public abstract int getWidthCm();
    /** Depth in Centimeters */
    public abstract int getDepthCm();
}
```

Figure 15.16: Part of a Java implementation of the abstract class LineItem.

Method	Intra funct	Intra struct	Inter funct	Inter struct
LineItem	$\langle TS_{LI1}, N\rangle$	$\langle TS_{LI2}, N\rangle$	$\langle TS_{LI3}, N\rangle$	$\langle TS_{LI4}, N\rangle$
validItem	$\langle TS_{vI1}, N\rangle$	$\langle -,-\rangle$	$\langle -,-\rangle$	$\langle -,-\rangle$
getUnitPrice	$\langle TS_{gUP1}, Y\rangle$	$\langle TS'_{gUP2}, Y\rangle$	$\langle TS_{gUP3}, Y\rangle$	$\langle TS'_{gUP4}, Y\rangle$
getExtendedPrice	$\langle TS_{gXP1}, N\rangle$	$\langle TS_{gXP2}, N\rangle$	$\langle TS_{gXP3}, N\rangle$	$\langle TS_{gXP4}, N\rangle$
getWeightGm	$\langle TS_{gWG1}, N\rangle$	$\langle -,-\rangle$	$\langle -,-\rangle$	$\langle -,-\rangle$
getHeightCm	$\langle TS_{gHC1}, N\rangle$	$\langle -,-\rangle$	$\langle -,-\rangle$	$\langle -,-\rangle$
getWidthCm	$\langle TS_{gWC1}, N\rangle$	$\langle -,-\rangle$	$\langle -,-\rangle$	$\langle -,-\rangle$
getDepthCm	$\langle TS_{gDC1}, N\rangle$	$\langle -,-\rangle$	$\langle -,-\rangle$	$\langle -,-\rangle$
CompositeItem	$\langle TS'_{CM1}, Y\rangle$	$\langle TS'_{CM2}, Y\rangle$	$\langle TS'_{CM3}, Y\rangle$	$\langle TS'_{CM4}, Y\rangle$

Table 15.6: Testing history for class CompositeItem. *New test sets are marked with a prime.*

abstract recursive methods do not need to be retested. Thus the old test sets are copied into the new table and marked as not-to-be-executed. Redefined and abstract redefined methods must be retested, so we add new test cases and mark them to be executed.

Table 15.6 shows the testing history for class CompositeItem that specializes class LineItem. The code of class CompositeItem is shown in Figure 15.17. Class CompositeItem adds a constructor, and thus we add a line to the testing history that indicates the four sets of test cases to be added and executed. It redefines method getUnitPrice, which was virtual in class LineItem: the functional test cases derived for class LineItem are thus executed, and new structural test cases are added. All other classes are inherited, and thus the testing history reports all test cases and marks them as not-to-be-executed.

The testing history approach reduces the number of tests to be executed, but requires extra effort of keeping track of testing activities. Effort is repaid mainly when it is possible to avoid *designing* new test cases, but when the cost of executing test cases is high (e.g., because the test requires interaction with an external device or a human) the savings in test execution cost can also be significant. If the cost of executing test cases is negligible, it may be cheaper to simply retest all classes regardless of the tests executed on the ancestors.

15.11 Genericity

Generics, also known as parameterized types or (in C++) as templates, are an important tool for building reusable components and libraries. A generic class (say, linked lists) is designed to be instantiated with many different parameter types (e.g., LinkedList<String> and LinkedList<Integer>). We can test only instantiations, not the generic class itself, and we may not know in advance all the different ways a generic class might be instantiated.

A generic class is typically designed to behave consistently over some set of permitted parameter types. Therefore the testing (and analysis) job can be broken into two parts: showing that some instantiation is correct and showing that all permitted instantiations behave identically.

```java
package Orders;
import Accounts.AccountType;
import Prices.Pricelist;
import java.util.*;

/**
* A composite line item includes a "wrapper" item for the whole
* bundle and a set of zero or more component items.
*/
public abstract class CompositeItem extends LineItem {

    /**
     * A composite item has some unifying name and base price
     * (which might be zero) and has zero or more additional parts,
     * which are themselves line items.
     */
    private Vector parts = new Vector();

    /**
     * Constructor from LineItem, links to an encompassing Order.
     */
    public CompositeItem(Order _order) {
        super(_order);
    }

    public int getUnitPrice(AccountType accountType) {
        Pricelist prices = new Pricelist();
        int price = prices.getPrice(sku, accountType);
        for (Enumeration e = parts.elements(); e.hasMoreElements(); )
            {
                LineItem i = (LineItem) e.nextElement();
                price += i.getUnitPrice(accountType);
            }
        return price;
    }
}
```

Figure 15.17: Part of a Java implementation of class CompositeItem.

Testing a single instantiation raises no particular problems, provided we have source code for both the generic class and the parameter class. Roughly speaking, we can design test cases as if the parameter were copied textually into the body of the generic class.

Consider first the case of a generic class that does not make method calls on, nor access fields of, its parameters. Ascertaining this property is best done by inspecting the source code, not by testing it. If we can nonetheless conjecture some ways in which the generic and its parameter might interact (e.g., if the generic makes use of some service that a parameter type might also make use of, directly or indirectly), then we should design test cases aimed specifically at detecting such interaction.

Gaining confidence in an unknowable set of potential instantiations becomes more difficult when the generic class does interact with the parameter class. For example, Java (since version 1.5) has permitted a declaration like this:

```
class PriorityQueue<Elem implements Comparable> {...}
```

The generic PriorityQueue class will be able to make calls on the methods of interface Comparable. Now the behavior of PriorityQueue<E> is not independent of E, but it should be dependent only in certain very circumscribed ways, and in particular it should behave correctly whenever E obeys the requirements of the contract implied by Comparable.

The contract imposed on permitted parameters is a kind of specification, and specification-based (functional) test selection techniques are an appropriate way to select representative instantiations of the generic class. For example, if we read the interface specification for java.lang.Comparable, we learn that most but not all classes that implement Comparable also satisfy the rule

```
(x.compareTo(y) == 0) == (x.equals(y))
```

Explicit mention of this condition strongly suggests that test cases should include instantiations with classes that do obey this rule (class String, for example) and others that do not (e.g., class BigDecimal with two BigDecimal values 4.0 and 4.00).

15.12 Exceptions

Programs in modern object-oriented languages use exceptions to separate handling of error cases from the primary program logic, thereby simplifying normal control flow. Exceptions also greatly reduce a common class of faults in languages without exception-handling constructs. One of the most common faults in C programs, for example, is neglecting to check for the error indications returned by a C function. In a language like Java, an exception is certain to interrupt normal control flow.

The price of separating exception handling from the primary control flow logic is introduction of implicit control flows. The point at which an exception is caught and handled may be far from the point at which it is thrown. Moreover, the association of exceptions with handlers is dynamic. In most object-oriented languages and procedural languages that provide exception handling, an exception propagates up the stack of calling methods until it reaches a matching handler.

Since exceptions introduce a kind of control flow, one might expect that it could be treated like other control flow in constructing program models and deriving test cases. However, treating every possible exception this way would create an unwieldy control flow graph accounting for potential exceptions at every array subscript reference, every memory allocation, every cast, and so on, and these would be multiplied by matching them to every handler that could appear immediately above them on the call stack. Worse, many of these potential exceptions are actually impossible, so the burden would not be just in designing test cases for each of them but in deciding which can actually occur. It is more practical to consider exceptions separately from normal control flow in test design.

We can dismiss from consideration exceptions triggered by program errors signaled by the underlying system (subscript errors, bad casts, etc.), since exercising these exceptions adds nothing to other efforts to prevent or find the errors themselves. If a method A throws an exception that indicates a programming error, we can take almost the same approach. However, if there are exception handlers for these program error exceptions, such as we may find in fault-tolerant programs or in libraries that attempt to maintain data consistency despite errors in client code, then it is necessary to test the error recovery code (usually by executing it together with a stub class with the programming error). This is different and much less involved than testing the error recovery code coupled with every potential point at which the error might be present in actual code.

Exceptions that indicate abnormal cases but not necessarily program errors (e.g., exhaustion of memory or premature end-of-file) require special treatment. If the handler for these is local (e.g., a Java try block with an exception handler around a group of file operations), then the exception handler itself requires testing. Whether to test each individual point where exceptions bound to the same handler might be raised (e.g., each individual file operation within the same try block) is a matter of judgment.

The remaining exceptions are those that are allowed to propagate beyond the local context in which they are thrown. For example, suppose method A makes a call to method B, within a Java try block with an exception handler for exceptions of class E. Suppose B has no exception handler for E and makes a call to method C, which throws E. Now the exception will propagate up the chain of method calls until it reaches the handler in A. There could be many such chains, which depend in part on overriding inherited methods, and it is difficult (sometimes even impossible) to determine all and only the possible pairings of points where an exception is thrown with handlers in other methods.

Since testing all chains through which exceptions can propagate is impractical, it is best to make it unnecessary. A reasonable design rule to enforce is that, if a method propagates an exception without catching it, the method call should have no other effect. If it is not possible to ensure that method execution interrupted by an exception has no effect, then an exception handler should be present (even if it propagates the same exception by throwing it again). Then, it should suffice to design test cases to exercise each point at which an exception is explicitly thrown by application code, and each handler in application code, but not necessarily all their combinations.

Open Research Issues

Many problems involved in test and analysis of object-oriented systems are still open. Most results about functional testing refer to a subset of UML and to algebraic specifications. Additional work is needed to complete the available methods to cope with all aspects of object-oriented systems and different specification approaches.

The few techniques for structural testing disclose a wide set of problems that need additional investigation. We need additional experimental data about the effectiveness of the available techniques and better ways to cope with interclass testing.

Test and analysis problems of many features that characterize object-oriented systems, such as exceptions, polymorphism, dynamic binding, and inheritance, have been investigated only partially and need additional work. Despite a good deal of experience with object-oriented design, we still have little information about common faults, and we lack fault taxonomies.

Further Reading

Many recent books on software testing and software engineering address object-oriented software to at least some degree. The most complete book-length account of current methods is Binder's *Testing Object Oriented Systems* [Bin00].

Structural state-based testing is discussed in detail by Buy, Orso, and Pezzè [BOP00]. The data flow approach to testing software with polymorphism and dynamic binding was initially proposed by Orso [Ors98]. Harrold, McGregor, and Fitzpatrick [HMF92] provide a detailed discussion of the use of testing histories for selecting test cases for subclasses.

Thévenod-Fosse and Waeselynck describe statistical testing using statechart specifications [TFW93]. An excellent paper by Doong and Frankl [DF94] introduces equivalent scenarios. Although Doong and Frankl discuss their application with algebraic specifications (which are not much used in practice), the value of the approach does not hinge on that detail.

Related Topics

Basic functional and structural testing strategies are treated briefly here, and readers who have not already read Chapters 10, 11, and 12 will find there a more thorough presentation of the rationale and basic techniques for those approaches. Chapters 13 and 14 likewise present the basic data flow and model-based testing approaches in more detail. As integration testing progresses beyond small clusters of classes to major subsystems and components, the interclass testing techniques described in this chapter will become less relevant, and component testing techniques presented in Chapter 21 more important. The system and acceptance testing techniques described in Chapter 22 are as appropriate to object-oriented software as they are to mixed and purely procedural software systems.

Exercises

15.1. The set of test cases given in Table 15.1 is not the smallest test suite that satisfies the *transition coverage* criterion for the finite state machine (FSM) of Figure 15.7.

(a) Derive a smaller set of test cases that satisfy the *transition coverage* criterion for the FSM.

(b) Compare the two sets of test cases. What are the advantages of each?

(c) Derive a suite of test cases that satisfies the simple transition coverage criterion but does not satisfy the transition coverage criterion.

15.2. The test cases given in Table 15.1 assume that transitions not given explicitly are "don't care," and thus we do not exercise them. Modify the test suite, first assuming that omitted transitions are "error" transitions. Next, modify the same test suite, but instead assuming that the omitted transitions are "self" transitions. Are the two modified test suites different? Why or why not?

15.3. Generate at least one equivalent and one nonequivalent scenario for at least one of the test cases $TC_A, \ldots, TC_E$ of Table 15.1.

15.4. A canonical representation is a unique representation of a set of equivalent objects. For example, $\{a,a,c,b\}$, $\{c,b,a\}$, and $\{a,b,c\}$ are all representations of the same mathematical set object. If we choose a lexicographically sorted representation without duplicates as a canonical representation, then we will use $\{a,b,c\}$ as the unique way of writing that set.

Imagine we are using the equivalent scenarios approach to test a hash table class. Why might we want a toString method that returns a canonical representation of the table? Give an example of a test case in which you might use it.

Chapter 16

Fault-Based Testing

A model of potential program faults is a valuable source of information for evaluating and designing test suites. Some fault knowledge is commonly used in functional and structural testing, for example when identifying singleton and error values for parameter characteristics in category-partition testing or when populating catalogs with erroneous values, but a fault model can also be used more directly. Fault-based testing uses a fault model directly to hypothesize potential faults in a program under test, as well as to create or evaluate test suites based on its efficacy in detecting those hypothetical faults.

Required Background

- Chapter 9
  The introduction to test case selection and adequacy sets the context for this chapter. Though not strictly required, it is helpful in understanding how the techniques described in this chapter should be applied.
- Chapter 12
  Some basic knowledge of structural testing criteria is required to understand the comparison of fault-based with structural testing criteria.

16.1 Overview

Engineers study failures to understand how to prevent similar failures in the future. For example, failure of the Tacoma Narrows Bridge in 1940 led to new understanding of oscillation in high wind and to the introduction of analyses to predict and prevent such destructive oscillation in subsequent bridge design. The causes of an airline crash are likewise extensively studied, and when traced to a structural failure they frequently result in a directive to apply diagnostic tests to all aircraft considered potentially vulnerable to similar failures.

Experience with common software faults sometimes leads to improvements in design methods and programming languages. For example, the main purpose of automatic memory management in Java is not to spare the programmer the trouble of releasing unused memory, but to prevent the programmer from making the kind of memory management errors (dangling pointers, redundant deallocations, and memory leaks) that frequently occur in C and C++ programs. Automatic array bounds checking cannot prevent a programmer from using an index expression outside array bounds, but can make it much less likely that the fault escapes detection in testing, as well as limiting the damage incurred if it does lead to operational failure (eliminating, in particular, the buffer overflow attack as a means of subverting privileged programs). Type checking reliably detects many other faults during program translation.

Of course, not all programmer errors fall into classes that can be prevented or statically detected using better programming languages. Some faults must be detected through testing, and there too we can use knowledge about common faults to be more effective.

The basic concept of fault-based testing is to select test cases that would distinguish the program under test from alternative programs that contain hypothetical faults. This is usually approached by modifying the program under test to actually produce the hypothetical faulty programs. Fault seeding can be used to evaluate the thoroughness of a test suite (that is, as an element of a test adequacy criterion), or for selecting test cases to augment a test suite, or to estimate the number of faults in a program.

16.2 Assumptions in Fault-Based Testing

The effectiveness of fault-based testing depends on the quality of the fault model and on some basic assumptions about the relation of the seeded faults to faults that might actually be present. In practice, the seeded faults are small syntactic changes, like replacing one variable reference by another in an expression, or changing a comparison from < to <=. We may hypothesize that these are representative of faults actually present in the program.

Put another way, if the program under test has an actual fault, we may hypothesize that it differs from another, corrected program by only a small textual change. If so, then we need merely distinguish the program from all such small variants (by selecting test cases for which either the original or the variant program fails) to ensure detection of all such faults. This is known as the *competent programmer hypothesis*, an assumption that the program under test is "close to" (in the sense of textual difference) a correct program.

Δ competent programmer hypothesis

Some program faults are indeed simple typographical errors, and others that involve deeper errors of logic may nonetheless be manifest in simple textual differences. Sometimes, though, an error of logic will result in much more complex differences in program text. This may not invalidate fault-based testing with a simpler fault model, provided test cases sufficient for detecting the simpler faults are sufficient also for detecting the more complex fault. This is known as the *coupling effect*.

Δ coupling effect hypothesis

The coupling effect hypothesis may seem odd, but can be justified by appeal to a more plausible hypothesis about interaction of faults. A complex change is equivalent

Fault-Based Testing: Terminology

Original program: The program unit (e.g., C function or Java class) to be tested.

Program location: A region in the source code. The precise definition is defined relative to the syntax of a particular programming language. Typical locations are statements, arithmetic and Boolean expressions, and procedure calls.

Alternate expression: Source code text that can be legally substituted for the text at a program location. A substitution is legal if the resulting program is syntactically correct (i.e., it compiles without errors).

Alternate program: A program obtained from the original program by substituting an alternate expression for the text at some program location.

Distinct behavior of an alternate program R for a test t: The behavior of an alternate program R is distinct from the behavior of the original program P for a test t, if R and P produce a different result for t, or if the output of R is not defined for t.

Distinguished set of alternate programs for a test suite T: A set of alternate programs are distinct if each alternate program in the set can be distinguished from the original program by at least one test in T.

to several smaller changes in program text. If the effect of one of these small changes is not masked by the effect of others, then a test case that differentiates a variant based on a single change may also serve to detect the more complex error.

Fault-based testing can guarantee fault detection only if the competent programmer hypothesis and the coupling effect hypothesis hold. But guarantees are more than we expect from other approaches to designing or evaluating test suites, including the structural and functional test adequacy criteria discussed in earlier chapters. Fault-based testing techniques can be useful even if we decline to take the leap of faith required to fully accept their underlying assumptions. What is essential is to recognize the dependence of these techniques, and any inferences about software quality based on fault-based testing, on the quality of the fault model. This also implies that developing better fault models, based on hard data about real faults rather than guesses, is a good investment of effort.

16.3 Mutation Analysis

Mutation analysis is the most common form of software fault-based testing. A fault model is used to produce hypothetical faulty programs by creating variants of the program under test. Variants are created by "seeding" faults, that is, by making a small change to the program under test following a pattern in the fault model. The patterns for changing program text are called *mutation operators*, and each variant program is called a *mutant*.

Δ mutation operator

Δ mutant

Mutation Analysis: Terminology

Original program under test: The program or procedure (function) to be tested.

Mutant: A program that differs from the original program for one syntactic element (e.g., a statement, a condition, a variable, a label).

Distinguished mutant: A mutant that can be distinguished for the original program by executing at least one test case.

Equivalent mutant: A mutant that cannot be distinguished from the original program.

Mutation operator: A rule for producing a mutant program by syntactically modifying the original program.

Mutants should be plausible as faulty programs. Mutant programs that are rejected by a compiler, or that fail almost all tests, are not good models of the faults we seek to uncover with systematic testing.

Δ valid mutant

Δ useful mutant

We say a mutant is valid if it is syntactically correct. A mutant obtained from the program of Figure 16.1 by substituting while for switch in the statement at line 13 would not be valid, since it would result in a compile-time error. We say a mutant is useful if, in addition to being valid, its behavior differs from the behavior of the original program for no more than a small subset of program test cases. A mutant obtained by substituting 0 for 1000 in the statement at line 4 would be valid, but not useful, since the mutant would be distinguished from the program under test by all inputs and thus would not give any useful information on the effectiveness of a test suite. Defining mutation operators that produce valid and useful mutations is a nontrivial task.

Since mutants must be valid, mutation operators are syntactic patterns defined relative to particular programming languages. Figure 16.2 shows some mutation operators for the C language. Constraints are associated with mutation operators to guide selection of test cases likely to distinguish mutants from the original program. For example, the mutation operator *svr* (scalar variable replacement) can be applied only to variables of compatible type (to be valid), and a test case that distinguishes the mutant from the original program must execute the modified statement in a state in which the original variable and its substitute have different values.

Many of the mutants of Figure 16.2 can be applied equally well to other procedural languages, but in general a mutation operator that produces valid and useful mutants for a given language may not apply to a different language or may produce invalid or useless mutants for another language. For example, a mutation operator that removes the "friend" keyword from the declaration of a C++ class would not be applicable to Java, which does not include friend classes.

```
/** Convert each line from standard input */
void transduce() {
  #define BUFLEN 1000
  char buf[BUFLEN];   /* Accumulate line into this buffer  */
  int   pos = 0;          /* Index for next character in buffer */

  char inChar; /* Next character from input */

  int atCR = 0; /* 0="within line", 1="optional DOS LF" */

  while ((inChar = getchar()) != EOF ) {
    switch (inChar) {
    case LF:
      if (atCR) {    /* Optional DOS LF */
        atCR = 0;
      } else {          /* Encountered CR within line */
        emit(buf, pos);
        pos = 0;
      }
      break;
    case CR:
      emit(buf, pos);
      pos = 0;
      atCR = 1;
      break;
    default:
      if (pos >= BUFLEN-2) fail("Buffer overflow");
      buf[pos++] = inChar;
    } /* switch */
  }
  if (pos > 0) {
    emit(buf, pos);
  }
}
```

Figure 16.1: Program transduce *converts line endings among Unix, DOS, and Macintosh conventions. The main procedure, which selects the output line end convention, and the output procedure* emit *are not shown.*

ID	Operator	Description	Constraint
Operand Modifications			
crp	constant for constant replacement	replace constant $C1$ with constant $C2$	$C1 \neq C2$
scr	scalar for constant replacement	replace constant C with scalar variable X	$C \neq X$
acr	array for constant replacement	replace constant C with array reference $A[I]$	$C \neq A[I]$
scr	struct for constant replacement	replace constant C with struct field S	$C \neq S$
svr	scalar variable replacement	replace scalar variable X with a scalar variable Y	$X \neq Y$
csr	constant for scalar variable replacement	replace scalar variable X with a constant C	$X \neq C$
asr	array for scalar variable replacement	replace scalar variable X with an array reference $A[I]$	$X \neq A[I]$
ssr	struct for scalar replacement	replace scalar variable X with struct field S	$X \neq S$
vie	scalar variable initialization elimination	remove initialization of a scalar variable	
car	constant for array replacement	replace array reference $A[I]$ with constant C	$A[I] \neq C$
sar	scalar for array replacement	replace array reference $A[I]$ with scalar variable X	$A[I] \neq X$
cnr	comparable array replacement	replace array reference with a comparable array reference	
sar	struct for array reference replacement	replace array reference $A[I]$ with a struct field S	$A[I] \neq S$
Expression Modifications			
abs	absolute value insertion	replace e by abs(e)	$e < 0$
aor	arithmetic operator replacement	replace arithmetic operator ψ with arithmetic operator ϕ	$e_1 \psi e_2 \neq e_1 \phi e_2$
lcr	logical connector replacement	replace logical connector ψ with logical connector ϕ	$e_1 \psi e_2 \neq e_1 \phi e_2$
ror	relational operator replacement	replace relational operator ψ with relational operator ϕ	$e_1 \psi e_2 \neq e_1 \phi e_2$
uoi	unary operator insertion	insert unary operator	
cpr	constant for predicate replacement	replace predicate with a constant value	
Statement Modifications			
sdl	statement deletion	delete a statement	
sca	switch case replacement	replace the label of one case with another	
ses	end block shift	move } one statement earlier and later	

Figure 16.2: A sample set of mutation operators for the C language, with associated constraints to select test cases that distinguish generated mutants from the original program.

16.4 Fault-Based Adequacy Criteria

Given a program and a test suite T, mutation analysis consists of the following steps:

Select mutation operators: If we are interested in specific classes of faults, we may select a set of mutation operators relevant to those faults.

Generate mutants: Mutants are generated mechanically by applying mutation operators to the original program.

Distinguish mutants: Execute the original program and each generated mutant with the test cases in T. A mutant is *killed* when it can be distinguished from the original program.

Figure 16.3 shows a sample of mutants for program Transduce, obtained by applying the mutant operators in Figure 16.2. Test suite TS

$$TS = \{1U, 1D, 2U, 2D, 2M, End, Long\}$$

kills M_j, which can be distinguished from the original program by test cases $1D$, $2U$, $2D$, and $2M$. Mutants M_i, M_k, and M_l are not distinguished from the original program by any test in TS. We say that mutants not killed by a test suite are *live*. live mutants

A mutant can remain *live* for two reasons:

- The mutant can be distinguished from the original program, but the test suite T does not contain a test case that distinguishes them (i.e., the test suite is not adequate with respect to the mutant).

- The mutant cannot be distinguished from the original program by any test case (i.e., the mutant is equivalent to the original program).

Given a set of mutants SM and a test suite T, the fraction of nonequivalent mutants killed by T measures the adequacy of T with respect to SM. Unfortunately, the problem of identifying equivalent mutants is undecidable in general, and we could err either by claiming that a mutant is equivalent to the program under test when it is not or by counting some equivalent mutants among the remaining live mutants.

The adequacy of the test suite TS evaluated with respect to the four mutants of Figure 16.3 is 25%. However, we can easily observe that mutant M_i is equivalent to the original program (i.e., no input would distinguish it). Conversely, mutants M_k and M_l seem to be nonequivalent to the original program: There should be at least one test case that distinguishes each of them from the original program. Thus the adequacy of TS, measured after eliminating the equivalent mutant M_i, is 33%.

Mutant M_l is killed by test case *Mixed*, which represents the unusual case of an input file containing both DOS- and Unix-terminated lines. We would expect that *Mixed* would also kill M_k, but this does not actually happen: Both M_k and the original program produce the same result for *Mixed*. This happens because both the mutant and the original program fail in the same way.[1] The use of a simple oracle for checking

[1]The program was in regular use by one of the authors and was believed to be correct. Discovery of the fault came as a surprise while using it as an example for this chapter.

Mutation Analysis vs. Structural Testing

For typical sets of syntactic mutants, a mutation-adequate test suite will also be adequate with respect to simple structural criteria such as statement or branch coverage. Mutation adequacy can simulate and subsume a structural coverage criterion if the set of mutants can be killed only by satisfying the corresponding test coverage obligations.

Statement coverage can be simulated by applying the mutation operator sdl (statement deletion) to each statement of a program. To kill a mutant whose only difference from the program under test is the absence of statement *S* requires executing the mutant and the program under test with a test case that executes *S* in the original program. Thus to kill all mutants generated by applying the operator sdl to statements of the program under test, we need a test suite that causes the execution of each statement in the original program.

Branch coverage can be simulated by applying the operator cpr (constant for predicate replacement) to all predicates of the program under test with constants *True* and *False*. To kill a mutant that differs from the program under test for a predicate *P* set to the constant value *False*, we need to execute the mutant and the program under test with a test case that causes the execution of the *True* branch of *P*. To kill a mutant that differs from the program under test for a predicate *P* set to the constant value *True*, we need to execute the mutant and the program under test with a test case that causes the execution of the *False* branch of *P*.

A test suite that satisfies a structural test adequacy criterion may or may not kill all the corresponding mutants. For example, a test suite that satisfies the statement coverage adequacy criterion might not kill an sdl mutant if the value computed at the statement does not affect the behavior of the program on some possible executions.

ID	Operator	line	Original/ Mutant	1U	1D	2U	2D	2M	End	Long	Mixed
M_i	ror	28	(pos >= BUFLEN−2) (pos == BUFLEN−2)	-	-	-	-	-	-	-	-
M_j	ror	32	(pos > 0) (pos >= 0)	-	x	x	x	x	-	-	-
M_k	sdl	16	atCR = 0 *nothing*	-	-	-	-	-	-	-	-
M_l	ssr	16	atCR = 0 pos = 0	-	-	-	-	-	-	-	x

Test case	Description	Test case	Description
1U	One line, Unix line-end	2M	Two lines, Mac line-end
1D	One line, DOS line-end	End	Last line not terminated with line-end sequence
2U	Two lines, Unix line-end	Long	Very long line (greater than buffer length)
2D	Two lines, DOS line-end	Mixed	Mix of DOS and Unix line ends in the same file

Figure 16.3: A sample set of mutants for program Transduce *generated with mutation operators from Figure 16.2.* x *indicates the mutant is killed by the test case in the column head.*

the correctness of the outputs (e.g., checking each output against an expected output) would reveal the fault. The test suite TS_2 obtained by adding test case *Mixed* to TS would be 100% adequate (relative to this set of mutants) after removing the fault.

16.5 Variations on Mutation Analysis

The mutation analysis process described in the preceding sections, which kills mutants based on the outputs produced by execution of test cases, is known as strong mutation. It can generate a number of mutants quadratic in the size of the program. Each mutant must be compiled and executed with each test case until it is killed. The time and space required for compiling all mutants and for executing all test cases for each mutant may be impractical.

The computational effort required for mutation analysis can be reduced by decreasing the number of mutants generated and the number of test cases to be executed. Weak mutation analysis decreases the number of tests to be executed by killing mutants when they produce a different intermediate state, rather than waiting for a difference in the final result or observable program behavior.

weak mutation analysis

With weak mutation, a single program can be seeded with many faults. A "meta-mutant" program is divided into segments containing original and mutated source code, with a mechanism to select which segments to execute. Two copies of the meta-mutant are executed in tandem, one with only original program code selected and the other with a set of live mutants selected. Execution is paused after each segment to compare the program state of the two versions. If the state is equivalent, execution resumes with the next segment of original and mutated code. If the state differs, the mutant is marked as dead, and execution of original and mutated code is restarted with a new selection of live mutants.

Weak mutation testing does not decrease the number of program mutants that must be considered, but it does decrease the number of test executions and compilations. This performance benefit has a cost in accuracy: Weak mutation analysis may "kill" a mutant even if the changed intermediate state would not have an effect on the final output or observable behavior of the program.

Like structural test adequacy criteria, mutation analysis can be used either to judge the thoroughness of a test suite or to guide selection of additional test cases. If one is designing test cases to kill particular mutants, then it may be important to have a complete set of mutants generated by a set of mutation operators. If, on the other hand, the goal is a statistical estimate of the extent to which a test suite distinguishes programs with seeded faults from the original program, then only a much smaller statistical sample of mutants is required. Aside from its limitation to assessment rather than creation of test suites, the main limitation of statistical mutation analysis is that partial coverage is meaningful only to the extent that the generated mutants are a valid statistical model of occurrençe frequencies of actual faults. To avoid reliance on this implausible assumption, the target coverage should be 100% of the sample; statistical sampling may keep the sample small enough to permit careful examination of equivalent mutants.

statistical mutation analysis

Estimating Population Sizes

Counting fish Lake Winnemunchie is inhabited by two kinds of fish, a native trout and an introduced species of chub. The Fish and Wildlife Service wishes to estimate the populations to evaluate their efforts to eradicate the chub without harming the population of native trout.

The population of chub can be estimated statistically as follows. 1000 chub are netted, their dorsal fins are marked by attaching a tag, then they are released back into the lake. Over the next weeks, fishermen are asked to report the number of tagged and untagged chub caught. If 50 tagged chub and 300 untagged chub are caught, we can calculate

$$\frac{1000}{\text{untagged chub population}} = \frac{50}{300}$$

and thus there are about 6000 untagged chub remaining in the lake.

It may be tempting to also ask fishermen to report the number of trout caught and to perform a similar calculation to estimate the ratio between chub and trout. However, this is valid only if trout and chub are equally easy to catch, or if one can adjust the ratio using a known model of trout and chub vulnerability to fishing.

Counting residual faults A similar procedure can be used to estimate the number of faults in a program: Seed a given number S of faults in the program. Test the program with some test suite and count the number of revealed faults. Measure the number of seeded faults detected, D_S, and also the number of natural faults D_N detected. Estimate the total number of faults remaining in the program, assuming the test suite is as effective at finding natural faults as it is at finding seeded faults, using the formula

$$\frac{S}{\text{total natural faults}} = \frac{D_S}{D_N}$$

If we estimate the number of faults remaining in a program by determining the proportion of seeded faults detected, we must be wary of the pitfall of estimating trout population by counting chub. The seeded faults are chub, the real faults are trout, and we must either have good reason for believing the seeded faults are no easier to detect than real remaining faults, or else make adequate allowances for uncertainty. The difference is that we cannot avoid the problem by repeating the process with trout — once a fault has been detected, our knowledge of its presence cannot be erased. We depend, therefore, on a very good fault model, so that the chub are as representative as possible of trout. Of course, if we use special bait for chub, or design test cases to detect particular seeded faults, then statistical estimation of the total population of fish or errors cannot be justified.

Hardware Fault-based Testing

Fault-based testing is widely used for semiconductor and hardware system validation and evaluation both for evaluating the quality of test suites and for evaluating fault tolerance.

Semiconductor testing has conventionally been aimed at detecting random errors in fabrication, rather than design faults. Relatively simple fault models have been developed for testing semiconductor memory devices, the prototypical faults being "stuck-at-0" and "stuck-at-1" (a gate, cell, or pin that produces the same logical value regardless of inputs). A number of more complex fault models have been developed for particular kinds of semiconductor devices (e.g., failures of simultaneous access in dual-port memories). A test vector (analogous to a test suite for software) can be judged by the number of hypothetical faults it can detect, as a fraction of all possible faults under the model.

Fabrication of a semiconductor device, or assembly of a hardware system, is more analogous to copying disk images than to programming. The closest analog of software is not the hardware device itself, but its design — in fact, a high-level design of a semiconductor device is essentially a program in a language that is compiled into silicon. Test and analysis of logic device designs faces the same problems as test and analysis of software, including the challenge of devising fault models. Hardware design verification also faces the added problem that it is much more expensive to replace faulty devices that have been delivered to customers than to deliver software patches.

In evaluation of fault tolerance in hardware, the usual approach is to modify the state or behavior rather than the system under test. Due to a difference in terminology between hardware and software testing, the corruption of state or modification of behavior is called a "fault," and artificially introducing it is called "fault injection." Pin-level fault injection consists of forcing a stuck-at-0, a stuck-at-1, or an intermediate voltage level (a level that is neither a logical 0 nor a logical 1) on a pin of a semiconductor device. Heavy ion radiation is also used to inject random faults in a running system. A third approach, growing in importance as hardware complexity increases, uses software to modify the state of a running system or to simulate faults in a running simulation of hardware logic design.

Fault seeding can be used statistically in another way: To estimate the number of faults remaining in a program. Usually we know only the number of faults that have been detected, and not the number that remains. However, again to the extent that the fault model is a valid statistical model of actual fault occurrence, we can estimate that the ratio of actual faults found to those still remaining should be similar to the ratio of seeded faults found to those still remaining.

Once again, the necessary assumptions are troubling, and one would be unwise to place too much confidence in an estimate of remaining faults. Nonetheless, a prediction with known weaknesses is better than a seat-of-the-pants guess, and a set of estimates derived in different ways is probably the best one can hope for.

While the focus of this chapter is on fault-based testing of software, related techniques can be applied to whole systems (hardware and software together) to evaluate fault tolerance. Some aspects of fault-based testing of hardware are discussed in the sidebar on page 323.

Open Research Issues

Fault-based testing has yet to be widely applied in software development, although it is an important research tool for evaluating other test selection techniques. Its limited impact on software practice so far can be blamed perhaps partly on computational expense and partly on the lack of adequate support by industrial strength tools.

One promising direction in fault-based testing is development of fault models for particular classes of faults. These could result in more sharply focused fault-based techniques, and also partly address concerns about the extent to which the fault models conventionally used in mutation testing are representative of real faults. Two areas in which researchers have attempted to develop focused models, expressed as sets of mutation operators, are component interfaces and concurrency constructs.

Particularly important is development of fault models based on actual, observed faults in software. These are almost certainly dependent on application domain and perhaps to some extent also vary across software development organizations, but too little empirical evidence is available on the degree of variability.

Further Reading

Software testing using fault seeding was developed by Hamlet [Ham77] and independently by DeMillo, Lipton, and Sayward [DLS78]. Underlying theories for fault-based testing, and in particular on the conditions under which a test case can distinguish faulty and correct versions of a program, were developed by Morell [Mor90] and extended by Thompson, Richardson, and Clarke [TRC93]. Statistical mutation using a Bayesian approach to grow the sample until sufficient evidence has been collected has been described by Sahinoglu and Spafford [SS90]. Weak mutation was proposed by Howden [How82]. The sample mutation operators used in this chapter are adapted from the Mothra software testing environment [DGK+88].

Exercises

16.1. Consider the C function in Figure 16.4, used to determine whether a misspelled word differs from a dictionary word by at most one character, which may be a deletion, an insertion, or a substitution (e.g., "text" is edit distance 1 from "test" by a substitution, and edit distance 1 from "tests" by deletion of "s").

Suppose we seed a fault in line 27, replacing `s1 +1` by `s1 + 0`. Is there a test case that will kill this mutant using weak mutation, but not using strong mutation? Display such a test case if there is one, or explain why there is none.

```c

/* edit1( s1, s2 ) returns TRUE iff s1 can be transformed to s2
 * by inserting, deleting, or substituting a single character, or
 * by a no-op (i.e., if they are already equal).
 */
int edit1( char *s1, char *s2) {
  if (*s1 == 0) {
    if (*s2 == 0) return TRUE;
    /* Try inserting a character in s1 or deleting in s2 */
    if ( *(s2 + 1) == 0) return TRUE;
    return FALSE;
  }
  if (*s2 == 0) { /* Only match is by deleting last char from s1 */
    if (*(s1 + 1) == 0) return TRUE;
    return FALSE;
  }
  /* Now we know that neither string is empty */
  if (*s1 == *s2) {
    return edit1(s1 +1, s2 +1);
  }

  /* Mismatch; only dist 1 possibilities are identical strings after
   * inserting, deleting, or substituting character
   */

  /* Substitution: We "look past" the mismatched character */
  if (strcmp(s1+1, s2+1) == 0) return TRUE;
  /* Deletion: look past character in s1 */
  if (strcmp(s1+1, s2) == 0) return TRUE;
  /* Insertion: look past character in s2 */
  if (strcmp(s1, s2+1) == 0) return TRUE;
  return FALSE;
}
```

Figure 16.4: C function to determine whether one string is within edit distance 1 of another.

16.2. We have described weak mutation as continuing execution up to the point that a mutant is killed, then restarting execution of the original and mutated program from the beginning. Why doesn't execution just continue after killing a mutant? What would be necessary to make continued execution possible?

16.3. Motivate the need for the competent programmer and the coupling effect hypotheses. Would mutation analysis still make sense if these hypotheses did not hold? Why?

16.4. Generate some invalid, valid-but-not-useful, useful, equivalent and nonequivalent mutants for the program in Figure 16.1 using mutant operators from Figure 16.2.

Chapter 17

Test Execution

Whereas test design, even when supported by tools, requires insight and ingenuity in similar measure to other facets of software design, test execution must be sufficiently automated for frequent reexecution without little human involvement. This chapter describes approaches for creating the run-time support for generating and managing test data, creating scaffolding for test execution, and automatically distinguishing between correct and incorrect test case executions.

Required Background

- Chapter 7
  Reasoning about program correctness is closely related to test oracles that recognize incorrect behavior at run-time.
- Chapters 9 and 10
  Basic concepts introduced in these chapters are essential background for understanding the distinction between designing a test case specification and executing a test case.
- Chapters 11 through 16
  These chapters provide more context and concrete examples for understanding the material presented here.

17.1 Overview

Designing tests is creative; executing them should be as mechanical as compiling the latest version of the product, and indeed a product build is not complete until it has passed a suite of test cases. In many organizations, a complete build-and-test cycle occurs nightly, with a report of success or problems ready each morning.

The purpose of run-time support for testing is to enable frequent hands-free reexecution of a test suite. A large suite of test data may be generated automatically from a more compact and abstract set of test case specifications. For unit and integration testing, and sometimes for system testing as well, the software under test may be combined with additional "scaffolding" code to provide a suitable test environment, which might, for example, include simulations of other software and hardware resources. Executing a large number of test cases is of little use unless the observed behaviors are classified as passing or failing. The human eye is a slow, expensive, and unreliable instrument for judging test outcomes, so test scaffolding typically includes automated test oracles. The test environment often includes additional support for selecting test cases (e.g., rotating nightly through portions of a large test suite over the course of a week) and for summarizing and reporting results.

17.2 From Test Case Specifications to Test Cases

If the test case specifications produced in test design already include concrete input values and expected results, as for example in the category-partition method, then producing a complete test case may be as simple as filling a template with those values. A more general test case specification (e.g., one that calls for "a sorted sequence, length greater than 2, with items in ascending order with no duplicates") may designate many possible concrete test cases, and it may be desirable to generate just one instance or many. There is no clear, sharp line between test case design and test case generation. A rule of thumb is that, while test case design involves judgment and creativity, test case generation should be a mechanical step.

Automatic generation of concrete test cases from more abstract test case specifications reduces the impact of small interface changes in the course of development. Corresponding changes to the test suite are still required with each program change, but changes to test case specifications are likely to be smaller and more localized than changes to the concrete test cases.

Instantiating test cases that satisfy several constraints may be simple if the constraints are independent (e.g., a constraint on each of several input parameter values), but becomes more difficult to automate when multiple constraints apply to the same item. Some well-formed sets of constraints have no solution at all ("an even, positive integer that is not the sum of two primes"). Constraints that appear to be independent may not be. For example, a test case specification that constrains both program input and output imposes a conjunction of two constraints on output (it conforms to the given output constraint *and* it is produced by the given input).

General test case specifications that may require considerable computation to produce test data often arise in model-based testing. For example, if a test case calls for program execution corresponding to a certain traversal of transitions in a finite state machine model, the test data must trigger that traversal, which may be quite complex if the model includes computations and semantic constraints (e.g., a protocol model in Promela; see Chapter 8). Fortunately, model-based testing is closely tied to model analysis techniques that can be adapted as test data generation methods. For example, finite state verification techniques typically have facilities for generating counter-examples to asserted properties. If one can express the negation of a test case specification, then treating it as a property to be verified will result in a counter-example from which a concrete test case can be generated.

17.3 Scaffolding

During much of development, only a portion of the full system is available for testing. In modern development methodologies, the partially developed system is likely to consist of one or more runnable programs and may even be considered a version or prototype of the final system from very early in construction, so it is possible at least to execute each new portion of the software as it is constructed, but the external interfaces of the evolving system may not be ideal for testing; often additional code must be added. For example, even if the actual subsystem for placing an order with a supplier is available and fully operational, it is probably not desirable to place a thousand supply orders each night as part of an automatic test run. More likely a portion of the order placement software will be "stubbed out" for most test executions.

Code developed to facilitate testing is called *scaffolding*, by analogy to the temporary structures erected around a building during construction or maintenance. Scaffolding may include test drivers (substituting for a main or calling program), test harnesses (substituting for parts of the deployment environment), and stubs (substituting for functionality called or used by the software under test), in addition to program instrumentation and support for recording and managing test execution. A common estimate is that half of the code developed in a software project is scaffolding of some kind, but the amount of scaffolding that must be constructed with a software project can vary widely, and depends both on the application domain and the architectural design and build plan, which can reduce cost by exposing appropriate interfaces and providing necessary functionality in a rational order.

test driver
test harness
stub

The purposes of scaffolding are to provide controllability to execute test cases and observability to judge the outcome of test execution. Sometimes scaffolding is required to simply make a module executable, but even in incremental development with immediate integration of each module, scaffolding for controllability and observability may be required because the external interfaces of the system may not provide sufficient control to drive the module under test through test cases, or sufficient observability of the effect. It may be desirable to substitute a separate test "driver" program for the full system, in order to provide more direct control of an interface or to remove dependence on other subsystems.

Consider, for example, an interactive program that is normally driven through a graphical user interface. Assume that each night the program goes through a fully automated and unattended cycle of integration, compilation, and test execution. It is necessary to perform some testing through the interactive interface, but it is neither necessary nor efficient to execute all test cases that way. Small driver programs, independent of the graphical user interface, can drive each module through large test suites in a short time.

When testability is considered in software architectural design, it often happens that interfaces exposed for use in scaffolding have other uses. For example, the interfaces needed to drive an interactive program without its graphical user interface are likely to serve also as the interface for a scripting facility. A similar phenomenon appears at a finer grain. For example, introducing a Java interface to isolate the public functionality of a class and hide methods introduced for testing the implementation has a cost, but also potential side benefits such as making it easier to support multiple implementations of the interface.

17.4 Generic versus Specific Scaffolding

The simplest form of scaffolding is a driver program that runs a single, specific test case. If, for example, a test case specification calls for executing method calls in a particular sequence, this is easy to accomplish by writing the code to make the method calls in that sequence. Writing hundreds or thousands of such test-specific drivers, on the other hand, may be cumbersome and a disincentive to thorough testing. At the very least one will want to factor out some of the common driver code into reusable modules. Sometimes it is worthwhile to write more generic test drivers that essentially interpret test case specifications.

At least some level of generic scaffolding support can be used across a fairly wide class of applications. Such support typically includes, in addition to a standard interface for executing a set of test cases, basic support for logging test execution and results. Figure 17.1 illustrates use of generic test scaffolding in the JFlex lexical analyzer generator.

Fully generic scaffolding may suffice for small numbers of hand-written test cases. For larger test suites, and particularly for those that are generated systematically (e.g., using the combinatorial techniques described in Chapter 11 or deriving test case specifications from a model as described in Chapter 14), writing each test case by hand is impractical. Note, however, that the Java code expressing each test case in Figure 17.1 follows a simple pattern, and it would not be difficult to write a small program to convert a large collection of input, output pairs into procedures following the same pattern. A large suite of automatically generated test cases and a smaller set of hand-written test cases can share the same underlying generic test scaffolding.

Scaffolding to replace portions of the system is somewhat more demanding, and again both generic and application-specific approaches are possible. The simplest kind of stub, sometimes called a *mock*, can be generated automatically by analysis of the source code. A mock is limited to checking expected invocations and producing precomputed results that are part of the test case specification or were recorded in a prior execution. Depending on system build order and the relation of unit testing to integration in a particular process, isolating the module under test is sometimes considered an advantage of creating mocks, as compared to depending on other parts of the system that have already been constructed.

mock

The balance of quality, scope, and cost for a substantial piece of scaffolding software — say, a network traffic generator for a distributed system or a test harness for a compiler — is essentially similar to the development of any other substantial piece of software, including similar considerations regarding specialization to a single project or investing more effort to construct a component that can be used in several projects.

The balance is altered in favor of simplicity and quick construction for the many small pieces of scaffolding that are typically produced during development to support

```
public final class IntCharSet {
...
  public void add(Interval intervall) {
...
}

package JFlex.tests;

import JFlex.IntCharSet;
import JFlex.Interval;
import junit.framework.TestCase;
...
public class CharClassesTest extends TestCase {
...
  public void testAdd1() {
    IntCharSet set = new IntCharSet(new Interval('a','h'));
    set.add(new Interval('o','z'));
    set.add(new Interval('A','Z'));
    set.add(new Interval('h','o'));
    assertEquals("{ ['A'-'Z']['a'-'z'] }", set.toString());
  }

  public void testAdd2() {
    IntCharSet set = new IntCharSet(new Interval('a','h'));
    set.add(new Interval('o','z'));
    set.add(new Interval('A','Z'));
    set.add(new Interval('i','n'));
    assertEquals("{ ['A'-'Z']['a'-'z'] }", set.toString());
  }
...
}
```

*Figure 17.1: Excerpt of JFlex 1.4.1 source code (a widely used open-source scanner generator) and accompanying JUnit test cases. JUnit is typical of basic test scaffolding libraries, providing support for test execution, logging, and simple result checking (*assertEquals *in the example). The illustrated version of JUnit uses Java reflection to find and execute test case methods; later versions of JUnit use Java annotation (metadata) facilities, and other tools use source code preprocessors or generators.*

unit and small-scale integration testing. For example, a database query may be replaced by a stub that provides only a fixed set of responses to particular query strings.

17.5 Test Oracles

It is little use to execute a test suite automatically if execution results must be manually inspected to apply a pass/fail criterion. Relying on human intervention to judge test outcomes is not merely expensive, but also unreliable. Even the most conscientious and hard-working person cannot maintain the level of attention required to identify one failure in a hundred program executions, little more one or ten thousand. That is a job for a computer.

Δ test oracle

Software that applies a pass/fail criterion to a program execution is called a *test oracle*, often shortened to *oracle*. In addition to rapidly classifying a large number of test case executions, automated test oracles make it possible to classify behaviors that exceed human capacity in other ways, such as checking real-time response against latency requirements or dealing with voluminous output data in a machine-readable rather than human-readable form.

Ideally, a test oracle would classify every execution of a correct program as passing and would detect every program failure. In practice, the pass/fail criterion is usually imperfect. A test oracle may apply a pass/fail criterion that reflects only part of the actual program specification, or is an approximation, and therefore passes some program executions it ought to fail. Several partial test oracles (perhaps applied with different parts of the test suite) may be more cost-effective than one that is more comprehensive. A test oracle may also give false alarms, failing an execution that it ought to pass. False alarms in test execution are highly undesirable, not only because of the direct expense of manually checking them, but because they make it likely that real failures will be overlooked. Nevertheless sometimes the best we can obtain is an oracle that detects deviations from expectation that may or may not be actual failures.

comparison-based oracle

One approach to judging correctness — but not the only one — compares the actual output or behavior of a program with predicted output or behavior. A test case with a comparison-based oracle relies on predicted output that is either precomputed as part of the test case specification or can be derived in some way independent of the program under test. Precomputing expected test results is reasonable for a small number of relatively simple test cases, and is still preferable to manual inspection of program results because the expense of producing (and debugging) predicted results is incurred once and amortized over many executions of the test case.

Support for comparison-based test oracles is often included in a test harness program or testing framework. A harness typically takes two inputs: (1) the input to the program under test (or can be mechanically transformed to a well-formed input), and (2) the predicted output. Frameworks for writing test cases as program code likewise provide support for comparison-based oracles. The assertEquals method of *JUnit*, illustrated in Figure 17.1, is a simple example of comparison-based oracle support.

Comparison-based oracles are useful mainly for small, simple test cases, but sometimes expected outputs can also be produced for complex test cases and large test suites. Capture-replay testing, a special case of this in which the predicted output or behavior

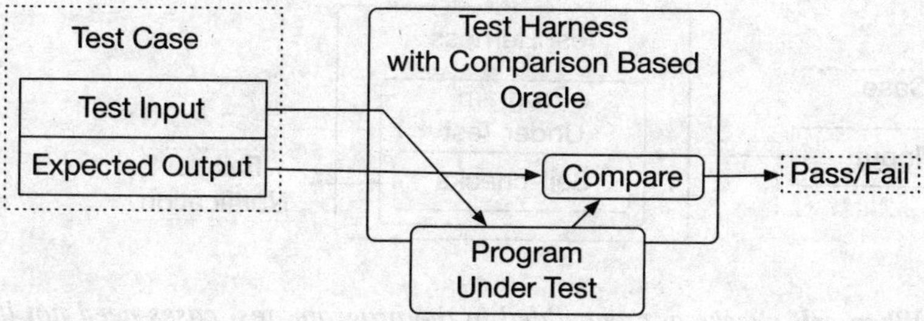

Figure 17.2: A test harness with a comparison-based test oracle processes test cases consisting of (program input, predicted output) pairs.

is preserved from an earlier execution, is discussed in this chapter. A related approach is to capture the output of a trusted alternate version of the program under test. For example, one may produce output from a trusted implementation that is for some reason unsuited for production use; it may too slow or may depend on a component that is not available in the production environment. It is not even necessary that the alternative implementation be *more* reliable than the program under test, as long as it is sufficiently different that the failures of the real and alternate version are likely to be independent, and both are sufficiently reliable that not too much time is wasted determining which one has failed a particular test case on which they disagree.

A third approach to producing complex (input, output) pairs is sometimes possible: It may be easier to produce program input corresponding to a given output than vice versa. For example, it is simpler to scramble a sorted array than to sort a scrambled array.

A common misperception is that a test oracle always requires predicted program output to compare to the output produced in a test execution. In fact, it is often possible to judge output or behavior without predicting it. For example, if a program is required to find a bus route from station *A* to station *B*, a test oracle need not independently compute the route to ascertain that it is in fact a valid route that starts at *A* and ends at *B*.

Oracles that check results without reference to a predicted output are often partial, in the sense that they can detect some violations of the actual specification but not others. They check necessary but not sufficient conditions for correctness. For example, if the specification calls for finding the optimum bus route according to some metric, a validity check is only a partial oracle because it does not check optimality. Similarly, checking that a sort routine produces sorted output is simple and cheap, but it is only a partial oracle because the output is also required to be a permutation of the input. A cheap partial oracle that can be used for a large number of test cases is often combined with a more expensive comparison-based oracle that can be used with a smaller set of test cases for which predicted output has been obtained.

partial oracle

Ideally, a single expression of a specification would serve both as a work assignment and as a source from which useful test oracles were automatically derived. Spec-

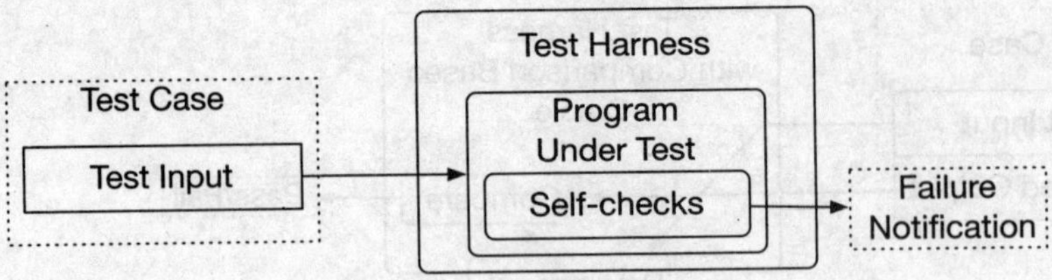

Figure 17.3: When self-checks are embedded in the program, test cases need not include predicted outputs.

ifications are often incomplete, and their informality typically makes automatic derivation of test oracles impossible. The idea is nonetheless a powerful one, and wherever formal or semiformal specifications (including design models) are available, it is worthwhile to consider whether test oracles can be derived from them. Some of the effort of formalization will be incurred either early, in writing specifications, or later when oracles are derived from them, and earlier is usually preferable. Model-based testing, in which test cases and test oracles are both derived from design models are discussed in Chapter 14.

17.6 Self-Checks as Oracles

A program or module specification describes *all* correct program behaviors, so an oracle based on a specification need not be paired with a particular test case. Instead, the oracle can be incorporated into the program under test, so that it checks its own work (see Figure 17.3). Typically these self-checks are in the form of assertions, similar to assertions used in symbolic execution and program verification (see Chapter 7), but designed to be checked during execution.

Self-check assertions may be left in the production version of a system, where they provide much better diagnostic information than the uncontrolled application crash the customer may otherwise report. If this is not acceptable — for instance, if the cost of a runtime assertion check is too high — most tools for assertion processing also provide controls for activating and deactivating assertions. It is generally considered good design practice to make assertions and self-checks be free of side-effects on program state. Side-effect free assertions are essential when assertions may be deactivated, because otherwise suppressing assertion checking can introduce program failures that appear only when one is *not* testing.

Self-checks in the form of assertions embedded in program code are useful primarily for checking module and subsystem-level specifications, rather than overall program behavior. Devising program assertions that correspond in a natural way to specifications (formal or informal) poses two main challenges: bridging the gap between concrete execution values and abstractions used in specification, and dealing in a reasonable way with quantification over collections of values.

Test execution necessarily deals with concrete values, while abstract models are indispensable in both formal and informal specifications. Chapter 7 (page 110) describes the role of abstraction functions and structural invariants in specifying concrete operational behavior based on an abstract model of the internal state of a module. The intended effect of an operation is described in terms of a precondition (state before the operation) and postcondition (state after the operation), relating the concrete state to the abstract model. Consider again a specification of the get method of java.util.Map from Chapter 7, with pre- and postconditions expressed as the Hoare triple

$$(|\langle k, v\rangle \in \phi(\text{dict})|)$$
$$o = \text{dict.get(k)}$$
$$(|o = v|)$$

ϕ is an abstraction function that constructs the abstract model type (sets of key, value pairs) from the concrete data structure. ϕ is a logical association that need not be implemented when reasoning about program correctness. To create a test oracle, it is useful to have an actual implementation of ϕ. For this example, we might implement a special observer method that creates a simple textual representation of the set of (key, value) pairs. Assertions used as test oracles can then correspond directly to the specification. Besides simplifying implementation of oracles by implementing this mapping once and using it in several assertions, structuring test oracles to mirror a correctness argument is rewarded when a later change to the program invalidates some part of that argument (e.g., by changing the treatment of duplicates or using a different data structure in the implementation).

In addition to an abstraction function, reasoning about the correctness of internal structures usually involves structural invariants, that is, properties of the data structure that are preserved by all operations. Structural invariants are good candidates for self checks implemented as assertions. They pertain directly to the concrete data structure implementation, and can be implemented within the module that encapsulates that data structure. For example, if a dictionary structure is implemented as a red-black tree or an AVL tree, the balance property is an invariant of the structure that can be checked by an assertion within the module. Figure 17.4 illustrates an invariant check found in the source code of the Eclipse programming invariant.

There is a natural tension between expressiveness that makes it easier to write and understand specifications, and limits on expressiveness to obtain efficient implementations. It is not much of a stretch to say that programming languages are just formal specification languages in which expressiveness has been purposely limited to ensure that specifications can be executed with predictable and satisfactory performance. An important way in which specifications used for human communication and reasoning about programs are more expressive and less constrained than programming languages is that they freely quantify over collections of values. For example, a specification of database consistency might state that account identifiers are unique; that is, *for all* account records in the database, there *does not exist* another account record with the same identifier.

It is sometimes straightforward to translate quantification in a specification statement into iteration in a program assertion. In fact, some run-time assertion checking

```
package org.eclipse.jdt.internal.ui.text;
import java.text.CharacterIterator;
import org.eclipse.jface.text.Assert;
/**
* A <code>CharSequence</code> based implementation of
* <code>CharacterIterator</code>.
* @since 3.0
*/
public class SequenceCharacterIterator implements CharacterIterator {
...
        private void invariant() {
                Assert.isTrue(fIndex >= fFirst);
                Assert.isTrue(fIndex <= fLast);
        }
...
        public SequenceCharacterIterator(CharSequence sequence, int first, int last)
            throws IllegalArgumentException {
                if (sequence == null)
                        throw new NullPointerException();
                if (first < 0 || first > last)
                        throw new IllegalArgumentException();
                if (last > sequence.length())
                        throw new IllegalArgumentException();
                fSequence= sequence;
                fFirst= first;
                fLast= last;
                fIndex= first;
                invariant();
        }
...
        public char setIndex(int position) {
                if (position >= getBeginIndex() && position <= getEndIndex())
                        fIndex= position;
                else
                        throw new IllegalArgumentException();

                invariant();
                return current();
        }
...
}
```

Figure 17.4: A structural invariant checked by run-time assertions. Excerpted from the Eclipse programming environment, version 3. © 2000, 2005 IBM Corporation; used under terms of the Eclipse Public License v1.0.

systems provide quantifiers that are simply interpreted as loops. This approach can work when collections are small and quantifiers are not too deeply nested, particularly in combination with facilities for selectively disabling assertion checking so that the performance cost is incurred only when testing. Treating quantifiers as loops does not scale well to large collections and cannot be applied at all when a specification quantifies over an infinite collection.[1] For example, it is perfectly reasonable for a specification to state that the route found by a trip-planning application is the shortest among all possible routes between two points, but it is not reasonable for the route planning program to check its work by iterating through all possible routes.

The problem of quantification over large sets of values is a variation on the basic problem of program testing, which is that we cannot exhaustively check all program behaviors. Instead, we select a tiny fraction of possible program behaviors or inputs as representatives. The same tactic is applicable to quantification in specifications. If we cannot fully evaluate the specified property, we can at least select some elements to check (though at present we know of no program assertion packages that support sampling of quantifiers). For example, although we cannot afford to enumerate all possible paths between two points in a large map, we may be able to compare to a sample of other paths found by the same procedure. As with test design, good samples require some insight into the problem, such as recognizing that if the shortest path from A to C passes through B, it should be the concatenation of the shortest path from A to B and the shortest path from B to C.

A final implementation problem for self-checks is that asserted properties sometimes involve values that are either not kept in the program at all (so-called ghost variables) or values that have been replaced ("before" values). A specification of noninterference between threads in a concurrent program may use ghost variables to track entry and exit of threads from a critical section. The postcondition of an in-place sort operation will state that the new value is sorted and a permutation of the input value. This permutation relation refers to both the "before" and "after" values of the object to be sorted. A run-time assertion system must manage ghost variables and retained "before" values and must ensure that they have no side-effects outside assertion checking.

17.7 Capture and Replay

Sometimes it is difficult to either devise a precise description of expected behavior or adequately characterize correct behavior for effective self-checks. For example, while many properties of a program with a graphical interface may be specified in a manner suitable for comparison-based or self-check oracles, some properties are likely to require a person to interact with the program and judge its behavior. If one cannot completely avoid human involvement in test case execution, one can at least avoid

[1] It may seem unreasonable for a program specification to quantify over an infinite collection, but in fact it can arise quite naturally when quantifiers are combined with negation. If we say "there is no integer greater than 1 that divides k evenly," we have combined negation with "there exists" to form a statement logically equivalent to universal ("for all") quantification over the integers. We may be clever enough to realize that it suffices to check integers between 2 and $\sqrt{k}$, but that is no longer a direct translation of the specification statement.

unnecessary repetition of this cost and opportunity for error. The principle is simple. The first time such a test case is executed, the oracle function is carried out by a human, and the interaction sequence is captured. Provided the execution was judged (by the human tester) to be correct, the captured log now forms an (input, predicted output) pair for subsequent automated retesting.

The savings from automated retesting with a captured log depends on how many build-and-test cycles we can continue to use it in, before it is invalidated by some change to the program. Distinguishing between significant and insignificant variations from predicted behavior, in order to prolong the effective lifetime of a captured log, is a major challenge for capture/replay testing. Capturing events at a more abstract level suppresses insignificant changes. For example, if we log only the actual pixels of windows and menus, then changing even a typeface or background color can invalidate an entire suite of execution logs.

Mapping from concrete state to an abstract model of interaction sequences is sometimes possible but is generally quite limited. A more fruitful approach is capturing input and output behavior at multiple levels of abstraction within the implementation. We have noted the usefulness of a layer in which abstract input events (e.g., selection of an object) are captured in place of concrete events (left mouse button depressed with mouse positioned at 235, 718). Typically, there is a similar abstract layer in graphical output, and much of the capture/replay testing can work at this level. Small changes to a program can still invalidate a large number of execution logs, but it is much more likely that an insignificant detail can either be ignored in comparisons or, even better, the abstract input and output can be systematically transformed to reflect the intended change.

Further amplification of the value of a captured log can be obtained by varying the logged events to obtain additional test cases. Creating meaningful and well-formed variations also depends on the abstraction level of the log. For example, it is simpler to vary textual content recorded in a log than to make an equivalent change to a recorded bitmap representation of that text.

Open Research Issues

Tools to generate some kinds of scaffolding from program code have been constructed, as have tools to generate some kinds of test oracles from design and specification documents. Fuller support for creating test scaffolding might bring these together, combining information derivable from program code itself with information from design and specification to create at least test harnesses and oracles. Program transformation and program analysis techniques have advanced quickly in the last decade, suggesting that a higher level of automation than in the past should now be attainable.

Further Reading

Techniques for automatically deriving test oracles from formal specifications have been described for a wide variety of specification notations. Good starting points in this literature include Peters and Parnas [PP98] on automatic extraction of test oracles from a specification structured as tables; Gannon et al. [GMH81] and Bernot et al. [BGM91] on derivation of test oracles from algebraic specifications; Doong and Frankl [DF94] on an approach related to algebraic specifications but adapted to object-oriented programs; Bochmann and Petrenko [vBP94] on derivation of test oracles from finite state models, particularly (but not only) for communication protocols; and Richardson et al. [RAO92] on a general approach to deriving test oracles from multiple specification languages, including a form of temporal logic and the Z modeling language.

Rosenblum [Ros95] describes a system for writing test oracles in the form of program assertions and assesses their value. Memon and Soffa [MS03] assesses the impact of test oracles and automation for interactive graphical user interface (GUI) programs. Ostrand et al. [OAFG98] describe capture/replay testing for GUI programs.

Mocks for simulating the environment of a module are described by Saff and Ernst [SE04]. Husted and Massol [HM03] is a guide to the popular JUnit testing framework. Documentation for JUnit and several similar frameworks for various languages and systems are also widely available on the Web.

Related Topics

Readers interested primarily in test automation or in automation of other aspects of analysis and test may wish to continue reading with Chapter 23.

Exercises

17.1. Voluminous output can be a barrier to naive implementations of comparison-based oracles. For example, sometimes we wish to show that some abstraction of program behavior is preserved by a software change. The naive approach is to store a detailed execution log of the original version as predicted output, and compare that to a detailed execution log of the modified version. Unfortunately, a detailed log of a single execution is quite lengthy, and maintaining detailed logs of many test case executions may be impractical. Suggest more efficient approaches to implementing comparison-based test oracles when it is not possible to store the whole output.

17.2. We have described as an ideal but usually unachievable goal that test oracles could be derived automatically from the same specification statement used to record and communicate the intended behavior of a program or module. To what extent does the "test first" approach of extreme programming (XP) achieve this goal? Discuss advantages and limitations of using test cases as a specification statement.

17.3. Often we can choose between on-line self-checks (recognizing failures as they occur) and producing a log of events or states for off-line checking. What considerations might motivate one choice or the other?

example include Peters and Parnas [PP98] on automatic extraction of test oracles from a specification structured as tables; Gannon et al. [GMH81] and Bernot et al. [BGM91] on derivation of test oracles from algebraic specifications; Doong and Frankl [DF94] on an approach related to algebraic specifications but adapted to object-oriented programs; Bochmann and Petrenko [vBP94] on derivation of test oracles from finite state models, particularly (but not only) for communication protocols; and Richardson et al. [RAO92] on a general approach to deriving test oracles from multiple specification languages, including a form of temporal logic and the Z modeling language.

Rosenblum [Ros95] describes a system for writing test oracles in the form of program assertions and assesses their value. Memon and Soffa [MS03] assesses the impact of test oracles and automation for interactive graphical user interface (GUI) programs. Ostrand et al. [OAFG98] describe capture/replay testing for GUI programs.

Mocks for simulating the environment of a module are described by Saff and Ernst [SE04]. Husted and Massol [HM03] is a guide to the popular JUnit testing framework. Documentation for JUnit and several similar frameworks for various languages and systems are also widely available on the Web.

Related Topics

Readers interested primarily in test automation or in automation of other aspects of analysis and test may wish to continue reading with Chapter 23.

Exercises

17.1. Voluminous output can be a barrier to naive implementations of comparison-based oracles. For example, sometimes we wish to show that some abstraction of program behavior is preserved by a software change. The naive approach is to store a detailed execution log of the original version as predicted output, and compare that to a detailed execution log of the modified version. Unfortunately, a detailed log of a single execution is quite lengthy, and maintaining detailed logs of many test case executions may be impractical. Suggest more efficient approaches to implementing comparison-based test oracles when it is not possible to store the whole output.

17.2. We have described as an ideal but usually unachievable goal that test oracles could be derived automatically from the same specification statement used to record and communicate the intended behavior of a program or module. To what extent does the "test first" approach of extreme programming (XP) achieve this goal? Discuss advantages and limitations of using test cases as a specification statement.

17.3. Often we can choose between on-line self-checks (recognizing failures as they occur) and producing a log of events or states for off-line checking. What considerations might motivate one choice or the other?

Chapter 18

Inspection

Software inspections are manual, collaborative reviews that can be applied to any software artifact from requirements documents to source code to test plans. Inspection complements testing by helping check many properties that are hard or impossible to verify dynamically. Their flexibility makes inspection particularly valuable when other, more automated analyses are not applicable.

Required Background

- Chapter 2
  This chapter discusses complementarities and trade-offs between test and analysis, and motivates the need for alternatives to testing.

18.1 Overview

Inspection is a low-tech but effective analysis technique that has been extensively used in industry since the early 1970s. It is incorporated in many standards, including the Capability Maturity Model (CMM and CMMI) and the ISO 9000 standards, and is a key element of verification- and test-oriented processes such as the Cleanroom, SRET and XP processes.[1]

Inspection is a systematic, detailed review of artifacts to find defects and assess quality. It can benefit from tool support, but it can also be executed manually. Inspection is most commonly applied to source code, but can be applied to all kinds of artifacts during the whole development cycle. It is effective in revealing many defects that testing cannot reveal or can reveal only later and at higher cost.

Inspection also brings important education and social benefits. Junior developers quickly learn standards for specification and code while working as inspectors, and expert developers under pressure are less tempted to ignore standards. The sidebar on page 342 summarizes the chief social and educational benefits of inspection.

[1] See the sidebars in Chapter 20 for additional information on Cleanroom, SRET, and XP.

Social and Educational Benefits of Inspection

While the direct goal of inspection is to find and remove defects, social and educational effects may be equally important.

Inspection creates a powerful social incentive to present acceptable work products, even when there is no direct tie to compensation or performance evaluation. The classic group inspection process, in which the author of the work under review is required to be a passive participant, answering questions but not volunteering explanation or justification for the work until asked, especially magnifies the effect; it is not easy to listen quietly while one's work is publicly picked apart by peers.

Inspection is also an effective way to form and communicate shared norms in an organization, not limited to rules that are explicit in checklists. The classic inspection process prohibits problem solving in the inspection meeting itself, but the necessity of such a rule to maintain momentum in the inspection meeting is evidence for the general rule that, given opportunity, developers and other technical professionals are quick to share experience and knowledge relevant to problems found in a colleague's work. When a new practice or standard is introduced in an organization, inspection propagates awareness and shared understanding.

New staff can be almost immediately productive, individually reviewing work products against checklists, accelerating their familiarization with organization standards and practices. Group inspection roles require some experience, but can likewise be more effective than traditional training in integrating new staff.

The social and educational facets of inspection processes should be taken into account when designing an inspection process or weighing alternatives or variations to an existing process. If the alternatives are weighed by fault-finding effectiveness alone, the organization could make choices that appear to be an improvement on that dimension, but are worse overall.

18.2 The Inspection Team

Inspections are characterized by roles, process, and reading techniques, i.e., who the inspectors are, how they organize their work and synchronize their activities, and how they examine the inspected artifacts.

Inspection is not a full-time job: Many studies indicate that inspectors' productivity drops dramatically after two hours of work, and suggests no more than two inspection sessions per day. Thus, inspectors are usually borrowed from other roles: junior and senior software and test engineers, project and quality managers, software analysts, software architects, and technical writers. The same studies highlight the delicate relation between inspectors and developers: The efficacy of inspection can vanish if developers feel they are being evaluated. In classic approaches to inspection, managers and senior engineers who participate in inspection sessions are often borrowed from other projects to avoid misinterpreting the goals of inspection.

Inspectors must be selected in a way that balances perspectives, background knowledge, and cost. A developer is most knowledgeable about his own work, and is an invaluable resource in inspection, but he cannot forget days or weeks of hard development work to see clearly all the details that are apparent to someone reading an artifact for the first time. Inspection can benefit from discussion among many inspectors with differing perspectives and expertise, but the cost of inspection grows with the size of the inspection team.

Classic inspection postulates groups from four to six inspectors, but recent studies question the efficacy advantages of large groups of inspectors over groups of two. Modern approaches prescribe different levels of inspection: simple checks performed by single inspectors and complex check performed by groups of two inspectors, reserving larger groups for inspections requiring special combinations of expertise.

Single inspectors are usually junior engineers not involved in development of the artifact under inspection. They combine inspection with training, learning basic standards for specification and programming by checking compliance of artifacts with those standards. Junior engineers are usually paired with senior engineers for checking complex properties. The senior engineer acts as moderator; he or she is in charge of organizing the inspection process and is responsible for the inspection results, while the junior engineer participates in the inspection and the discussion.

Large groups of inspectors (from four to six) balance junior and senior engineers, and may include the developer of the artifact under inspection. A senior engineer, usually a manager borrowed from a different project, plays the role of the moderator, organizing the process and being responsible for the results. Other software and test engineers, both senior and junior, are in charge of reading the inspected artifact, and of discussing the possible problems connected to the relevant elements. The developer is present when the inspection requires detailed knowledge that cannot be easily acquired without being involved in the development. This happens for example, when inspecting complex modules looking for semantics or integration problems.

Developers must be motivated to collaborate constructively in inspection, rather than hiding problems and sabotaging the process. Reward mechanisms can influence the developers' attitude and must be carefully designed to avoid perverse effects. For example, fault density is sometimes used as a metric of developer performance. An assessment of fault density that includes faults revealed by inspection may discourage developers from constructive engagement in the inspection process and encourage them to hide faults during inspection instead of highlighting them. At the very least, faults that escape inspection must carry a higher weight than those found during inspection. Naive incentives that reward developers for finding faults during inspection are apt to be counterproductive because they punish the careful developer for bringing a high-quality code to the inspection.

18.3 The Inspection Process

Inspection is not merely reading, but a systematic process that promotes efficiency and repeatability. Because inspection is expensive and not incremental (that is, reinspection after a change can be nearly as expensive as inspection of the original artifact), it must be placed to reveal faults as early as possible, but late enough to avoid excessive repetition. Consider, for example, source code inspection. Inspecting software still under construction may waste inspection effort on elements that are likely to change, but waiting until after integration and system test wastes testing effort on faults that could have been more cost-effectively removed by inspection.

Different inspection activities may be scheduled at distinct development phases. We can for example check for consistency and completeness of comments and coding standards before testing, and we can check for semantic consistency of the software after testing, to focus on key semantic aspects without being distracted by faults that can be easily identified by simple test cases.

The inspection process is usually composed of three main phases: preparatory, review, and follow-up. In the preparatory phase, inspectors check that the artifacts to be inspected are ready, assign inspection roles, acquire the information needed for inspections, plan individual inspection activities, and schedule inspection meetings.

In the review phase, inspectors review the artifact individually and in teams. Reviews follow a systematic and consistent process. The classic and most widely used inspection technique is based on following a checklist while reading the artifact, as described in Section 18.4. Other approaches include use-case and abstraction-driven reading techniques, designed to overcome delocalization in object-oriented programs, the many external references that make it difficult to inspect an individual class in an object-oriented program without global knowledge of the program structure.

In the follow-up phase, inspectors notify developers of inspection results and schedule additional inspection activities if needed. The results of the review phase are summarized in reports that indicate possible problems. Developers and test designers examine the reports to identify actual defects and schedule their removal. The team may schedule follow-up checks that could be as simple as ascertaining that a correction has been made or as complex as a full re-inspection. Simple checks may use the reports themselves as checklists. If, for example, a previous inspection reported missing elements in the code, they may simply check that the elements have been added. If the previous inspection reported logical problems, on the other hand, the team might schedule a new review after the corrective actions to ensure the quality of the new version.

18.4 Checklists

Checklists are a core element of classic inspection. They summarize the experience accumulated in previous projects, and drive the review sessions. A checklist contains a set of questions that help identify defects in the inspected artifact, and verify that the artifact complies with company standards. A good checklist should be updated regularly to remove obsolete elements and to add new checks suggested by the experience accumulated in new projects. We can, for example, remove some simple checks about coding standards after introducing automatic analyzers that enforce the standards, or we can add specific semantic checks to avoid faults that caused problems in recent projects.

Checklists may be used to inspect a large variety of artifacts, including requirements and design specifications, source code, test suites, reports, and manuals. The contents of checklists may vary greatly to reflect the different properties of the various artifacts, but all checklists share a common structure that facilitates their use in review sessions. Review sessions must be completed within a relatively short time (no longer than two hours) and may require teams of different size and expertise (from a single junior programmer to teams of senior analysts). Length and complexity of checklists must reflect their expected use. We may have fairly long checklists with simple questions for simple syntactic reviews, and short checklists with complex questions for semantic reviews.

Modern checklists are structured hierarchically and are used incrementally. Checklists with simple checks are used by individual inspectors in the early stages of inspection, while checklists with complex checks are used in group reviews in later inspection phases. The preface of a checklist should indicate the type of artifact and inspection that can be done with that checklist and the level of expertise required for the inspection.

The sidebar on page 346 shows an excerpt of a checklist for a simple Java code inspection and the sidebar on page 347 shows an excerpt of a checklist for a more complex review of Java programs.

A common checklist organization, used in the examples in this chapter, consists of a set of features to be inspected and a set of items to be checked for each feature. Organizing the list by features helps direct the reviewers' attention to the appropriate set of checks during review. For example, the simple checklist on page 346 contains checks for file headers, file footers, import sections, class declarations, classes, and idiomatic methods. Inspectors will scan the Java file and select the appropriate checks for each feature.

The items to be checked ask whether certain properties hold. For example, the file header should indicate the identity of the author and the current maintainer, a cross reference to the design entity corresponding to the code in the file, and an overview of the structure of the package. All checks are expressed so that a positive answer indicates compliance. This helps the quality manager spot possible problems, which will correspond to "no" answers in the inspection reports.

Inspectors check the items, answer "yes" or "no" depending on the status of the inspected feature, and add comments with detailed information. Comments are common when the inspectors identify violations, and they help identify and localize the

Java Checklist: Level 1 inspection (single-pass read-through, context independent)

FEATURES (where to look and how to check):
Item (what to check)

FILE HEADER: Are the following items included and consistent?	yes	no	comments
Author and current maintainer identity			
Cross-reference to design entity			
Overview of package structure, if the class is the principal entry point of a package			
FILE FOOTER: Does it include the following items?	**yes**	**no**	**comments**
Revision log to minimum of 1 year or at least to most recent point release, whichever is longer			
IMPORT SECTION: Are the following requirements satisfied?	**yes**	**no**	**comments**
Brief comment on each import with the exception of standard set: java.io.*, java.util.*			
Each imported package corresponds to a dependence in the design documentation			
CLASS DECLARATION: Are the following requirements satisfied?	**yes**	**no**	**comments**
The visibility marker matches the design document			
The constructor is explicit (if the class is not *static*)			
The visibility of the class is consistent with the design document			
CLASS DECLARATION JAVADOC: Does the Javadoc header include:	**yes**	**no**	**comments**
One sentence summary of class functionality			
Guaranteed invariants (for data structure classes)			
Usage instructions			
CLASS: Are names compliant with the following rules?	**yes**	**no**	**comments**
Class or interface: CapitalizedWithEachInternalWordCapitalized Special case: If class and interface have same base name, distinguish as ClassNameIfc and ClassNameImpl			
Exception: ClassNameEndsWithException			
Constants (final): ALL_CAPS_WITH_UNDERSCORES			
Field name: capsAfterFirstWord. name must be meaningful outside of context			
IDIOMATIC METHODS: Are names compliant with the following rules?	**yes**	**no**	**comments**
Method name: capsAfterFirstWord Local variables: capsAfterFirstWord. Name may be short (e.g., i for an integer) if scope of declaration and use is less than 30 lines.			
Factory method for X: newX			
Converter to X: toX			
Getter for attribute x: getX();			
Setter for attribute x: void setX			

Java Checklist: Level 2 inspection (comprehensive review in context)			
FEATURES (where to look and how to check): Item (what to check)			
DATA STRUCTURE CLASSES: Are the following requirements satisfied?	yes	no	comments
The class keeps a design secret			
The substitution principle is respected: Instance of class can be used in any context allowing instance of superclass or interface			
Methods are correctly classified as constructors, modifiers, and observers			
There is an abstract model for understanding behavior			
The structural invariants are documented			
FUNCTIONAL (STATELESS) CLASSES: Are the following requirements satisfied?	yes	no	comments
The substitution principle is respected: Instance of class can be used in any context allowing instance of superclass or interface			
METHODS: Are the following requirements satisfied?	yes	no	comments
The method semantics are consistent with similarly named methods. For example, a "put" method should be semantically consistent with "put" methods in standard data structure libraries			
Usage examples are provided for nontrivial methods			
FIELDS: Are the following requirements satisfied?	yes	no	comments
The field is necessary (cannot be a method-local variable)			
Visibility is protected or private, or there is an adequate and documented rationale for public access			
Comment describes the purpose and interpretation of the field			
Any constraints or invariants are documented in either field or class comment header			
DESIGN DECISIONS: Are the following requirements satisfied?	yes	no	comments
Each design decision is hidden in one class or a minimum number of closely related and co-located classes			
Classes encapsulating a design decision do not unnecessarily depend on other design decisions			
Adequate usage examples are provided, particularly of idiomatic sequences of method calls			
Design patterns are used and referenced where appropriate			
If a pattern is referenced: The code corresponds to the documented pattern			

violations. For example, the inspectors may indicate which file headers do not contain all the required information and which information is missing. Comments can also be added when the inspectors do not identify violations, to clarify the performed checks. For example, the inspectors may indicate that they have not been able to check if the maintainer indicated in the header is still a member of the staff of that project.

Checklists should not include items that can be more cost-effectively checked with automated test or analysis techniques. For example, the checklist at page 346 does not include checks for presence in the file header of file title, control identifier, copyright statement and list of classes, since such information is added automatically and thus does not require manual checks. On the other hand, it asks the inspector to verify the presence of references to the author and maintainer and of cross reference to the corresponding design entities, since this checklist is used in a context where such information is not inserted automatically. When adopting an environment that automatically updates author and maintainer information and checks cross references to design entities, we may remove the corresponding checks from the checklist, and increase the amount of code that can be inspected in a session, or add new checks for reducing different problems experienced in new projects.

Properties should be as objective and unambiguous as possible. Complete independence from subjective judgment may not be possible, but must be pursued. For example broad properties like "Comments are complete?" or "Comments are well written?" ask for a subjective judgment, and raise useless and contentious discussions among inspectors and the authors of an artifact undergoing inspection. Checklist items like "Brief comment on each import with the exception of standard set: java.io.*, java.util.*" or "One sentence summary of class functionality" address the same purpose more effectively.

Items should also be easy to understand. The excerpts in the sidebars on pages 346 and 347 list items to be checked, but for each item, the checklist should provide a description, motivations, and examples. Figure 18.1 shows a complete description of one of the items of the sidebars.

Checking for presence of comments is easy to automate, but checking contents for meaning and usefulness is apt to require human judgment. For example, we can easily automate a check that there is a comment for each import section or class, but we cannot automatically check that the comment is meaningful and properly summarizes the need for the import section or the functionality of the class.

Descriptions, motivations and examples may be lengthy, and displaying them directly in the checklist reduces an inspector's ability to quickly scan through the checklist to identify items relevant to each feature under review. Therefore, explanatory material is typically provided separately, linked to the inspection checklist by reference (e.g., a page number for printed documentation or a hyperlink in a Web-based display). Inexperienced inspectors and teams reviewing complex items may access the details to resolve questions and controversies that arise during inspection, but frequency of reference declines with experience.

Checklists can be used in many different contexts. The sidebar on page 350 shows an excerpt of a checklist for comprehensive review of test plans. That checklist assumes that the document includes a standard set of sections, whose presence can be easily checked automatically, and is suited for experienced testers.

Ref. Checklist D1A, page 1/1.

FEATURE: CLASS DECLARATION: Are the following requirements satisfied?

ITEM: The visibility of the Class is consistent with the design document

Detailed checklist item reference:

Description: The fields and methods exported by a class must correspond to those in the specification, which may be in the form of a UML diagram. If the class specializes another class, method header comments must specify where superclass methods are overridden or overloaded. Overloading or overriding methods must be semantically consistent with ancestor methods. Additional public utility or convenience methods may be provided if well documented in the implementation.

The class name should be identical to the name of the class in the specifying document, for ease of reference. Names of methods and fields may differ from those in the specifying document, provided header comments (class header comments for public fields, method header comments for public methods) provide an explicit mapping of implementation names to specification names. Order and grouping of fields and methods need not follow the order and grouping in the specifying document.

Motivations: Clear correspondence of elements of the implementation to elements of the specification facilitates maintenance and reduces integration faults. If significant deviations are needed (e.g., renaming a class or omitting or changing a public method signature), these are design revisions that should be discussed and reflected in the specifying document.

Examples: The code implementing the following UML specification of class CompositeItem should export fields and methods corresponding to the fields of the specification of class CompositeItem and its ancestor class LineItem. Implementations that use different names for some fields or methods or that do not redefine method getUnitPrice in class CompositeItem are acceptable if properly documented. Similarly, implementations that export an additional method compare that specializes the default method equal to aid test oracle generation is acceptable.

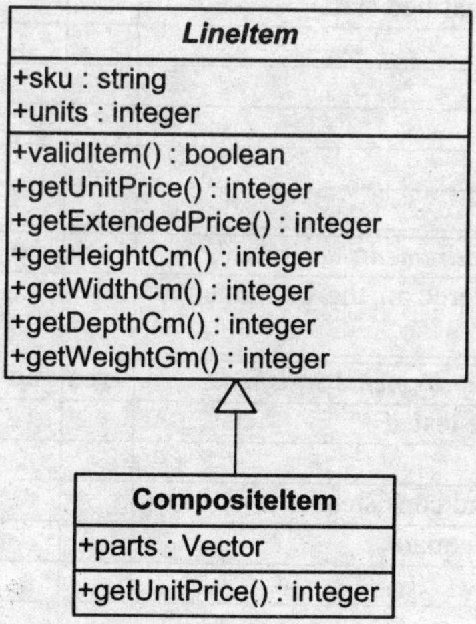

Figure 18.1: Detailed description referenced by a checklist item.

TEST PLAN CHECKLIST: Comprehensive review in context

FEATURES (where to look and how to check):
Item (what to check)

ITEMS TO BE TESTED OR ANALYZED: For each item, does the plan include:	yes	no	comments
A reference to the specification for the item			
A reference to installation procedures for the item, if any			

TEST AND ANALYSIS APPROACH: Are the following requirements satisfied?	yes	no	comments
The test and analysis techniques to be applied are cost-effective for items of this type			
The test and analysis techniques to be applied cover the relevant properties cost-effectively			
The description is sufficiently detailed to identify major tasks and estimate time and resources.			

PASS/FAIL CRITERIA: Are the following requirements satisfied?	yes	no	comments
The criteria clearly indicate the pass/fail conditions			
The criteria are consistent with quality standards specified in the test and analysis strategy			

SUSPEND/RESUME CRITERIA: Are the following requirements satisfied?	yes	no	comments
The criteria clearly indicate threshold conditions for suspending test and analysis due to excessive defects			
The criteria clearly indicate conditions for resuming test and analysis after suspension and rework			

RISKS AND CONTINGENCIES: Are the following risks addressed?	yes	no	comments
Personnel risks (loss or unavailability of qualified staff)			
Technology risks			
Schedule risks			
Development risks			
Execution risks			
Risks from critical requirements			

CONTINGENCY PLAN: Are the following requirements satisfied?	yes	no	comments
Each identified risk is adequately considered in the contingency plan			

TASK AND SCHEDULE: Are the following requirements satisfied?	yes	no	comments
The tasks cover all aspects that ought to be tested			
The description of the tasks is complete			
The relations among tasks are complete and consistent			
Resource allocation and constraints are adequate			
The schedule satisfies all milestones			
Critical paths are minimized			

18.5 Pair Programming

Pair programming is a practice associated with agile processes, particularly Extreme Programming (XP).[2] It can be viewed as a variation on program inspection. Two programmers work side-by-side at a computer, continuously collaborating on the same code. The two programmers alternate at the keyboard: While one programmer types new code, the other reviews and inspects the newly typed code. The programmer who is free from typing duties has more time for thinking about design and coding alternatives, evaluating the impact of design decisions, and checking for discrepancies with coding rules. In short, while the code is being written, the programmer who is not typing inspects the work of the other programmer, highlights possible problems and discusses alternative solutions. Thus, pair programming merges coding and inspection activities, eliminating the gap between classic coding and inspection phases.

In pair programming, the inspection activities are not driven by checklists, but are based on shared programming practice and style. Programmers frequently alternate roles, both at a fine grain (inspector and coder) and more generally in working on different parts of the code. Software components are not "owned" by individual programmers, but are the collective responsibility of the team.

The practice of inspection requires an attitude toward the inspected artifacts as public documents that must conform to group standards and norms. Pair programming makes a shared style and norms a collective asset of the development team. Ideally, this should result in an attitude known as *egoless programming*, in which criticism of artifacts is not regarded as criticism of the authors of those artifacts.

Pair programming is tied to a number of other practices that facilitate teamwork and concentration. As in conventional inspection, fatigue limits the amount of time that a pair can work together effectively, so joint activities are interleaved with pauses and individual activities that may occupy up to half the total programming time. In addition, in the XP approach, pair programming is to be carried out in normal (8-hour) work days, without excessive overtime and without severe or unrealistic schedule pressure. It has been observed that longer work days and working weekends do not improve productivity when extended beyond an occasional, brief "crunch" period, as concentration waivers and developers spend more time on unproductive activities.

Also as in conventional inspection, a constructive attitude must be nurtured for effective pair programming. In the classical group inspection process, the meeting convener acts as a mediator to keep comments constructive and avoid debates in which an author defends decisions that have been called into question. Since there is no mediator in pair programming, responsibility for an open, nonpersonal and nondefensive discussion of decisions and alternatives falls to the programmers themselves. Alternation of roles in pair programming emphasizes shared ownership of the artifact and discussion on the merits rather than on the basis of authority.

A superficial analysis of pair programming would suggest that using two programmers instead of one should halve productivity. The empirical evidence available so far suggests compensating effects of better use of time, better design choices and earlier detection of defects leading to less time lost to rework and overall better quality.

[2]For additional details on XP see the sidebar on page 381 in Chapter 20.

Open Research Issues

Active research topics in software inspection include adapting and extending inspection techniques for particular artifacts (e.g., object-oriented program code, specifications of real-time systems), automation to support inspection (e.g., remote and asynchronous inspections), and variations on process and procedures. Software inspection research is characterized by an emphasis on empirical research methods, including classic controlled experiments.

The most valuable empirical studies do not merely report on whether practice *A* is more or less effective than practice *B*, but rather help build up a more fundamental model of how each practice works. In other words, the empirical research that will matter in the long term is theory-based. Empirical research that addresses smaller questions (e.g., the effect of varying some small part of practice *A*) is likely to have more lasting value, as it reveals something about a principle that can be applied not only to *A* and to *B* but, at some future time, to a new practice *C*, and over the long term contributes to a coherent theory.

We have tried to indicate where some characteristics of effective inspection seem to cut across the particular inspection and review practices in use today, suggesting principles that will be equally important in variations on these approaches and on future approaches to inspection and review. To the extent that a body of general principles for designing inspection processes does develop, it will almost certainly draw from cognitive and social psychology and from management as well as from software engineering research.

Inspection techniques have an irreducible core of manual effort (otherwise they are reclassified as program analysis), but that does not mean that automated tools are irrelevant. Previous research on automated support for inspection has included tools to bring appropriate information quickly to hand (e.g., displaying the portions of an inspection checklist relevant to each portion of a program code as it is being inspected), supporting same-time and asynchronous meetings at a distance, and providing richer information about the artifact being inspected through static analyses. We expect research on tool support for inspection and review to continue alongside development of approaches to inspection and better understanding of the basic principles of inspection processes.

Further Reading

The classic group inspection process is known as Fagan inspections and is described by Fagan [Fag86]. Industrial experience with software inspections in a large software development project is described by Russell [Rus91] and by Grady and van Slack [GS94]. Gilb and Graham [GG93] is a widely used guidebook for applying software inspection.

Parnas and Weiss [PW85, HW01] describe a variant process designed to ensure that every participant in the review process is actively engaged; it is a good example of interplay between the technical and social aspects of a process. Knight and Myers' phased inspections [KM93] are an attempt to make a more cost-effective deployment of personnel in inspections, and they also suggest ways in which automation can be harnessed to improve efficiency. Perpich et al. [PPP+97] describe automation to facilitate asynchronous inspection, as an approach to reducing the impact of inspection on time-to-market.

There is a large research literature on empirical evaluation of the classic group inspection and variations; Dunsmore, Roper, and Wood [DRW03] and Porter and Johnson [PJ97] are notable examples. While there is a rapidly growing literature on empirical evaluation of pair programming as a pedagogical method, empirical evaluations of pair programming in industry are (so far) fewer and decidedly mixed. Hulkko and Abrahamsson [HA05] found no empirical support for common claims of effectiveness and efficiency. Sauer et al. [SJLY00] lay out a behavioral science research program for determining what makes inspection more or less effective and provide an excellent survey of relevant research results up to 2000, with suggestions for practical improvements based on those results.

Related Topics

Simple and repetitive checks can sometimes be replaced by automated analyses. Chapter 19 presents automated analysis techniques, while Chapter 23 discusses automatization problems.

Exercises

18.1. Your organization, which develops personal training monitors for runners and cyclists, has a software development team split between offices in Milan, Italy, and Eugene, Oregon. Team member roles (developers, test designers, technical writers, etc.) are fairly evenly distributed between locations, but some technical expertise is concentrated in one location or another. Expertise in mapping and geographic information systems, for example, is concentrated mainly in Eugene, and expertise in device communication and GPS hardware mainly in Milan. You are considering whether to organize inspection of requirements specifications, design documents, and program code primarily on a local, face-to-face basis, or distributed with teleconference and asynchronous communication support between sites. What are some of the potential advantages and pitfalls of each choice?

18.2. You have been asked to prepare a pilot study to measure the potential costs and benefits of inspection in your organization. You are faced with several questions in the design of this pilot study. Discuss these two:

(a) What specific costs-and-benefits will you try to measure? How might you measure and compare them?

(b) You could make cost-and-benefit comparisons within a single project (e.g., inspecting some documents and artifacts but not others), or you could compare two fairly similar ongoing projects, using inspection in one but not the other. What are the advantages and disadvantages of each approach?

18.3. Automated analysis should substitute for inspection where it is more cost-effective. How would you evaluate the cost of inspection and analysis to decide whether to substitute an analysis tool for a particular set of checklist items?

18.4. Inspection does not require tools but may benefit from tool support. Indicate three tools that you think can reduce human effort and increase inspectors' productivity. List tools in order of importance with respect to effort saving, explain why you ranked those tools highest, and indicate the conditions under which each tool may be particularly effective.

18.5. In classic inspection, some inspectors may remain silent and may not actively participate in the inspection meeting. How would you modify inspection meetings to foster active participation of all inspectors?

Chapter 19

Program Analysis

A number of automated analyses can be applied to software specifications and program source code. None of them are capable of showing that the specifications and the code are functionally correct, but they can cost-effectively reveal some common defects, as well as produce auxiliary information useful in inspections and testing.

Required Background

- Chapter 6
  This chapter describes data flow analysis, a basic technique used in many static program analyses.
- Chapter 7
  This chapter introduces symbolic execution and describes how it is used for checking program properties.
- Chapter 8
  This chapter discusses finite state verification techniques applicable to models of programs. Static analysis of programs is often concerned with extracting models to which these techniques can be applied.

19.1 Overview

Automated program analysis techniques complement test and inspection in two ways. First, automated program analyses can exhaustively check some important properties of programs, including those for which conventional testing is particularly ill-suited. Second, program analysis can extract and summarize information for inspection and test design, replacing or augmenting human effort.

Conventional program testing is weak at detecting program faults that cause failures only rarely or only under conditions that are difficult to control. For example, conventional program testing is not an effective way to find race conditions between concurrent threads that interfere only in small critical sections, or to detect memory

Concurrency Faults

Concurrent threads are vulnerable to subtle faults, including potential deadlocks and data races. Deadlocks occur when each of a set of threads is blocked, waiting for another thread in the set to release a lock. Data races occur when threads concurrently access shared resources while at least one is modifying that resource.

Concurrency faults are difficult to reveal and reproduce. The nondeterministic nature of concurrent programs does not guarantee the same execution sequence between different program runs. Thus programs that fail during one execution may not fail during other executions with the same input data, due to the different execution orders.

Concurrency faults may be prevented in several ways. Some programming styles eliminate concurrency faults by restricting program constructs. For example, some safety critical applications do not allow more than one thread to write to any particular shared memory item, eliminating the possibility of concurrent writes (write-write races). Other languages provide concurrent programming constructs that enable simple static checks. For example, protection of a shared variable in Java synchronized blocks is easy to check statically. Other constructs are more difficult to check statically. For example, C and C++ libraries that require individual calls to obtain and release a lock can be used in ways that resist static verification.

access faults that only occasionally corrupt critical structures.[1] These faults lead to failures that are sparsely scattered in a large space of possible program behaviors, and are difficult to detect by sampling, but can be detected by program analyses that fold the enormous program state space down to a more manageable representation.

Manual program inspection is also effective in finding some classes of faults that are difficult to detect with testing. However, humans are not good at repetitive and tedious tasks, or at maintaining large amounts of detail. If program analysis is not capable of completely replacing human inspection for some class of faults, it can at least support inspection by automating extraction, summarization, and navigation through relevant information.

Analysis techniques examine either the program source code or program execution traces. Techniques that work *statically* on the source code can exhaustively examine the whole program source code and verify properties of all possible executions, but are prone to false alarms that result from summarizing all possible and some impossible behaviors together. Techniques that work *dynamically* on actual execution states and traces do not suffer from the infeasible path problem, but cannot examine the execution space exhaustively.

19.2 Symbolic Execution in Program Analysis

Chapter 7 describes how symbolic execution can prove that a program satisfies specifications expressed in terms of invariants and pre and postconditions. Unfortunately, producing complete formal specifications with all the required pre and postconditions

[1] Concurrency and memory faults are further discussed in the sidebars on pages 356 and 357.

Memory Faults

Dynamic memory access and allocation are vulnerable to program faults, including null pointer dereference, illegal access, and memory leaks. These faults can lead to memory corruption, misinterpretation or illegal access to memory structures, or memory exhaustion. Common forms of these faults include the notorious buffer overflow problem in C programs (whether the dynamic access is through a pointer or an out-of-bounds array index), access through a "dangling" pointer to either dynamically allocated memory or the local memory of a procedure (C function), and slow leakage of memory in shared dynamic data structures where it is difficult to determine which portions of the structure are still accessible. These faults are difficult to reveal through testing because, in many cases, they do not cause immediate or certain failure. Programs may fail only in unusual circumstances (which may be exploited to subvert security), and typically execute without overt problems for some time before failing while executing code far from the original fault.

For example, program cgi_decode presented in Figure 12.1, page 213 increments the pointer eptr twice consecutively without checking for buffer termination:

```
    } else if (c == '%') {
      /* Case 2: '%xx' is hex for character xx */
      int  digit_high = Hex_Values[*(++eptr)];
      int  digit_low  = Hex_Values[*(++eptr)];
```

If executed with an input string terminated by `%x`, where *x* is an hexadecimal digit, the program incorrectly scans beyond the end of the input string and can corrupt memory. However, the failure may occur much after the execution of the faulty statement, when the corrupted memory is used. Because memory corruption may occur rarely and lead to failure more rarely still, the fault is hard to detect with traditional testing techniques.

In languages that require (or allow) a programmer to explicitly control deallocation of memory, potential faults include deallocating memory that is still accessible through pointers (making them dangerous *dangling pointers* to memory that may be recycled for other uses, with different data types) or failing to deallocate memory that has become inaccessible. The latter problem is known as a *memory leak*. Memory leaks are pernicious because they do not cause immediate failure and may in fact lead to memory exhaustion only after long periods of execution; for this reason they often escape unit testing and show up only in integration or system test, or in actual use, as discussed in the sidebar on page 409. Even when failure is observed, it can be difficult to trace the failure back to the fault.

Memory access failures can often be prevented by using appropriate program constructs and analysis tools. The saferC dialect of the C language, used in avionics applications, limits use of dynamic memory allocation (an application of the *restriction* principle of Chapter 3), eliminating the possibility of dangling pointers and memory leaks. Java dynamically checks for out-of-bounds array indexing and null pointer dereferences, throwing an exception immediately if access rules are violated (an application of the *sensitivity* principle). Many modern programming languages employ automatic storage deallocation (garbage collection), likewise preventing dangling pointers.

is rarely cost-effective. Moreover, even when provided with a complete formal specification, verification through symbolic execution may require solving predicates that exceed the capacity of modern constraint solvers.

Symbolic execution techniques find wider application in program analysis tools that aim at finding particular, limited classes of program faults rather than proving program correctness. Typical applications include checking for use of uninitialized memory, memory leaks, null pointer dereference, and vulnerability to certain classes of attack such as SQL injection or buffer overflow. Tools for statically detecting these faults make few demands on programmers. In particular, they do not require complete program specifications or pre- and postcondition assertions, and they range from moderately expensive (suitable for daily or occasional use) to quite cheap (suitable for instant feedback in a program editor).

In addition to focusing on particular classes of faults, making a static program analysis efficient has a cost in accuracy. As discussed in Chapter 2, the two basic ways in which we can trade efficiency for accuracy are abstracting details of execution to fold the state space or exploring only a sample of the potential program state space. All symbolic execution techniques fold the program state space to some extent. Some fold it far enough that it can be exhaustively explored, incurring some pessimistic inaccuracy but no optimistic inaccuracy. Others maintain a more detailed representation of program states, but explore only a portion of the state space. In that way, they resemble conventional testing.

19.3 Symbolic Testing

The basic technique of executing a program with symbolic values can be applied much like program testing. The values of some variables are summarized to elements of a small set of symbolic values. For example, if analysis is concerned with misuse of pointers, values for a pointer variable might be taken from the set

$$\{\text{null}, \text{notnull}, \text{invalid}, \text{unknown}\}$$

Values of other variables might be represented by a constraint or elided entirely. Since the representation of program state may not include enough information to determine the outcome of a conditional statement, symbolic execution can continue down either or both branches, possibly accumulating constraints in the program state. Unlike formal program verification using symbolic execution, symbolic testing does not follow every possible program execution path until all representations of all possible program states have been visited. It may explore paths to a limited depth or prune exploration by some other criterion, such as a heuristic regarding the likelihood that a particular path is really executable and leads to a potential failure.

Symbolic testing is a path-sensitive analysis: We may obtain different symbolic states by exploring program paths to the same program location. Usually it is also at least partly context sensitive, exploring execution through different procedure call and return sequences. The combination of path and context sensitivity is a key strength of symbolic testing, which can produce a warning with a detailed description of how a particular execution sequence leads to a potential failure, but it is also very costly. Often the ways in which the values passed to a procedure can affect execution are limited, and it is possible to build up a model of a procedure's effects by memoizing entry and exit conditions. A new path need be explored only when symbolic execution encounters an entry condition that differs from previously encountered conditions. Models of unchanged portions of a system, including external libraries, can be retained for future analysis.

Specializing the analysis to detect only a few classes of faults, and exploring a sample of program execution paths rather than attempting to summarize all possible behaviors, produce error reports that are more precise and focused than those that could be obtained from an attempt to verify program correctness. Nonetheless, abstraction in the symbolic representation of program state can lead to situations in which an apparent program fault is not actually possible. For example, a failure that appears to be possible when a loop body is executed zero times may actually be impossible because the loop always executes at least once. False alarms degrade the value of analysis, and a developer or tester who must wade through many false alarms (expending considerable effort on manually checking each one) will soon abandon the static checking tool. It is particularly frustrating to users if the same false alarm appears each time a program is re-analyzed; an essential facility of any static checking tool is suppression of warnings that have previously been marked as false or uninteresting.

A symbolic testing tool can simply prune execution paths whose execution conditions involve many constraints, suggesting a high likelihood of infeasibility, or it may suppress reports depending on a combination of likelihood and severity. A particularly useful technique is to order warnings, with those that are almost certainly real program faults given first. It is then up to the user to decide how far to dig into the warning list.

19.4 Summarizing Execution Paths

If our aim is to find *all* program faults of a certain kind (again focusing on a limited class of faults, such as pointer misuse or race conditions), then we cannot simply prune exploration of certain program paths as in symbolic testing. We must instead abstract far enough to fold the state space down to a size that can be exhaustively explored. This is essentially the approach taken in flow analysis (Chapter 6) and finite state verification (Chapter 8). A variety of useful and efficient program analyses can be constructed from those basic techniques.

A useful class of analyses are those in which all the represented data values can be modeled by states in a finite state machine (FSM), and operations in the program text trigger state transitions. For example, a pointer variable can be represented by a machine with three states representing an invalid value, a possibly null value, and a value that is definitely not null. Deallocation triggers a transition from the non-null state to the invalid state. Deallocation in the possibly null state is noted as a potential misuse, as is a dereference in the possibly null or invalid states. A conditional branch may also trigger a state transition. For example, testing a pointer for non-null triggers a transition from the possibly null state to the definitely non-null state.

An important design choice is whether and how to merge states obtained along different execution paths. Conventional data flow analysis techniques merge all the states encountered at a particular program location. Where the state obtained along one execution path is a state of an FSM, a summary of states reachable along all paths can be represented by a set of FSM states (the powerset lattice construct described in Chapter 6). Most finite state verification techniques, on the other hand, are path sensitive and never merge states. In fact, this is the primary difference between finite state verification and flow analysis.

Once again, modeling procedure call and return is particularly delicate. A complete path- and context-sensitive analysis is likely to be much too expensive, but throwing away all context information may cause too many false alarms. The compromise approach described here for symbolic testing, in which (entry, exit) state pairs are cached and reused, is again applicable.

19.5 Memory Analysis

The analyses described in the preceding sections are called *static* because they do not involve conventional program execution (although the line between symbolic testing and conventional testing is fuzzy). While only static analyses can fold the program state space in a way that makes exhaustive analysis possible, *dynamic* analyses based on actual program execution can amplify the usefulness of test execution. An example of this is dynamic memory analysis, which amplifies the sensitivity of test execution for detecting misuse of dynamically allocated or referenced memory structures.

As discussed in the sidebar on page 357, language support and disciplined programming can reduce the incidence of memory faults and leaks. Some programming languages, such as C, do not provide run-time protection against prevent memory faults. In these languages, faults in management of allocated memory can lead to unpredictable failures. Failure can occur when corrupted memory or references are used, far from the fault, making it difficult to diagnose the failure. Moreover, since observable failure may or may not occur, memory faults can be difficult to eliminate with testing.

Consider for example the C program in Figure 19.1 that invokes function cgi_decode presented in Figure 12.1 of Chapter 12 (page 213). The program translates cgi-encoded strings to ASCII strings. It invokes function cgi_decode with an output parameter outbuf of fixed length, and can overrun the output buffer if executed with an input parameter that yields an ASCII string longer than outbuf. The corrupted memory does not cause immediate or certain failure, and thus the fault can remain uncaught during testing.

Memory analysis dynamically traces memory accesses to detect misuse as soon as it occurs, thus making potentially hidden failures visible and facilitating diagnosis. For example, Figure 19.2 shows an excerpt of the results of dynamic analysis of program cgi_decode with the Purify dynamic memory analysis tool. The result is obtained by executing the program with a test case that produces an output longer than 10 ASCII characters. Even if the test case execution would not otherwise cause a visible failure, the dynamic analysis detects an array bounds violation and indicates program locations related to the fault.

Figure 19.3 shows states of a memory location relevant for detecting misuse. A dynamic memory analysis tool modifies the program (usually by instrumenting object

```
int cgi_decode(char *encoded, char *decoded);
/* Requirement: The caller must allocated adequate space for the output
    * string "decoded". Due to the nature of the CGI escaping, it is enough
    * for decoded to have the same size as encoded. Encoded is assumed
    * to be a null-terminated C string.
    */

int main (int argc, char *argv[]) {
        char sentinel_pre[] = "2B2B2B2B2B";
        char subject[]  = "AndPlus+%26%2B+%0D%";
    char sentinel_post[] = "26262626";
    char *outbuf = (char *) malloc(10); /* And just hope it's enough ... */
    int return_code;

    /* stub_init_table(); */
        printf("First test, subject into outbuf\n");
    return_code = cgi_decode(subject, outbuf);
    printf("Original:  %s\n", subject);
    printf("Decoded:   %s\n", outbuf);
    printf("Return code: %d\n", return_code);

        printf("Second test, argv[1] into outbuf\n");
        printf("Argc is %d\n", argc);
    assert(argc == 2);
    return_code = cgi_decode(argv[1], outbuf);
    printf("Original:  %s\n", argv[1]);
    printf("Decoded:   %s\n", outbuf);
    printf("Return code: %d\n", return_code);

}
```

Figure 19.1: A C program that invokes the C function cgi_decode of Figure 12.1 with memory for outbuf *allocated from the heap.*

```
[I] Starting main
[E] ABR: Array bounds read in printf {1 occurrence}
        Reading 11 bytes from 0x00e74af8 (1 byte at 0x00e74b02 illegal)
        Address 0x00e74af8 is at the beginning of a 10 byte block
        Address 0x00e74af8 points to a malloc'd block in heap 0x00e70000
        Thread ID: 0xd64
...
[E] ABR: Array bounds read in printf {1 occurrence}
        Reading 11 bytes from 0x00e74af8 (1 byte at 0x00e74b02 illegal)
        Address 0x00e74af8 is at the beginning of a 10 byte block
        Address 0x00e74af8 points to a malloc'd block in heap 0x00e70000
        Thread ID: 0xd64
...
[E] ABWL: Late detect array bounds write {1 occurrence}
        Memory corruption detected, 14 bytes at 0x00e74b02
        Address 0x00e74b02 is 1 byte past the end of a 10 byte block at 0x00e74af8
        Address 0x00e74b02 points to a malloc'd block in heap 0x00e70000
        63 memory operations and 3 seconds since last-known good heap state
        Detection location - error occurred before the following function call
            printf          [MSVCRT.dll]
...
        Allocation location
            malloc          [MSVCRT.dll]
...
[I] Summary of all memory leaks... {482 bytes, 5 blocks}
...
[I] Exiting with code 0 (0x00000000)
        Process time: 50 milliseconds
[I] Program terminated ...
```

Figure 19.2: Excerpts of Purify verification tool transcript. Purify has monitored memory allocation during execution and has detected buffer array out of bounds errors.

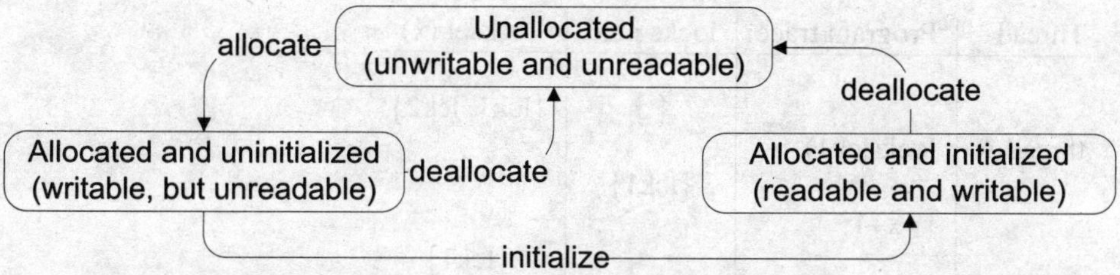

Figure 19.3: States of a memory location for dynamic memory analysis (adapted from Hastings and Joyce [HJ92]).

code) to trace memory access. The instrumented program records the state of each memory location and detects accesses incompatible with the current state. It detects attempts to access unallocated memory or read from uninitialized memory locations. For example, array bounds violations can be detected by adding a small set of memory locations with state unallocated before and after each array. Attempts to access these locations are detected immediately.

Memory leaks can be detected by running a *garbage detector*, which is the analysis portion of a *garbage collector*. Garbage collectors automatically identify unused memory locations and free them. Garbage detection algorithms implement the identification step by recursively following potential pointers from the data and stack segments into the heap, marking all referenced blocks, and thereby identifying allocated blocks that are no longer referenced by the program. Blocks allocated but no longer directly or transitively referenced are reported as possible memory leaks.

19.6 Lockset Analysis

Data races are hard to reveal with testing, due to nondeterministic interleaving of threads in a concurrent program. Statically exploring the execution space is computationally expensive, and suffers from the approximated model of computation, as discussed in Chapter 8. Dynamic analysis can greatly amplify the sensitivity of testing to detect potential data races, avoiding the pessimistic inaccuracy of finite state verification while reducing the optimistic inaccuracy of testing.

Data races are commonly prevented by imposing a locking discipline, such as the rule *every variable shared between threads must be protected by a mutual exclusion lock*. Dynamic lockset analysis reveals potential data races by detecting violation of the locking discipline.

Lockset analysis identifies the set of mutual exclusion locks held by threads when accessing each shared variable. Initially, each shared variable is associated with all available locks. When a thread accesses a shared variable v, lockset analysis intersects the current set of candidate locks for v with the locks held by that thread. The set of candidate locks that remains after executing a set of test cases is the set of locks that were always held by threads accessing that variable. An empty set of locks for a shared variable v indicates that no lock consistently protects v.

Thread	Program trace	locks held	lockset (x)
		{ }	{lck1, lck2}
thread A	lock(lck1)		
		{lck1}	
	x=x+1;		
			{lck1}
	unlock(lck1)		
		{ }	
thread B	lock(lck2)		
		{lck2}	
	x=x+1;		
			{ }
	unlock(lck2)		
		{ }	

Figure 19.4: Threads accessing the same shared variable with different locks. (Adapted from Savage et al. [SBN+97])

The analysis of the two threads in Figure 19.4 starts with two locks associated with variable x. When thread A locks lck1 to access x, the lockset of x is intersected with the locks hold by A. When thread B locks lck2 to access x, the intersection of the lockset of x with the current set of locks becomes empty, indicating that no locks consistently protect x.

This simple locking discipline is violated by some common programming practices: Shared variables are frequently initialized without holding a lock; shared variables written only during initialization can be safely accessed without locks; and multiple readers can be allowed in mutual exclusion with single writers. Lockset analysis can be extended to accommodate these idioms.

Initialization can be handled by delaying analysis till after initialization. There is no easy way of knowing when initialization is complete, but we can consider the initialization completed when the variable is accessed by a second thread.

Safe simultaneous reads of unprotected shared variables can also be handled very simply by enabling lockset violations only when the variable is written by more than one thread. Figure 19.5 shows the state transition diagram that enables lockset analysis and determines race reports. The initial *virgin* state indicates that the variable has not been referenced yet. The first access moves the variable to the *exclusive* state. Additional accesses by the same thread do not modify the variable state, since they are considered part of the initialization procedure. Accesses by other threads move to states *shared* and *shared-modified* that record the type of access. The variable lockset is updated in both *shared* and *shared-modified* states, but violations of the policy are reported only if they occur in state *shared-modified*. In this way, read-only concurrent accesses do not produce warnings.

To allow multiple readers to access a shared variable and still report writers' data races, we can simply distinguish between the set of locks held in all accesses from the

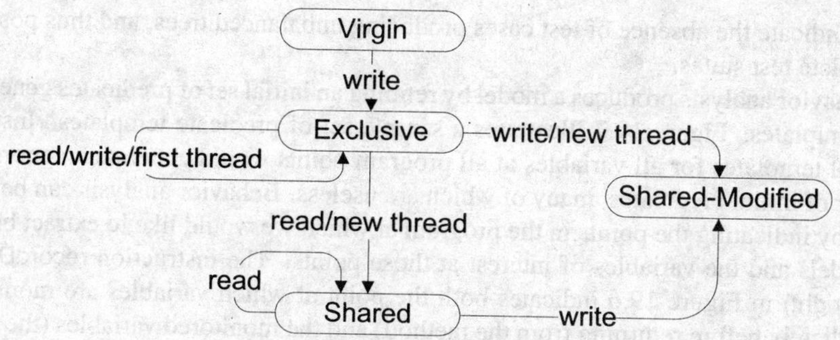

Figure 19.5: The state transition diagram for lockset analysis with multiple read accesses.

set of locks held in write accesses.

19.7 Extracting Behavior Models from Execution

Executing a test case reveals information about a program. Behavior analysis can gather information from executing several test cases and synthesize a model that characterizes those executions and, to the extent that they are representative, other executions as well.

Program executions produce information about the behavior of programs. Test case execution samples the program behavior but does not produce general models. Behavior analysis generalizes single executions and produces models of the behavior of the programs. Behavior models summarize the results of the analyzed executions, and approximate the overall behavior of the programs to the extent that the analyzed executions sample the execution spaces.

One kind of behavior model can be expressed as predicates on the values of program variables at selected execution points. For example, a behavior model computed at the exit point of AVL tree method insert, shown in Figure 19.6, could describe the behavior of the method with the following predicates:

father > left
father < right
diffHeight one of $\{-1, 0, 1\}$

These predicates indicate that, in all observed executions of the insert method, the AVL tree properties of node ordering and tree balance were maintained.

A model like this helps test designers understand the behavior of the program and the completeness of the test suite. We can easily see that the test suite produces AVL trees unbalanced both to the right and to the left, albeit within the AVL allowance. A predicate like

diffHeight == 0

would indicate the absence of test cases producing unbalanced trees, and thus possibly incomplete test suites.

Behavior analysis produces a model by refining an initial set of predicates generated from templates. Figure 19.7 illustrates a sample set of predicate templates. Instantiating all templates for all variables at all program points would generate an enormous number of initial predicates, many of which are useless. Behavior analysis can be optimized by indicating the points in the program at which we would like to extract behavior models and the variables of interest at those points. The instruction recordData(t, t.left, t.right) in Figure 19.6 indicates both the point at which variables are monitored (immediately before returning from the method) and the monitored variables (the fields of the current node and of its left and right children).

The initial set of predicates is refined by eliminating those violated during execution. Figure 19.9 shows two behavior models for the method insert shown in Figure 19.6. The models were derived by executing the two test cases shown in Figure 19.8. The model for test testCaseSingleValues shows the limitations of a test case that assigns only three values, producing a perfectly balanced tree. The predicates correctly characterize that execution, but represent properties of a small subset of AVL trees. The behavioral model obtained with test testCaseRandom provides more information about the method. This test case results in 300 invocations of the method with randomly generated numbers. The model indicates that the elements are inserted correctly in the AVL tree (for each node father, left < father < right) and the tree is balanced as expected (diffHeight one of $\{-1,0,1\}$). The models provide additional information about the test cases. All inserted elements are nonnegative (left >= 0). The model also includes predicates that are not important or can be deduced from others. For example, fatherHeight >= 0 can easily be deduced from the code, while father >= 0 is a consequence of left >= 0 and left < father.

As illustrated in the example, the behavior model is neither a specification of the program nor a complete description of the program behavior, but rather a representation of the behavior experienced so far. Additional executions can further refine the behavior model by refining or eliminating predicates.

Some conditions may be coincidental; that is they may happen to be true only of the small portion of the program state space that has been explored by particular set of test cases. We can reduce the effect of coincidental conditions by computing a probability of coincidence, which can be estimated by counting the number of times the predicate is tested. Conditions are considered valid if their coincidental probability falls below a threshold. For example, father >= 0 may occur coincidentally with a probability of 0.5, if it is verified by a single execution, but the probability decreases to 0.5^n, if it is verified by n executions. With a threshold of 0.05%, after two executions with father = 7, the analysis will consider valid the predicate father = 7, but not father >= 0 yet, since the latter still has a high probability of being coincidental. Two additional executions with different positive outcomes will invalidate predicate father = 7 and will propose father >= 0, since its probability will be below the current threshold. The predicate father >= 0 appears in the model obtained from testCaseRandom, but not in the model obtained from testCaseSingleValues because it occurred 300 times in the execution of testCaseRandom but only 3 times in the execution of testCaseSingleValues.

Behavior models may help in many ways: during testing to help validate the thor-

```java
/**
 * Internal method to insert into a subtree.
 *
 * @param x
 *        the item to insert.
 * @param t
 *        the node that roots the tree.
 * @return the new root.
 */
private AvlNode insert(Comparable x, AvlNode t) {
        if (t == null)
                t = new AvlNode(x, null, null);
        else if (x.compareTo(t.element) < 0) {
                t.left = insert(x, t.left);
                if (height(t.left) - height(t.right) == 2)
                        if (x.compareTo(t.left.element) < 0)
                                t = rotateWithLeftChild(t);
                        else
                                t = doubleWithLeftChild(t);
        } else if (x.compareTo(t.element) > 0) {
                t.right = insert(x, t.right);
                if (height(t.right) - height(t.left) == 2)
                        if (x.compareTo(t.right.element) > 0)
                                t = rotateWithRightChild(t);
                        else
                                t = doubleWithRightChild(t);
        } else
                ; // Duplicate; do nothing

        t.height = max(height(t.left), height(t.right)) + 1;

        recordData(t, t.left, t.right);

        return t;
}
```

*Figure 19.6: A Java method for inserting a node into an AVL tree [Wei07].**

Over any variable x:	
constant	$x = a$
uninitialized	$x = uninit$
small value set	$x = \{a,b,c\}$ for a small set of values
Over a single numeric variable x:	
in a range	$x \geq a$, $x \leq b$, $a \leq x \leq b$
nonzero	$x \neq 0$
modulus	$x \equiv a$ (mod b)
nonmodulus	$x \neg \equiv a$ (mod b)
Over two numeric variables x and y:	
linear relationship	$y = ax + b$
ordering relationship	$x \leq y$, $x < y$, $x = y$, $x \neq y$
functions	$x = fn(y)$
Over the sum of two numeric variables $x + y$:	
in a range	$x+y \geq a$, $x+y \leq b$, $a \leq x+y \leq b$
nonzero	$x + y \neq 0$
modulus	$x + y \equiv a$ (mod b)
nonmodulus	$x + y \neg \equiv a$ (mod b)
Over three numeric variables x, y and z:	
linear relationship	$z = ax + by + c$
functions	$z = fn(x,y)$
Over a single sequence variable:	
range	minimum and maximum sequence values, ordered lexicographically
element ordering	non-decreasing, non-increasing, equal
Over two sequence variables x and y:	
linear relationship	$y = ax + b$ elementwise
comparison	$x \leq y$, $x < y$, $x = y$, $x \neq y$ performed lexicographically
subsequence relationship	x is a subsequence of y
reversal	x is the reverse of y
Over a sequence of a numeric variable s:	
membership	$x \in s$

where a, b, and c denote constants, fn denotes a built-in function, and *uninit* denotes an uninitialized value. The name of the variable denotes its value at the considered point of execution; *origx* indicates the original value of variable x, that is, the value at the beginning of the considered execution.

Figure 19.7: A sample set of predicate patterns implemented by the Daikon behavior analysis tool.

```
private static void testCaseSingleValues() {
        AvlTree t = new AvlTree();
        t.insert(new Integer(5));
        t.insert(new Integer(2));
        t.insert(new Integer(7));
}

...

private static void testCaseRandom(int nTestCase) {
        AvlTree t = new AvlTree();

        for (int i = 1; i < nTestCase; i++) {
                int value = (int) Math.round(Math.random() * 100);
                t.insert(new Integer(value));
        }
}
```

Figure 19.8: Two test cases for method insert *of Figure 19.6.* testCaseSingleValues *inserts 5, 2, and 7 in this order;* testCaseRandom *inserts 300 randomly generated integer values.*

oughness of tests, during program analysis to help understand program behavior, during regression test to compare the behavior of different versions or configurations, during test of component-based software systems to compare the behavior of components in different contexts, and during debugging to identify anomalous behavior and understand its causes.

Open Research Issues

Program analysis research for fault detection and assurance is in a period of productive ferment, with every prospect of rapid advance for at least another decade. Some techniques initially introduced decades ago, now revisited or rediscovered, have become practical at last due to vastly increased computing resources and improvements in fundamental underlying algorithms, such as alias analysis and interprocedural data flow analysis.

One important thread of foundational research involves clarifying the relations among finite state verification techniques, techniques based on flow analysis, and type (or type and effect) systems. These once distinct approaches to verifying program properties now blur at the edges, and each is enriching the others. At the same time, research in the programming languages community and that in the software engineering research community are intertwining as much as at any time since they were one in the late 1970s.

Dynamic analysis (aside from conventional testing) was once relegated to debugging and performance analysis, but has recently become an important approach for

Behavior model for testCaseSingleValues
father one of $\{2, 5, 7\}$
left == 2
right == 7
leftHeight == rightHeight
rightHeight == diffHeight
leftHeight == 0
rightHeight == 0
fatherHeight one of $\{0, 1\}$

Behavior model for testCaseRandom
father >= 0
left >= 0
father > left
father < right
left < right
fatherHeight >= 0
leftHeight >= 0
rightHeight >= 0
fatherHeight > leftHeight
fatherHeight > rightHeight
fatherHeight > diffHeight
rightHeight >= diffHeight
diffHeight one of $\{-1, 0, 1\}$
leftHeight - rightHeight + diffHeight == 0

Figure 19.9: The behavioral models for method insert *of Figure 19.6. The model was obtained using Daikon with test cases* testCaseSingleValues *and* testCaseRandom *shown in Figure 19.8.*

constructing and refining models of program behavior. Synergistic combinations of static program analysis, dynamic analysis, and testing are a promising avenue of further research.

Further Reading

Readings on some of the underlying techniques in program analysis are suggested in Chapters 5, 6, 7, and 8. In addition, any good textbook on compiler construction will provide useful basic background on extracting models from program source code.

A recent application of symbolic testing described by Bush, Pincus, and Sielaff [BPS00] is a good example of the revival of an approach that found little practical application when first introduced in the 1970s. Aside from exploiting vastly greater computing capacity, the modern version of the technique improves on the original in several ways, most notably better managing communication of analysis results to the user. Coen-Porisini et al. [CPDGP01] describe a modern application of symbolic execution in constructing a rigorous demonstration of program properties by exploiting limitations of an application domain.

Savage et al. [SBN+97] introduced the lockset analysis technique, which has influenced a great deal of subsequent research in both static and dynamic analyses of multi-threaded software. The Daikon tool and its approach to behavioral model extraction were introduced by Ernst et al. [ECGN01].

Exercises

19.1. We claimed that Java synchronized(l) { *block* } is easier to check statically than separate lock(l) and unlock(l) operations.

Give an example of how it could be harder to verify that lock(l) and unlock(l) operations protect a particular variable access than to verify that the access is protected by a synchronized(l) { ... }.

19.2. Although Java synchronized blocks make analysis of locking easy relative to individual lock(l) and unlock(l) operations, it is still possible to construct Java programs for which a static program analysis will not be able to determine whether access at a particular program location is always protected by the same lock. Give an example of this, with an explanation. (Hint: Each lock in Java is identified by a corresponding object.)

19.3. A fundamental facility for symbolic testing and many other static analysis techniques is to allow the user to note that a particular warning or error report is a false alarm, and to suppress it in future runs of the analysis tool. However, it is possible that a report that is a false alarm today might describe a real fault sometime later, due to program changes. How might you support the "revival" of suppressed error reports at appropriate times and points? Discuss the advantages and disadvantages of your approach.

19.4. Suppose we choose to model a program execution state with four pieces of information — the program location (control point) and the states of four Boolean variables $w, x, y,$ and z — and suppose each of those variables is modeled by a finite state machine (FSM) with three states representing possible values (uninitialized, true, and false).

If we were modeling just the possible values of w, a natural choice would be to label each program location with an element from a powerset lattice in which each lattice element represents a subset of automaton states. If we model $w, x, y,$ and z, there are at least two different ways we could represent values at each program location: As a set of tuples of FSM states or as a tuple of sets of FSM states. What are the advantages and disadvantages of each of these representation choices? How might your choice depend on the property you were attempting to verify?

Part IV

Process

Chapter 20

Planning and Monitoring the Process

Any complex process requires planning and monitoring. The quality process requires coordination of many different activities over a period that spans a full development cycle and beyond. Planning is necessary to order, provision, and coordinate all the activities that support a quality goal, and monitoring of actual status against a plan is required to steer and adjust the process.

Required Background

- Chapter 4
  Introduction of basic concepts of quality process, goals, and activities provides useful background for understanding this chapter.

20.1 Overview

Planning involves scheduling activities, allocating resources, and devising observable, unambiguous milestones against which progress and performance can be monitored. Monitoring means answering the question, "How are we doing?"

Quality planning is one aspect of project planning, and quality processes must be closely coordinated with other development processes. Coordination among quality and development tasks may constrain ordering (e.g., unit tests are executed after creation of program units). It may shape tasks to facilitate coordination; for example, delivery may be broken into smaller increments to allow early testing. Some aspects of the project plan, such as feedback and design for testability, may belong equally to the quality plan and other aspects of the project plan.

Quality planning begins at the inception of a project and is developed with the overall project plan, instantiating and building on a quality strategy that spans several projects. Like the overall project plan, the quality plan is developed incrementally, beginning with the feasibility study and continuing through development and delivery.

Formulation of the plan involves risk analysis and contingency planning. Execution of the plan involves monitoring, corrective action, and planning for subsequent releases and projects.

Allocating responsibility among team members is a crucial and difficult part of planning. When one person plays multiple roles, explicitly identifying each responsibility is still essential for ensuring that none are neglected.

20.2 Quality and Process

A software plan involves many intertwined concerns, from schedule to cost to usability and dependability. Despite the intertwining, it is useful to distinguish individual concerns and objectives to lessen the likelihood that they will be neglected, to allocate responsibilities, and to make the overall planning process more manageable.

For example, a mature software project plan will include architectural design reviews, and the quality plan will allocate effort for reviewing testability aspects of the structure and build order. Clearly, design for testability is an aspect of software design and cannot be carried out by a separate testing team in isolation. It involves both test designers and other software designers in explicitly evaluating testability as one consideration in selecting among design alternatives. The objective of incorporating design for testability in the quality process is primarily to ensure that it is not overlooked and secondarily to plan activities that address it as effectively as possible.

An appropriate quality process follows a form similar to the overall software process in which it is embedded. In a strict (and unrealistic) waterfall software process, one would follow the "V model" (Figure 2.1 on page 16) in a sequential manner, beginning unit testing only as implementation commenced following completion of the detailed design phase, and finishing unit testing before integration testing commenced. In the XP "test first" method, unit testing is conflated with subsystem and system testing. A cycle of test design and test execution is wrapped around each small-grain incremental development step. The role that inspection and peer reviews would play in other processes is filled in XP largely by pair programming. A typical spiral process model lies somewhere between, with distinct planning, design, and implementation steps in several increments coupled with a similar unfolding of analysis and test activities. Some processes specifically designed around quality activities are briefly outlined in the sidebars on pages 378, 380, and 381.

A general principle, across all software processes, is that the cost of detecting and repairing a fault increases as a function of time between committing an error and detecting the resultant faults. Thus, whatever the intermediate work products in a software plan, an efficient quality plan will include a matched set of intermediate validation and verification activities that detect most faults within a short period of their introduction. Any step in a software process that is not paired with a validation or verification step is an opportunity for defects to fester, and any milestone in a project plan that does not include a quality check is an opportunity for a misleading assessment of progress.

The particular verification or validation step at each stage depends on the nature of the intermediate work product and on the anticipated defects. For example, anticipated defects in a requirements statement might include incompleteness, ambiguity, inconsistency, and overambition relative to project goals and resources. A review step might address some of these, and automated analyses might help with completeness and consistency checking.

The evolving collection of work products can be viewed as a set of descriptions of different parts and aspects of the software system, at different levels of detail. Portions of the implementation have the useful property of being executable in a conventional sense, and are the traditional subject of testing, but every level of specification and design can be both the subject of verification activities and a source of information for verifying other artifacts. A typical intermediate artifact — say, a subsystem interface definition or a database schema — will be subject to the following steps:

Internal consistency check: Check the artifact for compliance with structuring rules that define "well-formed" artifacts of that type. An important point of leverage is defining the syntactic and semantic rules thoroughly and precisely enough that many common errors result in detectable violations. This is analogous to syntax and strong-typing rules in programming languages, which are not enough to guarantee program correctness but effectively guard against many simple errors.

External consistency check: Check the artifact for consistency with related artifacts. Often this means checking for conformance to a "prior" or "higher-level" specification, but consistency checking does not depend on sequential, top-down development — all that is required is that the related information from two or more artifacts be defined precisely enough to support detection of discrepancies. Consistency usually proceeds from broad, syntactic checks to more detailed and expensive semantic checks, and a variety of automated and manual verification techniques may be applied.

Generation of correctness conjectures: Correctness conjectures, which can be test outcomes or other objective criteria, lay the groundwork for external consistency checks of other work products, particularly those that are yet to be developed or revised. Generating correctness conjectures for other work products will frequently motivate refinement of the current product. For example, an interface definition may be elaborated and made more precise so that implementations can be effectively tested.

20.3 Test and Analysis Strategies

Lessons of past experience are an important asset of organizations that rely heavily on technical skills. A body of explicit knowledge, shared and refined by the group, is more valuable than islands of individual competence. Organizational knowledge in a shared and systematic form is more amenable to improvement and less vulnerable to organizational change, including the loss of key individuals. Capturing the lessons of experience in a consistent and repeatable form is essential for avoiding errors, maintaining consistency of the process, and increasing development efficiency.

Cleanroom

The Cleanroom process model, introduced by IBM in the late 1980s, pairs development with V&V activities and stresses analysis over testing in the early phases. Testing is left for system certification. The Cleanroom process involves two cooperating teams, the development and the quality teams, and five major activities: specification, planning, design and verification, quality certification, and feedback.

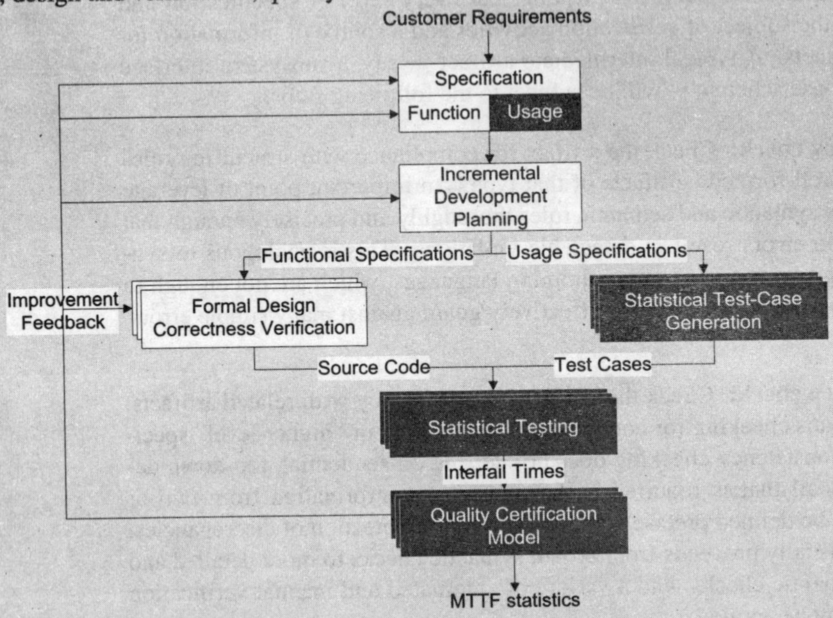

In the *specification* activity, the development team defines the required behavior of the system, while the quality team defines usage scenarios that are later used for deriving system test suites. The *planning* activity identifies incremental development and certification phases.

After planning, all activities are iterated to produce incremental releases of the system. Each system increment is fully deployed and certified before the following step. Design and code undergo formal inspection ("*Correctness verification*") before release. One of the key premises underpinning the Cleanroom process model is that rigorous design and formal inspection produce "nearly fault-free software."

Usage profiles generated during specification are applied in the *statistical testing* activity to gauge quality of each release. Another key assumption of the Cleanroom process model is that usage profiles are sufficiently accurate that statistical testing will provide an accurate measure of quality as perceived by users.[a] Reliability is measured in terms of mean time between failures (MTBF) and is constantly controlled after each release. Failures are reported to the development team for correction, and if reliability falls below an acceptable range, failure data is used for process improvement before the next incremental release.

[a]See Chapter 22 for more detail on statistical testing and usage profiling.

Software organizations can develop useful, organization-specific strategies because of similarities among projects carried out by a particular organization in a set of related application domains. Test and analysis strategies capture commonalities across projects and provide guidelines for maintaining consistency among quality plans.

A strategy is distinguished from a plan in that it is not specific to a single project. Rather, it provides guidance and a general framework for developing quality plans for several projects, satisfying organizational quality standards, promoting homogeneity across projects, and making both the creation and execution of individual project quality plans more efficient.

The quality strategy is an intellectual asset of an individual organization prescribing a set of solutions to problems specific to that organization. Among the factors that particularize the strategy are:

Structure and size: Large organizations typically have sharper distinctions between development and quality groups, even if testing personnel are assigned to development teams. In smaller organizations, it is more common for a single person to serve multiple roles. Where responsibility is distributed among more individuals, the quality strategy will require more elaborate attention to coordination and communication, and in general there will be much greater reliance on documents to carry the collective memory.

In a smaller organization, or an organization that has devolved responsibility to small, semi-autonomous teams, there is typically less emphasis on formal communication and documents but a greater emphasis on managing and balancing the multiple roles played by each team member.

Overall process: We have already noted the intertwining of quality process with other aspects of an overall software process, and this is of course reflected in the quality strategy. For example, if an organization follows the Cleanroom methodology, then inspections will be required but unit testing forbidden. An organization that adopts the XP methodology is likely to follow the "test first" and pair programming elements of that approach, and in fact would find a more document-heavy approach a difficult fit.

Notations, standard process steps, and even tools can be reflected in the quality strategy to the extent they are consistent from project to project. For example, if an organization consistently uses a particular combination of UML diagram notations to document subsystem interfaces, then the quality strategy might include derivation of test designs from those notations, as well as review and analysis steps tailored to detect the most common and important design flaws at that point. If a particular version and configuration control system is woven into process management, the quality strategy will likewise exploit it to support and enforce quality process steps.

Application domain: The domain may impose both particular quality objectives (e.g., privacy and security in medical records processing), and in some cases particular steps and documentation required to obtain certification from an external authority. For example, the RTCA/DO-178B standard for avionics software requires testing to the modified condition/decision coverage (MC/DC) criterion.

SRET

The software reliability engineered testing (SRET) approach, developed at AT&T in the early 1990s, assumes a spiral development process and augments each coil of the spiral with rigorous testing activities. SRET identifies two main types of testing: *development testing*, used to find and remove faults in software at least partially developed in-house, and *certification testing*, used to either accept or reject outsourced software.

The SRET approach includes seven main steps. Two initial, quick decision-making steps determine which systems require separate testing and which type of testing is needed for each system to be tested. The five core steps are executed in parallel with each coil of a spiral development process.

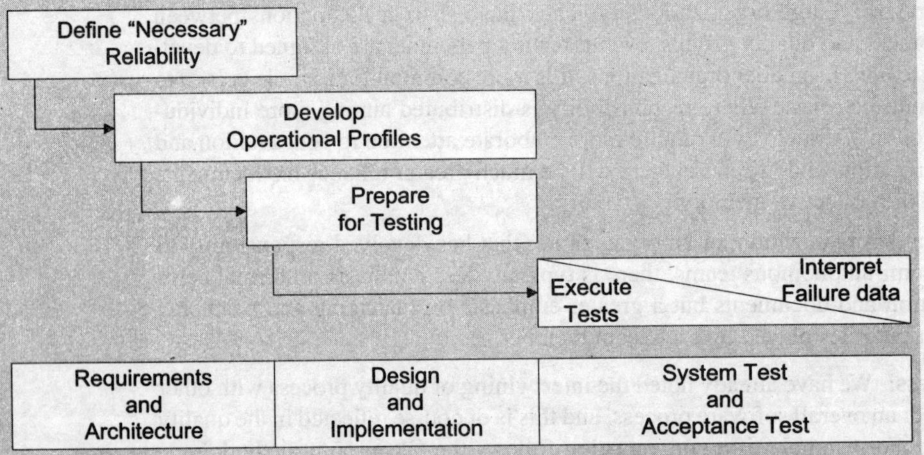

The five core steps of SRET are:

Define "Necessary" Reliability: Determine operational models, that is, distinct patterns of system usage that require separate testing, classify failures according to their severity, and engineer the reliability strategy with fault prevention, fault removal, and fault tolerance activities.

Develop Operational Profiles: Develop both overall profiles that span operational models and operational profiles within single operational models.

Prepare for Testing: Specify test cases and procedures.

Execute Tests

Interpret Failure Data: Interpretation of failure data depends on the type of testing. In development testing, the goal is to track progress and compare present failure intensities with objectives. In certification testing, the goal is to determine if a software component or system should be accepted or rejected.

Extreme Programming (XP)

The extreme programming methodology (XP) emphasizes simplicity over generality, global vision and communication over structured organization, frequent changes over big releases, continuous testing and analysis over separation of roles and responsibilities, and continuous feedback over traditional planning.

Customer involvement in an XP project includes requirements analysis (development, refinement, and prioritization of *user stories*) and acceptance testing of very frequent iterative releases. Planning is based on prioritization of user stories, which are implemented in short iterations. Test cases corresponding to scenarios in user stories serve as partial specifications.

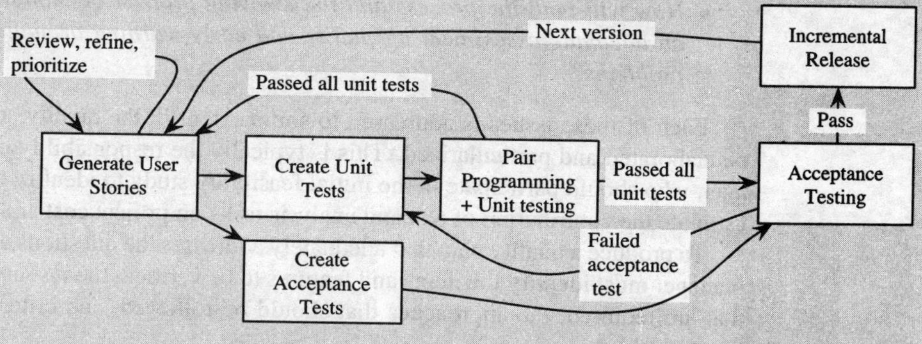

Test cases suitable for batch execution are part of the system code base and are implemented prior to the implementation of features they check ("test-first"). Developers work in pairs, incrementally developing and testing a module. Pair programming effectively conflates a review activity with coding. Each release is checked by running all the tests devised up to that point of development, thus essentially merging unit testing with integration and system testing. A failed acceptance test is viewed as an indication that additional unit tests are needed.

Although there are no standard templates for analysis and test strategies, we can identify a few elements that should be part of almost any good strategy. A strategy should specify common quality requirements that apply to all or most products, promoting conventions for unambiguously stating and measuring them, and reducing the likelihood that they will be overlooked in the quality plan for a particular project. A strategy should indicate a set of documents that is normally produced during the quality process, and their contents and relationships. It should indicate the activities that are prescribed by the overall process organization. Often a set of standard tools and practices will be prescribed, such as the interplay of a version and configuration control tool with review and testing procedures. In addition, a strategy includes guidelines for project staffing and assignment of roles and responsibilities. An excerpt of a sample strategy document is presented in Chapter 24.

20.4 Test and Analysis Plans

An analysis and test plan details the steps to be taken in a particular project. A plan should answer the following questions:

- *What quality activities will be carried out?*
- *What are the dependencies among the quality activities and between quality and development activities?*
- *What resources are needed and how will they be allocated?*
- *How will both the process and the evolving product be monitored to maintain an adequate assessment of quality and early warning of quality and schedule problems?*

Each of these issues is addressed to some extent in the quality strategy, but must be elaborated and particularized. This is typically the responsibility of a quality manager, who should participate in the initial feasibility study to identify quality goals and estimate the contribution of test and analysis tasks on project cost and schedule.

To produce a quality plan that adequately addresses the questions above, the quality manager must identify the items and features to be verified, the resources and activities that are required, the approaches that should be followed, and criteria for evaluating the results.

Items and features to be verified circumscribe the target of the quality plan. While there is an obvious correspondence between items to be developed or modified and those to undergo testing, they may differ somewhat in detail. For example, overall evaluation of the user interface may be the purview of a separate human factors group. The items to be verified, moreover, include many intermediate artifacts such as requirements specifications and design documents, in addition to portions of the delivered system. Approaches to be taken in verification and validation may vary among items. For example, the plan may prescribe inspection and testing for all items and additional static analyses for multi-threaded subsystems.

Quality goals must be expressed in terms of properties satisfied by the product and must be further elaborated with metrics that can be monitored during the course of the project. For example, if known failure scenarios are classified as critical, severe, moderate, and minor, then we might decide in advance that a product version may enter end-user acceptance testing only when it has undergone system testing with no outstanding critical or severe failures.

Defining quality objectives and process organization in detail requires information that is not all available in the early stages of development. Test items depend on design decisions; detailed approaches to evaluation can be defined only after examining requirements and design specifications; tasks and schedule can be completed only after the design; new risks and contingencies may be introduced by decisions taken during development. On the other hand, an early plan is necessary for estimating and controlling cost and schedule. The quality manager must start with an initial plan based on incomplete and tentative information, and incrementally refine the plan as more and better information becomes available during the project.

After capturing goals as well as possible, the next step in construction of a quality plan is to produce an overall rough list of tasks. The quality strategy and past experience provide a basis for customizing the list to the current project and for scaling tasks appropriately. For example, experience (preferably in the form of collected and analyzed data from past projects, rather than personal memory) might suggest a ratio of 3:5 for person-months of effort devoted to integration test relative to coding effort. Historical data may also provide scaling factors for the application domain, interfaces with externally developed software, and experience of the quality staff. To the extent possible, the quality manager must break large tasks into component subtasks to obtain better estimates, but it is inevitable that some task breakdown must await further elaboration of the overall project design and schedule.

The manager can start noting dependencies among the quality activities and between them and other activities in the overall project, and exploring arrangements of tasks over time. The main objective at this point is to schedule quality activities so that assessment data are provided continuously throughout the project, without unnecessary delay of other development activities. For example, the quality manager may note that the design and implementation of different subsystems are scheduled in different phases, and may plan subsystem testing accordingly.

Where there is a choice between scheduling a quality activity earlier or later, the earliest point possible is always preferable. However, the demand on resources (staff time, primarily) must be leveled over time, and often one must carefully schedule the availability of particular critical resources, such as an individual test designer with expertise in a particular technology. Maintaining a consistent level of effort limits the number of activities that can be carried on concurrently, and resource constraints together with the objective of minimizing project delays tends to force particular orderings on tasks.

If one has a choice between completing two tasks in four months, or completing the first task in two months and then the second in another two months, the schedule that brings one task to completion earlier is generally advantageous from the perspective of process visibility, as well as reduced coordination overhead. However, many activities demand a fraction of a person's attention over a longer period and cannot be compressed. For example, participation in design and code inspection requires a substantial investment of effort, but typically falls short of a full-time assignment. Since delayed inspections can be a bottleneck in progress of a project, they should have a high priority when they can be carried out, and are best interleaved with tasks that can be more flexibly scheduled.

While the project plan shows the expected schedule of tasks, the arrangement and ordering of tasks are also driven by risk. The quality plan, like the overall project plan, should include an explicit risk plan that lists major risks and contingencies, as discussed in the next section.

A key tactic for controlling the impact of risk in the project schedule is to minimize the likelihood that unexpected delay in one task propagates through the whole schedule and delays project completion. One first identifies the *critical paths* through the project schedule. Critical paths are chains of activities that must be completed in sequence and that have maximum overall duration. Tasks on the critical path have a high priority for early scheduling, and likewise the tasks on which they depend (which may not **critical paths** themselves be on the critical path) should be scheduled early enough to provide some schedule slack and prevent delay in the inception of the critical tasks.

critical dependence

A *critical dependence* occurs when a task on a critical path is scheduled immediately after some other task on the critical path, particularly if the length of the critical path is close to the length of the project. Critical dependence may occur with tasks outside the quality plan part of the overall project plan.

The primary tactic available for reducing the schedule risk of a critical dependence is to decompose a task on the critical path, factoring out subtasks that can be performed earlier. For example, an acceptance test phase late in a project is likely to have a critical dependence on development and system integration. One cannot entirely remove this dependence, but its potential to delay project completion is reduced by factoring test design from test execution.

Figure 20.1 shows alternative schedules for a simple project that starts at the beginning of January and must be completed by the end of May. In the top schedule, indicated as *CRITICAL SCHEDULE*, the tasks *Analysis and design*, *Code and Integration*, *Design and execute subsystem tests*, and *Design and execute system tests* form a critical path that spans the duration of the entire project. A delay in any of the activities will result in late delivery. In this schedule, only the *Produce user documentation* task does not belong to the critical path, and thus only delays of this task can be tolerated.

In the middle schedule, marked as *UNLIMITED RESOURCES*, the test design and execution activities are separated into distinct tasks. Test design tasks are scheduled early, right after *analysis and design*, and only test execution is scheduled after *Code and integration*. In this way the tasks *Design subsystem tests* and *Design system tests* are removed from the critical path, which now spans 16 weeks with a tolerance of 5 weeks with respect to the expected termination of the project. This schedule assumes enough resources for running *Code and integration*, *Production of user documentation*, *Design of subsystem tests*, and *Design of system tests*.

The *LIMITED RESOURCES* schedule at the bottom of Figure 20.1 rearranges tasks to meet resource constraints. In this case we assume that test design and execution, and production of user documentation share the same resources and thus cannot be executed in parallel. We can see that, despite the limited parallelism, decomposing testing activities and scheduling test design earlier results in a critical path of 17 weeks, 4 weeks earlier than the expected termination of the project. Notice that in the example, the critical path is formed by the tasks *Analysis and design*, *Design subsystem tests*, *Design system tests*, *Produce user documentation*, *Execute subsystem tests*, and *Execute system tests*. In fact, the limited availability of resources results in dependencies among *Design subsystem tests*, *Design system tests* and *Produce user documentation* that last longer than the parallel task *Code and integration*.

The completed plan must include frequent milestones for assessing progress. A rule of thumb is that, for projects of a year or more, milestones for assessing progress should occur at least every three months. For shorter projects, a reasonable maximum interval for assessment is one quarter of project duration.

Figure 20.2 shows a possible schedule for the initial analysis and test plan for the business logic of the Chipmunk Web presence in the form of a GANTT diagram. In the initial plan, the manager has allocated time and effort to inspections of all major artifacts, as well as test design as early as practical and ongoing test execution dur-

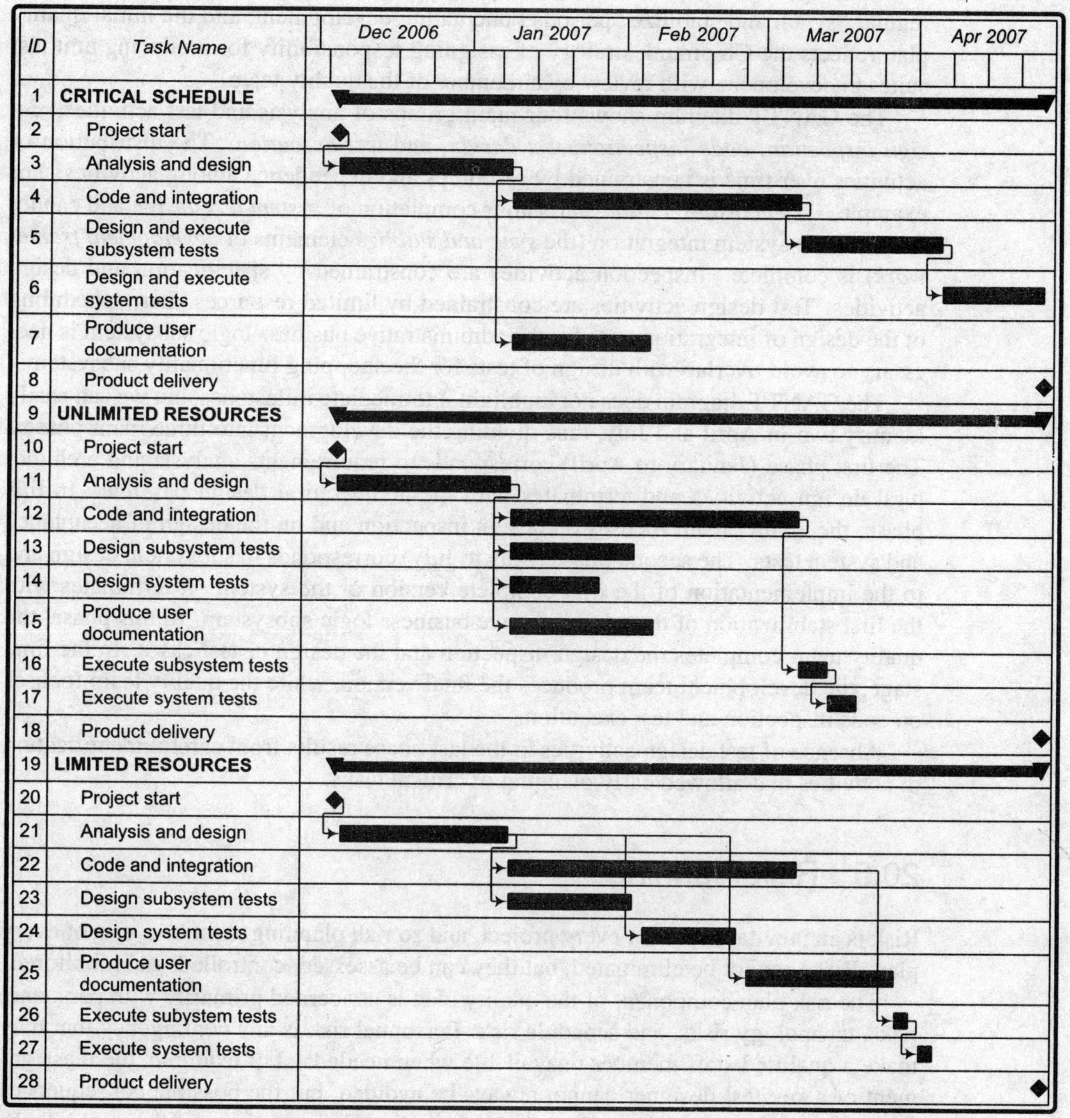

Figure 20.1: Three possible simple schedules with different risks and resource allocation. The bars indicate the duration of the tasks. Diamonds indicate milestones, and arrows between bars indicate precedence between tasks.

ing development. Division of the project into major parts is reflected in the plan, but further elaboration of tasks associated with units and smaller subsystems must await corresponding elaboration of the architectural design. Thus, for example, inspection of the shopping facilities code and the unit test suites is shown as a single aggregate task. Even this initial plan does reflect the usual Chipmunk development strategy of regular "synch and stabilize" periods punctuating development, and the initial quality plan reflects the Chipmunk strategy of assigning responsibility for producing unit test suites to developers, with review by a member of the quality team.

The GANTT diagram shows four main groups of analysis and test activities: *design inspection*, *code inspection*, *test design*, and *test execution*. The distribution of activities over time is constrained by resources and dependence among activities. For example, *system test execution* starts after completion of *system test design* and cannot finish before system integration (the *sync and stablize* elements of *development framework*) is complete. Inspection activities are constrained by specification and design activities. Test design activities are constrained by limited resources. Late scheduling of the design of integration tests for the administrative business logic subsystem is necessary to avoid overlap with design of tests for the shopping functionality subsystem.

The GANTT diagram does not highlight intermediate milestones, but we can easily identify two in April and July, thus dividing the development into three main phases. The first phase (January to April) corresponds to requirements analysis and architectural design activities and terminates with the architectural design baseline. In this phase, the quality team focuses on design inspection and on the design of acceptance and system tests. The second phase (May to July) corresponds to subsystem design and to the implementation of the first complete version of the system. It terminates with the first stabilization of the administrative business logic subsystem. In this phase, the quality team completes the design inspection and the design of test cases. In the final stage, the development team produces the final version, while the quality team focuses on code inspection and test execution.

Absence of test design activities in the last phase results from careful identification of activities that allowed early planning of critical tasks.

20.5 Risk Planning

Risk is an inevitable part of every project, and so risk planning must be a part of every plan. Risks cannot be eliminated, but they can be assessed, controlled, and monitored.

The risk plan component of the quality plan is concerned primarily with personnel risks, technology risks, and schedule risk. Personnel risk is any contingency that may make a qualified staff member unavailable when needed. For example, the reassignment of a key test designer cannot always be avoided, but the possible consequences can be analyzed in advance and minimized by careful organization of the work. Technology risks in the quality plan include risks of technology used specifically by the quality team and risks of quality problems involving other technology used in the product or project. For example, changes in the target platform or in the testing environment, due to new releases of the operating system or to the adoption of a new testing tool suite, may not be schedulable in advance, but may be taken into account in the

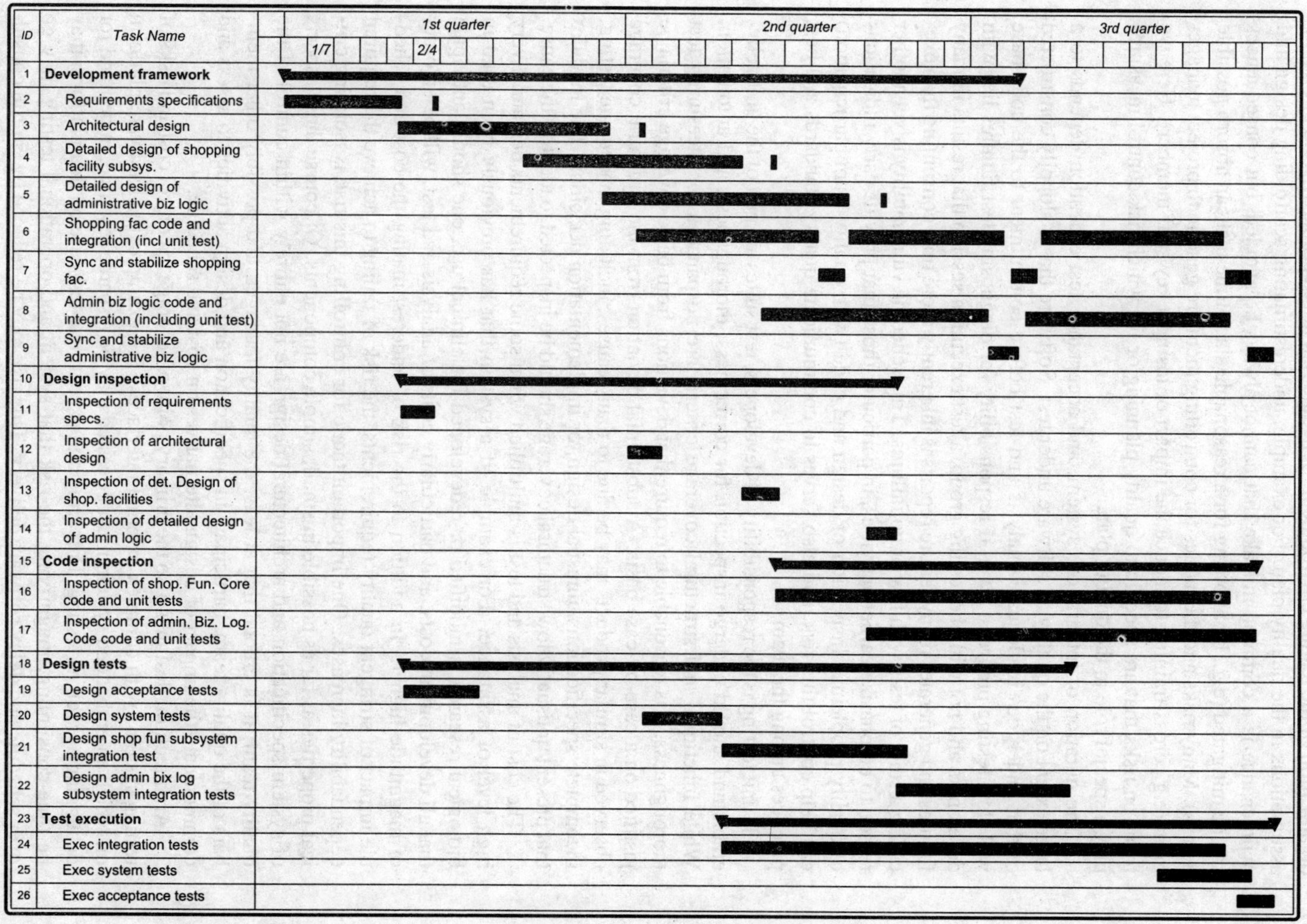

Figure 20.2: Initial schedule for quality activities in development of the business logic subsystem of the Chipmunk Web presence, presented as a GANTT diagram.

organization of the testing environment. Schedule risk arises primarily from optimistic assumptions in the quality plan. For example, underestimating scaffolding design and maintenance is a common mistake that cannot always be avoided, but consequences can be mitigated (e.g., by allowing for a reasonable slack time that can absorb possible delays). Many risks and the tactics for controlling them are generic to project management (e.g., cross-training to reduce the impact of losing a key staff member). Here we focus on risks that are specific to quality planning or for which risk control measures play a special role in the quality plan.

The duration of integration, system, and acceptance test execution depends to a large extent on the quality of software under test. Software that is sloppily constructed or that undergoes inadequate analysis and test before commitment to the code base will slow testing progress. Even if responsibility for diagnosing test failures lies with developers and not with the testing group, a test execution session that results in many failures and generates many failure reports is inherently more time consuming than executing a suite of tests with few or no failures. This schedule vulnerability is yet another reason to emphasize earlier activities, in particular those that provide early indications of quality problems. Inspection of design and code (with quality team participation) can help control this risk, and also serves to communicate quality standards and best practices among the team.

If unit testing is the responsibility of developers, test suites are part of the unit deliverable and should undergo inspection for correctness, thoroughness, and automation. While functional and structural coverage criteria are no panacea for measuring test thoroughness, it is reasonable to require that deviations from basic coverage criteria be justified on a case-by-case basis. A substantial deviation from the structural coverage observed in similar products may be due to many causes, including inadequate testing, incomplete specifications, unusual design, or implementation decisions. The modules that present unusually low structural coverage should be inspected to identify the cause.

The cost of analysis and test is multiplied when some requirements demand a very high level of assurance. For example, if a system that has previously been used in biological research is modified or redeveloped for clinical use, one should anticipate that all development costs, and particularly costs of analysis and test, will be an order of magnitude higher. In addition to the risk of underestimating the cost and schedule impact of stringent quality requirements, the risk of failing to achieve the required dependability increases. One important tactic for controlling this risk is isolating critical properties as far as possible in small, simple components. Of course these aspects of system specification and architectural design are not entirely within control of the quality team; it is crucial that at least the quality manager, and possibly other members of the quality team, participate in specification and design activities to assess and communicate the impact of design alternatives on cost and schedule.

Architectural design is also the primary point of leverage to control cost and risks of testing systems with complex external interfaces. For example, the hardware platform on which an embedded system must be tested may be a scarce resource, in demand for debugging as well as testing. Preparing and executing a test case on that platform may be time-consuming, magnifying the risk that system and operational testing may go over schedule and delay software delivery. This risk may be reduced by careful consideration of design-for-testability in architectural design. A testable design isolates and minimizes platform dependencies, reducing the portion of testing that requires access to the platform. It will typically provide additional interfaces to enhance controllability and observability in testing. A considerable investment in test scaffolding, from self-diagnosis to platform simulators, may also be warranted.

Risks related both to critical requirements and limitations on testability can be partially addressed in system specifications and programming standards. For example, it is notoriously difficult to detect race conditions by testing multi-threaded software. However, one may impose a design and programming discipline that prevents race conditions, such as a simple monitor discipline with resource ordering. Detecting violations of that discipline, statically and dynamically, is much simpler than detecting actual data races. This tactic may be reflected in several places in the project plan, from settling on the programming discipline in architectural design to checking for proper use of the discipline in code and design inspections, to implementation or purchase of tools to automate compliance checking.

The sidebars on page 390 and 391 summarize a set of risks both generic to process management and specific to quality control that a quality manager must consider when defining a quality plan.

20.6 Monitoring the Process

The quality manager monitors progress of quality activities, including results as well as schedule, to identify deviations from the quality plan as early as possible and take corrective action. Effective monitoring, naturally, depends on a plan that is realistic, well organized, and sufficiently detailed with clear, unambiguous milestones and criteria. We say a process is *visible* to the extent that it can be effectively monitored.

Successful completion of a planned activity must be distinguished from mere termination, as otherwise it is too tempting to meet an impending deadline by omitting some planned work. Skipping planned verification activities or addressing them superficially can seem to accelerate a late project, but the boost is only apparent; the real effect is to postpone detection of more faults to later stages in development, where their detection and removal will be far more threatening to project success.

For example, suppose a developer is expected to deliver unit test cases as part of a work unit. If project deadlines are slipping, the developer is tempted to scrimp on designing unit tests and writing supporting code, perhaps dashing off a few superficial test cases so that the unit can be committed to the code base. The rushed development and inadequate unit testing are nearly guaranteed to leave bugs that surface later, perhaps in integration or system testing, where they will have a far greater impact on project schedule. Worst of all, they might be first detected in operational use, reducing the real and perceived quality of the delivered product. In monitoring progress, therefore, it is essential to include appropriate metrics of the thoroughness or completeness of the activity.

Monitoring produces a surfeit of detail about individual activities. Managers need to make decisions based on an overall understanding of project status, so raw monitoring information must be aggregated in ways that provide an overall picture.

Risk Management in the Quality Plan: Risks Generic to Process Management

The quality plan must identify potential risks and define appropriate control tactics. Some risks and control tactics are generic to process management, while others are specific to the quality process. Here we provide a brief overview of some risks generic to process management. Risks specific to the quality process are summarized in the sidebar on page 391.

Personnel Risks	**Example Control Tactics**
A staff member is lost (becomes ill, changes employer, etc.) or is underqualified for task (the project plan assumed a level of skill or familiarity that the assigned member did not have).	Cross train to avoid overdependence on individuals; encourage and schedule continuous education; provide open communication with opportunities for staff self-assessment and identification of skills gaps early in the project; provide competitive compensation and promotion policies and a rewarding work environment to retain staff; include training time in the project schedule.

Technology Risks	**Example Control Tactics**
Many faults are introduced interfacing to an unfamiliar commercial off-the-shelf (COTS) component.	Anticipate and schedule extra time for testing unfamiliar interfaces; invest training time for COTS components and for training with new tools; monitor, document, and publicize common errors and correct idioms; introduce new tools in lower-risk pilot projects or prototyping exercises.
Test and analysis automation tools do not meet expectations.	Introduce new tools in lower-risk pilot projects or prototyping exercises; anticipate and schedule time for training with new tools.
COTS components do not meet quality expectations.	Include COTS component qualification testing early in project plan; introduce new COTS components in lower-risk pilot projects or prototyping exercises.

Schedule Risks	**Example Control Tactics**
Inadequate unit testing leads to unanticipated expense and delays in integration testing.	Track and reward quality unit testing as evidenced by low-fault densities in integration.
Difficulty of scheduling meetings makes inspection a bottleneck in development.	Set aside times in a weekly schedule in which inspections take precedence over other meetings and other work; try distributed and asynchronous inspection techniques, with a lower frequency of face-to-face inspection meetings.

Risk Management in the Quality Plan: Risks Specific to Quality Management

Here we provide a brief overview of some risks specific to the quality process. Risks generic to process management are summarized in the sidebar at page 390.

Development Risks	Example Control Tactics
Poor quality software delivered to testing group or inadequate unit test and analysis before committing to the code base.	Provide early warning and feedback; schedule inspection of design, code and test suites; connect development and inspection to the reward system; increase training through inspection; require coverage or other criteria at unit test level.
Executions Risks	**Example Control Tactics**
Execution costs higher than planned; scarce resources available for testing (testing requires expensive or complex machines or systems not easily available.)	Minimize parts that require full system to be executed; inspect architecture to assess and improve testability; increase intermediate feedback; invest in scaffolding.
Requirements Risks	**Example Control Tactics**
High assurance critical requirements.	Compare planned testing effort with former projects with similar criticality level to avoid underestimating testing effort; balance test and analysis; isolate critical parts, concerns and properties.

One key aggregate measure is the number of faults that have been revealed and removed, which can be compared to data obtained from similar past projects. Fault detection and removal can be tracked against time and will typically follow a characteristic distribution similar to that shown in Figure 20.3. The number of faults detected per time unit tends to grow across several system builds, then to decrease at a much lower rate (usually half the growth rate) until it stabilizes.

An unexpected pattern in fault detection may be a symptom of problems. If detected faults stop growing earlier than expected, one might hope it indicates exceptionally high quality, but it would be wise to consider the alternative hypothesis that fault detection efforts are ineffective. A growth rate that remains high through more than half the planned system builds is a warning that quality goals may be met late or not at all, and may indicate weaknesses in fault removal or lack of discipline in development (e.g., a rush to add features before delivery, with a consequent deemphasis on quality control).

A second indicator of problems in the quality process is faults that remain open longer than expected. Quality problems are confirmed when the number of open faults does not stabilize at a level acceptable to stakeholders.

The accuracy with which we can predict fault data and diagnose deviations from expectation depends on the stability of the software development and quality processes, and on availability of data from similar projects. Differences between organizations and across application domains are wide, so by far the most valuable data is from

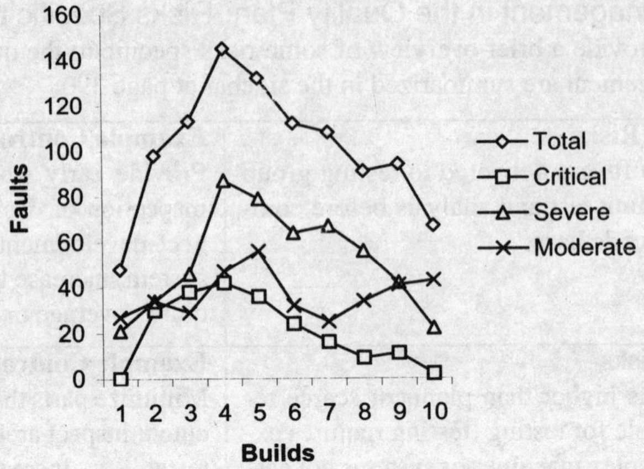

Figure 20.3: A typical distribution of faults for system builds through time.

similar projects in one's own organization.

The faultiness data in Figure 20.3 are aggregated by severity levels. This helps in better understanding the process. Growth in the number of *moderate* faults late in the development process may be a symptom of good use of limited resources concentrated in removing *critical* and *severe* faults, not spent solving *moderate* problems.

Accurate classification schemata can improve monitoring and may be used in very large projects, where the amount of detailed information cannot be summarized in overall data. The orthogonal defect classification (ODC) approach has two main steps: (1) fault classification and (2) fault analysis.

orthogonal defect classification (ODC)

ODC fault classification is done in two phases: when faults are detected and when they are fixed. At detection time, we record the *activity* executed when the fault is revealed, the *trigger* that exposed the fault, and the perceived or actual *impact* of the fault on the customer. A possible taxonomy for activities and triggers is illustrated in the sidebar at page 395. Notice that triggers depend on the activity. The sidebar at page 396 illustrates a possible taxonomy of customer impacts.

At fix time, we record *target*, *type*, *source*, and *age* of the software. The *target* indicates the entity that has been fixed to remove the fault, and can be *requirements*, *design*, *code*, *build/package*, or *documentation/development*. The *type* indicates the type of the fault. Taxonomies depend on the target. The sidebar at page 396 illustrates a taxonomy of types of faults removed from design or code. Fault types may be augmented with an indication of the nature of the fault, which can be: *missing*, that is, the fault is to due to an omission, as in a missing statement; *incorrect*, as in the use of a wrong parameter; or *extraneous*, that is, due to something not relevant or pertinent to the document or code, as in a section of the design document that is not pertinent to the current product and should be removed. The *source* of the fault indicates the origin of the faulty modules: *in-house*, *library*, *ported from other platforms*, or *outsourced* code.

The *age* indicates the age of the faulty element — whether the fault was found in *new*, *old (base)*, *rewritten*, or *re-fixed* code.

The detailed information on faults allows for many analyses that can provide information on the development and the quality process. As in the case of analysis of simple faultiness data, the interpretation depends on the process and the product, and should be based on past experience. The taxonomy of faults, as well as the analysis of faultiness data, should be refined while applying the method.

When we first apply the ODC method, we can perform some preliminary analysis using only part of the collected information:

Distribution of fault types versus activities: Different quality activities target different classes of faults. For example, algorithmic (that is, local) faults are targeted primarily by unit testing, and we expect a high proportion of faults detected by unit testing to be in this class. If the proportion of algorithmic faults found during unit testing is unusually small, or a larger than normal proportion of algorithmic faults are found during integration testing, then one may reasonably suspect that unit tests have not been well designed. If the mix of faults found during integration testing contains an unusually high proportion of algorithmic faults, it is also possible that integration testing has not focused strongly enough on interface faults.

Distribution of triggers over time during field test: Faults corresponding to simple usage should arise early during field test, while faults corresponding to complex usage should arise late. In both cases, the rate of disclosure of new faults should asymptotically decrease. Unexpected distributions of triggers over time may indicate poor system or acceptance test. If triggers that correspond to simple usage reveal many faults late in acceptance testing, we may have chosen a sample that is not representative of the user population. If faults continue growing during acceptance test, system testing may have failed, and we may decide to resume it before continuing with acceptance testing.

Age distribution over target code: Most faults should be located in new and rewritten code, while few faults should be found in base or re-fixed code, since base and re-fixed code has already been tested and corrected. Moreover, the proportion of faults in new and rewritten code with respect to base and re-fixed code should gradually increase. Different patterns may indicate holes in the fault tracking and removal process or may be a symptom of inadequate test and analysis that failed in revealing faults early (in previous tests of base or re-fixed code). For example, an increase of faults located in base code after porting to a new platform may indicate inadequate tests for portability.

Distribution of fault classes over time: The proportion of missing code faults should gradually decrease, while the percentage of extraneous faults may slowly increase, because missing functionality should be revealed with use and repaired, while extraneous code or documentation may be produced by updates. An increasing number of missing faults may be a symptom of instability of the product, while a sudden sharp increase in extraneous faults may indicate maintenance problems.

20.7 Improving the Process

Many classes of faults that occur frequently are rooted in process and development flaws. For example, a shallow architectural design that does not take into account resource allocation can lead to resource allocation faults. Lack of experience with the development environment, which leads to misunderstandings between analysts and programmers on rare and exceptional cases, can result in faults in exception handling. A performance assessment system that rewards faster coding without regard to quality is likely to promote low quality code.

The occurrence of many such faults can be reduced by modifying the process and environment. For example, resource allocation faults resulting from shallow architectural design can be reduced by introducing specific inspection tasks. Faults attributable to inexperience with the development environment can be reduced with focused training sessions. Persistently poor programming practices may require modification of the reward system.

Often, focused changes in the process can lead to product improvement and significant cost reduction. Unfortunately, identifying the weak aspects of a process can be extremely difficult, and often the results of process analysis surprise even expert managers. The analysis of the fault history can help software engineers build a feedback mechanism to track relevant faults to their root causes, thus providing vital information for improving the process. In some cases, information can be fed back directly into the current product development, but more often it helps software engineers improve the development of future products. For example, if analysis of faults reveals frequent occurrence of severe memory management faults in C programs, we might revise inspection checklists and introduce dynamic analysis tools, but it may be too late to change early design decisions or select a different programming language in the project underway. More fundamental changes may be made in future projects.

Δ root cause analysis

Root cause analysis (RCA) is a technique for identifying and eliminating process faults. RCA was first developed in the nuclear power industry and later extended to software analysis. It consists of four main steps to select significant classes of faults and track them back to their original causes: *What*, *When*, *Why*, and *How*.

What are the faults? The goal of this first step is to identify a class of important faults. Faults are categorized by severity and kind. The severity of faults characterizes the impact of the fault on the product. Although different methodologies use slightly different scales and terms, all of them identify a few standard levels, described in Table 20.1.

The RCA approach to categorizing faults, in contrast to ODC, does not use a predefined set of categories. The objective of RCA is not to compare different classes of faults over time, or to analyze and eliminate all possible faults, but rather to identify the few most important classes of faults and remove their causes. Successful application of RCA progressively eliminates the causes of the currently most important faults, which lose importance over time, so applying a static predefined classification would be useless. Moreover, the precision with which we identify faults depends on the specific project and process and varies over time.

ODC Classification of Triggers Listed by Activity

Design Review and Code Inspection

Design Conformance A discrepancy between the reviewed artifact and a prior-stage artifact that serves as its specification.

Logic/Flow An algorithmic or logic flaw.

Backward Compatibility A difference between the current and earlier versions of an artifact that could be perceived by the customer as a failure.

Internal Document An internal inconsistency in the artifact (e.g., inconsistency between code and comments).

Lateral Compatibility An incompatibility between the artifact and some other system or module with which it should interoperate.

Concurrency A fault in interaction of concurrent processes or threads.

Language Dependency A violation of language-specific rules, standards, or best practices.

Side Effects A potential undesired interaction between the reviewed artifact and some other part of the system.

Rare Situation An inappropriate response to a situation that is not anticipated in the artifact. (Error handling as specified in a prior artifact *design conformance*, not *rare situation*.)

Structural (White-Box) Test

Simple Path The fault is detected by a test case derived to cover a single program element.

Complex Path The fault is detected by a test case derived to cover a combination of program elements.

Functional (Black-Box) Test

Coverage The fault is detected by a test case derived for testing a single procedure (e.g., C function or Java method), without considering combination of values for possible parameters.

Variation The fault is detected by a test case derived to exercise a particular combination of parameters for a single procedure.

Sequencing The fault is detected by a test case derived for testing a sequence of procedure calls.

Interaction The fault is detected by a test case derived for testing procedure interactions.

System Test

Workload/Stress The fault is detected during workload or stress testing.

Recovery/Exception The fault is detected while testing exceptions and recovery procedures.

Startup/Restart The fault is detected while testing initialization conditions during start up or after possibly faulty shutdowns.

Hardware Configuration The fault is detected while testing specific hardware configurations.

Software Configuration The fault is detected while testing specific software configurations.

Blocked Test Failure occurred in setting up the test scenario.

ODC Classification of Customer Impact

Installability Ability of the customer to place the software into actual use. (Usability of the installed software is not included.)

Integrity/Security Protection of programs and data from either accidental or malicious destruction or alteration, and from unauthorized disclosure.

Performance The perceived and actual impact of the software on the time required for the customer and customer end users to complete their tasks.

Maintenance The ability to correct, adapt, or enhance the software system quickly and at minimal cost.

Serviceability Timely detection and diagnosis of failures, with minimal customer impact.

Migration Ease of upgrading to a new system release with minimal disruption to existing customer data and operations.

Documentation Degree to which provided documents (in all forms, including electronic) completely and correctly describe the structure and intended uses of the software.

Usability The degree to which the software and accompanying documents can be understood and effectively employed by the end user.

Standards The degree to which the software complies with applicable standards.

Reliability The ability of the software to perform its intended function without unplanned interruption or failure.

Accessibility The degree to which persons with disabilities can obtain the full benefit of the software system.

Capability The degree to which the software performs its intended functions consistently with documented system requirements.

Requirements The degree to which the system, in complying with document requirements, actually meets customer expectations

ODC Classification of Defect Types for Targets *Design* and *Code*

Assignment/Initialization A variable was not assigned the correct initial value or was not assigned any initial value.

Checking Procedure parameters or variables were not properly validated before use.

Algorithm/Method A correctness or efficiency problem that can be fixed by reimplementing a single procedure or local data structure, without a design change.

Function/Class/Object A change to the documented design is required to conform to product requirements or interface specifications.

Timing/Synchronization The implementation omits necessary synchronization of shared resources, or violates the prescribed synchronization protocol.

Interface/Object-Oriented Messages Module interfaces are incompatible; this can include syntactically compatible interfaces that differ in semantic interpretation of communicated data.

Relationship Potentially problematic interactions among procedures, possibly involving different assumptions but not involving interface incompatibility.

Level	Description	Example
Critical	The product is unusable.	The fault causes the program to crash.
Severe	Some product features cannot be used, and there is no workaround.	The fault inhibits importing files saved with a previous version of the program, and there is no way to convert files saved in the old format to the new one.
Moderate	Some product features require workarounds to use, and reduce efficiency, reliability, or convenience and usability.	The fault inhibits exporting in Postscript format. Postscript can be produced using the printing facility, but the process is not obvious or documented (loss of usability) and requires extra steps (loss of efficiency).
Cosmetic	Minor inconvenience.	The fault limits the choice of colors for customizing the graphical interface, violating the specification but causing only minor inconvenience.

Table 20.1: Standard severity levels for root cause analysis (RCA).

A good RCA classification should follow the uneven distribution of faults across categories. If, for example, the current process and the programming style and environment result in many interface faults, we may adopt a finer classification for interface faults and a coarse-grain classification of other kinds of faults. We may alter the classification scheme in future projects as a result of having identified and removed the causes of many interface faults.

Classification of faults should be sufficiently precise to allow identifying one or two most significant classes of faults considering severity, frequency, and cost of repair. It is important to keep in mind that severity and repair cost are not directly related. We may have cosmetic faults that are very expensive to repair, and critical faults that can be easily repaired. When selecting the target class of faults, we need to consider all the factors. We might, for example, decide to focus on a class of moderately severe faults that occur very frequently and are very expensive to remove, investing fewer resources in preventing a more severe class of faults that occur rarely and are easily repaired.

When did faults occur, and when were they found? It is typical of mature software processes to collect fault data sufficient to determine when each fault was detected (e.g., in integration test or in a design inspection). In addition, for the class of faults identified in the first step, we attempt to determine when those faults were introduced (e.g., was a particular fault introduced in coding, or did it result from an error in architectural design?).

Why did faults occur? In this core RCA step, we attempt to trace representative faults back to causes, with the objective of identifying a "root" cause associated with many faults in the class. Analysis proceeds iteratively by attempting to explain the

The *80/20* or *Pareto* Rule

Fault classification in root cause analysis is justified by the so-called *80/20* or *Pareto* rule. The Pareto rule is named for the Italian economist Vilfredo Pareto, who in the early nineteenth century proposed a mathematical power law formula to describe the unequal distribution of wealth in his country, observing that 20% of the people owned 80% of the wealth.

Pareto observed that in many populations, a few (20%) are vital and many (80%) are trivial. In fault analysis, the Pareto rule postulates that 20% of the code is responsible for 80% of the faults. Although proportions may vary, the rule captures two important facts:

1. Faults tend to accumulate in a few modules, so identifying potentially faulty modules can improve the cost effectiveness of fault detection.

2. Some classes of faults predominate, so removing the causes of a predominant class of faults can have a major impact on the quality of the process and of the resulting product.

The predominance of a few classes of faults justifies focusing on one class at a time.

error that led to the fault, then the cause of that error, the cause of that cause, and so on. The rule of thumb "ask why six times" does not provide a precise stopping rule for the analysis, but suggests that several steps may be needed to find a cause in common among a large fraction of the fault class under consideration.

Tracing the causes of faults requires experience, judgment, and knowledge of the development process. We illustrate with a simple example. Imagine that the first RCA step identified *memory leaks* as the most significant class of faults, combining a moderate frequency of occurrence with severe impact and high cost to diagnose and repair. The group carrying out RCA will try to identify the cause of memory leaks and may conclude that many of them result from *forgetting to release memory in exception handlers*. The RCA group may trace this problem in exception handling to lack of information: *Programmers can't easily determine what needs to be cleaned up in exception handlers*. The RCA group will ask *why* once more and may go back to a design error: *The resource management scheme assumes normal flow of control* and thus does not provide enough information to guide implementation of exception handlers. Finally, the RCA group may identify the root problem in an early design problem: *Exceptional conditions were an afterthought dealt with late in design.*

Each step requires information about the class of faults and about the development process that can be acquired through inspection of the documentation and interviews with developers and testers, but the key to success is curious probing through several levels of cause and effect.

How could faults be prevented? The final step of RCA is improving the process by removing root causes or making early detection likely. The measures taken may have a minor impact on the development process (e.g., adding consideration of exceptional conditions to a design inspection checklist), or may involve a substantial modification of the process (e.g., making explicit consideration of exceptional conditions a part of all requirements analysis and design steps). As in tracing causes, prescribing preventative or detection measures requires judgment, keeping in mind that the goal is not perfection but cost-effective improvement.

ODC and RCA are two examples of feedback and improvement, which are an important dimension of most good software processes. Explicit process improvement steps are, for example, featured in both SRET (sidebar on page 380) and Cleanroom (sidebar on page 378).

20.8 The Quality Team

The quality plan must assign roles and responsibilities to people. As with other aspects of planning, assignment of responsibility occurs at a strategic level and a tactical level. The tactical level, represented directly in the project plan, assigns responsibility to individuals in accordance with the general strategy. It involves balancing level of effort across time and carefully managing personal interactions. The strategic level of organization is represented not only in the quality strategy document, but in the structure of the organization itself.

The strategy for assigning responsibility may be partly driven by external requirements. For example, independent quality teams may be required by certification agencies or by a client organization. Additional objectives include ensuring sufficient accountability that quality tasks are not easily overlooked; encouraging objective judgment of quality and preventing it from being subverted by schedule pressure; fostering shared commitment to quality among all team members; and developing and communicating shared knowledge and values regarding quality.

Measures taken to attain some objectives (e.g., autonomy to ensure objective assessment) are in tension with others (e.g., cooperation to meet overall project objectives). It is therefore not surprising to find that different organizations structure roles and responsibilities in a wide variety of different ways. The same individuals can play the roles of developer and tester, or most testing responsibility can be assigned to members of a distinct group, and some may even be assigned to a distinct organization on a contractual basis. Oversight and accountability for approving the work product of a task are sometimes distinguished from responsibility for actually performing a task, so the team organization is somewhat intertwined with the task breakdown.

Each of the possible organizations of quality roles makes some objectives easier to achieve and some more challenging. Conflict of one kind or another is inevitable, and therefore in organizing the team it is important to recognize the conflicts and take measures to control adverse consequences. If an individual plays two roles in potential conflict (e.g., a developer responsible for delivering a unit on schedule is also responsible for integration testing that could reveal faults that delay delivery), there must be countermeasures to control the risks inherent in that conflict. If roles are assigned to different individuals, then the corresponding risk is conflict between the individuals (e.g., if a developer and a tester do not adequately share motivation to deliver a quality product on schedule).

An independent and autonomous testing team lies at one end of the spectrum of possible team organizations. One can make that team organizationally independent so that, for example, a project manager with schedule pressures can neither bypass quality activities or standards, nor reallocate people from testing to development, nor postpone quality activities until too late in the project. Separating quality roles from development roles minimizes the risk of conflict between roles played by an individual, and thus makes most sense for roles in which independence is paramount, such as final system and acceptance testing. An independent team devoted to quality activities also has an advantage in building specific expertise, such as test design. The primary risk arising from separation is in conflict between goals of the independent quality team and the developers.

When quality tasks are distributed among groups or organizations, the plan should include specific checks to ensure successful completion of quality activities. For example, when module testing is performed by developers and integration and system testing is performed by an independent quality team, the quality team should check the completeness of module tests performed by developers, for example, by requiring satisfaction of coverage criteria or inspecting module test suites. If testing is performed by an independent organization under contract, the contract should carefully describe the testing process and its results and documentation, and the client organization should verify satisfactory completion of the contracted tasks.

Existence of a testing team must not be perceived as relieving developers from responsibility for quality, nor is it healthy for the testing team to be completely oblivious to other pressures, including schedule pressure. The testing team and development team, if separate, must at least share the goal of shipping a high-quality product on schedule.

Independent quality teams require a mature development process to minimize communication and coordination overhead. Test designers must be able to work on sufficiently precise specifications and must be able to execute tests in a controllable test environment. Versions and configurations must be well defined, and failures and faults must be suitably tracked and monitored across versions.

It may be logistically impossible to maintain an independent quality group, especially in small projects and organizations, where flexibility in assignments is essential for resource management. Aside from the logistical issues, division of responsibility creates additional work in communication and coordination. Finally, quality activities often demand deep knowledge of the project, particularly at detailed levels (e.g., unit and early integration test). An outsider will have less insight into how and what to test, and may be unable to effectively carry out the crucial earlier activities, such as establishing acceptance criteria and reviewing architectural design for testability. For all these reasons, even organizations that rely on an independent verification and validation (IV&V) group for final product qualification allocate other responsibilities to developers and to quality professionals working more closely with the development team.

At the polar opposite from a completely independent quality team is full integration of quality activities with development, as in some "agile" processes including XP.

Communication and coordination overhead is minimized this way, and developers take full responsibility for the quality of their work product. Moreover, technology and application expertise for quality tasks will match the expertise available for development tasks, although the developer may have less specific expertise in skills such as test design.

The more development and quality roles are combined and intermixed, the more important it is to build into the plan checks and balances to be certain that quality activities and objective assessment are not easily tossed aside as deadlines loom. For example, XP practices like "test first" together with pair programming (sidebar on page 381) guard against some of the inherent risks of mixing roles.

Separate roles do not necessarily imply segregation of quality activities to distinct individuals. It is possible to assign both development and quality responsibility to developers, but assign two individuals distinct responsibilities for each development work product. Peer review is an example of mixing roles while maintaining independence on an item-by-item basis. It is also possible for developers and testers to participate together in some activities.

Many variations and hybrid models of organization can be designed. Some organizations have obtained a good balance of benefits by rotating responsibilities. For example, a developer may move into a role primarily responsible for quality in one project and move back into a regular development role in the next. In organizations large enough to have a distinct quality or testing group, an appropriate balance between independence and integration typically varies across levels of project organization. At some levels, an appropriate balance can be struck by giving responsibility for an activity (e.g., unit testing) to developers who know the code best, but with a separate oversight responsibility shared by members of the quality team. For example, unit tests may be designed and implemented by developers, but reviewed by a member of the quality team for effective automation (particularly, suitability for automated regression test execution as the product evolves) as well as thoroughness. The balance tips further toward independence at higher levels of granularity, such as in system and acceptance testing, where at least some tests should be designed independently by members of the quality team.

Outsourcing test and analysis activities is sometimes motivated by the perception that testing is less technically demanding than development and can be carried out by lower-paid and lower-skilled individuals. This confuses test execution, which should in fact be straightforward, with analysis and test design, which are as demanding as design and programming tasks in development. Of course, less skilled individuals *can* design and carry out tests, just as less skilled individuals *can* design and write programs, but in both cases the results are unlikely to be satisfactory.

Outsourcing can be a reasonable approach when its objectives are not merely minimizing cost, but maximizing independence. For example, an independent judgment of quality may be particularly valuable for final system and acceptance testing, and may be essential for measuring a product against an independent quality standard (e.g., qualifying a product for medical or avionic use). Just as an organization with mixed roles requires special attention to avoid the conflicts between roles played by an individual, radical separation of responsibility requires special attention to control conflicts between the quality assessment team and the development team.

The plan must clearly define milestones and delivery for outsourced activities, as well as checks on the quality of delivery in both directions: Test organizations usually perform quick checks to verify the consistency of the software to be tested with respect to some minimal "testability" requirements; clients usually check the completeness and consistency of test results. For example, test organizations may ask for the results of inspections on the delivered artifact before they start testing, and may include some quick tests to verify the installability and testability of the artifact. Clients may check that tests satisfy specified functional and structural coverage criteria, and may inspect the test documentation to check its quality. Although the contract should detail the relation between the development and the testing groups, ultimately, outsourcing relies on mutual trust between organizations.

Open Research Issues

Orthogonal defect classification (introduced in the 1990s) and root cause analysis (introduced in the 1980s) remain key techniques for deriving useful guidance from experience. Considering widespread agreement on the importance of continuous process improvement, we should expect innovation and adaptation of these key techniques for current conditions. An example is the renewed interest in fault-proneness models, exploiting the rich historical data available in version control systems and bug tracking databases.

Globally distributed software teams and teams that span multiple companies and organizations pose many interesting challenges for software development in general and test and analysis in particular. We expect that both technical and management innovations will adapt to these important trends, with increasing interplay between research in software test and analysis and research in computer-supported collaborative work (CSCW).

Further Reading

IEEE publishes a standard for software quality assurance plans [Ins02], which serves as a good starting point. The plan outline in this chapter is based loosely on the IEEE standard. Jaaksi [Jaa03] provides a useful discussion of decision making based on distribution of fault discovery and resolution over the course of a project, drawn from experience at Nokia. Chaar et al. [CHBC93] describe the orthogonal defect classification technique, and Bhandari et al. [BHC$^+$94] provide practical details useful in implementing it. Leszak et al. [LPS02] describe a retrospective process with root cause analysis, process compliance analysis, and software complexity analysis. Denaro and Pezzè [DP02] describe fault-proneness models for allocating effort in a test plan. DeMarco and Lister [DL99] is a popular guide to the human dimensions of managing software teams.

Exercises

20.1. Testing compatibility with a variety of device drivers is a significant cost and schedule factor in some projects. For example, a well-known developer of desktop publishing software maintains a test laboratory containing dozens of current and outdated models of Macintosh computer, running several operating system versions.

Put yourself in the place of the quality manager for a new version of this desktop publishing software, and consider in particular the printing subsystem of the software package. Your goal is to minimize the schedule impact of testing the software against a large number of printers, and in particular to reduce the risk that serious problems in the printing subsystem surface late in the project, or that testing on the actual hardware delays product release.

How can the software architectural design be organized to serve your goals of reducing cost and risk? Do you expect your needs in this regard will be aligned with those of the development manager, or in conflict? What other measures might you take in project planning, and in particular in the project schedule, to minimize risks of problems arising when the software is tested in an operational environment? Be as specific as possible, and avoid simply restating the general strategies presented in this chapter.

20.2. Chipmunk Computers has signed an agreement with a software house for software development under contract. Project leaders are encouraged to take advantage of this agreement to outsource development of some modules and thereby reduce project cost. Your project manager asks you to analyze the risks that may result from this choice and propose approaches to reduce the impact of the identified risks. What would you suggest?

20.3. Suppose a project applied orthogonal defect classification and analyzed correlation between fault types and fault triggers, as well as between fault types and impact. What useful information could be derived from cross-correlating those classifications, beyond the information available from each classification alone?

20.4. ODC attributes have been adapted and extended in several ways, one of which is including *fault qualifier*, which distinguishes whether the fault is due to missing, incorrect, or extraneous code. What attributes might *fault qualifier* be correlated with, and what useful information might thereby be obtained?

Exercises

20.1 Testing compatibility with a variety of device drivers is a significant cost and schedule factor in some projects. For example, a well-known developer of desktop publishing software maintains a test laboratory containing dozens of current and outdated models of Macintosh computer, running several operating system versions.

Put yourself in the place of the quality manager for a new version of this desktop publishing software, and consider in particular the printing subsystem of the software package. Your goal is to minimize the schedule impact of testing the software against a large number of printers, and in particular to reduce the risk that serious problems in the printing subsystem surface late in the project, or that testing on the actual hardware delays product release.

How can the software architectural design be organized to serve your goals of reducing cost and risk? Do you expect your needs in this regard will be aligned with those of the development manager, or in conflict? What other measures might you take in project planning, and in particular in the project schedule, to minimize risks of problems arising when the software is tested in an operational environment? Be as specific as possible, and avoid simply restating the general principles presented in this chapter.

20.2 Chipmunk Computers has signed an agreement with a software house for software development under contract. Project leaders are encouraged to take advantage of this agreement to outsource development of some modules and thereby reduce project cost. Your project manager asks you to analyze the risks that may result from this choice and propose approaches to reduce the impact of the identified risks. What would you suggest?

20.3 Suppose a project applied orthogonal defect classification and analyzed correlation between fault types and fault triggers, as well as between fault types and impact. What useful information could be derived from cross-correlating those classifications, beyond the information available from each classification alone?

20.4 ODC attributes have been adapted and extended in several ways, one of which is including fault qualifier, which distinguishes whether the fault is due to missing, incorrect, or extraneous code. What attributes might fault qualifier be correlated with, and what useful information might thereby be obtained?

Chapter 21

Integration and Component-based Software Testing

Problems arise in integration even of well-designed modules and components. Integration testing aims to uncover interaction and compatibility problems as early as possible. This chapter presents integration testing strategies, including the increasingly important problem of testing integration with commercial off-the-shelf (COTS) components, libraries, and frameworks.

Required Background

- Chapter 4
  Basic concepts of quality process, goals, and activities are important for understanding this chapter.
- Chapter 17
  Scaffolding is a key cost element of integration testing. Some knowledge about scaffolding design and implementation is important to fully understand an essential dimension of integration testing.

21.1 Overview

The traditional *V* model introduced in Chapter 2 divides testing into four main levels of granularity: module, integration, system, and acceptance test. Module or unit test checks module behavior against specifications or expectations; integration test checks module compatibility; system and acceptance tests check behavior of the whole system with respect to specifications and user needs, respectively.

An effective integration test is built on a foundation of thorough module testing and inspection. Module test maximizes controllability and observability of an individual unit, and is more effective in exercising the full range of module behaviors, rather than just those that are easy to trigger and observe in a particular context of other modules. While integration testing may to some extent act as a process check on module testing (i.e., faults revealed during integration test can be taken as a signal of unsatisfactory unit testing), thorough integration testing cannot fully compensate for sloppiness at the module level. In fact, the quality of a system is limited by the quality of the modules and components from which it is built, and even apparently noncritical modules can have widespread effects. For example, in 2004 a buffer overflow vulnerability in a single, widely used library for reading Portable Network Graphics (PNG) files caused security vulnerabilities in Windows, Linux, and Mac OS X Web browsers and email clients.

On the other hand, some unintended side-effects of module faults may become apparent only in integration test (see sidebar on page 409), and even a module that satisfies its interface specification may be incompatible because of errors introduced in design decomposition. Integration tests therefore focus on checking compatibility between module interfaces.

Integration faults are ultimately caused by incomplete specifications or faulty implementations of interfaces, resource usage, or required properties. Unfortunately, it may be difficult or not cost-effective to anticipate and completely specify all module interactions. For example, it may be very difficult to anticipate interactions between remote and apparently unrelated modules through sharing a temporary hidden file that just happens to be given the same name by two modules, particularly if the name clash appears rarely and only in some installation configurations. Some of the possible manifestations of incomplete specifications and faulty implementations are summarized in Table 21.1.

The official investigation of the Ariane 5 accident that led to the loss of the rocket on July 4, 1996 concluded that the accident was caused by incompatibility of a software module with the Ariane 5 requirements. The software module was in charge of computing the horizontal bias, a value related to the horizontal velocity sensed by the platform that is calculated as an indicator of alignment precision. The module had functioned correctly for Ariane 4 rockets, which were smaller than the Ariane 5, and thus had a substantially lower horizontal velocity. It produced an overflow when integrated into the Ariane 5 software. The overflow started a series of events that terminated with self-destruction of the launcher. The problem was not revealed during testing because of incomplete specifications:

> The specification of the inertial reference system and the tests performed at equipment level did not specifically include the Ariane 5 trajectory data. Consequently the realignment function was not tested under simulated Ariane 5 flight conditions, and the design error was not discovered. [From the official investigation report]

As with most software problems, integration problems may be attacked at many levels. Good design and programming practice and suitable choice of design and programming environment can reduce or even eliminate some classes of integration problems. For example, in applications demanding management of complex, shared

Integration fault	Example
Inconsistent interpretation of parameters or values Each module's interpretation may be reasonable, but they are incompatible.	Unit mismatch: A mix of metric and British measures (meters and yards) is believed to have led to loss of the Mars Climate Orbiter in September 1999.
Violations of value domains or of capacity or size limits Implicit assumptions on ranges of values or sizes.	Buffer overflow, in which an implicit (unchecked) capacity bound imposed by one module is violated by another, has become notorious as a security vulnerability. For example, some versions of the Apache 2 Web server between 2.0.35 and 2.0.50 could overflow a buffer while expanding environment variables during configuration file parsing.
Side-effects on parameters or resources	A module often uses resources that are not explicitly mentioned in its interface. Integration problems arise when these implicit effects of one module interfere with those of another. For example, using a temporary file "tmp" may be invisible until integration with another module that also attempts to use a temporary file "tmp" in the same directory of scratch files.
Missing or misunderstood functionality Underspecification of functionality may lead to incorrect assumptions about expected results.	Counting hits on Web sites may be done in many different ways: per unique IP address, per hit, including or excluding spiders, and so on. Problems arise if the interpretation assumed in the counting module differs from that of its clients.
Nonfunctional problems	Nonfunctional properties like performance are typically specified explicitly only when they are expected to be an issue. Even when performance is not explicitly specified, we expect that software provides results in a reasonable time. Interference between modules may reduce performance below an acceptable threshold.
Dynamic mismatches Many languages and frameworks allow for dynamic binding. Problems may be caused by failures in matchings when modules are integrated.	Polymorphic calls may be dynamically bound to incompatible methods, as discussed in Chapter 15.

This core taxonomy can be extended to effectively classify important or frequently occurring integration faults in particular domains.

Table 21.1: Integration faults.

structures, choosing a language with automatic storage management and garbage collection greatly reduces memory disposal errors such as dangling pointers and redundant deallocations ("double frees").

Even if the programming language choice is determined by other factors, many errors can be avoided by choosing patterns and enforcing coding standards across the entire code base; the standards can be designed in such a way that violations are easy to detect manually or with tools. For example, many projects using C or C++ require use of "safe" alternatives to unchecked procedures, such as requiring strncpy or strlcpy (string copy procedures less vulnerable to buffer overflow) in place of strcpy. Checking for the mere presence of strcpy is much easier (and more easily automated) than checking for its safe use. These measures do not eliminate the possibility of error, but integration testing is more effective when focused on finding faults that slip through these design measures.

21.2 Integration Testing Strategies

Integration testing proceeds incrementally with assembly of modules into successively larger subsystems. Incremental testing is preferred, first, to provide the earliest possible feedback on integration problems. In addition, controlling and observing the behavior of an integrated collection of modules grows in complexity with the number of modules and the complexity of their interactions. Complex interactions may hide faults, and failures that are manifested may propagate across many modules, making fault localization difficult. Therefore it is worthwhile to thoroughly test a small collection of modules before adding more.

A strategy for integration testing of successive partial subsystems is driven by the order in which modules are constructed (the build plan), which is an aspect of the system architecture. The build plan, in turn, is driven partly by the needs of test. Design and integration testing are so tightly coupled that in many companies the integration and the testing groups are merged in a single group in charge of both design and test integration.

Since incremental assemblies of modules are incomplete, one must often construct scaffolding — drivers, stubs, and various kinds of instrumentation — to effectively test them. This can be a major cost of integration testing, and it depends to a large extent on the order in which modules are assembled and tested.

One extreme approach is to avoid the cost of scaffolding by waiting until all modules are integrated, and testing them together — essentially merging integration testing into system testing. In this *big bang* approach, neither stubs nor drivers need be constructed, nor must the development be carefully planned to expose well-specified interfaces to each subsystem. These savings are more than offset by losses in observability, diagnosability, and feedback. Delaying integration testing hides faults whose effects do not always propagate outward to visible failures (violating the principle that failing always is better than failing sometimes) and impedes fault localization and diagnosis because the failures that are visible may be far removed from their causes. Requiring the whole system to be available before integration does not allow early test and feedback, and so faults that are detected are much more costly to repair. Big bang

big bang testing

Memory Leaks

Memory leaks are typical of program faults that often escape module testing. They may be detected in integration testing, but often escape further and are discovered only in actual system operation.

The Apache Web server, version 2.0.48, contained the following code for reacting to normal Web page requests that arrived on the secure (https) server port:

```
static void ssl_io_filter_disable(ap_filter_t *f)
{
    bio_filter_in_ctx_t *inctx = f->ctx;
    inctx->ssl = NULL;
    inctx->filter_ctx->pssl = NULL;
}
```

This code fails to reclaim some dynamically allocated memory, causing the Web server to "leak" memory at run-time. Over a long period of use, or over a shorter period if the fault is exploited in a denial-of-service attack, this version of the Apache Web server will allòcate and fail to reclaim more and more memory, eventually slowing to the point of unusability or simply crashing.

The fault is nearly impossible to see in this code. The memory that should be deallocated here is part of a structure defined and created elsewhere, in the SSL (secure sockets layer) subsystem, written and maintained by a different set of developers. Even reading the definition of the ap_filter_t structure, which occurs in a different part of the Apache Web server source code, doesn't help, since the ctx field is an opaque pointer (type void * in C) . The repair, applied in version 2.0.49 of the server, is:

```
static void ssl_io_filter_disable(SSLConnRec *sslconn, ap_filter_t *f)
{
    bio_filter_in_ctx_t *inctx = f->ctx;
    SSL_free(inctx->ssl);
    sslconn->ssl = NULL;
    inctx->ssl = NULL;
    inctx->filter_ctx->pssl = NULL;
}
```

This memory leak illustrates several properties typical of integration faults. In principle, it stems from incomplete knowledge of the protocol required to interact with some other portion of the code, either because the specification is (inevitably) incomplete or because it is not humanly possible to remember everything. The problem is due at least in part to a weakness of the programming language — it would not have occurred in a language with automatic garbage collection, such as Java. Finally, although the fault would be very difficult to detect with conventional unit testing techniques, there do exist both static and dynamic analysis techniques that could have made early detection much more likely, as discussed in Chapter 18.

integration testing is less a rational strategy than an attempt to recover from a lack of planning; it is therefore also known as the *desperate tester* strategy.

structural integration test strategy

Among strategies for incrementally testing partially assembled systems, we can distinguish two main classes: *structural* and *feature oriented*. In a structural approach, modules are constructed, assembled, and tested together in an order based on hierarchical structure in the design. Structural approaches include bottom-up, top-down, and a combination sometimes referred to as sandwich or backbone strategy. Feature-oriented strategies derive the order of integration from characteristics of the application, and include threads and critical modules strategies.

top-down and bottom-up testing

Top-down and *bottom-up* strategies are classic alternatives in system construction and incremental integration testing as modules accumulate. They consist in sorting modules according to the use/include relation (see Chapter 15, page 286), and in starting testing from the top or from the bottom of the hierarchy, respectively.

A top-down integration strategy begins at the top of the uses hierarchy, including the interfaces exposed through a user interface or top-level application program interface (API). The need for drivers is reduced or eliminated while descending the hierarchy, since at each stage the already tested modules can be used as drivers while testing the next layer. For example, referring to the excerpt of the Chipmunk Web presence shown in Figure 21.1, we can start by integrating *CustomerCare* with *Customer*, while stubbing *Account* and *Order*. We could then add either *Account* or *Order* and *Package*, stubbing *Model* and *Component* in the last case. We would finally add *Model*, *Slot*, and *Component* in this order, without needing any driver.

Bottom-up integration similarly reduces the need to develop stubs, except for breaking circular relations. Referring again to the example in Figure 21.1, we can start bottom-up by integrating *Slot* with *Component*, using drivers for *Model* and *Order*. We can then incrementally add *Model* and *Order*. We can finally add either *Package* or *Account* and *Customer*, before integrating *CustomerCare*, without constructing stubs.

Top-down and bottom-up approaches to integration testing can be applied early in the development if paired with similar design strategies: If modules are delivered following the hierarchy, either top-down or bottom-up, they can be integrated and tested as soon as they are delivered, thus providing early feedback to the developers. Both approaches increase controllability and diagnosability, since failures are likely caused by interactions with the newly integrated modules.

sandwich or backbone

In practice, software systems are rarely developed strictly top-down or bottom-up. Design and integration strategies are driven by other factors, like reuse of existing modules or commercial off-the-shelf (COTS) components, or the need to develop early prototypes for user feedback. Integration may combine elements of the two approaches, starting from both ends of the hierarchy and proceeding toward the middle. An early top-down approach may result from developing prototypes for early user feedback, while existing modules may be integrated bottom-up. This is known as the *sandwich* or *backbone* strategy. For example, referring once more to the small system of Figure 21.1, let us imagine reusing existing modules for *Model*, *Slot*, and *Component*, and developing *CustomerCare* and *Customer* as part of an early prototype. We can start integrating *CustomerCare* and *Customer* top down, while stubbing *Account* and *Order*. Meanwhile, we can integrate bottom-up *Model*, *Slot*, and *Component* with *Order*, using drivers for *Customer* and *Package*. We can then integrate *Account* with *Customer*,

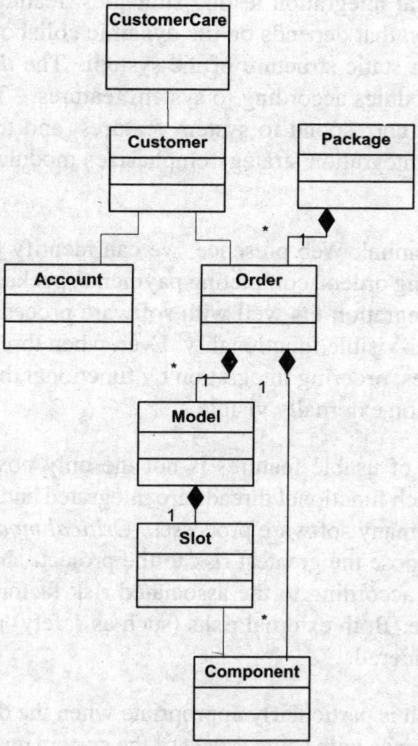

Figure 21.1: An excerpt of the class diagram of the Chipmunk Web presence. Modules are sorted from the top to the bottom according to the use/include relation. The topmost modules are not used or included in any other module, while the bottom-most modules do not include or use other modules.

and *Package* with *Order*, before finally integrating the whole prototype system.

The price of flexibility and adaptability in the sandwich strategy is complex planning and monitoring. While top-down and bottom-up are straightforward to plan and monitor, a sandwich approach requires extra coordination between development and test.

thread testing

In contrast to structural integration testing strategies, feature-driven strategies select an order of integration that depends on the dynamic collaboration patterns among modules regardless of the static structure of the system. The *thread* integration testing strategy integrates modules according to system features. Test designers identify threads of execution that correspond to system features, and they incrementally test each thread. The thread integration strategy emphasizes module interplay for specific functionality.

Referring to the Chipmunk Web presence, we can identify feature threads for assembling models, finalizing orders, completing payments, packaging and shipping, and so on. Feature thread integration fits well with software processes that emphasize incremental delivery of user-visible functionality. Even when threads do not correspond to usable end-user features, ordering integration by functional threads is a useful tactic to make flaws in integration externally visible.

critical module

Incremental delivery of usable features is not the only possible consideration in choosing the order in which functional threads are integrated and tested. Risk reduction is also a driving force in many software processes. *Critical module* integration testing focuses on modules that pose the greatest risk to the project. Modules are sorted and incrementally integrated according to the associated risk factor that characterizes the criticality of each module. Both external risks (such as safety) and project risks (such as schedule) can be considered.

A risk-based approach is particularly appropriate when the development team does not have extensive experience with some aspect of the system under development. Consider once more the Chipmunk Web presence. If Chipmunk has not previously constructed software that interacts directly with shipping services, those interface modules will be critical because of the inherent risks of interacting with externally provided subsystems, which may be inadequately documented or misunderstood and which may also change.

Feature-driven test strategies usually require more complex planning and management than structural strategies. Thus, we adopt them only when their advantages exceed the extra management costs. For small systems a structural strategy is usually sufficient, but for large systems feature-driven strategies are usually preferred. Often large projects require combinations of development strategies that do not fit any single test integration strategies. In these cases, quality managers would combine different strategies: top-down, bottom-up, and sandwich strategies for small subsystems, and a blend of threads and critical module strategies at a higher level.

21.3 Testing Components and Assemblies

Many software products are constructed, partly or wholly, from assemblies of prebuilt software components.[1] A key characteristic of software components is that the organization that develops a component is distinct from the (several) groups of developers who use it to construct systems. The component developers cannot completely anticipate the uses to which a component will be put, and the system developers have limited knowledge of the component. Testing components (by the component developers) and assemblies (by system developers) therefore brings some challenges and constraints that differ from testing other kinds of module.

Reusable components are often more dependable than software developed for a single application. More effort can be invested in improving the quality of a component when the cost is amortized across many applications. Moreover, when reusing a component that has been in use in other applications for some time, one obtains the benefit not only of test and analysis by component developers, but also of actual operational use.

The advantages of component reuse for quality are not automatic. They do not apply to code that was developed for a single application and then scavenged for use in another. The benefit of operational experience as a kind of *in vivo* testing, moreover, is obtained only to the extent that previous uses of the component are quite similar to the new use. These advantages are balanced against two considerable disadvantages. First, a component designed for wide reuse will usually be much more complex than a module designed for a single use; a rule of thumb is that the development effort (including analysis and test) for a widely usable component is at least twice that for a module that provides equivalent functionality for a single application. In addition, a reusable component is by definition developed without full knowledge of the environment in which it will be used, and it is exceptionally difficult to fully and clearly describe all the assumptions, dependencies, and limitations that might impinge upon its use in a particular application.

In general, a software component is characterized by a *contract* or *application program interface* (API) distinct from its implementation. Where a mature market has developed for components addressing a particular need, a single interface specification (e.g., SQL for database access or document object model (DOM) for access and traversal of XML data) can have several distinct implementations. The contract describes the component by specifying access points of the component, such as procedures (methods) and their parameters, possible exceptions, global variables, and input and output network connections. Even when the interface specification is bound to a single implementation, the logical distinction between interface and implementation is crucial to effective use and testing.

The interface specification of a component should provide all the information required for reusing the component, including so-called nonfunctional properties such as performance or capacity limits, in addition to functional behavior. All dependence of the component on the environment in which it executes should also be specified. In

[1] The term component is used loosely and often inconsistently in different contexts. Our working definition and related terms are explained in the sidebar on page 414.

Terminology for Components and Frameworks

Component A software component is a reusable unit of deployment and composition that is deployed and integrated multiple times and usually by different teams. Components are characterized by a *contract* or *interface* and may or may not have state.

Components are often confused with objects, and a component can be encapsulated by an object or a set of objects, but they typically differ in many respects:

- Components typically use persistent storage, while objects usually have only local state.
- Components may be accessed by an extensive set of communication mechanisms, while objects are activated through method calls.
- Components are usually larger grain subsystems than objects.

Component contract or interface The component contract describes the access points and parameters of the component, and specifies functional and nonfunctional behavior and any conditions required for using the component.

Framework A framework is a micro-architecture or a skeleton of an application, with hooks for attaching application-specific functionality or configuration-specific components. A framework can be seen as a circuit board with empty slots for components.

Frameworks and design patterns Patterns are logical design fragments, while frameworks are concrete elements of the application. Frameworks often implement patterns.

Component-based system A component-based system is a system built primarily by assembling software components (and perhaps a small amount of application-specific code) connected through a framework or ad hoc "glue code."

COTS The term commercial off-the-shelf, or COTS, indicates components developed for the sale to other organizations.

practice, few component specifications are complete in every detail, and even details that are specified precisely can easily be overlooked or misunderstood when embedded in a complex specification document.

The main problem facing test designers in the organization that produces a component is lack of information about the ways in which the component will be used. A component may be reused in many different contexts, including applications for which its functionality is an imperfect fit. A general component will typically provide many more features and options than are used by any particular application.

A good deal of functional and structural testing of a component, focused on finding and removing as many program faults as possible, can be oblivious to the context of actual use. As with system and acceptance testing of complete applications, it is then necessary to move to test suites that are more reflective of actual use. Testing with usage scenarios places a higher priority on finding faults most likely to be encountered in use and is needed to gain confidence that the component will be perceived by its users (that is, by developers who employ it as part of larger systems) as sufficiently dependable.

Test designers cannot anticipate all possible uses of a component under test, but they can design test suites for classes of use in the form of scenarios. Test scenarios are closely related to scenarios or use cases in requirements analysis and design.

Sometimes different classes of use are clearly evident in the component specification. For example, the W3 Document Object Model (DOM) specification has parts that deal exclusively with HTML markup and parts that deal with XML; these correspond to different uses to which a component implementing the DOM may be put. The DOM specification further provides two "views" of the component interface. In the flat view, all traversal and inspection operations are provided on node objects, without regard to subclass. In the structured view, each subclass of node offers traversal and inspection operations specific to that variety of node. For example, an Element node has methods to get and set attributes, but a Text node (which represents simple textual data within XML or HTML) does not.

Open Research Issues

Ensuring quality of components and of component-based systems remains a challenging problem and a topic of current research. One research thread considers how dynamic analysis of components and component-based systems in one environment can produce useful information for assessing likely suitability for using some of the same components in another environment (by characterizing the contexts in which a component has been used successfully). A related approach of characterizing a set of behaviors and recognizing changes or differences (whether or not those differences are failures) may be applicable in the increasingly important context of dynamically configurable and field-upgradable systems, which pose all the problems of component-based systems with the additional complication of performing integration in deployed systems rather than in the development environment. For these and other systems, self-monitoring and postdeployment testing in the field are likely to play an increasingly important role in the future.

Software design for testability is an important factor in the cost and effectiveness of test and analysis, particularly for module and component integration. To some extent model-based testing (Chapter 14) is progress toward producing modules and components with well-specified and testable interfaces, but much remains to be done in characterizing and supporting testability. Design for testability should be an important factor in the evolution of architectural design approaches and notations, including architecture design languages.

Further Reading

The buffer overflow problem in libpng, which caused security vulnerabilities in major Windows, Linux, and Mac OS X Web browsers and e-mail clients, was discovered in 2004 and documented by the United States Computer Emergency Readiness Team (CERT) in Vulnerability Note VU#388984 [Uni04]. The full report on the famous Ariane 5 failure [Lio96] is available from several sources on the Web. The NASA report on loss of the Mars Climate Orbiter [Ste99] is also available on the Web. Leveson [Lev04] describes the role of software in the Ariane failure, loss of the Mars Climate Orbiter, and other spacecraft losses. Weyuker [Wey98] describes challenges of testing component-based systems.

Exercises

21.1. When developing a graphical editor, we used a COTS component for saving and reading files in XML format. During integration testing, the program failed when reading an empty file and when reading a file containing a syntax error.

Try to classify the corresponding faults according to the taxonomy described in Table 21.1.

21.2. The Chipmunk quality team decided to use both thread and critical module integration testing strategies for the Chipmunk Web presence. Envisage at least one situation in which thread integration should be preferred over critical module and one in which critical module testing should be preferred over thread, and motivate the choice.

21.3. Can a backbone testing strategy yield savings in the cost of producing test scaffolding, relative to other structural integration testing strategies? If so, how and under what conditions? If not, why not?

Chapter 22

System, Acceptance, and Regression Testing

System testing can be considered a final step in integration testing, but encompassing systemwide properties against a system specification. Acceptance testing abandons specifications in favor of users, and measures how the final system meets users' expectations. Regression testing checks for faults introduced during evolution.

Required Background

- Chapter 4

  The concepts of dependability, reliability, availability and mean time to failure are important for understanding the difference between system and acceptance testing.

- Chapter 17

  Generating reusable scaffolding and test cases is a foundation for regression testing. Some knowledge about the scaffolding and test case generation problem, though not strictly required, may be useful for understanding regression testing problems.

22.1 Overview

System, acceptance, and regression testing are all concerned with the behavior of a software system as a whole, but they differ in purpose.

System testing is a check of consistency between the software system and its specification (it is a *verification* activity). Like unit and integration testing, system testing is primarily aimed at uncovering faults, but unlike testing activities at finer granularity levels, system testing focuses on system-level properties. System testing together with acceptance testing also serves an important role in assessing whether a product can be

System, Acceptance, and Regression Testing		
System test	Acceptance test	Regression test
Checks against requirements specifications	Checks suitability for user needs	Rechecks test cases passed by previous production versions
Performed by development test group	Performed by test group with user involvement	Performed by development test group
Verifies correctness and completion of the product	Validates usefulness and satisfaction with the product	Guards against unintended changes

released to customers, which is distinct from its role in exposing faults to be removed to improve the product.

Flaws in specifications and in development, as well as changes in users' expectations, may result in products that do not fully meet users' needs despite passing system tests. Acceptance testing, as its name implies, is a *validation* activity aimed primarily at the acceptability of the product, and it includes judgments of actual usefulness and usability rather than conformance to a requirements specification.

Regression testing is specialized to the problem of efficiently checking for unintended effects of software changes. New functionality and modification of existing code may introduce unexpected interactions and lead latent faults to produce failures not experienced in previous releases.

22.2 System Testing

The essential characteristics of system testing are that it is comprehensive, based on a specification of observable behavior, and independent of design and implementation decisions. System testing can be considered the culmination of integration testing, and passing all system tests is tantamount to being complete and free of known bugs. The system test suite may share some test cases with test suites used in integration and even unit testing, particularly when a thread-based or spiral model of development has been taken and subsystem correctness has been tested primarily through externally visible features and behavior. However, the essential characteristic of independence implies that test cases developed in close coordination with design and implementation may be unsuitable. The overlap, if any, should result from using system test cases early, rather than reusing unit and integration test cases in the system test suite.

Independence in system testing avoids repeating software design errors in test design. This danger exists to some extent at all stages of development, but always in trade for some advantage in designing effective test cases based on familiarity with the software design and its potential pitfalls. The balance between these considerations shifts at different levels of granularity, and it is essential that independence take priority at some level to obtain a credible assessment of quality.

In some organizations, responsibility for test design and execution shifts at a discrete point from the development team to an independent verification and validation team that is organizationally isolated from developers. More often the shift in emphasis is gradual, without a corresponding shift in responsible personnel.

Particularly when system test designers are developers or attached to the development team, the most effective way to ensure that the system test suite is not unduly influenced by design decisions is to design most system test cases as early as possible. Even in agile development processes, in which requirements engineering is tightly interwoven with development, it is considered good practice to design test cases for a new feature before implementing the feature. When the time between specifying a feature and implementing it is longer, early design of system tests facilitates risk-driven strategies that expose critical behaviors to system test cases as early as possible, avoiding unpleasant surprises as deployment nears.

For example, in the (imaginary) Chipmunk development of Web-based purchasing, some questions were raised during requirements specification regarding the point at which a price change becomes effective. For example, if an item's catalog price is raised or lowered between the time it is added to the shopping cart and the time of actual purchase, which price is the customer charged? The requirement was clarified and documented with a set of use cases in which outcomes of various interleavings of customer actions and price changes were specified, and each of these scenarios became a system test case specification. Moreover, since this was recognized as a critical property with many opportunities for failure, the system architecture and build-plan for the Chipmunk Web presence was structured with interfaces that could be artificially driven through various scenarios early in development, and with several of the system test scenarios simulated in earlier integration tests.

The appropriate notions of thoroughness in system testing are with respect to the system specification and potential usage scenarios, rather than code or design. Each feature or specified behavior of the system should be accounted for in one or several test cases. In addition to facilitating design for test, designing system test cases together with the system requirements specification document helps expose ambiguity and refine specifications.

The set of feature tests passed by the current partial implementation is often used as a gauge of progress. Interpreting a count of failing feature-based system tests is discussed in Chapter 20, Section 20.6.

Additional test cases can be devised during development to check for observable symptoms of failures that were not anticipated in the initial system specification. They may also be based on failures observed and reported by actual users, either in acceptance testing or from previous versions of a system. These are in addition to a thorough specification-based test suite, so they do not compromise independence of the quality assessment.

Some system properties, including performance properties like latency between an event and system response and reliability properties like mean time between failures, are inherently global. While one certainly should aim to provide estimates of these properties as early as practical, they are vulnerable to unplanned interactions among parts of a complex system and its environment. The importance of such global properties is therefore magnified in system testing.

Global properties like performance, security, and safety are difficult to specify precisely and operationally, and they depend not only on many parts of the system under test, but also on its environment and use. For example, U.S. HIPAA regulations governing privacy of medical records require appropriate administrative, technical, and physical safeguards to protect the privacy of health information, further specified as follows:

> Implementation specification: safeguards. A covered entity must reasonably safeguard protected health information from any intentional or unintentional use or disclosure that is in violation of the standards, implementation specifications or other requirements of this subpart. [Uni00, sec. 164.530(c)(2)]

It is unlikely that any precise operational specification can fully capture the HIPAA requirement as it applies to an automated medical records system. One must consider the whole context of use, including, for example, which personnel have access to the system and how unauthorized personnel are prevented from gaining access.

Some global properties may be defined operationally, but parameterized by use. For example, a hard-real-time system must meet deadlines, but cannot do so in a completely arbitrary environment; its performance specification is parameterized by event frequency and minimum inter-arrival times. An e-commerce system may be expected to provide a certain level of responsiveness up to a certain number of transactions per second and to degrade gracefully up to a second rate. A key step is identifying the "operational envelope" of the system, and testing both near the edges of that envelope (to assess compliance with specified goals) and well beyond it (to ensure the system degrades or fails gracefully). Defining borderline and extreme cases is logically part of requirements engineering, but as with precise specification of features, test design often reveals gaps and ambiguities.

Not all global properties will be amenable to dynamic testing at all, at least in the conventional sense. One may specify a number of properties that a secure computer system should have, and some of these may be amenable to testing. Others can be addressed only through inspection and analysis techniques, and ultimately one does not trust the security of a system at least until an adversarial team has tried and failed to subvert it. Similarly, there is no set of test cases that can establish software safety, in part because safety is a property of a larger system and environment of which the software is only part. Rather, one must consider the safety of the overall system, and assess aspects of the software that are critical to that overall assessment. Some but not all of those claims may be amenable to testing.

Testing global system properties may require extensive simulation of the execution environment. Creating accurate models of the operational environment requires substantial human resources, and executing them can require substantial time and machine resources. Usually this implies that "stress" testing is a separate activity from frequent repetition of feature tests. For example, a large suite of system test cases might well run each night or several times a week, but a substantial stress test to measure robust performance under heavy load might take hours to set up and days or weeks to run.

A test case that can be run automatically with few human or machine resources should generally focus on one purpose: to make diagnosis of failed test executions as

Unit, Integration, and System Testing			
	Unit Test	Integration Test	System Test
Test cases derived from	module specifications	architecture and design specifications	requirements specification
Visibility required	all the details of the code	some details of the code, mainly interfaces	no details of the code
Scaffolding required	Potentially complex, to simulate the activation environment (drivers), the modules called by the module under test (stubs) and test oracles	Depends on architecture and integration order. Modules and subsystems can be incrementally integrated to reduce need for drivers and stubs.	Mostly limited to test oracles, since the whole system should not require additional drivers or stubs to be executed. Sometimes includes a simulated execution environment (e.g., for embedded systems).
Focus on	behavior of individual modules	module integration and interaction	system functionality

clear and simple as possible. Stress testing alters this: If a test case takes an hour to set up and a day to run, then one had best glean as much information as possible from its results. This includes monitoring for faults that should, in principle, have been found and eliminated in unit and integration testing, but which become easier to recognize in a stress test (and which, for the same reason, are likely to become visible to users). For example, several embedded system products ranging from laser printers to tablet computers have been shipped with slow memory leaks that became noticeable only after hours or days of continuous use. In the case of the tablet PC whose character recognition module gradually consumed all system memory, one must wonder about the extent of stress testing the software was subjected to.

22.3 Acceptance Testing

The purpose of acceptance testing is to guide a decision as to whether the product in its current state should be released. The decision can be based on measures of the product or process. Measures of the product are typically some inference of dependability based on statistical testing. Measures of the process are ultimately based on comparison to experience with previous products.

Although system and acceptance testing are closely tied in many organizations, fundamental differences exist between searching for faults and measuring quality. Even when the two activities overlap to some extent, it is essential to be clear about the distinction, in order to avoid drawing unjustified conclusions.

Quantitative goals for dependability, including reliability, availability, and mean time between failures, were introduced in Chapter 4. These are essentially statistical measures and depend on a statistically valid approach to drawing a representative sample of test executions from a population of program behaviors. Systematic testing, which includes all of the testing techniques presented heretofore in this book, does not draw statistically representative samples. Their purpose is not to fail at a "typical" rate, but to exhibit as many failures as possible. They are thus unsuitable for statistical testing.

The first requirement for valid statistical testing is a precise definition of what is being measured and for what population. If system operation involves transactions, each of which consists of several operations, a failure rate of one operation in a thousand is quite different from a failure rate of one transaction in a thousand. In addition, the failure rate may vary depending on the mix of transaction types, or the failure rate may be higher when one million transactions occur in an hour than when the same transactions are spread across a day. Statistical modeling therefore necessarily involves construction of a model of usage, and the results are relative to that model.

Suppose, for example, that a typical session using the Chipmunk Web sales facility consists of 50 interactions, the last of which is a single operation in which the credit card is charged and the order recorded. Suppose the Chipmunk software always operates flawlessly up to the point that a credit card is to be charged, but on half the attempts it charges the wrong amount. What is the reliability of the system? If we count the fraction of individual interactions that are correctly carried out, we conclude that only one operation in 100 fails, so the system is 99% reliable. If we instead count entire sessions, then it is only 50% reliable, since half the sessions result in an improper credit card charge.

operational profile

Statistical models of usage, or *operational profiles*, may be available from measurement of actual use of prior, similar systems. For example, use of a current telephone handset may be a reasonably good model of how a new handset will be used. Good models may also be obtained in embedded systems whose environment is primarily made up of predictable devices rather than unpredictable humans. In other cases one cannot justify high confidence in a model, but one can limit the uncertainty to a small number of parameters. One can perform sensitivity testing to determine which parameters are critical. Sensitivity testing consists of repeating statistical tests while systematically varying parameters to note the effect of each parameter on the output. A particular parameter may have little effect on outcomes over the entire range of plausible values, or there may be an effect that varies smoothly over the range. If the effect of a given parameter is either large or varies discontinuously (e.g., performance falls precipitously when system load crosses some threshold), then one may need to make distinct predictions for different value ranges.

sensitivity testing

A second problem faced by statistical testing, particularly for reliability, is that it may take a very great deal of testing to obtain evidence of a sufficient level of reliability. Consider that a system that executes once per second, with a failure rate of one execution in a million, or 99.9999% reliability, fails about 31 times each year; this may require a great testing effort and still not be adequate if each failure could result in death or a lawsuit. For critical systems, one may insist on software failure rates that are an insignificant fraction of total failures. For many other systems, statistical measures of reliability may simply not be worth the trouble.

A less formal, but frequently used approach to acceptance testing is testing with users. An early version of the product is delivered to a sample of users who provide feedback on failures and usability. Such tests are often called *alpha* and *beta* tests. The two terms distinguish between testing phases. Often the early or alpha phases are performed within the developing organization, while the later or beta phases are performed at users' sites.

alpha and beta test

In alpha and beta testing, the user sample determines the operational profile. A good sample of users should include representatives of each distinct category of users, grouped by operational profile and significance. Suppose, for example, Chipmunk plans to provide Web-based sales facilities to dealers, industrial customers, and individuals. A good sample should include both users from each of those three categories and a range of usage in each category. In the industrial user category, large customers who frequently issue complex orders as well as small companies who typically order a small number of units should be represented, as the difference in their usage may lead to different failure rates. We may weigh differently the frequency of failure reports from dealers and from direct customers, to reflect either the expected mix of usage in the full population or the difference in consequence of failure.

22.4 Usability

A usable product is quickly learned, allows users to work efficiently, and is pleasant to use. Usability involves objective criteria such as the time and number of operations required to perform tasks and the frequency of user error, in addition to the overall, subjective satisfaction of users.

For test and analysis, it is useful to distinguish attributes that are uniquely associated with usability from other aspects of software quality (dependability, performance, security, etc.). Other software qualities may be necessary for usability; for example, a program that often fails to satisfy its functional requirements or that presents security holes is likely to suffer poor usability as a consequence. Distinguishing primary usability properties from other software qualities allows responsibility for each class of properties to be allocated to the most appropriate personnel, at the most cost-effective points in the project schedule.

Even if usability is largely based on user perception and thus is validated based on user feedback, it can be verified early in the design and through the whole software life cycle. The process of verifying and validating usability includes the following main steps:

Inspecting specifications with usability checklists. Inspection provides early feedback on usability.

Testing early prototypes with end users to explore their mental model (*exploratory test*), evaluate alternatives (*comparison test*), and validate software usability. A prototype for early assessment of usability may not include any functioning software; a *cardboard prototype* may be as simple as a sequence of static images presented to users by the usability tester.

Testing incremental releases with both usability experts and end users to monitor progress and anticipate usability problems.

System and acceptance testing that includes expert-based inspection and testing, user-based testing, comparison testing against competitors, and analysis and checks often done automatically, such as a check of link connectivity and verification of browser compatibility.

User-based testing (i.e., testing with representatives of the actual end-user population) is particularly important for validating software usability. It can be applied at different stages, from early prototyping through incremental releases of the final system, and can be used with different goals: exploring the mental model of the user, evaluating design alternatives, and validating against established usability requirements and standards.

exploratory testing

The purpose of *exploratory testing* is to investigate the mental model of end users. It consists of asking users about their approach to interactions with the system. For example, during an exploratory test for the Chipmunk Web presence, we may provide users with a generic interface for choosing the model they would like to buy, in order to understand how users will interact with the system. A generic interface could present information about all laptop computer characteristics uniformly to see which are examined first by the sample users, and thereby to determine the set of characteristics that should belong to the summary in the menu list of laptops. Exploratory test is usually performed early in design, especially when designing a system for a new target population.

The purpose of *comparison testing* is evaluating options. It consists of observing user reactions to alternative interaction patterns. During comparison test we can, for example, provide users with different facilities to assemble the desired Chipmunk laptop configuration, and to identify patterns that facilitate users' interactions. Comparison test is usually applied when the general interaction patterns are clear and need to be refined. It can substitute for exploratory testing if initial knowledge about target users is sufficient to construct a range of alternatives, or otherwise follows exploratory testing.

The purpose of *validation testing* is assessing overall usability. It includes identifying difficulties and obstacles that users encounter while interacting with the system, as well as measuring characteristics such as error rate and time to perform a task.

A well-executed design and organization of usability testing can produce results that are objective and accurately predict usability in the target user population. The usability test design includes selecting suitable representatives of the target users and organizing sessions that guide the test toward interpretable results. A common approach is divided into preparation, execution, and analysis phases. During the preparation phase, test designers define the objectives of the session, identify the items to be tested, select a representative population of end users, and plan the required actions. During execution, users are monitored as they execute the planned actions in a controlled environment. During analysis, results are evaluated, and changes to the software interfaces or new testing sessions are planned, if required.

Each phase must be carefully executed to ensure success of the testing session. User time is a valuable and limited resource. Well-focused test objectives should not be too narrow, to avoid useless waste of resources, nor too wide, to avoid scattering resources without obtaining useful data. Focusing on specific interactions is usually more effective than attempting to assess the usability of a whole program at once. For example, the Chipmunk usability test team independently assesses interactions for catalog browsing, order definition and purchase, and repair service.

The larger the population sample, the more precise the results, but the cost of very large samples is prohibitive; selecting a small but representative sample is therefore critical. A good practice is to identify homogeneous classes of users and select a set of representatives from each class. Classes of users depend on the kind of application to be tested and may be categorized by role, social characteristics, age, and so on. A typical compromise between cost and accuracy for a well-designed test session is five users from a unique class of homogeneous users, four users from each of two classes, or three users for each of three or more classes. Questionnaires should be prepared for the selected users to verify their membership in their respective classes. Some approaches also assign a weight to each class, according to their importance to the business. For example, Chipmunk can identify three main classes of users: individual, business, and education customers. Each of the main classes is further divided. Individual customers are distinguished by education level; business customers by role; and academic customers by size of the institution. Altogether, six putatively homogeneous classes are obtained: Individual customers with and without at least a bachelor degree, managers and staff of commercial customers, and customers at small and large education institutions.

Users are asked to execute a planned set of actions that are identified as typical uses of the tested feature. For example, the Chipmunk usability assessment team may ask users to configure a product, modify the configuration to take advantage of some special offers, and place an order with overnight delivery.

Users should perform tasks independently, without help or influence from the testing staff. User actions are recorded, and comments and impressions are collected with a post-activity questionnaire. Activity monitoring can be very simple, such as recording sequences of mouse clicks to perform each action. More sophisticated monitoring can include recording mouse or eye movements. Timing should also be recorded and may sometimes be used for driving the sessions (e.g., fixing a maximum time for the session or for each set of actions).

An important aspect of usability is accessibility to all users, including those with disabilities. Accessibility testing is legally required in some application domains. For example, some governments impose specific accessibility rules for Web applications of public institutions. The set of Web Content Accessibility Guidelines (WCAG) defined by the World Wide Web Consortium are becoming an important standard reference. The WCAG guidelines are summarized in the sidebar on page 426.

Web Content Accessibility Guidelines (WCAG)[a]

1. Provide equivalent alternatives to auditory and visual content that convey essentially the same function or purpose.

2. Ensure that text and graphics are understandable when viewed without color.

3. Mark up documents with the proper structural elements, controlling presentation with style sheets rather than presentation elements and attributes.

4. Use markup that facilitates pronunciation or interpretation of abbreviated or foreign text.

5. Ensure that tables have necessary markup to be transformed by accessible browsers and other user agents.

6. Ensure that pages are accessible even when newer technologies are not supported or are turned off.

7. Ensure that moving, blinking, scrolling, or auto-updating objects or pages may be paused or stopped.

8. Ensure that the user interface, including embedded user interface elements, follows principles of accessible design: device-independent access to functionality, keyboard operability, self-voicing, and so on.

9. Use features that enable activation of page elements via a variety of input devices.

10. Use interim accessibility so that assisting technologies and older browsers will operate correctly.

11. Where technologies outside of W3C specifications is used (e.g, Flash), provide alternative versions to ensure accessibility to standard user agents and assistive technologies (e.g., screen readers).

12. Provide context and orientation information to help users understand complex pages or elements.

13. Provide clear and consistent navigation mechanisms to increase the likelihood that a person will find what they are looking for at a site.

14. Ensure that documents are clear and simple, so they may be more easily understood.

[a]Excerpted and adapted from *Web Content Accessibility Guidelines 1.0*, W3C Recommendation 5-May 1999; used by permission. The current version is distributed by W3C at `http://www.w3.org/TR/WAI-WEBCONTENT`.

22.5 Regression Testing

When building a new version of a system (e.g., by removing faults, changing or adding functionality, porting the system to a new platform, or extending interoperability), we may also change existing functionality in unintended ways. Sometimes even small changes can produce unforeseen effects that lead to new failures. For example, a guard added to an array to fix an overflow problem may cause a failure when the array is used in other contexts, or porting the software to a new platform may expose a latent fault in creating and modifying temporary files.

When a new version of software no longer correctly provides functionality that should be preserved, we say that the new version *regresses* with respect to former versions. The *nonregression* of new versions (i.e., preservation of functionality), is a basic quality requirement. Disciplined design and development techniques, including precise specification and modularity that encapsulates independent design decisions, improves the likelihood of achieving nonregression. Testing activities that focus on regression problems are called *(non) regression testing*. Usually "non" is omitted and we commonly say *regression testing*.

A simple approach to regression testing consists of reexecuting all test cases designed for previous versions. Even this simple *retest all* approach may present nontrivial problems and costs. Former test cases may not be reexecutable on the new version without modification, and rerunning all test cases may be too expensive and unnecessary. A good quality test suite must be maintained across system versions.

retest all

Changes in the new software version may impact the format of inputs and outputs, and test cases may not be executable without corresponding changes. Even simple modifications of the data structures, such as the addition of a field or small change of data types, may invalidate former test cases, or outputs comparable with the new ones. Moreover, some test cases may be *obsolete*, since they test features of the software that have been modified, substituted, or removed from the new version.

test case maintenance

Scaffolding that interprets test case specifications, rather than fully concrete test data, can reduce the impact of input and output format changes on regression testing, as discussed in Chapter 17. Test case specifications and oracles that capture essential correctness properties, abstracting from arbitrary details of behavior, likewise reduce the likelihood that a large portion of a regression test suite will be invalidated by a minor change.

High-quality test suites can be maintained across versions by identifying and removing obsolete test cases, and by revealing and suitably marking redundant test cases. Redundant cases differ from obsolete, being executable but not important with respect to the considered testing criteria. For example, test cases that cover the same path are mutually redundant with respect to structural criteria, while test cases that match the same partition are mutually redundant with respect to functional criteria. Redundant test cases may be introduced in the test suites due to concurrent work of different test designers or to changes in the code. Redundant test cases do not reduce the overall effectiveness of tests, but impact on the cost-benefits trade-off: They are unlikely to reveal faults, but they augment the costs of test execution and maintenance. Obsolete test cases are removed because they are no longer useful, while redundant test cases are kept because they may become helpful in successive versions of the software.

Good test documentation is particularly important. As we will see in Chapter 24, test specifications define the features to be tested, the corresponding test cases, the inputs and expected outputs, as well as the execution conditions for all cases, while reporting documents indicate the results of the test executions, the open faults, and their relation to the test cases. This information is essential for tracking faults and for identifying test cases to be reexecuted after fault removal.

22.6 Regression Test Selection Techniques

Even when we can identify and eliminate obsolete test cases, the number of tests to be reexecuted may be large, especially for legacy software. Executing all test cases for large software products may require many hours or days of execution and may depend on scarce resources such as an expensive hardware test harness. For example, some mass market software systems must be tested for compatibility with hundreds of different hardware configurations and thousands of drivers. Many test cases may have been designed to exercise parts of the software that cannot be affected by the changes in the version under test. Test cases designed to check the behavior of the file management system of an operating system is unlikely to provide useful information when reexecuted after changes of the window manager. The cost of reexecuting a test suite can be reduced by selecting a subset of test cases to be reexecuted, omitting irrelevant test cases or prioritizing execution of subsets of the test suite by their relation to changes.

Test case prioritization orders frequency of test case execution, executing all of them eventually but reducing the frequency of those deemed least likely to reveal faults by some criterion. Alternate execution is a variant on prioritization for environments with frequent releases and small incremental changes; it selects a subset of regression test cases for each software version. Prioritization can be based on the specification and code-based regression test selection techniques described later in this chapter. In addition, test histories and fault-proneness models can be incorporated in prioritization schemes. For example, a test case that has previously revealed a fault in a module that has recently undergone change would receive a very high priority, while a test case that has never failed (yet) would receive a lower priority, particularly if it primarily concerns a feature that was not the focus of recent changes.

Regression test selection techniques are based on either code or specifications. Code-based selection techniques select a test case for execution if it exercises a portion of the code that has been modified. Specification-based criteria select a test case for execution if it is relevant to a portion of the specification that has been changed. Code-based regression test techniques can be supported by relatively simple tools. They work even when specifications are not properly maintained. However, like code-based test techniques in general, they do not scale well from unit testing to integration and system testing. In contrast, specification-based criteria scale well and are easier to apply to changes that cut across several modules. However, they are more challenging to automate and require carefully structured and well-maintained specifications.

Among code-based test selection techniques, control-based techniques rely on a record of program elements executed by each test case, which may be gathered from an instrumented version of the program. The structure of the new and old versions of the program are compared, and test cases that exercise added, modified, or deleted elements are selected for reexecution. Different criteria are obtained depending on the program model on which the version comparison is based (e.g., control flow or data flow graph models).

Control flow graph (CFG) regression techniques are based on the differences between the CFGs of the new and old versions of the software. Let us consider, for example, the C function cgi_decode from Chapter 12. Figure 22.1 shows the original function as presented in Chapter 12, while Figure 22.2 shows a revison of the program. We refer to these two versions as 1.0 and 2.0, respectively. Version 2.0 adds code to fix a fault in interpreting hexadecimal sequences `'%xy'`. The fault was revealed by testing version 1.0 with input terminated by an erroneous subsequence `'%x'`, causing version 1.0 to read past the end of the input buffer and possibly overflow the output buffer. Version 2.0 contains a new branch to map the unterminated sequence to a question mark.

control flow graph (CFG) regression test

Let us consider all structural test cases derived for cgi_decode in Chapter 12, and assume we have recorded the paths exercised by the different test cases as shown in Figure 22.3. Recording paths executed by test cases can be done automatically with modest space and time overhead, since what must be captured is only the set of program elements exercised rather than the full history.

CFG regression testing techniques compare the annotated control flow graphs of the two program versions to identify a subset of test cases that traverse modified parts of the graphs. The graph nodes are annotated with corresponding program statements, so that comparison of the annotated CFGs detects not only new or missing nodes and arcs, but also nodes whose changed annotations correspond to small, but possibly relevant, changes in statements.

The CFG for version 2.0 of cgi_decode is given in Figure 22.4. Differences between version 2.0 and 1.0 are indicated in gray. In the example, we have new nodes, arcs and paths. In general, some nodes or arcs may be missing (e.g., when part of the program is removed in the new version), and some other nodes may differ only in the annotations (e.g., when we modify a condition in the new version).

CFG criteria select all test cases that exercise paths through changed portions of the CFG, including CFG structure changes and node annotations. In the example, we would select all test cases that pass through node D and proceed toward node G and all test cases that reach node L, that is, all test cases except $TC1$. In this example, the criterion is not very effective in reducing the size of the test suite because modified statements affect almost all paths.

If we consider only the corrective modification (nodes X and Y), the criterion is more effective. The modification affects only the paths that traverse the edge between D and G, so the CFG regression testing criterion would select only test cases traversing those nodes (i.e., $TC2$, $TC3$, $TC4$, $TC5$, $TC8$ and $TC9$). In this case the size of the test suite to be reexecuted includes two-thirds of the test cases of the original test suite.

In general, the CFG regression testing criterion is effective only when the changes affect a relatively small subset of the paths of the original program, as in the latter case. It becomes almost useless when the changes affect most paths, as in version 2.0.

Data flow (DF) regression testing techniques select test cases for new and modi-

```
#include "hex_values.h"
/** Translate a string from the CGI encoding to plain ascii text.
 *    '+' becomes space, %xx becomes byte with hex value xx,
 *    other alphanumeric characters map to themselves.
 *    Returns 0 for success, positive for erroneous input
 *        1 = bad hexadecimal digit
 */
int cgi_decode(char *encoded, char *decoded) {
    char *eptr = encoded;
    char *dptr = decoded;
    int ok=0;
    while (*eptr) {
        char c;
        c = *eptr;
        if (c == '+') {            /* Case 1: '+' maps to blank */
            *dptr = ' ';
        } else if (c == '%') { /* Case 2: '%xx' is hex for character xx */
            int  digit_high = Hex_Values[*(++eptr)]; /* note illegal => -1 */
            int  digit_low  = Hex_Values[*(++eptr)];
            if ( digit_high == -1 || digit_low == -1 ) {
                /* *dptr='?'; */
                ok=1; /* Bad return code */
            } else {
                *dptr = 16* digit_high + digit_low;
            }
        } else {  /* Case 3: Other characters map to themselves */
            *dptr = *eptr;
        }
        ++dptr;
        ++eptr;
    }
    *dptr = '\0';                              /* Null terminator for string */
    return ok;
}
```

Figure 22.1: C function cgi_decode *version 1.0. The C function* cgi_decode *translates a cgi-encoded string to a plain ASCII string, reversing the encoding applied by the common gateway interface of most Web servers. Repeated from Figure 12.1 in Chapter 12.*

```
#include "hex_values.h"
/** Translate a string from the CGI encoding to plain ascii text.
 *   '+' becomes space, %xx becomes byte with hex value xx,
 *   other alphanumeric characters map to themselves, illegal to '?'.
 *   Returns 0 for success, positive for erroneous input
 *         1 = bad hex digit, non-ascii char, or premature end.
 */
int cgi_decode(char *encoded, char *decoded) {
  char *eptr = encoded;
  char *dptr = decoded;
  int ok=0;
  while (*eptr) {
    char c;
    c = *eptr;
    if (c == '+') {          /* Case 1: '+' maps to blank */
      *dptr = ' ';
    } else if (c == '%') { /* Case 2: '%xx' is hex for character xx */
      if (! ( *(eptr + 1)   && *(eptr + 2) )) {   /* \%xx must precede EOL */
        ok = 1; return;
      }
      /* OK, we know the xx are there, now decode them */
      int   digit_high = Hex_Values[*(++eptr)]; /* note illegal => -1 */
      int   digit_low  = Hex_Values[*(++eptr)];
      if (    digit_high == -1 || digit_low == -1 ) {
        /* *dptr='?'; */
        ok=1; /* Bad return code */
      } else {
        *dptr = 16* digit_high + digit_low;
      }
    } else {  /* Case 3: Other characters map to themselves */
      *dptr = *eptr;
    }
    if (! isascii(*dptr)) { /* Produce only legal ascii */
      *dptr = '?';
      ok = 1;
    }
    ++dptr;
    ++eptr;
  }
  *dptr = '\0';         /* Null terminator for string */
  return ok;
}
```

Figure 22.2: Version 2.0 of the C function cgi_decode *adds a control on hexadecimal escape sequences to reveal incorrect escape sequences at the end of the input string and a new branch to deal with non-ASCII characters.*

Id	Test case	Path
TC1	" "	A B M
TC2	"test+case%1Dadequacy"	A B C D F L ... B M
TC3	"adequate+test%0Dexecution%7U"	A B C D F L ... B M
TC4	"%3D"	A B C D G H L B M
TC5	"%A"	A B C D G I L B M
TC6	"a+b"	A B C D F L B C E L B C D F L B M
TC7	"test"	A B C D F L B C D F L B C D F L B C D F L
TC8	"+%0D+%4J"	A B C E L B C D G I L ... B M
TC9	"first+test%9Ktest%K9"	A B C D F L ... B M

Figure 22.3: Paths covered by the structural test cases derived for version 1.0 of function cgi_decode. Paths are given referring to the nodes of the control flow graph of Figure 22.4.

data flow (DF) regression test

fied pairs of definitions with uses (DU pairs, cf. Sections 6.1, page 77 and 13.2, page 236). DF regression selection techniques reexecute test cases that, when executed on the original program, exercise DU pairs that were deleted or modified in the revised program. Test cases that executed a conditional statement whose predicate was altered are also selected, since the changed predicate could alter some old definition-use associations. Figure 22.5 shows the new definitions and uses introduced by modifications to cgi_decode.[1] These new definitions and uses introduce new DU pairs and remove others.

In contrast to code-based techniques, specification-based test selection techniques do not require recording the control flow paths executed by tests. Regression test cases can be identified from correspondence between test cases and specification items. For example, when using category partition, test cases correspond to sets of choices, while in finite state machine model-based approaches, test cases cover states and transitions. Where test case specifications and test data are generated automatically from a specification or model, generation can simply be repeated each time the specification or model changes.

Code-based regression test selection criteria can be adapted for model-based regression test selection. Consider, for example, the control flow graph derived from the *process shipping order* specification in Chapter 14. We add the following item to that specification:

Restricted countries: A set of restricted destination countries is maintained, based on current trade restrictions. If the shipping address contains a restricted destination country, only credit card payments are accepted for that order, and shipping

[1]When dealing with arrays, we follow the criteria discussed in Chapter 13: A change of an array value is a definition of the array and a use of the index. A use of an array value is a use of both the array and the index.

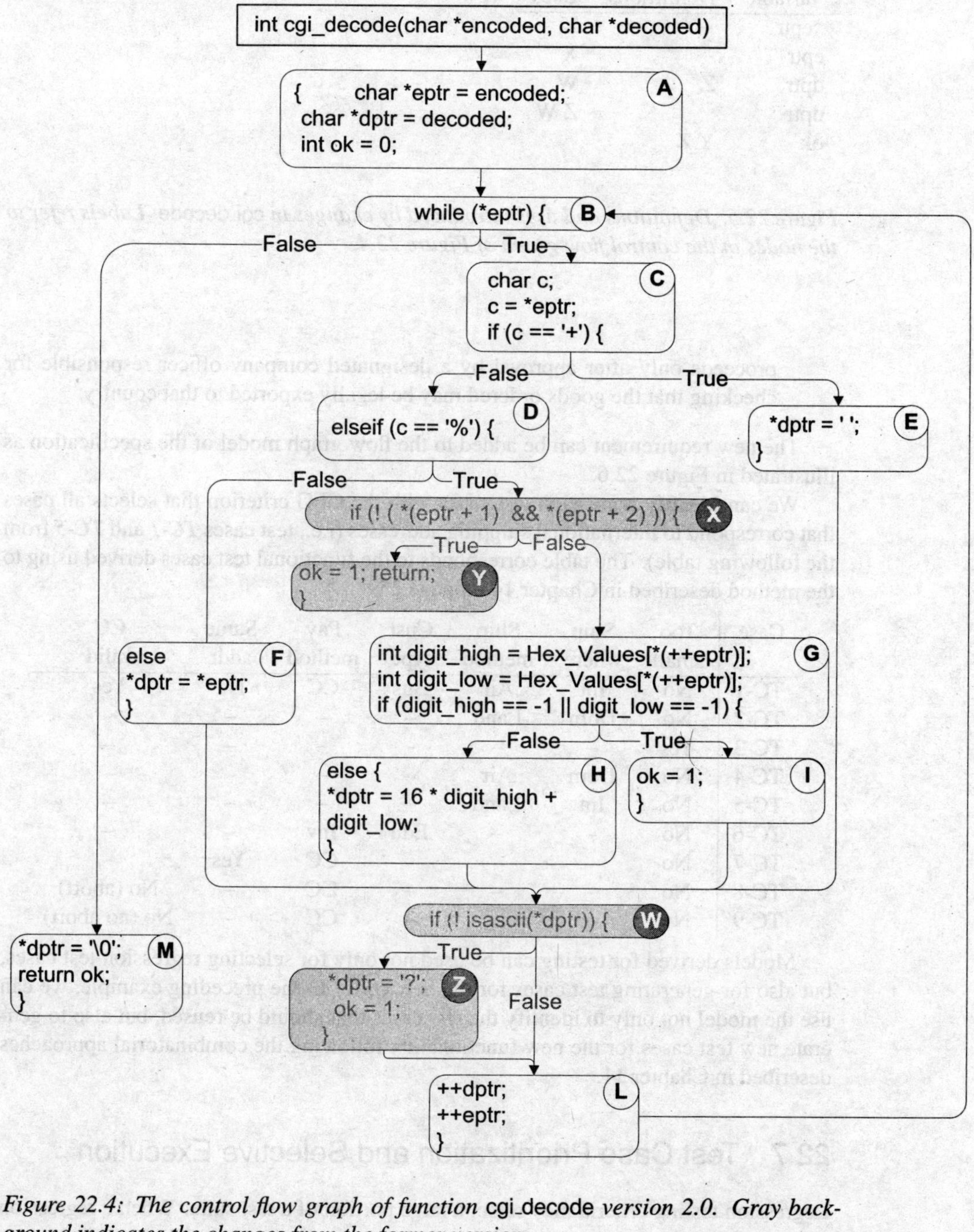

Figure 22.4: The control flow graph of function cgi_decode *version 2.0. Gray background indicates the changes from the former version.*

Variable	Definitions	Uses
*eptr		X
eptr		X
dptr	Z	W
dptr		Z W
ok	Y Z	

Figure 22.5: Definitions and uses introduced by changes in cgi_decode. *Labels refer to the nodes in the control flow graph of Figure 22.4.*

proceeds only after approval by a designated company officer responsible for checking that the goods ordered may be legally exported to that country.

The new requirement can be added to the flow graph model of the specification as illustrated in Figure 22.6.

We can identify regression test cases with the CFG criterion that selects all cases that correspond to international shipping addresses (i.e., test cases *TC-1* and *TC-5* from the following table). The table corresponds to the functional test cases derived using to the method described in Chapter 14 on page 259.

Case	Too small	Ship where	Ship method	Cust type	Pay method	Same addr	CC valid
TC-1	No	Int	Air	Bus	CC	No	Yes
TC-2	No	Dom	Land	–	–	–	–
TC-3	Yes	–	–	–	–	–	–
TC-4	No	Dom	Air	–	–	–	–
TC-5	No	Int	Land	–	–	–	–
TC-6	No	–	–	Edu	Inv	–	–
TC-7	No	–	–	–	CC	Yes	–
TC-8	No	–	–	–	CC	–	No (abort)
TC-9	No	–	–	–	CC	–	No (no abort)

Models derived for testing can be used not only for selecting regression test cases, but also for generating test cases for the new code. In the preceding example, we can use the model not only to identify the test cases that should be reused, but also to generate new test cases for the new functionality, following the combinatorial approaches described in Chapter 11.

22.7 Test Case Prioritization and Selective Execution

Regression testing criteria may select a large portion of a test suite. When a regression test suite is too large, we must further reduce the set of test cases to be executed.

Random sampling is a simple way to reduce the size of the regression test suite. Better approaches prioritize test cases to reflect their predicted usefulness. In a con-

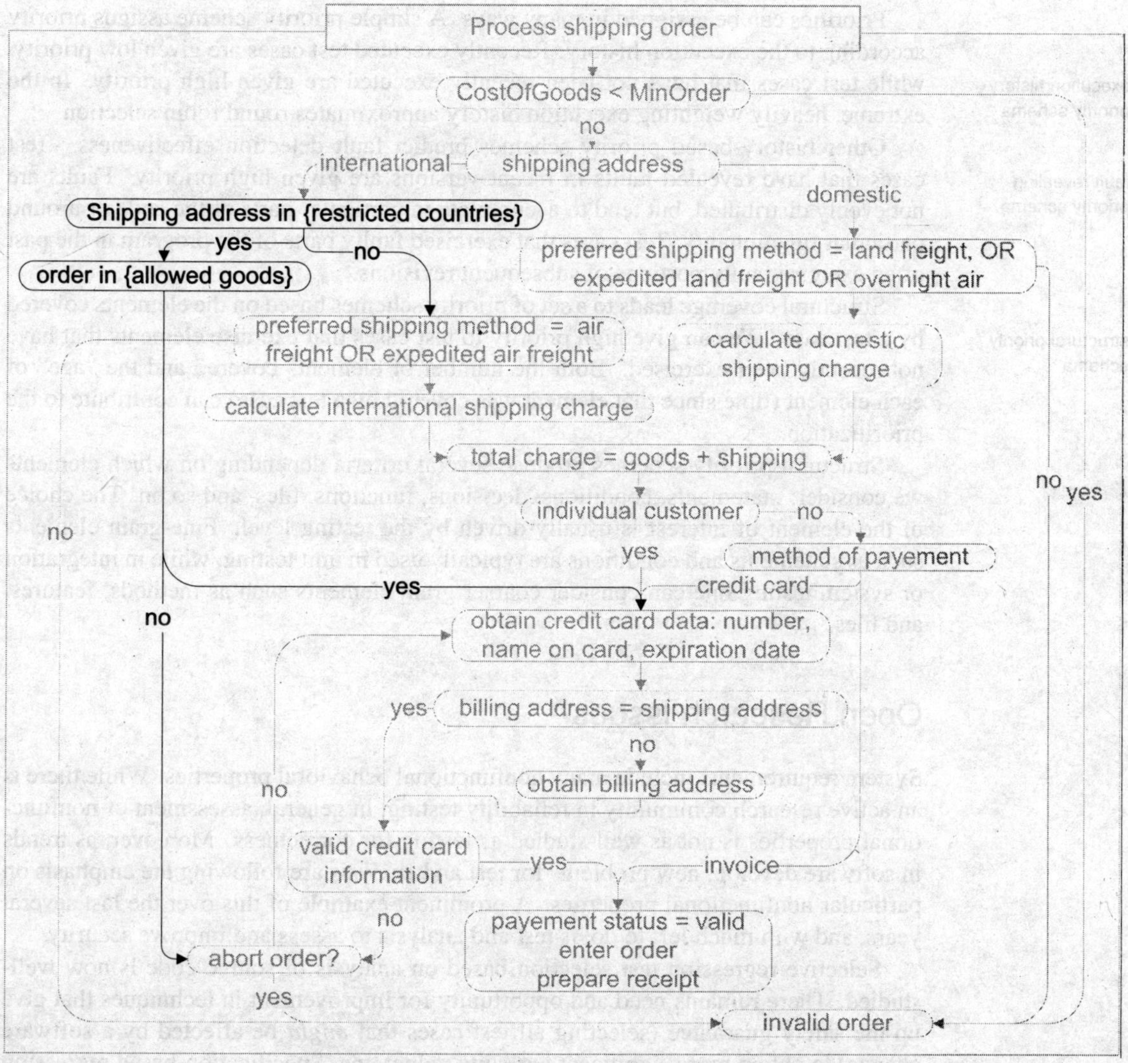

Figure 22.6: A flow graph model of the specification of the shipping order functionality presented in Chapter 14, augmented with the "restricted country" requirement. The changes in the flow graph are indicated in black.

tinuous cycle of retesting as the product evolves, high-priority test cases are selected more often than low-priority test cases. With a good selection strategy, all test cases are executed sooner or later, but the varying periods result in an efficient rotation in which the cases most likely to reveal faults are executed most frequently.

Priorities can be assigned in many ways. A simple priority scheme assigns priority according to the execution history: Recently executed test cases are given low priority, while test cases that have not been recently executed are given high priority. In the extreme, heavily weighting execution history approximates round robin selection.

execution history priority schema

Other history-based priority schemes predict fault detection effectiveness. Test cases that have revealed faults in recent versions are given high priority. Faults are not evenly distributed, but tend to accumulate in particular parts of the code or around particular functionality. Test cases that exercised faulty parts of the program in the past often exercise faulty portions of subsequent revisions.

fault revealing priority schema

Structural coverage leads to a set of priority schemes based on the elements covered by a test case. We can give high priority to test cases that exercise elements that have not recently been exercised. Both the number of elements covered and the "age" of each element (time since that element was covered by a test case) can contribute to the prioritization.

structural priority schema

Structural priority schemes produce several criteria depending on which elements we consider: statements, conditions, decisions, functions, files, and so on. The choice of the element of interest is usually driven by the testing level. Fine-grain elements such as statements and conditions are typically used in unit testing, while in integration or system testing one can consider coarser grain elements such as methods, features, and files.

Open Research Issues

System requirements include many nonfunctional behavioral properties. While there is an active research community in reliability testing, in general, assessment of nonfunctional properties is not as well-studied as testing for correctness. Moreover, as trends in software develop, new problems for test and analysis are following the emphasis on particular nonfunctional properties. A prominent example of this over the last several years, and with much left to do, is test and analysis to assess and improve security.

Selective regression test selection based on analysis of source code is now well-studied. There remains need and opportunity for improvement in techniques that give up the safety guarantee (selecting all test cases that *might* be affected by a software change) to obtain more significant test suite reductions. Specification-based regression test selection is a promising avenue of research, particularly as more systems incorporate components without full source code.

Increasingly ubiquitous network access is blurring the once-clear lines between alpha and beta testing and opening possibilities for gathering much more information from execution of deployed software. We expect to see advances in approaches to gathering information (both from failures and from normal execution) as well as exploiting potentially large amounts of gathered information. Privacy and confidentiality are an important research challenge in postdeployment monitoring.

Further Reading

Musa [Mus04] is a guide to reliability engineering from a pioneer in the field; ongoing research appears in the International Symposium on Software Reliability Engineering (ISSRE) conference series. Graves et al. [GHK+98] and Rothermel and Harrold [RH97] provide useful overviews of selective regression testing. Kim and Porter [KP02] describe history-based test prioritization. Barnum [Bar01] is a well-regarded text on usability testing; Nielsen [Nie00] is a broader popular introduction to usability engineering, with a chapter on usability testing.

Exercises

22.1. Consider the Chipmunk Computer Web presence. Define at least one test case that may serve both during final integration and early system testing, at least one that serves only as an integration test case, and at least one that is more suitable as a system test case than as a final integration test case. Explain your choices.

22.2. When and why should testing responsibilities shift from the development team to an independent quality team? In what circumstances might using an independent quality team be impractical?

22.3. Identify some kinds of properties that cannot be efficiently verified with system testing, and indicate how you would verify them.

22.4. Provide two or more examples of resource limitations that may impact system test more than module and integration test. Explain the difference in impact.

22.5. Consider the following required property of the Chipmunk Computer Web presence:

> Customers should perceive that purchasing a computer using the Chipmunk Web presence is at least as convenient, fast, and intuitive as purchasing a computer in an off-line retail store.

Would you check it as part of system or acceptance testing? Reformulate the property to allow test designers to check it in a different testing phase (system testing, if you consider the property checkable as part of acceptance testing, or vice versa).

Chapter 23

Automating Analysis and Test

Automation can improve the efficiency of some quality activities and is a necessity for implementing others. While a greater degree of automation can never substitute for a rational, well-organized quality process, considerations of what can and should be automated play an important part in devising and incrementally improving a process that makes the best use of human resources. This chapter discusses some of the ways that automation can be employed, as well as its costs and limitations, and the maturity of the required technology. The focus is not on choosing one particular set of "best" tools for all times and situations, but on a continuing rational process of identifying and deploying automation to best effect as the organization, process, and available technology evolve.

Required Background

- Chapter 20
  Some knowledge about planning and monitoring, though not strictly required, can be useful to understand the need for automated management support.

- Chapter 17
  Some knowledge about execution and scaffolding is useful to appreciate the impact of tools for scaffolding generation and test execution.

- Chapter 19
  Some knowledge about program analysis is useful to understand the need to automate analysis techniques.

23.1 Overview

A rational approach to automating test and analysis proceeds incrementally, prioritizing the next steps based on variations in potential impact, variations in the maturity, cost, and scope of the applicable technology, and fit and impact on the organization and process. The potential role of automation in test and analysis activities can be considered along three nonorthogonal dimensions: the value of the activity and its current cost, the extent to which the activity requires or is made less expensive by automation, and the cost of obtaining or constructing tool support.

Some test and analysis tasks depend so heavily on automation that a decision to employ a technique is tantamount to a decision to use tools. For example, employing structural coverage criteria in program testing necessarily means using coverage measurement tools. In other cases, an activity may be carried out manually, but automation reduces cost or improves effectiveness. For example, tools for capturing and replaying executions reduce the costs of reexecuting test suites and enable testing strategies that would be otherwise impractical. Even tasks that appear to be inherently manual may be enhanced with automation. For example, although software inspection is a manual activity at its core, a variety of tools have been developed to organize and present information and manage communication for software inspection, improving the efficiency of inspectors.

The difficulty and cost of automating test and analysis vary enormously, ranging from tools that are so simple to develop that they are justifiable even if their benefits are modest to tools that would be enormously valuable but are simply impossible. For example, if we have specification models structured as finite state machines, automatic generation of test case specifications from the finite state model is a sufficiently simple and well-understood technique that obtaining or building suitable tools should not be an obstacle. At the other extreme, as we have seen in Chapter 2, many important problems regarding programs are undecidable. For example, no matter how much value we might derive from a tool that infallibly distinguishes executable from nonexecutable program paths, no such tool can exist. We must therefore weigh the difficulty or expense of automation together with potential benefits, including costs of training and integration.

Difficulty and cost are typically entangled with scope and accuracy. Sometimes a general-purpose tool (e.g., capture and replay for Windows applications) is only marginally more difficult to produce than a tool specialized for one project (e.g., capture and replay for a specific Windows application). Investment in the general-purpose tool, whether to build it or to buy it, can be amortized across projects. In other cases, it may be much more cost-effective to create simple, project-specific tools that sidestep the complexity of more generic tools.

However industrious and well-intentioned, humans are slow and error-prone when dealing with repetitive tasks. Conversely, simple repetitive tasks are often straightforward to automate, while judgment and creative problem solving remain outside the domain of automation. Human beings are very good at identifying the relevant execution scenarios that correspond to test case specifications (for example, by specifying the execution space of the program under test with a finite state machine), but are very inefficient in generating large volumes of test cases (for example, by clicking combinations of menus in graphic interfaces), or identifying erroneous results within a large set of outputs produced when executing regression tests. Automating the repetitive portions of the task not only reduces costs, but improves accuracy as well.

23.2 Automation and Planning

One important role of a test strategy is to prescribe tools for key elements of the quality process used in the organization. Analysis and test strategies can include very detailed process and tool prescriptions, particularly in critical application domains where quality assurance procedures are imposed by certification agencies, as in avionics software. In general, however, a single detailed process and its supporting tools will not be a uniformly good fit for a diverse set of software projects. Rather, an analysis and testing strategy can recommend different tools contingent on aspects of a project including application domain, development languages, and size. Overall quality strategies often indicate tools for organizing test design and execution and for generating quality documents, for collecting metrics, and for managing regression test suites. They less often indicate tools for generating test cases from requirement and design specifications, or for dynamic analysis.

The quality plan for a particular project indicates tools inherited from the strategy as well as additional tools selected for that project. The quality manager should also evaluate needs and opportunities for acquiring or customizing existing tools or developing ad hoc solutions. For both organization-standard and project-specific tool choices, the plan must include related costs such as training, implied activities, and potential risks.

The quality strategy and plan must position tools within a development process and an analysis and test methodology. Tools are worthless and even harmful if not properly contextualized. For example, while tools for measuring code coverage are simple and inexpensive, if not preceded by careful consideration of the role of coverage metrics in the test process, they are at best an annoyance, producing data that are not put to productive use, and at worst a distorting influence that steers the process in unplanned ways.

23.3 Process Management

Managing a quality process involves planning a set of activities with appropriate cost and quality trade-offs, monitoring progress to identify risks as early as possible and to avoid delays, and adjusting the plan as needed. These tasks require human creativity and insight for which no tool can substitute. Nonetheless, tools can support process management, improving decision making by organizing and monitoring activities and results, facilitating group interaction, managing quality documents, and tracking costs.

Classic planning tools facilitate task scheduling, resource allocation, and cost estimation by arranging tasks according to resource and time constraints. They can be specialized to analysis and test management with features for automatically deriving relations among tasks, launching tasks, and monitoring completion of activities. For example, quality planning tools can schedule test generation and execution activities consistent with dependence among quality activities and between quality and development activities. They can recognize delivery of a given artifact, automatically schedule execution of a corresponding test suite, notify the test designer of test results, record the actual execution time of the activity, and signal schedule deviations to the quality manager. Quality planning tools are most useful when integrated in the analysis and test environment to react automatically to events with activation of other tools and procedures.

Analysis and testing involve complex relations among a large number of artifacts. A failure of a particular test case may be specific to a particular version of a module in some configurations of a system and to portions of a design specification that is in turn tied back to product requirements. An inspection may detect a fault indicated by a particular checklist item, which is applied by inspectors when they recognize a particular software design pattern, and that fault is also related to elements of the program, design, and version and configuration information. In most development projects, managing those relations, deriving useful information from them, and taking appropriate action are major tasks themselves.

Fortunately, managing the Web of relations among artifacts can be automated and managed by version control tools. Version and configuration control tools relate versions of software artifacts and are often used to trigger consistency checks and other activities. They can support analysis and testing activities in much the same manner as they control assembly and compilation of related modules, for example, triggering execution of the appropriate test suites for each software modification, associating version status with test reports, and tracking completion of follow-up activities for detected failures. In other words, artifacts and tasks related to quality are simply part of the product and development process, with the same requirements and opportunities for automated support. Also like other aspects of a development environment, integrated quality tracking improves efficiency in a well-structured process, but does not by itself bring order out of chaos.

Process management includes monitoring progress in terms of both schedule (comparing actual effort and completion times to a plan) and level of quality. Quality of the final product cannot be directly measured before its completion, but useful indications can be derived, for example, using the orthogonal defect classification discussed in Chapter 20. For both schedule and quality, the essential function of tracking is to recognize deviations from expectation, so that an alert manager can direct attention to understanding and dealing with problems before they are insurmountable.

Essential tasks that require human ingenuity include selecting or designing proxy measures that can be computed early, and interpreting those measures in a way that avoids misleading conclusions or distorted incentives. For example, counting lines of code is sometimes useful as a simple proxy for productivity, but must be carefully interpreted to avoid creating an incentive for verbosity or a disincentive for effective reuse of components. Similarly, the number of faults detected is a useful proxy measure if the goal is simply to detect deviations from the norm, but one should be as concerned about the causes of abnormally low numbers as high. Collection, summary, and presentation of data can be automated; design and interpretation cannot.

Effective management also involves coordinating people, who may work in different groups or even different companies, possibly distributed across time zones and continents. Several studies have indicated that a large proportion of a software engineer's time is devoted to communication. It is therefore important both to facilitate effective communication and to limit disruptions and distractions of unmanaged communication.

Where simple general-purpose tools like e-mail, chats, and forums are employed, a key factor in their efficiency is appropriately matching synchronous communication or asynchronous communication to tasks. When excessive interruptions slow progress, replacing synchronous communication by asynchronous or scheduled communication may be indicated. Conversely, asynchronous communication may be replaced or augmented with synchronous communication (e.g., messaging or chat) to improve the efficiency of discussions that have been splintered into many small exchanges punctuated by waits for reply.

Communication is most effective when all parties have immediate access to relevant information. In this regard, task-specific tools can improve on general-purpose communication support. For example, tools for distributed software inspections extend the familiar interfaces for chat (for synchronous inspection) or forum (for asynchronous inspection), adding managed presentation of the artifact to be inspected and appropriate portions of checklists and automated analysis results.

23.4 Static Metrics

Static metrics measure software properties, often to estimate other properties. Among the most basic properties of software is size, which is strongly correlated to schedule and cost, including the cost of testing. Even something as straightforward as counting lines of code turns out to have several possible variations, depending on whether and how one filters out variations in white space, comments, and programming style. Common metrics of code size include:

Size	Size of the source file, measured in bytes
Lines	All-inclusive count of lines in source code file
LOC	Lines of code, excluding comment and blank lines
eLOC	Effective lines of code, excluding comments, blank lines, and stand-alone braces or parenthesis
lLOC	Logical lines of code, that is, statements as identified by logical separators such as semicolons

Every programmer knows that there are variations in complexity between different pieces of code and that this complexity may be as important as sheer size. A number of attempts have been made to quantify aspects of complexity and readability:

CDENS	Comment density (i.e., comment lines/eLOC)
Blocks	Number of basic blocks (i.e., sequences of statements with one entry point, one exit point, and no internal branches)
AveBlockL	Average number of lines per basic block
NEST	Control structure nesting level (minimum, maximum, and average)
Loops	Number of loops
LCSAJ	Number of linear code sequences; see Chapter 5
BRANCH	Number of branches in the control flow graph

Size and complexity may also be estimated on a coarser scale, considering only interfaces between units:

Cyclomatic Complexity

Cyclomatic complexity is measured as $e-n+2$, where e is the number of edges of the control flow graph and n is the number of nodes in the graph.

Cyclomatic complexity does not depend on the size of the code but on branching in the control structure. For example, graphs $CFG1$ and $CFG2$, as follow, have the same cyclomatic complexity, despite their different sizes, while the cyclomatic complexity of $CFG3$ is higher than that of $CFG2$ despite having the same number of nodes.

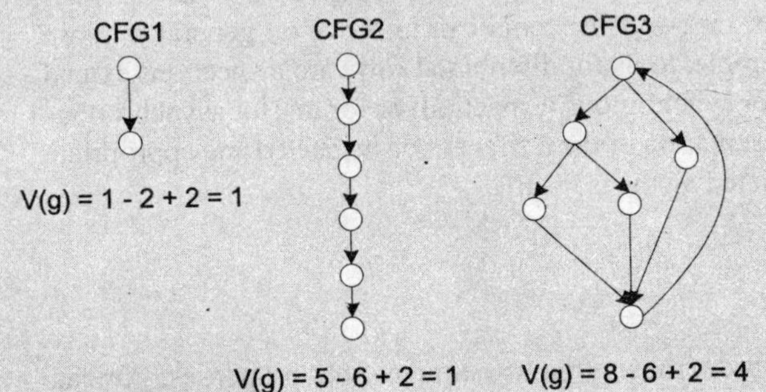

Low to moderate cyclomatic complexity (below 20) is interpreted as indicating a simple program; high cyclomatic complexity (above 20) indicates complex programs; very high cyclomatic complexity (above 50) characterizes programs that may be very difficult or impossible to thoroughly test.

Cyclomatic complexity is certainly a sign of complex control flow structure, but it does not capture other aspects of logical complexity that can lead to difficulty in testing. There is little evidence that cyclomatic complexity is a more reliable predictor of testing effort or quality than lines of code.

Functions	Number of defined functions (or methods, procedures, etc.)
FPar	Number of formal parameters of functions
FRet	Number of return points of functions
IComplex	Interface complexity (i.e., $FPar + FRet$)

All these metrics are proxies for size and complexity. Despite several attempts beginning in the 1970s, no proposed metric has succeeded in capturing intrinsic complexity in a manner that robustly correlates with effort or quality. Lines of code, despite its obvious shortcomings, is not much worse than other measures of size. Among attempts to measure complexity, only cyclomatic complexity ($V(g)$) is still commonly collected by many tools (see sidebar). Cyclomatic complexity is defined as the number of independent paths through the control flow graph.

Additional metrics have been introduced to capture complexity in structures unique to object-oriented programming:

WMC	Weighted methods per class, the sum of the complexities of methods in all classes, divided by the number of classes. This metric is parametric with respect to a measure of complexity in methods
DIT	Depth of the inheritance tree of a class
NOC	Number of children (subclasses) of a class
RFC	Response for a class, the number of methods that may be executed in response to a method call to an object of the class. The size of the transitive closure of the calling relation rooted at a class
CBO	Coupling between object classes, the number of classes with which the class is coupled through any relation (e.g., containment, method calls, subclassing)
LCOM	Lack of cohesion in methods, the number of methods with pairwise disjoint sets of instance variables referenced within their respective method bodies

All metrics discussed so far focus on code structure and can be measured only when the code is available, often late in the development process. A subset of the object-oriented metrics can be derived from detailed design, which still may be too late for many purposes.

Many standards define metrics. The well-known ISO/IEC 9126 standard (sidebar on page 446) suggests a hierarchy of properties to measure the quality of software. The six main high-level quality dimensions identified by the ISO/IEC 9126 standard describe quality properties as perceived by users.

23.5 Test Case Generation and Execution

Test case generation and execution can be a large fraction of overall cost for test and analysis, and if done poorly can become a scheduling bottleneck near product delivery deadlines. Although designing a test suite involves human creativity in the same degree as other kinds of design, instantiating and executing test cases is a repetitive and tedious task that can be largely automated, reducing overall cost and accelerating the test cycle.

Technical aspects of test case generation and execution are discussed in Chapter 17 and are not repeated here. Strategic aspects of automating test case generation and execution are much as for other quality activities: Essentially mechanical tasks should be factored out and automated, and essentially intellectual and creative tasks should be supported through cognitive aids, bookkeeping support, and communication support.

23.6 Static Analysis and Proof

Analysis of specifications and proof of properties span activities from simple checks to full proof of program correctness. Although analysis and proof are often related to formal methods, we can also analyze several aspects of semiformal and informal specifications, if they are precisely defined. For example, we can automatically check important syntactic properties of informal textual and diagrammatic notations.

ISO/IEC 9126 Properties

The ISO/IEC 9126 standard requires estimation of user-perceived quality on several dimensions. The standard defines only qualitative and subjective measures, but an organization can obtain more useful values by mapping them to objectively measurable criteria.

Functionality	Ability to meet explicit and implicit functional requirements
Suitability	Ability to provide functionality required to satisfy user goals
Accuracy	Ability to provide correct results
Interoperability	Ability to interact with other products
Security	Ability to protect access to private data and guarantee a level of service, preventing denial of service
Reliability	Ability to provide the required level of service when the software is used under appropriate conditions
Maturity	Ability to avoid failures that result from software faults
Fault Tolerance	Ability to maintain a suitable level of functionality even in the presence of external failures
Recoverability	Ability to recover data and resume function after a failure
Usability	Ease of understanding, teaching and using the software
Understandability	Ease of understanding the product
Learnability	Ease of training users
Operability	Ease of working with the product
Attractiveness	Degree of appreciation by users
Efficiency	Ability to guarantee required performance under given conditions
Time Behavior	Ability to satisfy average and maximum response time requirements
Resource Utilization	Amount of resources needed for executing the software
Maintainability	Ability to be updated, corrected, and modified
Analyzability	Ease of analyzing the software to reveal faults
Changeability	Ease of changing the software to remove faults and change existing and add new functionality
Stability	Ability to minimize the effects of changes on normal behavior
Testability	Ease of testing the software
Portability	Ability to be executed in different environments and interoperate with other software
Adaptability	Ability to be adapted to new operating environments
Installability	Ease of installing the software in different environments
Co-existence	Ability to share resources with other products
Replaceability	Ability to be replaced by other products

Automated analysis is effective both for quickly and cheaply checking simple properties, and for more expensive checks that are necessary for critical properties that resist cheaper forms of verification. For example, simple data flow analyses can almost instantaneously identify anomalous patterns (e.g., computing a value that is never used) that are often symptoms of other problems (perhaps using the wrong value at a different point in a program). At the other extreme, using a finite state verification tool to find subtle synchronization faults in interface protocols requires a considerable investment in constructing a model and formalizing the properties to be verified, but this effort is justified by the cost of failure and the inadequacy of conventional testing to find timing-dependent faults.

It may be practical to verify some critical properties only if the program to be checked conforms to certain design rules. The problem of verifying critical properties is then decomposed into a design step and a proof step. In the design step, software engineers select and enforce design rules to accommodate analysis, encapsulating critical parts of the code and selecting a well-understood design idiom for which suitable analysis techniques are known. Test designers can then focus on the encapsulated or simplified property. For example, it is common practice to encapsulate safety-critical properties into a safety kernel. In this way, the hard problem of proving the safety-critical properties of a complex system is decomposed into two simpler problems: Prove safety properties of the (small) kernel, and check that all safety-related actions are mediated by the kernel.

Tools for verifying a wide class of properties, like program verifiers based on theorem proving, require extensive human interaction and guidance. Other tools with a more restricted focus, including finite state verification tools, typically execute completely automatically but almost always require several rounds of revision to properly formalize a model and property to be checked. The least burdensome of tools are restricted to checking a fixed set of simple properties, which (being fixed) do not require any additional effort for specification. These featherweight analysis tools include type checkers, data flow analyzers, and checkers of domain specific properties, such as Web site link checkers.

Type-checking techniques are typically applied to properties that are syntactic in the sense that they enforce a simple well-formedness rule. Violations are easy to diagnose and repair even if the rules are stricter than one would like. Data flow analyzers, which are more sensitive to program control and data flow, are often used to identify anomalies rather than simple, unambiguous faults. For example, assigning a value to a variable that is not subsequently used suggests that either the wrong variable was set or an intended subsequent use is missing, but the program must be inspected to determine whether the anomaly corresponds to a real fault. Approximation in data flow analysis, resulting from summarization of execution on different control flow paths, can also necessitate interpretation of results.

Tools for more sophisticated analysis of programs are, like data flow analyses, ultimately limited by the undecidability of program properties. Some report false alarms in addition to real violations of the properties they check; others avoid false alarms but may also fail to detect all violations. Such "bug finders," though imperfect, may nonetheless be very cost-effective compared to alternatives that require more interaction.

Tools that provide strong assurance of important general properties, including model checkers and theorem provers, are much more "heavyweight" with respect to requirement for skilled human interaction and guidance. Finite state verification systems (often called model checkers) can verify conformance between a model of a system and a specified property, but require construction of the model and careful statement of the property. Although the verification tool may execute completely automatically, in practice it is run over and over again between manual revisions of the model and property specification or, in the case of model checkers for programs, revision of the property specification and guidance on program abstraction. Direct verification of software has proved effective, despite this cost, for some critical properties of relatively small programs such as device drivers. Otherwise, finite state verification technology is best applied to specification and design models.

The most general (but also the most expensive) static analysis tools execute with interactive guidance. The symbolic execution techniques described in Chapter 7, together with sophisticated constraint solvers, can be used to construct formal proofs that a program satisfies a wide class of formally specified properties. Interactive theorem proving requires specialists with a strong mathematical background to formulate the problem and the property and interactively select proof strategies. The cost of semi-automated formal verification can be justified for a high level algorithm that will be used in many applications, or at a more detailed level to prove a few crucial properties of safety-critical applications.

23.7 Cognitive Aids

Quality activities often require examining and understanding complex artifacts, from requirements statements to program code to test execution logs. Information clutter and nonlocality increase the cognitive burden of these tasks, decreasing effectiveness and efficiency. Even inherently manual tasks that depend on human judgment and creativity can be made more effective by cognitive aids that reduce cognitive burden by gathering and presenting relevant information in a task-appropriate manner, with a minimum of irrelevant and distracting details.

Information that requires a shift of attention (e.g., following a reference in one file or page to a definition on another) is said to be nonlocal. Nonlocality creates opportunities for human error, which lead to software faults, such as inconsistent uses of data values in a program, or inconsistent use of technical terms in a specification document. Not surprisingly, then, quality tasks often involve gathering and analyzing nonlocal information. Human analysis capability is amplified by bringing relevant information together. For example, where a human may be required to make a judgment about consistent use of technical terms, tools can support that judgment by gathering uses of terms together. Often tools synthesize a global view from scattered local information, as, for example, displaying a call graph extracted from many source code files.

Information required for a quality task is often obscured by a mass of distracting irrelevant detail. Tool support for focus and abstraction, delivering and drawing attention to relevant information while suppressing irrelevant detail, improve human effectiveness by reducing clutter and distraction. For example, an inspection tool that displays just the checklist items relevant to a particular inspection task and location in the artifact under inspection increases the efficiency and thoroughness of the human inspector. Similarly, an effective summary report of automated test executions quickly focuses attention on deviations from expected test behavior.

Cognitive aids for browsing and visualization are sometimes available as separate tools, but more often their features are embedded in other tools and customized to support particular tasks. Pretty-printing and program slicing,[1] for example, improve code readability and make it easier to identify elements of interest. Diagrammatic representations condense presentation of code properties, providing a summary view of nonlocal information.

Diagrammatic and graphical representations are often used to present the results of program analysis, such as data and control flow relations, structural test coverage, distribution of faults and corrections in a program, and source code metrics. Figure 23.1 shows a sample screen shot that visualizes some characteristics of a program. Nodes represent classes and edges inheritance between classes. Node size and background summarize various metrics of the corresponding class. In the diagram of Figure 23.1, width indicates the number of attributes of the class, height indicates the number of methods, and color indicates lines of code, where white represents the smallest classes, black represents the largest, and intermediate sizes are represented by shades of gray. The graphic provides no more information than a table of values, but it facilitates a quicker and fuller grasp of how those values are distributed.

23.8 Version Control

The quality process can exploit many general development tools not specifically designed for quality activities. Most fundamental among these are version control systems, which record versions and releases of each part of an evolving software system. In addition to maintaining test artifacts (plans, test cases, logs, etc.), the historical information kept in version control systems is useful for tracing faults across versions and collecting data for improving the process.

Test cases, scaffolding, and oracles are bound to the code: Changes in the code may result in incompatibilities with scaffolding and oracles, and test cases may not exercise new relevant behaviors. Thus, test suites must evolve with code. Test designers use version control systems to coordinate evolution of test artifacts with associated program artifacts. In addition to test and program artifacts, the status and history of faults is essential to project management, and many version control systems include functionality for supporting fault tracking.

23.9 Debugging

Detecting the presence of software faults is logically distinct from the subsequent tasks of locating, diagnosing, and repairing faults. Testing is concerned with fault detection,

[1]Program slicing is an application of static or dynamic dependence analysis (see Chapter 6) to identify portions of a program relevant to the current focus.

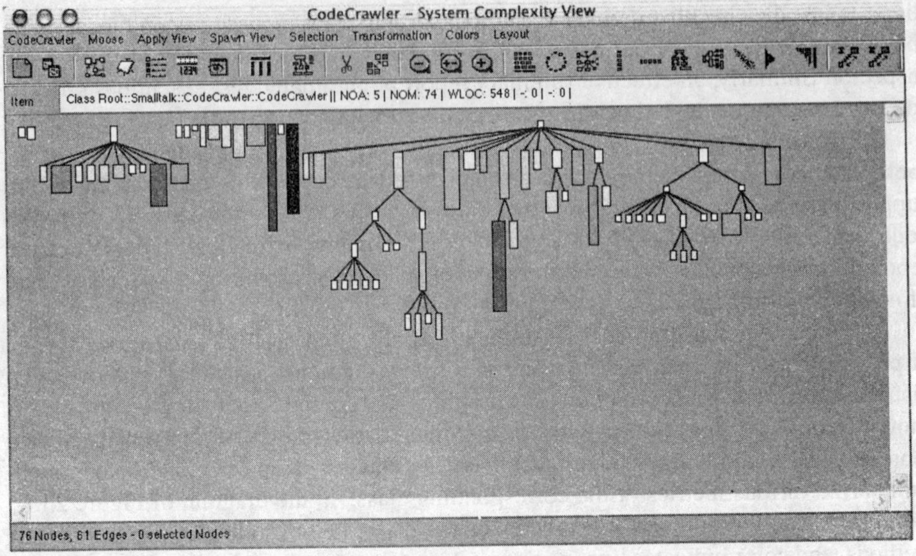

Figure 23.1: Visualization tools can summarize non-local information to facilitate understanding and navigation. The CodeCrawler tool, shown here, uses color, width, and height to represent three static measures of size (number of attributes, number of methods, and lines of code) with connections representing inheritance relations.

while locating and diagnosing faults fall under the rubric of debugging. Responsibility for testing and debugging typically fall to different individuals. Nonetheless, since the beginning point for debugging is often a set of test cases, their relation is important, and good test automation derives as much value as possible for debugging.

A small, simple test case that invariably fails is far more valuable in debugging than a complex scenario, particularly one that may fail or succeed depending on unspecified conditions. This is one reason test case generators usually produce larger suites of single-purpose test cases rather than a smaller number of more comprehensive test cases.

Typical run-time debugging tools allow inspection of program state and controls to pause execution at selected points (breakpoints), or when certain conditions occur (watchpoints), or after a fixed number of execution steps. Modern debugging tools almost always provide display and control at the level of program source code, although compiler transformations of object code cannot always be hidden (e.g., order of execution may differ from the order of source code). Specialized debugging support may include visualization (e.g., of thread and process interactions) and animation of data structures; some environments permit a running program to be paused, modified, and continued.

When failures are encountered in stress testing or operational use, the "test case" is likely to be an unwieldy scenario with many irrelevant details, and possibly without enough information to reliably trigger failure. Sometimes the scenario can be automatically reduced to a smaller test case. A test data reduction tool executes many variations on a test case, omitting portions of the input for each trial, in order to discover which parts contain the core information that triggers failure. The technique is not universally applicable, and meaningful subdivisions of input data may be application-specific, but it is an invaluable aid to dealing with large data sets. While the purpose of test data reduction is to aid debugging, it may also produce a useful regression test case to guard against reintroduction of the same program fault.

Not only the test case or cases that trigger failure but also those that execute correctly are valuable. Differential debugging compares a set of failing executions to other executions that do not fail, focusing attention on parts of the program that are always or often executed on failures and less often executed when the program completes successfully. Variations on this approach include varying portions of a program (to determine which of several recent changes is at fault), varying thread schedules (to isolate which context switch triggers a fatal race condition), and even modifying program data state during execution.

23.10 Choosing and Integrating Tools

Automation is a key lever for reducing cost and improving the effectiveness of test and analysis, but only if tools and approaches are a good fit with the development organization, process, application domain, and suitable test and analysis techniques.

A large software development organization in which a single software project is spread across several teams and functional areas has foremost a requirement for coordination and communication. We would typically expect to see process management and version and configuration control in a central role, with automation of other activities from programming to inspection to system testing arranged to fit smoothly into it. A large organization can typically afford to establish and maintain such a system, as well as to orient new employees to it. A smaller organization, or one divided into autonomous groups along project rather than functional lines, still benefits from integration of test and analysis tools with process management, but can afford to place a higher priority on other aspects of test and analysis automation.

A simple and obvious rule for automating test and analysis activities is to select tools that improve the efficiency of tasks that are significant costs (in money or schedule) for the organization and projects in question. For example, automated module testing is of little use for an organization using the Cleanroom process, but is likely to be important to an organization using XP. An organization building safety-critical software can justify investment (including training) in sophisticated tools for verifying the properties of specifications and design, but an organization that builds rapidly evolving mass market applications is more likely to benefit from good support for automated regression testing.

While automating what one is already doing manually is easiest to justify, one should not fail to consider activities that are simply impossible without automation. For example, if static source code analysis can efficiently detect a class of software faults that requires considerable testing effort, then acquiring or constructing tools to perform that analysis may be more cost-effective than automation to make the testing effort more efficient.

Investments in automation must be evaluated in a scope that extends beyond a single project and beyond the quality team. The advantage of reusing common tools across projects is savings not only in the cost of acquiring and installing tools, but also in the cost of learning to use them effectively and the consequent impact on project schedule. A continuing benefit for a one-time or declining investment becomes more attractive when tool use is considered over the longer term. Often a quality tool will have costs and benefits for other parts of the software organization (e.g., in the quality of diagnostic information produced), and the most successful tool adoptions are those that produce visible benefits for all parties.

Consider, for example, adoption of tools for recording and tracking faults. Tracking reported failures from the field and from system testing is easy to justify in most organizations, as it has immediate visible benefits for everyone who must deal with failure reports. Collecting additional information to enable fault classification and process improvement has at least equal benefits in the long term, but is more challenging because the payoff is not immediate.

Open Research Issues

Tools and automation are likely to remain an important part of research in all subareas of software analysis and test, particularly but not only for techniques that are essentially impossible to carry out manually. Where manual effort is central, as, for example, in software inspection or project planning, automation is equally important but depends more critically on fitting into the overall process and project context and human factors. For example, with version and configuration control systems playing a central role in team coordination and communication, we can expect to see innovations in the way test and analysis tasks exploit and are integrated with versioning repositories.

Nearly universal network connectivity has enabled a related trend, expanding the iterative cycle of software development and evolution beyond deployment. Regularly scheduled software field updates and automated transmission of crash logs and bug reports to developers is already commonplace for so-called desktop computers and seems inevitable for the growing tide of embedded systems. Research in software test and analysis is just beginning to address the kinds of automation this expansion enables and, in some cases, necessitates, such as rapid classification of error and crash logs. A natural extension into more sophisticated self-monitoring, diagnosis, and automatic adaptation in deployed software is sometimes included under the rubric of self-managed computing.

The current generation of integrated development environments is an architectural improvement of over its predecessors, particularly in provision of plug-in frameworks for tools. Nevertheless the distance from devising a useful technique to fielding a useful and well-integrated tool, particularly one with rich visualization capabilities, remains large. There is still a good deal of room for progress in approaches and techniques for quickly generating and integrating tools.

Further Reading

Surveys of currently available tools are available commercially, and reviews of many tools can be found in trade magazines and books. Since tools are constantly evolving, the research literature and other archival publications are less useful for determining what is immediately available. The research literature is more useful for understanding basic problems and approaches in automation to guide the development and use of tools. Zeller [Zel05] is a good modern reference on program debugging, with an emphasis on recent advances in automated debugging. A series of books by Tufte [Tuf01, Tuf97, Tuf90, Tuf06] are useful reading for anyone designing information-dense displays, and Nielsen [Nie00] is an introduction to usability that, though specialized to Web applications, describes more generally useful principles. Norman [Nor90] is an excellent and entertaining introduction to fundamental principles of usability that apply to software tools as well as many other designed artifacts. The example in Figure 23.1 is taken from Lanza and Ducasse [LD03], who describe a simple and adaptable approach to depicting program attributes using multiple graphical dimensions.

Related Topics

Chapter 19 describes program analysis tools in more detail.

Exercises

23.1. Appropriate choice of tools may vary between projects depending, among other factors, on application domain, development language(s), and project size. Describe possible differences in A&T tool choices for the following:

- Program analysis tools for a project with Java as the only development language, and for another project with major components in Java, SQL, and Python, and a variety of other scripting and special-purpose languages in other roles.
- Planning and monitoring tools for a three-month, three-person project in which all but acceptance testing is designed and carried out by developers, and for a two-year project carried out by a seven-person team including two full-time testers.
- A testing framework for an information system that archives international weather data, and for a weather forecasting system based on computer simulation.

23.2. Consider the following design rule: All user text (prompts, error messages, et al.) are made indirectly through tables, so that a table of messages in another language can be substituted at run-time. How would you go about partly or wholly automating a check of this property?

23.3. Suppose two kinds of fault are equally common and equally costly, but one is local (entirely within a module) and the other is inherently nonlocal (e.g., it could involve incompatibility between modules). If your project budget is enough to automate detection of either the local or the nonlocal property, but not both, which will you automate? Why?

Chapter 24

Documenting Analysis and Test

Mature software processes include documentation standards for all the activities of the software process, including test and analysis activities. Documentation can be inspected to verify progress against schedule and quality goals and to identify problems, supporting process visibility, monitoring, and replicability.

Required Background

- Chapter 20
  This chapter describes test and analysis strategy and plans, which are intertwined with documentation. Plans and strategy documents are part of quality documentation, and quality documents are used in process monitoring.

24.1 Overview

Documentation is an important element of the software development process, including the quality process. Complete and well-structured documents increase the reusability of test suites within and across projects. Documents are essential for maintaining a body of knowledge that can be reused across projects. Consistent documents provide a basis for monitoring and assessing the process, both internally and for external authorities where certification is desired. Finally, documentation includes summarizing and presenting data that forms the basis for process improvement. Test and analysis documentation includes summary documents designed primarily for human comprehension and details accessible to the human reviewer but designed primarily for automated analysis.

Documents are divided into three main categories: planning, specification, and reporting. *Planning documents* describe the organization of the quality process and include strategies and plans for the division or the company, and plans for individual projects. *Specification documents* describe test suites and test cases. A complete set of

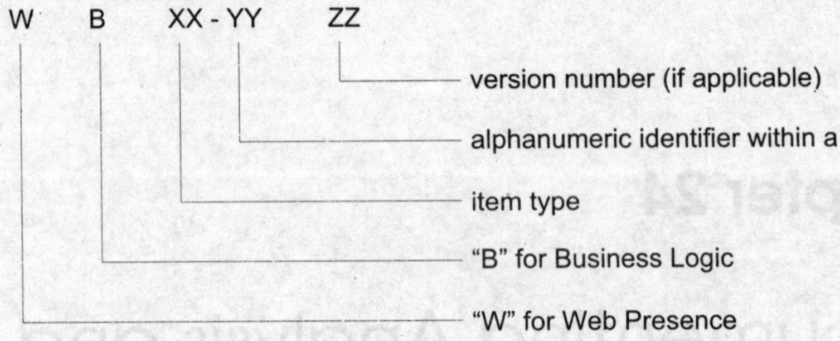

analysis and test documentation

WB05-YYZZ	analysis and test strategy
WB06-YYZZ	analysis and test plan
WB07-YYZZ	test design specifications
WB08-YYZZ	test case specification
WB09-YYZZ	checklists
WB10-YYZZ	analysis and test logs
WB11-YYZZ	analysis and test summary reports
WB12-YYZZ	other analysis and test documents

Figure 24.1: Sample document naming conventions, compliant with IEEE standards.

analysis and test specification documents include test design specifications, test case specification, checklists, and analysis procedure specifications. *Reporting documents* include details and summary of analysis and test results.

24.2 Organizing Documents

In a small project with a sufficiently small set of documents, the arrangement of other project artifacts (e.g., requirements and design documents) together with standard content (e.g., mapping of subsystem test suites to the build schedule) provides sufficient organization to navigate through the collection of test and analysis documentation. In larger projects, it is common practice to produce and regularly update a global guide for navigating among individual documents.

Mature processes require all documents to contain metadata that facilitate their management. Documents must include some basic information about its *context* in order to make the document self-contained, *approval* indicating the persons responsible for the document and *document history*, as illustrated in the template on page 457.

Naming conventions help in quickly identifying documents. A typical standard for document names would include keywords indicating the general scope of the document, its nature, the specific document, and its version, as in Figure 24.1.

Chipmunk Document Template

Document Title

Approvals

issued by	*name*	*signature*	*date*
approved by	*name*	*signature*	*date*
distribution status	*(internal use only, restricted, ...)*		
distribution list	*(people to whom the document must be sent)*		

History

version	description

Table of Contents

List of sections.

Summary

Summarize the contents of the document. The summary should clearly explain the relevance of the document to its possible uses.

Goals of the document

Describe the purpose of this document: Who should read it, and why?

Required documents and references

Provide a reference to other documents and artifacts needed for understanding and exploiting this document. Provide a rationale for the provided references.

Glossary

Provide a glossary of terms required to understand this document.

Section 1

. . .

Section N

. . .

24.3 Test Strategy Document

Analysis and test strategies (Chapter 20) describe quality guidelines for sets of projects, usually for an entire company or organization. Strategies, and therefore strategy documents, vary widely among organizations, but we can identify a few key elements that should be included in almost any well-designed strategy document. These are illustrated in the document excerpt on page 459.

overall quality

Strategy documents indicate common quality requirements across products. Requirements may depend on business conditions. For example, a company that produces safety-critical software may need to satisfy minimum dependability requirements defined by a certification authority, while a department that designs software embedded in hardware products may need to ensure portability across product lines. Some requirements on dependability and usability may be necessary to maintain brand image and market position. For example, a company might decide to require conformance to W3C-WAI accessibility standards (see Chapter 22) uniformly across the product line.

documentation quality

The strategy document sets out requirements on other quality documents, typically including an analysis and test plan, test design specifications, test case specifications, test logs, and test summary reports. Basic document requirements, such as naming and versioning, follow standards for other project documentation, but quality documents may have additional, specialized requirements. For example, testing logs for avionics software may be required to contain references to the version of the simulator used for executing the test before installing the software on board the aircraft.

24.4 Analysis and Test Plan

While the format of an analysis and test strategy vary from company to company, the structure of an analysis and test plan is more standardized. A typical structure of a test and analysis plan includes information about items to be verified, features to be tested, the testing approach, pass and fail criteria, test deliverables, tasks, responsibilities and resources, and environment constraints. Basic elements are described in the sidebar on page 461.

items to be verified

The overall quality plan usually comprises several individual plans of limited scope. Each test and analysis plan should indicate the items to be verified through analysis or testing. They may include specifications or documents to be inspected, code to be analyzed or tested, and interface specifications to undergo consistency analysis. They may refer to the whole system or part of it — like a subsystem or a set of units. Where the project plan includes planned development increments, the analysis and test plan indicates the applicable versions of items to be verified.

For each item, the plan should indicate any special hardware or external software required for testing. For example, the plan might indicate that one suite of subsystem tests for a security package can be executed with a software simulation of a smart card reader, while another suite requires access to the physical device. Finally, for each item, the plan should reference related documentation, such as requirements and design specifications, and user, installation, and operations guides.

A test and analysis plan may not address all aspects of software quality and testing

An Excerpt of the Chipmunk Analysis and Test Strategy

Document CP05-14.03: Analysis and Test Strategy

...

Applicable Standards and Procedures

Artifact	*Applicable Standards and Guidelines*
Web application	Accessibility: W3C-WAI ...
Reusable component (internally developed)	Inspection procedure: [WB12-03.12]
External component	Qualification procedure: [WB12-22.04]

...

Documentation Standards

Project documents must be archived according to the standard Chipmunk archive procedure [WB02-01.02]. Standard required documents include

Document	*Content & Organization Standard*
Quality plan	[WB06-01.03]
Test design specifications	[WB07-01.01] (per test suite)
Test case specifications	[WB08-01.07] (per test suite)
Test logs	[WB10-02.13]
Test summary reports	[WB11-01.11]
Inspection reports	[WB12-09.01]

...

Analysis and Test Activities

...

Tools

The following tools are approved and should be used in all development projects. Exceptions require configuration committee approval and must be documented in the project plan.

Fault logging	Chipmunk BgT [WB10-23.01]
...	

...

Staff and Roles

A development work unit consists of unit source code, including unit test cases, stubs, and harnesses, and unit test documentation. A unit may be committed to the project baseline when the source code, test cases, and test results have passed peer review.

...

References

[WB02-01.02] *Archive Procedure*

[WB06-01.03] *Quality Plan Guidelines*

[WB07-01.01] *Test Design Specifications Guidelines*

[WB08-01.07] *Test Case Specifications Guidelines*

[WB11-01.11] *Summary Reports Template*

[WB10-02.13] *Test Log Template*

[WB11-09.01] *Inspection Report Template*

[WB12-03.12] *Standard Inspection Procedures*

[WB12-22.04] *Quality Procedures for Software Developed by Third Parties*

[WB12-23.01] *BgT Installation Manual and User Guide*

...

activities. It should indicate the features to be verified and those that are excluded from consideration (usually because responsibility for them is placed elsewhere). For example, if the item to be verified includes a graphical user interface, the test and analysis plan might state that it deals only with functional properties and not with usability, which is to be verified separately by a usability and human interface design team.

features to be analyzed or tested

Explicit indication of features *not* to be tested, as well as those included in an analysis and test plan, is important for assessing completeness of the overall set of analysis and test activities. Assumption that a feature not considered in the current plan is covered at another point is a major cause of missing verification in large projects.

The quality plan must clearly indicate criteria for deciding the success or failure of each planned activity, as well as the conditions for suspending and resuming analysis and test.

suspend and resume criteria

test deliverables

Plans define items and documents that must be produced during verification. Test deliverables are particularly important for regression testing, certification, and process improvement. We will see the details of analysis and test documentation in the next section.

tasks and schedule

The core of an analysis and test plan is a detailed schedule of tasks. The schedule is usually illustrated with GANTT and PERT diagrams showing the relation among tasks as well as their relation to other project milestones.[1] The schedule includes the allocation of limited resources (particularly staff) and indicates responsibility for results.

resources and responsibilities

A quality plan document should also include an explicit risk plan with contingencies. As far as possible, contingencies should include unambiguous triggers (e.g., a date on which a contingency is activated if a particular task has not be completed) as well as recovery procedures.

environmental needs

Finally, the test and analysis plan should indicate scaffolding, oracles, and any other software or hardware support required for test and analysis activities.

24.5 Test Design Specification Documents

Design documentation for test suites and test cases serve essentially the same purpose as other software design documentation, guiding further development and preparing for maintenance. Test suite design must include all the information needed for initial selection of test cases and maintenance of the test suite over time, including rationale and anticipated evolution. Specification of individual test cases includes purpose, usage, and anticipated changes.

Test design specification documents describe complete test suites (i.e., sets of test cases that focus on particular aspects, elements, or phases of a software project). They may be divided into unit, integration, system, and acceptance test suites, if we organize them by the granularity of the tests, or functional, structural, and performance test suites, if the primary organization is based on test objectives. A large project may include many test design specifications for test suites of different kinds and granularity,

[1] Project scheduling is discussed in more detail in Chapter 20.

A Standard Organization of an Analysis and Test Plan

Analysis and test items:

The items to be tested or analyzed. The description of each item indicates version and installation procedures that may be required.

Features to be tested:

The features considered in the plan.

Features not to be tested:

Features not considered in the current plan.

Approach:

The overall analysis and test approach, sufficiently detailed to permit identification of the major test and analysis tasks and estimation of time and resources.

Pass/Fail criteria:

Rules that determine the status of an artifact subjected to analysis and test.

Suspension and resumption criteria:

Conditions to trigger suspension of test and analysis activities (e.g., an excessive failure rate) and conditions for restarting or resuming an activity.

Risks and contingencies:

Risks foreseen when designing the plan and a contingency plan for each of the identified risks.

Deliverables:

A list all A&T artifacts and documents that must be produced.

Task and schedule:

A complete description of analysis and test tasks, relations among them, and relations between A&T and development tasks, with resource allocation and constraints. A task schedule usually includes GANTT and PERT diagrams.

Staff and responsibilities:

Staff required for performing analysis and test activities, the required skills, and the allocation of responsibilities among groups and individuals. Allocation of resources to tasks is described in the schedule.

Environmental needs:

Hardware and software required to perform analysis or testing activities.

and for different versions or configurations of the system and its components. Each specification should be uniquely identified and related to corresponding project documents, as illustrated in the sidebar on page 463.

Test design specifications identify the features they are intended to verify and the approach used to select test cases. Features to be tested should be cross-referenced to relevant parts of a software specification or design document. The test case selection approach will typically be one of the test selection techniques described in Chapters 10 through 16 with documentation on how the technique has been applied.

A test design specification also includes description of the testing procedure and pass/fail criteria. The procedure indicates steps required to set up the testing environment and perform the tests, and includes references to scaffolding and oracles. Pass/fail criteria distinguish success from failure of a test suite as a whole. In the simplest case a test suite execution may be determined to have failed if any individual test case execution fails, but in system and acceptance testing it is common to set a tolerance level that may depend on the number and severity of failures.

A test design specification logically includes a list of test cases. Test case specifications may be physically included in the test design specification document, or the logical inclusion may be implemented by some form of automated navigation. For example, a navigational index can be constructed from references in test case specifications.

Individual test case specifications elaborate the test design for each individual test case, defining test inputs, required environmental conditions and procedures for test execution, as well as expected outputs or behavior. The environmental conditions may include hardware and software as well as any other requirements. For example, while most tests should be executed automatically without human interaction, intervention of personnel with certain special skills (e.g., a device operator) may be an environmental requirement for some.

A test case specification indicates the item to be tested, such as a particular module or product feature. It includes a reference to the corresponding test design document and describes any dependence on execution of other test cases. Like any standard document, a test case specification is labeled with a unique identifier. A sample test case specification is provided on page 464.

24.6 Test and Analysis Reports

Reports of test and analysis results serve both developers and test designers. They identify open faults for developers and aid in scheduling fixes and revisions. They help test designers assess and refine their approach, for example, noting when some class of faults is escaping early test and analysis and showing up only in subsystem and system testing (see Section 20.6, page 389).

A prioritized list of open faults is the core of an effective fault handling and repair procedure. Failure reports must be consolidated and categorized so that repair effort can be managed systematically, rather than jumping erratically from problem to problem and wasting time on duplicate reports. They must be prioritized so that effort is not

Functional Test Design Specification of check_configuration

Test Suite Identifier
WB07-15.01

Features to Be Tested
Functional test for check_configuration, module specification WB02-15.32.[a]

Approach
Combinatorial functional test of feature parameters, enumerated by category-partition method over parameter table on page 3 of this document.[b]

Procedure
Designed for conditional inclusion in nightly test run. Build target T02_15_32_11 includes JUnit harness and oracles, with test reports directed to standard test log. Test environment includes table MDB_15_32_03 for loading initial test database state.

Test cases[c]

WB07-15.01.C01	malformed model number
WB07-15.01.C02	model number not in DB
...	...
WB07-15.01.C09[d]	valid model number with all legal required slots and some legal optional slots
...	...
WB07-15.01.C19	empty model DB
WB07-15.01.C23	model DB with a single element
WB07-15.01.C24	empty component DB
WB07-15.01.C29	component DB with a single element

Pass/Fail Criterion
Successful completion requires correct execution of all test cases with no violations in test log.

[a] An excerpt of specification WB02-15.32 is presented in Figure 11.1, page 182.
[b] Reproduced in Table 11.1, page 187.
[c] The detailed list of test cases is produced automatically from the test case file, which in turn is generated from the specification of categories and partitions. The test suite is implicitly referenced by individual test case numbers (e.g., WB07-15.01.C09 is a test case in test suite WB07-15.01).
[d] See sample test case specification, page 464.

Test Case Specification for check_configuration

Test Case Identifier

WB07-15.01.C09[a]

Test items

Module check_configuration of the Chipmunk Web presence system, business logic subsystem.

Input specification

Test Case Specification:

Model No.	valid
No. of required slots for selected model (#SMRS)	many
No. of optional slots for selected model (#SMOS)	many
Correspondence of selection with model slots	complete
No. of required components with selection ≠ empty	= No. of required slots
No. of optional components with select ≠ empty	< No. of optional slots
Required component selection	all valid
Optional component selection	all valid
No. of models in DB	many
No. of components in DB	many

Test case:

Model number	Chipmunk C20
#SMRS	5
Screen	13"
Processor	Chipmunk II plus
Hard disk	30 GB
RAM	512 MB
OS	RodentOS 3.2 Personal Edition
#SMOS	4
External storage device	DVD player

Output Specification

return value valid

Environment Needs

Execute with ChipmunkDBM v3.4 database initialized from table MDB_15_32_03.

Special Procedural Requirements

none

Intercase Dependencies

none

[a]The prefix WB07-15.01 implicitly references a test suite to which this test case directly belongs. That test suite may itself be a component of higher level test suites, so logically the test case also belongs to any of those test suites. Furthermore, some additional test suites may be composed of selections from other test suites.

squandered on faults of relatively minor importance while critical faults are neglected or even forgotten.

Other reports should be crafted to suit the particular needs of an organization and project, including process improvement as described in Chapter 23. Summary reports serve primarily to track progress and status. They may be as simple as confirmation that the nightly build-and-test cycle ran successfully with no new failures, or they may provide somewhat more information to guide attention to potential trouble spots. Detailed test logs are designed for selective reading, and include summary tables that typically include the test suites executed, the number of failures, and a breakdown of failures into those repeated from prior test execution, new failures, and test cases that previously failed but now execute correctly.

In some domains, such as medicine or avionics, the content and form of test logs may be prescribed by a certifying authority. For example, some certifications require test execution logs signed by both the person who performed the test and a quality inspector, who ascertains conformance of the test execution with test specifications.

Open Research Issues

Many available tools generate documentation from test execution records and the tables used to generate test specifications, minimizing the extra effort of producing documents in a useful form. Test design derived automatically or semiautomatically from design models is growing in importance, as is close linking of program documentation with source code, ranging from simple comment extraction and indexing like Javadoc to sophisticated hypermedia systems. In the future we should see these trends converge, and expect to see test documentation fit in an overall framework for managing and navigating information on a software product and project.

Further Reading

The guidelines in this chapter are based partly on IEEE Standard 829-1998 [Ins98]. Summary reports must convey information efficiently, managing both overview and access to details. Tufte's books on information design are useful sources of principles and examples. The second [Tuf90] and fourth [Tuf06] volumes in the series are particularly relevant. Experimental hypermedia software documentation systems [ATWJ00] hint at possible future systems that incorporate test documentation with other views of an evolving software product.

Exercises

24.1. Agile software development methods (XP, Scrum, etc.) typically minimize documentation written during software development. Referring to the sidebar on page 381, identify standard analysis and test documents that could be generated automatically or semiautomatically or replaced with functionally equivalent, automatically generated documentation during an XP project.

24.2. Test documents may become very large and unwieldy. Sometimes a more compact specification of several test cases together is more useful than individual specifications of each test case. Referring to the test case specification on page 464, design a tabular form to compactly document a suite of similar test case specifications.

24.3. Design a checklist for inspecting test design specification documents.

24.4. The Chipmunk Web presence project is starting up, and it has been decided that all project artifacts, including requirements documents, documentation in English, Italian, French, and German, source code, test plans, and test suites, will be managed in one or more CVS repositories.[2] The project team is divided between Milan, Italy, and Eugene, Oregon. What are the main design choices and issues you will consider in designing the organization of the version control repositories?

[2] If you are more familiar with another version control system, such as Subversion or Perforce, you may substitute it for CVS.

Bibliography

[ABC82] Richards W. Adrion, Martha A. Branstad, and John C. Cherniavsky. Validation, verification, and testing of computer software. *ACM Computing Surveys*, 14(2):159–192, June 1982.

[ASU86] Alfred V. Aho, Ravi Sethi, and Jeffrey D. Ullman. *Compilers: Principles, Techniques, and Tools*. Addison-Wesley Longman, Boston, 1986.

[ATWJ00] Kenneth M. Anderson, Richard N. Taylor, and E. James Whitehead Jr. Chimera: Hypermedia for heterogeneous software development environments. *ACM Transactions on Information Systems*, 18(3):211–245, July 2000.

[Bar01] Carol M. Barnum. *Usability Testing and Research*. Allyn & Bacon, Needham Heights, MA, 2001.

[Bei95] Boris Beizer. *Black-Box Testing: Techniques for Functional Testing of Software and Systems*. John Wiley and Sons, New York, 1995.

[BGM91] Gilles Bernot, Marie Claude Gaudel, and Bruno Marre. Software testing based on formal specifications: A theory and a tool. *Software Engineering Journal*, 6(6):387–405, November 1991.

[BHC+94] Inderpal Bhandari, Michael J. Halliday, Jarir Chaar, Kevin Jones, Janette S. Atkinson, Clotilde Lepori-Costello, Pamela Y. Jasper, Eric D. Tarver, Cecilia Carranza Lewis, and Masato Yonezawa. In-process improvement through defect data interpretation. *IBM Systems Journal*, 33(1):182–214, 1994.

[BHG87] Philip A. Bernstein, Vassos Hadzilacos, and Nathan Goodman. *Concurrency Control and Recovery in Database Systems*. Addison-Wesley, Boston, 1987.

[Bin00] Robert V. Binder. *Testing Object-Oriented Systems, Models, Patterns, and Tools*. Addison-Wesley, Boston, 2000.

[Bis02] Matt Bishop. *Computer Security: Art and Science*. Addison-Wesley Professional, Boston, 2002.

[Boe81] Barry W. Boehm. *Software Engineering Economics*. Prentice Hall, Englewood Cliffs, NJ, 1981.

[BOP00] Ugo Buy, Alessandro Orso, and Mauro Pezzé. Automated testing of classes. In *Proceedings of the International Symposium on Software Testing and Analysis (ISSTA)*, pages 39–48, Portland, OR, 2000.

[BPS00] William R. Bush, Jonathan D. Pincus, and David J. Sielaff. A static analyzer for finding dynamic programming errors. *Software: Practice & Experience*, 30:775–802, 2000.

[BR01a] Thomas Ball and Sriram K. Rajamani. Automatically validating temporal safety properties of interfaces. In *SPIN '01: Proceedings of the 8th International SPIN Workshop on Model Checking of Software*, pages 103–122, Toronto, Ontario, Canada, 2001. Springer-Verlag.

[BR01b] Thomas Ball and Sriram K. Rajamani. Bebop: a path-sensitive interprocedural dataflow engine. In *PASTE '01: Proceedings of the 2001 ACM SIGPLAN-SIGSOFT Workshop on Program Analysis for Software Tools and Engineering*, pages 97–103, Snowbird, UT, 2001.

[Bry86] Randal E. Bryant. Graph-based algorithms for boolean function manipulation. *IEEE Transactions on Computers*, 35(8):677–691, 1986.

[Bry92] Randal E. Bryant. Symbolic boolean manipulation with ordered binary-decision diagrams. *ACM Computing Surveys*, 24(3):293–318, 1992.

[BSW69] K. A. Bartlett, R. A. Scantlebury, and P. T. Wilkinson. A note on reliable full-duplex transmission over half-duplex lines. *Communications of the ACM*, 12(5):260–261, May 1969.

[CBC+92] Ram Chillarege, Inderpal S. Bhandari, Jarir K. Chaar, Michael J. Halliday, Diane S. Moebus, Bonnie K. Ray, and Man-Yuen Wong. Orthogonal defect classification—A concept for in-process measurements. *IEEE Transactions on Software Engineering*, 18(11):943–956, 1992.

[CC77] Patrick Cousot and Radhia Cousot. Abstract interpretation: A unified lattice model for static analysis of programs by construction of approximation of fixpoints. In *ACM Symposium on Principles of Programming Languages*, pages 238–252, Los Angeles, CA, January 1977.

[CCD+80] Augusto Celentano, Stefano Crespi Reghizzi, Pier Luigi Della Vigna, Carlo Ghezzi, G. Granata, and F. Savoretti. Compiler testing using a sentence generator. *Software — Practice & Experience*, 10:897–918, 1980.

[CDFP97] David M. Cohen, Siddhartha R. Dalal, Michael L. Fredman, and Gardner C. Patton. The AETG system: An approach to testing based on combinatiorial design. *IEEE Transactions on Software Engineering*, 23(7):437–444, July 1997.

[CHBC93] Jarir Chaar, Michael J. Halliday, Inderpal S. Bhandari, and Ram Chillarege. In-process evaluation for software inspection and test. *IEEE Transactions on Software Engineering*, 19(11):1055–1070, November 1993.

[Cla76] Lori A. Clarke. A system to generate test data and symbolically execute programs. *IEEE Transactions on Software Engineering*, SE-2(3):215–222, September 1976.

[CPDGP01] Alberto Coen-Porisini, Giovanni Denaro, Carlo Ghezzi, and Mauro Pezzè. Using symbolic execution for verifying safety-critical systems. In *Proceedings of the 8th European Software Engineering Conference held jointly with the 9th ACM SIGSOFT International Symposium on Foundations of Software Engineering (ESEC/FSE-9)*, pages 142–151, Vienna, Austria, 2001.

[CPRZ89] Lori Clarke, Andy Podgurski, Debra Richardson, and Steven J. Zeil. A formal evaluation of data flow path selection criteria. *IEEE Transactions on Software Engineering*, 15(11):1318–1332, 1989.

[DCCN04] Matthew B. Dwyer, Lori A. Clarke, Jamieson M. Cobleigh, and Gleb Naumovich. Flow analysis for verifying properties of concurrent software systems. *ACM Transactions on Software Engineering and Methodologies*, 13(4):359–430, 2004.

[DF94] Roong-Ko Doong and Phyllis G. Frankl. The ASTOOT approach to testing object-oriented programs. *ACM Transactions on Software Engineering and Methodology*, 3(2):101–130, April 1994.

[DGK+88] Richard A. DeMillo, D.S. Guindi, Kim King, Mike M. McCracken, and A. Jefferson Offut. An extended overview of the Mothra software testing environment. In *Proceedings of the 2nd Workshop on Software Testing, Verification, and Analysis (TAV)*, Banff, Alberta, 1988.

[Dij72] Edsgar W. Dijkstra. Notes on structured programming. In O. J. Dahl, E. W. Dijkstra, and C. A. R. Hoare, editors, *Structured Programming*. Academic Press, London, 1972.

[DL99] Tom DeMarco and Timothy Lister. *Peopleware (2nd ed.): Productive Projects and Teams*. Dorset House, New York, 1999.

[DLS78] Richard A. DeMillo, Richard J. Lipton, and Frederick G. Sayward. Hints on test data selection: Help for the practicing programmer. *IEEE Computer*, 11(4):34–41, 1978.

[DN81] Joe W. Duran and Simeon Ntafos. A report on random testing. In *ICSE '81: Proceedings of the 5th International Conference on Software Engineering*, pages 179–183, San Diego, CA, 1981.

[DP02] Giovanni Denaro and Mauro Pezzè;. An empirical evaluation of fault-proneness models. In *Proceedings of the 24th International Conference on Software Engineering (ICSE)*, pages 241–251, Orlando, Florida, 2002.

[DRW03] Alastair Dunsmore, Marc Roper, and Murray Wood. The development and evaluation of three diverse techniques for object-oriented code inspection. *IEEE Transactions on Software Engineering*, 29(8):677–686, 2003.

[ECGN01] Michael D. Ernst, Jake Cockrell, William G. Griswold, and David Notkin. Dynamically discovering likely program invariants to support program evolution. *IEEE Transactions on Software Engineering*, 27(2):99–123, February 2001.

[Fag86] Michal E. Fagan. Advances in software inspections. *IEEE Transactions on Software Engineering*, 12(7):744–751, 1986.

[FHLS98] Phyllis Frankl, Richard Hamlet, Bev Littlewood, and Lorenzo Strigini. Evaluating Testing methods by Delivered Reliability. *IEEE Transactions on Software Engineering*, 24(8):586–601, 1998.

[FI98] Phyllis G. Frankl and Oleg Iakounenko. Further empirical studies of test effectiveness. In *Proceedings of the ACM SIGSOFT 6th International Symposium on the Foundations of Software Engineering (FSE)*, volume 23, 6 of *Software Engineering Notes*, pages 153–162, New York, November 3–5 1998. ACM Press.

[Flo67] Robert W. Floyd. Assigning meanings to programs. In *Proceedings of the Symposium on Applied Mathematics*, volume 19, pages 19–32, Providence, RI, 1967. American Mathematical Society.

[FO76] Lloyd D. Fosdick and Leon J. Osterweil. Data flow analysis in software reliability. *ACM Computing Surveys*, 8(3):305–330, 1976.

[FvBK+91] Susumu Fujiwara, Gregor von Bochmann, Ferhat Khendek, Mokhtar Amalou, and Abderrazak Ghedamsi. Test selection based on finite state models. *IEEE Transactions on Software Engineering*, 17(6):591–603, June 1991.

[FW93] Phyllis. G. Frankl and Elaine G. Weyuker. Provable improvements on branch testing. *IEEE Transactions on Software Engineering*, 19(10):962–975, October 1993.

[GG75] John B. Goodenough and Susan L. Gerhart. Toward a theory of test data selection. *IEEE Transactions on Software Engineering*, 1(2):156–173, 1975.

[GG93] Tom Gilb and Dorothy Graham. *Software Inspection*. Addison-Wesley Longman, Boston, 1993.

[GH99] Angelo Gargantini and Connie Heitmeyer. Using model checking to generate tests from requirements specifications. In *Proceedings of the 7th European Software Engineering Conference held jointly with the 7th ACM SIGSOFT Symposium on Foundations of Software Engineering (ESEC/FSE)*, pages 146–162, Toulouse, France, September 6–10 1999.

[GHK+98] Todd Graves, Mary Jean Harrold, Jung-Min Kim, Adam Porter, and Gregg Rothermel. An empirical study of regression test selection techniques. In *Proceedings of the 20th International Conference on Software Engineering (ICSE)*, pages 188–197. IEEE Computer Society Press, April 1998.

[GJM02] Carlo Gezzi, Mehdi Jazayeri, and Dino Mandrioli. *Fundamentals of Software Engineering*. Prentice Hall PTR, Upper Saddle River, NJ, 2nd edition, 2002.

[GMH81] John Gannon, Paul McMullin, and Richard Hamlet. Data abstraction, implementation, specification, and testing. *ACM Transactions on Programming Languages and Systems*, 3(3):211–223, 1981.

[Gou83] John S. Gourlay. A mathematical framework for the investigation of testing. *IEEE Transactions on Software Engineering*, 6(11):086–709, November 1983.

[GS94] Robert B. Grady and Tom Van Slack. Key lessons in achieving widespread inspection use. *IEEE Software*, 11(4):46–57, 1994.

[Gut77] John Guttag. Abstract data types and the development of data structures. *Communications of the ACM*, 20(6):396–404, 1977.

[HA05] Hanna Hulkko and Pekka Abrahamsson. A multiple case study on the impact of pair programming on product quality. In *Proceedings of the 27th International Conference on Software Engineering (ICSE)*, pages 495–504, St. Louis, MO, 2005.

[Ham77] Richard G. Hamlet. Testing programs with the aid of a compiler. *IEEE Transactions on Software Engineering*, 3(4):279–290, July 1977.

[Han70] Kenneth V. Hanford. Automatic generation of test cases. *IBM Systems Journal*, 4:242–257, 1970.

[HDW04] Mats P.E. Heimdahl, George Devaraj, and Robert J. Weber. Specification test coverage adequacy criteria = specification test generation inadequacy criteria? In *Proceedings of the Eighth IEEE International Symposium on High Assurance Systems Engineering (HASE)*, pages 178–186, Tampa, Florida, March 2004.

[Her76] P. Herman. A data flow analysis approach to program testing. *The Australian Computer Journal*, November 1976.

[Hin01] Michael Hind. Pointer analysis: haven't we solved this problem yet? In *Proceedings of the ACM SIGPLAN-SIGSOFT workshop on Program analysis for software tools and engineering*, pages 54–61, Snowbird, UT, 2001.

[HJ92] Reed Hastings and Bob Joyce. Purify: Fast detection of memory leaks and access errors. In *Proceedings of the Winter USENIX Conference*, pages 125–136. USENIX Association, January 1992.

[HJMS03] Thomas A. Henzinger, Ranjit Jhala, Rupak Majumdar, and Gregoire Sutre. Software verification with blast. In *Proceedings of the Tenth International Workshop on Model Checking of Software (SPIN)*, volume 2648 of *Lecture Notes in Computer Science*, pages 235–239. Springer-Verlag, 2003.

[HK76] Sidney L. Hantler and James C. King. An introduction to proving the correctness of programs. *ACM Computing Surveys*, 8(3):331–353, 1976.

[HM03] Ted Husted and Vincent Massol. *JUnit in Action.* Manning Publications, Greenwich, CT, 2003.

[HMF92] Mary Jean Harrold, John D. McGregor, and Kevin J. Fitzpatrick. Incremental Testing of Object-Oriented Class Structures. In *Proceedings of the 14th International Conference on Software Engineering*, pages 68–80, Melbourne, Australia, May 1992.

[Hoa69] C. A. R. Hoare. An axiomatic basis for computer programming. *Communications of the ACM*, 12(10):576–580, 1969.

[Hol97] Gerard J. Holzmann. The model checker SPIN. *IEEE Transactions on Software Engineering*, 23(5):279–295, 1997.

[Hol03] Gerard J. Holzmann. *The SPIN Model Checker: Primer and Reference Manual.* Addison-Wesley Professional, Boston, 2003.

[How75] William E. Howden. Methodology for the generation of program test data. *IEEE Transactions on Computers*, 24(5):554–560, May 1975.

[How76] William E. Howden. Reliability of the path analysis testing strategy. *IEEE Transactions on Software Engineering*, 2(3):208–215, 1976.

[How77] William E. Howden. Symbolic testing and the DISSECT symbolic evaluation system. *IEEE Transactions on Software Engineering*, SE–3(4):266–278, July 1977.

[How78] William E. Howden. An evaluation of the effectiveness of symbolic testing. *Software: Practice & Experience*, 8:381–397, 1978.

[How82] William E. Howden. Weak mutation testing and completeness of test sets. *IEEE Transactions on Software Engineering*, 8(4):371–379, July 1982.

[HR00] Michael R. A. Huth and Mark D. Ryan. *Logic in Computer Science: Modelling and Reasoning about Systems*. Cambridge University Press, 2000.

[HT90] Richard Hamlet and Ross Taylor. Partition testing does not inspire confidence. *IEEE Transactions on Software Engineering*, 16(12):206–215, December 1990.

[HW01] Daniel M. Hoffman and David M. Weiss, editors. *Software Fundamentals: Collected Papers by David L. Parnas*. Addison-Wesley Longman, Boston, 2001.

[Ins98] Institute of Electrical and Electronics Engineers. Software test documentation — IEEE Std 829-1998. Technical report, IEEE, New York, 1998.

[Ins02] Institute of Electrical and Electronics Engineers. IEEE standard for software quality assurance plans — IEEE Std 730-2002. Technical report, IEEE, New York, 2002.

[Jaa03] Ari Jaaksi. Assessing software projects: Tools for business owners. In *Proceedings of the 9th European Software Engineering Conference held jointly with 10th ACM SIGSOFT International Symposium on Foundations of Software Engineering (ESEC/FSE)*, pages 15–18, Helsinki, Finland, September 2003.

[Jac02] Daniel Jackson. Alloy: a lightweight object modelling notation. *ACM Transactions on Software Engineering and Methodology*, 11(2):256–290, 2002.

[JN95] Neil D. Jones and Flemming Nielson. Abstract interpretation: A semantics-based tool for program analysis. In S. Abramsky, Dov M. Gabbay, and T.S.E. Maibaum, editors, *Handbook of Logic in Computer Science*, volume 4, Semantic Modelling, pages 527–636. Clarendon Press, Oxford, UK, 1995.

[KE85] Richard A. Kemmerer and Steven T. Eckman. UNISEX: A UNIX-based symbolic EXecutor for Pascal. *Software: Practice & Experience*, 15(5):439–458, 1985.

[KM93] John C. Knight and E. Ann Myers. An improved inspection technique. *Commununications of the ACM*, 36(11):51–61, 1993.

[KP02] Jung-Min Kim and Adam Porter. A history-based test prioritization technique for regression testing in resource constrained environments. In *Proceedings of the 24th International Conference on Software Engineering*, pages 119–129, Orlando, FL, 2002.

[Lam89] Leslie Lamport. A simple approach to specifying concurrent systems. *Commununications of the ACM*, 32(1):32–45, 1989.

[LD03] Michele Lanza and Stephane Ducasse. Polymetric views - a lightweight visual approach to reverse engineering. *IEEE Transactions on Software Engineering*, 29(9):782–795, September 2003.

[Lev95] Nancy G. Leveson. *Safeware: System Safety and Computers*. Addison-Wesley, Boston, 1995.

[Lev04] Nancy G. Leveson. Role of software in spacecraft accidents. *Journal of Spacecraft and Rockets*, 41(4), July-August 2004.

[Lio96] Jacques-Louis Lions. ARIANE 5 flight 501 failure: Report of the inquiry board. European Space Agency press release. Originally appeared at `http://www.esrin.esa.it/htdocs/tidc/Press/Press96/ariane5rep.html`. Reproduced at `http://www.cs.berkeley.edu/~demmel/ma221/ariane5rep.html`, July 1996.

[LK83] Janusz Laski and Bogdan Korel. A data flow oriented program testing strategy. *IEEE Transactions on Software Engineering*, 9(5):33–43, 1983.

[LPS02] Marek Leszak, Dewayne E. Perry, and Dieter Stoll. Classification and evaluation of defects in a project retrospective. *The Journal of Systems and Software*, 61(3):173–187, April 2002.

[Mar97] Brian Marick. *The Craft of Software Testing: Subsystems Testing Including Object-Based and Object-Oriented Testing*. Prentice-Hall, Englewood Cliffs, NJ, 1997.

[McC83] Thomas McCabe. *Structured Testing*. IEEE Computer Society Press, 1983.

[Mea55] George H. Mealy. A method for synthesizing sequential circuits. *Bell System Technical Journal*, 34:1045–1079, 1955.

[MF96] Delia I. S. Marx and Phyllis G. Frankl. The path-wise approach to data flow testing with pointer variables. In *Proceedings of the 1996 International Symposium on Software Testing and analysis*, pages 135–146, New York, January 8–10 1996. ACM Press.

[Moo56] Edward F. Moore. Gedanken experiments on sequential machines. In *Automata Studies*, pages 129–153. Princeton University Press, Princeton, NJ, 1956.

[Mor90] Larry J. Morell. A theory of fault-based testing. *IEEE Transactions on Software Engineering*, 16(8):844–857, August 1990.

[MP43] Warren Sturgis McCulloch and Walter Harry Pitts. A logical calculus of the ideas immanent in nervous activity. *Bulletin of Mathematical Biophysics*, 5(115), 1943. Reprinted in *Neurocomputing: Foundations of Research*, 1988, MIT Press, Cambridge MA.

[MS03] Atif M. Memon and Mary Lou Soffa. Regression testing of GUIs. In *Proceedings of the 9th European Software Engineering Conference held jointly with 11th ACM SIGSOFT International Symposium on Foundations of Software Engineering (ESEC/FSE)*, pages 118–127, Helsinki, Finland, 2003.

[Mus04] John D. Musa. *Software Reliability Engineering: More Reliable Software Faster And Cheaper*. Authorhouse, second edition, 2004.

[Mye79] Glenford Myers. *The Art of Software Testing*. John Wiley and Sons, New York, 1979.

[Nie00] Jakob Nielsen. *Designing Web Usability: The Practice of Simplicity*. New Riders Publishing, Indianapolis, IN, 2000.

[Nor90] Donald A. Norman. *The Design of Everyday Things*. Doubleday/Currency ed., 1990.

[OAFG98] Thomas Ostrand, Aaron Anodide, Herbert Foster, and Tarak Goradia. A visual test development environment for GUI systems. In *Proceedings of the ACM SIGSOFT International Symposium on Software Testing and Analysis (ISSTA)*, volume 23,2 of *ACM Software Engineering Notes*, pages 82–92, New York, March 2–5 1998. ACM Press.

[OB88] Thomas J. Ostrand and Marc J. Balcer. The category-partition method for specifying and generating functional tests. *Communications of the ACM*, 31(6):676–686, June 1988.

[OO90] Kurt M. Olender and Leon J. Osterweil. Cecil: A sequencing constraint language for automatic static analysis generation. *IEEE Transactions on Software Engineering*, 16(3):268–280, 1990.

[OO92] Kurt M. Olender and Leon J. Osterweil. Interprocedural static analysis of sequencing constraints. *ACM Transactions on Software Engineering and Methodologies*, 1(1):21–52, 1992.

[Ors98] Alessandro Orso. *Integration Testing of Object-Oriented Software*. PhD thesis, Politecnico di Milano, 1998.

[PJ97] Adam A. Porter and Philip M. Johnson. Assessing software review meetings: Results of a comparative analysis of two experimental studies. *IEEE Transactions on Software Engineering*, 23(3):129–145, March 1997.

[PP98] Dennis K. Peters and David L. Parnas. Using Test Oracles Generated from Program Documentation. *IEEE Transactions on Software Engineering*, 24(3):161–173, 1998.

[PPP+97] James M. Perpich, Dewayne E. Perry, Adam A. Porter, Lawrence G. Votta, and Michael W. Wade. Anywhere, anytime code inspections: Using the web to remove inspection bottlenecks in large-scale software development. In *Proceedings of the International Conference on Software Engineering (ICSE)*, Boston, Massachusetts, 1997.

[PPW+05] Alexander Pretschner, Wolfgang Prenninger, Stefan Wagner, Christian Kühnel, M. Baumgartner, B. Sostawa, R. Zölch, and T. Stauner. One evaluation of model-based testing and its automation. In *Proceedings of the 27th international Conference on Software Engineering (ICSE)*, pages 392–401, St. Louis, MO, 2005.

[PTY95] Mauro Pezzè, Richard Taylor, and Michal Young. Graph models for reachability analysis of concurrent programs. *ACM Transactions on Software Engineering and Methodologies*, 4(2):171–213, April 1995.

[PW85] David L. Parnas and David M. Weiss. Active design reviews: principles and practices. In *Proceedings of the 8th International Conference on Software Engineering (ICSE)*, pages 132–136, London, England, 1985.

[PY99] Christina Pavlopoulou and Michal Young. Residual test coverage monitoring. In *Proceedings of the International Conference on Software Engineering (ICSE)*, pages 277–284, 1999.

[RAO92] Debra J. Richardson, Stephanie Leif Aha, and T. Owen O'Malley. Specification-based test oracles for reactive systems. In *Proceedings of the 14th International Conference on Software Engineering (ICSE)*, pages 105–118, Melbourne, Australia, 1992.

[RH97] Gregg Rothermel and Mary Jean Harrold. A safe, efficient regression test selection technique. *ACM Transactions on Software Engineering and Methodology*, 6(2):173–210, April 1997.

[Ros95] David S. Rosenblum. A practical approach to programming with assertions. *IEEE Transactions on Software Engineering*, 21(1):19–31, 1995.

[ROT89] Debra J. Richardson, Owen O'Malley, and Cynthia Tittle. Approaches to specification-based testing. In *Proceedings of the ACM SIGSOFT Symposium on Software Testing, Analysis, and Verification (ISSTA 89)*, 1989.

[RRL99] Atanas Rountev, Barbara G. Ryder, and William Landi. Data-flow analysis of program fragments. In *Proceedings of the 7th European Software Engineering Conference held jointly with the 7th ACM International Symposium on Foundations of Software Engineering(ESEC/FSE)*, pages 235–252, Toulouse, France, 1999. Springer-Verlag.

[Rus91] Glen W. Russell. Experience with inspection in ultralarge-scale development. *IEEE Software*, 8(1):25–31, 1991.

[RW85] Sandra Rapps and Elaine Weyuker. Selecting software test data using data flow information. *IEEE Transactions on Software Engineering*, 11(4):367–375, April 1985.

[SB99] Emin Gün Sirer and Brian N. Bershad. Using production grammars in software testing. In *Proceedings of the 2nd Conference on Domain-Specific Languages (DSL '99)*, pages 1–14, Austin, Texas, October 1999. USENIX, ACM Press.

[SBN+97] Stefan Savage, Michael Burrows, Greg Nelson, Patrick Sobalvarro, and Thomas Anderson. Eraser: A dynamic data race detector for multi-threaded programs. *ACM Transactions on Computer Systems*, 15(4):391–411, 1997.

[SC96] Phil Stocks and David Carrington. A framework for specification-based testing. *IEEE Transactions on Software Engineering*, 22(11):777–793, 1996.

[SE04] David Saff and Michael D. Ernst. Mock object creation for test factoring. In *Proceedings of the Workshop on Program Analysis for Software Tools and Engineering (PASTE '04)*, pages 49–51, Washington DC, 2004.

[SJLY00] Chris Sauer, D. Ross Jeffery, Lesley Land, and Philip Yetton. The effectiveness of software development technical reviews: A behaviorally motivated program of research. *IEEE Transactions on Software Engineering*, 26(1):1–14, 2000.

[SS90] Mehmet Sahinoglu and Eugene Spafford. Sequential statistical procedure in mutation-based testing. In *Proceedings of the 28th Annual Spring Reliability Seminar*, pages 127–148, Boston, April 1990. Central New England Council of IEEE.

[Ste96] Bjarne Steensgaard. Points-to analysis in almost linear time. In *Proceedings of the Symposium on Principles of Programming Languages*, pages 32–41, 1996.

[Ste99] Arthur G. Stephenson. Mars climate orbiter: Mishap investigation board report. Technical report, NASA, November 1999.

[TFW93] Pascale Thévenod-Fosse and Héléne Waeselynck. Statemate applied to statistical software testing. In *Proceedings of the International Symposium on Software Testing and Analysis (ISSTA)*, pages 99–109, Cambridge, MA, 1993.

[TRC93] Margaret C. Thompson, Debra J. Richardson, and Lori A. Clarke. An information flow model of fault detection. In *Proceedings of the International Symposium on Software Testing and Analysis (ISSTA)*, pages 182–192, 1993.

[Tuf90] Edward R. Tufte. *Envisioning Information*. Graphic Press, Cheshire CT, 1990.

[Tuf97] Edward R. Tufte. *Visual Explanations: Images and Quantities, Evidence and Narrative*. Graphic Press, Cheshire CT, 1997.

[Tuf01] Edward R. Tufte. *The Visual Display of Quantitative Information*. Graphic Press, Cheshire CT, 2nd edition, 2001.

[Tuf06] Edward R. Tufte. *Beautiful Evidence*. Graphic Press, Cheshire CT, 2006.

[Uni00] United State Department of Health and Human Services. Standards for privacy of individually identifiable health information (regulations pertaining to entities by the Health Insurance Portability and Accountability Act of 1996 (HIPAA). Text and commentary available at `http://www.hhs.gov/ocr/hipaa/finalreg.html`, Dec 2000.

[Uni04] United States Computer Emergency Response Team (CERT). libpng fails to properly check length of transparency chunk (tRNS) data. Vulnerability Note VU#388984, available at http://www.kb.cert.org/vuls/id/388984, November 2004.

[vBDZ89] Gregor von Bochman, Rachida Dssouli, and J. R. Zhao. Trace analysis for conformance and arbitration testing. *IEEE Transactions on Software Engineering*, 15(11):1347–1356, November 1989.

[vBP94] Gregor von Bochmann and Alexandre Petrenko. Protocol Testing: Review of Methods and Relevance for Software Testing. Technical Report IRO-923, Department d'Informatique et de Recherche Opérationnelle, Université de Montréal, 1994.

[Wei07] Mark Allen Weiss. *Data Structures and Algorithm Analysis in Java*. Addison-Wesley, Boston, 2nd edition, 2007.

[Wey98] Elaine J. Weyuker. Testing component-based software: A cautionary tale. *IEEE Software*, 15(5):54–59, September/October 1998.

[WHH80] Martin R. Woodward, David Hedley, and Michael A. Hennell. Experience with path analysis and testing of programs. *IEEE Transactions on Software Engineering*, 6(3):278–286, May 1980.

[WO80] Elaine J. Weyuker and Thomas J. Ostrand. Theories of program testing and the the application of revealing subdomains. *IEEE Transactions on Software Engineering*, 6(3):236–246, May 1980.

[YT89] Michal Young and Richard N. Taylor. Rethinking the taxonomy of fault detection techniques. In *Proceedings of the International Conference on Software Engineering (ICSE)*, pages 53–62, Pittsburgh, May 1989.

[Zel05] Andreas Zeller. *Why Programs Fail: A Guide to Systematic Debugging*. Morgan Kaufmann, San Francisco, 2005.

Index